Microeconomics
for
Managers

Microeconomics
for
Managers

David M. Kreps

Graduate School of Business, Stanford University, and
Berglas School of Economics, Tel Aviv University

W. W. Norton & Company • New York • London

W. W. Norton & Company has been independent since its founding in 1923, when William Warder and Mary D. Herter Norton first published lectures delivered at the People's Institute, the adult education division of New York City's Cooper Union. The Nortons soon expanded their program beyond the Institute, publishing books by celebrated academics from America and abroad. By mid-century, the two major pillars of Norton's publishing program—trade books and college texts—were firmly established. In the 1950s, the Norton family transferred control of the company to its employees, and today—with a staff of four hundred and a comparable number of trade, college, and professional titles published each year—W. W. Norton & Company stands as the largest and oldest publishing house owned wholly by its employees.

Manufacturing by the Maple-Vail Book Group.

Library of Congress Cataloging-in-Publication Data

Kreps, David M.
    Microeconomics for managers / David M. Kreps.
        p. cm.
    Includes bibliographical references and index.

    ISBN 0-393-97678-5

    1. Microeconomics. 2. Industrial management. I. Title.

HB172.K75 2003
338.5′024′658—dc21
                    2003054087

W. W. Norton & Company, Inc., 500 Fifth Avenue, New York, NY 10110
                www.wwnorton.com

W. W. Norton & Company Ltd., Castle House, 75/76 Wells Street, London W1T 3QT

1 2 3 4 5 6 7 8 9 0

To Joel S. Demski, Charles A. Holloway, Charles T. Horngren, and Robert K. Jaedicke

Four extraordinary educators
who taught me how to teach MBAs

Contents in Brief

Contents

Preface

This book is a textbook for an introductory microeconomics course, for MBA students. Chapter 1 answers the questions, What is microeconomics about? and Why should managers be interested in it? I will not repeat the answers here, except to say that microeconomics, applied with skill and with a judicious appreciation for what it can and cannot tell you, can be a very useful way of thinking for managers.

In U.S. terminology, this is an *intermediate-level* microeconomics text, at the more sophisticated end of the spectrum of such books. But in terms of content, the book is distinguished from standard intermediate micro texts in ways that increase its appeal to students of management:

- I emphasize applications of microeconomics to problems confronting managers, in particular, general managers. I try to capture the student's interest by leading many chapters with examples drawn from real life, before getting to the theory.

- In a number of places, I discuss the relationship between microeconomics and the functional fields of management: financial and managerial accounting, finance, marketing, operations, human resource management, and strategic management. I also link microeconomic models to models of behavior drawn from social psychology and sociology, which an MBA student is likely to encounter in courses on organizational behavior and the like.

- I shift the topical emphasis away from classical topics such as the theory of the consumer and perfect competition (although they are not abandoned) and toward topics such as uncertainty, information, reciprocity, credibility, reputation, and transaction costs.

- I provide an accompanying *Student's Companion* that gives, among other things, more complex exercises that emphasize calculations in closer-to-real-life settings.

- I emphasize the use of stylized models to gain qualitative insights as opposed to quantitative answers.

One of the important lessons of microeconomics is that the world is filled with trade-offs. In particular, a product or strategy well designed for one market or context is very likely to be ill suited for others. So let me be clear: this book is designed with MBA students in mind. In particular, it was crafted from a required course taught in the MBA program at Stanford University's Graduate School of Business. This specific group of students is fairly old (median age around 27) and experienced: students with at least 3 years of significant post-BA experience in the real world. The group is on average highly skilled analytically but with tremendous variation, ranging from PhDs in mathematical and scientific fields to those whose last organized math class was in high school. The students exhibit significant intellectual curiosity taken individually and in small groups, but in the larger "sections" of around 65 students in which the course is taught, the group ethic is that ideas that do not pay back in the first 5 months on the job are suspect and those that might not pay back in the first 5 years are a complete waste of time. Stanford MBA students tend to learn inductively and by analogy much more than deductively and by theory: The standard response after the course to the question What do you know about implicit collusion with noisy observables? is Huh? But if you ask them, What does the GE-Westinghouse case (the classic Harvard Business School case on the topic) have to say about this or that industry? you often get a sophisticated and nuanced answer.

Therefore, this book is strongly oriented toward people interested in general management. I assume a background knowledge about management and the functional tasks facing management. I use a modicum of calculus and some basic probability, but not a lot, and I generally take a lot of care to explain what the math means. I spend a lot of time justifying what I am doing, trying to convince the reader that the on-the-job payback is going to be relatively short, especially if the reader is willing to settle for a payback that takes the form of insight. While I present abstract ideas, I usually work in terms of examples first, and I believe the only place the word *theorem* appears is in a very loose and imprecise rendering of the folk theorem.

Because of the high average analytical skills of Stanford MBAs, I may have overreached for some MBA programs, but I hope this is not so: Owing to the enormous dispersion of those skills among the students at Stanford, I am quite deliberate throughout. Certainly, analytically adept Stanford students complain about the slow pace of the book, for the first few chapters, at least.

Because the use of calculus may prove a barrier in some places, I wrote the book so that it can be used without ever taking a derivative. In any case, calculus ceases to be used about halfway through the book, and, for the first half (which largely concerns the standard theories of the firm, consumer, and market), I set things up so that a student able to use spreadsheets (and a packaged optimizer, such as Solver for Excel) can skip all the sections with calculus. But calculus makes things a lot easier, and the level of calculus required is really quite minimal. (The *Student's Companion* contains an appendix that reviews the little bit of calculus needed.) Economics, with its intuitive use of margins (derivatives) is a good place to learn what calculus does; so students without calculus may get it more or less for free in this context, if they will only persevere.

The other mathematics requirements of the book are facility with basic graphs and, in particular, linear functions; the ability to solve simultaneous linear equations, especially two equations in two unknowns; moderate facility with a spreadsheet, including the use of an optimizer add-in such as Solver for Microsoft Excel;[1] and, near the end of the book, an understanding of basic probability theory. In a couple of places, I talk as if the student knows basic classical statistics to the level of one-equation, multiple (OLS) regression.

Especially in the asides that talk about the connections between microeconomics and the functions of management, I assume a general business background that students fresh from college may lack. For instance, I assume readers know a bit about income statements and balance sheets. (I assume, for instance, that readers know that asset depreciation is a charge against current income and that bad debts are generally written off quickly). I also assume the readers know about discounting. As for non-MBA audiences:

- Readers with a scientific or engineering background will find the math easy to swallow. The emphasis on micro applied to management is probably right for most scientists or engineers interested in economics, especially in professional MS programs at engineering schools.

- Undergraduates headed for professional schools may like the selection of topics, if they have the business background needed to cope. But the book has either light or nonexistent coverage of topics that are important for undergraduates headed for graduate study in economics, such as public sector economics and the theory of the consumer (nothing on income and substitution effects; Engel curves; or luxury, inferior, and Giffen goods).

- I have used chapters from the back of the book with considerable success in executive education programs (specifically, in the Stanford Executive Program, a 6-week general management program), although the first half of the book is probably too technical for such audiences.

Accompanying this textbook is a *Student's Companion*, which provides a few appendices of mathematical background, solutions to around half of the problems given in the book, a few longer caselike exercises, sets of review problems, and some supplementary material. Solutions to the other problems are provided at the instructor's Web site, as are other materials, including some suggestions for cases to teach in conjunction with the book. To gain access to this Web site, instructors should write to the publisher on letterhead giving details of their course.

My biggest debt of thanks is to the generations of Stanford GSB students who have taken this course from me. They contributed a lot to my understanding of economics and, even more, of how to teach them economics and convince them

---

[1] I use Microsoft Excel, and most of the spreadsheets used in the book are available in Excel for both Windows and the Mac. Spreadsheets appearing in the book can be downloaded from the book's Web site, www.wwnorton.com/web/kreps.

that this stuff is useful. My experiences with participants in the Stanford Executive Program leave me in their debt as well.

This book has been created from class notes that I've accumulated in over 10 years of teaching microeconomics (and 10 years before that teaching decision analysis) at Stanford. I had a succession of teaching assistants who have helped proofread these notes (and provided more general, valuable comments); I wish to acknowledge Dana Heller in this role, in particular.

I taught this course with a number of colleagues, many of whom have been gracious enough to use my notes and provide feedback. Two colleagues, Jeremy Bulow and Peter Reiss, have been particularly patient when I was obtuse and generous with ideas and specific materials. In particular, Bulow provided the wonderful GM truck coupon problem that serves as the lietmotif for the first half of the book, and Reiss, the Porsche story that appears in Chapter 6. Five others, Yossi Feinberg, Faruk Gul, Sven Rady, Andy Skrzypacz, and Dimitri Vayanos, also deserve specific mention for comments. Ronald Goettler at Carnegie-Mellon University provided useful feedback as he used preprint chapters at CMU. The appendices on probability and decision trees in the *Companion* were initially written for a course on decision making under uncertainty; my memory of those days is fading rapidly, but I do remember many helpful comments from Chuck Bonini, Michael Harrison, Chuck Holloway, and Evan Porteus. While Eddie Lazear has his own way of teaching micro, very different from mine, I benefited from teaching with him. Jim Baron, with whom I taught and then wrote a book about human resource management, taught me a lot of economics, even though he thinks it is sociology and social psychology. And I received more specific assistance from David Baron, David Brady, Don Brown, Rick Lambert, John Roberts, Garth Saloner, Andrea Shepard, Itamar Simonson, and Mark Wolfson; I'm grateful to them all.

Jack Repcheck of W. W. Norton has been both champion and critic, as warranted by circumstances. The book is much better than it would otherwise have been because of his efforts. The copyeditor Gnomi Schrift Gouldin and Marian Johnson and Ben Reynolds of W. W. Norton also contributed very significantly to the final product.

The economics in this book is neither original nor especially deep. But I hope it is pedagogically innovative and sound. If it is, this is due in large part to an extraordinary group of teachers who taught me both subject matter and, perhaps more important for current purposes, different ways to teach. I thought of dedicating this book to them as a group, but the list became too long, so I compromise as follows: The key, I believe, to first-rate management education is to combine rigorous disciplinary thought with a range of "applications," from models to real-world applications, that both motivate the student and show how the disciplinary thought can be used. Many of my senior colleagues at the GSB taught me to do this, but four had a particularly strong influence on my development as a teacher: Joel S. Demski, Charles A. Holloway, Charles T. Horngren, and Robert K. Jaedicke.

Microeconomics
for
Managers

1. Microeconomics? For Managers?

Each chapter in this book begins with a brief synopsis of what the chapter is about. Chapter 1 is part sales pitch, part definition, part description, and part warning:

- I try to convince you that microeconomics is worth your time and effort by providing real-life puzzles it helps solve.
- I define the subject fairly abstractly.
- The abstract definition uses the terms *model* and *modeling*. Using both definitions and examples, I describe what these all-important words mean to an economist.
- Finally, I tell you what it will take from you to learn microeconomics.

1.1. A Sales Pitch: Why Study Microeconomics?

Between 1973 and 1987, General Motors sold pickup trucks in the United States with gasoline tanks that sit outside the main structural frame of the truck.[1] In the summer of 1992, two groups founded by Ralph Nader filed a petition with the National Highway Traffic Safety Administration (NHTSA), alleging that these tanks were vulnerable to rupture if the truck was hit from the side, possibly leading to fire or an explosion. The petition asked that GM be compelled to recall the trucks and correct this problem. Passion on the subject reached fever pitch, when *Dateline NBC*, a television newsmagazine program, ran a story on these trucks in which toy rocket engines were secretly placed on the trucks to ignite any gas that did leak after a staged accident. Confronted with legal action by GM, NBC retracted the story, fired its producers, and apologized for the incident.

The NHTSA investigated the matter and, in 1993, requested a voluntary recall. GM declined, aggressively disputing the contention that the trucks in question were any more dangerous than trucks without this feature. In the end, GM avoided a mandatory recall. Simultaneously, however, GM faced a number of class-action lawsuits by owners of the vehicles, seeking compensation for the loss in value of their trucks or the cost of repairs. In contrast to its aggressive stand against the NHTSA, GM sought to settle the class-action suits, and in July 1993, GM and the lawyers for the class asked to presiding courts to approve a negotiated settlement.

---

[1] I am grateful to Jeremy Bulow, who first called this story to my attention and who has contributed enormously to the analysis that follows. Also, the real-life story gets complex in places, so I will simplify somewhat for expositional purposes.

In the proposed settlement, GM—without admitting any fault or liability—agreed to give each currently registered owner of these trucks a coupon worth $1000 toward the purchase of any new GM light truck, including minivans, full-sized vans, pickup trucks, and sport-utility vehicles, such as the Blazer and Suburban. The coupons could be used, at full value, by the registered owner of the old vehicle or by any member of the registered owner's immediate family. A coupon could also be transferred once to any third party, for whom it would be worth $500 off the purchase price of a new light truck. The coupons would be good for 15 months after being issued, with issuance initially set for the fall of 1993.

GM was quick to point out its generosity, given that many of the older trucks involved in the suit were up to 21 years old, had cost only $2000 or so new, and according to the *Kelly Bluebook*, the semi-official guide to market prices of used vehicles in the United States, had a retail value of around $1800. The newest of the affected vehicles had current retail values around $8000. GM emphasized that the old trucks were just as safe as other pickup trucks of similar vintages and that this wasn't an admission of liability or error but merely a matter of trying to appease loyal owners of GM products. "It does not affect the NHTSA case in any way, shape, or form," said a GM spokesperson, quoted in the *Wall Street Journal*.[2] "This is not a recall. There is absolutely no modification of the vehicle. This separates the customer satisfaction concerns from the technical concerns."

The *Wall Street Journal* seemed impressed by the settlement offer. Approximately 4.7 million of these trucks were still on the road, so GM would be issuing 4.7 million coupons. The *Journal* calculated that the potential liability of 4.7 million coupons at $1000 apiece is $4.7 billion. This is a lot of money, but GM didn't seem too worried; the same spokesperson pointed out that for each coupon cashed, GM would be selling a vehicle, "so there is a revenue component."

The judge to whom this settlement was proposed was less impressed, and did not approve the settlement, on the grounds that it provided very little value to members of the affected class. Following this setback, GM and the lawyers for the class continued their negotiations. In the summer of 1999, they reached agreement on terms of a revised settlement, which was tentatively approved by the presiding judge. The terms of the new settlement, simplified here, were as follows:

- 5.8 million coupons were to be mailed out to registered old-truck owners. The change from 4.7 to 5.8 million was because trucks manufactured from 1987 and 1991 were now included in the settlement.

---

[2] *Wall Street Journal*, July 20, 1993, A3.

- These coupons would provide a $1000 rebate to the original bearer or family members, or a $500 rebate to any third party to whom it was transferred, for a period of 15 months after the coupons were mailed out. Then, unless the original bearer was a fleet owner—defined as a registered owner of three or more of the vehicles—or a government agency, the coupons provided a $500 rebate for the original bearer and a $250 rebate if transferred, for an additional 18 months. For fleet owners and government agencies, the coupons would be worth a flat $250 if used by the original bearer for an additional 35 months, but these coupons could not be transferred after the first 15 months.

- The coupons provided rebates on any GM vehicles—not only GM light trucks—except for products produced by the Saturn Division.

- For original bearers, the $1000 rebate was in addition to any other rebate that GM might offer. But for third-party users, at least for the first 15 months, the use of other rebates offered by GM would reduce the rebate provided by this coupon; if the other rebates used totaled less than $250, the coupon would provide an additional rebate of $500 less the total of the others, so the total amount rebated would be $500. If the other rebates used amounted to more than $250, the coupon would provide an additional rebate of $250.

- In addition, GM would provide $4.1 million for a research project on fuel system safety in gasoline-powered vehicles.

Wrangling about this settlement didn't end at this point. In the summer of 1999, for instance, GM was upset that the lawyers for the affected class were proposing that when notifying members of the class about the settlement, they would include the information that the Certificate Redemption Group (CRG) of Houston, Texas, was willing to buy coupons from anyone at $100 apiece. Spokespersons at CRG, when interviewed, suggested that they expected to be able to sell the coupons at $150 to $200 apiece, so that, if 3 million coupons were tendered to them, they would make a tidy profit of $150 to $300 million. The *Wall Street Journal* of July 16, 1999, reported that GM was unhappy about this and had appealed to the courts to stop the inclusion of this statement in the notification to the class. Following this, the presiding court put the settlement on hold. The coupons were finally mailed to truck owners in the spring of 2001.

Why am I telling you all this? Consider the following three assertions:

- Back in 1994, the judge who refused to approve the original settlement was entirely correct to refuse. I estimate that the original proposed settlement would have cost GM tens of millions of dollars. That may seem like a lot of money, but it is pretty small potatoes to GM. More to the point, I estimate that the 1993 proposed settlement would have generated very little value to most of the injured class and less than $400 in value to those of the injured class willing to purchase a new GM light truck.

- The 1999 proposed settlement was far more costly to GM and far more generous to the bulk of the injured class members. I estimate that each member of the injured class would get at least $200 in value and the cost to GM would be on the order of $1.5 billion.

- Suppose that, under the terms of the 1999 proposed settlement, GM picked 11.6 million names out of the phone book and mailed each person a coupon, providing the same entitlement as given to the 5.8 million members of the affected class. In other words, suppose GM tripled the number of coupons in circulation. Would the cost of this program to GM then triple? Absolutely not! My guess is that the cost would go *down* to the neighborhood of $100 million, and most members of the injured class would be left with no discernible value.

You may be mystified by these assertions. You certainly don't have enough data to check my calculations and, if you are reading this book to learn economics, you probably wouldn't know what to do with the missing data had I supplied them. But after reading this book—in fact, after reading the first half of the book—you'll recognize that the key element in determining how costly this program will be to GM is, *What would it cost a third-party buyer of a GM vehicle—someone without a coupon who wants one—to purchase a coupon from an original holder?* The answer to that question depends on the answer to the question, *How many vehicles of the sort covered by the coupons would GM expect to sell over the period the coupons are valid?* I don't want to be mysterious, so here are the punchlines: In the 1993 proposed settlement, GM would normally sell far fewer light trucks than the 4.7 million coupons in circulation, hence the coupons have little value in the transferred-coupon market and the cost of the settlement to GM would be small. But, in the 1999 proposed settlement, GM would expect to sell more vehicles than there are coupons, hence the coupons would have substantial value and the cost to GM would be large. And if GM tripled the number of coupons, the number of coupons would far exceed their potential use, hence the coupons would command a low value in the transferred-coupon market and the program would cost GM very little.

Let me reiterate that all the *hences* in the preceding paragraph are unlikely to be clear to you—yet. But they will become clear after you make your way through this book. The reason for practicing and aspiring managers to learn economics is to understand the sort of story I've just related and to be able to do the analysis on your own.

Perhaps you aren't specially interested in the marketing of automobiles or in figuring out the economic value attached to proposed settlements of class action lawsuits. In case this story doesn't pique your interest, here are four less lengthy puzzlers to consider.

Price Protection Hurts Buyers

In the 1960s and 1970s, two American firms, General Electric and Westinghouse, were virtually the only manufacturers of large electric turbine generators, machines used by electric utilities to turn mechanical energy into electrical energy for the U.S. market.[3] In 1963, GE offered its customers "price protection." In short, GE published a price book that unambiguously determined a so-called book price for any generator it might produce, however customized. GE sold its generators on the basis of a discount from the book price: A customer would be offered a particular generator at, say, 78% of the generator's book price. Then, for the following 6 months, if GE sold any generator to any customer at a price less than 78% of book price for that generator, GE would retroactively refund the "difference" to the first customer. That is, the customer got a 6-month best-discount guarantee. GE retained the public accounting firm Peat, Marwick, Mitchell, and Company, to audit its compliance with this policy. Eventually Westinghouse responded by offering its customers virtually the same deal.

After a while, the Antitrust Division of the U.S. Department of Justice stepped in, claiming that price protection harmed the customers of GE and Westinghouse. They demanded that GE and Westinghouse refrain from this policy. The Antitrust Division was right to do so; price protection was being used in a way that harmed GE's and Westinghouse's customers enormously.

Giving Away a Monopoly

Developers of microprocessors for personal computers can, to some extent, patent their microprocessor designs. The manufacture of these chips is characterized by costs that fall with cumulative volume. So, it would seem, a

---

[3] This story is based on a Harvard Business School case, General Electric Vs. Westinghouse In Large Turbine Generators (A), Case No. 9-380-128, by Michael E. Porter. I refer to Harvard Business School and Stanford Business School cases from time to time; if you wish to order these cases, vist the Web sites http://gobi.stanford.edu/cases/ (for Stanford Business School cases) and http://harvardbusinessonline.hbsp.harvard.edu/b02/en/cases/cases_home.jhtml (for Harvard Business School cases).

developer of a microprocessor should keep a tight rein on the production of its chip. This logic was compelling to Motorola in the early days of PC manufacture; Motorola refused to license to other manufacturers the production of its family of microprocessors. In contrast, the Intel Corporation licensed the production of various of its '86 family of chips to other manufacturers, most notably Advanced Micro Devices. In some measure because Intel voluntarily gave up a cost-efficient monopoly position that it held, it won the microprocessor war against Motorola; Intel chips became the industry standard.

Flying Free to London

In 1991, it was cheaper to fly first class from San Francisco to Tokyo to London and back to San Francisco than it was to fly business class from San Francisco to Tokyo and then back to San Francisco. This was not a mistake, but part of a pricing strategy that almost certainly improved the profit of the airline involved.

Rice Imports to Japan

For many years, the Japanese government has resisted the free importation of rice from major rice producers such as the United States and Thailand. Most commentators believe this resistance is a matter of pressure-group politics. Rice farmers in Japan are an important and politically powerful constituency. It is clear that Japanese consumers have been hurt by these policies, paying much more for their rice than they would if free importation was allowed. And it is clear that Japanese rice farmers have benefited. But what is the impact on foreign rice producers? It takes a detailed look at the numbers and, in particular, at the amount of foreign rice that is allowed into Japan, but it is entirely possible that foreign rice producers are more profitable because of these restrictions.

My expectation is that, as a practicing or aspiring manager, you'd like to understand these stories and what lies behind some of their unsupported assertions. That's the point of this book. Microeconomics is a way of thinking—of organizing and studying real-life phenomena—that sheds light on each of these stories and many others we will encounter. In case you are curious,

- The GM coupons story involves *supply equals demand*, the subject of Chapters 2 and 11, *price discrimination*, from Chapter 7, and the impact of taxes on buyers and sellers, from Chapters 12 and 13.

- The GE–Westinghouse story is about implicit collusion, which is covered in Chapter 22.

- The Intel story is about credibility, covered in Chapter 23.

- Price discrimination—why it is cheaper to fly around the world than part way—is the topic of Chapter 7.

- The analysis of rice imports to Japan is discussed in Chapter 13.

If these examples don't sell you, I have a second line to try. As a practicing or aspiring manager, you are doubtless interested in understanding the various functions of management. In which case: Finance is virtually a wholly owned subsidiary of microeconomics, and Accounting is nearly so. Large chunks of Strategic Management and Marketing rely on economics. The chunks of Operations Management that use microeconomics are perhaps smaller but still significant. And Human Resource Management is at least half economics. In short, it's hard to find any important functional field of management that microeconomics doesn't touch, and in many, the touch is more like a bear hug. Understanding microeconomics is key to understanding the functions of management.

1.2. What Is Microeconomics?

A general and abstract definition of economics was offered by Paul A. Samuelson, one of leading economists of the 20th century, in a textbook that revolutionized teaching of the subject:

> Economics is the study of how men and society *choose*, with or without the use of money, to employ *scarce* productive resources, which could have alternative uses, to produce various commodities over time and distribute them for consumption, now and in the future, among various people and groups in society.[4]

Within this general definition, *micro*economics is concerned with the behavior of individual consumers and individual firms, acting and interacting in markets and in industry groups. *Macro*economics, in contrast, is concerned with the workings of national and international economies.

Since Samuelson wrote that general description, economics has evolved. His definition it still a good one, but nowadays economists increasingly emphasize "without money," nonmarket contexts, and decisions individuals

---

[4] Emphasis in the original, from P. A. Samuelson, *Economics, An Introductory Analysis*, 7th edition (New York: McGraw-Hill, 1955).

make for reasons other than consumption. In other words, the domain of economics is expanding.

Samuelson's definition is directed at the contextual subject matter of economics. But economics is equally a way of thinking; it can be characterized by answering the question, *By what means* does economics address its subject matter? A different definition that stresses means more than context is this:

> Economics is concerned with modeling the behavior of individuals and organizations—firms, nonprofit organizations, and so on—in market and nonmarket settings. Its models almost always assume that behavior is *purposeful*—directed at some clear goal—and it usually studies how diverse behaviors that have conflicting objectives are brought into *equilibrium* by market and nonmarket institutions This study is both *descriptive* (describing what happens) and *evaluative* (measuring what happens against some notion of an ideal outcome). After describing and evaluating particular institutions, economists often move on to policy *prescription*, considering how some objective might better be achieved if the institutions are modified.

That's quite a mouthful, so let's take it a piece at a time.

Purposeful Behavior

Economic models begin with entities that act purposefully. Purposeful behavior is modeled as striving to maximize some numerical measure of well-being, subject to constraints imposed by institutions and the actions of others. Among these entities can be individual consumers, firms, governments, political parties, and families, depending on the specific model and the purpose for which it is created. In this book, we spend a lot of time talking about *profit-maximizing firms* and *utility-maximizing consumers*.

Equilibrium

In most circumstances, the objectives of the different entities or actors come into conflict; resources are scarce; and more for one person means less for others. Economists model the balance that is achieved with the general notion of an *equilibrium*. Equilibria come in many different shapes and forms, which will be discussed later. For now you should understand that there is a lot more to equilibrium than "supply equals demand."

Equilibria take place within a model of an institutional setting. Most people associate economics with *market* institutions, but as already noted, economics is increasingly concerned with other institutional settings. Prominent in the list of other settings is the firm. This means that when economists model firms, the individual firm is sometimes a purposeful entity, while in other models it is the institutional setting within which diverse entities interact and come into equilibrium. Since this book is intended for managers, this duality is a major concluding theme of the book.

Evaluation and Improvement of Outcomes

Once economists identify what they think will happen in a particular context, they often examine how good or bad the outcome is and what might be done to make things better. Policy instruments they consider range from taxes and subsidies to administered prices to changing features of the institutional setting, including the provision of information.

We do relatively little of this in this book. However, managers face the pressure of public opinion and government intervention, so they, and you, should know how policy questions of this sort are addressed. For this reason, we spend time contrasting the concepts of *equity*, about which economists rarely have much to say that is useful; and *efficiency*, which economists discuss incessantly. But policy debates rarely are resolved on purely economic grounds; the forces that affect managers in this realm are more often and more powerfully political than economic. To do justice to this topic in a managerially relevant way would take another book, one that addresses political forces as well as economic arguments. So I leave this to others.[5]

1.3. Models and Analysis

Go back to the second description of economics, which began, "Economics is concerned with *modeling* the behavior of individuals and organizations—firms, nonprofit organizations, and so on—in market and nonmarket settings. Its *models* almost always assume . . ." The words *modeling* and *model* are italicized to make the point that economists work largely with models.

A dictionary definition of *model* is "a hypothetical or stylized representation of something." In economics, models can represent how people or institutions act: Firms maximize profits from a given set of feasible production plans; consumers maximize their utility subject to a budget constraint. Models can be of things like markets, for instance, the price of a good will rest at a point where supply equals demand. In all cases, models in economics are *analytical* and *simplified* depictions of reality.

The need for simplification is obvious. Models are built to help us understand very complex realities by focusing attention on what is important, so we can understand the essence or gist of the phenomenon being modeled.

---

[5] If you are interested in such a book, I recommend David Baron, *Business and Its Environment*, 4th edition (Englewood Cliffs, NJ: Prentice-Hall, 2003).

A model as complex as the reality it depicts is useless. Of course, intuiting what features are important and should therefore be built into the model takes considerable skill, which is crucial in applications: A model focused on unimportant features can be badly misleading.

Models in economics are invariably analytical. A dictionary definition is this: A model is *analytical* if it takes a whole and examines it by considering the pieces separately and then reassembles the pieces.

Suppose, for instance, you run a large chemical facility, say, an oil refinery. You have on hand various raw materials, with shipments due on various days and with some ability to buy others. You can manufacture various products, some to fill commitments but others to sell on the spot market. You face various constraints on processes and on storage capacity. The question is, How much of the various products should you make? Suppose your objective is to maximize the facility's contributions to profit made from products sold on the spot market, subject to meeting long-run constraints.

This sort of problem can be very difficult to solve, because of the complex interrelationships among the variables. But often it can be modeled fairly accurately as a linear programming problem, a mathematical model that looks separately at pieces like process constraints, raw material availability, and so forth. If modeled in this fashion, the problem can be easily solved on the computer to find the profit-maximizing plan. Moreover, it is a model that, once built, can be used to test the sensitivity of the "answer" to various assumptions; for example, what will happen if the tanker currently at sea is 36 hours late? What will happen if the spot-market price of aviation fuel falls by 5%? Because this type of model is often a very good approximation to reality, and sensitivity analysis permits the model maker to identify crucial variables so that they can be subjected to intense scrutiny, the numbers that emerge can be and are taken very seriously.

Economics also uses models so highly simplified and stylized that the numbers that emerge are not taken at all seriously. Instead, the point of the model is to sharpen intuition qualitatively, to learn "what is important and why."

Example: GM Truck Coupons—A Simple Model

It's hard to explain what this means in the abstract. But an example—a long example—makes the point vividly.

Go back to the story of GM and the truck coupons. I will build a simple model of the situation facing GM around 1993, when it proposed to issue coupons good for the purchase of its light trucks. As in all economic models, we begin with a list of simplifying assumptions:

- GM sells a single sort of light truck, costing $15,000 apiece to produce.

- GM posts a list price for this vehicle. I use P to denote this price.

Already you can see that this is going to be a highly simplified version of reality. GM sells many different sorts of light truck, whose costs of manufacture vary significantly. GM doesn't list prices for its vehicles; it sells them via a dealer network, through brokers, and nowadays via the Internet, and dealers bargain individually with individual customers.

Nonetheless, my model is based on these assumptions. This means that the numbers that emerge give, at best, a rough indication of what is going on. But the conclusion that I'll take from this model is not a number but a qualitative insight. After you become more comfortable with these sorts of models, you will agree, I expect, that replacing these assumptions with something more realistic wouldn't change this insight. To make that judgment you need to see more of the model, so back to making assumptions:

- GM has issued 4.7 million coupons that can be used in the purchase of this light truck. These coupons have been given to the owners of old GM pickups and provide, for 15 months, a discount of X for the original bearer of the coupon and x if transferred to some other buyer. In fact, $X = \$1000$ and $x = \$500$. But I'm going to build a model in which these values can be varied, so that later, in Problem 1.1, you can investigate how things change with changes in X and x.

- An organized market in these coupons is created, in which original bearers can sell their coupons to people without coupons who want to buy a GM light truck. In this market, called the *transferred-coupon market*, the seller of a coupon obtains a net Q for the coupon, while to get a coupon, a buyer must pay a net $Q + k$. The spread k between what a buyer of a coupon pays and what the seller of a coupon receives reflects things such as search costs and a broker's fee.

A key element of the model is a set of so-called demand functions, which say how many light trucks GM can expect to sell as a function of the price it posts P and the other variables just listed. The notion is that GM could choose to post a higher posted price P, but then more folks would buy from Toyota or Ford; the higher the prices GM sets for its light trucks, the fewer trucks it can sell.

When we study demand functions in detail in Chapter 4, you'll learn that, in specifying a demand function, you need to be clear about where the demand comes from and what is the market's extent, in time and geography. I assume that demand comes from any buyer of my hypothetical GM light truck, in the United States–Canadian market, for the 15-month period covered by the coupons.

In a more serious model of this situation, we might segment the demand for GM light trucks into individual buyers, fleet owners, and the government. Recall that GM, in the second proposed settlement, had different terms for these segments. You can be sure that this wasn't a matter of whimsy but done for specific reasons. However, the insights I'm building toward don't concern segmentation along these lines, so I can ignore this.

I can't ignore a different dimension of segmentation: Some potential buyers hold a coupon worth X off the purchase price or worth Q if sold— these are the owners of the old pickup trucks—while others must spend $Q+k$ to get a coupon worth x off. The second group of *third-party purchasers* may include some folks who don't realize that coupons are available and others who want a coupon but can't purchase one, because all the coupons have been used.

In my model, I assume that every original bearer of a coupon is aware of the opportunity to sell the coupon for Q if she doesn't use it and that every third-party buyer is aware that these coupons exist and is anxious to get his hands on one as long as the coupons are worth more than they cost; that is, as long as x exceeds $Q + k$. Once again, these are fairly strong assumptions, although there is some justification for them: Because the coupons are rebated by GM, individual dealers of GM light trucks are interested in getting coupons into the hands of all potential buyers. It is worth pointing out that, although my formal model ignores the existence of dealers—in the formal model, GM posts a price P and there is no haggling— the real-life existence of those dealers can and does justify some assumptions I make within the model. This happens in economic models fairly frequently: Institutional features of a market are ignored formally, but those features are nonetheless used informally to justify formal assumptions. For more on this point, see Chapter 2.

Therefore I'm down to three buyer segments: original bearers of the coupons; third-party buyers who find a coupon; and third-party buyers who do not find one because all the coupons are used up.

When members of each of those buyer segments think about buying a GM light truck, they face different *effective prices* for the GM product:

- Original bearers must pay the posted price P but get X back from their coupon. *In addition*, the original bearers of the coupons, by using their coupons in this fashion, give up the opportunity to sell their coupons for Q. So the effective price or cost to them of a GM light truck—the number they compare to the prices of Ford and Toyota products—is $P - X + Q$. (I assume that X exceeds Q; the original bearers who are going to purchase a GM light truck would rather use the coupon to purchase the truck than sell the coupon.)

In case the $+Q$ part isn't clear, let me say it differently: This represents the lost opportunity to sell the coupon rather than use it to purchase a GM light truck. Think of it this way: Suppose the alternative is a Ford light truck, the price of which is P'. In terms of out-of-pocket cash, the GM truck costs P less the rebate X, or $P - X$. The Ford, in comparison, costs P' for the truck, but a "rebate" of Q comes from selling the coupon, for a net out-of-pocket outlay of $P' - Q$. Rather than think about comparing $P - X$ with $P' - Q$, think in terms of comparing $P - X + Q$ with the (implicit to my model) price P' of the alternative product.

- Third-party buyers who find a coupon face an effective price of $P - x + Q + k$, or the posted price, less the amount of rebate the coupon provides, plus the cost of a coupon. This assumes x exceeds $Q + k$, which I need to justify.

- Third-party buyers who can't find a coupon must pay an effective price equal to the posted price P.

These effective prices determine the level of demand from each group. Now, to build the quantitative model, I have to specify the functional relationship between effective price for each group and the quantity the group purchases. More assumptions are needed:

- Over the 15-month period, if GM didn't have all these coupons to worry about, and the posted price was the effective price facing everyone, GM would expect to sell approximately 2 million light trucks. Of course, the actual level of sales depends on things like the general state of the economy; GM sells fewer trucks in a recession. That number also depends on the posted price. But I assume in my model that, if all the consumers faced an effective price of $20,000, GM would sell 2 million light trucks.

- Moreover, of those 2 million light trucks, around 30%, or 600,000, would go to the original-bearer segment, and 1.4 million would go to third-party purchasers.

- If GM raises the effective price by 1%, it can expect a 4% decline in sales. If it lowers its effective price by 1%, it can expect a 4% increase in sales. Moreover, these *elasticities of demand* apply to each segment of consumers, original-bearers and third-party buyers, separately.

- The 1%-price-change-gives-a-4%-quantity-change (in the other direction) ratio holds for all percentage changes in price from $20,000. So, for instance, a 1.5% fall in price means a 6% rise in quantity sold.

"Where," you are probably asking, "did all these numbers come from?" They are all ballpark estimates, based on a variety of sources. The 2 million vehicle figure is based on sales of GM light trucks at the time. The 1%-price-change-equals-4%-quantity-change ratio—what is called the *elasticity of demand*—is based on a simple calculation that you'll learn about in Chapter 4. The 30%-of-demand-from-original-bearers was plucked out of the air; after finishing up my model, I would want to see how sensitive my answers are to this number. Needless to say, if we worked at GM, these numbers could be obtained from the Marketing Department. As for the last of this set of assumptions, for those who know the terminology, I am assuming that demand is linear. If you don't know the terminology, you might be able to figure this out on your own, or you can wait for Chapter 4.

The last set of assumptions has made one thing clear: No third-party buyer is going to be disappointed in a search for a coupon. There are 4.7 million coupons in circulation, and at a price of $20,000, GM will sell only 2 million light trucks. To exhaust 4.7 million coupons, GM would have to increase the quantity sold by over 100%, which translates to a greater than 25% fall in price, which means a price below $15,000, at which point GM loses money on each light truck it sells. GM is unlikely to do that.

With these assumptions, we can proceed to build a quantitative model using a spreadsheet. See Figure 1.1, which depicts the Excel spreadsheet GM1.

In case you didn't read the Preface, I should warn you that this book assumes you are reasonably facile with Excel spreadsheets and, in particular, that you know how to use Solver. In places, it will make further demands on your mathematical and computing abilities; the Preface gives details. Also, all the spreadsheets I use are available in both Windows and Macintosh formats, at the Web site for this book, www.wwnorton.com/web/kreps. In case you are wondering, the pictures in the book are based on Excel 98 for the Mac.

The first block of numbers in the spreadsheet gives the variables of the model: the posted price P, the value of the coupon to an old-truck owner X, the value of a coupon to a third-party buyer x, the selling price of a coupon Q in the transferred-coupon market, and the additional amount k above Q that the buyer of a coupon must pay to get his hands on a coupon. In Figure 1.1, I entered the values $20,000, $1,000, $500, $200, and $50 for these five variables. These are trial values; they aren't necessarily the right ones.

The next piece of the spreadsheet pertains to the old-truck buyers. First

GM1

	A	B
5	P: Posted price	$20,000
6	X: value of coupon to original bearer	$1,000
7	x: value of coupon to third-party buyer	$500
8	Q: coupon price for seller in transferred-coupon market	$200
9	k: price spread in transferred-coupon market	$50
10		
11	OLD-TRUCK BUYERS	
12	Effective price they face	$19,200
13	% change in this price from $20,000	-4.00%
14	% change in quantity from 600,000	16.00%
15	total quantity bought (millions)	0.696
16	net profit to GM for one sale to this group	$4,000
17	net profit to GM for sales to this group ($ billions)	$2.78
18		
19	THIRD-PARTY BUYERS	
20	Effective price they face	$19,750
21	% change in this price from $20,000	-1.25%
22	% change in quantity from 1,400,000	5.00%
23	total quantity bought (millions)	1.47
24	net profit to GM for one sale to this group	$4,500
25	net profit to GM for sales to this group ($ billions)	$6.62
26		
27	GM SUMMARY FIGURES	
28	GM net profit for sales to both groups ($ billions)	$9.40
29	cost to GM of this program relative to benchmark	$0.60
30	($ billions)	
31		

Sheet 1 Sheet 2 Sheet 3

Figure 1.1 A spreadsheet model for GM truck coupons. This spreadsheet is used to evaluate the cost of the coupon program to GM, as a function of the variables: the price GM posts for its light truck, the rebates the coupons provide, the price to the seller of a coupon in the transferred-coupon market, and the additional amount buyers of coupons must pay in the transferred-coupon market.

we have the effective price they face for a GM light truck, or $P - X + Q$. The next cell calculates how much of a percentage change this price is from $20,000. In the next cell, we multiply by 4 and reverse the sign, to give the percentage change in the quantity this group will buy. Then we have the number of light trucks this segment of the consumer population will purchase, measured in millions. If you are unsure about the formulas that give rise to these entries, get the spreadsheet and examine them closely. The cell after that gives GM's net profit per light truck sold to these consumers; GM gets revenues of $P - X$ and has costs of $15,000. We then compute GM's net profit from sales to this segment, or profit per vehicle times the number of vehicles sold. This final entry is computed in billions of dollars.

Next, we redo these calculations for third-party buyers. Of course, the effective price for them is $P - x + Q + k$, and GM's profit per vehicle is $P - x - 15{,}000$.

Finally, we sum GM's net profits from the two segments. And, for reasons that will be supplied momentarily, we subtract this from $10 billion and call the result the *Cost to GM* of the coupon program.

Why $10 billion? Suppose there were no coupons. That is, suppose that $X = x = Q = k = 0$. Plug those values, together with $P = \$20,000$ into the spreadsheet, and you'll find that GM makes a $10 billion profit. Moreover, if we imagine GM trying different posted prices, it turns out that a posted price of $20,000 maximizes GM's profit. You can verify this with the spreadsheet by trying different posted prices (keeping $X = x = Q = k = 0$), or you can invoke Solver and ask it to maximize GM's net profit (cell B29) by varying the cell (B5) that contains P. Therefore $10 billion is GM's benchmark, and once it sets X and x above zero, to settle the class-action lawsuit, we can compute the cost of this settlement to GM by seeing how far its profit falls below this benchmark.

The variables X and x are certainly under the control of GM; they are parameters of the settlement GM is offering: $X = \$1000$ and $x = \$500$. So from here on, we use those values only. You can play around with other values for X and x in the spreadsheet; or see Problem 1.1 for some more structured play.

The variables Q and k, on the other hand, are not controlled by GM, at least not entirely. These variables are set by conditions in the market for unused coupons, a market GM might influence but can't control. In what follows, I focus on Q, and so I assume throughout that $k = \$50$; in Problem 1.2, you are asked to investigate how the value of k affects GM's profit.

Since GM can't control Q, I build three scenarios: How does GM fare if $Q = \$400$, which means that the coupons go for 80% of their face value? How does GM fare if $Q = \$200$? And how does GM fare if $Q = \$10$, which means that the coupons have almost no value in the unused coupon market?

Figure 1.2 shows the basic spreadsheet copied three times, into three successive columns. This is Sheet 2 in spreadsheet GM1. In all three columns, we set the posted price of a GM light truck to $20,000, we set $X = \$1000$, $x = \$500$, and $k = \$50$. And then we try the three values of Q.

What a difference. If $Q = \$400$, the cost of these coupons to GM according to this model is $950 million. If $Q = \$200$, the cost is only $600 million. And if $Q = \$10$, the cost is a paltry $270 million.

We're almost ready to extract the moral of this story, but not quite. So far, we've kept the posted price P at $20,000. Of course, with all these coupons flying around, the effective price to the consumer is less than $20,000. I asserted that $20,000 was the profit-maximizing price for GM to charge with no coupons; take my word for this if you don't run the numbers in the spreadsheet. But there is no reason to believe that $20,000 is best for GM

	A	B	C	D
	GM1			
7				
8	P: Posted price	$20,000	$20,000	$20,000
9	X: value of coupon to original bearer	$1,000	$1,000	$1,000
10	x: value of coupon to third-party buyer	$500	$500	$500
11	Q: coupon price for seller in transferred-coupon market	$400	$200	$10
12	k: price spread in transferred-coupon market	$50	$50	$50
13				
14	OLD-TRUCK BUYERS			
15	Effective price they face	$19,400	$19,200	$19,010
16	% change in this price from $20,000	-3.00%	-4.00%	-4.95%
17	% change in quantity from 600,000	12.00%	16.00%	19.80%
18	total quantity bought (millions)	0.672	0.696	0.7188
19	net profit to GM for one sale to this group	$4,000	$4,000	$4,000
20	net profit to GM for sales to this group ($ billions)	$2.69	$2.78	$2.88
21				
22	THIRD-PARTY BUYERS			
23	Effective price they face	$19,950	$19,750	$19,560
24	% change in this price from $20,000	-0.25%	-1.25%	-2.20%
25	% change in quantity from 1,400,000	1.00%	5.00%	8.80%
26	total quantity bought (millions)	1.414	1.47	1.5232
27	net profit to GM for one sale to this group	$4,500	$4,500	$4,500
28	net profit to GM for sales to this group ($ billions)	$6.36	$6.62	$6.85
29				
30	GM SUMMARY FIGURES			
31	GM net profit for sales to both groups ($ billions)	$9.05	$9.40	$9.73
32	cost to GM of this program relative to benchmark	$0.95	$0.60	$0.27
33	($ billions)			

| Sheet1 | **Sheet2** | Sheet4 | Sheet3 |

Figure 1.2. Three different prices for coupons in the transferred-coupon market. The results for GM depend crucially on the price of coupons in the transferred-coupon market. If the coupons command a price of $400 in that market, the cost to GM is $950 million. But, if they cost only $10 in this market, GM's net costs of the program are a mere $270 million.

under the three scenarios in Figure 1.2. So for each of these scenarios, let's answer the question, *What is the best price for GM to post?*

This is easy enough to do with Solver. First ask Solver to maximize cell B31 by varying B8. Then ask it to maximize cell C31 by varying C8. And then ask it to maximize D31 by varying D8. If you do this, you'll wind up with the spreadsheet in Figure 1.3.

This decreases the costs of the program in each case. The decrease is largest, on a percentage basis, in column D, where $Q = \$10$. In this case, GM posts a price of $20,628, and the program costs it a mere $110 million. Now the differences in cost across the three columns are even more pronounced. The cost of the program to GM if $Q = \$400$ is nearly eight times the cost if $Q = \$10$.

What's the moral? What do we learn from this extraordinarily stylized model of the light truck market? We learn that, as far as GM is concerned, a big influence on the cost of the program is Q, the price for coupons in the transferred-coupon market. GM's costs are low when Q is low and high

	A	B	C	D
7				
8	P: Posted price	$20,432	$20,532	$20,628
9	X: value of coupon to original bearer	$1,000	$1,000	$1,000
10	x: value of coupon to third-party buyer	$500	$500	$500
11	Q: coupon price for seller in transferred-coupon market	$400	$200	$10
12	k: price spread in transferred-coupon market	$50	$50	$50
13				
14	OLD-TRUCK BUYERS			
15	Effective price they face	$19,832	$19,732	$19,638
16	% change in this price from $20,000	-0.84%	-1.34%	-1.81%
17	% change in quantity from 600,000	3.36%	5.36%	7.24%
18	total quantity bought (millions)	0.62016	0.63216	0.64344
19	net profit to GM for one sale to this group	$4,432	$4,532	$4,628
20	net profit to GM for sales to this group ($ billions)	$2.75	$2.86	$2.98
21				
22	THIRD-PARTY BUYERS			
23	Effective price they face	$20,382	$20,282	$20,188
24	% change in this price from $20,000	1.91%	1.41%	0.94%
25	% change in quantity from 1,400,000	-7.64%	-5.64%	-3.76%
26	total quantity bought (millions)	1.29304	1.32104	1.34736
27	net profit to GM for one sale to this group	$4,932	$5,032	$5,128
28	net profit to GM for sales to this group ($ billions)	$6.38	$6.65	$6.91
29				
30	GM SUMMARY FIGURES			
31	GM net profit for sales to both groups ($ billions)	$9.13	$9.51	$9.89
32	cost to GM of this program relative to benchmark	$0.87	$0.49	$0.11
33	($ billions)			

Sheet1 \ **Sheet2** / Sheet4 / Sheet3 /

Figure 1.3. If GM optimizes the posted price of its light truck. When GM optimizes (maximizes its profit on) the posted price of its light truck, the costs of the coupon program decline. The decline is most dramatic when the coupons cost $10 in the transferred-coupon market; GM optimally posts of price of $20,628, and the cost of the program drops to $110 million.

when Q is high. If GM is interested in reducing the cost of this program, it wants to set things up so that Q is as low as possible.

And what about the judge, to whom the 1993 proposed settlement was first broached? He was probably looking at something like column D in Figure 1.3, seeing that, for the old truck owners, GM was giving out coupons that would have little value in the resale market and that, if the individual was willing to buy a new GM light truck, would provide an effective price of $19,638 rather than $20,000, a $362 price reduction for around 14% of the affected class (643,000 out of 4.7 million), and virtually nothing for everyone else.

Why did the judge think that column D was relevant? Why should the transferred-coupon market settle on a price of $10 or some other tiny figure? The answer is another bit of economic modeling, supply equals demand. In short, in the initial proposed settlement, GM would put 4.7 million coupons into circulation. Some 600,000 or so of those coupons would be used by the original bearers, leaving 4 million or so to be sold in the transferred-coupon market. But, at the prices GM charges for its light truck, around 1.4 million third-party buyers would want a coupon. That's a lot of supply—4 million coupons—chasing a pretty small demand—1.4 million buyers—and this means a lot of competition among sellers for a buyer. Sellers compete by undercutting one another in price, which means a very low Q and a very cheap program for GM.

So what changes in 1998? Now, there are 5.8 million coupons. But the coupons are worth dollars off any GM vehicle, except products of the Saturn Division, for a longer period of time. It's true that the coupons are worth only $250 for third-party buyers after the first 15 months. But if you look at the balance of demand for those coupons given their much wider applicability, in terms of both type of vehicle and time, you see that now demand for the coupons outstrips supply, and we expect a market price for the coupons in the neighborhood of $200 to $250. This means substantial value for the injured class at substantial cost to GM.

If you understand all this after less than 10 pages of analysis, you have a great future in economics: This story involves a lot of what is going to happen in the next 400 pages or so of this book. Don't feel bad if you don't quite get the whole story. It will make a lot more sense when you've finished Chapter 13. For now, I hope for two things:

- I hope this story and example show how, from a model that makes incredibly simplifying assumptions, you can still gain important insights. No matter how we complicate this model to make it more realistic, the basic insight will remain: For GM, the cost of this program is going to be hugely affected by the value of Q, the transferred-coupon market price of a coupon, with GM hoping for and taking actions that lead to low values of Q.

- I hope that the example whets your appetite for what is to come, by giving you a sense of the sort of real-world insights you can glean from applying economics.

1.4. Learning Economics

The final issue for this chapter is: How can you learn microeconomics efficaciously? What will it take from you?

Consider as an analogy learning how to play tennis. Assume that your objective in learning to play tennis is not simply recreational; you hope to find yourself one day at Centre Court, Wimbledon. You certainly don't begin to learn the game at Wimbledon, you don't even begin in a local tournament. Instead, you might begin by reading some material that explains the rules of the game, basic tactics, and the mechanics of the different sorts of strokes. Then you hit the courts with an instructor, who begins teaching you the basic strokes. You might hit 50 backhands in succession and then 50 forehands. At some point, you begin to rally with your instructor who, if she is a good instructor, will hit to your backhand for a while, then to your forehand, and so forth. Slowly, the rallys will become more and more realistic. You begin to play some points and then games. Meanwhile, you begin playing others recreationally, and at some point, you start entering tournaments, with Wimbledon looming off in the distance.

Of course, it isn't so linear or cut and dried as this. After your first tournament, it may be back to the practice courts to rework your backhand. The point is that, between your first purchase of a racquet and your confident stride onto Wimbledon Centre Court, you pass through a number of steps, increasing in complexity and similarity to what you do when, eventually, you play for pay.

While the analogy is strained, learning to apply economics is similar. You begin with the basics, which includes basic concepts and simple exercises. Once you have the basics down, you can move to more complex problems and cases. Eventually, you apply what you learned in the real world, recognizing that even tennis pros sometimes return to the practice court and their teachers, going back to basics from time to time.

The basic concepts and simple exercises are often best learned in terms of ultrasimple, simplistic contexts. Take the GM truck coupon story, for instance. The reason a significant price for coupons in the transferred-coupon market is so costly to GM is that this price acts "like a tax" on GM and its customers. This remains true in much more complex models and, in fact, is true in reality; it is one of the most important insights you will glean from this model. But first you have to understand how taxes work, and why and when they impose substantial costs on buyers and sellers. The GM truck coupon model, while relatively simple, is still too complex for this to be clear. So to show you what I have in mind—when we get to this point in Chapter 13—I illustrate with a tax imposed on some entirely mythical producer of an entirely mythical commodity. Once you understand the basic and somewhat abstract idea—best communicated without real-world complications, in what amounts to a parable—it is relatively easy to see the basic idea at work in the more complex but still highly simplified model of GM. Having learned the basic idea in an ultrasimple and wholly imaginary context and seen the idea adapted to the model of GM, you'll probably understand why the effect would remain in more complex models and, ultimately, in reality.

Students of economics are sometimes put off by mythical models that involve commodities called widgets or poiuyts. "This," they will say, "proves

how unrealistic economics is. Poiuyts and widgets insult my intelligence."
But, you learn basic ideas best by seeing them first in stark, simple contexts,
and the use of fictitious commodities signals that the model in question is
more a parable than a the depiction of a real-world situation. The key to
whether such parables work is whether, when you turn to real-world situations such as the GM truck coupon story, your ability to understand the
basic forces at work has been honed by studying those fictitious parables. It
will be.

"Nobody Does It That Way!"

In many of the parables we study, we suppose firms decide how much to produce by maximizing algebraic representations of their profit functions. At
one point, later in the book, we study a model of an insurance company priv-
ileged to know everything there is to know about its clients' risk-proneness
and attitudes toward risk. Inevitably when I reach these points in class,
some student, probably expressing the opinion of many in the classroom,
objects that no firm really "does it" that way, because no firm has the sort
of information the firm in my model possesses. If no firm really does it that
way, why bother to study the model? Why not tell you how it's really done?

The reason why not is simple. How it is really done is usually extraordinarily complex, reflecting the immense complexities of the real world. If
we leapt immediately to a real-life application, you would have no clue as to
what was going on or what basic forces were at work. By first studying the
effect in parable form, you can learn the basics. Then, in real-life settings,
you can apply what you now understand.

While you are learning to play tennis, a match against the reigning Wimbledon champion isn't going to teach you much except how to lose. Hitting
50 consecutive forehands is the way to start. I have yet to see a match at
Wimbledon where a player hits 50 consecutive forehands. Nobody "does
it" that way on Wimbledon Centre Court. But to get to Centre Court, hitting
50 consecutive forehands is a very useful exercise.

Reading versus Doing: The *Student's Companion*

Imagine your tennis instructor had you read about the theory of backhand
and forehand, the rules of the game, and strategy and tactics. To supplement
this, she had you watch some matches involving tennis greats. In fact, she
played tapes of those matches for you and spent time going over particular
points in slow motion, dissecting both the mechanics and the strategems
employed. Then she sent you out to play in a tournament.

You can learn a lot from reading theory, and you can learn more by
reading about the analyses and actions of others. But watching economics is

like watching tennis. It is nowhere near a substitute for doing it. You should learn theory, read about applications, and then work on some "problems" yourself, ranging from simple exercises to more complex problems to, finally, trying your hand at quite complex exercises. Eventually, you are ready to take on the real world.

In this textbook, you don't take on the real world. No book can do that. But the jump from reading to the real world is large, and you can bridge the gap with simple problems, complex problems, and even a case study or two.

This book has the theory—and a few real-life analyses as well as a selection of problems at the end of each chapter. Accompanying this book is a *Student's Companion*, which provides you with solutions to some of those problems. The *Companion* also provides some "bonus" material—things omitted from the text because they are digressions or not quite the thing for a first-time reader—and an appendix which reviews—or teaches you—the small amount of calculus required. I can't imagine learning microeconomics from this textbook without doing the problems at the end of each chapter or going step-by-step over their solutions in the *Companion*. Get a copy of the *Companion* and complement your reading of the theory here by doing the problems.

Executive Summary

- Economics is concerned with modeling the behavior of individuals and organizations, such as firms, nonprofit organizations, and so on, in market and nonmarket settings. Its models almost always assume that behavior is *purposeful*—directed at some clear goal—and it usually studies how diverse behaviors that have conflicting objectives are brought into *equilibrium* by market and nonmarket institutions This study is both *descriptive* and *evaluative*. And after describing and evaluating particular institutions, economists often move on to policy *prescription*, considering how some objective might better be achieved if the institutions are modified.

- Examples as well as the list of functional specialties that use economics show that this subject should be of enormous interest to managers.

- Economics works through analytical models, simplified depictions of reality that take a situation, examine and model its pieces, and then reassemble. Sometimes those models result in numerical "answers," where the numbers are meant to be taken seriously. Sometimes—for more highly stylized models—the model generates a qualitative rather than a quantitative insight. Other models are purely parables—stories about made-up commodities bought and sold in made-up markets—that illustrate some basic concept in a stark setting.

- In the parable sort of model, firms sometimes solve problems in ways that are beyond the capabilities of real-life firms. Real firms don't always "do it" in the fashion some of our models suppose, but the models are still useful if real firm behavior approximates the assumed behavior and if the model teaches something about the fundamental economics of the situation being modeled.

- Reading is fine, but doing simple exercises, more complex problems, really complex problems, and full-blown cases is essential to mastering this subject. In addition to reading the theory, you must actively consume the problems at the end of chapters and their solutions in the *Student's Companion*.

Problems

Before giving you the problems, a warning: In Problems 1.1 and 1.2, as well as in many other places in this book, you are asked to optimize some measure of performance, such as profit, in terms of one or more variables, such as the posted price P, for a variety of different parameterizations of the model. Using Solver to do the optimizing would seem to mean running Solver as many times as you vary the parameters. You often can employ a neat trick that allows you to call up Solver only once and optimize in all the different scenarios simultaneously. The trick is described at the start of the section *Solutions to Problems—Chapter 1* in the *Student's Companion*; to save time, look at this before you tackle these two problems.

1.1 Using the basic spreadsheet GM1, consider the impact of different face values for the coupons on GM. Specifically, consider the following three scenarios, in addition to the case considered in the text, where the coupon was worth $1000 off to original bearers and $500 off to third-party buyers:

- Scenario 1: The coupons are worth $1000 off for all parties.

- Scenario 2: The coupons are worth $2000 off for original holders and $1500 off for third-party buyers.

- Scenario 3: The coupons are worth $1000 off for original holders and $200 off for third-party buyers.

You may assume that Q, the price in the transferred-coupon market, is $10 in all cases and k, the extra cost of transferring a coupon, is $50. Also, when you do your analysis, assume that GM is able to optimize the posted price P; that is, it can always choose the level P that maximizes its profit. After you conclude your analysis, you should be able to fill in the following sentences:

> Assuming the cost of transferred-coupons in the transferred-coupon market is close to 0, in terms of the two face values X and x of the

coupons, what matters to GM is _____, because _____. And, in terms of the values of X and x, the cost to GM of the coupon program increases when _____.

1.2 Using the basic spreadsheet GM1, consider the impact on GM of different values of the parameter k, the extra or frictional cost of transferring a coupon. Do this by assuming Q = $10, X = $1000, and x = $500, and varying k. Look at the three cases k = $5, k = $50, and k = $100. As in Problem 1.1, assume that GM can optimize the posted price P. Can you offer a qualitative explanation of the pattern you see here?

2. The Most Famous Picture in Economics

Supply equals demand is the most famous expression in economics, and the picture that goes with it is economics' most famous picture. This fame is well deserved. The expression and picture encapsulate powerful and empirically relevant concepts. In this chapter, we explore the expression and picture (1) because of their cardinal importance, (2) because they will allow us to continue the discussion from the last chapter about how economists build and use models, and (3) to advance your understanding of the GM truck coupon story.

In Chapter 1, we learned that a key variable affecting the cost to GM of the truck coupons was the price Q the coupons would command in the transferred-coupon market. If Q were small, the cost of the program to GM would be relatively small. If Q increased, so would the cost of the program to GM.

We asserted that, under the conditions of the original proposal of 1993, Q would be quite low; therefore the judge was right to reject the proposal. The judge was probably more interested in the value to the plaintiffs of the settlement than in the cost to GM, but in this case, the two go hand in hand.

This second assertion—that the price of a coupon in the transferred-coupon market would be quite low—is justified by comparing the large number of coupons in circulation and the significantly smaller number of uses to which they could be put. This is a simple application of one of the most famous and powerful tools in the economist's arsenal, the invocation of the maxim that, in a competitive market, price will settle where supply equals demand or, in shortened form, that *supply equals demand*.

Most people exposed to economics come away with the strong impression that this maxim is the heart and soul of microeconomics. This overstates the case, but supply equals demand and its "picture," Figure 2.1, are fundamental to economics.

I don't think it is a good idea to use this bit of economics until you understand where supply and demand come from and what they represent. Getting to that point will take a few hundred pages. But I found, in writing this book, that students and some instructors get nervous if the picture isn't discussed right up front. Doing so gives me the opportunity to say a few more things about models in economics, and we already have the GM truck coupon story on the table, so it won't hurt to spend some time on this subject.

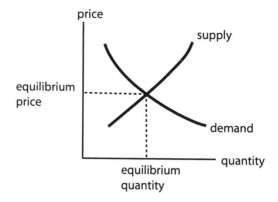

Figure 2.1. Supply, demand, and equilibrium.

2.1. Supply and Demand

There can be little doubt that Figure 2.1 is the most famous picture in economics. It is what every semi-knowledgeable person thinks of when he or she thinks of economics. If you've never seen this picture before, you've led a sheltered life. But what does it mean?

This picture graphs two functions, the *supply* and *demand functions*. Imagine some commodity, such as wheat, is bought and sold by many people. The good in question is sufficiently uniform in characteristics so that we are comfortable thinking that a standard amount of it is the same from one buyer or seller to the next. Also, all buyers and sellers are aware of the best available price for the item; either trades take place in a single centralized market, or lots of information is available about the price of wheat in the local or regional markets that make up the whole. We have to delimit this market in time and space, so think about the market for wheat in, say, the European Community during a particular week. The time and spatial limits can't be so large that they do violence to the ideas that the good is a commodity—wheat traded in January isn't the same as wheat traded in July, so six months would be too long—and that there is a single price for the good.

Of course, the notions that the good in question is completely uniform and has a uniform price are modeling abstractions that rarely, if ever, match reality perfectly. The model is valuable only to the extent that it gives useful insights or predictions, even if its assumptions hold only approximately.

The demand function, then, is a function that records, for each possible price of the good, the total amount buyers of the good would choose to purchase. We write $D(p)$ for this function. The notion is that, as the price changes, the amount that buyers want to buy changes; presumably the higher the price, the less buyers want to purchase, either going without or substituting other products.

For each possible price, the supply function records the total amount that sellers of the good would choose to sell. Presumably, the higher the price, the more sellers would choose to sell. We write $S(p)$ for this function.

These two functions are superimposed on a single set of axes, as in Figure 2.1. You are probably used to graphing functions where the independent variable is graphed on the abscissa (horizontal axis) and the value of the function, or the dependent variable, is graphed on the ordinate (vertical axis). But in economics, tradition always puts price on the vertical axis. So, in reading Figure 2.1 as a picture of the demand and supply functions, you have three choices: (1) Turn your head 90°, (2) turn the book 90°, or (3) get used to reading functions where the variable appears on the ordinate and the value of the function on the abscissa.

2.2. Equilibrium

Suppose that, somehow, a price for the good was set. Where could it be set that would leave everyone happy? If this price p is at a point where supply exceeds demand, or $S(p) > D(p)$, more would be offered for sale than would be bought. Some of the good would sit on shelves or in warehouses or silos, unwanted and unpurchased. Sellers with excess supply on their shelves would try to unload this merchandise by holding a sale, and prices would fall. On the other hand, if the price p is at a point where demand exceeds supply, or $D(p) > S(p)$, then the shelves would empty and customers would still come in looking for the good. Some buyers might go to the sellers and offer to pay more than p, to guarantee that they get some of this good. Some sellers might get the bright idea that they could charge a slightly higher price and still sell the amount they want. So the price p would rise. Only if the price p is at a level where supply equals demand, or $S(p) = D(p)$, would markets clear. At that price, just as much would be desired for purchase as would be supplied. We call this price p the *equilibrium price* and the corresponding quantity $x = S(p) = D(p)$ the *equilibrium quantity*. Note well, if supply is an increasing function of price and demand is a decreasing function, then there will be at most one equilibrium price and quantity.

2.3. (How) Does It Really Work?
Market Institutions and Figure 2.1

Do markets really reach a price where supply equals demand? Do they work in the way just described? If not, how do they work? How do the answers to these questions vary with the institutional features of the market?

Put it this way. The demand function records how much buyers want to buy at each price, once they know the price. The supply function records how much sellers want to sell at each price, once they know the price. But which comes first, the equilibrium price or supply and demand decisions by sellers and buyers? The first two sentences of this paragraph seem to say that the price comes first; folks see the price and decide how much to supply and demand. But the price is the result of supply and demand decisions of individuals. Presumably, there is some dynamic process of equilibration in the market. Whatever it is, Figure 2.1 tells us nothing about it.

Economists have enormous faith in markets. They believe that in most cases, *if* a large number of people want to purchase the item and a large number of people want to sell, *if* the item is a commodity item in the sense that it doesn't matter to buyer/seller from whom/to whom the item is bought/sold, and *if* buyers and sellers have access to relatively good information about what is happening with other buyers and sellers, *then* most transactions will take place at or near the price where supply equals demand. The source of their faith is sometimes the result of their upbringing as economists; that's what the books say, so it must be true. But substantial empirical evidence supports this belief. The evidence doesn't suggest that *price will reach a point where supply equals demand* is a law of nature, but it does suggest that, when the preceding conditions are met, it comes close to being a law of nature.

The evidence comes from both real life and experimentally staged markets. Here is a taste of what the experimental data look like.[1]

An Experimental Market

Some number of participants, on the order of 10 to 20, are seated in cubicles in front of computer terminals. It is explained to them that they are about to participate in a market for a mythical good, known as a *poiuyt*. Some of them are given poiuyts to sell, and others are given incentives to buy and hold poiuyts. All are given money with which to undertake transactions, and the market is opened.

If you looked at the computer terminal of one of the participants at a given point in time, you would find two sorts of data. The computer tells the participant how much money she has and how many poiuyts she owns. The computer also tells the participant what are the highest *bid* and the lowest *ask* for a poiuyt currently on the books. A bid is an offer by some participant

---

[1] To keep the discussion simple, I concoct a simplified version of real experimental markets here. If you want to see what the real thing looks like, try the article referenced in Figure 2.3 or C. R. Plott and V. L. Smith, "An Experimental Examination of Two Exchange Institutions," *Review of Economic Studies*, Vol. 45, 1978, 133–53.

to buy a poiuyt; an ask is the amount the owner of a poiuyt requires to sell that poiuyt. The computer prevents each participant from bidding more money than he or she has and from entering an ask with no poiuyt to sell.

The participants have up to four options, besides doing nothing. Someone who wishes to buy a poiuyt and has enough money on account to increase the current bid may type B and the amount he wishes to bid. If he has the resources to make this bid and if his bid is higher than the current high bid, his bid replaces the high bid on all the screens. If the participant has a poiuyt in inventory and is willing to ask for less than the currently posted ask, she can type A and the amount she is asking, and the new, lower ask is recorded on all the screens. If she wishes to sell and has at least one poiuyt, she can also type S for sell, and one of her poiuyts is sold to whoever posted the currently posted bid; her inventory is reduced by one and the bidder's is increased by one, while her cash level is increased and his is decreased by the bid amount. Finally, someone who wishes to buy and is willing and able to pay the current ask can type P for purchase; and the computer records the shift in poiuyts and money. After any transaction—after someone sells or purchases—the current bid and ask on all the screens go blank, and they remain that way until someone restarts the process by typing A and an asked amount or B and a bid amount.

This continues for some time. In some experiments, a time limit is imposed, in which case the computer may include a countdown clock so that participants can keep track. In other cases, the market stays open until some set length of time, like 30 seconds, passes with no activity; no one improves the current bid and ask and no one purchases or sells.

At the outset, some participants are given an initial endowment of money. Some are given endowments of poiuyts: Some may be given six poiuyts, others two, and still others none. Those with poiuyts have no incentive to hold on to them; at the end of the trading session, they take home whatever money they have accumulated through trading. Those who are not given poiuyts are given incentives to hold them, in messages of the following sort:

> At the start of trading you are credited with $5.00 with which you may begin to buy and later, if you wish, sell poiuyts. You start with no poiuyts. If, at the end of the trading session, you hold one poiuyt you will be given $1 in addition to your final money balance. If you hold two poiuyts, you will be given $1.50 in addition to your money balance. If you hold three or more, you will be given $1.75 in addition to your money balance.

For completeness, let me also give an example of the type of message that is given to a seller of poiuyts:

At the start of trading you are credited with $1.00 with which you may begin to buy and sell poiuyts. You also start with four poiuyts. At the end of the trading session, you will be given the amount of your final money balance—poiuyts are worthless to you except insofar as you can sell them to someone else for money.

Participants are told only the general "rules" of the market and their own characteristics as a buyer or seller. They do not know how many poiuyts are outstanding in the market, or what values others may attach to poiuyts. With just this much information, they are told to engage in computer-mediated trading for, say, 15 minutes. The market is then restarted; each participant is restored to his or her initial endowment, and they trade again. And again, and again. At the end of each 15-minute period, the participants are paid according to how they did in that period, by the schemes just outlined.

This is a fairly complex marketplace. Perhaps the quick explanation given doesn't convey precisely what is going on. In actual stagings of this sort of marketplace, the explanations given to participants beforehand are much longer and clearer, and it still takes a few trading periods before some of the participants understand how the system works.

In this context, Figure 2.1 can be used to help predict what would happen if we let the market run. Figure 2.1 has nothing to do with the institutional details of this market: It says nothing about the fact that there will be bids and asks or that participants will have to decide on their own when to make a transaction. It doesn't relate to the fact that the transactions are computer mediated. Even so, as an adherent to the doctrine of economics, I am prepared to hypothesize:

> Several rounds of trading may be necessary for participants to learn the rules of the market and, at the same time, get a sense of the range of prices at which purchases and sales can be made. After several rounds, however, almost all trades will take place at very close to a single price, the price predicted by a model resembling Figure 2.1 and based on the data of the market; virtually all poiuyts will change hands, bought by subjects who value the poiuyts at more than this single price.

To make this hypothesis precise, let me explain how we would build a model of the sort in Figure 2.1 from data on this type of market. To keep matters simple, suppose that there are only six participants in the market. Three of the six are given a positive number of poiuyts; one is given one poiuyt, one is given two, and the third is given four. Three of the six are given no poiuyts, but instead are told:

You begin with $5. One poiuyt held at the end is worth $1 to you, two are worth $1.50, three are worth $1.80, and four or more are worth $1.85.

You begin with $5. One poiuyt held at the end is worth $1 to you, two are worth $1.30, three are worth $1.50, and four or more will be worth $1.60.

You begin with $5. One poiuyt held at the end is worth $.50 to you, two are worth $1.00, three or more are worth $1.50.

Note that we have three different statements here, one for each of the three participants who begin with no poiuyts to sell.

From these data, we wish to construct supply and demand schedules of the sort in Figure 2.1. Supply is the easiest: The question is, How many poiuyts would the three sellers be willing to sell if the price of each poiuyt were, say, $1? Since each poiuyt left unsold is worthless to any seller, the answer is all seven. What if the price per poiuyt were $.50? Same answer, all seven. And all seven would willingly be sold if the price per poiuyt were $.10. At any (positive) price, the three sellers would wish to sell their poiuyts, since unsold poiuyts are worthless to them. Hence the *supply schedule* for this market is as given in Figure 2.2(a); a vertical line at the quantity seven, interpreted as, No matter what is the price, seven poiuyts are supplied.

What about demand? Suppose the price per poiuyt is $0.90. How many poiuyts would the three demanders wish to buy? Take them one by one. The first would buy one poiuyt at this price, because the first poiuyt she purchases is worth $1.00 to her—she'll be ahead by $0.10 if she buys this poiuyt for $0.90. But, if she buys two poiuyts for $1.80 total, together they are worth only $1.50, and she'll be $0.30 behind. The second buyer will also purchase one poiuyt at a price of $0.90, and the third won't purchase any. At the price of $0.90, two poiuyts are demanded.

Suppose the price per poiuyt is $0.45. Now the first buyer computes: "If I buy one poiuyt at $0.45, I'm ahead by $0.55; if I buy two, at a total cost of $0.90, I'm ahead by $1.50 − $0.90 = $0.60. If I buy three, I'm ahead by $1.80 − (3)($0.45) = $1.80 − $1.35 = $0.55, and if I buy four, I'm ahead by $1.85 − (4)($0.45) = $0.05." So at a price per poiuyt of $0.45, the first buyer will optimally purchase two. The second buyer will purchase one, and the third will purchase three. So total demand at a price per poiuyt of $0.45 is $2 + 1 + 3 = 6$.

See if you can conclude that at a price of $0.15, demand will be for nine units. The logic is the same for every possible price, giving us the demand function shown in Figure 2.2(b). (A problem arises with prices such as $0.30, at which the quantity demanded is indeterminate because one or more of

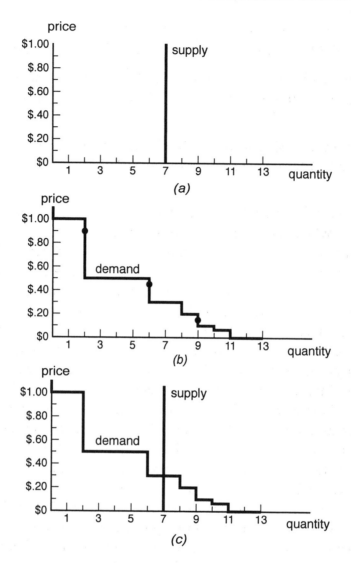

Figure 2.2. Supply and demand in an experimental market. Supply and demand functions constructed from the data in the text are shown in panels a and b, and superimposed in panel c. We see the prediction of supply equals demand: Seven poiuyts should change hands, at a price of $0.30 each.

the buyers is indifferent between buying a unit or not at that price. The flat spots in the demand curve record these points; at $0.30, say, demand could be seven units or eight.)

Now in accordance with the model of Figure 2.1, I superimpose Figures 2.2(a) and 2.2(b), in Figure 2.2(c). Note that the equilibrium prediction—the points of intersection of the supply and demand schedules—is at the price $0.30 per poiuyt and a quantity of seven poiuyts. If our general hypothesis about this sort of market is correct, then in this particular market we would make the following prediction:

> After a few rounds of trading in which participants learn both about this market mechanism and the characteristics of this market, trades will take place at prices around $0.30 apiece, all seven poiuyts will change hands, and moreover, the first demander will purchase two or three poiuyts, the second will purchase two or one, and the third will purchase three.

What do you think? Will this work? Will the hypothesis be borne out or will it be rejected by the data?

I made up the data in this example, so I can't offer a definitive answer to these questions. But markets of these sorts have been staged, under rules like those given here and under many different rules, such as allowing only sellers to post asking prices or only buyers to post bids, where the auction is conducted orally instead of via computers, and so on. And— what is one of the strongest findings in experimental economics—Figure 2.1 works, over and over again, in all sorts of environments, with all sorts of subjects. A typical picture from papers that report on this sort of experiment is reproduced in Figure 2.3. On the left of the figure are the supply and demand curves that Vernon Smith induced experimentally. Note that unlike in the previous example, in Smith's experiment the supply schedule is not perfectly vertical. Supply intersects demand at a price of $6.85 per item, with an equilibrium quantity of 11 or 12 units. Moving on, you see the results of eight periods of trading. (Ignore the numbers in the second row for a moment.) For each of the eight periods, you see a succession of dots. These record the prices at which trades took place, for the number of trades that took place in the period. So, in the first period, the first trade was at a price

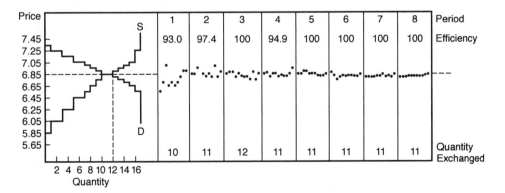

Figure 2.3. Typical experimental results. (Source: V. L. Smith, "Markets as Economizers of Information: Experimental Examination of the 'Hayek Hypothesis,'" *Economic Inquiry*, Vol. 20, April 1982, 165–79, Fig. 2. Reprinted here by permission of Oxford University Press.)

of $6.55, the second at $6.70, the third at $6.95, the fourth at $6.65, and so on. There are 10 dots, meaning that 10 units changed hands during this period; this is indicated by the number 10 at the bottom of the column. In the second period prices bounced around a bit—note that the fourth trade took place at around $6.20—and in the third, fourth, and sixth periods there is a bit of dispersion, but by period 8 the equilibrium prediction of *all trades close to $6.85 and 11 or 12 trades per period* is clearly borne out. The second row of numbers gives a numerical measure of whether the units that changed hands wound up in the right hands; a level of 100 means that they did, while the other levels (93.0, 97.4, 94.9) reflect less than ideal exchanges. While this is but one experiment with one group of subjects, one trading environment, and one set of "endowments and incentives," the picture shown in Figure 2.3 is entirely typical of what appears in lots of experiments of this sort.

Real-Life Examples

At some point in the preceding subsection, it may have occurred to you that experimental markets aren't all that interesting, unless they replicate what happens in real life. They do. Figure 2.1 also works in real-life markets. Prominent examples include commercial and retail rental markets in major metropolitan areas and markets in commodity foods and metals. These are particularly interesting cases because they are markets subject to sudden and dramatic swings in equilibrium prices as conditions of supply or demand shift. For instance, in commercial real estate, the "arrival" of a large downtown office building project can dramatically decrease office rental rates as the market moves from a condition of tight supply to over-supply. In commodity foodstuffs markets, a suddenly failed harvest or large negotiated export agreement can send prices skyrocketing.

The Harvard Business School case, "The Oil Tanker Shipping Industry,"[2] gives details of another interesting example. The "item" being bought and sold is the transportation of crude oil from the Persian Gulf to northern European ports such as Rotterdam. Some crude oil shipped along this route is carried by major oil refining companies in ships that they own, maintain, and manage. More is carried by so-called time-chartered shipping; a major refiner charters, for a period of time, an independently operated vessel. But a sizeable residual of the trade is carried in so-called spot charters: If you wish to ship a load of crude, brokers will match you with an independent vessel looking for cargo. The cost of shipping is a relatively small portion of the value of the cargo, so someone looking for a charter is usually willing to pay whatever it takes to move that cargo from the Persian Gulf to northern

---

[2] Harvard Business School case HBS 9-394-034

Europe. Demand for shipping moves around somewhat unpredictably; a sudden cold snap in Europe can temporarily increase demand dramatically. Supply is more complex; crewed ships will take on cargoes as long as the fee covers their marginal costs of making the voyage, largely the cost of fuel and voyage-specific insurance. Ship operators have some ability to increase supply by speeding up. Speeding up a ship leads to higher voyage costs, mainly from increased fuel consumption, but if fees rise enough, it becomes worthwhile to increase speed, allowing for more voyages and more fees. If fees rise high enough, there is also a reserve of laid-up ships that can be brought back into service.

It is impossible to do justice in a single paragraph to this fascinating industry. But if you wish to see a real-life example where supply equals demand is clearly on view, the case is highly recommended. (Warning: This is not a simple case, and most readers will be better able to tackle it after completing Chapter 11. Instructors interested in covering this case in class should visit the *Instructors' Website.*)

Institutions of the Marketplace

To reiterate, the model of Figure 2.1, supply equals demand, is simultaneously based on and entirely misses important institutional details of the marketplace. In the oil tanker shipping industry, the so-called market makers are shipping brokers in New York City who run up enormous phone bills from keeping in close contact with and making matches between clients who need to move shipments of crude oil and operators of independent tankers. Someone wishing to move a load of crude might call several brokers in search of the best deal—although it is a small percentage of the value of the cargo, tens of thousands of dollars are at stake—and competition among the brokers keeps information available and markets cleared.

In other cases, markets are made through different means; information might be collected and diffused by a central agency, through classified ads in newspapers, or by flyers on supermarket bulletin boards. Securities and futures markets, which are exemplars of supply equals demand, include many sorts of institutions: The New York Stock Exchange uses a so-called specialist system where, with a few exceptions, a single trader is charged with the task of making a liquid market; the Chicago Board of Trade uses open outcry; and NASDAQ uses a computer-driven marketplace. (Financial markets are complex exemplars of supply equals demand, because the value of the object being traded depends on expectations of future prices. That's one reason that Finance is a subject in its own right.) In the gross prediction of Figure 2.1, that price will settle to a point where supply equals demand, all these market institutions do fairly well.

This is not to say that the institutions of a marketplace don't matter or are unimportant. They affect whether the market functions smoothly and achieves the theoretical ideal of getting a price where supply equals demand. Even in cases where the ideal is achieved, it is achieved only approximately, and those who make the market—who bring buyers and sellers together at approximately a single price—can make a very good living by their brokerage or market-making activities.

2.4. Back to the GM Truck Coupons

In our analysis of the GM truck coupons in the last chapter, we built a model in which the coupons had a price-to-transfer Q, and we concluded that the cost to GM of the program would depend crucially on the level of Q. Specifically, if Q is at or near 0, the program would cost GM very little, but if Q is substantial, the program is quite costly. Having arrived at that conclusion, I asserted that the difference between the 1993 proposal and the eventual settlement is the value of Q; in the 1993 proposal, Q would have been close to 0; in the settlement, it will be substantial. The eventual settlement, where the rebate provided by the coupon changes as time passes, complicates the story somewhat, so in what follows I will concentrate on my model of what would have been, had the 1993 proposal gone into effect.

The assertion that Q would have been close to 0 compounds a lot of assumptions. One assumption that is so implicit it may have escaped your notice is that a market in transferred-coupons would be established; both the original bearers of the coupons and third-party buyers of the relevant GM vehicles would know where to buy and sell these pieces of paper.

Of course my model also made very strong simplifying assumptions, such as that GM sells a single generic light truck, GM posts a price for the truck P for the entire period, the cost of manufacture of this generic truck is $15,000, and so forth. But these were simplifying assumptions only; the main conclusions of the model wouldn't change very much if we built a more realistic model along these lines. This is different than my assumptions that a market in coupons will be established, with a recognized price Q for a coupon. Those assumptions are basic to my analysis.

Why do I believe that a market in coupons would be established? The coupons have no value to original truck owners, unless they are used to purchase a truck or are transferred. They are worth $500 to folks who want to buy a GM light truck. Economists believe, on the basis of both doctrine and evidence, that when someone owns something that is of less value to him than it is to someone without the item, a way will be found to realize the gains from trade. Well, that's going too far. Later in the book, especially in Chapters 18 and 19, we see why this might fail. But those reasons do not apply to GM truck coupons. Few economists will disagree with the assertion that someone, and probably several someones, is going to create a market in GM truck coupons. There is just too much in the way of gains from trade for this not to happen. And, since that someone will benefit by increasing the size of the market she creates, she will be sure to advertise its existence effectively. In the end, something approximating a market price Q for coupons will be established.

Having made the assumptions that a market in coupons will be created and that a price Q per coupon will emerge at which supply of coupons will approximate the demand for them, we can enlist Figure 2.1 to predict what Q will be. In other words, we can establish, based on conditions of supply and demand, whether Q will be close to 0 or a substantial positive amount.

Both supply and demand depend on Q and on two other parameters, the price P that GM posts for its light trucks, and the transaction cost k that buyers of coupons must pay in addition to Q to secure a coupon. To use Figure 2.1, we treat P and k as fixed parameters of the model. We are in essence finding what Q will be as a function of P and k, after which we will try to figure out, as we did in the last chapter, what price P GM will set and, to the extent anyone controls k, what value of k is likely to emerge.

Assume P and k are given. Demand is easier. A third-party buyer holding a coupon pays $P - 500 + Q + k$ for his light truck. Alternatively, he pays P if he buys without a coupon. So he will want a coupon as long as $Q + k < \$500$ or $Q < \$500 - k$. Of course, if the reverse inequality holds, he has no desire for a coupon. Thus *demand for coupons is 0 if $Q > \$500 - k$, and it equals the number of third-party sales of GM light trucks, if $Q < \$500 - k$.* Assuming $Q < \$500 - k$, the number of third-party sales of trucks depends on P, Q, and k. The bigger any of these numbers is, the more a truck costs a buyer, so the smaller is the number of trucks purchased. Because I know how this story is going to come out, I know that the crucial number to figure out is an upper bound on the number of third-party sales. Therefore we want to determine demand for GM light trucks by third-party buyers for low values of P, Q, and k. There is no way that GM will set P below \$15,500—given the rebates, it would lose money on every truck sold if P went any lower— and Q and k can't get any lower than 0, so an upper bound on demand for coupons is the number of sales of GM light trucks to third-party buyers if $P = \$15,500$, $Q = 0$, and $k = 0$, which, the spreadsheet GM1 can tell you, is 2.8 million.

In a picture, the demand function looks like Figure 2.4(a): Fixing P and k, demand is 0 if Q exceeds $\$500 - k$; and demand is strictly positive if Q is less than $\$500 - k$, rising somewhat as Q falls. The level of demand at

$Q = 0$, denoted by D_0, depends on the precise values of P and k, but as long as $P \geq \$15,\!500$, this value is no larger than 2.8 million. For the more reasonable value of $P = \$20,\!500$ and for $k = 0$, it is 1.4 million.

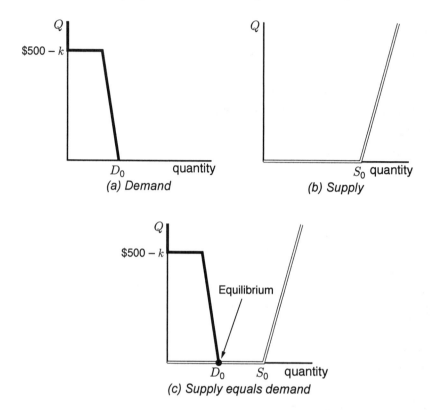

Figure 2.4. *Supply equals demand in the transferred-coupon market, under the terms of the 1993 proposed settlement.* Panels a and b depict demand for and supply of coupons to the transferred-coupon market as a function of the price of the coupons Q, for fixed values of the price GM charges for its light trucks P and the extra cost k that buyers of coupons must pay to procure a coupon. See the text for explanation of and bounds on the quantities D_0 and S_0. Superimposing supply and demand gives panel c and the conclusion: The equilibrium price for coupons in the transferred-coupon market will be $Q = 0$.

As for supply, at any price $Q > 0$, the holder of a coupon is either going to sell it or use it to buy a GM light truck. With 4.7 million coupons in circulation, the number of coupons supplied, given P and as a function of Q, is 4.7 million less the demand for GM light trucks by old truck owners, as a function of Q and P. This holds until Q exceeds \$1000, at which point all the holders of coupons want to sell them instead of using them for a rebate. Demand for GM light trucks falls as either Q or P rises, and it is is maximized—and supply of coupons to the transferred-coupon market is miminized—when $Q = 0$ and P is as small as it reasonably can be. We stick to the lower bound on P used before, $P = \$15,500$, on the grounds that GM would never post a price lower than this. At $Q = 0$ and $P = \$15,500$, the spreadsheet tells us that demand by original truck owners for GM light trucks is 1.26 million. Therefore supply at this Q and P is $4.7 - 1.26 = 3.44$ million. Of course, this is just a lower bound on supply. For instance, if P is the eminently more reasonable \$20,500 and $Q = 0$, demand for GM light trucks by original truck owners is 660,000 according to the spreadsheet, so supply of coupons to the transferred-coupon market is $4.7 - 0.66 = 4.04$ million. The picture of supply, then, is Figure 2.4(b).

To find where supply equals demand, we superimpose Figures 2.4(a) and 2.4(b), getting 2.4(c). The two bounds we established tell the tale: Demand at any price won't exceed 2.8 million—a figure of 1.4 million is a lot more reasonable—and supply at any positive price will never be less than 3.44 million, with 4.04 million a lot more reasonable. For supply to equal demand, we need $Q = 0$, which, when combined with the analysis we performed in the last chapter, justifies the ruling of the judge in 1993 that the original terms of the settlement gave virtually no value to the original truck owners.

What changes with the alterations in the proposed settlement? Because more coupons are put in circulation, supply may go up. Supply could go down, because there is a greater likelihood that old truck owners will want to use the coupons themselves, but because the coupons can be used for a longer period of time and for any GM product except Saturns, demand for the coupons really soars. The picture of the demand function is complex, because the value of the coupon changes after 15 months. But, if a careful analysis is undertaken, it is clear that under the new terms, supply equals demand predicts a price Q substantially above 0 and, in fact, at $\$250 - k$ or more.

2.5. Supply Equals Demand as a Model

Supply equals demand, illustrated in Figure 2.1, is a perfect example of an economic model. It is a simplified description of a much more complex reality that leads to predictions, albeit at a somewhat gross level, about that reality. Indeed, when it comes to the institutions of the marketplace, Figure 2.1 isn't so much a simplified description as a shoulder shrug concerning those institutions; it simply takes the institutions for granted.

So, to return to the fundamental question, if levels of supply and demand are conditioned on equilibrium price, and equilibrium price depends on supply and demand, which comes first? The answer is a definite deep sigh. In many markets, *something* gets the price to adjust to a level where supply equals demand. But Figure 2.1 tells us nothing about what that something is.

More precisely, Figure 2.1 depends crucially on that something, whatever it is, while having absolutely nothing to say to resolve the mystery. Whenever we use Figure 2.1, for instance in the case of GM and the truck coupons, we must ask ourselves: *Are the detailed conditions—market institutions, availability of information, uniformity of the item for sale, numbers of buyers and sellers— such that we can trust a simple-minded application of the picture?* And, if the conditions seem propitious, does the model work, empirically? The answers are *Yes* in a surprisingly wide variety of markets, which is why Figure 2.1 is indeed the most famous picture in economics.

Executive Summary

- The most famous picture in economics is the picture of supply equals demand, Figure 2.1.

- The picture is made up of two functions, supply and demand, which are the subject of the next few hundred pages.

- Supply equals demand as a model doesn't have a thing to say about the process by which an equilibrium price emerges.

  - It works well, empirically, in situations with many buyers, many sellers, a commodity item, and lots of freely available information.

  - It has proven to work empirically in the laboratory, in carefully controlled experimental markets.

  - It can be observed to work in many real-life markets.

  - But, while the prediction that the price will find the level where supply equals demand depends on the institutional details of how the market is made—to be more precise, it depends on the market functioning somehow—it doesn't say what those institutions are. To know when it is safe to use this model, you need to have a feel for whether the unmodeled market institutions are adequate to the task, which they will be in a remarkable number of specific contexts.

Problems

This chapter is concerned much more with concepts than with computations. Once you get the concepts, you can perform lots of computations on examples with specific supply and demand functions. Many instructors want you to do these sorts of exercises at this point. But, as noted at the outset of this chapter, I don't believe you get much out of such computations until you understand where supply and demand functions come from, which we spend a while developing. So I limit myself to two relatively straightforward problems. The first makes sure you understand the connections between the spreadsheet GM1 and the supply and demand function pictures we've been constructing in this chapter. The second gives you an example of supply equals demand done algebraically.

2.1 In the General Motors analysis, suppose that $P = $ \$20,630, $X = $ \$1000, $x = $ \$500, and $k = $ \$50. In the supply-equals-demand picture for the transferred-coupon market, what are the levels of supply and demand for $Q = $ \$10? What are the levels of supply and demand for $Q = $ \$300?

2.2 This problem concerns a market for a commodity item in which there are many sellers, all firms that produce the item, and many buyers, who are consumers. Supply of the product depends on the price received by the firms and increases as that price increases. If firms receive p per unit, they will supply (in total) $S(p) = 1000(p - 4)$ units of the good for $p \geq 4$. (If the price is less than 4, they will supply none.) Consumer demand depends on the price that consumers must pay per unit for the good. Calling the price per unit to consumers q, consumer demand is given by the demand function $D(q) = 2000(10 - q)$ for $q \leq 10$. If the price exceeds 10, consumers demand no units of the good.

(a) Suppose this good is sold in a market where consumers pay an amount that exactly equals the amount (per unit) taken in by producers. That is, suppose that $p = q$. Where does supply equal demand? (You might want to draw a picture of supply and demand in this market, just to get the practice.)

(b) Suppose that this good is sold in a region where there is a 10% sales tax. That is, if the posted price per unit of the good is p (which is what the sellers of the good receive, free and clear), then for each unit of the good purchased, a consumer must remit $q = 1.1p$. What is the equilibrium in this market? How much tax revenue does the government take in?

(c) Suppose that this good is sold in a region where sellers must pay the government 10% of their gross revenues (but no sales tax is imposed on buyers). That is, if purchasers of the good pay q per unit purchased, the seller receives q gross, but only $p = 0.9q$ net of the mandatory payment to the government. What is the equilibrium in this market? How much tax revenue does the government take in?

3. Marginal This and Marginal That

This chapter explains why economists love the adjective *marginal*.

- I explain what an economist means by the term.
- I show why it is so important to economics.
- I use marginal analysis in a sequence of increasingly complex situations: unconstrained optimization with a single variable, discrete optimization, unconstrained optimization with multiple variables, and constrained optimization.

This chapter solves four puzzles.

Puzzle 1. Luxury Boxes

Among the many decisions facing designers of American sports stadiums is the number of luxury boxes—plush suites that look out onto the playing field—to build. Suppose that, for a particular stadium under construction, luxury boxes will be sold outright to local businesses and can be constructed at a cost of $300,000 apiece. The designer of this stadium plans to build 25 boxes and expects, at this number, to sell each for $1 million, for a net profit of $700,000 × 25 = $17.5 million. An associate asserts that this is crazy. Since boxes can be built at $300,000 and sold for around $1 million apiece, building only 25 leaves money on the table, even if a small price reduction is needed if more are built. This associate is not necessarily correct. Why?

Puzzle 2. Selling Seats for a Soccer Game

A soccer promoter must allocate 40,000 seats in the stadium among the supporters of the two competing teams, the Wolverton Gladabouts and Manteca United. This promoter can set different prices for seating in the Wolverton and Manteca sections of the stands. If she sells W seats to Wolverton supporters, she will receive £20 − $W/2000$ for each, while she can get £10 per ticket from Manteca supporters, regardless of the number of tickets she sells to them. Her objective is to allocate the 40,000 seats she has available to maximize her gate receipts. A friend suggests that an equal allocation of 20,000 seats to each side is best, since this will mean that the price of each ticket is the same, £10; at any other division, she would be making more per ticket on one team than on the other. Why is this friend wrong?

Puzzle 3. Profitability of a Product Line

Imagine a firm that is engaged in manufacturing and marketing three products: widgets, gidgets, and gadgets. Its highly simplified income statement is given by Figure 3.1. Note that overhead, consisting of items such as general and administrative expense, is allocated equally among the three products. Top management of this firm, looking at Figure 3.1, decides to stop producing gadgets, since gadgets are sustaining a loss on a full-cost basis. Why is this an error?

Income Statement				
	Widgets	Gidgets	Gadgets	TOTAL
Sales	$120	$160	$70	$350
Less:				
variable costs	70	90	55	215
allocated overhead	40	40	40	120
Net contribution to profits:	10	30	(25)	15

Figure 3.1. An income statement. The firm is sustaining a net loss on gadgets. Should it discontinue their production?

Puzzle 4. Should Freedonia Export Steel?

In a mythical land called Freedonia, in a time before trade liberalization became the norm, a small domestic steel manufacturing industry, consisting of a single firm, produces and sells steel at $680 per ton, well above the world price of $375 per ton. This firm is protected against foreign competition by incredibly high tariffs that effectively bar all imports. There is no possibility that these tariffs will be dropped; the steel manufacturer contributes heavily to both major political parties as well as several smaller parties.

This firm has never exported steel: Why export at $375 per ton, when they sell steel at $680 per ton domestically? And, to clinch the argument that there is no reason to export steel, executives at the company note that the average cost of manufacturing steel, which varies with the rate at which the firm produces steel, is never below $400 per ton. This company simply cannot make positive profits selling steel for $375 per ton. Notwithstanding everything just said, this firm might increase profits by exporting steel. Why?

3.1. Think Like an Economist: Think Margins

The suggested logic in each puzzle is flawed because it fails to consider *marginal effects* or *marginal trade-offs*. An analogy explains this crucial term.

Imagine yourself standing on a hill in a dense fog. You cannot see more than one step in any direction. The question is, Are you on top of the hill?

You cannot tell for sure that you *are* on top, but you sometimes can tell that you are *not*. Ask yourself, Does the hill slope up *on the margin* in any direction? Can you get higher with a small step in any direction? When the answer is yes, then you aren't on top of the hill.

The italicized *on the margin* in the question is superfluous; the question would mean exactly the same thing had I not included it. But I put it there to indicate that the question *Does the hill slope up?* is a question about things in your immediate neighborhood. In general, the term *a marginal change* means a small change.

This test can tell you only that you are not on top of the hill. It cannot assure you that you are on top. Anyone familiar with climbing hills knows that hillsides have what economists, mathematicians, and perhaps hikers call *local peaks*, peaks in their immediate neighborhood that nonetheless are not *global peaks*, or peaks overall. On the surface of the Earth, Mt. Everest is a global peak, while Mont Blanc is just a very impressive local peak. If you were standing atop Mont Blanc and you ran the test *Can I get higher in a single step?* you would conclude that you could not. But that does not mean that you had reached the top of the highest mountain on Earth.

This test of *local maximization* is, in part, why *marginal* is one of the most useful words in economics. In economic models, we assume that entities—firms and consumers—purposefully strive to make themselves as well off as possible. We model this purposeful behavior as the act of maximizing some numerical function of "well-offness." In the spirit of the top-of-the-hill test, we constantly ask whether the entities involved can improve their situation by making a small—marginal—change in their activities. They have maximized their situation only when they have exhausted all possible marginal improvements.

The test seems almost trivial. Yet economists use the adjective *marginal* to a nearly unbelievable extent. For instance, the index of Parkin's *Economics*, an excellent principles-of-economics textbook, lists as primary entries that begin with the adjective *marginal* the following:[1]

> marginal analysis; marginal benefit; marginal cost; marginal cost pricing rule; marginal grade and grade point average; marginal product; marginal product of labor; marginal propensity to consume; marginal propensity to import; marginal propensity to save; marginal rate of substitution; marginal revenue; marginal revenue product; marginal social benefit and marginal social cost; marginal tax rate; marginal utility; marginal utility in action; marginal utility per dollar spent; and marginal utility theory.

---

[1] *Economics*, 6th edition (Reading, MA: Addison-Wesley, 2003).

That is a lot of uses for an extremely simple idea. But simple or not, the idea is extremely powerful because it reminds economists, and henceforth you, to think hard about the marginal impacts of small changes in some decision.

For instance, take the fourth puzzle that started this chapter, concerning Freedonian steel. The discussion asked, *Why export at $375 per ton, when they are selling steel at $680 per ton domestically?* and *Why export steel at $375 per ton when the average cost of production is never less than $400 per ton?* But those are the wrong questions. The domestic price of $680 per ton is an average amount received per ton and the $400 figure is an average cost. The Freedonian steel manufacturer needs to stop thinking about averages and start thinking about margins.

3.2. A Simple Example

The problem facing the Freedonian steel manufacturer is not the simplest possible problem of this sort. So instead of tackling Freedonian steel (an opportunity you have in Problem 3.3), begin with an even simpler problem. A firm that produces poiuyts, shown in Figure 3.2, is trying to determine how many poiuyts to make and sell.

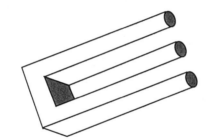

Figure 3.2. A square-base, tri-slot poiuyt.

Let x be the number of poiuyts this firm makes. The firm believes that the more poiuyts it tries to sell, the less it will receive per poiuyt. More specifically, the firm believes that if it manufactures and sells x poiuyts, then the price it will receive per poiuyt is given by the function

$$P(x) = 6 - \frac{3}{5000}x.$$

If the firm sells x poiuyts, therefore, its total revenue will be $x \times P(x)$, or

$$TR(x) = x\left(6 - \frac{3}{5000}x\right) = 6x - \frac{3}{5000}x^2,$$

where TR is an acronym for *total revenue*. This firm has also computed that its *total cost* to make x poiuyts is

$$\text{TC}(x) = 1000 + x + \frac{x^2}{5000}.$$

Thus, if the firm makes x poiuyts, its profit, equal to its total revenue less its total cost, is

$$\pi(x) = \text{TR}(x) - \text{TC}(x) = \left(6x - \frac{3}{5000}x^2 \right) - \left(1000 + x + \frac{x^2}{5000} \right)$$

$$= 5x - \frac{4}{5000}x^2 - 1000.$$

The firm wishes to select the production level x that maximizes its profit.

This problem contains a lot of economics, so without losing too much momentum, let me record what just happened:

- We imagine a firm that is choosing a production rate or level, x.

Is x a rate—x units per day or month or year—or a production level, meaning x poiuyts produced? The distinction is irrelevant to the objectives of this chapter, and so I am not careful about it in my language. But the distinction will become very relevant in Chapter 10. For the sake of definiteness in this example, suppose x means x poiuyts produced per month, so that revenue is revenue per month, total cost is total cost per month, profit is profit per month, and so forth.

- We imagine that, as a function of x, the firm receives revenue given by the function $\text{TR}(x)$, which in turn is derived from a function $P(x)$ that records what price the firm can set as a function of how much it sells per month. The function $P(x)$, called *inverse demand function* facing the firm, is the co-star of Chapter 4.

- We imagine that, to produce x units of output per month, the firm must incur a total cost per month given by the total cost function $\text{TC}(x)$.

- The firm's *profit function*, or profit per month as a function of output rate, is the function $\pi(x) = \text{TR}(x) - \text{TC}(x)$. And the firm is presumed to choose its production rate x to maximize its profit.

Using a Spreadsheet and Solver to Solve the Problem

What level of x maximizes $\pi(x)$? This is easy to answer with a spreadsheet, such as Microsoft's Excel, together with optimization add-ins, such as Solver.

First, build a spreadsheet that captures the model. The spreadsheet depicted in Figure 3.3(a), which is sheet 1 of CHAP3-1, does the trick. In column B, you have, successively,

- In row 2, the rate of production x, entered as a constant. In Figure 3.3(a), I entered 1000, just to get things started.

- In row 3, the price per unit received as a function of x, given by the Excel formula = 6 − 3*B2/5000.

- In row 4, the total revenue received as a function of x, given by the Excel formula = B2*B3.

- In row 5, the total cost incurred as a function of x, given by the Excel formula = 1000 + B2 + B2^ 2/5000.

- In row 6, the firm's profit, given by the Excel formula = B4 − B5.

You can see in Figure 3.3(a) that, if $x = 1000$, the profit computed by the spreadsheet is $3200.

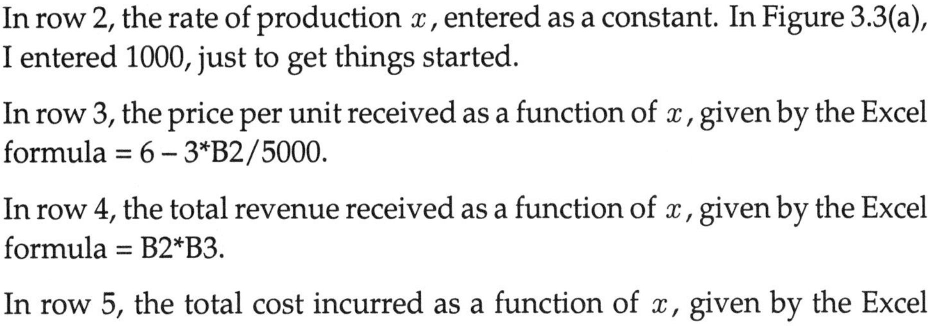

	CHAP3-1			CHAP3-1	
	A	B		A	B
2	value of x	1000	2	value of x	3125
3	price per poiuyt	$5.40	3	price per poiuyt	$4.13
4	total revenue	$5,400.00	4	total revenue	$12,890.63
5	total cost	$2,200.00	5	total cost	$6,078.13
6	profit	$3,200.00	6	profit	$6,812.50
7			7		
Sheet1			Sheet1		

(a)   (b)

Figure 3.3. Spreadsheet CHAP3-1, Sheet 1. This is the basic spreadsheet for finding the profit-maximizing number of poiuyts. Panel a shows the spreadsheet, computed for 1000 poiuyts. Panel b shows the spreadsheet after you ask Solver to maximize cell B6 by varying B2; Solver returns with the answer that the profit-maximizing number of poiuyts is 3125.

To optimize, ask Solver to maximize cell B6, by varying cell B2. Solver does its stuff and returns the solution shown in Figure 3.3(b): The optimal quantity is 3125, giving a profit of $6812.50.

Discrete Marginal Profit, Marginal Revenue, Marginal Cost

Suppose you have access to Excel but not Solver. How could you find the solution to the problem? This is where the magic word *marginal* comes in.

The adjective *marginal* when attached by an economist to a function of one variable means, more or less, the rate of change in the value of the function per unit change in the variable. One way to make this idea precise is to define the *discrete margin* function, where you see how much the function changes when the argument is increased by 1. So, for instance, the firm's *discrete marginal profit* at the production rate $x = 1000$ is the amount $\pi(1001) - \pi(1000)$. *Discrete marginal revenue* is TR(1001) − TR(1000). *Discrete marginal cost* is TC(1001) − TC(1000).

On sheet 2 of the spreadsheet CHAP3-1, shown in Figure 3.4, I add eight more rows to the basic spreadsheet from sheet 1, to calculate the discrete marginal profit, marginal revenue, and marginal cost figures for the rates of production x specified in row 2. First, I copy the basic spreadsheet into rows 8 through 12, except that, in the entry for the rate of production, I take the level in row 2 and add 1. Now I have total revenue, total cost, and total profit if x is increased by 1. And then, in rows 14, 15, and 16, I do the subtractions needed to find the three discrete margins.

	A	B
1		
2	value of x	1000
3	price per poiuyt	$5.40
4	total revenue	$5,400.00
5	total cost	$2,200.00
6	profit	$3,200.00
7		
8	one more x	1001
9	new price	$5.40
10	new revenue	$5,404.80
11	new cost	$2,201.40
12	new profit	$3,203.40
13		
14	discrete marginal revenue	$4.80
15	discrete marginal cost	$1.40
16	discrete marginal profit	$3.40
17		

Figure 3.4. Spreadsheet CHAP3-1, sheet 2: Computing discrete marginal profit, revenue, and cost. After recomputing total revenue, cost, and profit for $x + 1$, subtractions are performed to get discrete marginal revenue, cost, and profit.

What is the point? Look at row 16 and the discrete marginal profit. At $x = 1000$, this is $3.40. If the firm chooses $x = 1001$, profit will rise by $3.40. The ground slopes upward in the direction of increasing x, so (1) we are not at the maximizing value of x and (2) the direction to go is increasing x. Try $x = 2000$ and you will discover that discrete marginal profit is still positive, so we still want to increase x. Next try $x = 5000$. (I urge you to get the spreadsheet and do these things.) You'll find that marginal profit is -3.00.

At this point, the hill slopes up in the direction of less x, so you might try $x = 4000$ next.

The marginal profit figure tells you whether you might be on top of the hill—you are not if it is negative or positive; you might be if it were $0—and in which direction to go, to move up the hill. Without Solver, your job is to keep searching until you get marginal profit equal to $0.

If you do this, you will find that numbers in the neighborhood of 3125 make the marginal profit equal to $0. These look like the top of the hill. Of course, Excel is doing some rounding here; if you want more accuracy, expand the number of digits after the decimal point. But, if you do this, when you are at the top of the hill, precisely at $x = 3125$, discrete marginal profit is -0.0008. This does not tell you to decrease x, even a bit; total profit would decline if you decreased x. This is the consequence of computing margins discretely; when you reach the top of a hill, a small but discrete step in any direction takes you down a bit.

You might worry, when you reach $x = 3125$ (or so) and a marginal profit of $0, that you might be at a local peak, instead of the global profit-maximizing point. This is a valid worry, and margin-based tests on their own can never resolve it. But when we solve this problem with calculus, I show how to be certain that 3215 is the global maximum.

Looking back at Figure 3.4, you see that at $x = 1000$, marginal revenue is $4.80 and marginal cost is $1.40. This means that if we change from $x = 1000$ to $x = 1001$, total revenue will increase by $4.80 and total cost by $1.40. This is, in fact, where the marginal profit of $3.40 comes from: *Marginal profit equals marginal revenue less marginal cost*. So instead of trying to find x such that marginal profit is $0, it is equivalent to try to find where marginal revenue equals marginal cost. Where marginal revenue exceeds marginal cost, you should increase x, while where marginal revenue is less than marginal cost, decrease x.

Once More, with Calculus

The use of calculus in this book is optional, in the sense that you can skip all sections or subsections that use calculus and still learn the basic ideas. But do not skip pieces that use calculus because you do not know calculus. The calculus used is not very difficult, and if you do not know calculus, you will probably never have a better opportunity to learn. The uses of calculus in microeconomics are very intuitive, because they are so completely tied up with marginal analysis, which is at the heart of a lot of microeconomics. To learn calculus well takes more than you will find here and in the Appendix to the *Student's Companion*—if you've never seen the subject, you might need some help. But, as strongly as I can, I urge you to read on. While the point of this book is to teach you microeconomics, learning basic calculus along the way is a bonus.

The analysis in the previous subsection was based on discrete margins; we saw how much the function in question—profit, total revenue, or total cost—changes when we increase the variable by 1. In terms of the hill-climbing analogy, we compute the elevation change if you take precisely one step.

As long as you can see the ground under your feet, however, why not simply look at the slope of the terrain where you stand?

For functions such as profit, total revenue, and total cost, the "slope where you stand" is just the derivative of the function. The derivative of the function f at the value x, written $f'(x)$, is usually well approximated by the discrete margin $f(x + 1) - f(x)$, although it is better approximated, in most cases, by

$$\frac{f(x + 0.1) - f(x)}{0.1,}$$

and the approximation is usually better still if we replace 0.1 in this display by 0.01 or by 0.001.

An economist who refers to marginal profit, or marginal revenue, or marginal cost, without the adjective *discrete*, generally means the derivative of the profit, total revenue, or total cost function; that is, the slope of the function at the value in question. Then everything said in the previous section remains true:

- Profit rises where marginal profit is positive and falls where marginal profit is negative. The optimal level of production, in terms of maximizing profit, is where marginal profit turns from positive to negative, assuming it does so only once.

- Marginal profit equals marginal revenue less marginal cost.

- Where marginal revenue exceeds marginal cost, increasing output causes profit to rise. Where marginal revenue is less than marginal cost, decreasing output causes profit to rise. Profit is maximized by producing to the point where marginal revenue just falls to equal marginal cost, assuming marginal revenue starts above marginal cost, equals marginal cost, and then falls to below marginal cost only once.

The advantage of working with calculus—essentially, taking derivatives—is that, in a lot of the models we will create, the computation of the marginal *whatever* function is simple, as long as we have a nice algebraic formula for *whatever*. For instance, in this simple problem,

$$\pi(x) = 5x - \frac{4}{5000}x^2 - 1000, \quad TR(x) = 6x - \frac{3}{5000}x^2, \text{ and}$$

$$TC(x) = 1000 + x + \frac{x^2}{5000}.$$

Thus marginal profit, marginal revenue, and marginal cost are

$$\pi'(x) = 5 - \frac{8x}{5000}, \quad MR(x) = 6 - \frac{6x}{5000}, \quad \text{and} \quad MC(x) = 1 + \frac{2x}{5000}.$$

For readers whose calculus is rusty or new, the mysterious part of calculus just happened. We are employing well-established rules for computing the derivatives of functions expressed algebraically, rules found in the Appendix to the *Companion*. So, in this example:

- Marginal profit, $\pi'(x)$, is a linear function with a negative slope. It is positive for $x = 0$, stays positive for a while, and then hits 0 and immediately turns and stays negative. Thus, profit rises for a while, then peaks, and falls thereafter. Profit is maximized where marginal profit goes from positive to negative, which is the solution to $5 - 8x/5000 = 0$, or $x = 25000/8 = 3125$.

- Marginal revenue is a linear function with a negative slope. Marginal cost is a linear function with a positive slope. At $x = 0$, marginal revenue is above marginal cost—that is, $MR(0) = 6 > 1 = MC(0)$—and so marginal revenue stays above marginal cost for a while. They cross precisely once, after which marginal cost exceeds marginal revenue. Thus, profit is maximized where marginal revenue equals marginal cost, which is the solution to $6 - 6x/5000 = 1 + 2x/5000$, which is $x = 3125$.

If you are new to this stuff, do not be impressed by the fact that the two points came to the same answer. Because $\pi(x) = TR(x) - TC(x)$, it follows that $\pi'(x) = MR(x) - MC(x)$. Therefore, where $\pi'(x) = 0$, $MR(x) - MC(x) = 0$, which is to say that $MR(x) = MC(x)$.

Discrete Margins and Exact Margins Are Approximately Equal

I asserted that discrete margins and exact margins are approximately equal. Take the case of MR(2000). The exact marginal calculation, using calculus, is

$$MR(2000) = 6 - 6 \times 2000/5000 = 6 - \frac{12}{5} = \$3.60.$$

If you plug in 2000 for the quantity in sheet 2 of CHAP3-1, this is exactly what you get.

Or do you? Plug in the value 2000 for x in sheet 2 of CHAP3-1. Then go to the cell in question, B14, and ask for more digits after the decimal point. You will find that the precise discrete margin is $3.5994. The discrete and exact marginal revenue at $x = 2000$ differ by six one-hundredths of a cent.

The point is not to impress you with the outstanding quality of the approximation, but to help you understand that the discrete margin computed by Excel, or by other means, only approximates the value of the exact margin, computed using calculus.

Please note that this approximation works for other relatively small discrete changes in the variable. If I wanted to compute TR(2032) − TR(2000) for any reason, I know that this will be approximately $32 \times \$3.60$, or the amount of change in the variable times the slope of the function at 2000. My approximation computed by this means is $115.20. But the precise value of TR(2032) − TR(2000) is $114.5856. And, by the same logic of approximation, TR(1998.5) − TR(2000) is approximately $(-1.5)(\$3.60) = \$-5.40$. In fact, this difference is exactly $\$-5.40135$.

3.3. Recalling Why We Are Doing This: Margins Are Not Always What You First Think

If you are among the category of readers for whom calculus is an old friend, you probably wonder why a book with *Microeconomics* in the title is turning out to be a text in introductory calculus. And if you are among the category of readers for whom calculus is new or otherwise a distant memory, you probably wonder the same thing, although with different emotions.

This is no calculus textbook, and the point of all this is not to impress you with the fact that a function is increasing when it slopes up and is decreasing when it slopes down. Economists talk about marginal this and marginal that, because thinking in these terms forces them to think about marginal effects. And the marginal impact of some variable isn't always obvious.

For instance, both the spreadsheet and the formula tell you that MR(8000) = $-3.60. That is, if the firm sells 8001 instead of 8000 units, its total revenue *decreases* by $3.60. But the price per unit sold, if it sells 8000 or 8001 units, is (approximately) $1.20. So why does total revenue decrease?

While the price, when $x = 8000$, is $1.20, the price per poiuyt when $x = 8001$ is slightly less. It is not much less; if you use the formula for price and force Excel to report things without rounding, you will find that the price at $x = 8001$ is $1.1994. Increasing from 8000 to 8001 decreases the price per unit by $0.0006, or six one-hundreths of a cent.

This explains why marginal revenue is negative. When the firm sells 8001 instead of 8000 units, two things happen to its revenue. It gets about $1.20 for the one extra unit sold. But the price per unit on the first 8000 it sells decreases by $0.0006. So, on those 8000 units, it "loses" $0.0006×8000 = $4.80. The two effects net out as a $1.20 gain for the 8001st unit, less $4.80 for the decreased price on the others, or a net loss of $3.60—which is the marginal revenue.

Go back to puzzle 1 from the start of this chapter. Luxury boxes cost $300,000 apiece to build. Assume that this is marginal cost. The puzzle states that if 25 luxury boxes are built, each can be sold for $1 million. So why, the puzzle asks, stop at 25?

Now the puzzle should be a puzzle no longer. That $1 million figure is, presumably, the price per box if the stadium builder creates and sells 25 boxes. If he adds one more, to sell 26, he *might* have to lower their price, to sell all 26. Of course, it is possible that he can sell different boxes for different prices, depending on their location. Perhaps his marginal revenues for moving from 25 to 26 boxes is just the revenue he takes in for box 26, because he need not lower the price of the first 25 at all. But if, for any reason, he needs to keep a single price for all the boxes, in figuring out whether to build box 26, he has to consider the marginal effect this will have on his total revenue. Knowing that box 26 sells for more than it costs is only part of the story. At this point, try Problem 3.4.

That is pretty much the point of this chapter. Economists talk about marginal this and that because economists model the behavior of entities such as firms as maximizing some function, such as profit. When you maximize a function, marginal effects are your first-line consideration. This isn't much of an insight. It says no more than that you cannot be on top of a hill if the ground under your feet slopes up one way or the other. But it alerts economists, and you, to think through the marginal impact of various decisions.

What's left to do? In principle, nothing is left. But practically, I want to explore with you three increasingly complex examples of this basic idea.

3.4. Discrete Optimization and "Margins"

Calculus is used in economics along with the modeling assumption that variables are infinitely divisible; that is, they can be split into any fractional parts. In real life, fractions of units can pose a problem. If marginal profit is equal to $0 at the level of production $n = 3127.886$ poiuyts, how would we make that last 0.886 of a poiuyt?

We cannot make fractional units of poiuyts, but this is unlikely to be of consequence. If calculus says to make 3127.886 poiuyts, then making 3127 or 3128 will probably give very close to the maximal level of profit. In fact, we probably lose little if we round up or down to 3130 or 3120. If we absolutely needed to know, we could compute the level of profit at 3127 and 3128 and see which is larger, but that would be taking the model much too seriously.

On some problems in economics, however, no amount of straining will let us get away with modeling choices as infinitely divisible. When the choice is between doing something or not with no intermediate options or when we have only a handful of intermediate options, to find the optimum we must evaluate profit for each of the discrete options and compare them.

We can, however, often use the *logic* of marginal analysis in cases of discrete choice. An example of this, a classic problem of cost allocation, is puzzle 3 from the start of this chapter. A firm that manufactures and sells three products, widgets, gidgets, and gadgets, has the income statement shown in Figure 3.5(a). Overhead is allocated equally among the three products. Top management of this firm, seeing that gadgets sustain a loss on a full-cost basis, decides to get rid of gadgets. But, when the production of gadgets ceases, the income statement becomes Figure 3.5(b). Now, widgets are showing a fully costed loss. So widgets are eliminated, and the income statement changes to Figure 3.5(c). At this point, the firm is losing money. It is time to liquidate the firm.

We started out with a profitable firm, made a sequence of decisions to eliminate unprofitable lines, and wound up with no firm and consequently no profit. Something is wrong here.

The problem is that fully allocated costs are not marginal costs. Ending the production and sale of a product does not reduce overhead by the amount that is allocated to that product. When the firm did away with gadgets, its overhead had to be reallocated to the other two product lines. The decision whether to do away with gadgets, or any other product line, should be done in terms of the *marginal* or *incremental impact* of that decision on total profit. If overhead is unaffected by the product lines the firm keeps or kills, the marginal or incremental profit of a product line consists of sales revenue less variable costs. Eliminating gadgets makes no sense; the marginal or incremental impact on profit will be to *reduce* profit by $70 − $55 = $15.

Income Statement				(period 1)
	Widgets	Gidgets	Gadgets	TOTAL
Sales	$120	$160	$70	$350
Less: variable costs allocated overhead	70 40	90 40	55 40	215 120
Net contribution to profits:	10	30 (a)	(25)	15

Income Statement			(period 2)
	Widgets	Gidgets	TOTAL
Sales	$120	$160	$280
Less: variable costs allocated overhead	70 60	90 60	160 120
Net contribution to profits:	(10)	10 (b)	0

Income Statement		(period 3)
	Gidgets	TOTAL
Sales	$160	$160
Less: variable costs allocated overhead	90 120	90 120
Net contribution to profits:	(50) (c)	(50)

Figure 3.5. Three income statements. These three income statements depict a three-product firm that eliminates product lines that are not profitable on a fully allocated cost basis. Initially profitable overall, this decision rule leads the firm to eliminate first gadgets, then widgets, and finally gidgets, turning positive profit into a defunct firm. Moral: Fully costed profit contributions are not necessarily the marginal contributions to profit by the products.

Managerial Accounting and Economics

(When appropriate, I try to highlight the connections between microeconomics and the various functions of management, such as Accounting, Finance, Information Systems, Human Resources, Marketing, Operations and

Purchasing, and Strategy. Sometimes the connections are made in the main flow of the chapter; occasionally, as in this instance, something of a digression is required.)

While this example is transparent, it is rarely easy to trace the consequences of real-life decisions of this sort, when all sorts of things change together with the decision to drop a product line. Great care is required when evaluating product lines, divisions, and such, when using profitability or internal accounting numbers.

The production of such numbers is the management function of *cost* or *managerial accounting*. Although managerial accounting may at times seem like the application of fixed and arbitrary recipes for allocating cost, there is much more to it. To answer the question *How should internal accounts be kept?* first you must answer *Why are accounts being kept?*

Internal accounts are kept first to evaluate the performance of products, managers, services, and so on. If the firm is run in top-down fashion by a central decision maker, then this evaluation is done to inform the decision maker about what things cost, to improve his or her decisions. This is closest to what is going on in the example we just considered, in which the income statement was (mis)used to decide which product lines to keep and which to drop. When accounts are kept to inform a single decision maker, then as the example shows, accounting procedures should reflect the incremental costs and benefits of the decisions that will be taken.

Most large firms and organizations are decentralized, with different decision makers (heads of divisions or business units), who make independent decisions about things in their domain of responsibility. In such firms, accounting measures are used to provide incentives to the autonomous decision makers, either retrospectively, where the firm promotes division heads whose divisions did well, or prospectively, where a manager's annual bonus is explicitly tied to how well his or her division does, according to internal accounts. When the numbers are used in this fashion, answers to the questions *Should fixed costs be allocated?* and *If so, how?* change from when the numbers are used for top-down decision making. As you might anticipate, answering these questions in a decentralized context is more difficult. (See Problem 3.12 for the simplest example.)

In addition to keeping accounting numbers for internal purposes, firms keep them for a host of reasons having to do with parties external to the firm, such as tax authorities, regulators, legal authorities, large investors, and potential acquirers. Each of these answers to *Why?* suggests different answers to *How?* For instance, when accounts are used by tax authorities, *How?* calls up answers such as *Delay the realization of accounting earnings* and *Use transfer pricing to "transfer" profits to low-tax localities.* Moreover, the question *Why are internal accounts being kept?* often has more than one answer. And the answers to *How?* corresponding to different answers to *Why?* conflict with one another. Since firms usually do not wish to keep different sets of internal accounts, answers to *How?* must be found that balance the different demands the firm puts on its accounting numbers.

Economics enters into all these considerations. The simplest story shows that accounting numbers kept for top-down decision making should reflect incremental costs. The stories for decentralization and appropriate incentives are a good deal more complex, because they involve the separate decisions of many different entities, but they still fall in substantial part inside the domain of economics. As for tax or regulatory considerations, accountants often look for ways to beat a given system, while the Cost Accounting Standards Board and the government or regulator look for accounting procedures that are "fair" and reflect to some extent the economic value of activities while being hard for the accountants to manipulate.

We examine the use of internal accounts, and in particular the use of transfer prices, in Chapter 14. (The role of financial accounting is discussed in Chapter 18, and ethical considerations connected to financial accounting are discussed in Chapter 24.) This is a fairly specialized subject, however, and your accounting instructors will have to fill in most of the details.

3.5. Multivariable Optimization

In our basic example, the firm made a single product, poiuyts. To complicate the story, suppose that the firm produces two goods, poiuyts and qwerts. These two goods are substitutes, which is fancy talk for, If the firm sells a lot of poiuyts, this depresses the price it can get for qwerts. (A real-life example of substitute products is beef and chicken sold by a butcher. If the butcher sells more chicken and keeps the price of beef constant, less beef is sold. So to keep the quantity of beef sold the same, the price of beef must be lowered.) Specifically, suppose that, if the firm decides to sell x_p poiuyts and x_q qwerts, the price per poiuyt that it will receive is

$$P_p(x_p, x_q) = 90 - \frac{x_p}{100} - \frac{x_q}{300},$$

and the price per qwert that it will receive is

$$P_q(x_p, x_q) = 120 - \frac{x_q}{100} - \frac{x_p}{150}.$$

We assume a very simple cost function: If the firm makes n_p poiuyts and n_q qwerts, the total cost will be $TC(n_p, n_q) = 10x_p + 20x_q + 1000$; that is, a fixed cost of \$1000, plus \$10 per poiuyt and \$20 per qwert. If the firm wants to maximize profit, what number of poiuyts and qwerts should it produce?

A Spreadsheet

The firm's level of profit of is composed of three parts:

- The revenue accrued from selling poiuyts, or $x_p[90-(x_p/100)-(x_q/300)]$.
- Plus the revenue accrued from selling qwerts, $x_q[120-(x_q/100)-(x_p/150)]$.
- Less total cost, $10x_p + 20x_q + 1000$.

Using these formulas, it is quite easy to create a spreadsheet to compute profit as a function of x_p and x_q. Sheet 1 of the spreadsheet CHAP3-2, depicted in Figure 3.6(a), does this, with the trial values of $x_p = 1000$ and $x_q = 5100$.

Discrete Margins and Solver

The obvious next step is to enlist Solver or calculus to find the answer. But before doing either, we can use this spreadsheet to compute discrete margins. There are two variables, x_p and x_q, so for each of the five values—revenue from poiuyts, revenue from qwerts, total revenue, total cost, profit—in the spreadsheet, we have two discrete margins, one where we increase x_p by 1 and the other where we increase x_q by 1. For the values $x_p = 1000$ and $x_q = 5100$, sheet 2 of CHAP3-2, depicted in Figure 3.6(b) provides these discrete margins.

The numbers in Figure 3.6(b) tell us that if we increase the number of poiuyts by 1, so $x_p = 1001$, leaving $x_q = 5100$, revenue from poiuyts will increase by \$52.99 while revenue from qwerts will *decrease* by \$34.00. That decrease in revenue from qwerts bears close scrutiny; it reflects the fact that if you raise the number of poiuyts, the price of qwerts must decrease to keep the number of qwerts the same. Hence a one-unit increase in the number of poiuyts raises total revenue by \$18.99. Cost is increased by \$10, hence the marginal impact on profit of the marginal poiuyt is an increase of \$8.99. On the other hand, raising the number of qwerts by 1 raises revenue from qwerts by \$11.32 while lowering revenue from poiuyts by \$3.33; marginal revenue for both products is \$7.99. Cost rises by \$20.00, so the discrete marginal profit for qwerts is a \$12.01 decrease.

What if we changed the numbers of poiuyts and qwerts at the same time and by numbers other than 1? As long as the changes are small, the net impact on any of the quantities will be approximately additive. For instance,

CHAP3-2

	A	B
2		
3		Basic values
4		
5	number of poiuyts	1000
6	number of qwerts	5100
7		
8	price of a poiuyt	$63.00
9	price of a qwert	$62.33
10		
11	revenue from poiuyts	$63,000.00
12	revenue from qwerts	$317,900.00
13	total revenue	$380,900.00
14		
15	total cost	$113,000.00
16		
17	profits	$267,900.00
18		

Sheet1 | Sh

(a) The basic spreadsheet (which is all Solver needs)

CHAP3-2

	A	B	C	D	E	F	G	H
1								
2				discrete margins	discrete margins		values for	values for
3		Basic values		in poiuyts	in qwerts		one more poiuyt	one more qwert
4								
5	number of poiuyts	1000					1001	1000
6	number of qwerts	5100					5100	5101
7								
8	price of a poiuyt	$63.00					$62.99	$63.00
9	price of a qwert	$62.33					$62.33	$62.32
10								
11	revenue from poiuyts	$63,000.00		$52.99	-$3.33		$63,052.99	$62,996.67
12	revenue from qwerts	$317,900.00		-$34.00	$11.32		$317,866.00	$317,911.32
13	total revenue	$380,900.00		$18.99	$7.99		$380,918.99	$380,907.99
14								
15	total cost	$113,000.00		$10.00	$20.00		$113,010.00	$113,020.00
16								
17	profits	$267,900.00		$8.99	-$12.01		$267,908.99	$267,887.99

Sheet1 | Sheet2 | Sheet3

(b) Discrete margins for $x_p = 1000$ and $x_q = 5100$

Figure 3.6. Spreadsheet CHAP3-2: The poiuyt–qwert example. These two spreadsheets give the basic model and marginal value calculations for the poiuyt–qwert example. They depict the case of 1000 poiuyts and 5100 qwerts. The marginal profit figures are not \$0, so profit can be improved: Since the marginal profit in poiuyts is positive, more poiuyts should be produced and sold; and since the marginal profit in qwerts is negative, profit will increase with fewer qwerts.

if we raise the number of poiuyts by 10 to 1010 and we raise the number of qwerts by 5, to 5105, the net impact on profit will be, approximately, an increase of

$$(10)(8.99) + (5)(-12.01) = \$29.85.$$

In fact, if you run the numbers, the exact change is an increase of \$28.25.

It is clear that profit is not maximized if $x_p = 1000$ and $x_q = 5100$. We make more profit by increasing x_p, by decreasing x_q, or by doing both simultaneously. Try doing both at once: Increase x_p to 1200 and decrease x_q to 4800. If you run the numbers, you will find that this improves profit; now the discrete margins on profit are $7.99 for poiuyts and $-8.01 for qwerts. So more poiuyts and fewer qwerts is still a good idea.

Where do we stop? As long as either discrete margin is significantly different from $0, profit can be increased. This is just the hill-in-the-fog story again, and in fact, it is a better analogy to the hill: On a hill, you can move north–south or east–west; here you can move poiuyts up or down and qwerts up or down. We maximize profit when the discrete profit margins are both approximately $0. With this criterion for finding the optimum and the guidance provided by the marginal profit figures—increase a variable if its marginal profit is positive and decrease if the marginal profit is negative—it is not that hard to work with the spreadsheet to find that the optimum seems to occur at $x_p = 2000$ and $x_q = 4000$. Or, at least, at those values, the marginal profit figures are both $-0.01. See Figure 3.7. This is indeed the optimum but take heed:

- As in the one-variable problem, the discrete margins are very slightly negative at the top of the hill. This is not a signal to decrease the variables; it simply reflects that, atop a hill, a discrete step in any direction loses altitude.

- We do not know for sure that this point is the global maximizer, only that a small step in any direction does not improve matters. In other words, this could be a local but not a global peak.

Of course, we could use Solver to find the answer once we had the basic spreadsheet put together. If you go back to the initial values of $x_p = 1000$ and $x_q = 5100$ and ask Solver to maximize cell B17 by varying B5 and B6, you will get the answer $x_p = 2000$ and $x_q = 4000$ quick as a flash. But, by doing this by hand, so to speak, we glean the following takeaways:

- With two basic variables, x_p and x_q, we have two discrete margins for each "value."
- When profit is maximal, marginal profit in each variable must be (nearly) $0.

- At the optimum, marginal revenue equals marginal cost for each variable. We didn't remark on this before now, but if you look at Figure 3.7, you will see that cell D13 approximately equals D15 and cell E13 approximately equals E15.

	A	B	C	D	E	F	G	H
1								
2				discrete margins	discrete margins		values for	values for
3		Basic values		in poiuyts	in qwerts		one more poiuyt	one more qwert
4								
5	number of poiuyts	2000					2001	2000
6	number of qwerts	4000					4000	4001
7								
8	price of a poiuyt	$56.67					$56.66	$56.66
9	price of a qwert	$66.67					$66.66	$66.66
10								
11	revenue from poiuyts	$113,333.33		$36.66	-$6.67		$113,369.99	$113,326.67
12	revenue from qwerts	$266,666.67		-$26.67	$26.66		$266,640.00	$266,693.32
13	total revenue	$380,000.00		$9.99	$19.99		$380,009.99	$380,019.99
14								
15	total cost	$101,000.00		$10.00	$20.00		$101,010.00	$101,020.00
16								
17	profits	$279,000.00		-$0.01	-$0.01		$278,999.99	$278,999.99

Figure 3.7. Spreadsheet CHAP3-2: The optimizing values for the poiuyt–qwert example. You can use Solver to find the profit-maximizing production quantities, or you can search for them "by hand," using the rule that you should increase the production of a product that has a positive marginal profit and decrease the production of a product that has a negative marginal product. When you have found the optimum production plan, the spreadsheet appears as in this figure.

An important economic point is buried in the last point. What is the marginal revenue from a poiuyt? Unless you remember that raising the number of poiuyts decreases the price of qwerts and thus the revenue received from qwerts, you might be misled into thinking that the marginal revenue of a poiuyt is the impact an additional poiuyt has on the revenue accrued from the sale of poiuyts only. Not so. The marginal revenue from an additional poiuyt is the marginal impact on *total revenue*, including the impact on the revenue from qwerts. Therefore when we maximize profit, we find cell D13, and not cell D11, roughly equals D15.

And with Calculus: Partial Derivatives

To solve this problem with calculus, we mimic what we just did discretely. First write profit as a function of x_p and x_q:

$$\pi(x_p, x_q) = x_p\left(90 - \frac{x_p}{100} - \frac{x_q}{300}\right) + x_q\left(120 - \frac{x_q}{100} - \frac{x_p}{150}\right) - \left(10x_p + 20x_q + 1000\right).$$

Multiply through and collect similar terms. You get

$$\pi(x_p, x_q) = 80x_p + 100x_q - \frac{x_p^2}{100} - \frac{x_q^2}{100} - \frac{3x_p x_q}{300} - 1000.$$

For each variable, compute marginal profit. These are the rates at which the profit function changes in each of the variables separately, which are the two partial derivatives of the profit function. That is,

$$\text{marginal profit in } x_p \text{ is } \frac{\partial \pi}{\partial x_p} = 80 - \frac{2x_p}{100} - \frac{3x_q}{300}, \quad \text{and}$$

$$\text{marginal profit in } x_q \text{ is } \frac{\partial \pi}{\partial x_q} = 100 - \frac{2x_q}{100} - \frac{3x_p}{300}.$$

The profit function is maximized where these two marginal profit functions are $0, or where

$$80 - \frac{2x_p}{100} - \frac{3x_q}{300} = 0 \quad \text{and} \quad 100 - \frac{2x_q}{100} - \frac{3x_p}{300} = 0.$$

Solve these two equations in two unknowns, and the solution is $x_p = 2000$ and $x_q = 4000$.

The takeaways are the same, which should not be surprising, since a discrete margin is a discrete approximation to a derivative and a derivative gives a continuous approximation to a discrete margin or difference. In particular,

- *To have maximized a function of several variables, the function's partial derivatives all have to equal 0.* So, to find where a function of several variables is maximized, find its partial derivatives and set them simultaneously equal to 0.

- *In this problem, you can either set the two marginal profit functions to $0 or equate marginal revenue in each variable to marginal cost in that variable.* But be sure, if you use marginal cost and marginal revenue, to use the full marginal revenue functions—the partial derivatives of total revenue from both products—and not, for instance, the partial derivative of revenue from poiuyts taken with respect to poiuyts.

- *Setting partial derivatives equal to 0 is necessary but not sufficient to know you are at the maximum.* This is the hill-climbing-in-the-fog phenomenon: You know you are not on top of the hill when the ground under your feet slopes up in some direction, but when the ground is flat, you cannot be sure you are on the peak. Indeed, you might even be at the bottom of a local depression.

    If this worries you—how can you be sure you solved the problem when you set the partial derivatives to 0?—mathematical techniques can be employed to give you some assurances in some cases. We won't cover those techniques—this isn't a math book—so you'll need to look elsewhere for them. The key words are *second-order conditions* and *convex optimization* problems.

3.6. Puzzle 2: Constrained Maximization

In poiuyt and poiuyt–qwert examples, the firm is not constrained in setting its production quantities. But many economic problems come with constraints on the variables; the problem is to find the maximizing choice of variables while respecting the constraints.

There are mathematical methods for solving constrained maximization problems using things called Lagrangians and Hamiltonians, but their use often obscures what is really going on. We take a more intuitive approach to constrained maximization in this book. To begin, recall puzzle 2:

> A soccer promoter must allocate 40,000 seats in her stadium among the supporters of two teams, the Wolverton Gladabouts and Manteca United. The promoter can set different prices for seating in the Wolverton and Manteca sections of the stands. If she sells W seats to Wolverton supporters, she will receive £20 − W/2000 for each, while she can get £10 per ticket from Manteca supporters, regardless of the number of tickets she sells them. Her objective is to allocate the 40,000 seats she has available in whatever manner maximizes her gate receipts.

One way to solve this problem is to turn it into (essentially) a one-variable problem without constraints, by assuming that the promoter wishes to allocate all 40,000 seats. Then, if W is the number of seats allocated to Wolverton supporters, $40000 - W$ seats are left for supporters of Manteca, and gate receipts are

$$W\left(20 - \frac{W}{2000}\right) + 10(40000 - W).$$

The variable W is in fact constrained—W cannot be negative and cannot exceed 40,000—but if you use either Solver or calculus to maximize gate receipts in W while ignoring these constraints, you will find that they are satisfied at the answer.

This works but does not generalize easily, and it hides rather than reveals intuition. So let me suggest a different way to attack the problem. Begin, once again, with a spreadsheet. The basic spreadsheet, depicted in Figure 3.8(a), is sheet 1 of CHAP3-3. The two variables, W and M, are in cells B2 and B3.

CHAP3-3

	A	B
1		
2	W--seats for Wolverton	15,000
3	M--seats for Manteca	25,000
4		
5	total number of seats	40,000
6		
7	price of a Wolverton seat	£13
8	price of a Manteca seat	£10
9		
10	gate receipts, Wolverton	£187,500
11	gate receipts, Manteca	£250,000
12		
13	total gate receipts	£437,500
14		

(a) The basic spreadsheet

CHAP3-3

	A	B	C	D	E	F	G	H
1				margins in W	margins in M		one more W	one more M
2	W--seats for Wolverton	15,000					15,001	15,000
3	M--seats for Manteca	25,000					25,000	25,001
4								
5	total number of seats	40,000					40,001	40,001
6								
7	price of a Wolverton seat	£12.5000					£12.4995	£12.5000
8	price of a Manteca seat	£10.0000					£10.0000	£10.0000
9								
10	gate receipts, Wolverton	£187,500		£4.9995	£0.0000		£187,505	£187,500
11	gate receipts, Manteca	£250,000		£0.0000	£10.0000		£250,000	£250,010
12								
13	total gate receipts	£437,500		£4.9995	£10.0000		£437,505	£437,510
14								

(b) Discrete margins for W = 15,000 and M = 25,000

Figure 3.8. Spreadsheet CHAP3-3: The Wolverton–Manteca seat allocation problem. To find the optimal allocation of seats between the supporters of Wolverton and Manteca, we first build the basic spreadsheet shown in panel a. We can use Solver on this, asking it to maximize cell B13 by varying B2 and B3, subject to the constraint that B5 is less than or equal to 40,000. Or we can use marginal analysis: Supplement the basic spreadsheet with discrete marginal values as shown in panel b and begin to hunt, using the rule that we reallocate seats from one set of supporters to the other if the first group's discrete marginal gate receipts are less than that of the second.

Cell B5 contains the sum $W + M$. Cells B7 and B8 give the prices per seat of seats sold to Wolverton and Manteca supporters, respectively; and cells B10 and B11 give the gate receipts from these two sets of supporters. Finally, B13 contains the total gate receipts. I start out with the values W = 15,000 and M = 25,000.

You could, at this point, ask Solver to maximize B13 by varying B2 and B3, subject to the constraints that cell B5 cannot exceed 40,000 and that B2 and

B3 must be nonnegative. If you have never used Solver with a constraint, I suggest you do this.

Rather than use Solver, I want to think in terms of margins. So, in Figure 3.8(b), you see the spreadsheet once more, but with some more columns. Column D gives marginal values if the number of seats allocated to Wolverton is increased by 1. And column E gives marginal values for one more seat for Manteca.

Note very carefully that the discrete margins in columns D and E are computed without respecting the constraint on the total number of seats. That is, cell E13 tells us that, if the stadium had 40,001 seats, allocated 15,000 to Wolverton and 25,001 to Manteca, the promotor would make £10 more than if the stadium has 40,000 seats, allocated 15,000 and 25,000.

What else do the numbers in Figure 3.8(b) tell us? On the margin, one more seat allocated to Wolverton supporters would mean £5 more in gate receipts. One more seat allocated to Manteca supporters would mean £10 more in gate receipts. Pretty clearly, if the stadium had 40,0001 seats, the promoter would be better off allocating the last seat to Manteca supporters.

But the stadium has only 40,000 seats. So the question is not *To which team to allocate a marginal seat?* but *On the margin, should seats be reallocated between the two teams' supporters?* And the marginal gate receipt figures make it fairly clear that one more seat for a Manteca supporter means £10 more in gate receipts, while one less for a Wolverton supporter means £5 or so less in gate receipts, a net gain of £5.

There is a trade-off between allocating seats to Manteca and to Wolverton. So whenever the marginal gate receipts for an extra Manteca seat exceed the marginal gate receipts for an extra Wolverton seat, it makes sense to reallocate seats from Wolverton to Manteca. If the marginal gate receipts from a Wolverton seat exceed the marginal gate receipts from a Manteca seat, it makes sense to reallocate seats from Manteca to Wolverton. *To be maximized, the marginal gate receipts from one more Manteca supporter must equal the marginal gate receipts from one more fan of Wolverton.*

You can still ask Solver to find the answer. Or, using the rules just enunciated, you can use the spreadsheet to find the answer on your own. Keep substituting supporters of the team with higher marginal gate receipts for supporters of the team with lower marginal gate receipts until the two marginal gate receipts figures are equalized.

You will find the allocation of seats that equalizes the two marginal gate receipt figures is $W = 10,000$ and $M = 30,000$. Or you might find $W = 9999$ and $M = 30,001$. It makes very little difference to the bottom line. Just so you know what to look for, Figure 3.9 shows how my spreadsheet looked at this point. Note that the two marginal gate receipt figures are not quite

	A	B	C	D	E	F	G	H	
1				margins in W	margins in M		one more W	one more M	
2	W--seats for Wolverton	10,000					10,001	10,000	
3	M--seats for Manteca	30,000					30,000	30,001	
4									
5	total number of seats	40,000					40,001	40,001	
6									
7	price of a Wolverton seat	£15.0000					£14.9995	£15.0000	
8	price of a Manteca seat	£10.0000					£10.0000	£10.0000	
9									
10	gate receipts, Wolverton	£150,000		£9.9995	£0.0000		£150,010	£150,000	
11	gate receipts, Manteca	£300,000		£0.0000	£10.0000		£300,000	£300,010	
12									
13	total gate receipts	£450,000		£9.9995	£10.0000		£450,010	£450,010	
14									

Figure 3.9. Spreadsheet CHAP3-3: The optimal allocation of seats between Wolverton and Manteca supporters. At the optimal allocation, the discrete marginal gate receipts are (virtually) equalized, telling you that a one-for-one reallocation from one side to the other does not improve gate receipts.

equal: Discrete marginal gate receipts for Wolverton are £0.0005 less than for Manteca, which is close enough.

Now it should be clear why the friend's logic—equalize ticket prices—does not work. Equalizing price per tickets between the two groups equalizes *average* gate receipts per seat. That may be a fair thing to do, but to maximize gate receipts in this world of one-for-one trade-offs, you need to equalize marginal gate receipts.

And with Calculus

Gate receipts are given by the formula

$$R(W, M) = W\left(20 - \frac{W}{2000}\right) + 10M.$$

The marginal gate receipt functions are the partial derivatives of this function in W and in M:

$$\frac{\partial R}{\partial W} = 20 - \frac{2W}{2000} \quad \text{and} \quad \frac{\partial R}{\partial M} = 10.$$

For the reason just given—because there is a one-for-one trade-off between W and M in terms of the seating constraint—gate receipts will not be maximized unless the two marginal gate receipt figures are equal. So the solution to the promoter's problem is found where

$$20 - \frac{2W}{2000} = 10,$$

which is easily solved as $W = 10,000$. (See Problem 3.10 for a slightly harder version of this.)

Finally, just as you cannot tell a local peak from a global peak on a hill in the fog, equalizing the marginal gate receipts does not guarantee the correct answer. But, in this problem, we can use the logic of margins to conclude that we have the answer. The marginal gate receipt function for Wolverton seats is a linear function with a negative slope. That is, the marginal gate receipts for the first seat given to a Wolverton supporter is (approximately) £20 and the margins decrease from there. The marginal gate receipts for Manteca supporters is a constant £10. So we should allocate the first, second, and third seats to Wolverton supporters, and we should keep doing this until the marginal contribution to gate receipts for Wolverton supporters falls to £10. At which point, every seat that comes along should go to Manteca.

That is, if the stadium has fewer than 10,000 seats but the same ticket-price functions hold, every seat should go to a Wolverton supporter. If the stadium has 11,000 seats, 10,000 go to Wolverton and 1000 to Manteca. If the stadium has 12,000 seats, 10,000 go to Wolverton and 2000 to Manteca, and if the stadium has, say, 200,000 seats and the same ticket-price functions hold, 10,000 seats go to Wolverton, and 190,000 to Manteca. Wolverton supporters gets the "first" 10,000 seats. And they never get another, no matter how big the stadium grows, at least for these two ticket-price functions.

Executive Summary

- Marginal this and marginal that appear frequently in economic discussions for the following two-step reason:

    1. In economic models, entities are assumed to act purposefully; purposeful action is modeled as *maximizing some one-dimensional measure*, such as profit or utility; and a necessary test for achieving the maximum is that no marginal improvement in one's current position is possible.

    2. Once reminded to look at the marginal impact of various actions or decisions, economists know to think carefully about what the marginal impacts might be.

- A discrete margin is the amount a quantity of interest—such as profit, revenue, or cost—changes for a one-unit increase in a particular variable. Using calculus, continuous margins are just (partial) derivatives. The two typically approximate one another, and analysis can be conducted using discrete margins and a spreadsheet, or using calculus.

- For a single-product firm choosing its output rate or level, profit rises where marginal profit is positive or, equivalently, when marginal revenue exceeds marginal cost, and profit falls where marginal profit is negative or, equivalently, where marginal cost exceeds marginal revenue. Hence, to find a profit-maximizing level of production, set marginal profit to $0 or set marginal revenue to marginal cost.

- Marginal revenue is *not* generally the price obtained for the last good sold. It is generally less than this, reflecting the loss in revenue that occurs because the unit price must be lowered to sell the extra unit.

- For multiproduct firms, the same basic slogans for profit-maximization apply, as long as you recall that marginal anything measures the rate of change of that thing as one variable changes, the others being held fixed. And marginal cost and revenue means the rate of change of total cost and total revenue, summed across all the firm's activities.

- For discrete maximization problems, you can't take derivatives. But the logic of thinking about marginal or, more properly in this sort of problem, incremental impact, still applies.

- For constrained maximization problems, the general rule is more complex (we'll be developing it in stages), but the seat-allocation problem indicates that thinking in terms of margins—in particular, thinking about marginal contributions of different activities that can be traded off against one another—is the way to go.

Problems

The *Students' Companion* contains the solutions of some, but not all, of the following problems.

3.1 Suppose a firm that produces a single product can sell its output for $p = 100 - x/100$ for each unit that it produces, where x is its level of output. Its total cost function is $TC(x) = 200 + 20x + x^2/300$. What is the profit-maximizing level of production for this firm?

3.2 A firm that produces a single product sells its output for $p = 20 - x/1000$, where x is the quantity that it produces and sells. Its total cost function is $TC(x) = 5000 + 4x$. What is its profit-maximizing level of production?

3.3 Imagine that the sole manufacturer of steel in the country Freedonia, Chiccolini Heavy Industries (CHI), has a total cost function given by

$$TC(x) = \$10,000,000 + 200x + \frac{x^2}{1000},$$

where x is the rate of steel production per year (measured in tons). If this company sells x tons of steel domestically (to Freedonian firms), the price per ton that it can charge is

$$P(x) = 1000 - \frac{x}{250}.$$

The world price of steel is $375, but domestic consumers of steel are barred from buying imported steel because of incredibly high tariffs on steel imported into Freedonia.

(a) The average cost function of CHI, written $AC(x)$, is total cost divided by quantity:

$$AC(x) = \frac{TC(x)}{x} = \frac{10{,}000{,}000}{x} + 200 + \frac{x}{1000}.$$

What is the shape of this function? At what rate of production x is average cost minimized? (Use calculus or Excel and Solver. Look at sheet 1 of the spreadsheet FREEDONIAN STEEL if you don't know how to begin.) What is the level of average cost at this rate of production?

(b) Suppose that CHI decides to ignore utterly the world market in steel and instead sells steel only domestically. What rate of steel production maximizes CHI's profit? You can use either calculus or a spreadsheet and Solver to solve this problem.

(c) Should CHI export steel? To answer this question, create a spreadsheet with two variables, domestic steel sales and international sales. Compute, from these two variables, total cost of production, domestic price, revenue from domestic sales, revenue from international sales, total revenue, and total profit. Ask Solver to maximize total profit by varying the two variables. You can do this with calculus, if you prefer, but this is a case in which I think you are better off trying a spreadsheet first. If you get stuck, look at sheet 3 of the spreadsheet FREEDONIAN STEEL.

(d) You should conclude in part (c) that CHI does indeed want to sell steel internationally. To figure out the economic intuition here, take your spreadsheet from part (c) and add columns for marginal revenue and cost figures in the two variables. (Or see sheet 4.) Use this spreadsheet and logic to explain why CHI wants to export steel, even though the domestic price of steel is way above the international price and even though CHI's average costs of production are never less than $400 per ton.

3.4   Return to puzzle 1. Recall that the stadium builder is able to sell 25 luxury boxes for $1 million apiece, while they cost $300,000 apiece to build. Suppose that the builder is constrained by law to sell all luxury boxes for the same price, and to sell 26 boxes, he must price all 26 at $950,000 apiece. Will he make more money selling 25 or 26?

3.5   In Figure 3.10, you see the marginal profit function for a firm with a single output. What will be the shape of the profit function of this firm? Assume that profit at zero production level is $0. (Why is this last piece of information important?)

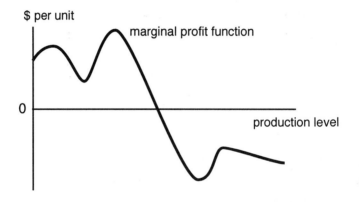

Figure 3.10. Problem 3.5: A marginal profit function.

3.6 In Figure 3.11, you see the marginal revenue and marginal cost functions for a firm with a single output. Where do you think will be the profit maximizing level of production for the firm? Why do you think this? (Assume that both total revenue and total cost at zero production level are $0. Is this assumption necessary?)

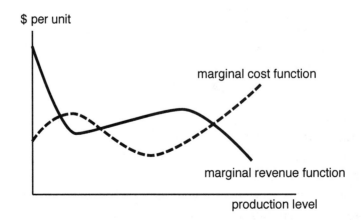

Figure 3.11. Problem 3.6: Marginal revenue and marginal cost.

3.7 (For people interested in cost accounting) In our simple example of why you shouldn't take seriously full-cost contributions, overhead was allocated equally among all product lines. You might think that this is the problem, since this clearly makes product lines with small sales volumes look pretty bad; they have to carry a disproportionate share of the overhead. Suppose, therefore, that we allocated overhead in proportion to revenue for each product line. That is, if widgets generate $100 in revenue, gidgets generate $200, and gadgets generate $300, then fixed costs are allocated in the ratio of 1:2:3 over the three product lines. Will allocating overhead in this more sophisticated manner solve the problem we saw before? (Hint: What happens if you allocate overhead in this manner for the numbers in the example we looked at earlier?)

3.8 (Here is a slightly harder version of the poiuyt–qwert problem from the text) Let x_p be the number of poiuyts the firm sells and x_q the number of qwerts. The two inverse demand functions are

$$P_p = 100 - \frac{x_p}{100} - \frac{x_q}{400} \quad \text{and} \quad P_q = 80 - \frac{x_q}{50} - \frac{x_p}{200}.$$

Total costs are given by

$$TC(x_p, x_q) = 300 + 20x_p + 10x_q + \frac{(3x_p + x_q)^2}{1200}.$$

Find the profit-maximizing production rates.

3.9 A firm that produces red and blue bobbleheads can sell red bobbleheads for $20 - x_r/1000$ apiece and blue bobbleheads for $17 - x_b/2000$ apiece, if it sells x_r red bobbleheads and x_b blue. The total cost of producing $x = x_r + x_b$ bobbleheads is $4x + x^2/4000$. What are the profit-maximizing quantities of red and blue bobbleheads for this firm to make and sell?

3.10 (a) Suppose that, in the stadium problem, the data are changed as follows. The stadium holds 30,000 people. If W seats are allocated to Wolverton supporters, each can be sold for £$20 - W/2000$. And if M seats are allocated to Manteca supporters, each can be sold for £$24 - M/3000$. What division of seats maximizes gate receipts?

(b) If you like a bit of a challenge, suppose the stadium held 60,000 instead of 30,000 seats. What would be the answer then?

3.11 Redo Problem 3.8, but under the constraint that the sum of x_p and x_q cannot exceed 2000. If you know about Lagrange multipliers, try not to use them, but reason this out using the logic of marginal analysis.

3.12 The poiuyt–qwert example of Section 3.5 can be used to address managerial accounting issues, where accounting numbers are used in a multidivisional firm. Specifically, imagine that the firm in question has two divisions, the Poiuyt Division and the Qwert Division. Imagine that top management, having had a good course in managerial accounting, knows better than to allocate the $1000 fixed cost when evaluating the performance of the two divisions. So top management, in evaluating how well the Poiuyt Division has done, looks at revenue from poiuyts less variable costs of producing poiuyts, where the latter is $10x_p$, and similarly for the Qwert Division. Imagine finally that the decisions of how many poiuyts and qwerts to produce are left to the division heads, each of whom is motivated to maximize his or her own divisional (variable) profit. What happens? There is no pat answer to this; since it involves two interacting division heads, it involves techniques we won't get to until Chapter 21. But try your best and, as you do, reflect on why, in this decentralized context, looking at divisional (variable) profit as divisional revenue less divisional variable cost is very problematic.

4. Demand Functions

After a bit of preparation for the next seven chapters, this chapter focuses on demand functions, especially as they bear on profit-maximizing firms. We begin with a thorough discussion of demand functions and then turn to the heart of this chapter, the concept of *elasticity* and its use in economic models.

The model employed in the first half of the last chapter, concerning the firm that manufactures poiuyts, was built from several important pieces of microeconomics:

- A firm has to decide how much of a product to make and sell.

- The cost of making and selling x units is given by a *total cost function* $TC(x)$.

- The revenue obtained from selling x units is given by a *total revenue function* $TR(x)$, which in turn is computed as the product of the quantity x times the price per unit $P(x)$ that could be obtained, if x units were sold.

- The firm chooses x to maximize its profit, or $\pi(x) = TR(x) - TC(x)$.

Think of a firm divided into three functions. For each possible production quantity x, operations decides how to make x most cost effectively, which determines $TC(x)$. Marketing sells the stuff to get as much revenue as possible, determining $TR(x)$. Top management consults with operations and marketing, learns about TC and TR, and chooses x to maximize profit.

If you think about the firm in this ultrasimple fashion, you have a road map to the next seven chapters. The marketing side of the firm is the subject of this chapter and the next three. Moreover, in this chapter, marketing is particularly simple-minded: The firm sells all its output for a single price. Alternative, more creative marketing arrangements will be the subject of Chapters 6 and 7, after we spend some time on the ultimate destination of output, the consumer, in Chapter 5. Throughout these chapters, we assume that the operations side of the firm is very simple, characterized by a linear total cost function $TC(x) = kx$ for some constant k, the firm's marginal cost. We explore the operations side of the firm in Chapters 8, 9, and 10.

This leaves top management, which is supposed to choose x to maximize profit. *Is this a reasonable model of what real firms do?* I assume that many readers of this book have spent time in real-life firms and are likely to know what the rest of you probably suspect. This is not how real firms or their top managers act. Or, if you prefer to hear this from a top manager, I can quote John Reed, head of Citibank and, after its merger with Travelers, cohead of Citigroup. As a banker, Reed had a pretty good window on the workings of many firms that banked at Citibank. He offers this opinion:

> [The] objective in running [a] business is the long-term, evolutionary success of the firm. . . Most of my colleagues and I have come to understand that profit is not a robust model and that we need, in fact, a broader vision of what it is we are trying to do.[1]

Notwithstanding Reed's opinion and the opinions of most folks who have managed firms, large and small, economists persist in modeling firms as profit-maximizing entities whose decision makers are endowed with an amazing understanding of what their firm can do and an amazing ability to implement their decisions. How can this be defended?

- Once adapted to the real world, the hypothesis is not as ludicrous as it may seem. In the real world of firms that exist for many years, profit maximization means the maximization of the value of equity. And, while it is a stretch to say that top managers maximize shareholder equity to the exclusion of all other goals, in the United States at least, the consensus is that managers *do* pay a lot of attention to increasing shareholder equity.

- Even if managers do not consciously maximize profits, their actions approximate profit maximization. This "positive economics" defense says that it doesn't matter whether economic actors consciously behave as they are assumed to do in models; what matters is that their actions are consistent with those assumptions. To take a standard analogy—offered first, I believe, by Milton Friedman—a tree setting its leaf canopy in the spring most certainly does not solve the complex problem of maximizing its exposure to sunlight, taking into account the cost in energy of creating leaves. This very difficult optimization problem is well beyond the capabilities of the average tree, which typically has problems with simple sums. Yet, to a first approximation, the leaf canopy of a tree solves this problem, and as a model that predicts the tree's leaf canopy, modeling the tree as a "constrained exposure to the sun" maximizer does fairly well. The same, goes this defense, is true of firms and their managers. John Reed may not consciously have maximized profit—he may even have thought that this was beyond his capabilities—but, meaning no offense

---

[1] From "Citigroup's John Reed and Stanford's James March on Management Research and Practice," *Academy of Management Executive*, Vol. 14, No. 1, 2000.

to John Reed, do you think a tree, if asked, would understand that it was maximizing sun exposure?

The reasons that trees act in this "as-if" fashion have to do with evolutionary pressures. A tree good at setting its leaf canopy will, presumably, produce more seeds and have more offspring. Similarly, profit maximization may be a good positive model of what firms do because of competitive pressures on firms. More profitable firms presumably attract more capital and grow larger. Firms run at less than full profitability are good candidates for takeovers or management buyouts. If managers tend to imitate the actions of their more profitable peers, the result looks like natural selection in favor of profit maximization.

Ultimately, the positive economics defense rests on the strength of empirical evidence. Owing to the importance of the hypothesis of profit maximization, this empirical issue has attracted substantial attention. A reasonable rough summary of the empirical studies that have been done is that the data are generally consistent with the hypothesis of profit maximization, suitably adapted to the real world.

- A final defense is that, for many purposes, the precise objectives of management are not important to the conclusions we draw from the models we build. Even if management does not *maximize* profit, it is still interested in increasing profit and decreasing cost. Or, to quote Reed again, "Profits and price earnings on stock and things of that sort are significant and important contributors to our evolutionary success." To assume in our models that profit maximization is the single and single-minded goal of management is surely too extreme; but when we are trying to understand how price discrimination might increase revenue (Chapter 7), how the experience curve affects production volumes (Chapter 10), or the mechanics of implicit collusion (Chapter 22), the conclusions we draw would still hold if management's objectives are only partly to increase profit. Some of our conclusions—especially those around Chapters 12 and 13 concerning the efficiency of markets—depend strongly on the full profit-maximization assumption. We need to watch out for results and insights tightly tied to this assumption. But, for the conclusions that are of most interest and relevance to managers, this is usually no problem.

This is not the end of this story. In particular, in Chapter 24, where we return to economic conceptions of the firm, we get a good deal closer to reality in modeling and understanding what firms do. But, for the time being and notwithstanding its deficiencies, we stick to this simple conceptualization of the profit-maximizing firm.

4.1. Demand and Inverse Demand Functions

Demand functions say how much of some given product would be purchased at each price for the item. We use the symbols $D(p)$; the usual graph is as in the supply-equals-demand picture, Figure 2.1 of Chapter 2, with price placed on the vertical axis.

In Chapter 3, we dealt with a different sort of function that contains the same information. There a function, typically labeled $P(x)$, gave the price per unit that could be charged if x units of the good were sold. The typical picture has quantity, the variable, on the horizontal axis and price, the value of the function, on the vertical axis.

The pictures of these functions for the same market look identical on the page. If the demand function says that at a price $13, 4000 units will be sold, then the price at which 4000 units can be sold is $13. Mathematically, these two functions are inverses of one another, and so the function $P(x)$ is called an *inverse demand function*.

- When I say that the pictures of a demand function and an inverse demand function look identical on the page, this does not mean they are the same function. They are inverses of one another, and only the economist's habit of putting price on the vertical axis, even if price is the variable, which it is for demand functions, causes them to look the same.

- For demand to be invertible, we need to know that a single price is not consistent with two different levels of demand. For inverse demand to be invertible, a single quantity sold cannot be consistent with two different prices. As long as we assume both demand and inverse demand are decreasing functions—higher prices go with lower quantities and vice versa—both functions are invertible.

- In the models we explore, we constantly do the inversion algebraically. That is, for a given market, if the demand function is $D(p) = 1000(105-p)$, then algebra tells us that the inverse demand function is $P(x) = 105 - (x/1000)$. And, conversely, if the inverse demand function for some other market is $P(x) = 12 - 0.002x$, I expect you to compute without strain that the demand function for this market is $D(p) = 6000 - 500p$.

Demand Facing a Firm versus Facing an Industry

The concept of a demand function gets used in two different ways: It can be the demand facing an entire industry or it can represent demand facing a particular firm within an industry. For instance, we might wish to discuss the demand for automobiles in the United States; in other cases, we might discuss the demand facing General Motors for the same period. The distinction is unimportant for industries that contain a single firm—in which case, we call the industry and the single firm in it a *monopoly*—but it becomes important in multifirm industries.

Usually, the demand facing a single firm in the industry is much more responsive to price than the demand facing the industry as a whole. If every laptop manufacturer raised its price by, say, 10%, demand for laptops would fall. But the demand for Dell laptops would fall a lot more (proportionately) if Dell raised its prices 10%, while all other manufacturers held their prices fixed.

Product Differentiation and Commodities

The concept of industrywide demand implicitly presumes that the good sold and the prices charged are uniform enough across producers that all this makes sense. Given the wide variety of computers, we do not speak of a demand function for the computer industry as a whole. We speak instead of the industry demand for Wintel (Windows–Intel) desktops or for Wintel laptops, and even this is a stretch given the variety of such machines.

These considerations apply as well to single firms that sell a type of product in a number of different varieties related to specification, quality, and so on. For instance, Honda sells different models and types of automobiles, and it sells the same basic model with different engine sizes, suspensions, and trims. The market for Honda Civics is not the same as the market for Honda Preludes, and we do not put the two on to a single demand function.

When a good being sold comes in several varieties that are distinguished enough that the purchasers do not view the varieties as perfect substitutes, the products are *differentiated*. When purchasers make no distinction among the goods being sold by different producers, viewing them as more or less identical and perfect substitutes, the good is a *commodity*.

Notwithstanding what I just said, sometimes it makes modeling sense to treat differentiated products as a single commodity. For instance, in Chapters 1 and 2, we built a model in which the various light trucks produced by General Motors—including vans, minivans, full-sized pickups, and compact pickups, produced by the various divisions of GM—were treated as a single generic light truck, with a single demand function. Marketing analysts at GM almost surely would find this too simplified for their purposes, but as long as we are after qualitative insights about what determines the cost to GM of various coupon programs, it suffices. It takes experience to make wise modeling choices of this sort. But, when aiming for intuitive insights, simpler is usually better: It is hard enough to figure out what is going on in the spreadsheet model of Chapters 1 and 2; it would be a lot harder if I began with a model that took into account the wide variety of GM light trucks.

Competitive Firms and Firms with Market Power

Especially in commodity markets, the differences in demand facing the industry and facing a single producer can be dramatic. For instance, industry demand for spot (immediate) shipping of crude oil from the Persian Gulf to northwest Europe is not very sensitive to price. The cost to refiners of shipment is a small part of the overall cost of the crude oil, and during a cold snap in northern Europe, refiners, whose stocks of heating oil are dwindling quickly, are prepared to pay whatever is the market price of shipment to move crude from the Persian Gulf to refineries. But the services offered by owner–operators of so-called very large crude carriers (VLCCs) on the spot-shipping market are pretty close to undifferentiated, and brokers (people who match demand with supply) have superb information networks about available VLCCs. Hence, a small spot shipper, someone who operates a small fleet of tankers, faces a lot of competition. This individual ship operator can get all the cargo his tankers can handle if he is willing to ship a bit more cheaply than competitors. But an operator who demands a price higher than that of competitors will have tankers circling the Persian Gulf aimlessly, without cargo or anywhere to go.

In essence, the owner–operator of a VLCC is a *price taker*. The market has a prevailing price, determined by industrywide forces of supply and demand, and the individual owner–operator has to do business at that price or not at all. There is no point in charging less than the prevailing market price, and there is no business at any higher price. In *Economese*, the language of economics, when everyone in an industry is a price taker, we say that the industry is *competitive* or *perfectly competitive* and firms in the industry are *perfectly competitive*.

This is one place where standard English usage and Economese diverge sharply. A journalist who writes that a company, by making major investments in new technology, has become more competitive on the world market does not mean that the company has lost the ability to control the price of its output. When an economist says that a market has become more competitive, however, she means precisely that firms inside the industry are closer to price takers than to price setters.

A firm that chooses the price of its output, selling an amount determined by its demand function, is called *imperfectly competitive* or *a firm with market power*. The distinction here is more a matter of degree than a dichotomy. Apple Computer can raise the price of Macintosh computers and not suffer from a calamitous decline in sales, because consumers perceive that Macs are fairly differentiated from standard Wintel computers. The manufacturer of a well-established brand of Wintel machines (Dell Computer, say) has somewhat less market power than Apple, but it still has some. And an East-Asian manufacturer of generic Wintel machines approaches being competitive.

The notion of a perfectly competitive firm—one that has absolutely no market power—is an important economic abstraction. Taken literally, such a firm faces a constant inverse demand function $P(x) = p_m$, where p_m is the prevailing market price. This is depicted as in Figure 4.1. This function has no inverse—turned $90°$, Figure 4.1 does not depict a function—and so a perfectly competitive firm does not face a demand function.

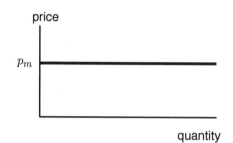

price

p_m

quantity

Figure 4.1. "Demand" facing a perfectly competitive firm. A perfectly competitive firm is unable to affect the price it gets for its output—it faces some market price p_m and can sell as much or as little as it wants at this price. It has a constant inverse demand function, $P(x) = p_m$.

A *supply function*—essential to the story of supply equals demand—tells how much suppliers in an industry would supply as a function of the prevailing market price. This construction therefore only makes sense for firms that are perfectly competitive. We avoid perfectly competitive firms until Chapter 11, so we also avoid supply equals demand. But, in Chapter 11, competitive firms become the stars of the story, and the ideas of Chapter 2 return to center stage.

Do Firms with Market Power Choose Price or Quantity?

A perfectly competitive firm has no power over the price it receives for its output; its decision is simply one of choosing the output level or rate. What about a firm with market power? Does it choose price or quantity? Most people find it more intuitive to imagine such a firm choosing the price it charges and then selling the quantity that corresponds to that price, according to the firm's demand function.

But, if we assume, as we always do in our simple models, that the firm knows its demand function, it is equivalent to think of the firm choosing the quantity it will sell and then adjusting the price so that it is able to sell that quantity. Perhaps the most satisfactory way to say this is that a firm with market power picks a price–quantity *pair* that lies along its demand/inverse demand functions. In choosing either price or quantity, it implicitly chooses the other, so in effect it simultaneously chooses both.

When studying these simple models, you have a choice. You can make quantity the driving variable: Express profit as a function of quantity, then maximize, with either Excel or calculus. Or you can make price the driving variable: Express profit or revenue and cost in terms of the price the firm chooses and maximize. Either will work perfectly well, as long as you are careful to choose one or the other as the variable to work with. Problem 4.1 gives you the opportunity to solve a profit-maximization problem both ways, to see that they give the same answer.

Is it better to work in terms of price or quantity? This is a matter of algebraic convenience. For a variety of reasons, it is more typical to work in terms of quantity, and therefore the terms *total revenue, total cost, marginal revenue*, and *marginal cost* almost always mean these things expressed as functions of the quantity the firm chooses to sell.

Questions about Units

Demand for wheat at $4.00 per bushel is 4 million bushels. What does this mean? About the only clear thing is that the price is a dollar price per bushel. We must specify precisely what we mean by wheat, the geographic scope of the market, and the time period involved.

- There are many different types of wheat, coming in many different grades. In the models of economics, we usually simplify and speak of the demand for wheat as a composite commodity. For some applications, this simplification can be too significant a concession and it becomes necessary to deal separately with different types and varieties of wheat; one must be guided by the extent to which this sort of composition gives useful models. Also, wheat delivered today is not the same as wheat delivered six months hence, which distinguishes *spot* from *futures* markets in wheat.

- Demand, whether for a single seller or industrywide, is usually delimited by geographical region, such as *demand for wheat in the United States* or *in California*. It rarely makes sense to speak of demand in very narrow regions such as *in Palo Alto* or in very broad regions such as *worldwide*, the former because demand in Palo Alto is radically affected by prices in the neighboring town of Menlo Park, and the latter because the conditions of a single price rarely hold worldwide. But, for some commodity items, such as crude oil, speaking of worldwide demand is entirely natural and often done.

- Demand is also sometimes delimited by buyer group. An electric utility might consider separately household, commercial, and industrial demand for electricity. A consumer marketing firm may decompose the demand it faces into demographic groups, distinguished by age, sex, family income, and so on.

- A period of time must be specified: Is the demand for wheat at $4.00 per bushel over a period of a day, a week, or a month?

For most of the models in this book, we rarely are so precise as to specify all these things, largely because the models we build are usually constructed as parables and not as models of real markets. But, in a few instances where we look at real markets, we have to be specific along these lines, and you will discover that this is easier to say than do.

Ceteris Paribus: What Is Held Fixed?

A demand function records how the quantity of a certain good demanded changes as a function of the price of the good. But the amount demanded depends on much more than the price of the good alone. The demand for wheat depends on the price of substitutes, such as corn and rice, and to some extent on things like the state of the economy. The demand for Chevrolets depends on the price of Fords and Hondas and very much on the state of the economy. The demand for Macintosh laptops depends on the price of other Macintosh compatible laptops, the price of other desktop Macs, the price of other (Wintel) laptops, and even consumer anticipations concerning the price of Mac laptops over the next 18 months.

When we work with a demand function, we look at the effect on demand of one variable, its own price, among many that determine overall demand. To do this, we have to do something with the values of those other variables. Economists usually incant *ceteris paribus*, which is Latin for "everything else held equal," and proceed holding fixed at some levels all those other variables. Don't think of there being a single demand function for Mac laptops in the United States over the next month, but rather a family of these functions, parameterized by the values of those other variables.

Ceteris paribus is easy enough to say, but less easy to do. For instance:

- When constructing the demand function for American Airlines' flights from Chicago to San Francisco, what should be assumed about the price charged by United Airlines on the same route? We can hold fixed the price charged by United, but if we are constructing the demand function to model the pricing decisions of American Airlines and if management at American Airlines believes that United will match any price cuts, the relevant demand function facing American should presume United's price-matching.

- Demand for a new line of Macintosh computers depends on consumer expectations about how Macintosh will price those computers in the relatively near future. If Apple Computer drops the price of the computers today, consumers might expect even larger price drops in the future, depressing immediate demand. Apple Computer, by its price policies today, affects consumer expectations; it makes little sense to hold those expectations fixed in constructing today's demand function.

- When constructing the marketwide demand function for wheat, should we hold fixed the current price of corn? Before you answer Yes, let me ask a second question: Should we hold fixed the market supply of corn? The point is, you cannot hold both the price and the supply of corn fixed, if you are varying the price of wheat. If, say, the price of wheat falls, demand for corn decreases. Holding fixed the supply of corn requires a fall in the price of corn. Holding fixed the price of corn requires a fall in the supply of corn. When constructing the demand function for wheat, should we fix the price or the supply of corn?

None of these situations is easy to deal with. In the case of United and American Airlines, economists would usually formulate demand functions with both prices explicitly included and use techniques from Chapters 20 through 23 to analyze the competitive interactions. In the second story, marketing specialists would have to be consulted, to see what sort of reputation Apple has among consumers and how they might construe a price change today. In formulating the demand for wheat, if a short-run analysis is being contemplated, it is probably better to hold the supply of corn fixed; while for a longer-run analysis, it is probably better to hold the price of corn fixed. Do not be alarmed if you do not see the basis for these assertions; a lot of economics that you have yet to see goes into each one. The point for now is, When you hear an economist say ceteris paribus, do not think of it as trivial.

Do Demand Functions Slope Downward?

In virtually every example we discuss in this book, demand slopes downward: The higher the price, the less is the amount demanded. (For perfectly competitive firms, demand is not defined, and inverse demand is flat.) Assuming that demand is downward sloping makes life easy in several respects. For instance, whenever demand slopes downward, we can think and work interchangeably with the demand and inverse demand functions. But we do not want to be guided by analytical convenience alone.

Do demand functions slope downward? Most economists would answer, Normally yes, but the possibility exists that demand slopes upward, at least for some ranges of prices and especially if we are speaking of the demand by a single purchaser or a subset of the population. Exceptions, when they arise, usually arise because purchasers are unsure about the quality of the good and assume that the posted price signals something about quality. A potentially very important example concerns financial securities, such as shares of equity: If the price of shares in a company begins to rise, investors may suddenly take notice, decide that someone must know something good about the company, and so increase demand. Of course, this would have to stop at some price level, but the possibility exists that, at least for a while, demand increases in price, especially for less well-informed investors.

Such possibilities should be carefully considered, especially in a context as important as equity markets, but for the remainder of this book, we follow economic orthodoxy and assume that demand functions slope downward.

4.2. Do Firms Know Their Demand Functions?

In just a few pages, we start imagining profit-maximizing firms that decide what price to charge and how much to produce based on the demand function they face. So how do real-life sellers discover the demand functions they face, if they do so at all?

To state the obvious, no firm knows the demand curve it faces to the mathematical precision we assume in models. Experience and savvy sometimes give a manager an idea how many units more or less he can expect to sell if he lowers or raises his prices a bit. In other words, he may have a reasonable idea what his demand function looks like around the prices he has been charging. But the further he moves from prices where he has recent experience, the less he knows. General Motors probably has a reasonable idea what would happen to the number of cars it would sell if it moved prices up or down a percentage point or so. But it would be a lot harder to guess how much it might sell if, say, it cut its price by 20%.

Firms that engage in large-scale consumer marketing do more than guess at their demand functions. These firms engage in systematic statistical estimation of the demand they face. The data they need can be gathered in many ways: Some firms ask panels of consumers hypothetical questions, such as, How much would you buy if the price of our product was X? How much if it was Y? Or, rather than rely on responses to hypothetical questions, the firms can test market the product, selling it in one region at one price and in a second region at a somewhat different price.

Two technological advances make this sort of marketing experiment a lot easier to do. The first advance is the supermarket scanner, which records and stores, consumer by consumer, precisely what the particular consumer has purchased. The second advance is the Internet and the phenomenon of Internet marketing. Imagine, for instance, that Amazon.com, the Internet bookseller, is curious how demand for a particular book would respond to a deeper discount than Amazon currently offers. It is easy for Amazon to randomly offer consumers different prices over the Web—one consumer is quoted a standard price, while a second is offered a discount—and then the results in sales made are analyzed statistically (see Problem 4.15).

The bottom line is that firms don't know the demand functions they face, but they often know how demand varies in a neighborhood of the prices they have been charging, so they can undertake marginal analysis, at least.

4.3. Elasticity

Elasticity is a general term economists use to describe how responsive one quantity is to changes in a second quantity. In this chapter, we are concerned with the elasticity of demand.

> *The elasticity of demand along a demand function $D(p)$ at a given price is the rate of percentage change in quantity demanded per 1% change in the price, starting from that price.*

Calculating Elasticity with Discrete Changes

That is quite a mouthful, but a formula will, I hope, clarify. Start with a demand function $D(p)$ and a price p_0. Let x_0 be the corresponding quantity; that is, $x_0 = D(p_0)$.

- If the price changes slightly, from p_0 to $p_0 + \Delta p$, the percentage change in price is $100 \times \Delta p / p_0$.

- When price changes to $p_0 + \Delta p$, the quantity demanded changes to $D(p_0 + \Delta p)$. The change in quantity is $\Delta x = D(p_0 + \Delta p) - x_0$, giving a percentage change in quantity of $100 \times \Delta x / x_0$.

- Elasticity is the ratio of the percentage change in quantity to the percentage change in price. Cancelling the 100's and letting $\nu(p_0)$ denote the elasticity of demand at the price p_0, this gives

$$\nu(p_0) = \frac{\Delta x / x_0}{\Delta p / p_0}.$$

We'll also be dealing with the elasticity of demand along a given *inverse* demand function $P(x)$, at the quantity x_0. This is also the rate of percentage change in quantity per 1% change in price. Denoted by $\hat{v}(x_0)$ it is given by exactly the formula just shown.

Four questions need to be addressed:

1. If $\hat{v}(x_0)$ is given by exactly the same formula and is exactly the same thing as $v(p_0)$, what is the point of the hat in $\hat{v}$?

2. Does it matter how big is the small change in price Δp?

3. Why are we looking at the ratios of *percentage* changes?

4. What is the point of this whole thing, anyway?

The answers take a few pages, but they are coming. It is easiest to address them and clarify what is going on with an example. Consider the demand function $D(p) = 1000(20 - p)$. Fix the price $p_0 = 15$. The corresponding quantity is $x_0 = 1000(20 - 15) = 5000$. To find the elasticity of demand at this price–quantity pair along this demand function, we calculate demand at a slightly different price. For instance, we might take the price 15.30, at which point demand is $1000(20 - 15.30) = 4700$. The change in price, 0.30, is a 2% increase on a base of 15, while the fall in demand, from 5000 to 4700, is a 6% decrease on a base of 5000. Hence, the elasticity of demand, along this demand function, at this price–quantity pair is $-6\%/2\% = -3$.

- This is just the formula in action: $p_0 = 15$, $q_0 = 5000$, $\Delta p = 0.30$, and $\Delta x = -300$, so the formula says to compute

$$\frac{-300/5000}{0.30/15} = \frac{-0.06}{0.02} = -3.$$

- Elasticity is negative. Both p_0 and x_0 are positive, and since demand is downward sloping, the sign of Δx is the reverse of the sign of Δp. One is positive and the other, negative.

- We could have started with a baseline quantity of $x_0 = 5000$ and the inverse demand function $P(x) = 20 - x/1000$, to find that the corresponding price is $20 - 5000/1000 = 15$. And we could have chosen a change in quantity, from 5000 to 4700, or $\Delta x = -300$, with a corresponding change in price $\Delta p = [20 - 4700/1000] - 15 = 15.30 - 15 = 0.30$. Then, applying the formula, we would get the same -3 for the elasticity of demand.

What is the point of the hat in $\hat{v}$? Elasticity is a property of the demand function at a particular price–quantity pair along the demand function. When we want to signal that we are specifying the price–quantity pair by fixing the price, we write $\nu(p)$, without the hat. When we want to signal that we are specifying the price–quantity pair by fixing the quantity, we write $\hat{\nu}(x)$. But, for a given demand function and price–quantity pair (p_0, x_0) along the demand function, the elasticity of demand is the same thing. Or, in symbols, if $x_0 = D(p_0)$, then $\nu(p_0) = \hat{\nu}(x_0)$. In particular, in this example, $\nu(15) = \hat{\nu}(5000) = -3$.

Does it matter in computing elasticity what is the small change in price Δp? Starting with the same demand function and the same base price $p_0 = 15$, suppose we had used as the second price 15.15 or 15.03 or 14.70. This changes the answer we get for elasticity in general, but not in this specific example. To see this, rewrite the formula for elasticity as follows:

$$\frac{\Delta x / x_0}{\Delta p / p_0} = \frac{\Delta x}{\Delta p} \times \frac{p_0}{x_0}.$$

In this example, the fraction $\Delta x / \Delta p$ is constant, because this demand function is linear. But, for a nonlinear demand function, this ratio changes as Δp changes.

Formulas for Elasticity That Use Calculus

Having said that, we can also say that as long as the demand function is smooth at p_0, if Δp is small, it does not matter much what value of Δp you pick. The reason is that $\Delta x / \Delta p$, for small values of Δp, is approximately $D'(p_0)$, the derivative of the demand function at the value p_0. Hence, if the demand function is given algebraically and you can take its derivative at p_0, you need not mess with small changes in price or quantity to find the elasticity. Instead, use the formula

$$\nu(p_0) = D'(p_0) \times \frac{p_0}{x_0} = D'(p_0) \times \frac{p_0}{D(p_0)}.$$

For instance, if the demand function is $D(p) = 1000(20 - p)$, then $D'(p)$ is the constant -1000, and so the elasticity of demand at $p = 15$ is

$$-1000 \times \frac{15}{5000} = -3.$$

Or, if you are working with the inverse demand function $P(x)$ instead of with the demand function $D(p)$, rewrite $\hat{\nu}(x_0)$ as follows :

$$\hat{\nu}(x_0) = \frac{\Delta x / x_0}{\Delta p / p_0} = \frac{1}{\Delta p / \Delta x} \times \frac{p_0}{x_0}.$$

For small values of Δx, $\Delta p / \Delta x$ is approximately $P'(x_0)$, the derivative of inverse demand at the value x_0. Hence

$$\hat{v}(x_0) = \frac{1}{P'(x_0)} \times \frac{p_0}{x_0} = \frac{1}{P'(x_0)} \times \frac{P(x_0)}{x_0}.$$

For instance, for the inverse demand function $P(x) = 20 - x/1000$, at $x_0 = 5000$ the corresponding price is 15. The derivative of inverse demand is the constant $-1/1000$ (constant because inverse demand is linear), and so the formula tells us that

$$\hat{v}(5000) = \frac{1}{-1/1000} \times \frac{15}{5000} = -1000 \times \frac{15}{5000} = -3.$$

In summary, the basic definition of elasticity is the ratio of the percentage change in quantity demanded to the percentage change in price for a given demand function and price–quantity pair along that demand function. Elasticity is expressed as a function of price as $v(p)$, or as a function of quantity $\hat{v}(x)$. To compute elasticity, you can use the "discrete changes" formula or either of the two formulas that use the derivatives of demand and inverse demand: These formulas can be written in one line as

$$v(p_0) = D'(p_0) \times \frac{p_0}{D(p_0)} \approx \frac{\Delta x/x_0}{\Delta p/p_0} \approx \frac{1}{P'(x_0)} \times \frac{P(x_0)}{x_0} = \hat{v}(x_0), \qquad (4.1)$$

where it is implicit that $D(p)$ and $P(x)$ are inverses of one another, and the price–quantity pair (p_0, x_0) lies along the given demand/inverse demand functions. Note that I use equals signs at the first and last steps in this progression, but approximately equal signs in the middle: The term *elasticity of demand* conventionally goes with the precise, calculus-based formulas, while the discrete measures of elasticity give approximations, which are better the smaller are Δp and Δx.

Changing Elasticity and Constant Elasticity

I still have two questions to go—Why use percentage changes? and What is this good for?—but before turning to those, I want to note that elasticity in general changes along a given demand function. For instance, in our example $D(p) = 1000(20 - p)$, we computed that, at the price 15 and quantity 5000, the elasticity of demand is -3. What about the price 5, which corresponds to a quantity of 15,000? I leave it to you to do the math—you have a choice of using a discrete change in price, or using calculus and one of the formulas in equation (4.1)—you'll find that $\nu(5) = \hat{\nu}(15000) = -1/3$. Or try the price 10 and corresponding quantity 10,000: You'll discover that $\nu(10) = \hat{\nu}(10,000) = -1$.

Some special demand functions have constant elasticity of demand. These demand functions take the form $D(p) = Cp^k$, for some constants $C > 0$ and $k < 0$: Note that, for this demand function, $D'(p) = Ckp^{k-1}$, so the calculus formula for $\nu(p)$ tells us that

$$\nu(p) = D'(p) \times \frac{p}{D(p)} = Ckp^{k-1} \times \frac{p}{Cp^k} = k.$$

That is, the elasticity of this demand function is the constant k.

Why Percentage Changes?

Why are we looking at ratios of percentage changes? If we want to measure how responsive quantity is to changes in price, why not use the plain old derivative of the demand function?

These questions are best answered with an example. Suppose we are studying the demand for wheat in the European Community. At a price of 2.5 euros per bushel, demand might be for 60 million kilograms over a period of a month. Suppose demand falls to 58 million kilograms if price increases to 2.6 euros. Using this discrete change, the impact of a 0.1 euro change in price is a 2 million kg change in quantity. The derivative is 20 million. But suppose we measure wheat not in kilograms but in metric tons. And instead of a month, we use a week for the time period. Further, instead of measuring prices in euros, we use deutsche marks. All these changes in units mean a dramatic change in the derivative. To say that the derivative is 20 million is to say very little, and, in particular, that number gives us no guidance whether demand for wheat is "very responsive to price," or "moderately responsive," or "not at all responsive."

But if we look at ratios of percentage changes, none of the units matter. A 2 million decline on a base of 60 million, is a 3.33% decline whether quantity is measured in kilograms or metric tons or even ounces. And assuming reasonable stability in demand through time, it does not matter if we measure demand by the month or the week. At the same time, a 4% rise in price, from 2.5 to 2.6 euros, remains a 4% rise in price whether prices are denominated in euros, deutsche marks, or French francs.

Moreover, if a 4% rise in the price of wheat leads to a 3.33% decline in demand, while a 4% rise in the price of veal leads to an 8% decline in demand, it makes sense to say that the demand for veal is more responsive to price changes than the demand for wheat. In terms of demand facing firms, suppose a 5% rise in the price of Macintosh computers would lead to an 8% decline in demand for Macs, a 5% rise in the price of Dell desktops would lead to a 20% decline in demand for Dells, and a 5% rise in the price of a generic Wintel machine made in East Asia would lead to a 50% decline in demand for those computers. Then we would say that Apple has more market power than Dell, which in turn has more market power than the East Asian manufacturer.

Relating Price and Marginal Revenue via Elasticity

We can see this most clearly if we go back to an issue raised in the last chapter. Recall that marginal revenue is, in general, less than price. The change in total revenue (marginal revenue) when $x + 1$ units are sold instead of x has two components. First is the added revenue from selling the $x+1$st unit, $P(x+1)$. Offsetting this is the loss in revenue on the first x units, incurred because instead of selling them at $P(x)$ apiece, they are sold for the (presumably slightly) lower price $P(x + 1)$. This offsetting loss is $x[P(x) - P(x + 1)]$. Expressing this algebraically,

$$\text{MR}(x) = (x + 1)P(x + 1) - xP(x) = P(x + 1) + x[P(x + 1) - P(x)].$$

(Of course, this is a discrete measure of marginal revenue. We redo this with calculus momentarily.) In most cases, x is a fairly big number, and so $P(x + 1)$ is approximately the same as $P(x)$. Therefore we can replace the first term $P(x + 1)$ with $P(x)$ and have the approximate equation

$$\text{MR} = P(x) + x[P(x + 1) - P(x)] = P(x)\left[1 + x\frac{P(x + 1) - P(x)}{P(x)}\right].$$

I can hear the objections: "If $P(x)$ is approximately the same as $P(x+1)$, then the second piece of this, involving the difference in prices $P(x + 1) - P(x)$, is approximately 0. So, in the spirit of approximation, can't we drop the second term?" We cannot, because, while $P(x + 1) - P(x)$ is generally a small number, this small difference is multiplied by the large number x. Especially when dealing with x measured in thousands of units or more, the product $x[P(x + 1) - P(x)]$ is usually something significant.

The point of all this algebra is that $x[P(x+1) - P(x)]/P(x)$ is just $1/\hat{\nu}(x)$, at least insofar as we are using discrete measures of elasticity. If this confuses you, remember that, in this case, Δx is 1. So we have

$$\text{MR}(x) = P(x)\left[1 + \frac{1}{\hat{\nu}(x)}\right]. \tag{4.2}$$

With calculus, we get the formula (4.2) quickly and directly from the product rule for derivatives. Since TR$(x) = xP(x)$,

$$\frac{\mathrm{dTR}(x)}{\mathrm{d}x} = \frac{\mathrm{d}xP(x)}{\mathrm{d}x} = P(x) + xP'(x) = P(x)\left[1 + \frac{xP'(x)}{P(x)}\right] = P(x)\left[1 + \frac{1}{\hat{\nu}(x)}\right],$$

where the last equation uses the definition of elasticity from inverse demand.

Memorize formula (4.2). It tells us that the elasticity of demand determines the degree to which marginal revenue falls short of price:

- The knife-edge case is an elasticity of -1. Then the formula says that MR$(x) = 0$: The revenue from selling another unit is precisely offset by the loss in revenue from a lower price for the first x units.

The case of $\hat{\nu}(x) = -1$, called *unit elasticity*, separates cases where $\hat{\nu}(x) < -1$, called *elastic demand*, from cases where $\hat{\nu}(x) > -1$, called *inelastic demand*. Formula (4.2) shows that:

- Where demand is elastic, or $\hat{\nu}(x) < -1$, marginal revenue is positive. The more elastic is demand, the closer marginal revenue is to price.

- Where demand is inelastic, or $\hat{\nu}(x) > -1$, marginal revenue is negative. The more inelastic is demand, the more negative is marginal revenue, for a fixed price.

We already noted that, in general, elasticity changes as you move along a given demand function, unless the demand function is of the constant elasticity variety. In particular, for linear demand functions, demand is elastic (that is, $\hat{\nu}(x) < -1$) for high-price–low-quantity pairs and inelastic ($\hat{\nu}(x) > -1$) for low prices and large quantities. The formula says that this means positive marginal revenue for low quantity levels and negative marginal revenue for high quantities. I suggest you try Problem 4.3 to reinforce all this.

Using the Formula

Formula (4.2) can be used in a variety of ways. In particular, it can be used for problems of the following sort:

> Based on market experimentation, a firm believes that, for prices for its product in the range \$10–\$15, its elasticity of demand is approximately -2.5. The firm currently charges a price near the upper end of this range, $p = \$14$. At this price, the firm sells 30,000 units per month. The firm's cost function is TC$(x) = \$7.50x$. (a) Is the firm currently profit maximizing? (b) If not, how much should it charge to maximize profit?

To answer these questions, we first compute that the marginal revenue of the firm, charging a price of $14 and selling 30,000 units, is

$$\text{MR}(30{,}000) = \$14 \times \left(1 + \frac{1}{\hat{\nu}(30{,}000)}\right) = 14\left(1 + \frac{1}{-2.5}\right)$$

$$= 14 \times (1 - 0.4) = 14 \times 0.6 = \$8.40.$$

Since its marginal cost is only $7.50, the firm would increase profit by selling more units.

As for part b, if elasticity stays at −2.5 as the price changes, the profit-maximizing price is where marginal cost (of $7.50) equals marginal revenue, or the price p that solves

$$\$7.50 = p \times \left(1 + \frac{1}{-2.5}\right) = 0.6p.$$

The solution to this equation is $p^* = \$7.50/0.6$, or $p^* = \$12.50$. Note that this is within the range for which the firm believes that elasticity is −2.5, so based on what we are told, this is a good candidate for profit maximization.

Problems 4.4 through 4.8 give you practice in using formula (4.2).

Other Elasticities

We do not pursue the matter of the elasticity of demand much further; but note that everything discussed above concerns *own-price elasticity*, a measure of the responsiveness in percentage terms of the demand for a good to a change in its own price. Economists also worry about elasticities such as *cross-price elasticities*, which measure the responsiveness of demand for product A to the price of product B; *advertising elasticities*, which measure the responsiveness of demand to changes in advertising budgets, and *income elasticities*, which measure the responsiveness of demand to changes in the level of income or wealth of the buyers.

4.4. Demand by Groups and in the Aggregate

Sometimes we work with demand functions that record the demand coming from each of several groups of customers. For instance, an electric utility might wish to think separately of demand from residential, commercial, and industrial customers; a consumer-marketing firm might wish to think separately about demand from different demographic groups.

Imagine, for instance, a firm selling some consumer good. The firm considers demand from three groups, segmented by age: customers 25 years old or less, those 26–55 years old, and those above 55 years old. It charges the same price p to all three groups, and demand functions for the three are, respectively, $D_y(p)$, $D_m(p)$, and $D_s(p)$, where the subscripts y, m, and s represent *youth*, *middle-aged*, and *seniors*, respectively. If the firm fixes its price at p_0, its total demand is the sum of the amount it sells to youths, $D_y(p_0)$; the amount it sells to middle-aged consumers, $D_m(p_0)$; and the amount it sells to seniors, $D_s(p_0)$. Thus, the total demand *function* it faces is the sum of the three component demand functions, or

$$D_{\text{TOTAL}}(p) = D_y(p) + D_m(p) + D_s(p).$$

As you read this paragraph, it probably seems that nothing could be more natural. But, in models and problems, a lot of confusion arises at this point, on two grounds.

1. If you graph total demand, remember that the price goes on the vertical axis, so this summing of functions is *horizontal* summing. To see what this means, look at Figure 4.2, in which I assume that each of the three component pieces of demand is linear. (See Problem 4.9 for the functions assumed in this figure.)

2. Suppose you were given *inverse* demand functions for each of the three groups, as $P_y(x_y)$, $P_m(x_m)$, and $P_s(x_s)$. To find total inverse demand, do you sum these three functions? *No!* Inverse demand gives the price it takes to excite a certain level of demand. If we fix a level of demand, say $x = 3000$, and sum $P_y(3000) + P_m(3000) + P_s(3000)$, we are summing the prices it takes to sell 3000 units to each group. This sum is likely to be a price at which no sales are made to any of the three groups. Summing prices makes no sense.

   To find total or aggregate inverse demand, if you have inverse demand functions for each group, first invert them to get demand functions for each group. Next sum the demand functions to get total or aggregate demand. And then invert the sum, to get aggregate inverse demand.

As strongly as I can, I urge you to work your way very carefully through Problem 4.9, which gives an example of all this. Until you do, you are unlikely to understand fully what you just read.

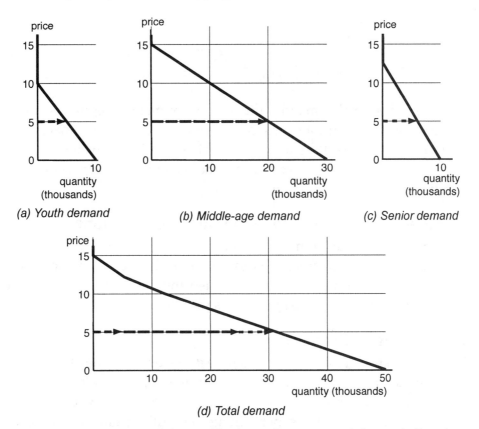

(a) Youth demand   *(b) Middle-age demand*   *(c) Senior demand*

(d) Total demand

Figure 4.2. Add pieces of demand horizontally to get total demand. Panels a, b, and c of the figure depict demand by youths, the middle-aged, and seniors, respectively. To get total demand, at a given price p, we find the quantity demanded by each group at the price and sum. In a picture, this translates to *horizontal* summing, as shown in panel d.

Elasticity of Total Demand from Elasticities of Pieces

Suppose we have demand broken into pieces, as in the example of the consumer-marketing firm that looks at demand by youths, middle-aged consumers, and seniors. Recall the notation

$$D_{\text{TOTAL}}(p) = D_y(p) + D_m(p) + D_s(p).$$

Suppose that we know the elasticities for each of the three pieces; that is,

$$\nu_y(p) = D'_y(p)\frac{p}{D_y(p)}, \quad \nu_m(p) = D'_m(p)\frac{p}{D_m(p)}, \quad \text{and} \quad \nu_s(p) = D'_s(p)\frac{p}{D_s(p)}.$$

Simple algebra tells us that

$$\nu_y(p)D_y(p) + \nu_m(p)D_m(p) + \nu_s(p)D_s(p)$$
$$= (D'_y(p) + D'_m(p) + D'_s(p))p = D'_{\text{TOTAL}}(p)p,$$

and thus

$$\nu_{\text{TOTAL}}(p) = D'_{\text{TOTAL}}(p)\, \frac{p}{D_{\text{TOTAL}}(p)} = \frac{\nu_y(p)D_y(p) + \nu_m(p)D_m(p) + \nu_s(p)D_s(p)}{D_y(p) + D_m(p) + D_s(p)}.$$

In words, when total demand is the sum of a number of segments or pieces, summed over demographic groups, different classes of customers, or even individual customers, the elasticity of total demand is the weighted average of the elasticities of the pieces, where the weights are proportional to the amounts demanded by each piece.

Marginal Revenue for Aggregate Demand Functions

We deal with several examples in the book where demand is the sum of demand by different demographic groups and where the demand functions for the different groups are linear. When this happens, be warned that marginal revenue is "interesting." Please see Problem 4.10.

Disaggregating Demand

Firms often have an incentive to *disaggregate* the demand they face, charging different sectors or groups of consumers different prices. When you see the local cheese store giving senior citizens a 10% discount, you are not necessarily observing a storekeeper willing to sacrifice profit to help feed the poor. "Helping to feed the poor" can be quite consistent with profit maximization. If you've ever wondered why manufacturers incur sizeable expense to distribute discount coupons or establish outlet stores at which they sell their product at drastically lower prices than at standard retail outlets, these actions arise from a desire to disaggregate demand. This topic—price discrimination—belongs to Chapter 7. But you now have sufficient tools to deal with it, and in Problems 4.13 and 4.14, you get a preview.

Executive Summary

- Demand functions encode the quantity that can be sold at each price; inverse demand, the price that can be charged for each quantity sold. Both are conventionally graphed with price on the vertical axis and quantity on the horizontal axis.

- Demand functions can encode the demand facing an entire industry and the demand facing a single firm. Demand facing an entire industry makes most sense for commodity items and less sense for differentiated products.

- Demand functions for real-life problems require specification of the breadth of the market in terms of the products included and the geographic and temporal scope of the market.

- Demand functions, which give the quantity demanded as a function of the price of a particular good, are constructed with *all other relevant parameters* (such as the prices of substitute and complementary goods *held fixed*. But in real life, holding these other things fixed can involve subtleties.

- We usually assume overall demand slopes downward, but no law says that this must be so.

- While it seems unlikely that a firm would ever know precisely the entire demand curve it faces, especially for prices far removed from the firm's experiences, firms—whether out of general experience or more careful empirical investigation—often have a good sense of how their demand varies locally; that is, what elasticity of demand they face around the prices with which they have experience.

- Elasticity—more precisely, own-price elasticity—is the percentage change in quantity demanded per 1% change in price, measured at different points along the demand curve. Elasticity can be computed based on (small) discrete changes in price and quantity or (using calculus) using derivatives. The relevant formulas are

$$\nu(p_0) = D'(p_0) \times \frac{p_0}{D(p_0)} \approx \frac{\Delta x/x_0}{\Delta p/p_0} \approx \frac{1}{P'(x_0)} \times \frac{P(x_0)}{x_0} = \hat{\nu}(x_0), \qquad (4.1)$$

- Elasticity determines how much marginal revenue falls short of price. The key formula is

$$\text{MR}(x) = P(x)\left(1 + \frac{1}{\hat{\nu}(x)}\right). \qquad (4.2)$$

- We sometimes deal with demand for a particular product by different demographic groups or classes of customers. When it comes to summing up these different pieces of overall demand, a price should be fixed and the quantities demanded summed; that is, sum horizontally.

Problems

4.1 Consider a firm with the demand function $D(p) = 2000(50 - p)$ and the total cost function $\text{TC}(x) = 10{,}000 + 10x$.

(a) Use a spreadsheet to find the price–quantity pair that maximizes profit for this firm.

(b) Use calculus to find the profit-maximizing quantity (and price) for this firm, by working with quantities and equating marginal revenue to marginal cost. Are you sure that this gives the profit-maximizing point? Why?

(c) Use calculus to find the profit-maximizing price (and quantity) for the firm to charge, by expressing profit as a function of price and setting the derivative equal to 0. Are you sure that this gives the profit-maximizing point? Why?

4.2 What is the inverse demand function for the demand function $D(p) = 1000(12 - p)$? (Assume that demand is 0 for prices greater than 12.) What quantity corresponds to the price $p = \$8$ along this demand function? Compute the elasticity of demand at the price–quantity pair ($\$8, 4000$), using the discrete change in price from $\$8$ to $\$8.04$. Using the inverse demand function, compute the elasticity of demand at the quantity–price pair ($4000, \$8$), using the discrete change in quantity from 4000 to 4080. If you have calculus in your arsenal, recompute the elasticity of demand at the price–quantity pair first using the derivative of the demand function and then using the derivative of the inverse demand function.

4.3 (a) Consider the demand function $D(p) = 1000(12 - p)$. Either use discrete changes to find the elasticity of demand at prices $p = 1, 2, 3, \ldots, 11$ or use calculus to find the elasticity-of-demand functions $\nu(p)$ and $\hat{\nu}(x)$.

(b) Using calculus, find the elasticity-of-demand functions for the general linear demand function, $D(p) = A - Bp$, for positive constants A and B. You should find elasticity both as a function of price, for prices between 0 and A/B, and as a function of quantity, for quantities between 0 and A. Also find the total revenue function TR(x). Where in terms of quantity x is marginal revenue positive? Where is it negative?

4.4 A firm sells its product for $\$8$ apiece and sells 10,000 units per month at that price. It estimates that for small changes in price, a 1% change in price means a 3% change in the quantity sold (in the opposite direction).

(a) What would be the change in total revenues or receipts for this firm if it lowered its price by $\$0.10$?

(b) What would be the change in total revenues or receipts for this firm if it lowered the quantity it sells by 150 units?

4.5 A profit-maximizing firm sells its goods at a price of $\$40$ apiece. Its marginal cost of production at its profit-maximizing level of production is $\$10$. For this firm, what is $\nu(\$40)$?

4.6 General Motors, a profit-maximizing firm, produces a single variety of light truck. It sells this truck for $20,000, at which price it sells approximately 1.6 million light trucks per year. GM estimates that, at this price–quantity pair, the elasticity of demand for its light truck is -4. Given that all this is true, what is the marginal cost of a GM light truck?

4.7 Go back to pages 90–91 and the problem discussed there. We said that $14 was not profit maximizing but, per the information given, $12.50 would be. How much would the firm's profit increase if it lowered its price to $12.50? (Warning: This is not easy.)

4.8 Firms that engage in so-called mark-up pricing set prices as follows. They determine how much, on the margin, is the cost of the goods they sell, then take that figure and add a fixed percentage to get the price.

Suppose a firm has a production technology with a constant marginal cost. This firm always marks up its marginal cost by 20% to get the price it charges; that is, if a product costs c on the margin, the firm charges the price $p = 1.2c$ for the good. If we believe that this firm is a profit maximizer, what implications does this have for the elasticity of demand of the firm's various products?

4.9 Go back to page 92 and the firm selling to the three consumer groups mentioned there. Suppose that the inverse demand functions facing this firm for the three groups are, respectively, $P_y(x_y) = 10 - x_y/1000$, $P_m(x_m) = 15 - x_m/2000$, and $P_s(x_s) = 12.5 - x_s/800$. Find the aggregate or total demand and inverse demand functions facing this firm.

4.10 Consider a firm that sells to two groups of customers. Demand by group 1 is $D_1(p) = 5000(20 - p)$, with no demand at prices above $20. Demand by group 2 is $D_2(p) = 10000(14 - p)$, with no demand at prices above $14. This firm's marginal cost of production is a constant $10. What price maximizes its profits?

4.11 Imagine a firm that sells a product, a light truck, to customers at a price of $20,000 apiece. At this price, it sells 1.5 million light trucks per year. Of these trucks, 450,000 are sold to past owners of light trucks from this firm. This group's elasticity of demand at the $20,000 price is -1.667. The other 1.05 million trucks (at the price $20,000) go to individuals who are not past owners. Their elasticity of demand at $20,000 is -5. What is the overall elasticity of demand facing this firm at the price $20,000?

4.12 (a) A consumer marketing firm has been test marketing a new product in a number of markets. This firm believes that demand for its product comes entirely from women aged 15–35, and that demand by the 15–25 year-old group is quite different from consumers in the 26–35 year-old segment. Specifically, per 1000 women between 15 and 25 in a market, the firm would sell $X_1 = 500(10 - P)$ units at the price P (to those women), while it would sell $X_2 = 250(15 - P)$ per 1000 women between 26 and 35. What demand function would this firm face in a market that has 40,000 women in the age group 15–25 and 25,000 women in the age group 26–35?

(b) It is unlikely that a real firm would have the sort of knowledge assumed in part a. It is much more realistic that the firm would know "local" data about the demand by various segments, local in the sense that the data are for small changes in price only. For example, the firm might know, on the basis of consumer surveys or test marketing, that at a price of $8:

- Per 1000 women aged 15–20, it can expect to sell 600 units of the good, with a price elasticity of -1.0.

- Per 1000 women aged 21–25, it can expect to sell 500 units of the good, with a price elasticity of -1.2;

- Per 1000 women aged 26–30, it can expect to sell 600 units of the good, with a price elasticity of -1.5.

- Per 1000 women aged 31–35, it can expect to sell 300 units of the good, with a price elasticity of -2.0.

(Note that these data are not consistent with the data given in part a.) In a market with 25,000 women aged 15–20, 15,000 aged 21–25, 10,000 aged 26–30, and 5,000 aged 31–35, how many units can the firm expect to sell at a price of $8 per unit? Approximately how many can it expect to sell at a price of $8.16?

(c) Suppose this firm has a constant marginal cost of production of $c = \$2$ per unit. Assuming the firm faces falling marginal revenues, is the price of $8 per unit too high, too low, or just right for profit maximization, based on the demand data given in part b?

4.13 A bakery in the seaside resort town of Malvino sells freshly baked bread to two categories of customers: residents of the town and tourists. The weekly demand from tourists is given by the demand function

$$X_T = 120(5 - P)$$

for prices P between $0 and $5. (There is no demand at prices above $5.00

per loaf.) The weekly demand from local residents is

$$X_L = 180(3 - P)$$

for prices P between $0 and $3. (There is no demand from locals at prices above $3.00 per loaf.) The bakery's marginal cost per loaf is a constant $1.20.

(a) Suppose the Acme Bakery could somehow set different prices for locals and for tourists. What prices would it set for each group? What profit would it earn from the two groups?

(b) If Acme had to charge the same price to both locals and tourists, what price would it set? What would be its level of profit?

(c) The Acme Bakery has come to the Malvino Town Council with a request for a zoning variance that will permit it to sell bread inside the residential district of the town. This will permit it to sell bread at the optimal price for tourists at its store on Main Street and sell bread at the optimal price for locals in this new outlet. The geography of the town is such that no tourist could buy bread at the store intended for locals (they would be unable to find it and, since the locals in Malvino are very taciturn and suspicious of strangers, no local will tell any tourist of its existence) and no local would buy from the Main Street store unless the price on Main Street were lower than the price in the residential district. Acme's argument in favor of this is that it would promote the profits of local industry. As a member of the Malvino Town Council, you are concerned about the profits of the bakery—it makes generous contributions to your reelection campaign—but you also need votes, and so you are very concerned with the welfare of local consumers. Should you favor this zoning variance?

4.14 Suppose a manufacturer with a constant marginal cost production technology sells 10,000 units at a price of $10 per unit. The elasticity of demand facing this manufacturer at this price is -3. The price of $10 is profit maximizing.

The manufacturer decides to engage in a coupon campaign. In this campaign, coupons offering an instant discount of $0.50 per unit purchased to anyone holding a coupon would be distributed to a segment of the entire buying public. (In real life, you need a separate coupon for each unit purchased. If you think of coupons as operating in this fashion, imagine that that members of this segment of the population will have access to as many coupons as they wish to use.) Marketing specialists determine that the segment of the buying public that would obtain a coupon purchases 3000 units at a net per-unit price of $10 per unit and has an elasticity of demand of -6

at that price per unit. The remaining 70% of the population have no access to coupons and so must pay the full price, which—until part c—is $10 per unit.

(a) How would this coupon campaign affect the firm's profit? (There are several steps to solving this, so you might need to consult the solutions, to see how to proceed. Also, check your solution to part a before going on with the rest of the problem.)

(b) Suppose the manufacturer keeps the noncoupon price at $10 and optimizes over the coupon value. What coupon value should be selected, and what is the impact on profit?

(c) Suppose the manufacturer optimizes over both the noncoupon price and the coupon value. That is, the $10 price may change as well as the amount off provided by the coupon. What noncoupon price and what coupon value should be chosen, and what is the impact on profit?

(d) Suppose that an alternative coupon program would get the coupons into the hands of 40% of the consuming population, but this 40% has an (average) elasticity of demand of -5.2. Only one of the two coupon programs can be used. Which is better for the manufacturer?

So that your computations are the same as mine, compute changes in quantity demanded given price changes in the following "simpleminded" fashion: If a group has a price elasticity of -6 and its price falls by $x\%$, then its quantity demanded rises by $6x\%$. I suggest, very strongly, that you solve this problem with Excel. Part a isn't too bad done by hand, but the rest gets to be quite an algebraic mess. (The spreadsheet I use to solve this is PROBLEM 4-14, in case you need help getting started.)

4.15 (You need to know how to do ordinary least squares regression for this problem.) An Internet marketing company that sells clothing exclusively over the Internet has decided to do some test marketing. When customers inquire about a particular article of clothing, for which it has been charging $50, for a period of 6 weeks, it randomly quotes prices of $48, $49, $50, $51, and $52. (It quotes each of these five prices an equal number of times. You can assume that the firm has ways to make sure that once it quotes one of these prices to a customer, it continues to quote that price to the customer if he or she returns to the firm's website. Actually, this is a bit of a problem in real life, although with cookies, many wonderful things approaching this are possible.) Over the 6 week period, the firm recorded the sales data shown in Table 4.1. (You can extract these data from the spreadsheet PROBLEM 4-15, sheet 1.) Estimate the demand function facing this firm.

	week 1	week 2	week 3	week 4	week 5	week 6	total
$48	458	447	424	429	419	412	2589
$49	422	435	400	400	438	428	2523
$50	420	386	414	417	381	404	2422
$51	400	367	404	375	399	365	2310
$52	369	363	378	375	357	402	2244

Table 4.1. Data for problem 4.15. (Data available in spreadsheet PROBLEM 4-15.)

4.16 (Avoid this problem if you feel shaky on the material in this chapter.) In the text, the very useful formula

$$\text{MR}(x) = P(x)\left(1 + \frac{1}{\hat{\nu}(x)}\right)$$

was derived. Suppose we want to make price p the driving variable, rather than quantity x. That is, we begin with a demand function $D(p)$ and write $TR(p)$ for the amount $p \times D(p)$, which is total revenue or receipts as a function of p. Using the demand function $D(p)$ and the elasticity-of-demand function $\nu(p)$, derive a formula for the derivative in p of $TR(p)$ analogous to the formula just displayed. How does the sign (positive, negative, or zero) of this derivative relate to the elasticity of demand?

4.17 (This problem is for students with time on their hands and a love of high school algebra.) In Problem 4.1, we saw that solving the firm's profit-maximization problem can be done using either price or quantity as the driving variable. Because of the simple total cost function in that problem, you may have decided that it was easier to work with price than with quantity. Economists, however, almost always think in terms of quantity as the driving variable, at least when it comes to solving simple algebraic examples (such as in Problem 4.1), and in fact, the terms *marginal revenue* and *marginal cost* are reserved for the derivatives of total revenue and cost, expressed as functions of quantity.

In part, this preference for quantity arises because of the special case of perfect competition, where price is taken by the firm as given and quantity is the firm's sole decision variable. But this also reflects analytical ease for problems that are a step less simple than in Problem 4.1. To see what I mean, repeat Problem 4.1 with one amendment: Imagine that this firm has the total cost function $\text{TC}(x) = 10000 + 10x + .001x^2$. You'll find that the spreadsheet method of finding the answer is quite simple, and it is relatively easy to work in quantity. But—the point of this problem—have fun working through the analytic (calculus-based) solution of this problem using price as the driving variable.

5. Modeling Consumer Behavior

This chapter concerns the economic model of the utility-maximizing consumer, which is arguably *the* cornerstone of microeconomics:

- Section 5.1 introduces the basic model.
- In Section 5.2, the heart of the chapter, the model is used to solve the so-called consumer's problem of maximizing utility subject to a budget constraint.
- Pictures of this, using indifference curve diagrams, are described in Section 5.3.
- Demand functions for single consumers are created in Section 5.4.
- Section 5.5 presents the justification for this model.

In the models we've explored so far, the only entities making conscious choices have been firms, which have chosen production levels to maximize profits. But, in economic contexts, other sorts of "actors" make choices. Preeminent among these are persons, who choose how much to buy and consume, how much to save, how to invest those savings, where to work, how hard to work, and so forth. For a variety of purposes, including a better understanding what firms really do, we want to model the choice behavior of individuals.

This chapter introduces the model of the *utility-maximizing consumer*, which economists use for this purpose. Note carefully; we, eventually, use this basic model as the foundation for modeling savings and investment choices, effort choices on the job, and so forth. It would better suit the variety of applications we have in mind to call this the model of the *utility-maximizing person*, but economists use the term *consumer* instead of *person* and we follow suit. Indeed, in this chapter, all our illustrative examples concern a consumer choosing what to eat for lunch and, in places, how much money to leave in her pocket for future purchases. So, as far as our examples are concerned, the term *consumer* is entirely appropriate. But do not be misled by this; we apply this model much more broadly in later chapters.

5.1. The Model: Utility Maximization

The model of the utility-maximizing consumer is quite simple. A set of consumption bundles are offered to the consumer, from which she must choose. Let X denote the set of all consumption bundles that might ever be available. Then, a choice problem for the consumer is, Choose one x from a subset A of X, where A represents the set of *available* bundles. The consumer's behavior in the face of any choice problem is modeled as follows.

Every bundle x in X has a numerical value $u(x)$, called the *utility* of x. When faced with the problem of choosing from the set A, the consumer chooses whichever element x of A has the highest utility among all elements x of A.

Each consumer has her own subjective utility function, reflecting her own preferences and tastes. If Consumer H likes apples more than pears, bundles with more apples and fewer pears have higher utility, *according to H's utility function*, than otherwise identical bundles with more pears and fewer apples.

For instance, imagine a world in which there are only three different goods: bread, cheese, and salami. We fix units for each good, say, loaves of bread, kilos of cheese, and kilos of salami. A *bundle* of goods is an amount of bread, cheese, and salami, such as three loaves of bread, three-quarters of a kilo of cheese, and a kilo of salami. Listing bread first, cheese second, and salami third, we write this bundle compactly as the vector $(3, 0.75, 1)$. Another bundle would be $(1.5, 1, 0)$, meaning a bundle consisting of one and a half loaves of bread, a kilo of cheese, and no salami.

This can be confusing, so be careful. Do not think of x as a number, standing for a number of loaves of bread or kilos of cheese, so that the consumer chooses to fill her shopping basket with several points from X. Instead, x is a consumption *bundle*, a three-dimensional vector that describes everything in the consumer's shopping basket; and the consumer chooses a single x from X as a result of her trip to the market.

Imagine a consumer who has to choose between the following four bundles of goods:

$$(3, 3, 2), \quad (2, 1, 6), \quad (5, 0.1, 0.1), \quad (1, 4, 0.5).$$

Imagine as well that this consumer is modeled as having the *utility function*

$$u(b, c, s) = 3\ln(b) + \ln(c) + 0.5\ln(s),$$

where b, c, and s are the levels of bread, cheese, and salami, respectively, in the bundle (b, c, s), and $\ln(\cdot)$ is the natural logarithm function. (Important properties of the natural logarithm function are reviewed at the start of Chapter 5 material in the *Student's Companion*, for readers who need a review.) To the nearest 0.01, the utilities of the four bundles are

$$u(3, 3, 2) = 3\ln(3) + \ln(3) + 0.5\ln(2) = 4.74,$$

$$u(2, 1, 6) = 3 \ln(2) + \ln(1) + 0.5 \ln(6) = 2.98,$$
$$u(5, 0.1, 0.1) = 3 \ln(5) + \ln(0.1) + 0.5 \ln(0.1) = 1.37, \text{ and}$$
$$u(1, 4, 0.5) = 3 \ln(1) + \ln(4) + 0.5 \ln(0.5) = 1.04.$$

Thus, a consumer with the utility function we assume chooses $(3, 3, 2)$ from among these four bundles. If the choice were among (2,1,6), (5,0.1,0.1), and (1,4,0.5), then the chosen bundle would be (2,1,6), and so on. The point is that, once we know the utility function of the consumer, her behavior in every choice situation is clear: Her choice behavior is completely described by (1) her utility function and (2) the assertion that she always picks whichever bundle ranks most highly according to it.

Comments on the Basic Model

1. The essence of the model is that each consumer has a single utility function that works for all subsets A from which the consumer might choose. We do not allow the consumer's utility function to change depending on the range of choices available to her; if we did, the model would have no content. This is a real restriction, and, we see at the end of the chapter, it can be controversial in some contexts.

2. In some cases, more than one bundle in the set of bundles on offer may have the highest utility. In this case, we imagine that the consumer is happy to take any of the bundles that have highest utility, without a further care about which of those bundles she gets. Also, when two bundles give the same utility so that, according to the model, the consumer does not care which bundle she gets, she is said to be *indifferent* between the two bundles.

3. The numerical utility function is not what matters, but rather the order this function establishes among bundles. Suppose we took three other consumers, whose utility functions are

$$v_1(b, c, s) = 6 \ln(b) + 2 \ln(c) + \ln(s) + 2701,$$
$$v_2(b, c, s) = [3 \ln(b) + \ln(s) + 0.5 \ln(s)]^3, \text{ and}$$
$$v_3(b, c, s) = b^3 c s^{0.5}.$$

These functions establish exactly the same order among bundles as u, in the sense that, for any two bundles (b, c, s) and $(b', c's')$,

$$u(b, c, s) \geq u(b', c', s') \text{ if and only if } v_i(b, c, s) \geq v_i(b', c', s'),$$

for i = 1, 2, or 3. (Depending on the amount of math you know, you may need to take my word for this.) Thus, these three consumers' choices in any situation would be exactly the same as that of our original consumer. Put somewhat differently, in terms of our model of consumer choice behavior, it does not matter whether we think of our original consumer having the utility function u or one of the three v_i functions.

4. This is not to say that every utility function gives the same choice behavior, of course. Two utility functions that establish different orders over consumption bundles lead to different choice behaviors. For example, a consumer whose utility function is $v(b, c, s) = b + c + s$ would choose the bundle (2,1,6) from among the four we are considering, rather than (3,3,2), and someone with utility function $w(b, c, s) = 3b + c + s$ would choose (5,0.1,0.1). (Be sure you understand these two assertions.) Different consumers may order bundles differently and therefore make different choices, at least in some situations.

5. With respect to the particular utility function $u(b, c, s) = 3\ln(b) + \ln(c) + 0.5\ln(s)$, note that $\ln(x) < 0$, for $x < 1$, and so, $u(0.5, 0.5, 0.5) = 3\ln(0.5) + \ln(0.5) + 0.5\ln(0.5) < 0$. Does this mean that half a loaf of bread, half a kilo of cheese, and half a kilo of salami is worse than nothing at all?

   It absolutely *does not* mean that. The numerical quantities of utility have no particular meaning, and this is as true for the number 0 as it is for any other number. Thinking of 0 utility as being the utility of "nothing at all" makes as much sense as it does to think of $0°$ C or $0°$ F as meaning "no temperature at all." Presumably, you think that more bread or cheese or more salami is better than less. That is, if (b, c, s) is one bundle and (b', c', s') is another and if $b > b'$, $c > c'$, and $s > s'$, then you expect (b, c, s) to be higher in utility than (b', c', s'). Sure enough, since the natural logarithm function is increasing, that is the case; at least for the function $u(b, c, s) = 3\ln(b) + \ln(c) + 0.5\ln(s)$.

6. A "problem" with the utility function $u(b, c, s) = 3\ln(b) + \ln(c) + 0.5\ln(s)$ concerns bundles where one or more of the quantities $b, c,$ or s is 0. Look, for instance, at a bundle $(10, 10, 0)$, or 10 loaves of bread, 10 kilos of cheese, and no salami. Because $\ln(0) = -\infty$, $u(10, 10, 0) = -\infty$. What do we make of this, in terms of our consumer?

   A consumer whose utility function $u(b, c, s)$ is $3\ln(b) + \ln(c) + 0.5\ln(s)$ needs positive quantities of each of the three goods; she cannot make do with none of any one. Any positive amount, however small, of all three is better than any bundle of goods that has none of one or more of the three commodities. You may decide that this is a silly utility function, that consumers can usually stand to be without salami and would willingly choose, say, (100,100,0) over (0.001,0.001,0.001). But this is just saying that you do not find the particular utility function $u(b, c, s) = 3\ln(b) + \ln(c) + 0.5\ln(s)$ to be very believable; you want instead a function where $u(100, 100, 0) > u(0.001, 0.001, 0.001)$. For instance, the function $w(b, c, s) = 3\ln(b) + \ln(c+3) + 0.5\ln(s+5)$ describes a consumer who must have some positive amount of bread—any consumption bundle (b, c, s) where $b = 0$ gives utility $-\infty$—but who will survive quite nicely without any cheese or salami: For this utility function $w(100, 100, 0) = 3\ln(100) + \ln(103) + 0.5\ln(5) = 19.255$, while $w(0.001, 0.001, 0.001) = 3\ln(0.001) + \ln(3.001) + 0.5\ln(5.001) = -18.82$.

That is the model. The rest of this chapter is devoted to working with the model algebraically and graphically and to connecting it to demand functions. I proceed to this analysis directly. But this leaves hanging a question you may be asking yourself: Why would anyone put any credence in this model?

I will not answer that question fully until the very end of the chapter, but let me give you a fast justification.

Imagine someone dining at a roadside cafe who, when it is time for dessert, asks the waiter if they have any pie. "Yes we do," is the reply. "We have apple pie and cherry."

Customer: "I'll have apple pie, please."

The waiter goes to the kitchen to get a slice of apple pie but returns to declare, "We also have blueberry pie. Would you prefer that?"

To which the customer responds, "So you have blueberry pie, too! Well in that case, bring me a slice of cherry pie!"

Essentially, the model of the utility-maximizing consumer "works" for any consumer who never behaves in the manner of the customer in my story. That sort of behavior, and only that sort of behavior, is excluded.

5.2. The Consumer's Problem: Equating Bangs for the Buck

One context in which the model of the utility-maximizing consumer is frequently used is called *the consumer's problem*:

- The object being chosen is a consumption bundle, which is a vector listing amounts of various commodities. That is, a commodity bundle is a vector

$(x_1, x_2, \ldots, x_k)$, where k is the number of commodities, representing x_1 units of the first commodity, x_2 units of the second commodity, and so on, to x_k units of the kth commodity. It is fine to continue to think in terms of $k = 3$, with the three commodities being bread (in loaves), cheese (in kilos), and salami (in kilos), although keep in the back of your mind that the story is meant for much more general situations.

- Each commodity has a market price; p_j denotes the market price of the jth good on the list, measured in dollars per unit of the jth good. Imagine, for example, that bread costs $1.60 per loaf, cheese is $5.00 per kilo, and salami is $8.00 per kilo. Then, $p_1 = \$1.60$, $p_2 = \$5.00$, and $p_3 = \$8.00$.

- The consumer has an amount of wealth she can spend on her consumption bundle. In the abstract, we denote this amount of money by the variable y. But you can think, concretely, about our consumer having $160 to spend.

The consumer's problem is to purchase the *best* bundle she can afford. She can afford any bundle $(x_1, x_2, \ldots, x_k)$ whose total cost is less than her wealth y. We assume that her purchase activities have no impact on the prices of commodities—these stay fixed at the levels p_1, p_2, and so on—so that the total cost to her of the bundle $(x_1, x_2, \ldots, x_k)$ is $p_1 x_1 + p_2 x_2 + \ldots + p_k x_k$. Therefore, she can afford any bundle $(x_1, x_2, \ldots, x_k)$ that satisfies her *budget constraint*

$$p_1 x_1 + p_2 x_2 + \ldots + p_k x_k \leq y.$$

In our example, she can spend all her $160 on bread, which will give her 100 loaves of bread, no cheese, and no salami, or the bundle $(100, 0, 0)$. Or she can spend all her money on cheese, getting 32 kilos of cheese, no bread, and no salami, or the bundle (0,32,0). Or she can spend all her money on salami, getting 20 kilos of salami, no bread, and no cheese, the bundle $(0, 0, 20)$. These are the extreme purchases she might make. But she can also, for example, purchase 45 loaves of bread, 8 kilos of cheese, and 6 kilos of salami. This will cost her

$$\$1.60 \times 45 + \$5 \times 8 + \$8 \times 6 = \$72 + \$40 + \$48 = \$160,$$

which is just what she has to spend.

She can, if she wishes, spend less than all her money. That is, one of the bundles she can afford is the bundle $(40, 5, 5)$, or 40 loaves of bread (total cost $64), 5 kilos of cheese (total cost $25), and 5 kilos of salami (total cost $40), for a total expenditure of $64 + $25 + $40 = $129. If this turns out to be best for her, then this is what she will buy.

How is "best" to be judged? This is where the model of the utility-maximizing consumer comes in: The consumer has a utility function u whose arguments are consumption bundles $(x_1, x_2, \ldots, x_k)$ and whose values are numbers. The consumer chooses whichever bundle maximizes her utility, among those she can afford. To summarize then, the consumer's problem is to

$$\text{maximize } u(x_1, x_2, \ldots, x_k)$$
$$\text{subject to } p_1 x_1 + p_2 x_2 + \ldots + p_k x_k \leq y.$$

Nonnegativity?

In the formulation of the consumer's problem just given, the consumer is not restricted to choosing nonnegative levels of the commodities. But it is natural to assume that she cannot consume a negative amount of some commodity, so constraints to this effect are almost always added.

Finding the Answer with Excel and Solver

It is relatively easy to use Excel and Solver to solve specific examples of this problem. Take our example,

$$\text{maximize } 3\ln(b) + \ln(c) + 0.5\ln(s))$$
$$\text{subject to } 1.60b + 5c + 8s \leq 160.$$

The spreadsheet CHAP5-1, shown in Figure 5.1(a), sets up the problem. The first three entries are the variables: the amount of bread b, cheese c, and salami s consumed. Then I compute the consumer's total expenditure and finally her utility. In Figure 5.1(a), I start with the values $b = c = s = 1$, which gives a total expenditure of $14.60.

Now I call up Solver. I want Solver to maximize utility, in cell B8, by varying the three consumption amounts in cells B2, B3, and B4, subject to the constraint that the amount spent, in cell B6, remains less than or equal to 160. I give Solver these specs, let it do its stuff, and it comes back with the answer shown in Figure 5.1(b). (If you look at the innards of CHAP5-1, you'll find something strange going on in how I define utility levels. It turns out that Solver and logarithmic utility are not very compatible, unless

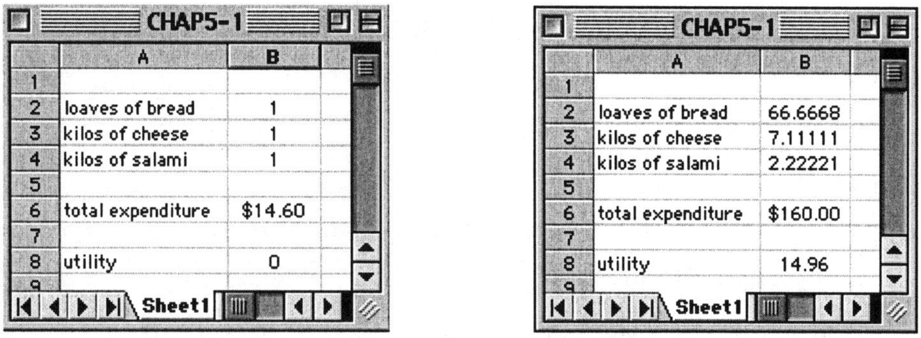

	CHAP5-1	
	A	B
1		
2	loaves of bread	1
3	kilos of cheese	1
4	kilos of salami	1
5		
6	total expenditure	$14.60
7		
8	utility	0

	CHAP5-1	
	A	B
1		
2	loaves of bread	66.6668
3	kilos of cheese	7.11111
4	kilos of salami	2.22221
5		
6	total expenditure	$160.00
7		
8	utility	14.96

(a)   (b)

Figure 5.1. *Solving the consumer's problem with Excel.* Panel a shows the basic spreadsheet (sheet 1 of CHAP5-1) with initial values of $b = c = s = 1$, and panel b shows the optimized values, obtained by Solver.

you are careful. The details are all about Solver and not at all about utility-maximizing consumers, so I leave the discussion of this to the *Companion*. If you try to create CHAP5-1 on your own, please see this discussion.)

Equalized Bangs for the Buck

To interpret the answer that Solver found, I asked Excel to compute the marginal utilities of the three consumption variables. You can see them in Figure 5.2, computed for the results obtained by Solver; this is sheet 2 of CHAP5-1. Because 1 loaf of bread, 1 kilo of cheese, and 1 kilo of salami are all pretty substantial changes, I computed discrete margins using increases of 0.01 in each commodity, instead of increases of one unit. Let me be clear here on two points:

- I am violating the expenditure constraint for my marginal value calculations. That is, column B has levels of b, c, and s that require the full $160. In column I, for instance, I increase c by 0.01, so the bundle in this column costs more than $160 (see cell I6).

- Marginal utilities, in row 8, are computed by taking the rate of increase in utility, per unit increase in the variable. That is, the formula for the entry in cell E8 is $= (I8 - B8)/0.01$, since cell I8 involves a 0.01 increase in c from the entries in B8.

It is evident that the marginal utility from a loaf of bread *does not* equal the marginal utility from a kilo of cheese nor does it equal the marginal utility from a kilo of salami.

The reason why the marginal utilities are not equal is that a loaf of bread is cheaper than a kilo of cheese, which in turn is cheaper than a kilo of salami. With the money it takes to buy a kilo of cheese, you can buy more than three

	A	B	C	D	E	F	G	H	I	J
1				margin in b	margin in c	margin in s		0.01 more b	0.01 more c	0.01 more s
2	loaves of bread	66.6668						66.6767556	66.6667556	66.6667556
3	kilos of cheese	7.11111						7.11110882	7.12110882	7.11110882
4	kilos of salami	2.22221						2.22220576	2.22220576	2.23220576
5										
6	total expenditure	$160.00		1.6	5	8		$160.02	$160.05	$160.08
7										
8	utility	14.96		0.04499657	0.14052626	0.22449692		14.9604775	14.9614328	14.9622725
9										

Figure 5.2. The marginal values of utility in the three commodities, for the answer obtained to the consumer's problem. We add to the basic spreadsheet computations that tell us the marginal expenditure (row 5) and marginal utility (row 8) figures for each of the three commodities. Note that the three marginal utilities have not been equalized. This is not unexpected: The three commodities have different prices, so they are not traded off one unit against one unit.

loaves of bread. So, if the marginal utility of a loaf of bread were equal to the marginal utility of a kilo of cheese, it would make sense to buy less cheese—say a tenth of a kilo less—and spend the money saved on three tenths and more of a loaf of bread.

So what in terms of margins is equalized at the solution? The answer is, the *bang for the buck* of each of the three commodities.

The bang for the buck of a commodity is the rate of increase in utility obtained by consuming more of the commodity, measured not per unit of the commodity but instead per dollar spent on the commodity.

Figure 5.3 shows the computation of bangs for the buck by the spreadsheet CHAP5-1, for the example. For instance, by subtracting the entry in cell B8 from the entry in cell I8, we compute that an extra 0.01 kg of cheese increases utility by 0.001405. An extra 0.01 kg of cheese, at $5 per kg, costs $0.05. Hence, utility rises at the rate of 0.001405 units per $0.05, or 0.001405/0.05 = 0.0281 per dollar. In Figure 5.3, this is computed in cell E10.

In fact, if you look at the innards of CHAP5-1, you'll find that the formula for cell E10 is = E8/E6, or the (discrete) marginal utility of cheese, in cell E8, divided by the price of cheese. But since the entry in E8 is the increase in utility divided by the 0.01 increase in the amount of cheese, the computation is precisely as in the previous paragraph.

In general, the bang for the buck of a commodity is the marginal utility of that commodity divided by its price. In symbols, writing MU_i for the marginal utility of commodity i (the rate at which utility rises per unit

	A	B	C	D	E	F	G	H	I	J
1				margin in b	margin in c	margin in s		0.01 more b	0.01 more c	0.01 more s
2	loaves of bread	66.667						66.6767556	66.6667556	66.6667556
3	kilos of cheese	7.1111						7.11110882	7.12110882	7.11110882
4	kilos of salami	2.2222						2.22220576	2.22220576	2.23220576
5										
6	total expenditure	$160.00		1.6	5	8		$160.02	$160.05	$160.08
7										
8	utility	14.96		0.04499657	0.14052626	0.22449692		14.9604775	14.9614328	14.9622725
9										
10	bangs for the buck			0.02812285	0.02810525	0.02806212				
11										

Sheet1　Sheet2　**Sheet3**

Figure 5.3. Adding bangs for the buck to the spreadsheet. We add to the spreadsheet in Figure 5.2 a final row, which computes bangs for the buck for each commodity, or marginal utility divided by price. Since the consumption levels in the spreadsheet are optimal, the bangs for the buck are equal.

increase in the commodity) and p_i for the price per unit of good i,

$$\text{the bang for the buck of good } i \text{ is } \frac{\text{MU}_i}{p_i}.$$

At the solution of the consumer's problem, the bangs for the buck must be equal. The reason is this: If the bang for the buck of good i exceeds the bang for the buck of good j, the consumer can get more utility while keeping to her budget constraint by spending a marginal bit of money less on good j, using that little bit of money to buy more of good i.

Just to check, in Figure 5.3 the three bangs for the buck are approximately equal. (They are only approximately equal because the margins in the spreadsheets are computed using discrete changes in the amounts of the three commodities.)

Nonnegativity Constraints and Bangs for the Buck

One caveat must be made here. Suppose the bang for the buck of commodity i exceeds that of commodity j, but that x_j, the level of consumption of good j, is 0. The way the consumer is supposed to get more utility while maintaining her budget constraint is to consume a bit less of good j, using the money saved to buy more i. But the consumer cannot consume less j if the level of good j is already at 0. Taking this into account, we get the following rule:

At the solution of the consumer's problem, the bangs for the buck of all commodities being consumed in strictly positive amounts must be equal to each other, and they must be at least as large as the bang for the buck of any commodity whose level of consumption is 0.

And, Now, Calculus

The rule just derived is the basis for solving these sorts of problems with calculus. Take the example we have been working with. The consumer's utility function is

$$u(b, c, s) = 3\ln(b) + \ln(c) + 0.5\ln(s).$$

Marginal utilities in bread, cheese, and salami are just the partial derivatives of this function in each of the three variables, or

$$\mathrm{MU}_b = \frac{3}{b}, \qquad \mathrm{MU}_c = \frac{1}{c}, \qquad \text{and} \qquad \mathrm{MU}_s = \frac{0.5}{s}.$$

The three prices are, respectively, $p_b = 1.6$, $p_c = 5$, and $p_s = 8$, so the bangs for the buck are

$$\mathrm{bfb}_b = \frac{3/b}{1.6} = \frac{3}{1.6b}, \quad \mathrm{bfb}_c = \frac{1/c}{5} = \frac{1}{5c}, \quad \text{and} \quad \mathrm{bfb}_s = \frac{0.5/s}{8} = \frac{0.5}{8s}.$$

Apply the rule: These bangs for the buck must be equal if the levels of consumption of all goods are strictly positive. Since this particular utility function gives utility $-\infty$ if any good is set at 0, all three must be strictly positive at the solution. So, from the rule, we know that

$$\mathrm{bfb}_b = \frac{3}{1.6b} \quad = \quad \mathrm{bfb}_c = \frac{1}{5c} \quad = \quad \mathrm{bfb}_s = \frac{0.5}{8s}.$$

Invert these fractions. The rule tells us that, at the solution,

$$\frac{1.6b}{3} \quad = \quad 5c \quad = \quad \frac{8s}{0.5}.$$

That is almost it; we have three unknowns and two equations. To find the answer, we resort to one more piece of logic: We know that the solution must respect the constraint $1.6b + 5c + 8s \leq 160$. But, in fact, the consumer is sure to spend all of her \$160 at the solution; we know this because money left over gives her no utility, while money spent on any commodity increases utility. (Would someone really would blow \$160 on a simple lunch of bread, cheese, and salami? Of course not, and we deal with this over the next several subsections.) So, in addition to equal bangs for the buck, we have the budget equation

$$1.6b + 5c + 8s = 160.$$

From the equation $1.6b/3 = 5c$, we can replace $5c$ in the budget constraint with $1.6b/3$. And from $1.6b/3 = 8s/0.5 = 16s$, we can replace $8s$ with $0.8b/3$. So combining the equal bangs for the buck with the budget constraint (as an equation), we get

$$1.6b + 1.6b/3 + 0.8b/3 = 160,$$

which after simplifying is $2.4b = 160$, or $b = 66.67$ loaves of bread. Since $1.6b/3 = 5c$ or $c = 1.6b/15$, we get $c = (1.6 \times 66.67)/15 = 7.111$ kilos of cheese. And from $1.6b/3 = 8s/0.5$, we get $s = 2.222$ kilos of salami. Compare with Figure 5.1(b).

Is the Rule Sufficient?

In what follows, you are asked to solve the consumer's problem by finding a consumption bundle that satisfies the rule. Satisfying the rule is passing the hill-in-the-fog test (Is there a direction you can go in, along which the hill slopes up?) with the added proviso that this hill has fences that you cannot cross—the nonnegativity constraints and the budget constraint—and the rule is constructed to provide the equivalent of, If the hill slopes upward in a direction that involves crossing a fence, you are still okay.

But, as we know from Chapter 3, hill-in-the-fog tests do not check for global optimality. You can take my word for the following: Unless you are told otherwise explicitly, any consumption bundle for a consumer that satisfies this rule is indeed a global optimum, a solution to the consumer's problem. In case you are interested, I know this because I present only problems where the consumer's utility function is concave and for which the feasible consumption set is convex. But you need to consult an advanced textbook in microeconomics or optimization theory to see why this is enough.

Will the Consumer Spend All Her Wealth?

In the general formulation of the consumer's problem, the budget constraint reads $p_1 x_1 + p_2 x_2 + \ldots + p_k x_k \leq y$. The consumer is allowed to spend less than all her money, if doing so gives her higher utility. What does it take to conclude that the consumer will indeed spend all her money?

Suppose some commodity, say, good i, is always desirable. That is, no matter what else the consumer is consuming, as long as we hold the levels of consumption of goods other than i fixed, more of good i gives higher utility. In this case, the consumer will never stop short of spending all her money; any money left over can be used to purchase a bit more of good i, improving her situation.

Putting Money in the Utility Function

On the other hand, I imagine that on most trips to the deli to buy lunch, you leave with lunch *and* some money in your pocket. You do not spend every penny on food, and this is so even though you are not completely satiated: At least one good, if increased in your lunch menu, would increase your utility. The reason you leave with money in your pocket is that you plan to spend that money sometime in the future. Money is worth something to you outside of its use in buying lunch.

The utility functions we looked at so far fail to capture this, because money left over does not enter as an argument. And anything that is not an argument of the utility function cannot be something that is, in the model, desirable. The key, then, is to think in terms of utility functions that have as arguments things like bread, cheese, salami, *and* money left over. As long as money left over has high enough marginal utility, the consumer being modeled will choose a bundle with money left in her pocket.

An example illustrates the point. To model the idea that a consumer buying a lunch of bread, cheese, and salami also values money left over, we can employ the utility function

$$u(b, c, s, m) = 3\ln(b) + \ln(c) + 0.5\ln(s) + m^{1/2},$$

where the new variable m is money left over. Her budget constraint, which previously was $1.60b + 5c + 8s \leq 160$, becomes $1.60b + 5c + 8s + m = 160$ or, what may be easier to understand,

$$160 - (1.60b + 5c + 8s) = m.$$

Written this second way, the budget constraint says that the money she has left over is what she begins with, $160, less the cost of her purchases, $1.60b + 5c + 8s$. You can solve this example with calculus, although because of the mix of logs and power functions, it is not easy. So I solve it with Excel and Solver: Ask Solver to maximize this utility function subject to the budget constraint, and the answer is 33.47 loaves of bread, 3.57 kilos of cheese, 1.12 kilos of salami, and $79.67 in money left over.

In general, whenever the consumer's utility is increasing in money left over, which is in virtually every case, the consumer's budget constraint is satisfied with an equality; anything the consumer does not spend, she puts back in her pocket.

It is appropriate to constrain money left over to be nonnegative, if the consumer can't borrow funds. We assume for current purposes that she cannot borrow, so $m \geq 0$ is assumed. But in some applications, such as the purchase of graduate education, it is entirely appropriate to allow for the possibility of borrowing.

A Particularly Convenient Form of Utility Function

Consider a consumer whose utility function for bread, cheese, salami, and money left over takes the form

$$u(b, c, s, m) = 20 \ln(b) + 8 \ln(c + 1) + 5 \ln(s + 2) + m.$$

Imagine that this consumer faces prices $p_b = \$2$, $p_c = \$4$, and $p_s = \$10$ and has \$100 in her pocket. Which consumption choices maximize her utility, subject to her budget constraint?

Hypothesize that, when she solves her problem, the consumer will have money left over in her pocket; she will not spend the whole \$100 on lunch. (We check this hypothesis later.) Then the rule says that the bang for the buck of money must equal the bangs for the buck of other commodities that are consumed in positive amounts and it must equal or exceed the bangs for the buck of commodities whose consumption level is 0.

The bang for the buck of money left over, for this utility function, is remarkably simple. As always, it is the marginal utility of money left over, divided by the price of money left over. The marginal utility of money left over for this utility function is 1. And the price of money left over—the amount of money it takes to "buy" another dollar in the consumer's pocket as she leaves the deli—is 1. So her bang for the buck in money is 1.

Now go on to the three food commodities:

- The bang for the buck of bread is its marginal utility, $20/b$, divided by its price, \$2, or $10/b$. This, the rule says, must equal the bang for the buck of money left over, which is 1, so at the solution to the consumer's problem, $10/b = 1$, or $b = 10$.

- For cheese, we get $[8/(c+1)]/4 = 2/(c+1)$ as its bang for the buck. Setting this equal to the bang for the buck of money gives $2/(c+1) = 1$, or $c = 1$.

- The bang for the buck of salami is $[5/(s+2)]/10 = 1/(2s+4)$. When $s = 0$, this is $1/4$, and it decreases as s gets larger, because the marginal utility of salami decreases. Therefore, the bang for the buck in salami is never going to equal 1, for nonnegative amounts of salami.

We conclude that the consumer maximizes her utility, subject to her budget constraint, if she consumes 10 loaves of bread, 1 kilo of cheese, and no salami. At these consumption levels, the bang for the buck in bread equals the bang for the buck in cheese equals the bang for the buck in money left over (all equal 1) and all exceed the bang for the buck of salami. The rule is satisfied, and so this is the solution.

Now we confirm the hypothesis that this bundle leaves the consumer with money left over: 10 loaves of bread cost $20, and 1 kilo of cheese costs $4, so the consumer spends $24 out of her initial $100, leaving $76 in her pocket.

As consumer problems go, this one is remarkably easy to solve, because the consumer's utility function, defined for a string of "real" commodities x_1, x_2, and so on, and for money left over m, takes the form

$$u(x_1, x_2, \ldots, m) = v_1(x_1) + v_2(x_2) + \ldots + m.$$

In words, the contribution of each of the "real" commodities to utility is a function of the amount of that commodity alone added to the total, and the contribution of money left over is simply the amount of money left over.

In Economese, we say that this utility function is additively separable by commodities and quasi-linear in money left over. But regardless of terminology, this form of utility is so convenient analytically that we use it incessantly in examples and to illustrate basic ideas in what follows.

For this special utility function, once the consumer is rich enough, her consumption of the "real" commodities does not depend on her level of wealth, y. In the example, we saw that, with the prices given and with $y = \$100$ in her pocket, the consumer purchased 10 loaves of bread, 1 kilo of cheese, and no salami, at a cost of $24, leaving $m = \$76$. Suppose that, instead, the consumer had $1000 in her pocket. Then, as long as the prices are the same, she would choose 10 loaves of bread, 1 kilo of cheese, and no salami, leaving $m = \$976$ in her pocket. If she has any amount of money exceeding $24, she consumes 10 loaves of bread, 1 kilo of cheese, and no salami, with any money left after these purchases going to money left over.

Why is this? You can get some intuition by looking at the marginal utilities of the various goods. Since money left over enters the utility function as $\ldots + m$, it has a constant marginal utility of 1 unit of utility per dollar. The other commodities have decreasing marginal utility, in this case because the logarithm function is concave. So the consumer, in matching bangs for the buck, consumes each commodity to the point where its marginal utility divided by its price equals the constant marginal utility of money, 1, divided by its price $1. To consume any more of the commodity would reduce its bang for the buck below that of money left over. Consuming any less would be consuming too little. And since the bang for the buck of money never diminishes, this remains true no matter how rich the consumer becomes.

Is this a reasonable model of human preferences? Does the marginal value of money, measured on a scale where the marginal values of other commodities decreases, stay constant? Would your purchases of commodities remain constant, once your wealth rose to some level, no matter how much richer you became? The answer to all these questions is probably No, in general, but Yes in specific cases. When you walk into a cafeteria or deli to purchase lunch, you probably do not consider your bank account balance, to see what food to buy. If I increased your bank balance by, say, 10%, it would not affect what you buy for lunch. Now if I doubled or tripled your bank balance, you might buy a different lunch—lobster salad and caviar, instead of turkey and swiss on rye—but when you purchase lunch, you do not contemplate purchases that would take half your bank account balance, so what you choose with half or double your current wealth really is not at issue. Therefore, this ultra-convenient utility function is probably adequate for modeling consumers—relatively well-to-do consumers, perhaps—who are in the market for lunch, a week's groceries, or other such minor, day-to-day purchases. But this sort of utility function is not a good model when we discuss the purchase of a house, investments, or education, things that do take an appreciable fraction of one's income.

In summary, we use this ultra-simple form for utility in examples and to illustrate some concepts because it is so convenient. But it involves implicit assumptions that are not always valid.

Two final comments:

- The preceding discussion concerned the $\ldots + m$ part of the utility function. The "additive separability" assumptions (that the rest of the utility function looks like $v_1(x_1) + v_2(x_2) + \ldots$) also involve implicit assumptions. But these are beyond the scope of this book; consult a more advanced economics textbook to learn about them. For most economic purposes, the $\ldots + m$ part is a more restrictive assumption, which is why I concentrate on it.

- Earlier in this chapter I said that the numerical quantities of utility don't have any particular meaning. With this special form of utility, that is no longer true: Utility is measured on a scale where $1 more left over provides precisely one unit of utility more. For this utility function, utility is measured on a dollar scale.

5.3. Pictures: Indifference Curves and Budget Sets

Economists love to draw pictures of their concepts, and the theory of the consumer is no exception. Unhappily, these pictures are limited by the talents of the artist, and economists typically are not artists, especially when it comes to diagrams with more than two dimensions. So the pictures are limited to examples where there are two commodities, which for this discussion will be bread and cheese.

Indifference Curves

The first step is to draw a "map" of the consumer's utility function. Figure 5.4 is typical. This depicts the *indifference curves* or level sets of the consumer's utility function u. Two bundles are on the same indifference curve if they have the same utility. The arrow in the picture, which typically is not drawn, indicates that moving up and to the right—more c or more b—puts you on indifference curves with greater utility, which just means that this particular utility function increases if either b or c increases.

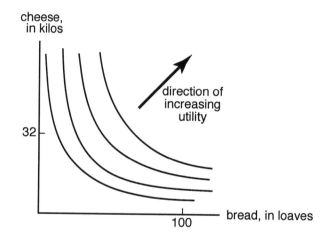

Figure 5.4. A typical set of indifference curves.

Think in terms of a topographical relief map. The coordinates, measured north–south and east–west, give the amounts of b and c. Imagine coming up out of the page is a mountain, whose height at coordinates (b, c) is $u(b, c)$. This mountain rises (perpetually) as you move north or east. Figure 5.4 shows the topographical contours, or families of bundles that are at the same height or utility.

The four functions graphed in Figure 5.4 are *not* the utility function u. They represent sets of points (b, c) such that, along each curve, $u(b, c)$ equals a constant, with the constant changing for each curve; the constants get larger as we move northeast. For example, if $u(b, c) = 3 \ln(b) + \ln(c)$, then one indifference curve would be the set of points (b, c) that satisfy $3 \ln(b) + \ln(c) = 5$. A second curve, further to the north and east, would be all the points (b, c) that satisfy $3 \ln(b) + \ln(c) = 5.6$, and so on.

The Shape of Indifference Curves

The shapes you see in Figure 5.4, indifference curves that proceed more or less from the northwest to the southeast and are convex to the origin, are standard. The northwest–southeast character is a consequence of the assumption that utility strictly increases in the two goods. As for the convexity, pick a point (b, c) along an indifference curve. Decrease the amount of bread by some amount to, say, $b - 0.1$, then to remain on the indifference curve, you must increase the amount of cheese by some amount in compensation. Decrease the amount of bread a second time by the same amount, to $b - 0.2$, and again the amount of cheese must be increased to compensate, to stay on the indifference curve. The convexity of indifference curves simply says that, as you decrease bread by some fixed amount, say, 1/10th of a loaf, from b to $b - 0.1$ to $b - 0.2$ and so forth, the amount that you must increase cheese in compensation, to stay on the same indifference curve, increases with each step.

While this is the typical picture, no natural law says that preferences should conform to these properties. In particular, for some goods, such as a very sweet dessert, the utility eventually declines as the amount of the good increases. In Problems 5.6 and 5.10, we examine indifference curves for this sort of good.

Consumer Choice from Indifference Curves

Imagine a consumer choosing from among the five points shown in heavy dots in Figure 5.5(a). If we have handy the consumer's indifference curve

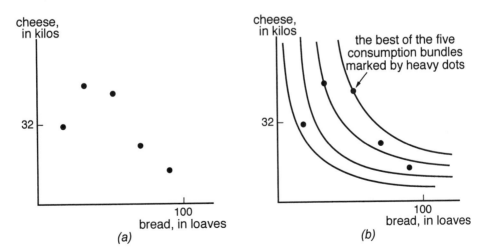

Figure 5.5. Choosing among five consumption bundles. To choose among the five bundles shown as heavy dots in panel a, you first lay on the graph the consumer's indifference curves. The point on the highest (most northeastern) indifference curve is the winner, as shown in panel b.

map, it is easy to figure out what our model of the consumer predicts she will do. We superimpose the indifference curves on the five points, as shown in Figure 5.5(b), and whichever of the five points is on the indifference curve of highest elevation is what she is meant to pick.

Now try a harder problem. Suppose that the price of bread is $1.60 per loaf, the price of cheese is $5.00 per kilo, and the consumer has $160 to spend. What will the consumer choose?

Look first at Figure 5.6(a) and the line segment connecting the points $(100, 0)$ and $(0, 32)$. This represents all bundles (b, c) that the consumer could buy at these prices and just exhaust her wealth. The budget-exhaustion equation $1.60b + 5c = 160$ defines a straight line. To draw in that line, we find two points on it. It is easiest to find the two end points: If the consumer spends all $160 on bread, she can have 100 loaves and no cheese. If she spends all $160 on cheese, she can have 32 kilos of cheese and no bread. Given these two points, we have the line.

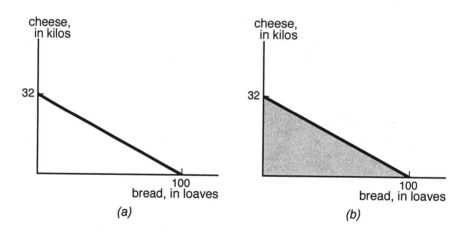

Figure 5.6. *A budget-exhaustion line segment and a budget set.* If bread costs $1.60 a loaf, cheese costs $5 a kilo, and the consumer has $160 to spend, we get the budget line (a) and budget set (b) shown here.

In Figure 5.6(b), I shade in the triangle formed by this line segment and the point $(0, 0)$. This is the *budget set* of the consumer, representing all the consumption bundles (b, c) she can afford; that is, that satisfy the inequality $1.60b + 5c \leq 160$.

In Figure 5.7, I superimpose Figures 5.4 and 5.6(b). The consumer's problem is to find that point in the shaded triangle, her budget set, that gives her the highest utility, or that lies on the highest (most northeast) of her indifference curves. You see this point and its indifference curve marked in Figure 5.7.

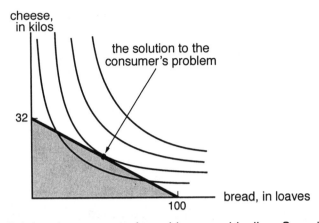

Figure 5.7. *Solving the consumer's problem graphically.* Superimposing the consumer's indifference curves on her budget set, the bundle she chooses is the bundle from her budget set that lies on the highest (most northeast) indifference curve. The indifference curve through this point is tangent to the budget line, which is the graphical manifestation of equal bangs for the buck.

Equal Bangs for the Buck in the Picture

Note in particular that, at the optimal consumption bundle, the budget line and the indifference curve are tangent. This is the graphical manifestation of the equal-bangs-for-the-buck rule. Here is why:

- An indifference curve for a two-commodity world is a curve given by the equation $u(x_1, x_2) = k$, for some constant k. Suppose x_1 increases by a small amount, ϵ. This increases utility by approximately ϵMU_1, where MU_1 is shorthand for the marginal utility of good 1. If x_2 simultaneously decreases by some amount δ, utility falls by δMU_2. If δ and ϵ are chosen so that the net effect of the two changes is to stay on a single indifference curve, then

$$\epsilon MU_1 - \delta MU_2 = 0, \quad \text{or} \quad \frac{\delta}{\epsilon} = \frac{MU_1}{MU_2}.$$

Recalling that δ is the amount of decrease of commodity 2, the slope of the indifference curve at the point is $-\delta/\epsilon$, so that

$$\text{the slope of an indifference curve at a point is} \quad -\frac{MU_1}{MU_2},$$

where the marginal utilities are measured at that point.

- The budget line is the line $p_1 x_1 + p_2 x_2 = $ constant. So the slope of this line, viewed as defining x_2 as a function of x_1, is $-p_1/p_2$.

- Hence, the tangency of the budget line and the indifference curve implies

$$-\frac{MU_1}{MU_2} = -\frac{p_1}{p_2} \quad \text{which can be rewritten as} \quad \frac{MU_1}{p_1} = \frac{MU_2}{p_2},$$

which is the equal-bangs-for-the-buck condition.

5.4. Individual Demand Functions

The previous two sections concern the consumer's problem at a given set of prices. Suppose we solve that problem for all possible prices. More specifically, suppose we fix the prices of all the goods except good i and answer the question, What amount of good i is chosen by this consumer as a function of p_i, holding fixed the consumer's wealth and the prices of all other goods? This function is the consumer's demand function for good i.

In general, this is a very hard problem to solve algebraically. But for some special utility functions, it can be done. One example is found in Problem 5.11. A second example follows.

Demand for Money-Left-Over Utility Functions

(This discussion requires calculus. Readers who dogmatically avoid calculus get the rest of this section off.)

Consider a consumer whose utility function is given by

$$u(x_1, \ldots, x_k, m) = v_1(x_1) + \ldots + v_k(x_k) + m.$$

Assume that v_i is a concave function, which means that v_i', the marginal utility function, is a decreasing function.

Recall that, as long as the consumer has enough money at the start to have money left over at the end, the optimal level of good j to consume at price p_j is given by

$$\frac{v_i'(x_i)}{p_i} = 1, \quad \text{or} \quad v_i'(x_i) = p_i.$$

Graph the function v_i' with its argument x_i on the horizontal axis. Find p_i on the vertical axis and move across until you hit v_i'. The quantity at which you hit v_i' solves the equation $v_i'(x_i) = p_i$, which is this consumer's demand at price p_i.

In fact, draw this picture and you discover that, subject to a caveat coming up, the graph of v_i' is the "same" as the graph of the demand function. Look at Figure 5.8. Think of this first as the marginal utility function $v_i'(x_i)$; that is, the argument runs on the horizontal or quantity axis and the value of the function is measured on the vertical axis. Now turn the page $90°$. If the argument of the function is price p_i, the value of this function—keep the page turned $90°$—is the demand at that price.

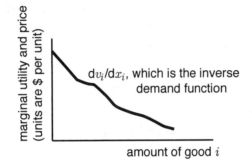

Figure 5.8. *The consumer's demand curve for good* i. For a consumer with utility function $u(x_1, \ldots, x_k, m) = v_1(x_1) + \ldots v_k(x_k) + m$ and enough initial wealth that, after choosing her optimal consumption bundle, she has money left over, her demand for good i is given by the equation $v_i'(x_i) = p_i$. If we graph the function $v_i'(x_i)$, we see her (inverse) demand function.

Why are there quotes around "same" in the preceding paragraph? Looking at this as the graph of the function v_i', the argument of the function x_i runs from 0 to infinity. In Figure 5.8, I drew things so that $v_i'(0)$ is finite and $v_i'(x_i)$ is always strictly positive, no matter how large is x_i. Turn the page $90°$, so that price is the argument and the function is demand, and we see something slightly different: Price runs from 0 to infinity, and demand at high enough prices is 0. (How high? Demand is 0 whenever the price $p_i \geq v_i'(0)$.) On the other end of the price spectrum, demand is not really defined for the price $p_i = 0$. In this case, if the good is being given away, the consumer would ask for infinite quantities of it.

This is a utility function where $v_i'(0)$ is finite and v_i' does not hit 0 for any finite level of consumption. Problem 5.13 explores a number of other possibilities.

There are two more things to say about this special case:

- Everything just derived is based on the assumption that demand is given by $v_i'(x_i) = p_i$, which in turn depends on the consumer being rich enough that, after all her purchases are made, she has some money left over. You have to verify that this is so in applications, at least for the range of prices you are interested in. On this point, see Problems 5.4 and 5.5.

- Suppose the consumer is offered as much of good i as she wishes to purchase at price p_i. How does this opportunity to buy good i at a price p_i affect her utility, vis-à-vis a situation where she could not buy any good i? With this special sort of utility function, the inability to buy good i does not affect her demand for other goods as long as she is wealthy enough to have money left over, so the net effects are these: If she could participate in the market for good i, she would buy the amount x_i^* that solves $v_i'(x_i^*) = p_i$, which increases her utility of consuming commodity i from $v_i(0)$ up to $v_i(x_i^*)$. But she would have less money in her pocket as a result; more precisely, her money left over would decrease by $p_i x_i^*$. So, on net, her utility would increase by

$$v_i(x_i^*) - v_i(0) - p_i x_i^*.$$

Because her demand function is the graph of $v_i'(x_i)$, this gain in utility is

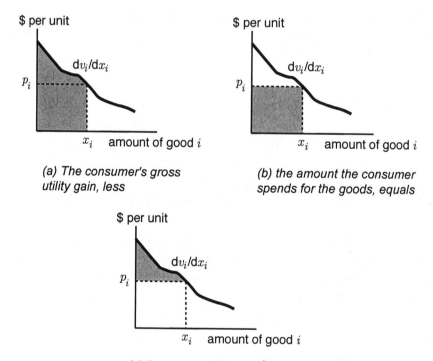

(a) *The consumer's gross utility gain, less*

(b) *the amount the consumer spends for the goods, equals*

(c) *the consumer's net utility gain*

Figure 5.9. Consumer surplus. Suppose the consumer from Figure 5.8 were offered good i at a price p_i. She would choose to consume x_i^*, the solution of $v_i'(x_i^*) = p_i$. By consuming x_i^* instead of 0 of good i, her utility gain is the shaded area in panel a. This costs her the shaded rectangle in panel b. Therefore, her net gain from the opportunity to purchase good i at this price is the shaded area in panel c, her *consumer surplus*.

the area shaded in Figure 5.9(a) less the area shaded in Figure 5.9(b), which gives the area shaded in Figure 5.9(c). This area is called the *consumer surplus* from the good; we meet it again in Chapters 12 and 13.

5.5. (Why) Are You Supposed to Believe This Model of Behavior?

The model of the utility-maximizing consumer is a cornerstone, perhaps the biggest cornerstone, of economic modeling and thought. But most people encountering it for the first time are very skeptical. Have you every stopped in the middle of shopping for lunch to equate bangs for the buck?

Economists defend the use of this model by proclaiming that it is an as-if model. Consumers behave *as if* they were maximizing utility. Just like the tree setting its leaf canopy at the start of Chapter 4, it isn't necessary that consumers actually do the computations, as long as their actions are consistent with this sort of computation.

So what does it take for a consumer's actions to be consistent with utility maximization? To answer this question, imagine an individual who is asked to choose from sets of objects she is offered. To be very concrete, imagine some large set X of conceivable choices (the set of all possible consumption bundles or baskets of groceries plus money in the consumer's pocket) and ask the consumer, From every subset of X, what do you choose? Consider the following two properties of her choices:

- From any finite subset A of X, the consumer is ready to make a choice. She might say that several elements of A are tied for best and she is willing to have any one of those, but she is never so flummoxed by the situation that she freezes with indecision.

- Suppose x and y are two bundles in some set of bundles A, and the consumer says she is willing to have x out of A. Then, for any other set of bundles B that contains both x and y, if the consumer is willing to take y out of B, she must be happy to take x as well.

The first of these should present no problem. But the second takes a bit of thought. You can think of the second as, more or less, eliminating the sort of choices described at the start of the chapter, concerning an individual choosing dessert at a diner. If apple pie is chosen when the only choices are apple and cherry, then cherry can't be chosen in preference to apple when the choices are apple, cherry, or blueberry.

These two properties seem pretty reasonable. And, up to some technical conditions that would interest only a Ph.D. student, they are what it takes:

Any consumer whose choice behavior obeys these two rules chooses *as if* she were maximizing some utility function. That is a mathematical result that I do not expect you to see through—the proof isn't easy and, in fact, some technical problems must be dealt with that do not change the economic intuition at all—so you have to take my word for it.[1]

But looks can be deceiving. In particular, the second property says, in as many words, that the consumer cannot be tricked by how a set of options is framed. She knows what she likes—how she ranks the options she might have—and her relative likes and dislikes are not affected by the set of objects from which she is allowed to choose.

Designers of mail order catalogs do not believe that real consumers are quite so rational. They sometimes put two versions of a given item on the same page. Version 1 is a standard model, with a price of, say, $40. Version 2 is a very slightly enhanced model, with a price of $60. The mail order house wants to sell the first version; the purpose of the very steeply priced version 2 is to try to convince you that version 1 is fairly priced. Or the catalog designer may put on the page with the $40 model a much inferior model at a price only slightly below $40. Again, the idea is to convince the reader that the $40 model is a good deal. This sort of stuff works, and to the extent that it does, it constitutes a violation of the second property.

More generally, a lot of advertising is an attempt to frame items in ways that cause consumers to change their purchase behavior, something that the standard economic model of the utility-maximizing consumer rules out. We observe violations of the standard model in the real world that are systematic enough that people make sizeable incomes creating violations that benefit sellers of goods.

Notwithstanding this, economic models are almost invariably populated by utility-maximizing consumers. As with the profit-maximizing firm, this is done with one of two rationales in mind: The violations that occur are not sufficiently important empirically to worry about; or, in terms of the conclusions drawn, those violations we do see have insignificant impact. The best attitude to have is one of informed skepticism. Studying consumer marketing, especially those pieces that rely on social and cognitive psychology, will alert you to egregious and systematic violations. But, as long as you are alert to those violations, the model is still useful. You'll be alert to applications that are dubious and able to judge when the systematic violations we sometimes observe are not all that relevant to the conclusions being drawn.

---

[1] If you do not want to take my word for it, see David M. Kreps, *Notes on the Theory of Choice* (Boulder, CO: Westview Press, 1988).

Executive Summary

- In the economic model of the utility-maximizing consumer, the consumer's utility function associates a numerical value to each conceivable choice. Given any feasible set of choices, the consumer chooses that option from the feasible set which maximizes her utility.

  - The utility function establishes an order among the consumer's possible options. Two utility functions that establish the same order are equivalent in the sense that they give the same choice behavior by consumers.

  - In models of some choices by individuals, money left over is included as an argument of the utility function, where the "utility" from money left over is derived from the value of things that might be purchased (outside the model) with the money left over.

- The consumer's problem is to choose the best (utility-maximizing) bundle from among all those she can afford, given prices and her monetary resources.

  - At the solution of the consumer's problem, the bangs for the buck of commodities at strictly positive levels must be equal and must be at least as large as the bangs for the buck of commodities that are not consumed.

  - This rule is typically very easy to apply in models where money left over enters the utility function linearly.

- The model of the utility-maximizing consumer is rationalized by economists as an as-if model. No one believes that consumers actually maximize a utility function. But, if the consumer's choice behavior conforms to two relatively simple rules, the consumer acts as if she maximizes utility.

  - Unhappily, systematic violations of one of these simple rules can be observed in real life. Consumer marketers and advertising executives are well compensated for their skills in manipulating how consumers frame their choices.

  - Economists continue to use the model of the utility-maximizing consumer, in the belief that the violations are usually insignificant or in the hope that the conclusions drawn from models so constructed are not grossly affected by violations.

Problems

5.1 Three consumers rank bundles consisting of b loaves of bread, c kilos of cheese, and s kilos of salami according to the following three utility functions: Consumer 1 ranks them according to the utility function $u_1(b, c, s) = \ln(b) + 0.5 \ln(c) + 0.5 \ln(s)$. Consumer 2 ranks them according to the utility function $u_2(b, c, s) = b^4 c^2 s$. And consumer 3 ranks them according to the utility function $u_3(b, c, s) = b + 2c + 2\ln(s)$. Suppose these three consumer are given their choice from the following three bundles:

Bundle 1: $(b, c, s) = (4, 0.5, 0.25)$

Bundle 2: $(b, c, s) = (2, 1.25, 0.5)$

Bundle 3: $(b, c, s) = (1, 0.5, 2.5)$

Which bundle will each consumer choose?

5.2 Suppose that a particular consumer has utility function (for bundles of bread, cheese, and salami) given by

$$u(b, c, s) = 6\ln(b) + 3\ln(c) + \ln(s),$$

and the consumer has $20 to spend. The prices of bread, cheese, and salami are, respectively, $1.20 per loaf, $3 per kilo, and $4 per kilo. What amounts of bread, cheese, and salami will this consumer choose, if she chooses in a way that maximizes her utility, subject to the constraint that she spend no more than $20?

5.3 Suppose a consumer with $160 to spend has the utility function (for bundles of bread, cheese, salami, and money left over) given by

$$u(b, c, s, m) = 6\ln(b) + 2\ln(c) + \ln(s) + m.$$

What choices maximize this consumer's utility? Assume $p_b = \$1.20$, $p_c = \$3$, and $p_s = \$4$.

5.4 (a) Solve the consumer's problem for a consumer with the utility function $u(b, c, s) = 8\ln(b+2)+6\ln(c+1)+2\ln(2s+1)$, if the prices are $p_b = \$1$, $p_c = \$2$, and $p_s = \$4$, and the consumer has $18 to spend.

(b) Solve the consumer's problem for a consumer with the utility function $u(b, c, s) = 8\ln(b+2)+6\ln(c+1)+2\ln(2s+1)$, if the prices are $p_b = \$1$, $p_c = \$2$, and $p_s = \$4$, and the consumer has $6.50 to spend.

(c) Solve the consumer's problem for a consumer with the utility function $u(b, c, s) = 8\ln(b+2)+6\ln(c+1)+2\ln(2s+1)+m$, where m is money left over, if the prices are $p_b = \$1$, $p_c = \$2$, and $p_s = \$4$, and the consumer has $50 to spend. What if the consumer has $500 to spend? What if the consumer has $18 to spend? What if the consumer has $6.50 to spend?

5.5 (a) Solve the consumer's problem for a consumer with utility function $u(b, c, s) = 10 \ln(b) + \ln(c + 1) + 0.5 \ln(s + 4)$, if the prices are $p_b = \$2, p_c = \$5$, and $p_s = \$10$, and if the consumer has $83 to spend.

(b) Solve the consumer's problem for a consumer with the utility function $u(b, c, s) = 10 \ln(b) + \ln(c) + 0.5 \ln(s + 4) + m$, where m is money left over, if the prices are $p_b = \$2, p_c = \$5$, and $p_s = \$10$, and the consumer has $83 to spend. What if the consumer has only $6.60 to spend?

5.6 Imagine a consumer who wants to purchase some cotton candy. This consumer's choice behavior (in terms of her purchase of cotton candy) is described by utility maximization for the utility function $u(c, m) = 4c - c^2 + m$, where c is the amount of cotton candy consumed (measured in sticks) and m is the amount of money the consumer has left over (measured in dollars). Note that, past the level $c = 2$, this function decreases in c; this consumer is decreasingly well off if she consumes more than two sticks of cotton candy.

(a) Suppose we graph the indifference curve of this individual through the point ($5.00, 1 stick). At what dollar value m^* does this indifference curve pass through the 1.5 stick level? That is, for what value of m^* is (m^*, 1.5 sticks) on the same indifference curve as ($5.00, 1 stick)?

(b) Graph this consumer's entire indifference curves through the points ($5.00, 1 stick) and ($6.00, 1 stick).

5.7 Go back to Figure 5.5(a) and number the five dots consecutively, moving from left to right. Then, for the consumer whose indifference curves are shown in Figure 5.5(b), what is the rank order of these five in terms of consumer well-being? (To get you started: The leftmost dot is worst, and the rightmost dot is second worst.)

5.8 Suppose that a consumer has $24 to spend for bread and cheese, where bread costs $1.20 per loaf and cheese costs $3 per kilo. On a piece of graph paper, draw the budget set of this consumer.

5.9 In Figure 5.10, I depict four indifference curves for an individual trying to decide how much wine to buy (where we consider money left over as the second good).

(a) Suppose the price of wine is $10 per bottle, and the consumer has $40 to spend. How many bottles of wine will he buy? (Do not try to be too precise about this.)

(b) If the consumer has $40 to spend and the price of wine is $30 per bottle, how many bottles will the consumer purchase?

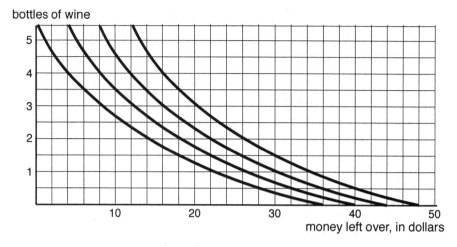

bottles of wine

money left over, in dollars

Figure 5.10. Problem 5.9: Some indifference curves.

5.10 Imagine a consumer choosing bundles consisting of an amount of cotton candy and an amount of double chocolate fudge. The consumer has a certain amount she can spend on these two confections and she forfeits any money she does not spend on them. Her preferences can be described (very roughly and descriptively) as follows. She likes both confections but only in limited amounts. If we write (c, f) for the bundle consisting of c sticks of cotton candy and f pounds of double chocolate fudge, then her most preferred bundle out of any conceivable bundle is $(2, 3)$, or two sticks of cotton candy and 3 pounds of fudge.

Try to draw indifference curves for this consumer that are consistent with the statements just made. One example will do. Try to make these as "realistic" as you can; that is, as much in accord as possible with the general tenor of the brief description given.

5.11 A consumer with $10 to spend on bread, cheese, and salami has the utility function $u(b, c, s) = 4\ln(b) + \ln(c+1) + 0.5\ln(s)$. Describe as completely as you can the demand function of this consumer for cheese, if the price of bread is $2 per loaf and the price of salami is $2.50 per kilo.

5.12 (a) Suppose a consumer has utility function

$$u(b, c, f, m) = \ln(b) + \ln(c + 3) + (2f - f^2) + m,$$

where b is loaves of bread, c is kilos of cheese, f is kilos of fudge, and m is money left over. The consumer has $100 to spend, which (you may assume) leaves him with money left over after purchasing the optimal amounts of bread, cheese, and fudge, at any prices for those three goods. What are his demand functions (or, if it is easier, his inverse demand functions) for the three goods?

(b) What is the most he will spend on the three goods? To answer this question, you have to find prices for the three goods that maximize his expenditures on each. (This is a little tricky when it comes to cheese.)

5.13 (This problem is primarily for readers who love math.) Figure 5.8 depicts a demand function that hits quantity 0 at a finite price and that (seemingly) goes to infinity as the price approaches 0. This is not the only possibility. Imagine a consumer choosing the amount x to consume, where the alternative to purchasing x is to leave money in her pocket. More specifically, imagine a consumer with the utility function $u(x, m) = v(x) + m$ for a concave function v. For each of the four possibilities for v that follow, find the consumer's demand function for the good x as a function of its price p.

(a) $v(x) = x^{1/2}$

(b) $v(x) = 10 \ln(x + 1)$

(c) $v(x) = 6x - x^2$

(d)

$$v(x) = \begin{cases} \ln(x), & \text{for } x \leq 1, \text{ and} \\ 3x - x^2, & \text{for } x \geq 1. \end{cases}$$

Using these examples as guides, complete the following sentences. For this sort of problem, in which the utility for x and money left over has the form $v(x) + m$ (where, to be fastidious, v is a strictly concave function),

Demand is strictly positive no matter how high price gets if _____, but if _____, demand hits zero when price rises to _____.

Demand approaches ∞ as price declines to 0 if _____. But if _____, then demand stops at the level _____ when price goes to 0.

6. Channels of Distribution and the Problem of Double Marginalization

Manufactured goods are typically sold via multilayered channels of distribution, from manufacturer to wholesalers to retailers to consumers. This chapter uses some of the concepts and techniques we have developed to study this situation. In particular, it studies the problem of *double marginalization*, the loss in overall profit that takes place because each party in the distribution chain, to get its share of the pie, marks up the price of the goods. The chapter goes on to show how so-called two-part tariffs, or dealership or franchise fees, can ameliorate the problem.

Chapter 5 concerns one sort of customer for goods and services, consumers. But customers come in other shapes and sizes. Goods and services are sold to other firms, governments, not-for-profit organizations, and so on. To understand completely the intricacies of marketing, you need to understand the process of marketing to all these different customers.

And, of course, they are different. Look at the course catalogs of business schools, and you find distinct courses in consumer and industrial marketing.

In most cases, industrial customers buy goods and services as inputs to their own production processes, and therefore understanding the characteristics of industrial demand requires an understanding of production. We are still two chapters away from production, so we do not go down that path in this chapter. Instead, we take the simplest case of industrial marketing: A manufacturer produces a good at a fixed marginal cost and sells it to one or more retailers, which sell it to the consuming public. What sorts of issues arise in this simple setting?

- Retailers often sell competitive products. Supermarkets sell a variety of ready-to-eat cereals made by various manufacturers, a variety of cleaning products, and so forth. Manufacturers' marketing strategies must therefore be designed to capture the retailers' efforts and attention.

- A second problem concerns powerful retailers. In this book so far, manufacturers that face downward-sloping demand name the price they charge and customers meekly respond. But powerful retailers will bargain over wholesale prices.

We do not deal with these issues here, however. We assume that the retailers in question purchase and resell from a single manufacturer. And we assume that the manufacturer has all the bargaining power in its relationships with its retailers: It sets the terms of its transactions, and its retailers maximize their own profits, taking those terms as an unalterable fact of life.

So what does this leave of interest? A very important and interesting issue remains, which is best motivated by a story.[1]

6.1. A Story about Porsche

Through 1984, Porsches were sold in the United States through the Volkswagon–Audi dealership network. Usually, a dealer would sell Porsches and Audis, although sometimes a dealer would sell all three lines of cars. But, in 1984, the marketing agreement between Porsche and Volkswagon USA that resulted in VW USA wholesaling Porsches to its dealers was about to expire. Porsche took this opportunity to rethink it basic marketing arrangements in the United States

Automobile Retailing in the United States

In 1984 in the United States, automobile retailing was done largely by independent dealers, which bought cars from auto manufacturers and resold the cars to the public. Stock trading among the dealers was common. Dealerships were "authorized franchises" of the major manufacturers. It was becoming increasingly common, at least in urban areas, for a dealer to sell more than one brand of car. And many dealerships were owned or controlled by large holding corporations; in northern California, for example, many dealerships were part of either the Mike Harvey Group or the Lucas Group. Dealers and manufacturers had arm's length relationships; a manufacturer sold its cars wholesale to its dealers, which then got the best prices they could selling cars to consumers.

Dealers could usually get a very good price from consumers. The invoice that a dealer would show the customer, however reluctantly, was (and is) often an overstatement of what the dealer would wind up paying for the car. This is so in particular because dealers are sometimes given an off-invoice "rebate" for cars that move quickly through the dealership. Moreover, many cars were sold for an amount greatly in excess of the invoice price. Dealers guard this sort of information closely, but it is asserted that, at the time, over 90% of the sales were at amounts within $1000 of the manufacturer's suggested retail price (MSRP), a figure that represents the highest and most glorious aspirations of dealers.

---

[1] My sources for this story are clippings from *Automotive News* (February 20, 1984; February 27, 1984; March 12, 1984; and March 19, 1984) and *Fortune* (April 16, 1984). This example was suggested to me by Peter C. Reiss.

Dealers, while independent of manufacturers, have certain responsibilities as part of their franchise agreement. They must contribute to cooperative national and regional advertising. They must maintain repair and servicing facilities and an inventory of spare parts.

This manner of marketing presents substantial problems of incentives. Most notably, while the manufacturer wants the independent dealer to sell a large number of cars by taking a smaller-percentage profit, dealers are more interested in holding back cars, waiting for the customer who would pay the sticker (MSRP) price. Since dealers carry the cost of inventory, they have some incentive to sell cars quickly. And some special arrangements between the manufacturer and dealers increase each dealer's incentive to sell cars quickly. But, in general, dealers' incentives do not align with those of the manufacturer.

Given these problems of incentives, we might wonder why automobiles are retailed in this fashion. The institution of independent dealerships goes back to when Alfred P. Sloan was building General Motors, and the most widely accepted explanation is that Sloan felt that independent dealers would have a better chance of building a loyal customer base and a better sense of the local conditions in the market, especially as it related to trade-ins.

For whatever reason, independent dealerships became the norm. And, since dealers are an easily organized group, with strong ties to local government, many laws were passed at the level of state government to protect the interests of dealers from exploitation by manufacturers. These laws, which are usually posed more generally to apply to all franchiser–franchisee relationships, essentially prohibit the franchiser from ever changing the nature of its economic relationship with the franchisee, except with the agreement of the franchisee. The economic relationship, in other words, is essentially fixed by its initial form, except for changes that benefit both parties.

Back to Porsche

In 1984, as its arrangement with VW was winding down, Porsche announced its intention of marketing Porsches in the United States by an entirely novel scheme. Dealers would become independent agents who booked orders. Inventory would be held exclusively by the parent corporation, Porsche USA, which would also do vehicle preparation work. Prices would be nonnegotiable, set by Porsche USA. The agencies, which previously were dealerships, would be encouraged to maintain their repair and maintenance operations, although Porsche owners would be given ample opportunity to communicate directly with Porsche USA regional centers in the event of maintenance problems. The agencies would not be required to contribute to cooperative advertising. They would be given around an 8% commission on sales they booked, compared to an estimated margin of 18% or so over their cost for cars they sold in the traditional manner.

This did not make the Porsche dealers happy. Invoking state laws concerning franchises, many lawsuits were filed. Porsche maintained that it was not in violation of those laws, because the Porsche–Audi dealers had franchise arrangements with VW and not with Porsche; as Porsche was no longer being sold through VW USA, new arrangements were unconstrained by the prior arrangements. VW, fearing that it would be named as a party to these lawsuits, itself initiated a suit against Porsche, claiming that *its* relationship was covered by franchise laws.

When the dust settled, Porsche retreated from its proposed new way of marketing cars. It continued to assert that its legal case was strong, but there was insufficient time for it to establish the sort of agency network it wanted, and so it would undertake traditional dealership relationships. Of course, whatever the standing of its legal position, once it did this, it was stuck.

The question is, Under the assumption that Porsche could anticipate the resistance it would meet, why would it want to establish the new way of selling cars? Note especially that, by fixing the price, Porsche loses the ability to charge higher prices to those who, for whatever reason, shop less. (The dealers benefit directly from this ability, but Porsche benefits indirectly because, if dealers make higher profits, Porsche can get away with higher wholesale prices.) What problem was Porsche addressing?

6.2. A Simple Model of Two-Step Distribution

To answer this question, we analyze a very simple and stylized model of a manufacturer, her, and an arm's-length retailer, him. Imagine a manufacturer who produces a product at constant marginal cost, say, $11 per unit. This manufacturer sells the good to the retailer, at a price set by the manufacturer, denoted by p. The retailer then turns around and sells the good to the public, at a price denoted by P. The retailer, we assume, holds the monopoly right to sell this good to the public. To keep the math and pictures simple, assume a zero marginal cost of retailing, other than the cost of goods sold, so the marginal cost to the retailer is p, the wholesale price set by the manufacturer. Although the numbers are hardly suggestive of the marginal cost or demand function for Porsche automobiles, I refer to this item as a *car*.

Suppose the retailer faces the inverse demand function

$$P(x) = 131 - \frac{x}{100},$$

where x is the number of units the retailer sells, and $P(x)$ is the price he gets per unit. We tackle the following questions:

- What wholesale price p should the manufacturer set, to maximize her profit? What retail price will be set by the retailer, how much will be sold, and what will be the profit of the two firms?

- Suppose that the manufacturer could retail cars on her own, without the middleman, and at no additional cost of retailing. What happens then?

- Suppose the manufacturer could retail cars on her own, but at a marginal cost of k per vehicle sold, as compared to 0 marginal cost for the retailer. That is, the retailer has a cost advantage in retailing. At what levels of k does the manufacturer prefer to deal through the retailer and at what levels would she prefer to sell direct? At what levels of k would the public prefer that sales come through the retailer?

- Suppose the manufacturer decides that she must market her cars through the retailer, say, because she is much less capable at consumer marketing than the retailer. Is there any sort of scheme she might employ in her dealings with the retailer, that would enable her to do better than by simply charging a wholesale price p?

We answer these questions, then take our analysis back to the Porsche story, to see what this model teaches us. If you wish to try your analytical skills, try to answer these questions for the model on your own, and see what you think the answers are saying about the real-world problem of Porsche. Then proceed to read the analysis that follows.

The Best Wholesale Price to Charge

We begin with the question, What is the best wholesale price p for the manufacturer to set? The manufacturer's profit per vehicle in this simple model is $p - 11$, since the constant marginal cost of production is $11. This must be multiplied by the number of cars the retailer chooses to buy, which in turn depends on p; the lower is p, the more cars the retailer purchases for resale. So, to find the optimal value of p, we need to know the number of cars the retailer would purchase for resale, as a function of p.

Excel and Solver are quite handy for finding out how many cars the retailer would purchase, for a given number for p. For instance, suppose the manufacturer sets $p = \$51$. The retailer chooses his purchase level or, equivalently, the retail price P he would charge, to maximize his profit. If he sets a retail price P, he would buy and resell $100(131 - P)$ vehicles, for a profit of $(P - \$51) \times [100(131 - P)]$. The one-line spreadsheet shown in Figure 6.1, which is sheet 1 of the spreadsheet PORSCHE, is employed. Column A contains the wholesale price p, which is $51 in this case. Column B contains the retail price P, which in panel a is set at the starting value of $101. Column C computes the level of retail demand corresponding to the retail price in column B, and column D computes the retailer's profit.

We ask Solver to maximize column D, varying the entry in column B. Figure 6.1(b) shows the results: If p = $51, the retailer would optimally set P = $91 or, equivalently, buy (and sell) 4000 vehicles, for a profit of $160,000.

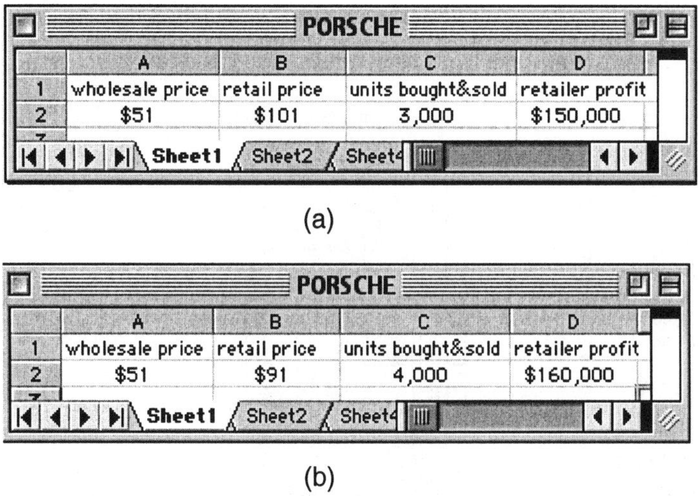

	A	B	C	D
1	wholesale price	retail price	units bought&sold	retailer profit
2	$51	$101	3,000	$150,000

Sheet1 / Sheet2 / Sheet4

(a)

	A	B	C	D
1	wholesale price	retail price	units bought&sold	retailer profit
2	$51	$91	4,000	$160,000

Sheet1 / Sheet2 / Sheet4

(b)

Figure 6.1. PORSCHE, sheet 1: Solving the retailer's problem. The retailer takes the wholesale price as given and chooses a retail price. From the retail price, demand and then the retailer's profit are computed. For a wholesale price of $51, panel a shows the basic spreadsheet for a retail price of $101. Solver is used to maximize cell D2 by varying B2, with the results shown in panel b.

So we know that, if p = $51, the manufacturer would sell 4000 vehicles. But what if p = $61? What if p = $41? We need to run Solver for each of these values put in cell A2, to find how the number of cars sold to the retailer varies with p. And then, once we have those numbers, we need to maximize the manufacturer's profit.

Solver isn't great at this sort of problem, but in this case, we can push through to an answer. Look at the top half of Figure 6.2, which is sheet 2 of PORSCHE. I copied the single row, from sheet 1, 13 times, and in successive rows of column A, I put in the values p = $11, $21, $31 ..., $131. I set P = $101 in all 13 rows to begin and summed the entries in column D, putting the sum in cell D16. Then I asked Solver to maximize D16, by varying B2 through B14; the result, shown in Figure 6.2, is the simultaneous solution of the retailer's problem for the 13 values of p in column A.

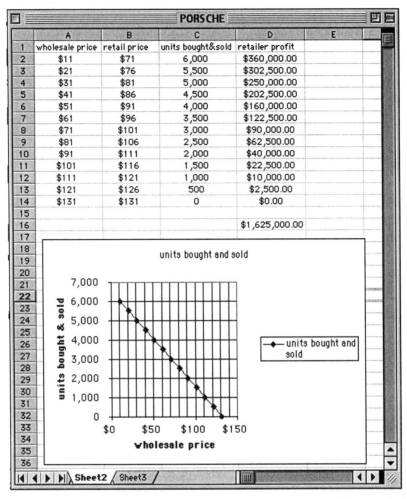

	A	B	C	D	E
	wholesale price	retail price	units bought&sold	retailer profit	
1					
2	$11	$71	6,000	$360,000.00	
3	$21	$76	5,500	$302,500.00	
4	$31	$81	5,000	$250,000.00	
5	$41	$86	4,500	$202,500.00	
6	$51	$91	4,000	$160,000.00	
7	$61	$96	3,500	$122,500.00	
8	$71	$101	3,000	$90,000.00	
9	$81	$106	2,500	$62,500.00	
10	$91	$111	2,000	$40,000.00	
11	$101	$116	1,500	$22,500.00	
12	$111	$121	1,000	$10,000.00	
13	$121	$126	500	$2,500.00	
14	$131	$131	0	$0.00	
15					
16				$1,625,000.00	

Figure 6.2. PORSCHE, sheet 2: The retailer's response to different wholesale prices. For a variety of wholesale prices, we find the retailer's optimal response in terms of retail price to set and number of units to buy and resell. Both the optimal retail price and the number of units bought and resold are linear functions of the wholesale price; in the bottom of the spreadsheet, we graph the relation between wholesale price and number of units.

A graph of the entries in column A against the entries in column C is shown in the bottom half of Figure 6.2. Clearly, this is a linear function. You can try other values of p—say, $p = \$34.56$—and find that this linear relationship holds up: The retailer's order quantity is a linear function of the wholesale price p. Moreover, we can use the numbers in the spreadsheet to work out the coefficients of this linear function; do this and you'll find that $x = 50(131 - p)$.

With calculus, which allows us to deal in symbols such as p, this can be done much more quickly: Fixing p, the formula for the retailer's profit as a function of the quantity of cars bought and sold x is

$$\left(131 - \frac{x}{100} - p\right)x,$$

this being price less cost times volume. To maximize this expression over x, we multiply through the x to get $(131 - p)x - x^2/100$, differentiate, and set the derivative to 0:

$$131 - p - \frac{2x}{100} = 0 \quad \text{or} \quad x = 50(131 - p),$$

which is precisely the linear function we see in Figure 6.2.

To finish with Excel, we move to sheet 3 of PORSCHE, shown in Figure 6.3. We have, in different rows, the wholesale price p, the quantity of cars the manufacturer can expect to sell to the retailer as a function of p, and the manufacturer's profit. I also include a calculation for the retail price P that the retailer sets; this is obtained by plugging the quantity into the retail inverse demand function. We want to maximize the manufacturer's profit by varying p, and Solver has no problem with that: In Figure 6.3, you see the spreadsheet that results after Solver has done its stuff, which is $p = \$71$. This entails the manufacturer selling 3000 cars at a retail price of \$101. The manufacturer's profit is $(71 - 11)(3000) = \$180,000$, while the retailer's profit is $(101 - 71)(3000) = \$90,000$. (If you download PORSCHE from the website, you'll find that sheet 3 has the trial value $p = \$51$; the optimization has not been run there yet.)

	A	B
1	wholesale price p	$71
2		
3	number of cars sold	3,000
4	retail price P	$101
5		
6	profits of manufacturer	$180,000
7		

Figure 6.3. PORSCHE, sheet 3 after optimization: Finding the optimal wholesale price for the manufacturer to set. For a given wholesale price in row 1, we use the formula found from sheet 2 (or by calculus) to compute the number of units the retailer would buy for resale and the corresponding retail price. Then we compute the profit of the manufacturer. Use Solver to maximize cell B6 by varying B1. The result, shown here, is a wholesale price of $71, leading to 3000 units bought and sold, a retail price of $101, and manufacturer profit of $180,000.

Or just use calculus. The manufacturer's profit as a function of p is $(p - 11) \times 50(131 - p)$. We work in p instead of in x, but as we learned in Chapter 3, that is legitimate: To maximize, first expand the polynomial to get $50(142p - p^2 - 1441)$. The derivative is $50(142 - 2p)$. Set this to 0, and you get $p = \$71$. From here, you can work out all the numbers in the previous paragraph. (If you absolutely had to work in terms of the quantity sold x instead of the wholesale price p, how would you do this? See Problem 6.2.)

Marketing Directly to the Public

The next step is to work out what the manufacturer would do if she could sell directly to the public. I include in these calculations the value k, a marginal cost incurred by the manufacturer if she sells directly to the public. Sheet 4 of PORSCHE shows the basic spreadsheet: We have the value of k in column A, the retail price set by the manufacturer in column B, the number of units sold in column C, and the manufacturer's profit in column D. Note that the formula for column D is $= Cn * (Bn - 11 - An)$, where n is the row number.

If you download the spreadsheet PORSCHE and turn to sheet 4, you'll find the trial value of $101 for the retail price in column B. But the manufacturer wants to set the retail price to maximize her profit, so the next step is to call Solver and ask it to maximize manufacturer profit, varying retail price. Using the trick of summing the profits in the different rows and asking Solver to maximize the sum, varying the different retail prices, we can do all this with one pass of Solver. The results are shown in Figure 6.4.

- If she could sell directly with no additional marginal cost (line 2), the manufacturer would set a retail price of $71, sell 6000 units, and make a profit of $360,000. Note that this is *more* than the combined profit of manufacturer and retailer in the optimal (for the manufacturer) two-step distribution scheme from the previous subsection.

- In the two-step distribution scheme, the manufacturer optimally made a profit of $180,000. It takes an additional marginal cost of k greater than $35 to get the manufacturer to prefer two-step distribution to selling directly to the public.

- Customers prefer direct-to-the-public distribution for values of k less than $60, since with such distribution and $k < \$60$, the retail price is lower and more units are sold than with two-step distribution.

- It goes without saying that, no matter what is k, the retailer does not like the manufacturer selling directly to the public because this puts the retailer out of business.

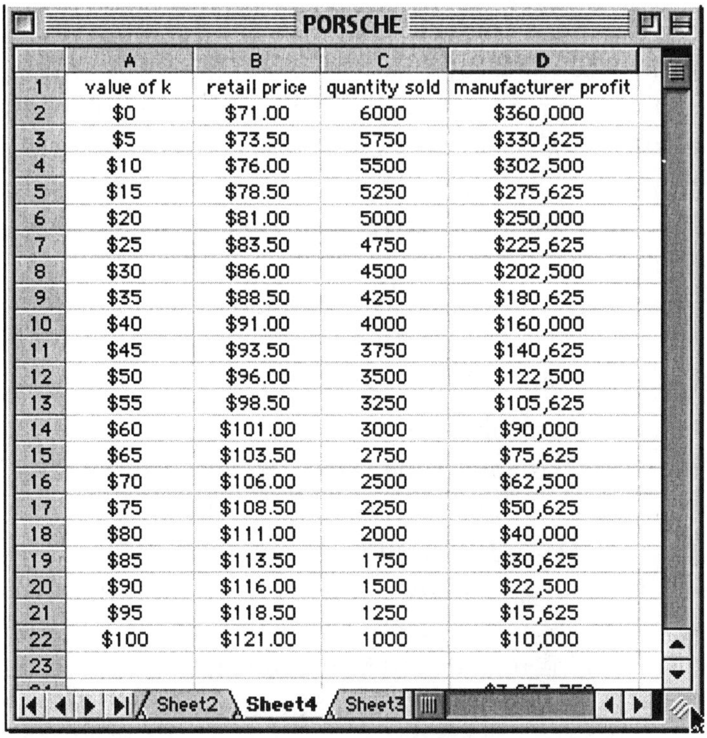

	A	B	C	D
1	value of k	retail price	quantity sold	manufacturer profit
2	$0	$71.00	6000	$360,000
3	$5	$73.50	5750	$330,625
4	$10	$76.00	5500	$302,500
5	$15	$78.50	5250	$275,625
6	$20	$81.00	5000	$250,000
7	$25	$83.50	4750	$225,625
8	$30	$86.00	4500	$202,500
9	$35	$88.50	4250	$180,625
10	$40	$91.00	4000	$160,000
11	$45	$93.50	3750	$140,625
12	$50	$96.00	3500	$122,500
13	$55	$98.50	3250	$105,625
14	$60	$101.00	3000	$90,000
15	$65	$103.50	2750	$75,625
16	$70	$106.00	2500	$62,500
17	$75	$108.50	2250	$50,625
18	$80	$111.00	2000	$40,000
19	$85	$113.50	1750	$30,625
20	$90	$116.00	1500	$22,500
21	$95	$118.50	1250	$15,625
22	$100	$121.00	1000	$10,000
23				

Sheet2 Sheet4 Sheet3

Figure 6.4. PORSCHE, Sheet 4, optimized: The manufacturer's optimal strategies for direct-to-the-public marketing. Suppose the manufacturer sells directly to the public but subject to an additional marginal cost of k (per unit) for doing so. Solver was used to optimize over the retail price the manufacturer would set. In this figure, you see those retail prices, the number of units sold, and the manufacturer's profit, as we parametrically vary the extra marginal cost k.

That is how to do this with a spreadsheet. For those who prefer calculus, if the manufacturer sells directly to the public with marginal costs of $11+k$, she equates her marginal revenue to this marginal cost. Since inverse demand is $131 - x/100$, total revenue is $131x - x^2/100$ and marginal revenue is $131 - 2x/100$. So marginal revenue = marginal cost is

$$131 - \frac{2x}{100} = 11 + k, \quad \text{or} \quad x = 50(120 - k).$$

This gives a retail price of

$$131 - \frac{50(120 - k)}{100} = 71 + \frac{k}{2},$$

and so a manufacturer profit of

$$\left(71 + \frac{k}{2} - 11 - k\right)\left(50(120 - k)\right) = 50\left(60 - \frac{k}{2}\right)\left(120 - k\right) = 25(120 - k)^2.$$

To discover where the manufacturer prefers direct-to-the-public distribution, you need to find the values of k for which $25(120-k)^2 \geq \$180,000$, this being the manufacturer's profit if she sells via the retailer. A bit of algebra shows that this is true for $k \leq 35.148$. Consumers, on the other hand, compare the retail price \$101 they pay with two-step distribution to the retail price $71 + k/2$ that they pay with direct-to-the-public distribution; they prefer such distribution for $k \leq \$60$.

Sometimes calculus is a lot less work than messing with spreadsheets.

What Does It All Mean? The Costs of Double Marginalization

To understand what is going on here, focus on the case of $k = 0$, where the manufacturer is just as able as the retailer to sell the product to consumers. The model says that, in this case, selling directly to the public results in a \$71 retail price, 6000 units sold, and a profit of \$360,000. But, with two-step distribution, the retail price is \$101, only 3000 units are sold, and total profit—the sum of the retailer's and the manufacturer's profits—is only \$270,000, divided \$90,000 to the retailer and \$180,000 to the manufacturer.

As long as the retailer has no cost advantage in retailing, it is not hard to see why total profit with two-step distribution is no larger than profit from selling directly to the public. Whatever distribution system is used, some quantity x is produced and sold to the public. Revenue earned from consumers is $xP(x)$, and the cost to manufacture x units is $TC(x)$. If the costs of retailing are 0, then total profit—the sum of the two firms' profits in two-step distribution—is $xP(x)-TC(x)$. In direct-to-the-public distribution, the manufacturer chooses x to maximize $xP(x) - TC(x)$. So, whatever x is chosen in two-step distribution, total profit can be no larger in two-step distribution than in selling directly to the public. And, to the extent that two-step distribution results in a quantity different from the profit-maximizing quantity for the direct-to-the-public system, total profit with the two-step distribution system must be less.

Moreover, two-step distribution definitely results in a lower quantity x than selling directly to the public. *For the manufacturer to make a profit, she must set her wholesale price p at a level that exceeds her marginal cost.* But her wholesale price is the marginal cost of the retailer. So, *the marginal cost of the retailer exceeds the marginal cost of the manufacturer.* With direct-to-the-public distribution, the manufacturer equates her marginal cost to retail marginal revenue. With two-step distribution, the quantity is set by the retailer, who equates his higher marginal cost to retail marginal revenue. Since his marginal cost is higher, his profit-maximizing quantity is less than hers. (This conclusion does not depend on marginal revenue being a decreasing function of quantity. It is true for any continuous marginal revenue function, although the argument is a bit tricky.)

To summarize, two-step distribution means a lower quantity than direct-to-the-public distribution, and therefore it means higher prices for consumers. And it yields a smaller total profit.

But, let me reiterate, this is true *only* as long as the manufacturer is not at a cost disadvantage to the retailer in retailing. We find two-step distribution precisely because retailers have lower costs of retailing than manufacturers or because retailers, being closer to the market, are better able to engage in the sort of price-discrimination strategies we study in Chapter 7.

The Economese term for this phenomenon is *double marginalization*. To explain this terminology, see Figure 6.5. In panel a, the solid line is retail market (inverse) demand, $P(x) = 131 - x/100$. Retail total revenue is $TR(x) = 131x - x^2/100$ and retail marginal revenue is $MR_R(x) = 131 - 2x/100$, depicted by the dashed line.

Suppose the manufacturer sets a wholesale price of \$51. This is the retailer's marginal cost, and to maximize profit, he equates this wholesale price to his retail marginal revenue. So, as shown in panel b, a wholesale price of \$51 gives the quantity where $MR_R(x) = \$51$. And, in general, a wholesale price of p gives the quantity where $MR_R(x) = p$. But this means that wholesale demand—the amount the manufacturer could expect to sell as a function of wholesale price—is traced out by retail marginal revenue. In other words, wholesale inverse demand *is* retail marginal revenue.

Wholesale marginal revenue is the marginal revenue curve obtained from the wholesale inverse demand curve = retail marginal revenue curve = $131 - 2x/100$. Do the math, and you'll find that this means that wholesale marginal revenue is $131 - 4x/100$, the double-dashed line in panel c of Figure 6.5.

Panel d finishes the story. Given manufacturer marginal cost, the manufacturer sets her wholesale price to sell the quantity where her marginal cost equals her wholesale marginal revenue. The retail price is then read off the retail inverse demand function at this quantity.

Hence, the terminology *double marginalization*: We begin with retail inverse demand and "marginalize" it for each step in the distribution chain—that is, twice in two-step distribution—to get the marginal revenue curve equated to manufacturer marginal cost.

Having Your Cake and Eating It, Too:
Charging the Retailer an Up-Front Fee

Of course, the analysis just completed does not imply that we never see retailers. Retailers exist. And, in fact, we have already seen one reason why: Retailers may have a cost advantage over manufacturers in retailing.

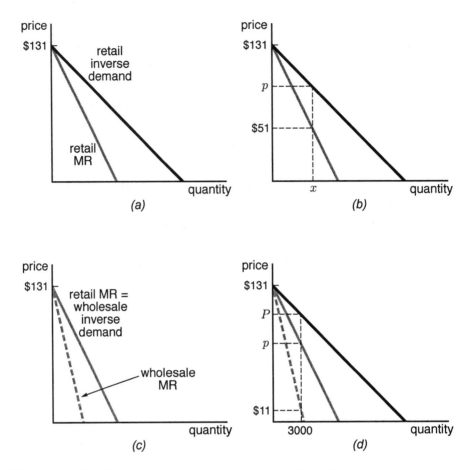

Figure 6.5. Double marginalization in a picture. Panel a shows retail inverse demand and retail marginal revenue. Panel b shows how, given a wholesale price p, such as $p = \$51$, the retailer equates this, his marginal cost, to retail marginal revenue to find the quantity x to buy, marking up the retail price to P. Hence, wholesale inverse demand is retail marginal revenue. In panel c, we see the "second marginalization": Retail inverse demand is marginalized once to get retail marginal revenue = wholesale inverse demand, which is marginalized a second time to get wholesale marginal revenue. Finally, in panel d, we see that manufacturer marginal cost ($11) is equated to the wholesale marginal revenue to get the quantity (3000 units) sold; this determines the wholesale price p and the retail price P. Of course, this is a much smaller quantity—in this linear example, half—than we would get with direct distribution, if the manufacturer's marginal cost of distribution is 0.

So, based on the issues we've discussed, it would seem that the choice between two-step and direct-to-the-public distribution turns on the cost of double marginalization versus the retailing cost advantages possessed by dedicated retailers. Manufacturers can have their cake or they can eat it, but they cannot do both—or so it might seem.

To be very concrete about things, suppose the retailer has a marginal cost of $0 for retailing, and if the manufacturer retails directly to the public, her marginal cost of retailing is $30. With these numbers, our earlier calculations tell us that the manufacturer would rather sell directly to the public, setting a retail price of $86 and making a profit of $202,500.

Suppose someone in the marketing department of the manufacturer comes up with the idea of charging the retailer an up-front fee in addition to a per-unit cost. In other words, the manufacturer will tell the retailer:

> "You can buy as many units as you wish at a cost to you of p per unit, and you can retail them at any price you wish. But before you buy any, you must pay me an up-front fee of F."

What is the manufacturer's profit-maximizing combination of F and p? Does it do better than marketing directly to the public? To answer these questions, we have to answer the question, Which combinations of F and p will the retailer accept?

In real life, this takes us into some psychological considerations. Suppose the retailer accepts this offer and pays F. That payment is now a *sunk cost* for the retailer, meaning nothing he does is going to get this money back, so he may as well forget that he paid it and optimize in what remains. And then, with a per-unit cost of p as his marginal cost, he would choose to buy and resell $50(131 - p)$ units—see the second display on page 139—setting a retail price of $131 - 50(131 - p)/100 = (131 + p)/2$, for a profit gross of F equal to

$$50(131 - p)\left(\frac{131 + p}{2} - p\right) = 25(131 - p)^2.$$

Will he pay F to make a gross profit of $25(131 - p)^2$? This is where, in real life, the psychology of the situation enters. Clearly he will not do so if F exceeds $25(131 - p)^2$. But suppose F is $1 less than $25(131 - p)^2$. Would he accept the offer then, to make a net profit of $1? Will he accept only if F is at least $1000 less than $25(131 - p)^2$, so that he makes a net $1000? How much net profit must the manufacturer leave on the table for the retailer, to induce him to accept the offer?

This is a hard question. It has to do with the retailer's next best profit opportunity as well as his psychology; would he spurn a profitable offer net of his opportunity cost, if he thought he was being exploited by the manufacturer? These issues have little to do with the current topic, so I make the modeling assumption that the retailer accepts the offer as long as F leaves him with a net profit of at least $100. That is, F must be less than $25(131 - p)^2 - 100$, to induce the retailer to say yes.

But if, as we assume, the manufacturer knows this $100 figure and, as we also assume, the manufacturer is able to calculate that, facing a wholesale price of p, the retailer's gross profit would be $25(131 - p)^2$, *then* the manufacturer has no reason to make F any less than $25(131 - p)^2 - 100$. Why leave the retailer more net profit than is necessary to induce him to say Yes?

So, assume that, if the manufacturer sets a wholesale price of p, she will set $K = 25(131 - p)^2 - 100$. And then her net profit will be

$$25(131 - p)^2 - 100 \quad + \quad 50(131 - p)(p - 11).$$

Let me take this formula a term at a time: The first piece is the up-front fee F received by the manufacturer. The second piece is the quantity she sells, $50(131 - p)$, times her profit margin $p - 11$ on each unit she sells.

The manufacturer, then, wants to set p, and so $F = 25(131 - p)^2 - 100$, to maximize this expression. You have a choice of Excel or calculus; I employ calculus. First, simplify the expression

$$25(131-p)^2-100+50(131-p)(p-11) = 25(131-p)[(131-p)+2(p-11)]-100 =$$
$$25(131 - p)(109 + p) - 100 = 25(131 \times 109 + 22p - p^2) - 100.$$

Take the derivative of this expression and set it equal to 0:

$$25(22 - 2p) = 0 \quad \text{or} \quad p = 11.$$

With this sort of fixed fee plus per-unit (wholesale) price scheme, it is optimal for the manufacturer to set the wholesale price p at $11, which is her marginal cost, and to set the franchise fee at

$$25(131 - 11)^2 - 100 = \$360,000 - \$100.$$

Note that in this scheme, the manufacturer is making all her profit on the up-front fee; she is selling her goods at her marginal cost.

This allows the manufacturer to have her cake and consume all but $100 of it: She gets the retailer to do the retailing, an activity at which he is more efficient, but she makes (almost) as much profit as she would have made selling directly to the public, had she the more efficient retailing technology of the retailer. The parenthetic *almost* refers to the $100 net profit she must leave the retailer to get him to accept. But $360,000 less $100 is a whole lot better than $202,500, the best she can do distributing directly.

What is going on here? Why does the answer come out with a per-unit wholesale cost equal to the manufacturer's marginal cost? This is actually very intuitive. The key is to recognize that, with the ability to set an up-front fee, the manufacturer is, essentially, going to realize all the profit made (gross) by her production operations and the retailer's retail operations. She will drain the retailer of all his profit, except for the $100.

How much profit will there be? Some amount x will be manufactured, sold to the retailer, and resold to the public; and the retail price for this amount x must be $131 - x/100$, read right off the retail inverse demand curve. To manufacture x units costs $11x$, and as long as the retailer is doing the retailing, the cost of retail operations is $0. So sum of the manufacturer's and retailer's profits must be $(131 - x/100)x - 11x$. Since all but $100 of this is going into the manufacturer's pocket, she wants to make this as large as possible. And we know that the way to do this is to sell 6000 cars, obtained from equating manufacturing marginal cost to retail marginal revenue.

The retailer is going to pick x in this scheme. So, from the manufacturer's perspective, the thing to do is to induce him to choose $x = 6000$, which is easy to do: He is going to equate his marginal cost, p, with retail marginal revenue. So set $p = 11$, and he will pick $x = 6000$. In other words, pass along to him the manufacturer's marginal cost, and he will choose the quantity that is optimal in terms of maximizing the sum profit. This is great for the manufacturer because, in the end, she gets everything except for the $100.

Multiple Retailers

To take this simple model a step closer to Porsche, imagine that the manu-facturer deals with not one retailer but several. To be exact, suppose there are three markets, each with its own monopolist retailer. In the first mar-ket, retail inverse demand is $P_1(x_1) = 131 - x_1/100$. In the second, it is $P_2(x_2) = 151 - x_2/200$. And in the third, it is $P_3(x_3) = 171 - x_3/50$. Sup-pose that these three retail markets are indeed distinct; they are separated geographically enough that different retail prices can be sustained in them. Each distinct retailer (one per region) has a marginal cost of retailing of $0. Marginal costs of retailing for the manufacturer are $30 in the first market, $20 in the second, and $50 in the third. The marginal cost of manufacturing the cars remains a constant $11.

You should have no problem repeating the earlier analysis for the two new markets. (The first market is precisely the case we already analyzed.) For the fixed fee and per-unit cost scheme for two-step distribution, assume that in each market, the retailer must be given $100 in profit. If you do this, the results you obtain should match those in Table 6.1.

Direct-to-the-public distribution beats simple wholesale-price-only, two-

	market 1	*market 2*	*market 3*
PARAMETERS			
intercept of inverse demand	131	151	171
slope of inverse demand	-0.01	-0.005	-0.02
cost of retailing	30	20	50
TWO-STEP DISTRIBUTION WITH A WHOLESALE PRICE ONLY			
wholesale price p	$71	$81	$91
retail price P	$101	$116	$131
quantity bought & sold	3000	7000	2000
manufacturer profit	$180,000	$490,000	$160,000
retailer profit	$90,000	$245,000	$80,000
DIRECT-TO-THE-PUBLIC DISTRIBUTION			
retail price	$86	$91	$116
quantity bought & sold	4500	12000	2750
manufacturer profit	$202,500	$720,000	$151,250
TWO-STEP DISTRIBUTION WITH FIXED FEE AND PER-UNIT CHARGE			
fixed fee	$359,900	$979,900	$319,900
per-unit charge = wholesale price	$11	$11	$11
retail price	$71	$81	$91
quantity bought & sold	6000	14000	4000
manufacturer profit	$359,900	$979,900	$319,900
retailer profit	$100	$100	$100

Table 6.1. Three separate retail markets. This table gives the data for three distribution schemes and three markets. (Parameters are given in the text.) If the choice is between two-step distribution with wholesale-price-only or direct-to-the-public distribution, direct distribution is better for the manufacturer in markets 1 and 2. But because of the high (relative) costs of retailing for the manufacturer in market 3, the manufacturer prefers two-step distribution here. (Consumers prefer direct marketing in all cases, but no one asks their opinion.) Best of all, in all cases, is two-step distribution with a fixed fee and per-unit charges: The manufacturer realizes (almost) full profit, while taking advantage of the superior marketing cost structure of the retailers.

step distribution in markets 1 and 2, but because of the high costs of distribution for the manufacturer in market 3, she prefers using the retailer in this case and suffers the costs of double marginalization.

For the manufacturer, two-step distribution with a fixed fee and per-unit charge is always the best option of the three. With this scheme, the manufacturer takes all but $100 of the profit she could earn with direct distribution *if* she had the superior distribution cost structure of the retailer. Note that, in this scheme, each retailer is charged the same per-unit price $11, because this per-unit price is the manufacturer's marginal cost of manufacture.

This is fairly important. Go back to the two-step distribution scheme, where the manufacturer charges only a wholesale price. Suppose the manufacturer's cost of retailing is such that she uses retailers in all three markets. We suppose that these three different markets can sustain different retail prices, presumably because the markets are geographically separated and no consumer living in a region with a high retail price is willing or able to move that demand to a region with lower retail price. But, even if moving demand from one region to another is unrealistic for individual consumers, the three retailers might see it in their interest to have the retailer in region 1 make substantial purchases and then transfer units to the retailers in the two other regions, if the wholesale price charged retailer 1 is substantially less than the wholesale prices quoted retailers 2 and 3.

But, in the fixed fee and per-unit charge scheme, the per-unit charge is the same in all regions. Now the three retailers have no incentive to move units from one region to another.

6.3. Back to Porsche

While I cannot be certain, my guess is that Porsche's attempt to restructure its distribution system was an attempt to avoid the cost of double marginalization. A natural question to ask is, Why now? One possible answer is that the expiration of the agreement with Volkswagon gave Porsche a natural opportunity to try a restructuring. At the same time, it is not hard to imagine that Porsche, a very well-established brand with a loyal following, felt that, with those advantages, it could sell directly to consumers at costs comparable to those incurred by retailers. Improved communication systems made a centralized repair and service system increasingly cost effective. Finally, the cost of double marginalization rises as the elasticity of demand for the product falls relative to fixed costs incurred in direct-to-the-public distribution, and it is not hard to imagine that Porsche believed that its cars, with a very loyal established customer base, faced increasingly inelastic demand.

The scheme Porsche attempted is, essentially, direct distribution. The old dealers remain as order takers and service providers, but Porsche USA sets the price. Why not take advantage of any distribution-cost advantage the retailers have and use a fixed-fee scheme? It is worth noting that, although dealers in cars can move stock from one dealer to another, because the per-unit charge is the same for all dealers, Porsche would not give the dealers an incentive to take advantage of this in the fixed-fee scheme.

I do not know for certain why Porsche did not attempt a scheme of fixed fees plus per-unit (wholesale) price. Perhaps the idea did not occur to Porsche. But two more substantial explanations are worthy of mention:

- Had Porsche attempted this scheme, it could reasonably assume that the dealers would initiate lawsuits contending that large up-front fees violated the no-change provision of franchise laws. Porsche may have decided that its prospects of winning such a suit were worse than the chance of successfully defending the changes it did attempt. After all, maintaining a dealership network where dealers retain autonomy but must pay new up-front fees is less of break with the past than what was proposed, and so the courts may have been more likely to see up-front fees as a modification of an existing relationship.

- Our simple model presumes that the retail demand function is certain and known to retailer and manufacturer alike. But, in real life, the demand for cars over a period of, say, a year is quite uncertain. Many exogenous factors impinge, such as the state of the national economy. And local factors affect local dealers. For instance, I expect that the period 1998–2000 was remarkably profitable for the Porsche dealership in Silicon Valley, as the dot-com revolution led to exploding wealth in the region, but that, in 2001, the Porsche dealership in the area did a good deal less business.

  The point is that, if Porsche were to charge a fixed yearly up-front fee, dealers would carry almost all the risks in year-end profits. This takes us into material that is not covered until Chapters 15 through 17, but this is very likely to be very inefficient in terms of the sharing of risk. Porsche USA is probably in a lot better shape to shoulder at least some of this risk. We might imagine fancier schemes, where the size of the fixed fee a dealer owes Porsche at the end of the year is tied to the state of the national and local economies, but such schemes are hard to administer. The one thing Porsche cannot do is to tie the fixed fee to the dealer's actual annual profit; the fixed fee and per-unit charge scheme works precisely because the dealer's marginal cost is set equal to the manufacturer's marginal cost. Tieing the fixed fee to the actual dealer's profit destroys this.

6.4. Why Do Laws to Protect Franchisees Exist?

A final comment about this story is worth making. Porsche did not get the change it desired in its distribution system because of the legal difficulties it faced. These difficulties arise because, in the United States, at least, laws protect franchisees from changes in the terms of their franchise arrangement, unless the franchisees agree to the changes.

Why are these laws on the books? In part, this is a matter of pure interest-group politics. Franchisees are an easily organized group; they are easy to find and very concerned with laws affecting their economic status. And, as small- to medium-size business owners, the owners of franchises are the sort of interest group that can have substantial influence, through contributions they make, on local legislators.

But there is more to the story than this. To do justice to this question, we need ideas that we reach only in the last few chapters of the book. But, since the topic has come up, let me take a very quick pass at explaining.

Most franchisees, when they establish their franchise, incur substantial fixed costs. Car dealers invest in lavish showrooms and repair facilities. Fast food franchisees often invest in their "restaurant." Very often, many of these fixed costs are sunk, meaning that the franchise owner who decides to get out of the business cannot easily or completely recoup the initial investment.

If a franchiser could freely change the terms of the franchise agreement, this would put the franchisee in an untenable position: The franchisee presumably makes the initial sunk-cost investment in the expectation of a stream of profits from the franchise. If the franchiser can, say, suddenly impose a substantial fixed annual franchise fee, the initially forecast stream of profits might disappear. Whether it is in the interest of the franchiser to take advantage in this fashion is a complex question; we discuss precisely this sort of matter in Chapter 23, when we get to the issue of credibility. But it is easy to see why a potential franchisee would be reluctant to make any sunk-cost investments without protection against subsequent exploitation of this sort. (It does not work to have the franchiser make the sunk cost investment because of incentive issues of the sort we address in Chapter 19.)

Therefore these laws may actually be in the interest of franchisers, insofar as they provide the assurance franchisees need, to convince the franchisees to invest in franchises.

Executive Summary

This chapter is quite different from earlier chapters in this book and so it rates a different sort of Executive Summary. Rather than exploring some very general ideas or techniques, we focus on exploring a particular story, Porsche's attempt to restructure its distribution system in the United States, and a model that sheds light on that story. In understanding the Porsche story, we come to grips with an important aspect of multistep marketing and distribution, the problem of multiple marginalization; and we see how, at least potentially, pricing schemes other than charging a simple per-unit price can lead to higher profits.

If you understand where the costs of multiple marginalization come from and how the fixed fee and per-unit charge scheme allows the manufacturer to have its cake and eat most of it, you have the main points of this chapter. The model also provides some practice at working with the model of the profit-maximizing firm. It is the first example of a model where more than one party is explicitly optimizing and one participant, the manufacturer, to optimize, has to take into account the optimizing decisions of other entities, the retailers.

Multistep distribution is a fact of life in all sorts of businesses, and understanding both the problem of multiple marginalization and the potential cure is very useful per se. This is especially true for firms that manufacture in one country and depend on local retailers in other countries to distribute their products. Beyond being important in its own right, this chapter serves as well as an extended introduction to Chapter 7. The fixed fee and per unit charge scheme is the tip of a very large iceberg known as *price discrimination.* With this appetizer, we proceed to the main course.

Problems

6.1 Redo the analysis of this chapter with the following assumptions: Retail inverse demand is $131 - x/100$. The total cost of manufacturing x units is $TC(x) = 10{,}000 + 11x$. If the retailer is used, his cost of retailing x units is $1000 + 10x$. If the manufacturer sells directly to consumers, her cost of retailing x units is $5000 + 30x$. To get the retailer to sign an agreement to pay a fixed fee F and a per-unit price of p, the retailer must be left with a net profit of \$100.

6.2 On page 140, we found the manufacturer's best wholesale price to charge, for two-step, wholesale-price-only distribution, working with the wholesale price as the variable. If we absolutely insisted on working in terms of the quantity sold the retailer, how would the analysis go?

7. Price Discrimination (and Surplus Extraction)

Firms selling goods do not limit themselves to charging every customer the same price for every unit of the good they sell. Using a variety of techniques that fit under the general rubric of *price discrimination*, they are able to improve the revenue they receive from selling a given amount of output. This chapter discusses the two main ideas of these schemes—charging higher prices to people who will pay higher prices and extracting from customers the surplus they obtain from consuming the good—as it describes a number of the methods used:

- Discrimination by group membership, such as discounts for seniors.
- Discrimination by self-selection, such as buyers' clubs and coupons.
- Third-degree price discrimination: product differentiation.
- Second-degree price discrimination: entry fees, quantity discounts, and so on.
- First-degree price discrimination: what Porsche should have tried.

This chapter concerns the following phenomena:

- Hard-cover and soft-cover editions of the same book sell for very different prices. This is particularly true of textbooks. For instance, I know of a text that sells in Europe for around $30 for a soft-cover edition and around $80 for hard cover. Of course, some of the difference in price is accounted for by the difference in the costs of producing a soft-cover vs. a hard-cover book. But not too much; it costs about $0.50 more to make a book with a hard cover than one with a soft cover. Why, then, is the retail price of a hard-cover book $50 more?

- In October 2000, the cheapest round-trip ticket from San Francisco to Chicago, departing Sunday morning and returning Tuesday morning, cost over $2300. But the same itinerary, with a departure time shifted 15 hours earlier, cost less than $450.

- Manufacturers of packaged foods such as ready-to-eat cereals distribute coupons for their products in so-called advertising mailers, which are freely available. These coupons effectively reduce the profit margin of the company by up to 40%, *and* they are costly to prepare, distribute, and administer. Why not save the administrative expense and simply sell the goods at the cheaper price?

- Order phone service for a new business and you will be amazed at the array of billing plans available. The choice can be so bewildering that phone companies have sometimes offered to compute a customer's bill, on a month by month basis, according to whichever scheme the company offers that would be cheapest for the customer. What are phone companies trying to accomplish with all this?

- If two individuals, one a man and the second a woman, bargain separately with a new car dealer for the purchase of a new car and the two follow precisely the same bargaining script, on average, the man will be offered the better deal. Why?

All these phenomena are examples of or closely related to price discrimination. The term *price discrimination* is used because, at their heart, all these phenomena involve discriminating among customers, charging different customers different prices, to exploit differences in the demand characteristics of the customers.

Why would a firm want to charge different customers different prices? Consider the two individuals depicted in Figure 7.1. The first says that he is not very sensitive to the price being charged. He wants some amount of the good, and if the price he is charged doubles, he will decrease his demand, but only by a bit. The second says that he is sensitive to price; lower the price a bit, for him, and he will respond with a substantial increase in his level of purchases. I have two questions regarding these individuals:

- If you could charge them different prices, which one would you charge a lower price and which one a higher price?

- The names of these two individuals are Mr. Pretty-elastic-demand and Mr. Not-very-elastic-demand. Who is who?

Figure 7.1. Two consumers. If you can charge one of these two a higher price and one a lower, which will get the higher price? And, given what they have to say, which one has more-elastic and which less-elastic demand?

Of course, you want to charge a high price to the individual who is not sensitive to price—he pays through the nose for his stuff—and you want to charge a relatively low price to the other individual, to get him to buy a substantial quantity. The first is Mr. Not-very-elastic-demand; the second is Mr. Pretty-elastic-demand.

Firms can rarely charge each individual a custom-tailored price. But sometimes they can separate their customers into *groups*, where the different groups have different elasticities of demand, charging the more-inelastic-demand group a higher price, thus increasing revenues. The impact can be substantial: Imagine a firm selling a product whose marginal cost is a constant $40. The firm finds that it maximizes profits at a price of $60. Imagine that the firm can divide its customer group into two, with one group having constant elasticity of demand equal to -2 and the other equal to -5. Then, if it can charge the two groups different prices, it optimally charges the first group a price of $80 and the second group a price of $50, which improves its profit by 14.14%. (For the derivation of these numbers, see Problem 7.10 and its solution in the *Companion*.)

The question is, How do firms accomplish this neat trick of marketing?

7.1. Discrimination by Group Membership

The simplest sort of price discrimination is discrimination by demographic group membership. For instance, a food store might give senior citizens, defined by age, a percentage discount on their purchases. Theaters sometimes offer discounts for seniors; symphony orchestras give students a discount on subscriptions. A very common example is when public transportation systems have special prices for seniors and students.

Why? One possible reason is a sense of social justice: Seniors often live on restricted or fixed incomes, and the local cheese store may feel is socially just to supplement the meager diets that seniors can afford. A second reason is to develop loyalty; symphony orchestras may offer cut-price subscriptions to students in the hope that the students will become long-term subscribers after they have left school.

But this sort of "price break for the disadvantaged poor" may also be a simple matter of profit maximization. Senior citizens and students may be disadvantaged, but at the same time and connected to their disadvantages, they probably have more elastic demand regarding food items and symphony tickets than is typical in the public at large. So purely on profit-maximization grounds, it makes sense—if you can get away with it—to charge them lower prices.

Three remarks concerning this basic idea are in order.

- Not every senior citizen has more elastic demand than every nonsenior. Discrimination by group membership works because seniors have more elastic demand than nonseniors *on average*.

- If the local deli cuts prices by 10% for seniors, what prevents an enterprising senior from walking into the store, buying a thousand sandwiches, then selling them outside the deli for 5% more than she paid, which is, more or less, 5% less than the deli's regular price? For one thing, the deli probably does not offer the senior discount for large-quantity orders. This example is fanciful but the problem is not: Discriminatory schemes can fail if the good in question can be resold and if a low-price customer can purchase at the low price and sell to customers who would otherwise pay the high price. For this reason, discrimination of this sort, as with other sorts to be discussed, is most often found in cases of things that cannot be resold so easily, such as services.

- In many states in the United States, drivers under the age of 25 pay more for car insurance than drivers over this age, at least among men. This is not because the demand for insurance among young drivers is relatively more inelastic, but that young male drivers have, on average, a lot more accidents. This is not price discrimination but rather charging different classes of customer different prices for a service, insurance, based on the actuarially determined expected cost of providing that service.

Discrimination by group membership raises significant legal and ethical questions. Concerning, say, price discounts for senior citizens, recognize that this means price hikes for everyone else. If overall demand has elasticity, say, -3, and a subgroup of the population has elasticity -5, so that it rates a discount, the remaining group of customers has elasticity between -3 and 0—how much closer depends on the relative size of the groups—and if the more-elastic demand group gets a lower price, profit maximization means the other group faces higher prices.

Even so, most people feel that senior citizens deserve this sort of break. But discrimination by group membership is not always so benign. For instance, legal scholar Ian Ayers[1] sent trained investigators to new car dealerships in the Chicago area armed with very precise scripts about how to negotiate the purchase of a new car. The investigators were dressed uniformly; appearance and behavior, except for gender and race, were kept as

---

[1] In Ayers, "Fair Driving: Gender and Race Discrimination in Retail Car Negotiations," *Harvard Law Review*, Vol. 104, 1991, 817–71. I have elected to use the terms that Ayers uses, namely *white* and *black* for race and *male* and *female* for gender.

uniform as possible. Ayers's investigators kept track of the progress of their negotiations, noting the levels of price concessions they got from the dealer. The question Ayers addressed with the data collected was, Would dealership salespersons respond differently to customers who were following the same script and were dressed similarly, depending on the customer's race and sex? He found that white males received significantly greater concessions from dealers than white females, black males, and black females: In terms of the final offer they received, white females, on average, were offered 40% higher mark-ups than white males. Black males were offered around twice the mark-up of white males. Black females were offered around three times the mark-up offered to white males. Of course, none of the deals were consummated—Ayers's research budget did not stretch that far—so perhaps the females and black males would have gotten the same deals being offered to white males had they been a bit more patient. But if females and black males have to negotiate longer to get the same deal, this is still a form of discrimination. Why might this be?

One possible explanation is pure prejudice, meaning actions in the face of countervailing economic considerations, to serve some noneconomic goal such as harming people of color and women. Ayers considered this possibility, and he asserts that the data he collected do not support it. Instead, he asserts that this is a case of economic discrimination based on group membership. White females, black males, and especially black females have more inelastic demand for new cars than white males. For economic or social or some other reason, females and black males are less likely to haggle *on average* than white males. Please note the "on average" in this sentence. A black female who is also ready and willing to drive a hard bargain might, in the end, get the concessions offered a white male. But she has to wait longer and work harder to get those concessions.

Suppose Ayers is right about this. Suppose that, on average, it makes economic sense, *meaning it increases profits*, for new car dealers to discriminate in this fashion against females and black males. Should such discrimination be legal? And since it might be hard to enforce a law against it if it is illegal, is it ethical? Most individuals with whom I discussed these questions believe both that it should not be permitted under law and, even absent an effective and enforceable law against it, that such behavior is ethically reprehensible. I share these judgments. But, assuming you agree, let me challenge you: Should discounts for seniors be legal? Are they ethical? And if you answer Yes to both questions, what is the philosophical or ethical basis for the distinction?

This is a textbook in economics, not law and not ethics. So I will not try to answer those questions. My point is that economic discrimination by group membership is based on the simple idea that profits may be increased if you charge inelastic-demand customers higher prices and more elastic-demand customers lower prices. To the extent that elasticity is correlated with group membership, charging different groups different prices can improve your bottom line. But just because it improves your bottom line does not mean that it is legal or, where it is legal, ethical to do so.

7.2. Discrimination (Nearly) by Group Membership: From Buyers' Clubs to Coupons

In a scheme of discrimination by group membership, different demographic groups, who cannot do anything about their membership status, face different prices. It is often impossible or illegal to discriminate between demographic groups in this fashion, even when, because the groups have different elasticities of demand, it would increase profit to do so. But schemes can sometimes be devised that permit this sort of discrimination: In theory, everyone has access to the discounts offered, but in practice, only a subset, the more elastic segment of the population, takes advantage. A sampler of such schemes follows:

- Go into a supermarket near a tourist area on one of the islands of Hawaii, and you will find that the posted prices of various goods are very high by mainland standards. Market managers, when asked about this, are quick to point out how everything has to be flown in from the mainland. But for a lot of the items, a second and substantially lower price is given for, well, I don't know the word, but I believe it is Hawaiian for "local residents' club members." To be a member of this club, you need a membership card. And the store will be happy to give you an application form for the club, but unhappily, the card will have to be mailed to your home address and it will take a few weeks. "Only going to be here in the Islands for a week? Oh, that's too bad."

  What is going on here? Tourists on vacation have less elastic demand for food items than the locals, especially those tourists renting a vacation condominium so that they can cook their own meals to avoid the cost and hassle of restaurants. It probably would not do—it might even be illegal—to offer discounts to anyone with a state of Hawaii driver's license. But the club membership scheme works almost as well.

- Fine restaurants often offer a number of fixed or semi-fixed menus— you might get no choices, or you might get your choice of one of two appetizers, one of two main courses, and one of three desserts—priced at

significant savings relative to ordering à la carte. The lower prices may
be cost related: Perhaps the ingredients were obtained at lower cost in
the markets, which is why they appear on one of the menus. Spoilage of
ingredients for à la carte items is presumably higher, since order levels
for specific à la carte items are more variable. Certainly, it eases strain
on the kitchen staff to have a less diverse list of items to prepare. But,
especially for very fine restaurants, where the semi-fixed menus change
almost daily, this could be a way to discriminate between regulars, who
are happy to eat at reduced cost whatever is on the menu today, as long
as the menu does change frequently, and the occasional diner, who will
want to take the opportunity of this one-time or infrequent visit to order
the chef's particular specialties.

- The Stanford Shopping Center, located next to Stanford University, is a
luxury shopping mall filled with branded boutiques such as Ann Taylor. About 60 minutes from Stanford, along a highway in the town of
Gilroy, the world's largest producer of garlic, is an outlet center, a spe-
cialty shopping mall that has outlets of some of the same boutiques as
you find at the Stanford Shopping Center, including an outlet of Ann
Taylor. At the outlet stores in Gilroy, you can find "seconds," goods with
slight imperfections, selling at dramatically lower prices than would be
charged for "firsts." And you can find slightly out-of-fashion or out-of-
date merchandise, moved no doubt from the Stanford outlet. But you
can also find some of the same items found in the Stanford outlet, at substantially reduced prices. The relative costs of running the two different
outlets might explain some of the price differences: Rents in the Stanford
Shopping Center are probably astronomical relative to those in Gilroy.
And this in turn explains the differences in merchandise selection: Only
premium goods—firsts and currently fashionable goods—generate the
sorts of margins that can justify floor space in the high-rent Stanford
Shopping Center. But it is also undoubtedly the case that the clienteles
attracted to the two different outlets have very different price elasticities
for the goods, with the more inelastic demand turning up at Stanford
and the more elastic demand taking the trouble to drive to Gilroy.

- The time to buy sheets, pillowcases, and towels in the United States is late
January, when the January white sales take place. (Sheets, pillowcases,
and towels are known as "white goods.") Why does anyone buy any of
these goods in, say, November, paying the higher prices? If you need
new towels or if waiting for the sales to come is just too inconvenient, you
buy now. This doubtless means that your demand, and more generally
the demand of people who buy these goods in November, is less elastic

than the demand of people who are willing to wait for the sales.

- Advertisements for vendors heard on the radio, read by a radio personality, sometimes end with the tag line, "Tell them [the vendor] that Joe Radio-guy [the radio personality] sent you and they'll pay the sales tax," or "... they'll take 5% off," or "... they'll give you a free waffle iron." Why does the mention of Joe Radio-guy's name get you favored treatment? In part—when the add-on is relatively cheap, such as a waffle iron—this is a way for the seller to gauge the success of its advertisements. But when the price break offered is large—sales taxes can be on the order of 8% in the United States—another explanation is that Joe Radio-guy's audience has more elastic demand for the goods being sold than the population as a whole. This offer allows the vendor to charge this more elastic demand segment of the population a lower price.

- Sunday newspapers in the United States are full of inserts that contain coupons for all sorts of goods, coupons that allow the bearer reductions in the price paid for specific goods. You can undoubtedly anticipate what comes next: Consumers who go through these inserts looking for coupons they can use, have, on average, more elastic demand for the goods than the consumers who do not.

To reiterate, each of these is nearly discrimination by group membership. The only distinction from, say, discounts for seniors is that consumer X is or is not a senior. X can do nothing about it. But any individual consumer X, if he or she so chooses, can hunt through the Sunday papers for coupons, mention Joe Radio-guy's name, wait for the sale, drive to Gilroy, order the semi-fixed menu, or even—if given enough time—join the buyers' club. Some consumers do and others—whether because of the time and effort involved, out of ignorance of the possibility, or because the logistics of doing so make it nearly impossible—do not. As long as those who take advantage of the lower prices have more elastic demand than those who do not, these techniques are profit-enhancing price discrimination.

These techniques have some substantial drawbacks, which parallel the notion that offering senior citizens discounts means offering a discount to seniors whose demand is inelastic. When a discount is offered for anyone saying "Joe Radio-Guy sent me," this discount is given to individuals who would have bought the particular item or service anyway. Sales of white goods in early January can be quite slow because individuals who would otherwise purchase sheets or pillowcases at white-sale prices—and would have done so in October—are willing to wait the week or so until the January white sales begin. The basic problem is perhaps most acute when it comes to coupons. Since manufacturers pay for the coupons, retailers have an incentive to get the coupons into the hands of all customers, and cases are not unknown where stores will get coupons in bulk and "display" them right alongside the goods for which the coupons are valid, guaranteeing that every purchaser of the goods gets the discounted price. Indeed, cases are not unknown where the clerk at the checkout stand will direct the customer's attention to the coupons, in the rare case where the customers has missed them but is buying the goods anyway.

In fact, coupons add an interesting general twist to this. Imagine a situation in which every customer for a given good buys more than one unit of the good; think, for example, of buying pints of ice cream. Suppose that the manufacturer is able to get the coupons into the hands of a particular segment of the market, whose demand for the product is very elastic. But to control the cost of the couponing program, the manufacturer limits coupons so that each customer can use only one coupon; that is, the discount applies to only one pint of ice cream. In this case, in terms of price discrimination, the coupon program is worse than an utter failure. No additional demand for the product is stimulated by the coupons, since the marginal cost to a customer is the posted price of the good. Customers with a coupon simply get the face value of the coupon back for the purchase of a pint of ice cream they would have made in any case. The key to a successful coupon program, at least in the terms of price discrimination, is that it lowers for a high-elasticity segment of the population the marginal cost to that segment of the good being sold, stimulating increased demand. Coupons, to work, must induce sales that would not have happened otherwise.

So why do we see "limit one per customer" clauses in some coupons?

- "Limit one per customer" is a way to introduce new customers to a product, without giving old and established customers, who are buying in bulk, a discount for all their units. If the good being sold is one that, once experienced, will "hook" customers, then this is a good marketing technique for getting the hook in.

- "Limit one per customer" is a form of second-degree price discrimination, which is discussed at length later this chapter.

7.3. Third-Degree Price Discrimination: Product Differentiation

(First- and second-degree price discrimination are coming, but on expositional grounds, it makes sense to start with third-degree price discrimination and work up.)

The packages of dried pasta in a Hawaiian supermarket that I buy for $4.59 and a member of the locals' club buys for $2.19 are identical, costing the supermarket the same amount. A pint of ice cream bought with a $0.50 coupon is precisely the same as a pint of ice cream bought without the coupon.

But when a consumer pays more for sheets and pillowcases in December than in January, the goods are not quite the same. The sheets bought in December are bought, presumably, in a more timely fashion, and they are useful for the month of December. A garment bought at the Stanford Shopping Center is not quite the same as the same garment bought from an outlet in Gilroy, in terms of the cost of getting to the store, the ambiance of the shopping center, and especially, the level of service customers receive in selecting their purchases.

For this reason, some of the schemes described last section begin to approach *third-degree price discrimination*, where the manufacturer or seller of the good sells the same "basic" good in different forms or with different conditions attached, using the forms and conditions to discriminate among buyers' groups.

A relatively simple example involves textbooks outside the United States. While most textbooks sold in the United States are sold in hard cover, in many other locations students buy soft-cover editions, sometimes explicitly labeled as *International Student Edition* and the like, while libraries purchase hard-cover editions. As noted at the start of the chapter, the costs of production may differ; a hard-cover edition of a 600-page book costs about $0.50 more than a soft-cover edition of the same book. But the differences in price swamp the differences in cost: It is common to find soft-cover editions that cost half or less of the cost of hard-cover editions, differences on the order of $50.00.

Hard-cover editions are bought by libraries. I do not know why libraries do not buy soft-cover books and put their own hard covers on, but, at least until recently, they have not. So demand for textbooks can be thought of as coming from two sources: from libraries and institutional buyers, who will not purchase a soft-cover book at any price, and from individuals, especially students, for whom a hard-cover book is more valuable, but only a bit more valuable. How should publishers respond?

A simple model, which ignores a number of real-life features such as the used-book market and reeditioning the same basic book, runs as follows.

The demand curve for a soft-cover textbook overseas is usually held to have the sort of shape shown in Figure 7.2. There is a maximum potential quantity that could be sold, and then a range of prices over which demand is fairly elastic. Demand responds to price by two means: The decision by an instructor to adopt a particular book depends on its price, and even if a book is adopted by an instructor, individual students may decide not to purchase a copy if the price is too high. Profit maximization gives around 2800 copies sold at a price of $30. (I place the marginal cost curve around the absolute level of $10. While the $0.50 difference between hard- and soft-cover production costs is a bona fide figure, my source requests that I not reveal his absolute costs of production. I am allowed to say, however, that this $10 figure is substantially higher than is true in reality.)

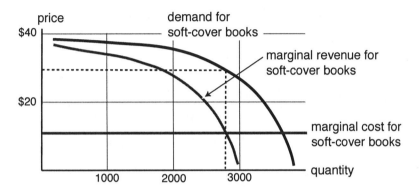

Figure 7.2. Pricing a soft-cover textbook.

Now we bring a hard-cover edition into the story. Assume for the moment that there is no interaction between the two markets; a completely separate demand curve for hard-cover books arises entirely from library sales. I superimpose on the picture in Figure 7.2 the demand, marginal revenue, and marginal cost curves for this hard-cover edition in Figure 7.3, and by equating marginal cost to marginal revenue for hard covers, we get a hard-cover price of $80 and demand for around 600 books.

With these numbers, and with marginal costs of $10 and $10.50, say, for soft- and hard-cover editions, the publisher makes profits of $69.50 × 600 = $41,700 on the hard-cover edition and $20 × 2800 = $56,000 on the soft-cover edition, for a total profit of $97,700.

Of course, there are interactions between the two markets. If the price of hard-cover books gets down to the $50 range, hard-cover books take market share from soft-cover books, depending on the difference in price. This effect becomes very noticeable if the hard-cover price is within around $5 of the soft-cover price. Let me suppose that any soft-cover customer is willing to pay $5 more for a hard cover than for a soft cover. Then the publisher could lower the hard-cover price to, say, $35, and sell 2800 additional hard-cover books. This increases the profit margin on those 2800 books from $20 to $24.50, which increases profits by $12,500. But, instead of selling 600

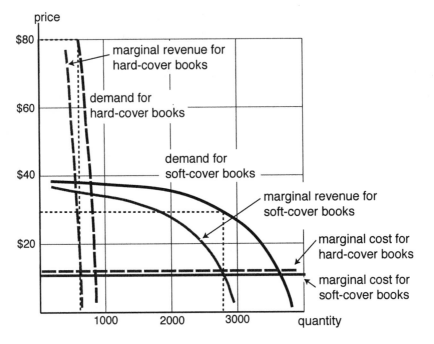

Figure 7.3. Pricing hard-cover and soft-cover books.

books to libraries at $80, this would mean selling around 720 books at $35, giving a fall in profit on sales to libraries of $24,060. It is better to have a soft-cover edition for nonlibrary sales and a hard-cover for library sales and really exploit the libraries, even though the publisher could sell hard-cover editions to nonlibrary users at around $4.50 more profit per book.

Using Time to Discriminate

A much-used tool in third-degree price discrimination is time. Roughly speaking, if you want the good now, you pay a high price, while if you are willing to wait, the price is substantially lower. The key to such schemes is that impatient customers tend to have more inelastic demand, while those willing to wait have relatively more elastic demand. A wide variety of such schemes can be found:

- In the publication of popular books, best-sellers and the like, cheaper paperback editions are often issued substantially after the time that the original hard-cover edition is published.

- Periodic sales, such as the January white sales, are essentially based on this idea.

- Electronic equipment and other high-priced consumer durables are often very high priced when first released, but then prices decline as time passes. This effect is sometimes hidden by using different marketing channels; for instance, a new model camera may be available only from retail outlets that charge close to list price for a while, only later becoming available through discounters. Often it is not hidden at all; list prices decline as time passes. Manufacturers will sometimes explain these declines as the result of competition or costs that decline due to experience curve effects (see Chapter 10), and this may account for some of the decline in price. But third-degree price discrimination is likely to be at work as well.

- Telephone rates decline at night. Business users, whose demand for telephone services is relatively inelastic, make most of their phone calls during the business day. Personal users are more able to shift their demand to evenings and nights; and their demand is relatively more elastic.

The example of telephone rates deserves two comments. First, the cost structure of telephone networks is such that cost depends heavily on the *peak load* that the network must handle, with a marginal cost equal to 0 for times other than when the load on the network is at its peak. Lower prices at night may be a simple attempt to shift demand from daytime to night, to lower the peak load on the network and reduce costs.

Second, it will be evident in this case, and indeed in all these cases, that *demand shifting* makes it difficult to find the optimal ways to price discriminate using time. That is, in the simple example of hard- and soft-cover books in the previous subsection, we could work things out because we assumed that the markets for the two varieties of books were independent of one another. This is similar to the case of discrimination by groups, in which we specified separate and independent demand functions for each demographic segment of the market. But, in all the examples just given—lowering the price for a paperback edition of a best-seller, selling sheets cheap in January, selling electronic equipment at a discount nine months after it has first been released, or having cheaper rates for phone calls at night—to some extent cannabalizes the market for the hard-cover first edition, sheets in December, newly released electronic equipment, and calls made in the daytime. In practice, dealing with this sort of demand shifting requires sophisticated analysis.

Airline Pricing

Third-degree price discrimination as practiced by passenger airlines, so-called revenue or yield management, is extraordinarily sophisticated. The basic ideas are well known: Advanced purchase requirements, overnight stay requirements, cancellation privileges, upgrade privileges, and seat comfort and meal quality are ways of differentiating the basic item (a seat on a particular flight) where passengers with more inelastic demand pay a very large premium for the "higher-quality" terms and conditions. Examples illustrating the dramatic price differences that can result are mentioned at the start the book and the start of this chapter; I mention another example here. When I first wrote these lines, in September 2001, I was pricing a round-trip from San Francisco to Paris. My travel agent gave me three different coach fares—$520, $1230, and $2671—depending largely on cancellation and upgrade privileges. And, to finish off the possibilities, a round-trip business class ticket would have cost $6610, while first class cost $8652. It is true that the food is better in, say, business class than in coach and there is more room to stretch out, but $6000 better? Who is willing to pay that sort of premium?

The answer is, business people. They do not pay the fare themselves— their employers do—and if the employer has a policy of sending people business class, the exorbitant fare is paid. If ever there was a recipe for inelastic demand, that is it.

Now, consider the problem facing the airline. There are 49 seats in the business class cabin of the flight in question. When I wrote this, about 6 weeks before the flight, 9 of the 49 seats in business class were sold for the outbound leg and 10 out of 49 were sold on the return flight. This leaves a lot of seats in business class to sell. When the plane in question takes off, if a seat is empty, the airline loses the ability to ever sell that seat on that flight. Some marginal costs are associated with a full versus an empty seat—the cost of the little gift pack the passenger gets and food and wine—perhaps this comes to $100, although that probably is an overestimate. So the airline wants to fill those seats.

Of course, it isn't necessary to pay $6000 to get a business class seat. You can pay $1230 and give up 40,000 frequent flier miles, or you can pay $2671 and give up 20,000 frequent flier miles. Give up enough frequent flier miles, and you can have one of those seats for $0. Or, rather, this might be possible. You can upgrade in this fashion *if* the airline makes some seats in the business class cabin available for upgrade. And, although I have no way of telling, I bet that most of the business cabin seats sold for these two flights with 6 weeks to go were upgrades or to passengers using frequent-flier miles only. But when I wrote this, with 6 weeks to go and most of the 49 seats unsold, there was no current availability of upgrade seats. Someone at the airline watches these flights' business class cabin, together with all the other categories of seats on these flights and all the other seats on all the other flights of this airline. With, perhaps, 3 weeks to go, if most of the business class cabin is still empty, the airline might make more seats available for upgrade. (In fact, it did.) But if, with 3 weeks to go, only a few seats remain in the business class cabin, the airline is likely to hold back, hoping that, at the last moment, they can sell a seat or two to some business traveler at $6610. After all, as a last resort, the airline can and often does upgrade some passengers willing to part with their frequent flier miles at the departure gate, 15 minutes prior to the flight.

I hope the point is clear. Revenue and yield management is third-degree price discrimination at a level of extraordinary dynamic complexity. The methods actually used bear almost no resemblance to our simple exercise concerning how to price soft- and hard-cover books. But the basic principle—high prices for inelastic demanders, low prices for elastic demanders, and goods that are differentiated to achieve the desired separation—is precisely the same.

Keeping the Markets Separate by Product Differentiation

Keeping the relatively inelastic-demand customers from buying the low priced goods is the key to success in these schemes. While this goes without saying, one spectacular example may help fix the idea: A particular material, developed by a chemicals and plastics firm, could be used both as a dental filling material and for construction purposes. The relatively inelastic demand application was dentistry; the problem the firm faced was to keep dentists from getting a friendly building contractor to buy a few hundred pounds at the low price charged contractors. The firm in question hit on a magnificent scheme for achieving this; they added to the material sold for construction purposes a small amount of an "impurity" that, if introduced into someone's mouth, would slowly poison the individual. This very effectively stopped crossover sales.

7.4. Second-Degree Price Discrimination

In second-degree price discrimination, each customer is offered a *nonlinear* price schedule. Discounts for purchases made in bulk is second-degree price discrimination, as are price schedules where the individual customer gets a discount for the first few items purchased, but has to pay full price for any units beyond the first few. A very common form of second-degree price discrimination consists of schemes in which the customer pays an "entry fee" for the right to buy anything at all and then pays a per-unit price, as in the standard form of pricing. At an extreme, only the entry fee is charged; for instance, the Disney theme parks charge an entry fee only; the customer pays nothing more no matter how many rides he or she takes. (Customers pay for food consumed and entry fees are not uniform; one-day, three-day, and season passes are available. Not to miss a trick, Disney also offers special services for premium entry fees and discount coupons, and members of organizations such as the American Automobile Association qualify for extra discounts.)

Telephone service providers and utility companies are probably the masters of second-degree price discrimination, with their very complex nonlinear price packages and deals. And they typically offer consumers a variety of nonlinear price packages. For instance, cell telephone service providers offer customers a bewildering array of choices, with different levels of "free" minutes per month, for a fixed monthly fee, and then different prices for minutes used above the packaged free minutes.

The practice of setting nonlinear pricing schemes is, in general, very complex. No hard and fast rules describe the structure of optimal schemes. Discounts for large-scale purchases might be optimal, or discounts for the first few items purchased might be optimal. It all depends on the specific demand characteristics of the customers.

A couple of simple examples illustrate why this is. Suppose a particular product is sold to two different types of customers, A and B types. Suppose that demand by the A types is relatively inelastic, while demand by the Bs is relatively elastic. If the firm in question could engage in discrimination by group membership, discriminating between the groups A and B, profit maximization would lead it to charge the members of group A a higher price than members of B. For purposes of illustration, suppose that those prices are $15 per unit for A and $10 per unit for B. But, we suppose discrimination by group membership is not feasible.

Suppose further that the members of group A purchase small quantities of the item in question (say, no more than 5 items) while members of group B purchase large quantities (say, no fewer than 20). Then, the firm in question would like to offer discounts for large-lot purchases; for instance, it might say that customers can purchase up to 5 units apiece at $15 per unit, but for any purchases beyond this by the customer, a price per unit of $10 will prevail. Members of group A buy their up-to-five units for $15 apiece, and those in B face a price on the margin of $10 apiece, just what we wanted in for the discrimination-by-group solution.

In fact, it is not quite so easy as this. For one thing, a member of group A, facing a per-unit price of $10 beyond the fifth unit, might be inclined to buy a sixth or seventh unit. This is presumably good for the firm selling the good. But what about group B? Will its members be happy paying $75 for their first five units? To know the answer to this question, we need to know their utility functions. If we suppose that they swallow this and make the same level of purchases as if they faced a flat $10 per-unit price—and notice that this is not entirely unreasonable, if you look at marginal costs and marginal utilities for them—then the firm can only be better off than in the discrimination-by-groups scheme.

The story turns around if, on the other hand, it is members of group A who buy in lots no smaller than 20, while those in B buy no more than 5 units apiece, at respective prices of $15 for A and $10 for B. The firm in question should offer goods at $15 apiece, with a $5 "price break" for the first five units the consumer purchases. Group B members effectively face a $10 per-unit price; they were not interested in more than five units at a flat price of $10, so they are hardly likely to increase their purchases when the price rises beyond the fifth unit purchased. Members of group A, looking at the marginal cost of $15 for units when the total quantity purchased is beyond 20, make purchase decisions approximating those they would make if they faced a flat $15 per unit price schedule. The firm selling the good pays a bit for this sort of nonlinear price scheme relative to discrimination by groups— members of group B save $25 on the first five units each purchases—but the firm gets to charge them a high price for units beyond the fifth one.

Real-life examples of each case are not hard to find. Utilities often offer "life-line" options, where a small level of service can be obtained for a very low price per unit, but prices rise for units purchased beyond the life-line quantities. Regulators sometimes compel utilities to offer such life-line prices, so that the relatively poor can afford at least a basic level of service. But it also seems reasonable to suppose that consumers who purchase massive levels of water, gas, or electricity tend to be quite well-to-do and so have fairly inelastic demand; these are precisely the people for whom a high price is optimal.

Consider, on the other hand, that theme parks such as Disneyland offer season passes at not much more than the entry fees for a few days' entry. Think of the A group—the relatively inelastic demand group—as tourists coming a great distance for a once-in-a-lifetime vacation at Disneyland. The B group—the relatively elastic demand group—are, for Disneyland, residents of Los Angeles and the surrounding areas. Members of group A (relatively inelastic) buy only a few days' admission, while if the marginal price is low enough, members of group B, who have relatively elastic demand, will buy "in bulk" by buying a season pass. (Moreover, the B group tends to come when crowds are relatively light, so the marginal cost of providing services to them—there is a lot of peak load to Disneyland—is relatively low.) These are just the conditions that make discounts for volume purchases the right thing to do.

Nonlinear price schemes can face implementation problems. The problems are different, depending on whether there are price breaks or price hikes as the number of units purchased increases:

- If the price per unit falls with the quantity of units bought, the problem of resale must be confronted. Simply put, a single customer might buy the item in very large quantities and resell to other customers who want only small lots of the good.

- If the price per unit rises with the quantity of units bought, the problem is one of fictitious customers purchasing for a single real customer. In the story where the price is $10 per unit for the first five units and $15 thereafter, what stops a customer wishing to buy, say, 25 units, from buying 5 himself, and having his brother, sister, aunt, and uncle each buy 5 more, which they turn over to him?

The ability to control resale of the good solves the first problem. If you buy a season pass to Disneyland, your photo goes on your season pass, making it difficult if not impossible to transfer the privilege of free entry. And an ability to monitor the amount of the good consumed by the individual customer solves the second problem; when selling electricity, say, to a private residence, the electric company can read the meter that is the sole entry point to the residence's electric circuits.

7.5. The Extraction of Surplus

So far, our discussion of price discrimination has concerned the notion that different groups of customers have different elasticities of demand. Assuming they can be charged different prices, it enhances profit to do so. But with second-degree price discrimination—that is, nonlinear prices—a second basic notion comes into play: the extraction of consumer surplus.

To see what this means is to consider a case in which a firm sells to a large number of identical customers. Note that, with this assumption, we eliminate the previous motivation for price discrimination: If all consumers are identical, why sort them into groups?

When a firm offers a consumer her choice of quantity at a price p per unit and the consumer chooses to consume x^* units, paying px^* for them, that consumer usually is better off than if she keeps all her money and gets none of the good. In symbols, suppose her utility for x units of the good and money left over for other purchases takes the simple form $u(x)+m$. (The use of this sort of utility function is for purposes of exposition only. Everything can be generalized to general utility functions.) The consumer begins with none of the good and, say, m_0 dollars in her pocket, so she begins with base utility level $u(0) + m_0$. She leaves with x^* units of the good and $m_0 - px^*$

in her pocket, for an after the shopping trip level of utility $u(x^*) + m_0 - px^*$. My point is that, in most cases, she is strictly better off as she leaves:

$$u(x^*) + m_0 - px^* > u(0) + m_0.$$

Indeed, a weak inequality, $\geq$, is certain, since among the choices the consumer could make is to buy 0 units, paying \$0 and ending up with base utility $u(0) + m_0$. If she purchases some positive amount of the good, it must be because she is better off with x^* units of the good and with px^* dollars less than when she started, with none of the good and all her money. Let me name this increase in her utility the *surplus* she takes from this transaction; that is, the surplus she takes from the transaction is

$$[u(x^*) + m_0 - px^*] - [u(0) + m_0] = u(x^*) - u(0) - px^*.$$

Now, suppose the firm selling the good to this consumer goes in for a bit of nonlinear pricing. In particular, it offers the consumer as many units of the good as she wants, at the old price per unit p. But it insists that, if she buys anything at all, she must pay an up-front fee of F. Will she pay the up-front fee?

Because of the simple sort of utility I assume, we can answer this question quite easily. If she pays the the up-front entry fee F, she enters the store poorer by F. But for the sort of utility functions we assume here, her purchase level is not affected by her level of initial wealth, as long as, after paying F, the amount of money left in her pocket is px^* or more. So if she pays F and enters the store, she buys x^* units of the good, winding up with utility $u(x^*) + m_0 - F - px^*$. She pays the up-front fee then, as long as this final level of utility exceeds her utility if she chooses not to buy, $u(0) + m_0$. In other words (symbols, really) she pays the up-front fee if

$$u(x^*) + m_0 - F - px^* > u(0) + m_0, \quad \text{or} \quad u(x^*) - u(x) - px^* > F.$$

In words, she would pay the up-front fee F as long as F is smaller than the surplus she would take from the transaction, if there were no up-front fee.

Of course, if the firm charges this fee F, it raises its own profit by F and it lowers the consumer's utility (or surplus) by F. So, from the point of view of the firm, this is a good deal: *The up-front fee, if not made so large that the consumer decides not to pay it at all, extracts some of the surplus the consumer gains from the transaction and transfers that surplus into profit earned by the firm.*

Take-It-or-Leave-It Offers

We get back to entry fees in just a bit, but first a small excursion into something that will seem like fantasy land.

We continue to think of a firm that faces a single sort of consumer, whose utility function for the good in question takes the form $u(x) + m$, where x is the amount of the good in question consumed and m is money left over. Assume that the firm has constant marginal cost of production c.

The fantasy land part comes here: Suppose the firm knows all of this and, in particular, knows the consumer's utility function. Suppose further that the firm is able to make any take-it-or-leave-it offer it chooses to the consumer, where a take-it-or-leave-it offer takes the following form: "Mr. Consumer. You may, if you wish, purchase $\hat{x}$ units of the good from me, if you pay me $\hat{Q}$ in total. Take it or leave it." Suppose finally that the consumer believes the firm will stick to this offer, so he must either take it or leave it.

The consumer takes it as long as it gives him at least as much utility as if he leaves it. That is, the offer is taken as long as

$$u(\hat{x}) + m_0 - \hat{Q} \geq u(0) + m_0, \quad \text{or} \quad u(\hat{x}) - u(0) \geq \hat{Q}.$$

Right? Well, there are two good grounds on which to object to this conclusion. First, if the inequality is actually an equation—if the deal leaves the consumer at precisely the same utility level as when he turns it down—the consumer might just turn down the deal. Second, a consumer with even a particle of self-respect is likely to turn the deal down, just to spite the firm, if it leaves him with just a little more utility than he starts with. That is, there is probably some threshold utility gain, $u_t > 0$ such that the consumer will accept the deal only if

$$u(\hat{x}) + m_0 - \hat{Q} \geq u(0) + m_0 + u_t, \quad \text{or} \quad u(\hat{x}) - u(0) - u_t \geq \hat{Q}_t.$$

So suppose this is how the consumer decides whether to take the deal. The question I want to answer is then, From the perspective of the firm, what is the best take-it-or-leave-it offer to make to the consumer?

It is possible that the best offer to make is one that is turned down, leaving the firm with no profit. But, if we look at offers that will be accepted, it is clear that the firm should ask for as much money $\hat{Q}$ as it can, consistent with the offer being accepted. That is, if the firm offers the consumer $\hat{x}$ units of the good, the money part of the offer should be

$$\hat{Q} = u(\hat{x}) - u(0) - u_t.$$

This gives the firm a net profit of

$$\hat{Q} - c\hat{x} = u(\hat{x}) - u(0) - u_t - c\hat{x}.$$

And then, to finish this off, if the firm is going to make an offer that will be accepted, it will want to choose $\hat{x}$ to make this last expression as large as possible. To maximize this expression in $\hat{x}$, take its derivative in $\hat{x}$ and set the derivative to 0. This gives $u'(\hat{x}) = c$, where u' is the derivative of the function u.

To paraphrase, if the firm produces and sells $\hat{x}$ for this consumer, the consumer's gross gain in utility, not including any monetary transfer back to the firm, is $u(\hat{x}) - u(0)$. This gross gain in surplus for the consumer can be recouped by the firm, except for the u_t that must be left to the consumer to induce him to accept. Thus the firm's best *net* revenue, fixing the quantity at $\hat{x}$, is $u(\hat{x}) - u(0) - u_t$, generating a profit of $u(\hat{x}) - u(0) - u_t - c\hat{x}$. Profit is maximized by the $\hat{x}$ that solves the equation $u'(\hat{x}) = c$ or, in words, when the consumer's marginal utility equals the firm's marginal cost of production.

I think, at this point, a reminder is in order. That last sentence, equating marginal utility and marginal cost, may sound a bit funny. Marginal utility is measured in units of "utils per amount of the good." Marginal cost is measured in dollars per amount of the good. So equating these two seems to say that utility is measured on a dollar scale. We are saying precisely that. By looking at the special case of a utility function of the form $u(x) + m$, where m is money left over, we measure utility on a dollar scale. If we did not assume this special form for utility, the story would be more complex. But the basic economic insights would change very little.

So, we know what is the best take-it-or-leave-it offer for the firm to make to the consumer, where *best* means the offer that maximizes profit for the firm. The quantity of the good, in this deal, $\hat{x}$, is found by solving $u'(\hat{x}) = c$. The dollar part of the deal, $\hat{Q}$, is just $u(\hat{x}) - u(0) - u_t$. (At this point, try Problems 7.5 and 7.6.)

It may be overdoing it, but let me repeat what just happened, using a discrete example. Suppose a particular consumer is willing to pay up to $15 for the first unit of some good he buys. The second unit gives him a lower dollar-measured marginal utility; it is worth only $12 to him. The third unit has marginal utility $10, and then, successively, the marginal utilities, measured in dollars, are $8, $6, $5, $4, and so forth. Meanwhile, the firm has marginal cost of production equal to $5.50. In this case, if the firm chooses to sell one unit to the consumer, it can charge him, say, $14.95 for it, if to get him to make the deal, it has to leave him with $0.05 worth of surplus. If it makes him a take-it-or-leave-it offer of two units, it can effectively charge him $15 for the first and $11.95 for the second, or $26.95 in total. For three units, it can charge him $15 + $12 + $9.95 = $36.95. Each additional unit it sells him costs the firm $5.50 to produce, so it will choose to sell him until the marginal utility to the consumer of the next unit (what the firm can recoup) is less than its marginal cost. This means, in this discrete example, selling him five units, for a total of $15 + $12 + $10 + $8 + $6 = $51 less the $0.05 it takes to make the deal go. Finally, recognize that summing these marginal utilities of the first unit, the second, and so forth, to some level at which we stop, just gives the overall utility of the number of units offered to the consumer less his starting utility, when he has no units. That is what we just derived with calculus.

One more thing and we can leave this fantasy land of take-it-or-leave-it offers. The firm can offer the consumer no deal that will do better for the firm than this best take-it-or-leave-it offer, unless the firm somehow tricks the consumer into accepting a deal that leaves him less than u_t ahead of where he starts. This is so because, however the firm structures the deal, in the end the deal results in some quantity going to the consumer and some amount of money going to the firm. The firm can match this with the corresponding take-it-or-leave-it offer, and we found the best of those. Short of tricking the consumer—something we do not study here—we know the very best the firm can do, in terms of making a deal with this consumer.

Getting the Consumer to Choose This Deal
without Making a Take-It-or-Leave-It Offer

Of course, this was fantasy land. Firms rarely make take-it-or-leave-it offers to consumers. Consumers usually expect choice in the quantity they buy, except when they buy single objects such as cars or houses or packages such as cable TV subscriptions. But suppose the firm in question makes an offer taking the form of an entry fee F and a per-unit charge p, leaving it to the consumer to decide (1) whether to pay the entry fee and, if he does, (2) how much to buy at p per unit. Suppose, in particular, the firm makes this sort of offer setting $F = u(\hat{x}) - u(0) - u_t - c\hat{x}$ and $p = c$, where $\hat{x}$ solves $u'(\hat{x}) = c$.

Assuming the consumer chooses to pay the entry fee, once he has done so, he chooses the quantity to purchase by equating his marginal utility to the price per unit of the good. That is, the consumer chooses to consume x^* solving $u'(x^*) = c$, since c is the per-unit price. Which means the consumer chooses $x^* = \hat{x}$. And the consumer pays the entry fee as long as his net utility from all this, which is $u(\hat{x}) + m_0 - F - c\hat{x}$ exceeds or equals $u(0) + m_0 + u_t$, assuming the same utility gain threshhold u_t applies. But F was defined so that the first of these equals the second. (Do the algebra if you don't see it.) So the consumer will pay the entry fee. And the firm's profit is the sum of the entry fee and the money the consumer pays for the goods he buys, less the cost of production of the goods, or

$$u(\hat{x}) - u(0) - u_t - c\hat{x} \quad + \quad c\hat{x} \quad - \quad c\hat{x} \quad = \quad u(\hat{x}) - u(0) - u_t - c\hat{x}.$$

Surely this rates a Wow! The consumer, facing this particular choice of $F = u(\hat{x}) - u(0) - u_t - c\hat{x}$ and $p = c$ replicates, by his own free will, precisely the firm's optimal take-it-or-leave-it offer.

It's time to insert a small measure of reality. In dealing with this consumer, the firm needs to set an entry fee and a per-unit price. The per-unit price chosen is c, the firm's marginal cost of production. That isn't a hard thing for the firm to do. But the entry fee is $u(\hat{x}) - u(0) - u_t$. To get this right, the firm has to anticipate how much the consumer will choose to buy, what is the gross surplus gain (in dollar terms) the consumer obtains from this quantity, and what is the consumer's threshhold utility gain, for consummating a deal. Unless the firm knows the consumer's utility function, it is unlikely to be able to do this.

On the other hand, the firm, given time and the ability to experiment, can try various entry fees on its customers, seeking to find the largest entry fee it can set without causing consumers to reject its business, if the per-unit cost to the consumer once he has paid the entry fee is the firm's level of marginal cost. That "largest acceptable entry fee" is the F the firm is looking for. And that is the way to use nonlinear prices, to extract from the consumer all the surplus he takes from the deal and, even more, to set up the surplus extraction in a way that gives the firm the maximum level of profit it could ever take from this consumer, whatever deal it proposes.

7.6. First-Degree Price Discrimination

Imagine, then, a firm selling to a population of customers, each of whom has his or her own utility function, possibly different from the utility functions of other customers. Imagine, and this takes a vivid imagination, that as any specific customer walks through the door where sales are made, the firm's sales representative can look at the customer and "see" his or her utility function. Imagine that the firm's sales rep is able, in an instant, to compute for each customer (!) the amount of the good the customer will purchase at the per-unit price c, the firm's marginal cost, and (2) the amount of gross surplus the consumer gets from consuming that amount of the good versus consuming none. In symbols, for each customer, the sales rep is able to "see" the solution to $u'(\hat{x}) = c$ and, for that $\hat{x}$, the value of $u(\hat{x}) - u(0)$, where u is the utility function of the consumer coming through the door.

Further imagine that the sales rep sidles over to the customer and says, "Howdy pardner." (This sales rep is from Texas.) "You can buy as much of this good as you want at a price of c per unit. But to buy any, you first have to pay an entry fee of $u(\hat{x}) - u(0) - c\hat{x} - u_t$." To be clear, the sales rep does not read all those symbols. He evaluates the symbols, and if, say, $u(\hat{x}) - u(0) - c\hat{x} - u_t = 23$, he says, "an entry fee of \$23."

That is first-degree price discrimination. A deal is proposed separately for each customer that extracts virtually all the surplus the customer would take from the deal and, moreover, sets the terms so that the quantity bought by the customer gives the firm the most profit is could get from that particular customer. The sales spiel just given implements first-degree price discrimination using entry fees and a per-unit charge of c, allowing the customer to choose how much to buy. The firm could use take-it-or-leave-it offers instead, where the sales rep says, "Howdy Pardner. You can buy $\hat{x}$ units of the good for a total dollar amount of $u(\hat{x}) - u(0) - u_t$, take it or leave it." What makes this first-degree price discrimination is that almost every bit of surplus is sucked out of each customer, and moreover, the terms are set so that the firm makes the most it could possibly make, because the consumer winds up with $\hat{x}$ solving $u'(\hat{x}) = c$, the quantity that maximizes the total surplus in the deal.

Pretty good stuff, if possible. But of course, in real life, there are problems:

- Obviously, this is going to require offering different terms to different customers, which may be illegal.

- There is the danger of resale. A customer may walk in, pay her entry fee, and proceed to buy a ton of the stuff at c per unit; then exit and start (re)selling the stuff in competition with the firm's store.

- Customers, being dealt with individually, may decide that this is not a simple matter of taking the firm's announced terms. What if a customer, hearing the offer from the sales rep, responds, "Just hold on there. I'll pay you an entry fee of \$0.25, and I'll pay you c per unit for every unit I want. That'll leave you with a clear profit of \$0.25, which is more than you'll make from me if I walk. What do you say?" The sales rep probably won't say, "Yes," but once bargaining commences, the firm could wind up doing a lot worse than first-degree price discrimination supposes.

- Of course, sales representatives sometimes have pretty good skills at figuring out the most an individual client will pay—that's what makes a good sales rep—but even a really good sales rep cannot do quite as well as this story supposes.

So, for the most part, first-degree price discrimination is an idealization; a benchmark against which to measure practical discriminatory schemes.

First-Degree Price Discrimination and Porsche

Before giving up on first-degree price discrimination as a hopeless ideal, however, return a final time to Porsche and the analysis we did in Chapter 6 concerning a franchise fee plus fixed wholesale cost. I hope that for the last few pages, some voice in the back of your brain was saying, "This sure sounds like the last part of Porsche. What's the connection?" This is a case where, except for the restraints imposed by franchise law, the seller, Porsche, can get close to the ideal of first-degree price discrimination. To understand why Porsche can do this or, rather, why it could have, if not for its legal difficulties due to preexisting franchise agreements, let us go down the list of reasons why first-degree price discrimination is difficult:

- *It takes a really good sales rep to ascertain the utility function of each consumer.* We spent the entire chapter thinking of price discrimination in the business-to-consumer world. But Porsche is in the world of business-to-business (B-to-B) transactions. And in B to B, the "utility function" of the buyer or retail dealer is the profit function of the client, which relates the client's profit as a function of how much of the product the client purchases. In the Porsche case, this profit function is essentially determined by the demand function for Porsche automobiles in the market served by the retail dealer. Porsche has both historical data and the capability of generating fresh market research data about demand by geographical regions, so this knowledge is largely available to it.

- *Discrimination of this sort is often illegal.* Note that the discrimination comes entirely in terms of the franchise fee. Porsche, like any first-degree discriminator, wants to set the per-unit price equal to its marginal cost; that is, the same for every dealer. And, in principle, if Porsche were setting up a franchised-dealer network from scratch, it could vary the franchise fee according to variables such as size of the market, concentration of competing dealers, regional average income, and other variables that play a large role in determining how profitable a dealership will be. The legal problems Porsche encountered were not due to the illegality of varied franchise fees per se but the problems of trying to change the terms of an existing franchise contract.

- *Clients may bargain back.* As a practical matter, unless bound by earlier franchise arrangements, Porsche probably has a lot of bargaining leverage with its potential franchisees. We see why this is—what about the

Porsche story makes this so—in Chapter 23.

- *Schemes of this sort will not work if the good in question can be resold.* Note that Porsche wants to have the same wholesale price for its cars, adjusting for different transportation fees and the cost of special emissions control devices and the like that might be needed on, say, California cars. It is not resale of the cars between dealers that is a problem. Rather, the "resale" problem would arise if a dealer in, say, Portland, Oregon, were to buy a lot of cars to sell to an *unfranchised* dealer in West Los Angeles. Insofar as Porsche can control what its retailers do—for instance, allow them to sell only for local delivery, except for swaps among franchised dealers—it has no resale problem. I am not sure about the law on this point, but it is certainly credible that Porsche can control this sort of resale enough to get away with different franchise fees based on geography.

Other Examples of (Almost) First-Degree Price Discrimination

Porsche is not the only case where first-degree price discrimination might be possible. In many cases of service providers, such as lawyers, accountants, consultants, and doctors, fees are set with the customer's ability and willingness to pay in mind. No serious problem with resale arises, because it is hard to resell a service. Since the "service" is typically tailor-made to the customer, legal problems of charging different customers different prices can be avoided. The controlling factor on whether these schemes approximate first-degree price discrimination is the extent to which the service provider is willing and able to run the numbers; willing in the sense that it is worthwhile to compute fees on a customer-by-customer basis and able in the sense that the service provider can work out how much value—dollar-valued utility or profit enhancement—the customer gets from the service provided.

The Internet offers real potential along these lines. Repeat sales to single customers might allow a firm, such as Amazon.com, to learn a lot about that customer's utility function. And since they are quoted "over the computer," prices can be tailored to the consumer. In fact, in the year 2000, Amazon.com was caught charging different customers different prices for the same book. Amazon said that it wasn't attempting to engage in price discrimination but to "sample the market," to see what the full market demand curve might be, in the sense discussed in Chapter 5. You have to judge on your own what you think Amazon.com was doing, but the potential for something approximating first-degree price discrimination is certainly there.

An Unfortunate Fact about Optimal
Second-Degree Price Discrimination

In first-degree price discrimination implemented with entry fees, the per-unit cost paid by customers is the firm's marginal cost. This is true for every customer; only the entry fee varies according to the specific customer and his or her utility (or profit, in B to B) function.

Students sometimes see this and conclude, erroneously, that this must be true for optimal second-degree price discrimination, which takes the form of an entry fee and per-unit price. That is, although in second-degree price discrimination, every customer must face the *same* entry fee and per-unit price, we *at least* know that the optimal per-unit price is the firm's marginal cost; all that is left is to find the optimal entry fee. Unhappily, life is not that simple. If every customer must be charged the same entry fee, the optimal per-unit price can, and generally does, differ substantially from the firm's marginal cost. And finding it can be quite a task. You get the opportunity to try this in some of the problems.

7.7. Closing Remarks

The discussion in this chapter does not exhaust the bag of tricks firms have for sorting among customers and, simultaneously, extracting surplus from them to improve the firm's bottom line. For instance, firms use bundling strategies for these purposes; a sports team, for instance, will sell season tickets at a price substantially less than what it would cost to purchase a full suite of single game tickets. And the local opera will often sell "package deals" for various subsets of the opera's full season, package deals that might be structured to appeal to fans of Wagner, Mozart, Italian opera, and so forth. (But if the public does not like, say, Wagner, the optimal bundling strategy may be to put a Wagnerian opera in each bundle that otherwise specializes in Mozart or Italian opera.) If you want to learn more about both the sorts of schemes discussed and some of the techniques not touched on here, there is a substantial literature to consult.

Executive Summary

- Price discrimination schemes of various sorts, including discrimination by group membership; schemes where groups are self-selected; third-degree price discrimination, using product differentiation; second-degree product differentiation, using nonlinear prices; and first-degree price discrimination, whether with take-it-or-leave-it offers or entry fee plus per-unit price offers, all chase two basic objectives.

1. Find ways to get different customers paying different prices and, in particular, get the more inelastic customers paying more and the more elastic customers paying less, at least on the margin.

2. Find ways to extract from individual customers the "surplus" they would otherwise obtain from trading or, more to the point, find ways to move that surplus from consumers into the firm's coffers.

- In general, these schemes are difficult to design "optimally" and, in fact, many of the most sophisticated companies plying these schemes—airlines, telephone service providers, and so forth—make no pretense of finding the optimal scheme. Instead, they use very sophisticated schemes aimed at improving profit, while chasing these twin goals.

  1. The specific cases of discrimination by groups, and some of the self-selection schemes, are simple enough to afford simple optimization techniques.

  2. At the other end of the spectrum, first-degree price discrimination is fairly simple, if the discriminator has the information necessary, because it involves personalized entry fees and a per-unit cost equal to its marginal cost.

- Most discrimination schemes face problems associated with knowing the customer, resale, legality and ethicality of discriminatory schemes, and customers who bargain back.

Problems

Problems 4.13 and 4.14 already introduced you to the mechanics of discrimination by group membership and couponing. If you did not do those problems previously, try them now.

7.1 Here is another example (along with Problem 4.13) of discrimination by group membership. Suppose that for some item, the marginal cost of production is $5. Demand comes from two sources, senior citizens and the rest of the population. Senior citizen demand is given by the inverse demand function $P_S(y) = 15 - y/500$. Demand by the rest of the population is given by the inverse demand function $P_R(y) = 20 - y/2000$.

(a) If a monopolist facing these two demands must set a single price for the good, what price would it optimally set? What would be its profit?

(b) Suppose this monopolist could set two prices, one for seniors and another for regulars. What prices maximize profit and what is that level of profit?

7.2 Suppose a firm sells to senior citizens and others at a single price of $10 per unit. At this price, it sells 10,000 units in total; 2,000 to seniors and 8,000 to the others. At the price of $10, demand by seniors has elasticity −3, while demand by the others has elasticity −1.5.

(a) Suppose the firm decided to raise the price it charges nonseniors by $0.10. At the same time, it will lower the price facing seniors. If it wants to lower the price charged to seniors so that it sells (approximately) the same 10,000 units (so that the decrease in demand from nonseniors is balanced by an increase in demand by seniors), by how much should it decrease its price to seniors?

(b) (The answer to part a is that it should lower the price to seniors by $0.20. Use this number even if you cannot solve part a.) What will be the (approximate) impact on the firm's profits if it simultaneously raises its price to nonseniors to $10.10 and lowers the price to seniors to $9.80?

(c) Note that I say nothing about the marginal costs of production of this firm. Why don't you need to know this to answer part b?

7.3 In the spreadsheet model of GM and the truck coupons from Chapter 1, suppose that Q, the price of coupons in the transferred coupon market, is $0, and k, the transaction cost associated with this market is also $0. Suppose that GM sets X = $1000 and x = $500. Even if GM optimizes over the posted price it can set, in the model, the program is costly to GM. Why is this? What is the source of this cost? This cost rises in the difference $X - x$; why is this? Under what assumptions about the two groups of customers— original truck owners and third-party sellers—might this couponing scheme (with these values for Q, k, X, and x) result in higher profit for GM than if the coupons did not exist?

7.4 On October 10, 2000, a particular book about human resource management was being sold by Amazon.com for $102.75. At precisely the same time, this book could be purchased at the Amazon.uk website for the sterling equivalent of $36.29. (This is not an international student edition or anything like that. It is the same book, published by the same publisher, in the same format.) What do you think is going on here?

7.5 A firm that produces a good with a constant marginal cost of $3 is able to engage in first-degree price discrimination: It has the uncanny ability to look at any customer and discern his or her utility function; it is willing to do the math necessary; it faces no legal difficulties; and it can control resale of its product. One of its customers has utility function $u(x, m) = 16x^{1/3} + m$, where x is the amount of good this consumer consumes and m is her money left over. (This consumer has substantial financial resources, so you need not worry about her money running out.) What offer should the firm make to this consumer? Answer this question twice, first using a take-it-or-leave-it offer and then with a fixed fee plus per-unit price offer.

7.6 Suppose a firm faces four consumers: Larry, Mae, Curly, and Shepp. Each of these consumers has the utility function $u(x)+m$, where x is the level of consumption of the good produced by the firm and m is money left over for other purchases. (You may assume that each consumer has lots of cash to begin with, so that the constraint that "money left over is nonnegative" is never a problem.) For Larry, the function u is given by $u(x) = 10x - x^2$. For Mae, it is $u(x) = 8\ln(x + 1)$. For Curly, it is $u(x) = 8x^{1/2}$. And for Shepp, it is $u(x) = 8x - x^2$.

(a) This firm has constant marginal costs equal to 2. For each of the four consumers, what is the best (first-degree price-discriminating, profit-maximizing) take-it-or-leave-it offer to make to that consumer? What is its total profit from dealing with the four?

(b) Suppose the firm sets an entry fee plus per-unit price for each consumer. It can tailor the entry fee and the per-unit price to the individual consumer. What are the best (profit-maximizing) entry fees and per-unit prices for it to set? What is its total profit in this case?

(c) Suppose the firm must charge a single linear price for its output, in nondiscriminatory fashion. What is the best (profit-maximizing) price for it to charge? What is its total profit? (While you should solve parts a and b analytically, for this part and part d proceed numerically, using Excel or some other spreadsheet program.)

(d) (This is not easy.) Suppose the firm can set an entry fee and a per-unit price for its output, but both the entry fee and the per-unit price must be the same for all four consumers. (The firm can control resale of the good.) What is the best combination of entry fee and per-unit price?

7.7 Imagine we have a good that can be consumed only in integer units and that cannot be resold. The good costs the manufacturer $3 on the margin to produce. There are three customers, indexed 1, 2, and 3, and each has a utility function of the form $v_i(x)+m$, where x is the integer number of units of the good consumed and m is money left over. For the first consumer,

$$v_1(0) = 0, \quad v_1(1) = 10, \quad v_1(2) = 18, \quad v_1(3) = 23, \quad v_1(4) = 25, \quad v_1(5) = 26, \quad \ldots,$$

and so the (discrete) marginal utilities of the successive units for this consumer are, respectively, $MU_1(1) = 10$, $MU_1(2) = 8$, $MU_1(3) = 5$, $MU_1(4) = 2$, $MU_1(5) = 1, \ldots$ The second and third customers have, respectively,

$$v_2(0) = 0, \ v_2(1) = 20, \ v_2(2) = 39, \ v_2(3) = 44, \ v_2(4) = 48, \ v_2(5) = 50, \ \ldots, \text{and}$$
$$v_3(0) = 0, \ v_3(1) = 30, \ v_3(2) = 50, \ v_3(3) = 60, \ v_3(4) = 62, \ v_3(5) = 61, \ \ldots$$

(a) The optimal single (linear) price for this firm is $p = 19$. Why?

(b) If we use a fixed entry fee plus constant per-unit pricing scheme where the per-unit price is the firm's marginal cost of production, \$3, why is $F = 36$ the optimal fixed fee?

(c) If we use a fixed fee plus constant marginal-cost pricing scheme, where the marginal cost is \$5, what is the optimal fixed fee?

7.8 Consider selling a good to a large population of consumers. The good must be consumed in integer amounts and cannot be transferred or resold. The marginal cost of production is 3. All consumers have utility functions of the form $v(x) + m$, where m is money left over. Of these consumers, 90% have marginal-utility valuations $MU(1) = 20$, $MU(2) = 1$, $\ldots$ and 10% have marginal valuation $MU(1) = 30$, $MU(2) = 29$, $MU(3) = 1$, $\ldots$ What is the optimal single-price scheme? What is the optimal first-degree discriminatory scheme for these customers? It has been claimed that the optimal second-degree discriminatory scheme offers the first unit a consumer buys for \$20 and all subsequent units for \$29. Is this correct?

7.9 Boogle College, the last all-male college in the United States, has a very large football stadium, which is rarely filled for football games. The Athletic Department, noting this, has decided to offer students discounted tickets, but with a limit of two discounted tickets per student. Moreover, the discounted tickets, if purchased, must be used by the student himself and someone accompanying him; this is enforced using student IDs. Students can buy more than two tickets, of course, but they must pay full price for any tickets beyond the first two that they buy. In general terms, what do you think is going on here?

7.10 Derive the numbers given in the second paragraph on page 155.

8. Averages and Margins

This fairly short chapter concerns average cost and its relationship to marginal and total cost. Along the way, I introduce the concept of efficient scale, which takes center stage in Chapter 11.

Now we turn our attention to the production side of the firm. In all the stories so far, except for the retailer in Porsche, the firm's production technology was summed up in its total cost function TC, telling us how much it would cost to produce each production level x. Moreover, in most of the stories so far, marginal cost was constant and total cost was, at its most complex, some fixed cost plus this marginal cost times x.

Of course, for most firms, "obtaining" a level of output x takes more than spending a given amount of money. Firms buy raw materials or inputs and transform those inputs into outputs, where the word *transform* has an incredibly wide meaning. Even retailers, who simply buy goods from wholesalers and resell them to consumers, provide marketing services, such as selection of stock, transportation, display, sales assistance, and so forth. Put it this way; both Costco, a warehouse-style retailer, and Balducci's, a posh New York delicatessen, sell smoked salmon. But their manner of doing so, the managerial problems that arise therefrom, and their total cost of selling some given volume are quite a bit different.

While some managers spend their time determining what prices to set and how much to sell, a lot of attention—a lot *more* managerial attention—is paid to the details of managing plant, equipment, vendor relations, and most important, employees. Courses in operations and human resource management testify to the importance of these details.

Moreover, these details are anything but mundane. In the 1980s, U.S. industry was getting its brains beat out—or so the business press reported—by the superior manufacturing technique and human resource management style of Japanese and, to a lesser extent, German industry. Twenty years later, the shoe was claimed to be on the other foot: The so-called U.S. style of deploying and employing people and capital was supposedly winning, and the Europeans and Japanese were exhorted to learn from the United States.

You would expect, therefore, that a book entitled *Microeconomics for Managers* would dive headfirst into details of turning input into output. You might anticipate that these details are complex; if they were straightforward, there would have been much less uncertainty and confusion about the relative merits of Japanese, European, and American styles of management. In fact, the details are so complex that we cannot talk intelligently about operations, human resource management, and the like, until nearly the end of this book. But we can get to some issues right now:

- Chapter 9 introduces the basic economic model of technology and cost minimization. How do economists model technology? Given a choice of methods for turning input into output, prices for the input, and a target level of output, what is the cheapest way to get that level of output?

- In most firms, production takes time and involves dynamic factors. Production facilities cannot be turned on or off; frictions are involved. A lot of the "stuff" used in production is durable, so that terms like *depreciation* and *net present value* enter the conversation. And, as the Total Quality Manufacturing movement has shown us, a firm's technology is not static but evolves, depending on what the firm does. Chapter 10 introduces these issues of dynamic production technology.

- Before getting to these ideas, this chapter discusses average cost and its relationship to marginal cost. Managers have a mistaken tendency to think in terms of averages instead of margins, and by being very explicit about the connections between margins, averages, and totals, I hope you will not fall prey to thinking solely in terms of averages.

8.1. Average Cost for a Single-Product Firm

For a firm that produces a single product, average cost is easy enough to define: Writing $AC(x)$ for the average cost of a unit of production at production level x, we define

$$AC(x) = \frac{TC(x)}{x}.$$

Note that, as x is in the denominator, the function AC is not well defined at $x = 0$; if $TC(0) = 0$, we have $0/0$, while if $TC(0) > 0$, average cost is infinite.

Profit Margin

Assume that the firm in question does not engage in price discrimination, so that its total revenue is the price per unit it obtains times the volume it sells. The firm's *profit margin* is the price obtained for the product less its average cost, and profit equals profit margin times quantity. In symbols,

$$\pi(x) = TR(x) - TC(x) = xP(x) - xAC(x) = x[P(x) - AC(x)].$$

Don't look for anything profound here; this is purely an accounting identity.

Marginal and Average Cost

Suppose you go down a line of individuals, asking each for his or her height. As you do this, you compute a running average of the heights so far. Suppose when you get to the 1076th individual, the average height of the first 1075 is 69.322 inches, and the 1076th person has height 74.25 inches. Is the average after this individual is averaged in going to be larger or smaller than 69.322? If the 1076th person has height 64.5 inches, will the new average be larger or smaller than 69.322?

These are easy questions to answer. If the next person in line has height greater than that of the average so far, this person pulls the average up. If this person's height is less than the average so far, he or she pulls the average down. And if the $(n + 1)$st person in line has a height precisely equal to the average of the first n, averaging this person does not change the average.

This is true for costs, revenues, and everything else. In particular:

> Average cost falls whenever marginal cost is less than average cost. Average cost rises whenever marginal cost exceeds average cost. Average cost is flat whenever marginal cost equals average cost.

Note that these implications run in both directions: If marginal cost is less than average cost, average cost falls. And if average cost is falling, marginal cost is less than average cost.

The analogy to a line of people probably convinces you of the truth of these assertions, but in case you need something a bit more formal, here are two proofs. The first uses discrete margins, and the second uses calculus and continuous margins.

- Write $(x + 1)\mathrm{AC}(x + 1) = \mathrm{TC}(x + 1) = \mathrm{TC}(x) + \mathrm{MC}(x) = x\mathrm{AC}(x) + \mathrm{MC}(x)$, where by $\mathrm{MC}(x)$ we mean the discrete marginal cost of going from x to $x+1$ units. The first and last terms in this progression are $(x+1)\mathrm{AC}(x+1) = x\mathrm{AC}(x) + \mathrm{MC}(x)$. Subtract $(x + 1)\mathrm{AC}(x)$ from both sides and divide both sides by $x + 1$. This gives

$$\mathrm{AC}(x + 1) - \mathrm{AC}(x) = \frac{\mathrm{MC}(x) - \mathrm{AC}(x)}{x + 1}. \tag{8.1}$$

- Take the derivative of average cost: $d(\mathrm{AC}(x))/dx = d[\mathrm{TC}(x)/x]/dx$ which, by the product rule, $= (1/x)(d\mathrm{TC}(x)/dx) - (\mathrm{TC}(x)/x^2) = (\mathrm{MC}(x)/x) - (\mathrm{AC}(y)/x)$. This is

$$\frac{d\mathrm{AC}(x)}{dx} = \frac{\mathrm{MC}(x) - \mathrm{AC}(x)}{x}. \tag{8.2}$$

Equations (8.1) and (8.2) say the same thing: AC rises precisely when MC > AC, and AC falls precisely when MC < AC.

An Example

It may help to work our way slowly through a "typical" example. Figure 8.1(a) shows a total cost function. Note that, for this particular total cost function, TC(0) = 0.

Consider the point marked x on the quantity axis in Figure 8.1(a) and the corresponding level of total cost, TC(x). Is AC(x) or MC(x) greater at that point? It is easy to see that average cost is greater: Figure 8.1(b) shows both the chord joining $(0,0)$ to $(x, \mathrm{TC}(x))$, the solid line, and the tangent to the total cost curve at $(x, \mathrm{TC}(x))$, which is dashed. Average cost at level x is the slope of the chord, while marginal cost is the slope of the tangent, so AC(x) exceeds MC(x).

We can discern from the figure the shape of the marginal cost function. Marginal cost, the slope of the total cost function, decreases at first and then increases, turning around, from decreasing to increasing, at the point of inflection, marked by x^* in Figure 8.1(a).

As for the shape of the average cost function, AC(x) is the slope of the chord from $(0,0)$ to $(x, \mathrm{TC}(x))$. Figures 8.1(c) and 8.1(d) show these chords for increasingly larger levels of x. In Figure 8.1(c), we have levels of x less than x^{**}, and in Figure 8.1(d) levels greater than x^{**}. Note that, as x increases up to x^{**}, the slopes of the chords fall; then they rise as x increases beyond x^{**}. Hence AC(x) falls until x^{**} and then rises.

Note one more thing. At x^{**}, the chord joining $(0,0)$ to $(x^{**}, \mathrm{TC}(x^{**}))$ is tangent to the total cost function; at this point, marginal cost equals average cost.

Putting everything together, we have the average and marginal cost curves shown in Figure 8.1(e). (The figure shows AC and MC coming together as we get close to $x = 0$. I explain this in a bit.) Marginal cost is indeed below average cost whenever average cost is falling, above average cost when average cost is rising, and MC(x) = AC(x) when average cost is at its minimum. (Both the marginal- and average-cost functions are U-shaped in Figure 8.1. This is not general to all cost functions but arises from the particular shape of total cost in Figure 8.1.)

Average Cost Near Zero

Before seeing some other shapes, let us settle matters about the behavior of the average cost function near $x = 0$. AC(0) is not properly defined, because it involves a 0 in the denominator of a fraction. But we can think through how average cost behaves for x approaching 0. To avoid mathematical pathology,

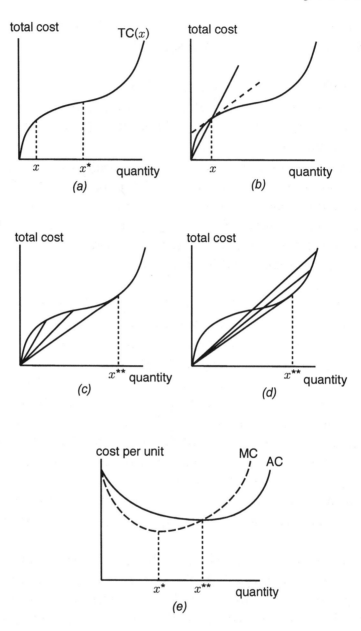

Figure 8.1. *Building marginal and average cost curves from total cost.* For the total cost function shown in panel a and any production level x, the marginal cost at x is the slope of a tangent to the total cost function and the average cost is the slope of a chord from $(0,0)$ to $(x, \mathsf{TC}(x))$ (see panel b). Panels c and d show how average cost progresses as x increases: The slopes of the chords first decrease, until the quantity reaches x^{**}, then increase. Note that, at x^{**}, the chord is also tangent to the total cost function, so that MC equals AC at this point. The slope of TC also decreases and then increases as x increases; the minimum slope (or MC) is reached at the point of inflection of total cost, denoted by x^*, which is less than x^{**}. Putting all this together, we have the picture in panel e.

I assume that TC and MC are continuous functions near 0. Then there are two cases to think through: TC(0) = 0, or no fixed cost; and TC(0) > 0, or positive fixed cost. (The case TC(0) < 0 is uncommon and so not worth the worry.)

- If TC(0) = 0, then the average cost approaches MC(0) as the quantity approaches 0.

- If TC(0) > 0, then the average cost explodes as x approaches 0.

The second of these is easy to see. If TC(0) > 0, then for small values of x, AC(x) = TC(x)/x must diverge to infinity: You are dividing numbers bounded away from 0 by a smaller and smaller amount x. In more economic language, when the fixed cost is positive, amortizing that fixed cost over a very small volume results in a very high level of average cost.

The first point is a bit harder. A discrete argument is that TC(1) = MC(0), where MC(0) is the discrete marginal cost of going from $x = 0$ to $x = 1$. But AC(1) = TC(1)/1, so AC(1) = MC(0).

Or, to put this in terms of a line of people whose heights are being averaged, the statement that marginal cost is continuous near 0 is analogous, in this context, to the statement that the first few people in the line have nearly identical heights. In this case, common sense suggests that the average heights for those first few people are very close to the height of any one of them. Only after the individual heights vary somewhat does the average begin to be different from the marginal person's height.

When confronted with these discrete arguments, students sometimes complain that the arguments are inconsistent with Figure 8.1. We just said that AC(1) = TC(1) = MC(0), when TC(0) = 0. But, if we compare Figure 8.1(a) with Figure 8.1(e), it looks like TC(1) is far less than MC(0): TC(1) looks to be very near 0, while MC(0) is a substantially positive number. This is no inconsistency, however, because the vertical scale in Figure 8.1(e) is quite different from the scales in the other panels of Figure 8.1. Think, for example, of General Motors building cars. Average cost is in the neighborhood of $15,000 per car. When we graph total cost, for quantities in the millions of cars that GM produces annually, the vertical scale must be set so that a total cost on the order of $75 *billion* (for 5 million cars) can be plotted. On a scale where we can plot $75 billion, the total cost of a single car (around $15,000) looks a lot like 0.

For a more mathematical justification that AC(x) converges toward MC(0) for small values of x when TC(0) = 0, write

$$TC(x) = \int_0^x MC(y)\, dy + TC(0) = \int_0^x MC(y)\, dy,$$

since, by assumption, TC(0) = 0. As long as the marginal cost function is continuous, for small values of x, this gives us the approximation

$$TC(x) \approx xMC(0), \quad \text{and thus} \quad AC(x) = \frac{TC(x)}{x} \approx MC(0),$$

where the approximation is valid for small values of x. (If you know L'Hôpital's rule, you can apply it to $AC(x) = TC(x)/x$ as x approaches 0, for another proof.)

Three More Cases

Figure 8.1, with no fixed cost and marginal costs that fall and then rise, is only one of many possibilities. I give here the three other possibilities that are most used in this book; to explore still others, try Problem 8.4.

The first is the easiest: no fixed cost and constant marginal cost. Total cost is a linear function, $TC(x) = kx$, for some constant k. Both the average and the marginal cost functions are constants: $AC(x) = MC(x) = k$. Figure 8.2 gives the picture.

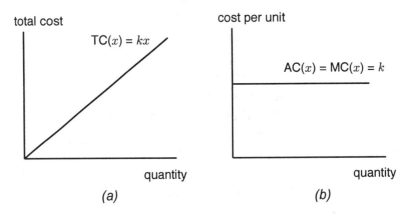

Figure 8.2. Linear total cost. If $TC(x) = kx$ for some constant k, then $AC(x)$ and $MC(x)$ are both the constant function k.

The second case combines a strictly positive fixed cost with a constant marginal cost, or $TC(x) = K + kx$ for constants K (the fixed cost) and k (the constant marginal cost). We have $MC(x) = k$ and $AC(x) = K/x + k$; the picture is in Figure 8.3. Note that the average cost function explodes to infinity for very small values of x, and it approaches the marginal cost k as the fixed cost K is amortized over an increasingly large level of production.

The third case has a strictly positive fixed cost and rising marginal cost. (I assume that marginal cost rises without bound to keep things simple.) The total cost function is concave. Average cost drops down from infinity,

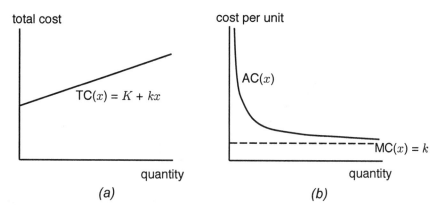

Figure 8.3. *Fixed plus constant marginal cost.* When $TC(x) = K + kx$ for $K > 0$, marginal cost is the constant k and average cost descends from very large numbers, staying above and approaching the marginal cost as x gets large.

but the rising marginal cost eventually pulls it back up, so the average cost function is bowl shaped. Of course, marginal cost cuts through average cost where average cost is minimized. Figure 8.4 gives the picture.

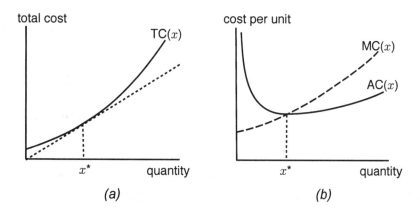

Figure 8.4. *Fixed plus rising marginal cost.* When marginal costs rise and the fixed cost is strictly positive, you get a bowl-shaped average cost function, which bottoms out precisely where MC cuts AC from below to above.

8.2. Adding Average Revenue (Inverse Demand) and Marginal Revenue to the Picture

Now superimpose the average and marginal revenue functions onto the average and marginal cost functions. We will restrict attention to the traditional *set a per-unit price and let customers choose the quantity*. Therefore, *average revenue* or $AR(x) = TR(x)/x$ is just the inverse demand function.

All four functions are depicted in Figure 8.5. The cost structure in this figure is a hybrid of Figures 8.1(e) and 8.4: Since average cost shoots off to

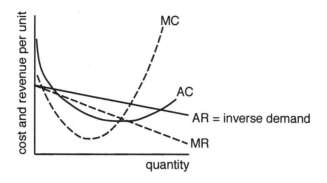

Figure 8.5. Marginal and average cost with marginal and average revenue. To the previous pictures of the marginal and average cost functions, we add the average revenue (or inverse demand) and marginal revenue functions. Given these functions, where is profit positive? Where is profit rising?

infinity for small values of x, fixed cost is positive; marginal cost falls and then rises; hence average cost is bowl shaped.

In this figure, for which levels of production x is the firm's profit positive? For which levels of production x is its profit rising? The answers are

- Profit is positive wherever average revenue (inverse demand) exceeds average cost.

- Profit is increasing wherever marginal revenue exceeds marginal cost.

The region of positive profit is shaded in Figure 8.6(a), while in Figure 8.6(b), the region of rising profit is shaded. Neither region contains the other, although there are some obvious connections: Since profit begins negative, if profit never rose it could never become positive; and once profit becomes positive, it can become negative only after a region in which it falls.

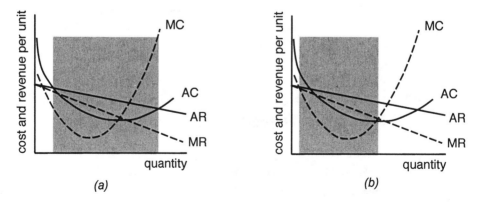

Figure 8.6. Regions of positive and increasing profit. Profit is positive where AR exceeds AC (shaded in panel a). Profit is increasing where MR exceeds MC (shaded in panel b).

The corresponding profit function is shown in Figure 8.7(a), while Figure 8.7(b) reproduces Figure 8.6. Note where profit is positive and negative, where it rises and falls, and where profit is maximized, which is where *marginal revenue equals marginal cost*.

Note that, in Figure 8.7, profit is maximized at a level of output greater than the level of output that has the largest profit margin (average profit per unit, or AR − AC). This is true generally: As long as the average cost and average revenue functions have no kinks and profit is positive at some level of production, profit maximization always occurs at a higher quantity than the quantity that maximizes profit margin. The rough intuition is that, at the point where profit margin is largest, increasing quantity a bit allows the firm to "make it up in volume." If you know sufficient calculus, you can prove this for yourself (see Problem 8.11).

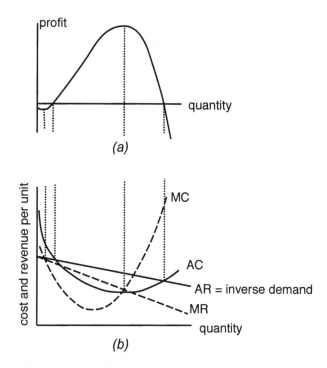

Figure 8.7. *Adding the profit function to the picture.* The average and marginal cost and revenue functions shown in Figure 8.6 and reproduced here in panel b give the profit function graphed in panel a.

8.3. From Average to Marginal Cost but Not Back

Given a picture such as Figure 8.5, you can draw, on a different set of axes, the corresponding profit function, picking out where profit is positive, where it increases, and where it is maximized. Please practice these skills on Figure 8.8, and when you run into difficulties, return to the text.

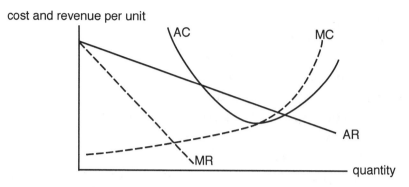

Figure 8.8. What profit function goes with these average and marginal costs and revenues? (You'll find that something is wrong here.)

Something is not right here. Profit is negative as long as average cost exceeds average revenue. It is positive where average revenue exceeds average cost. Hence profit starts negative, becomes positive, and then becomes negative again. Profit rises where marginal revenue exceeds marginal cost and falls where marginal cost exceeds marginal revenue. According to Figure 8.8, profit first rises and then falls. Of course, where marginal cost equals marginal revenue, profit is maximized. The problem is that, according to Figure 8.8, profit is maximized at a level of production x where it is still negative. And at a higher level of production, profit is positive. This cannot be true.

The point of this is that one cannot simply draw four curves and call them marginal and average cost and marginal and average revenue, even though wherever marginal X is below average X, the average falls, and wherever marginal X is above average X, the average rises. The connection between marginal X and average X is much tighter than that. Indeed, if you draw a function and call it the average X curve, then the position of the marginal X curve is completely determined.

I illustrate with average cost. I use calculus, but you could equally well use the formula (8.1) to justify my graphical procedure. The key is the formula (8.2), $AC'(x) = [MC(x) - AC(x)]/x$. (The prime in AC' denotes the derivative.) Solving this for $MC(x)$ gives $MC(x) = xAC'(x) + AC(x)$. Begin with a graph of the average cost function (follow along on Figure 8.9).

Step 1. Choose the production level x for which you wish to compute $MC(x)$. Mark on the vertical axis the level of $AC(x)$.

Step 2. Draw the tangent to $AC(x)$ at the point you are interested in and go back along that tangent to the point where it intersects the vertical axis. This point of intersection is $AC(x) - xAC'(x)$.

Step 3. Hence the distance between the point you marked on the vertical axis in step 1 and the point of intersection found in step 2 is $-x\mathrm{AC}'(x)$. Move that distance in the other direction from $\mathrm{AC}(x)$, and you are at $\mathrm{AC}(x) + x\mathrm{AC}'(x)$, which is $\mathrm{MC}(x)$.

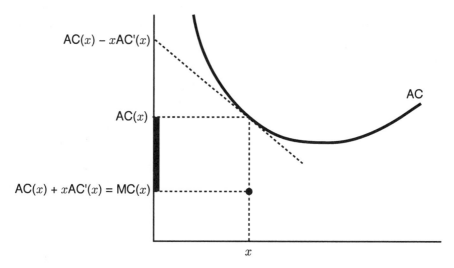

Figure 8.9. Computing marginal cost from the average cost function. Given the average cost function shown and a production level x, mark $\mathrm{AC}(x)$ on the vertical axis, extend the tangent to the average cost function at x back to the vertical axis, and on the other side of $\mathrm{AC}(x)$, move the same distance from $\mathrm{AC}(x)$ as the point where the tangent intersects. This is $\mathrm{MC}(x)$; the marginal cost curve passes through the heavy dot shown. ($\mathrm{AC}'(x)$ denotes the derivative of $\mathrm{AC}(x)$.)

How about the reverse? Can we get from a marginal cost function to the corresponding average cost function? Not without knowing at least one value of total cost or average cost. You cannot even tell whether average cost is above or below marginal cost, in general, without some idea of the size of the fixed cost. And even if that problem is resolved—for example, if you are told that $\mathrm{TC}(0) = K$ for some constant K—it is generally quite a chore to figure out where $\mathrm{AC}(x)$ is from a graph of $\mathrm{MC}(x)$. Why? Roughly, because it is a lot easier to see a derivative on a graph than an integral. If a neat way of doing it exists, I do not know it.

8.4. Efficient Scale

The scale of production x at which average cost is lowest—if one exists—is called the *(technologically) efficient scale* of production. Find it using Solver, with calculus by setting the derivative of average cost to 0, or by solving $\mathrm{MC}(x) = \mathrm{AC}(x)$. This is an important skill in Chapter 11; practice with Problems 8.1, 8.2, and 8.9.

Any time an economist puts the adjective *efficient* in front of something, suspect that it is important. Efficient scale is important in Chapter 11 but not now. In the single-firm perspective we take for now, efficient scale is not connected to the profit-maximizing level of production. Profit-maximization may be at a level of production below or above efficient scale, as illustrated by Figures 8.10(a) and (b). The marginal cost function is omitted from both figures, and I leave it to you, in Problem 8.10, to prove that marginal cost equals marginal revenue to the left of efficient scale in Figure 8.10(a) and to the right of efficient scale in Figure 8.10(b). It is possible that profit maximization is precisely at efficient scale, but this requires that marginal revenue cuts through marginal cost at efficient scale, which is precisely where marginal cost cuts through average cost, as in Figure 8.10(c). This could happen, but it would be quite a coincidence, since in general there is no connection between the positions of the average cost and marginal revenue curves.

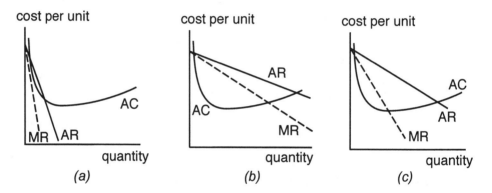

Figure 8.10. *Profit maximization and efficient scale.* In panel a, the profit-maximizing quantity is less than efficient scale. In panel b, it is more than efficient scale. And in panel c, it is at efficient scale.

8.5. Multiproduct Firms and Cost Functions

Most firms produce more than one product. How does the concept of average cost extend to such cases?

Defining a total cost function for a multiproduct firm is simple in principle: Enumerate the products of the firm by $k = 1, 2, \ldots, K$, and let $TC(x_1, \ldots, x_K)$ denote the total cost to the firm of producing x_1 units of the first product, x_2 units of the second, and so on, up to x_K units of the Kth product. As long as you are comfortable with partial derivatives, notions of marginal cost are also easy to work with in principle; in particular, if $TR(x_1, \ldots, x_K)$ denotes the firm's total revenue from the output vector

$(x_1, \ldots, x_K)$, then MR = MC becomes

$$\frac{\partial \mathrm{TR}(x_1, \ldots, x_K)}{\partial x_k} = \frac{\partial \mathrm{TC}(x_1, \ldots, x_K)}{\partial x_k},$$

for each of the K products. But what about notions of average cost?

In some cases, the cost of producing the vector of outputs $(x_1, \ldots, x_K)$ can be broken into the cost of each piece separately. That is, there are individual-product cost functions, $\mathrm{TC}_k(x_k)$, one for each $k = 1, 2, \ldots, K$, such that

$$\mathrm{TC}(x_1, x_2, \ldots, x_K) = \mathrm{TC}_1(x_1) + \mathrm{TC}_2(x_2) + \ldots + \mathrm{TC}_K(x_K).$$

When this happens, and when total revenue can similarly be additively composed of independent pieces, one for each product, we can apply everything we did in this chapter to each product in turn. It does not really matter that this is a multiproduct firm, since nothing would change in terms of costs and revenues if the firm split into K divisions or even K separate firms, one for each product.

Of course, the reason that multiproduct firms do not split along product lines is that costs, revenues, or both cannot be additively composed of independent pieces in this fashion. On the revenue side, the amount of one product sold may affect, for better or worse, the revenue obtained for a second. On the cost side, synergies or the reverse may be found in the production of outputs. For example, there are synergies in the production of lawnmowers and snowblowers; the machines and labor force needed for these products is roughly the same, and a firm that produces all these products can save on storage costs by producing lawnmowers in the winter and spring for sale in the spring and summer and snowblowers in the summer and fall for sale in the fall and winter. To take a less patent example, the manufacture of, say, Pontiacs and Chevrolets involves some synergies on the cost side, insofar as the development costs of engines, bodies, and other parts can be shared among different "varieties" of car. At the very least, some expenses in a firm, for administration and basic R&D, for example, are shared among several products. A particularly simple model of this would be to think of the firm's cost function as looking like

$$\mathrm{TC}(x_1, x_2, \ldots, x_K) = \mathrm{OC} + \mathrm{VTC}_1(x_1) + \mathrm{VTC}_2(x_2) + \ldots + \mathrm{VTC}_K(x_K),$$

where OC is a fixed overhead cost unaffected by the level of production of the individual products, and all other costs can be individually assigned to single products. (The V in front of TC connotes *variable* total cost, that portion of total cost that varies with the scale of output.)

As soon as these complications arise and the total cost function becomes more complex than

$$TC(x_1, x_2, \ldots, x_K) = TC_1(x_1) + TC_2(x_2) + \ldots + TC_K(x_K),$$

the notion of the average cost of a product more or less flies out the window.

One thing that cost accountants do is allocate all the firm's costs to its products. At least, when product lines are organized by divisions, they try to allocate interdivisional shared costs among the divisions. This does *not* mean that they are finding some way of writing total cost in the form

$$TC(x_1, x_2, \ldots, x_K) = TC_1(x_1) + TC_2(x_2) + \ldots + TC_K(x_K).$$

In general, the allocation of costs to, say, product 1 depends on the amount of other products made. For example, if fixed cost is allocated proportionally to sales revenue of the individual products, then the amount allocated to product 1 decreases the more revenue accrues from the sale of goods 2 through K. Most cost allocation schemes can be thought of as fancy ways of taking $TC(x_1, \ldots, x_K)$ and writing this as

$$TC(x_1, \ldots, x_K) = TC_1(x_1, \ldots, x_K) + \ldots + TC_K(x_1, \ldots, x_K).$$

Indeed, when costs are allocated on the basis of product–sales figures, the "decomposition" of costs is even worse than this; it depends on the position of demand curves for the products. Depending on how this is done, there may be some meaning in the cost-allocation exercise. But, as noted by an example in Chapter 3, the use of average-cost figures or profit margins derived from cost-allocation schemes can lead to some fairly silly decisions. To reiterate what was said there, before you can ask how shared costs *should* be shared among different products or divisions—or whether they should be at all—you have to know to what use these cost allocations are put.

8.6. Why Spend All This Time on Average Cost?

Because most firms are multiproduct firms, most multiproduct cost functions involve some shared costs; and because average cost is at least difficult and sometimes nonsensical in these cases, you may wonder why we spent an entire chapter on the concept of average cost.

First, thinking carefully through the context of one-product firms teaches us some specific and valuable lessons, such as

- Profit maximization does not generally entail producing at the efficient scale, where average cost is minimized. It can come at a larger or smaller scale.

- Profit-maximization does not occur where the profit margin is largest. In general, it involves producing at a level greater than that which maximizes profit margin.

Second, to reiterate from the introduction, by being explicit about the connections between margins, averages, and totals, I hope to keep you from falling into the trap of thinking blindly in terms of averages.

Third, we see in Chapter 11 that the concepts of average cost and efficient scale play an important role in economics, when equilibrium considerations of supply and demand are brought into the story.

Executive Summary

- Average cost for a single-product firm is defined as $AC(x) = TC(x)/x$.

- AC rises wherever MC exceeds AC and falls wherever MC is less than AC. Therefore, when AC has a bowl shape, MC starts below AC and cuts through it where AC is minimized.

- When $TC(0) = 0$, MC and AC start out together. When $TC(0) > 0$, AC explodes to infinity for small levels of output.

- Commonly used "pictures" of marginal and average cost are presented in Figures 8.1(e) and 8.2 through 8.4.

- Profit is positive where AR = inverse demand exceeds AC. Profit rises where MR exceeds MC.

- Given an average cost or average revenue function, simple graphical procedures allow you to find marginal cost or revenue at specific quantity levels.

- The level of production where AC is minimized is called *efficient scale*, found by setting $AC'(x) = 0$ or by solving $AC(x) = MC(x)$ (see Problems 8.1 and 8.2).

- Profit maximization is not related to efficient scale, except by coincidence (see Problem 8.10).

- Multiproduct firms give us problems with the notion of average cost, but the concepts of marginal cost and marginal revenue are still there and MC = MR for each product remains the mantra of profit maximization (see Problem 8.12).

Problems

8.1 Imagine a firm with the total cost function $TC(x) = 10,000,000 + 50x + x^2/16,000$. This means that its marginal cost function is $MC(x) = 50 + x/8000$.

(a) Based on this information, will the graph of this firm's average and marginal cost functions look like Figure 8.1(e), 8.2, 8.3, or 8.4? Why?

(b) What is this firm's average cost function? For which values of x is marginal cost less than average cost, and for which values of x is marginal cost greater than average cost?

(c) What is efficient scale for this firm? What is the average cost of the firm at its efficient scale?

(d) Suppose this firm faces the inverse demand function $P(x) = 250 - x/4000$. For which values of x does this firm have positive profit? (You need to know the quadratic formula to answer with algebra. Do not expect the answer to be in nice round numbers.) For which values of x does this firm have increasing profit? What level of x maximizes this firm's profit?

8.2 Answer all parts of Problem 8.1 for firms with the following total cost functions:

(a) $TC(x) = 40,000 + 55x + x^2/9000$

(b) $TC(x) = 60x$

(c) $TC(x) = 250,000 + 60x$ (efficient scale is tricky)

(d) $TC(x) = 55x + x^2/9000$

(e) $TC(x) = 20x - x^2/20,000$ for $x \leq 50,000$ and $TC(x) = 10x + x^2/20,000 + 250,000$ for $x \geq 50,000$

8.3 (To answer this problem, you may need to evaluate an integral.) The cost functions in Problems 8.1 and 8.2(a) are of a sort we use a lot in this book: a positive fixed cost F and linear (and increasing) marginal cost $MC(x) = a + bx$, where F, a, and b are all strictly positive. What is the "picture" for this case in terms of F, a, and b, and what is the efficient scale of production?

8.4 Figures 8.1 through 8.4 give the most common cases of average and marginal cost functions that we see in this book, but there are other possibilities. What does the "picture" look like for each of the following cases?

(a) No fixed cost and increasing marginal cost.

(b) No fixed cost and decreasing marginal cost.

(c) Strictly positive fixed cost and decreasing marginal cost.

(d) Strictly positive fixed cost and marginal cost that falls for a while and then rises (where, to avoid pathology, you can assume that marginal cost is not bounded above).

8.5 Figure 8.11 provides two examples of marginal and average cost and revenue curves. For each of these, draw the corresponding profit function. Find where profit is positive, where it is negative, where it increases, where it decreases, and where it is maximized. (In Figure 8.11(a), both average revenue and average cost are linear functions. What is the precise shape of the total profit function?)

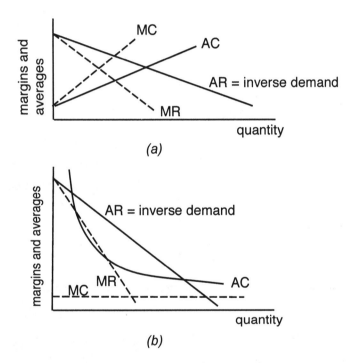

Figure 8.11. Problems 8.5 and 8.6: Two sets of four functions.

8.6 For the cost functions shown in Figure 8.11(b), total cost has the form $TC(x) = K + kx$ for constants K and k.

(a) Suppose K increases. How does the picture for profit change? Specifically, how do the profit-maximizing point and the region in which profit is positive change as K increases?

(b) Suppose k increases. How does this picture for profit change? How do the profit-maximizing point and the region of positive profits change?

(c) For some value of K (larger than that depicted in the figure), AC will exceed AR for all but a single level of production at which AC will equal AR. At this level of K, the average cost curve will be tangent to the inverse demand (average revenue) curve. For this level of K, at which level of production does the tangency occur?

8.7   Figure 8.12 depicts the average cost and inverse demand functions facing a firm. So there is no ambiguity, let me state categorically that inverse demand is a linear function and average cost is constant at $10 up to 160 units, and then increases.

(a) Copy Figure 8.12 and draw on your copy the firm's marginal revenue function as accurately as you can.

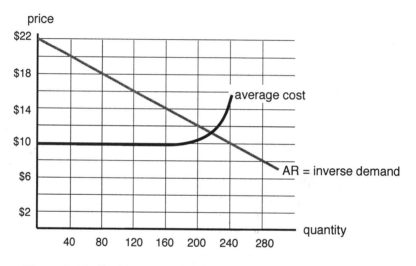

Figure 8.12. Problem 8.7: Average cost and inverse demand.

(b) What is the value of marginal cost at a level of production of 130 units?

(c) Can you tell what level of production maximizes this firm's profit? If so, what is that level? If not, to what extent can you pin down this level?

8.8 Figure 8.13 shows the average revenue and average cost functions facing a particular firm. At the quantity 100, what are its levels of marginal cost and marginal revenue? (Do this graphically.)

8.9   Consider again the total cost function of Chiccolini Heavy Industries (CHI), the sole manufacturer of steel in Freedonia, which is $TC(x) =$ $\$10,000,000 + 200x + x^2/1000$. Find the efficient scale and minimum average cost for this company (which we did back in Problem 3.3) using the characterization that marginal cost equals average cost at the efficient scale.

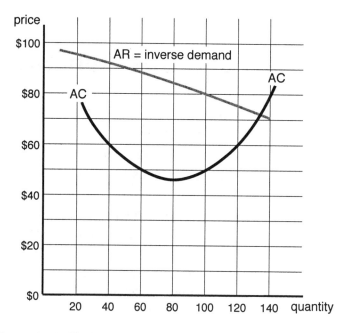

Figure 8.13. Problem 8.8: Average revenue and average cost.

8.10 In the discussion surrounding Figure 8.10, I claim that profit maximization would occur at less than efficient scale in panel a, at more than efficient scale in panel b, and precisely at efficient scale in panel c. Give precise, one- or two-sentence arguments (for each case) why this is so. You may assume (if you wish) that marginal cost is an increasing function in these figures.

8.11 In the text, I claim that, as long as positive profits can be obtained, profit maximization takes place at a level of production greater than where the profit margin is maximized. Prove this using calculus. (Hint: Compute the first derivate of profit margin and set it equal to 0. Assume that the profit function has a derivative and, for those who are very careful in mathematics, that both the profit function and the profit-margin function attain a maximum value.)

8.12 A firm produces two products, skets and plorts. The firm's inverse demand function for skets is $P_s = 200 - s$, the inverse demand curve for plorts is $P_p = 200 - 2p$. The firm's total cost function is given by $TC(s, p) = 50(s + p) + (s + p)^2$. What levels of sket and plort production by the firm maximizes its profit? (Note that p here stands for the number of plorts, not the price of anything. We use uppercase Ps in this problem for prices.)

9. Technology and Cost Minimization

This chapter concerns economic models of production technology and the connection between these models and the total cost function:

- Technology is modeled graphically, with isoquant diagrams, and algebraically, with production functions. Concepts such as flexibility and returns to scale are discussed.
- Given a model of technology and prices for the inputs to production, we find the cheapest way the firm can attain a given level of output, which provides us the total cost function.
- A second cost-minimization problem studied concerns the allocation of a desired amount of production among a number of cost-independent sources.
- To conclude, threads about constrained maximization problems in general are pulled together.

This is a long chapter, full of material. It might be prudent to read it in two or three sittings.

9.1. Modeling Technology

In this chapter, we envision firms as enterprises with the ability to turn various combinations of input into various levels of output. The *technology* of the firm is, essentially, a complete description of the firm's abilities in this regard. We use two models of production technology: isoquant diagrams and the production function.

Isoquant Diagrams

Isoquant diagrams are employed for a firm that produces one output, using two other goods as inputs. (*Iso* is the Greek prefix for "equal," so *isoquant* is meant to be read as "equal quantity.")

Imagine a firm that makes widgets out of labor hours and sheet metal. For each given number of widgets, we graph the combinations of labor and sheet metal sufficient to make that number of widgets. The axes in Figure 9.1 represent, respectively, amounts of labor and amounts of sheet metal in some chosen units, so the point marked with the heavy dot represents 10 units of labor and 5 units of sheet metal. Suppose that, from 10 units of labor and 5 units of sheet metal, the firm is able to produce six widgets. Suppose as well that six widgets can be made up out of 7 units of labor and 8 units of sheet metal, the point marked with the open circle. The *six-widget isoquant* passes through both these points, like the curve so labeled in Figure 9.1. Note that the point (5 units of labor, 12 units of sheet metal) is a third point on this isoquant, meaning that this combination of inputs also produces six widgets.

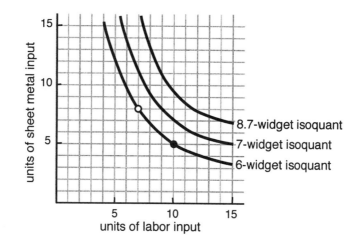

Figure 9.1. Isoquant diagrams. For a good produced out of two inputs, we graph, for various levels of output, all the combinations of the two inputs that give that level of output.

The 7-widget isoquant and the 8.7-widget isoquant are also shown on Figure 9.1. Note that the 7-widget isoquant is to the northeast of the 6-widget isoquant, and the 8.7-widget isoquant is to the northeast of the 7-widget isoquant; this reflects the idea that it takes more of the inputs to make more output.

Convex Isoquants and Marginal Rates of Substitution

Most isoquant diagrams have convex isoquants, which means that they bend away from the origin, as in Figure 9.1. This corresponds to the following property: Pick an isoquant and a point along that isoquant. Moving along the isoquant, decrease the amount of one input by some fixed amount, call it δ. To compensate, the other input must be increased by some amount, ϵ_1. Reduce the first input by δ once more; to stay on the isoquant, the amount of the second input must be increased again by some amount, ϵ_2. Isoquants are convex when, every time we do this, from any starting point, for either input, and for any δ, the amount ϵ_1 that compensates for δ less of input 1 the first time is no larger than the amount ϵ_2 needed to compensate for the second decrease in the first output by δ.

The notion that inputs can substitute for one another, holding fixed the output level, is an important one, and some terminology goes with it. Starting from the first point, the ratio ϵ_1/δ is called the (discrete) *marginal rate of substitution* (MRS) of input 2 to input 1. As δ goes to 0, and we get the slope of a tangent to the isoquant at the base point, the so-called (continuous) MRS. In terms of MRSs, convexity of isoquants means that, moving along any isoquant, decreasing one input and increasing the other, the MRS of the second for the first is nondecreasing.

Technological Flexibility and Isoquants

Technological flexibility can mean many things. For instance, a firm's technology might be said to be flexible if the firm can change its rate of output quickly and without substantial cost. For a multiproduct firm, flexibility might mean the ability to shift production among different products quickly and cheaply. But in terms of isoquants, flexibility refers to changes in MRSs. Consider the following extreme cases:

- *No-substitutions technologies.* Suppose every level of output x requires a minimum amount of each input, with no possibility of substituting one input for the other. For instance, imagine a production technology that, to produce x units of output, requires $3x$ units of input 1 and $x + x^2/4$ units of input 2, with no possibility of substitution. Two units of output requires 6 units of input 1 and 3 units of input 2. If you have, say, 6 units of input 1 and 10 units of input 2, you can make no more than 2 units of output; the 6 units of input 1 suffices to make two units of output and no more; the unneeded 7 units of input 2 go to waste. This sort of production technology has right-angle isoquants, as depicted in Figure 9.2(a).

- *Fixed-coefficients technology.* In the no-substitutions technology just given, the ratio of input 1 to input 2 required to produce x units of output changes with changes in the level of output x. To produce 2 units of output requires 6 units of input 1 and 3 units of input 2, a ratio of 2:1, while 3 units of output requires 9 units of input 1 and 5.25 units of input 2, a 1.714:1 ratio. In many no-substitutions technologies, the ratio of the required levels of inputs does not change as the level of output changes; this type of technology is called a *fixed-coefficients technology*. Being a special case of a no-substitution technology, we still have right-angle isoquants, but now the vertices of the right angles lie along a single ray coming out of $(0, 0)$. See Figure 9.2(b), for an example where the ratio of input 1 to input 2 is 1 to 2.

- *Constant marginal rates of substitution technology.* In a constant marginal rate of substitution technology, we can always swap a set amount of input 2 for 1 unit of input 1; the marginal rate of substitution is constant.

This gives isoquants that are parallel lines, as in Figure 9.2(c), where we have a 2:1 (constant) marginal rate of substitution of input 2 for input 1.

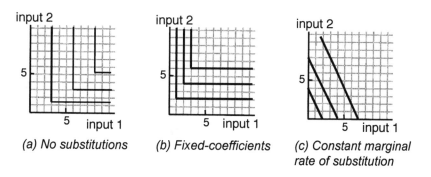

(a) No substitutions   (b) Fixed-coefficients   (c) Constant marginal rate of substitution

Figure 9.2. Three special types of isoquants.

The first two of these technologies are inflexible in terms of the ability to swap inputs, while the third is quite flexible. In general, the closer isoquants are to right angles, the less flexible is the technology in this sense; the closer isoquants are to straight lines, the more flexible is the technology.

A technology's degree of flexibility in this sense usually depends on the time scale of the analysis. General Motors, in its day-to-day operations, has remarkably little ability to shift labor and capital inputs, where capital means things like robots, material transfer equipment, and so forth. Once the production line is established and tasks on the line are assigned, each car coming down the line requires a more-or-less fixed amount of labor. But when planning a production facility or adapting an existing facility to a new model, production engineers have considerable flexibility in this regard; they can substitute robots for labor and vice versa. This is to say that isoquant diagrams, especially as they relate to this sort of flexibility, are drawn differently depending on whether we analyze day-to-day operations at a plant or the design of the plant in the first place.

Production Functions

Production functions give the same data as isoquant diagrams but in the form of a function. A production function f gives, for every set of inputs, the most output we can get from those inputs. So, for example, in the technology represented by Figure 9.1,

$$f(10 \text{ units of labor, } 5 \text{ units of sheet metal}) = 6$$

and similarly, $f(7, 8) = 6$, $f(6, 14) = 7$, and $f(12, 8) = 8.7$.

To distinguish between input to the firm's production process and output from it, we use x to denote output and y to denote input. Therefore $f(y_1, y_2) = x$ means that output level x is obtained from y_1 units of the first input and y_2 units of the second. Prices for output are denoted by p, while prices for input are denoted by the letter r. So, for instance, output level x, produced from inputs y_1 and y_2 yields revenue px, at a cost of $r_1 y_1 + r_2 y_2$.

An isoquant diagram and the corresponding production function tell you the same things, but there are advantages to each:

- Isoquant diagrams are often a more transparent representation of the technology; the old saw that a picture is worth 1000 words or, in this case, algebraic symbols, applies. You can look at isoquants and quickly get a rough sense of technological flexibility, for instance, something that is very hard to do with a production function. (The extreme cases of no-substitutions, fixed-coefficients, and constant MRS technologies can be encoded algebraically, however; see Problem 9.3.)

- Because it is impossible to draw on a graph the isoquants for all possible levels of output, production functions give the data more completely.

- When we proceed to solve the firm's cost-minimization problem, having the technology encoded in a production function allows us to use either a spreadsheet or calculus.

- While isoquant diagrams limit us to cases of one output and two inputs, production functions enable us to encode production technologies for one output and as many inputs as desired. If we have, say, four inputs—in order, labor, sheet metal, time on a metal lathe, and electricity—then $f(4, 5, 3, 2) = 8$ means that 8 units of output can be produced from 4 units of labor, 5 units of sheet metal, 3 units of metal lathe time, and 2 units of electricity.

Regarding the last point, whether isoquant diagrams or production functions are used, they are rarely used at the level of detail of each separate input. Economists usually use them instead for aggregates of input. A production function for automobiles, for instance, might list as inputs skilled blue-collar labor hours, white-collar labor hours, raw materials, capital equipment, and energy, without going into the detail of different forms of labor, material, capital, and energy. And, to be fair to isoquant diagrams here, even in a production technology that involves more than two broad aggregates of input, isoquant diagrams can be used to depict the trade-offs between two of those input aggregates. For instance, in the manufacture of cars, we might draw isoquant diagrams that depict the trade-offs between skilled blue-collar labor and capital equipment, with the understanding that raw materials are used in (rough) proportion to the number of vehicles produced, and energy requirements depend on both the total number of vehicles and the amount of energy-intensive capital used.

More than One Output?

Production functions allow many inputs, but they are limited to a single output. How do we represent technologies for multiproduct firms?

In cases where the production processes of different outputs are technologically independent—the amount of output 1 derived from some combinations of inputs does not depend on the amounts of other outputs produced—there are no problems: Simply treat each output independently, with its own production function. But very often outputs generate *production externalities* for one another, meaning the menus of input needed to get x units of output 1 will depend on the production levels of other output. These externalities can be positive, where more of one output makes it easier to get more of another; for instance, if the technology for output 1 generates excess heat, that heat might help in producing output 2 or if different outputs share productive resources or know-how. The externalities also can be negative; for instance, if two outputs rely on river water for cooling, supplemented as needed by refrigeration, then more of output 2, by raising the water temperature, can increase the amount of supplemental refrigeration needed in the production of output 1.

When they exist, externalities complicate the representation of the production technology of the firm. Formal models are not impossible in such cases, but they are not simple, so we do not deal with them here.

Returns to Scale

Suppose we increase all the inputs in some production technology by 10%. What happens to the amount of output? In particular, does the amount of output increase by more than, less than, or precisely 10%? The technology's *returns to scale* are the issue here.

The following terminology is used when the answer to this question—more than, less than, precisely equal—is the same regardless of the baseline production quantity and the scale increase in input:

- The production function f has *increasing returns to scale* when, assuming there are n inputs, for all sets of inputs y_1 through y_n and all scale factors $a > 1$, $f(ay_1, ay_2, \ldots, ay_n) \geq af(y_1, y_2, \ldots, y_n)$.

- The production function f has *decreasing returns to scale* when, for all sets of inputs y_1 through y_n and all scale factors $a > 1$, $f(ay_1, ay_2, \ldots, ay_n) \leq af(y_1, y_2, \ldots, y_n)$.

- The production function f has *constant returns to scale* when, for all sets of inputs y_1 through y_n and for all scale factors $a > 0$, $f(ay_1, ay_2, \ldots, ay_n) = af(y_1, y_2, \ldots, y_n)$.

Two clarifying remarks are in order:

1. In the first two of these definitions, $a > 1$ means that we are looking at how output reacts to scale increases in the inputs. In the third, since we have an equals sign, we can get away with scaling inputs up *or down* proportionately.

2. In the first two definitions, we have weak inequalities in terms of output. So the first would be more accurately termed *nondecreasing* returns to scale and the second, *nonincreasing* returns. Moreover, constant returns to scale, for this reason, is a special case of both increasing and decreasing returns. Sorry about that, but that is how things are defined in Economese.

The most important remark is that each of these definitions requires the inequality (or equation) to hold for *every* set of inputs and *every* proportional scaling of those inputs. To understand this remark, begin by answering the questions: *Why might a technology have increasing returns to scale?* and *Why might it have decreasing returns?*

- One set of reasons for increasing returns—what most people think of first—is purely technological. Making steel in blast furnaces, generating electricity by burning coal, and shipping cargo by both road and sea are all examples where, at least up to some fairly large scale, processes are more efficient at larger and larger scale.

- Another set of reasons for increasing returns appeals to specialization of labor and mass production. An artisan who makes every part of a car and then assembles the pieces is likely to be less efficient than a team that produces cars at a scale sufficient to have specialists in motor assembly, casting, bumper attachment, and so forth.

- Some expenses relative to production need not increase proportionally with the scale of production, especially expenses that are knowledge-related. The knowledge derived from a fixed amount of R&D expenditure can be used in production plant A just as well as in plant B, even if A is twice the size of B. So if we double all the inputs, including the amount of R&D, we get more knowledge, which might then more than double the output.

- The standard stories for decreasing returns concern the costs of coordination and management. With increases in scale, management is less able to monitor and coordinate what is going on. Incentives for individual workers are less effective in larger and larger facilities. So an increase in all input means a smaller than proportional increase in output.

All these can be true, and in some technologies, *all* are true; but they do not apply uniformly. The first three forces are typically more powerful at low levels of output, giving "increasing returns," and the last predominates at high levels of output, giving "decreasing returns."

The quotes in the previous sentence explain the remark begun just prior to the four bullet points. The formal definitions of increasing, decreasing, and constant returns to scale require satisfaction of the appropriate inequality for all scale changes and all baseline vectors of inputs. A technology that has increasing returns for low levels and decreasing returns for higher levels of output satisfies none of these definitions, and so the terms *increasing* and *decreasing returns* don't apply, formally. But they certainly apply informally, and we use them informally in the fashion of the final sentence of the previous paragraph, in some of the discussion to come.

9.2. From Technology to Cost Functions: The Cost-Minimization Problem

Imagine a firm whose technology is given by the production function f. Suppose also that the price of input j is r_j dollars per unit, for $j = 1, \ldots, n$, regardless of how much or little this firm purchases. Then the cheapest, most cost-efficient way for the firm to produce x or more units of output is the solution to the following problem, called the *cost-minimization problem*:

$$\text{minimize } r_1 y_1 + r_2 y_2 + \ldots + r_n y_n$$
$$\text{subject to } f(y_1, \ldots, y_n) \geq x, \quad \text{and} \quad y_1 \geq 0, \ y_2 \geq 0, \ \ldots, \ y_n \geq 0.$$

The output constraint is written with an inequality, but if it always takes more input to produce more output and the production function is continuous, an equality would give the same answer.

This cost-minimization problem is a part of the firm's overall profit-maximization problem. The firm, seeking to maximize profits, can be thought of as tackling that problem in two steps. First, for each possible level of output x, it solves the cost-minimization problem, finding the cheapest way it can make x. This gives us the total cost function $TC(x)$. Then, once $TC(x)$ is computed, the firm chooses the optimal level of output x by looking at total revenues less total costs. This is where $MC = MR$ comes in.

Deriving Total Cost Graphically

For the case of two-input production technology, we can use an isoquant diagram to solve the firm's cost-minimization problem graphically.

Consider the firm of Figure 9.1, turning labor and sheet metal into widgets. Suppose that 1 unit of labor costs $2 and 1 unit of sheet metal costs $3. Then, on the grid of Figure 9.1, we draw *iso-cost* lines, the various input combinations that have a single cost. For example, the $12 iso-cost line is the line segment of pairs (l, m) (for labor and metal, respectively) satisfying $2l + 3m = 12$. This iso-cost line and the $24 iso-cost line are shown in Figure 9.3(a).

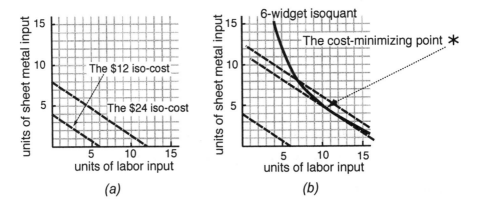

(a)   (b)

Figure 9.3. Determining total cost graphically. To find the cheapest way to make 6 units of output, find the cheapest iso-cost line—the one most to the southwest—that touches the 6-unit isoquant curve. This gives you the *bill of materials* for the least-cost production method—here 10.5 units of labor and 4.5 units of sheet metal—and hence the least-cost total cost, $2 \times 10.5 + \$3 \times 4.5 = \$34.50$.

In Figure 9.3(b) we add the six-widget isoquant. What is the cheapest way to make six widgets? We want to find the point along the six-widget isoquant on the lowest iso-cost line possible. We can make six widgets with 7 units of labor and 8 units of sheet metal, putting us on the $2 \times 7 + \$3 \times 8 = \$38$ iso-cost line, as shown. But, if we increase the amount of labor employed and decrease the amount of sheet metal while keeping on the isoquant, we can move to a lower iso-cost line and decrease costs. This process terminates when we get to the point marked with the star in Figure 9.3(b), the point at which the six-widget isoquant is tangent to an iso-cost. Reading from the graph, the coordinates of this cost-minimizing point are approximately 10.5 units of labor and 4.5 units of sheet metal; this means a total cost of ($2)(10.5) + ($3)(4.5) = $21 + $13.50 = $34.50, which is thus the total cost of making six widgets as cheaply as possible, at these input prices.

So TC(6) = $34.50. To find TC($x$) for some other value of x, repeat the exercise, using the x-unit isoquant.

Solving the Cost-Minimization Problem on a Spreadsheet

To solve the cost-minimization problem using a spreadsheet, we need an Excel-executable formula for the firm's production function. Suppose, for instance, the firm uses three inputs, capital, labor, and material, denoted by k, l, and m, respectively; and its production function is

$$f(k, l, m) = k^{1/2}l^{1/8}m^{1/4}.$$

Suppose that the prices of the three inputs are $r_k = 1$, $r_l = 2$, and $r_m = 2$. What is the cheapest way to make 100 units of output?

Refer to Figure 9.4(a), which depicts sheet 1 of CHAP9. Rows 2, 3, and 4 contain the three input levels. The corresponding level of output and total cost of the inputs are computed in rows 6 and 8. Panel a contains the initial values $k = m = l = 100$, which give 56.234 units of output at a cost of $500.

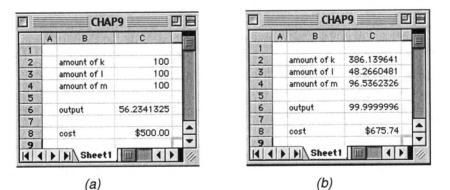

(a)   (b)

Figure 9.4. Solving the cost minimization problem with a spreadsheet. Panel a shows the spreadsheet CHAP9, sheet 1, which computes from a bundle of inputs the amount of output obtained and the cost of the bundle. Solver is asked to minimize C8 by varying C2, C3, and C4, subject to the constraint that C6 ≥ 100. The result is shown in panel b.

Call up Solver and ask it to minimize the cost of the mix of inputs, subject to the constraint that the output level is at least 100. The answer Solver provides is shown in Figure 9.4(b). We read from this that TC(100) = $675.74.

How do we interpret this answer? On sheet 2 of CHAP9, depicted in Figure 9.5, I compute margins in each of k, l, and m. I increase each of the variables separately by 0.001 and find the marginal impact of these increases on both the amount of output and the cost of the mix of inputs. Note that in computing the margins, I normalize to get rates per unit change in the inputs. That is, the entry in cell E6 is $= (I6 - C6)/0.001$. Of course, the marginal impact on the cost of the mix of inputs is in each case the price of the input. (Think this through if it isn't obvious.)

	A	B	C	D	E	F	G	H	I	J	K
1					margin in k	margin in l	margin in m		.001 more k	.001 more l	.001 more m
2		amount of k	386.139641						386.140641	386.139641	386.139641
3		amount of l	48.2660481						48.2660481	48.2670481	48.2660481
4		amount of m	96.5362326						96.5362326	96.5362326	96.5372326
5											
6		output	99.9999996		0.12948675	0.25897887	0.25896912		100.000129	100.000259	100.000259
7											
8		cost	$675.74		1	2	2		$675.75	$675.75	$675.75
9											
10			ratios:		7.72279784	7.72263773	7.72292864				

Figure 9.5. *Interpreting the solution to the cost-minimization problem.* This spreadsheet, sheet 2 of CHAP9, adds the calculation of (discrete) margins in output and cost, for small increases in k, l, and m. So, for instance, output increases at a rate of 0.12948 units of output per unit increase in k; that is, the marginal physical product of k, or MPP$_k$, is 0.12948. At the solution, the ratios of the input prices to these marginal physical products are equal. See the text for the explanation why.

The margins on the production function f in the different inputs record the rates at which a unit increase in a given input increases the amount of output. Economists typically call these the *marginal physical products* of the inputs, where the adjective *physical* reminds us that output here is measured in physical and not monetary terms. The notation used is MPP$_l$ for the marginal physical product of l, and so forth.

Finally, in row 10, I compute for each input the ratios of the marginal impact on the cost of the bundle of inputs—that is, the input's price—to the input's marginal physical product. That is, the entry in cell E10 is $= E8/E6$, which is r_k/MPP_k. Remarkably, at the optimal solution, these three ratios are nearly equal.

In fact, this is not remarkable, and they are not precisely equal only because of the approximate nature of discrete margin calculations. They must be equal at the solution to the cost-minimization problem. To see why, suppose the firm has settled on input levels k, l, and m, which lead to output level 100, but where these ratios are not equal. Suppose, in particular, that this ratio for k is less than the ratio for l.

Imagine increasing k by some small amount, say, by $0.001/\mathrm{MPP}_k$. This raises the amount of output we have by $[0.001/\mathrm{MPP}_k] \times \mathrm{MPP}_k = 0.001$, this being the product of the amount of change in the variable times the rate at which output changes per unit change in the variable. At the same time that we increase k by $[0.001/\mathrm{MPP}_k]$, we lower l by $[0.001/\mathrm{MPP}_l]$. This change lowers the level of output back down to 100. Let me highlight this:

> If we simultaneously raise k by $0.001/\mathrm{MPP}_k$ and lower l by $0.001/\mathrm{MPP}_l$, the net effect is to keep the level of output at 100.

But $0.001/\mathrm{MPP}_k$ more of input k costs $[0.001/\mathrm{MPP}_k] \times r_k$, while $0.001/\mathrm{MPP}_l$ less of input l saves $[0.001/\mathrm{MPP}_l] \times r_l$. The net impact on costs is

$$\frac{0.001}{\mathrm{MPP}_k} \times r_k - \frac{0.001}{\mathrm{MPP}_l} \times r_l = 0.001 \left[\frac{r_k}{\mathrm{MPP}_k} - \frac{r_l}{\mathrm{MPP}_l} \right],$$

which is a negative number under our assumption that the ratio is smaller for k than for l. Of course, if the ratio for l were smaller, we would go the other way, lowering the amount of k and raising the amount of l. And similarly for l versus m and for k versus m. *Equality of the ratios of the inputs' prices to their marginal physical products, for each pair of inputs, is necessary, at any solution of the firm's cost-minimization problem.*

Well, that is almost true. Watch out for one complication. Suppose, for instance, $r_m/\mathrm{MPP}_m < r_k/\mathrm{MPP}_k$, but the level of k is 0. Given the ratio of input prices to marginal physical products, we want to increase the amount of m used and decrease the amount of k used. But, if k is at 0, we cannot decrease the amount of k. So the correct rule is this:

> At the solution of the firm's cost-minimization problem, the ratios of input prices to marginal physical products should be equalized for each pair of inputs in which both are used in strictly positive amounts, and these equal ratios should be less than or equal to the ratio for any input not used.

Solving the Cost-Minimization Problem with Calculus

The rule just uncovered is approximately true for discrete margins but precisely true for calculus-based margins, where an input's marginal physical product is the partial derivative of the production function in the input.

Let me illustrate with the example just done in Excel, where the firm's production function is $f(k, l, m) = k^{1/2}l^{1/8}m^{1/4}$ and the inputs' prices are $r_k = 1$, $r_l = 2$, and $r_m = 2$. In fact, I will do better than we did with Excel; I will solve the firm's cost-minimization problem *for every level of output x* simultaneously, emerging with the entire function $\mathrm{TC}(x)$.

First note that, for any amount of output $x > 0$, we need strictly positive amounts of all three inputs, because this particular production function equals 0 if any one of the inputs is 0. This means that, at the solution of the cost-minimization problem, the ratios of the input prices to the marginal physical products of the different inputs must be equal. That is, according to the rule, at the optimal solution,

$$\frac{r_k}{\text{MPP}_k} = \frac{r_l}{\text{MPP}_l} = \frac{r_m}{\text{MPP}_m}. \qquad (9.1)$$

The three marginal physical product functions are

$$\text{MPP}_k = \frac{\partial f(k,l,m)}{\partial k} = \frac{\partial k^{1/2} l^{1/8} m^{1/4}}{\partial k} = \frac{1}{2} k^{-1/2} l^{1/8} m^{1/4},$$

and, similarly,

$$\text{MPP}_l = \frac{1}{8} k^{1/2} l^{-7/8} m^{1/4} \quad \text{and} \quad \text{MPP}_m = \frac{1}{4} k^{1/2} l^{1/8} m^{-3/4}.$$

Therefore (9.1) can be rewritten

$$\frac{1}{\frac{1}{2} k^{-1/2} l^{1/8} m^{1/4}} = \frac{2}{\frac{1}{8} k^{1/2} l^{-7/8} m^{1/4}} = \frac{2}{\frac{1}{4} k^{1/2} l^{1/8} m^{-3/4}}.$$

Take the first of these two equalities, cancel the common $m^{1/4}$, and flip the two fractions over. This results in

$$\frac{k^{-1/2} l^{1/8}}{2} = \frac{k^{1/2} l^{-7/8}}{16}.$$

Now collect all the ks on the right and the ls on the left. The equation becomes

$$\frac{l}{2} = \frac{k}{16} \quad \text{or} \quad 8l = k.$$

At the optimal production point, we use eight times as many units of k as l. Similar manipulation of the second equality gives

$$\frac{m}{16} = \frac{l}{8} \quad \text{or} \quad 2l = m,$$

and if you equate the first and last terms, you get $4m = k$.

Do not get too excited about how, magically, everything suddenly became so simple. This sort of production function has a name, a Cobb-Douglas production function, because things work out so well for it: Independent of the level of production x, at the input prices we assume, the optimal ratio of k to l is 8:1, the optimal ratio of l to m is 1:2, and the optimal ratio of k to m is 4:1. (The first two imply the third; we did a little more work than is necessary.)

To finish, we now know that, whatever x is, at the solution of the cost-minimization problem, the ratios of l to m to k are 1:2:8. If we use l^* units of input l, then $m^* = 2l^*$ and $k^* = 8l^*$. Hence the total output is

$$f(k^*, l^*, m^*) = f(8l^*, l^*, 2l^*) = (8l^*)^{1/2}(l^*)^{1/8}(2l^*)^{1/4} = 8^{1/2}2^{1/4}(l^*)^{7/8}.$$

If we want x units of output, we need

$$x = f(k^*, l^*, m^*) = 8^{1/2}2^{1/4}(l^*)^{7/8}, \quad \text{or} \quad x^{8/7} = 8^{4/7}2^{2/7}l^*, \quad \text{or}$$

$$x^{8/7} = 2^{12/7}2^{2/7}l^* = 2^{14/7}l^* = 4l^*, \quad \text{or} \quad \frac{x^{8/7}}{4} = l^*.$$

Therefore,

$$k^* = 8l^* = 2x^{8/7}, \quad \text{and} \quad m^* = 2l^* = \frac{x^{8/7}}{2}.$$

Having solved the cost-minimization problem for any value of x, it is easy to write $\text{TC}(x)$:

$$\text{TC}(x) = k^* + 2l^* + 2m^* = 2x^{8/7} + \frac{x^{8/7}}{2} + x^{8/7} = 3.5x^{8/7}.$$

That went by rather quickly, but do not worry too much if you did not get it all on a first reading. You can try your hand at other examples in Problems 9.5 and 9.6.

Figure 9.3 and the Rule

We now have seen two ways to solve the firm's cost-minimization problem: graphically, using iso-cost lines and isoquant curves, and algebraically, with the rule. In the graphical treatment, the solution is found where the isoquant curve and the iso-cost line are tangent. That tangency is, essentially, the rule.

The iso-cost line is $r_1y_1 + r_2y_2$ = constant. Calling the constant k, and expressing y_2 as a function of y_1, we get $y_2 = k/r_2 - (r_1/r_2)y_1$, so the slope of the iso-cost line is $-r_1/r_2$. As for the slope of the isoquant, this measures how much of input 2 needs to be added on the margin, to counteract in terms of output a decline in input 1. From the argument I gave as we were deriving the rule, we know that an increase of δ/MPP_2 of input 2 just counteracts a decrease of δ/MPP_1 in input 1, for small values of δ. Therefore, the slope of the isoquant is the ratio of these two with a minus sign, since one goes up and the other down. After cancelling the δs and simplifying, this slope is $-\text{MPP}_1/\text{MPP}_2$. The tangency of iso-cost and isoquant is hence $-r_1/r_2 = -\text{MPP}_1/\text{MPP}_2$. Rearrange terms, and this is the rule.

The Rule and Isoquants with Kinks

I may have made it seem as if the calculus approach (using production functions) is superior to the graphical approach (using isoquants) except that the graphical approach may be more intuitive by virtue of being graphical. If I left you with that impression, let me issue one caveat.

The calculus approach, at least as presented here, depends on the production function being smooth or, in math-speak, differentiable. If it is not, we can make no sense out of all those MPPs, which are, after all, partial derivatives of f. And, for some pretty standard technologies, the production function f is not differentiable. For instance, a no-substitutions technology does not have a differentiable production function. More generally, any production technology whose isoquants have kinks does not have a differentiable production function.

So if you tried to apply the rule to, say, a no-substitutions technology, you would be stumped. If you think about it, this one particular example isn't too bad, since if you have a no-substitutions technology, it is *easy* to go from input prices to the total cost function. (How? See Problem 9.4(b).) But some other technologies with kinked isoquants take more thinking. See, for instance, Problem 9.14. In such cases, unless your math skills extend to things like right- and lefthand derivatives, the graphical approach is required.

Inputs Without Clearly Defined Prices

We have been assuming that the total cost of a list of quantities of inputs is clear. Each input has a price r_j, and the bill for the list of inputs $(y_1, \ldots, y_n)$ is $r_1y_1 + r_2y_2 + \ldots + r_ny_n$.

Things are not so easy in real life. Sometimes it is hard to ascribe a price to each input. One important class of difficulties, which we'll deal with next chapter, concerns inputs that are durable. For example, suppose one input is time on a metal lathe. If the firm rents its metal lathes, then there is no problem; $r_{\text{metal lathes}}$ is just the rental rate of a lathe. But most firms purchase equipment like metal lathes and use them for more than a single production period. How should the cost of such durable inputs be computed? See Chapter 10.

A second class of difficulties concerns inputs for which there is no clearly established market price, because the item in question is one of a kind. The typical example here is managerial time, especially the labor input of owner–managers. Most owner–managers are paid a wage by the firm, and it might seem appropriate to say that the cost of the owner–manager to the firm is just the wage paid. But, for a variety of reasons including both tax and financing considerations, it is rare that the wages an owner–manager pays herself equals the "economic cost" her time represents. In principle, the correct economic cost of her time is the opportunity cost of her time; that is, what she could earn in her best alternative opportunity. This represents the economic cost of her time, because if the firm did not employ her in supervising and managing its operations, she could instead earn this amount of money and contribute it to the firm's income. But, while the principle is fairly clear, in practice it is often difficult and sometimes impossible to compute opportunity costs. And, whether easy, difficult, or impossible, firms rarely keep their books in this fashion.

The message is a double-edged caution. First, we simplify unrealistically when we assume we can easily associate a cost to every input. Second, the accounting that firms do will not always correspond precisely to the appropriate economic costs of different inputs; so that economic profits and accounting profits are different, for this reason and for more to come in the next two chapters.

Returns to Scale and Average Cost

Suppose a firm's technology has increasing returns to scale. Fix a level of output x and suppose that $(y_1^*, \ldots, y_n^*)$ is the vector of inputs that gives output x most cheaply, so that

$$\text{TC}(x) = r_1 y_1^* + \ldots + r_n y_n^*.$$

Suppose the firm wishes to increase its production to the level ax, for $a > 1$. Because the firm has increasing returns to scale, we know that the vector of inputs $(ay_1^*, \ldots, ay_n^*)$ produces at least output ax. Therefore, the cost of producing ax can be no more than

$$r_1 \times ay_1^* + \ldots + r_n \times ay_n^* = a \times [r_1 y_1^* + \ldots + r_n y_n^*] = a\text{TC}(x).$$

That is, if the firm has increasing returns to scale in its technology, then for all levels of output x and constants $a > 1$,

$$TC(ax) \leq aTC(x).$$

Take two levels of output, x and x', such that $x' > x$. Let $a = x'/x$, so that $a > 1$. Since $TC(x') = TC(ax) \leq aTC(x)$, if we divide both ends of this inequality by $x' = ax$, we get $AC(x') = TC(x')/x' \leq aTC(x)/(ax) = TC(x)/x = AC(x)$. Therefore, the average cost function is nonincreasing. Similar arguments work for decreasing and constant returns to scale:

- A firm with increasing returns to scale has a nonincreasing average cost function.

- A firm with decreasing returns to scale has a nondecreasing average cost function.

- A firm with constant returns to scale has a constant average cost function, thus a linear total cost function.

And what about the "typical" firm that, loosely speaking, has increasing returns to scale for low levels of output but decreasing returns to scale when output levels are large? This sort of pattern in technology implies a U- or bowl-shaped average cost function. Which is why bowl shapes for average cost functions are so popular in economic examples.

9.3. Allocating Production among Cost-Independent Production Processes

We are done with isoquants and production functions and about to start a new subject. This is a good place to break your reading of this chapter, if you need to do so.

Imagine a firm that produces a particular product. This firm has two facilities at which it can produce the product. At facility 1, producing x_1 units of the good costs $TC_1(x_1) = 10x_1 + x_1^2/1000$. At facility 2, producing x_2 units of the good costs $TC_2(x_2) = 9x_2 + 3x_2^2/2000$. The firm wishes to produce 15,000 units of the good in total, dividing that production quantity between the two facilities in a way that minimizes the sum of total costs at the two facilities. How should it proceed? What will be the minimized total cost?

This is a special case of a more general problem of allocating "production" among several cost-independent sources. In general, we imagine a firm that wishes to obtain x units of some good. A number of possible sources (say,

N of them) can be employed. The total cost to procuring x_n units from facility n is independent of the costs incurred using the other sources—this is the "cost-independent" part of the formulation—and is given by a total cost function $TC_n(x_n)$. The different sources could be different facilities or different technologies; one source might be direct purchase from another firm. The cost-minimization problem facing the firm is to

Minimize $TC_1(x_1) + TC_2(x_2) + \ldots + TC_N(x_N)$,

subject to $x_1 + x_2 + \ldots + x_N = x$ and $x_1 \geq 0, \ x_2 \geq 0, \ \ldots, \ x_N \geq 0$.

Solving this problem in full generality can be quite difficult—see Problem 9.16—so we make two simplifying assumptions: All the marginal cost functions corresponding to the N total cost functions are nondecreasing. And all the total cost functions are continuous; in particular, if any total cost function involves a fixed cost, this fixed cost cannot be avoided by producing no units at that facility.

A Different Problem

To solve this problem, shift attention to a different problem but one that, ultimately, is very closely connected. The setting is the same. A firm can source a product from any of N sources, each of which has a cost-independent total cost function. We write $MC_n(x_n)$ for the marginal cost function associated with source n. Then,

fix a level of marginal cost c. How many units can be obtained from source n, at a marginal cost of c or less? How many units can be obtained in total from the N sources, at a marginal cost of c or less?

We write $X_n^*(c)$ for the answer to the first question and $X^*(c)$ for the answer to the second question. Of course,

$$X^*(c) = X_1^*(c) + \ldots + X_N^*(c).$$

Answering these questions for our example indicates the technique. Corresponding to the two total cost functions in the example are the marginal cost functions $MC_1(x_1) = 10 + x_1/500$ and $MC_2(x_2) = 9 + 3x_2/1000$. Take facility 1 first. If $c < 10$, then we cannot source any units from facility 1 at a cost of c or less. But if $c \geq 10$, since marginal cost is rising, we produce all the units up to the last one that has this marginal cost. That is, we solve the equation

$$c = MC_1(x_1) = 10 + \frac{x_1}{500}, \quad \text{or} \quad x_1 = 500(c - 10), \quad \text{thus} \quad X_1^*(c) = 500(c - 10).$$

And, by the same logic,

$$X_2^*(c) = \begin{cases} 0, & \text{if } c < 9, \text{ and} \\ 1000(c-9)/3, & \text{if } c \geq 9. \end{cases}$$

Adding these two,

$$X^*(c) = \begin{cases} 0, & \text{for } c < 9, \\ 1000(c-9)/3, & \text{for } 9 \leq c < 10, \text{ and} \\ 1000(c-9)/3 + 500(c-10) = 833.333c - 8000, & \text{for } c \geq 10. \end{cases}$$

In general, $X_n^*(c)$ is the solution of $MC_n(x_n) = c$, with the proviso that, for costs c less than $MC_n(0)$, $X_n^*(c) = 0$. (Special cases are where marginal cost is constant for an interval of quantities, marginal cost jumps discontinuously, and for some values of c, marginal cost never rises as high as c. The most important of these special cases, where $MC_n(x_n)$ is constant for one source, in encountered in Problem 9.11.)

Graphs of This: $X^*(c)$ Is the Horizontal Sum of the Marginal Cost Functions

A key graphical insight comes next: The picture of $X_n^*(c)$ is (almost) precisely the picture of $MC_n(x_n)$, except that cost is the argument and quantity is the value of the function. And $X^*(c)$ is just the horizontal sum of the (inverse) marginal cost functions.

Let me explain. To find $X_n^*(c)$, you solve $MC_n(x_n) = c$. This means, in a picture, that you find c on the vertical (cost or price) axis; move horizontally until you hit the marginal cost function; then drop down. So regarding cost as the argument and quantity as the value of the function, the graph of X_n^* is the same as the graph of marginal cost. The parenthetical *almost* refers to costs c less than $MC_n(0)$; for these, $X_n^*(c) = 0$. And then, since $X^*(c) = X_1^*(c) + \ldots + X_N^*(c)$, X^* is indeed just the horizontal sum of these functions, much like summing demand functions. Figure 9.6 provides the picture.

Back to the Cost-Minimization Problem

We began this section asking for the cost-minimizing way for the firm with the two facilities to get 15,000 units in total. Let me first show you how to do it, and then explain why this is the answer.

Step 1 *Compute $X^*(c)$*. We already did this; the formula is displayed at the top of this page.

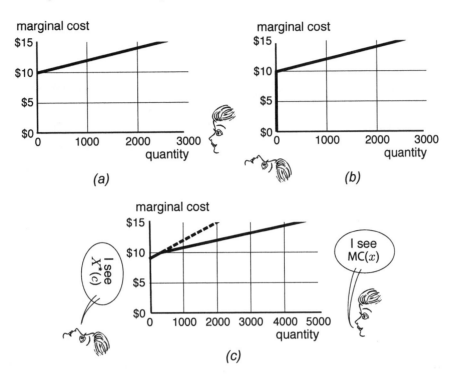

Figure 9.6. Finding the $X^*(c)$ and $MC(x)$ functions by horizontal summing. Panel a shows the marginal cost function for the first facility in the example. Think of c as the variable and quantity as the value and fill in 0 quantity for marginal costs less than $10, and you have $X_1^*(c)$, as in panel b. Sum X_1^* and X_2^* horizontally to derive X^*. Now go back to thinking of quantity as the variable and cost as the value: You are looking at the firm's overall marginal cost function.

Step 2 *Solve the equation $X^*(c) = x$ for c, using for x the desired quantity.* We want 15,000 units. The $X^*(c)$ function comes in two branches, and we do not know which branch will give us 15,000. But it is easy to find out. When $c = 10$, where we move from the $1000(c - 9)/3$ branch to the $833.333c - 8000$ branch, $X^*(10) = 333.33$. We need a much higher marginal cost to call forward 15,000 units. So we solve

$$833.333c - 8000 = 15,000, \quad \text{or} \quad c = \frac{23,000}{833.333} = \$27.60.$$

Step 3 *Use this value of c to read the answer from the X_n^* functions.* The answer is to source $X_1^*(27.6) = 500(27.6 - 10) = 8800$ units from facility 1 and $X_2^*(27.6) = 1000(27.6 - 9)/3 = 6200$ units from facility 2.

Why is this the answer? Under the assumptions we made—no unavoidable fixed costs and nondecreasing marginal costs from each source—the cheapest way to produce some number of units is to start with whatever source gives you the marginally cheapest units and keep adding from whatever source is cheapest on the margin, until you get to the quantity you want. The function $X^*(c)$ tells you how many units can be gotten at a marginal cost of c or less, so the only question is, What level of marginal cost would be reached, when we have the units we need? Since $X^*(27.6) = 15{,}000$ in the example, this means that, when marginal cost reaches \$27.60, the number of units with that marginal cost or less will total precisely 15,000. Those are the ones we want, and it remains only to source them by going source by source—facility by facility, in the example—and finding how many come from the first source, how many from the second, and so forth. In other words, we solve $X^*(c) = x$ for c, to find the cutoff level of marginal cost needed to get x units in total. And then, for each source, compute $X_n^*(c)$ to find how many come from source n.

The Inverse of $X^*(c)$ Is the Firm's Overall Marginal Cost Function

We receive a bonus here. Suppose we wanted to produce 15,001 units. What would be the marginal cost of the 15,001st unit? To get 15,000 units, we exhausted the supply of units that have marginal costs of \$27.60 or less. Every facility we use—and in the example, at this point both are actively producing—is ready to contribute its next unit at a cost of \$27.60. So the 15,001st unit will cost \$27.60 or, for the discrete margin, a tiny bit more.

But this means that, if $X^*(c) = x$, the marginal cost for the firm at x units, $MC(x)$, is c. Invert the function $X^*(c)$ and you have the firm's marginal cost function, assuming it sources its units in cost-minimizing fashion. Or, if you prefer the graphical version of this, the X^* function graphed in Figure 9.6(c), obtained by horizontally summing, is (almost) the firm's marginal cost function, where the parenthetical *almost* refers to the fact that, for the marginal cost function, quantity is the variable and cost is the value of the function.

For the example, we invert $X^*(c)$, and you know how this goes from inverting similar "in sections" demand functions back in Chapter 5: The cost ranges of the pieces are from \$9 to \$10 and \$10 and up, corresponding to quantity ranges 0 to 333.33 and 333.33 on up. The first segment is $X^*(c) = 1000(c-9)/3$, which, solving for c as a function of x, gives $c = 9 + 3x/1000$. The second segment is $X^*(c) = 833.333c - 8000$, which, solving for c as a function x, gives $c = (8000 + x)/833.33$. So, putting the pieces together, this firm's marginal cost function, assuming it allocates production between the two facilities in a cost-minimizing fashion, is

$$MC(x) = \begin{cases} 9 + 3x/1000, & \text{for } 0 \le x \le 333.333, \text{ and} \\ (8000 + x)/833.333, & \text{for } x \ge 333.333. \end{cases}$$

To find the firm's total cost function, integrate this marginal cost function and add any fixed cost. But this is rarely necessary. For most problems, the marginal cost function is what is needed. For instance, suppose I had asked you, *For this two-facility firm, how much should it produce at each facility, if it faces inverse demand function* $P(x) = 20 - x/3000$? Marginal revenue is $MR(x) = 20 - x/1500$, and the marginal cost function is as just given, so the answer is a very few steps away (see Problem 9.10).

The Rule

We have solved constrained maximization problems, of which this is certainly one, using various "rules" that have to hold at the solution. In case my somewhat indirect means for solving this problem obscures its rule, let me give the rule and a very quick justification. Remember, we assume that marginal cost functions at each facility are nondecreasing and that any fixed costs are unavoidable.

If $(x_1^*, x_2^*, \ldots, x_N^*)$ is the cost-minimizing way to produce x units in total, then it must be that

$$x_1^* + x_2^* + \ldots + x_N^* = x,$$

$MC_i(x_i^*) = MC_j(x_j^*)$ for i and j such that $x_i^* > 0$ and $x_j^* > 0$, and

$MC_i(x_i^*) = MC_i(0) \geq MC_j(x_j^*)$ for i and j such that $x_i^* = 0$ and $x_j^* > 0$.

Of course, the first equation is required; we must make x units in total. As for the second part of the rule, suppose the firm is using sources i and j— that is, both x_i^* and x_j^* are strictly positive—but their marginal costs are not equal. Suppose, in particular, that $MC_i(x_i^*) > MC_j(x_j^*)$. Then the firm can get a bit more from source j and a bit less from source i. If the amounts more and less are equal and equal to, say, δ, this means the total amount produced does not change. But the costs change: δ more from source j costs $MC_j(x_j^*)\delta$ more, while δ less from source i saves $MC_i(x_i^*)\delta$. The net impact on total cost is

$$MC_j(x_j^*)\delta - MC_i(x_i^*)\delta = \delta\left[MC_j(x_j^*) - MC_i(x_i^*)\right],$$

which, since $MC_i(x_i^*) > MC_j(x_j^*)$, is negative. Total cost is lower, showing that we were not cost-minimizing before.

Do not get lost in the symbols. The idea is simple. In fact, we explored this rule in Chapter 3, although in the context of revenue maximization rather than cost minimization. Since units trade off one for one in this problem—one more unit from source j offsets one fewer from source i—if the marginal costs are not equal, the firm should obtain more low-marginal-cost units and fewer with higher marginal cost. Of course, the equal marginal cost at every active source is the value of c that solves $X^*(c) = x$; that is, c is this "cut-off" marginal cost.

The only caveat to this occurs if some source is not being used. Its marginal cost, at 0 units of output, could be larger than the marginal costs at the sources being used, because we cannot decrease the number of units being obtained from a source where 0 is the current quantity. This is line 3 of the rule.

Final Comments

Our assumptions of no unavoidable fixed costs and nondecreasing marginal costs are a bit limiting. We cannot quite do without them without making a few somewhat complex changes in the rule and the procedures outlined. But, if you are interested in what has to be done, try Problem 9.16.

Meanwhile, do not dismiss this as merely technical. Behind these ideas, as you'll discover in Chapter 12, is one of the most important reasons for the triumph of free-market capitalism over communism.

9.4. Constrained Maximization: Pulling Threads Together

We have discussed four examples of constrained maximization: Chapter 3 presented the problem of allocating seats between Manteca and Wolverton supporters. Chapter 5 concerned the consumer's problem of maximizing utility subject to a budget constraint. This chapter concerned the firm's cost-minimization problem (minimize the cost of inputs, subject to a constraint on the level of output) and the problem of minimizing the total cost of producing a given amount of output, allocating production to different cost-independent facilities.

In each problem, an objective function is optimized, subject to a single constraint. The examples we've seen are:

- Maximize gate receipts, where the total number of seats to be divided between the supporters of the two teams is fixed.

- Maximize utility, where the consumer has a maximum amount she can spend.

- Minimize the cost of the inputs, while producing a given amount of output.

- Minimize the sum of total costs, while producing or procuring a given amount of output.

Each of these is a constrained optimization problem with a single constraint. You may someday encounter optimization problems with multiple constraints—you are virtually sure to do so if you take a course in linear programming—which complicates the situation.

For each problem, we use marginal analysis to find a rule or principle for finding the solution. You should carry away from these four examples the notion that, notwithstanding slight differences, the nature of the rule or principle is always the same:

> At the solution, the ratio of the marginal effect of a decision variable on the objective function to the marginal effect of this variable on the constraint must equal the same ratio for other decision variables.

Why? If these ratios are not equal, then by increasing one decision variable while decreasing another, we can continue to respect the constraint while improving the objective function. The reason the rule has the marginal impact of the variable on the constraint in the denominator of these ratios is so that, when we increase one and decrease the other, we do so in a ratio that keeps the constraint satisfied. With that sort of scaling of the increases and decreases, the marginal impact of the variable on the objective shows up in the numerator, because that is how we know that the net impact on the objective function is to improve the objective.

In these problems, we must qualify this general statement to deal with decision variables—amount of goods consumed, amount of inputs used, amount of output assigned to a particular source—up against nonnegativity constraints. Our argument about increasing one thing while decreasing another cannot be applied if the thing to be decreased is already at 0. But except for that qualification, the basic principle is as stated.

Why harass you with all this? Because, although the four specific applications are interesting, you should not miss the general principle and logic that cuts across them. If you understand the basic logic, then when you meet some other constrained optimization problem, you'll have a good start on thinking through how to solve it. You'll see at least two more examples before the book is done.

Executive Summary

- The technology of a two-input, one-output firm can be displayed graphically, with *isoquants*. Three important shapes correspond to technologies with no substitutions, fixed coefficients, and constant marginal rates of substitution. Greater flexibility cum substitutibility, corresponding to isoquants that bend less, naturally goes with a longer time horizon for organizing production.

- The technology of any one-output firm can be represented algebraically by a *production function*.

- Three ways to solve the firm's cost-minimization problem are

  1. Graphically, using isoquants and iso-cost lines.

  2. With a spreadsheet.

  3. With calculus, using the rule

  $$\frac{r_i}{\text{MPP}_i} = \frac{r_j}{\text{MPP}_j} \leq \frac{r_k}{\text{MPP}_k} \quad \text{for } y_i, y_j > 0, \; y_k = 0,$$

  where MPP_i is shorthand for $\partial f / \partial y_i$, input i's marginal physical product.

- Returns to scale concern assumptions about the production technology and, more specifically, how much output increases as input levels are increased proportionally. The "natural" pattern is increasing returns—reflecting technological efficiencies, the benefits of specialization, and amortization of fixed costs—up to some level and then decreasing returns as coordination and incentive inefficiencies take over.

- Constant returns to scale implies constant average (and marginal) cost, increasing returns to scale implies nonincreasing average cost, and decreasing returns to scale implies nondecreasing average cost. Thus, the "natural" pattern of returns to scale just described implies bowl-shaped average costs.

- To minimize the total cost when allocating production among several cost-independent sources, answer the question, For a given marginal cost c, how many units can be procured at the marginal cost c or less? In this problem, the marginal cost function for the entire enterprise is the horizontal sum of the marginal cost functions of the different sources.

- The four examples of constrained maximization that we have seen employ marginal analysis in the same way: The key is to think about ratios of the marginal impact of a decision variable on the objective function to the marginal impact of the variable on the constraint.

Problems

9.1 In the production of a particular type of chair, a firm uses both labor hours and lathe hours. To make the chair requires at least 2 labor hours and at least 1 lathe hour. Also, the total number of hours must be 6 in any combination. That is, 5 labor hours and 1 lathe hour suffice to produce a chair, as do 4 and 2, 3 and 3, and so on. But 5 lathe and 1 labor hour are insufficient, as it takes a minimum of 2 labor hours. The firm has a constant-returns-to-scale technology.

(a) What do the isoquants of the firm look like? Draw in isoquants for four chairs and then for six.

(b) Suppose labor costs $10 per hour and lathe time costs $15 per hour. What combination of inputs would the firm use to produce six chairs?

(c) With the same information as in part b, what do the firm's cost functions (total, average, and marginal) look like? Draw the total cost function on one graph and the average and marginal cost functions together on a second.

9.2 Imagine a firm with the following very simple technology for making wadgets. Each wadget requires precisely 1.5 units of sheet metal and some labor time. One wadget requires precisely 3 hours of labor, 2 wadgets require 4.5 hours, 3 wadgets require 5.5, 4 wadgets require 6 hours, 5 wadgets require 7 hours, 6 wadgets require 8.5 hours, 7 wadgets require 10.5 hours, 8 wadgets require 13 hours, 9 wadgets require 16 hours, and 10 wadgets require 19.5 hours. (For intermediate levels of wadget production, you may interpolate between these values if you wish.) In wadget production, sheet metal cannot be substituted for labor hours; if you wish to make 8 wadgets, you need 13 hours of labor and 12 units of sheet metal, with no exceptions.

(a) What does the isoquant diagram for this firm look like?

(b) Suppose the wage rate for labor is $10 per hour and the price of sheet metal is $2 per unit. What will be the cost of producing each integer level of wadgets, from 2 to 10?

(c) If each wadget can be sold for $30, how many wadgets should this firm produce (between 2 and 10, integer values only) to maximize its profits?

9.3 (a) A firm producing a single output from n inputs has the production function

$$f(y_1, \ldots, y_n) = \min\{g_1(y_1), \ g_2(y_2), \ \ldots, \ g_n(y_n)\},$$

where each function g_i is a strictly increasing function of one variable. Is this a no-substitutions, fixed-coefficients, or constant-marginal-rate-of-substitution technology?

(b) Answer question a, but for the production function

$$f(y_1, \ldots, y_n) = G\left(\min\left\{\frac{y_1}{a_1}, \ldots, \frac{y_n}{a_n}\right\}\right),$$

for positive constants a_1 through a_n and a strictly increasing function G.

(c) Answer question a, but for the production function

$$f(y_1, \ldots, y_n) = G\left(\frac{y_1}{a_1} + \ldots + \frac{y_n}{a_n}\right).$$

9.4   One way to specify a no-substitutions technology is to give, for each level of output x, the minimum amount of each input needed to produce x units of output. That is, if there are n inputs, we specify the technology with n functions $y_1(x)$, $y_2(x)$, $\ldots$, $y_n(x)$, where $y_i(x)$ is the amount of input i needed to make x units of output. Naturally, we assume that each of these functions is nondecreasing.

(a) Problem 9.2 gives an example of this. There are two inputs, sheet metal and labor. Index these with 1 and 2, respectively (so that $y_2(4)$ will be the amount of labor hours needed to produce 4 wadgets). What is $y_1(10)$? What is the function $y_1(x)$? What is $y_2(10)$?

(b) In general, with n inputs and input-requirement functions $y_i(x)$ for $i = 1, \ldots, n$, suppose input prices are r_1 through r_n. What is TC(x) for this firm?

(c) What is the connection between this problem and Problem 9.3?

9.5   Figure 9.7 shows the 100-unit isoquant of a firm that makes a single product, utemkos, out of labor and materials. This isoquant comes from the production function

$$f(l, m) = l^{1/2}m^{1/2}.$$

(The isoquant is as exact as I could make it, exact enough for this problem, but it probably is not perfectly matched with this production function.) The production technology that goes with this production function has constant

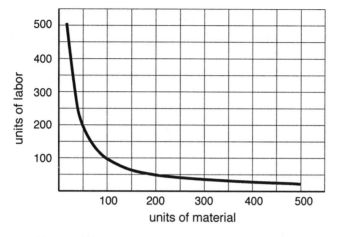

Figure 9.7. Problem 9.5: The 100-unit isoquant.

returns to scale. The price of materials is $1 per unit. The price of labor is $4 per unit.

(a) First using the graph of the 100-unit isoquant, then using a spreadsheet, and finally using the production function algebraically, find the value of TC(100).

(b) Suppose the firm faces an inverse demand curve of the form $P(x) = 12 - (x/2000)$, where x is the number of utemkos produced and sold and $P(x)$ is their price. What price will the firm charge to maximize its profits and how many units will it make? (Hint: If you chose to work graphically in part a, you can still answer this question, if you use the fact that this production technology has constant returns to scale.)

9.6 A firm makes a patented product, called xillip, out of two inputs, raw material and labor. Letting x stand for the amount of xillip produced, m be the amount of raw material, and l the amount of labor input, the firm's production function is given by $x = m^{1/3}l^{1/6}$. In addition, the firm must have a license to produce xillip, which costs it $300 per production period, regardless of how much xillip it produces. The price of a unit of raw material is $1, and the price of a unit of labor is $4. The (inverse) demand function for xillip is $P = 160 - 2x$. Find the profit-maximizing production plan for this firm in two steps. First, find the total cost function for this firm. Then, find the profit-maximizing production level by equating marginal cost to marginal revenue.

9.7 Recall the example from the text in which the firm's production function was $f(k, l, m) = k^{1/2}l^{1/8}m^{1/4}$. Does this firm have increasing, decreasing, or constant returns to scale? (It is one of these.) What about the production function of Problem 9.5. (I told you that this was a constant-returns-to-scale production function; now I ask you to verify this.) Suppose another firm had production function $f(k, m) = k^{1/2}m^{2/3}$. Does this firm have increasing, decreasing, or constant returns to scale? What is the general rule at work here?

9.8 Look at the isoquant diagram in Figure 9.8. In this figure, I give you the ten-unit isoquant only.

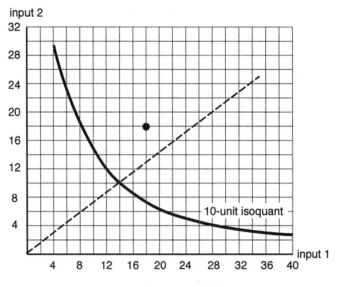

Figure 9.8. Problem 9.8: An isoquant diagram.

(a) Suppose I told you this firm has constant returns to scale. Where would the 20-unit isoquant pass through the dashed line shown? Mark the appropriate point on the graph with an X.

(b) Suppose I told you that the firm has decreasing returns to scale. On which of the following isoquants might the heavy dot lie: the 12-unit isoquant, the 14-unit isoquant, the 16-unit isoquant, the 18-unit isoquant? More than one of these might be correct—note that I ask you for isoquant(s) on which the dot *might* lie.

9.9 Figure 9.9 illustrates the 10-unit isoquant for a firm that produces rewps. The two inputs are labor and raw material. Labor costs $10 per unit, and raw material costs $2 per unit.

(a) What is the cost to the firm of producing 10 rewps as cheaply as it can?

(b) Suppose you know that this firm has decreasing returns to scale. Finish the following sentence by choosing one of the three italicized choices and

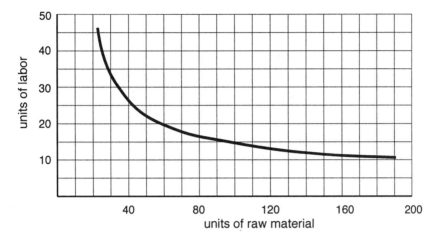

Figure 9.9. Problem 9.9: The 10-unit isoquant.

filling in the blank:

The total cost of producing 15 rewps is $\begin{cases} no\ more\ than \\ exactly \\ no\ less\ than \end{cases}$ _____ .

9.10 Finish the problem posed on page 225: For this two-facility firm, how much should it produce at each facility, if it faces inverse demand function $P(x) = 20 - x/3000$?

9.11 Consider a one-product firm that has access to three sources for its output. If x_1 units are produced by the first source, the total cost is $TC_1(x_1) = x_1^2/1000 + 4x_1$. If x_2 units are produced by the second source, the total cost is $TC(x_2) = 3x_2^2/1000 + x_2$. The third source is direct purchase from another firm at a price of $6 apiece. The firm can produce its output using any mix of the three sources it chooses. Suppose the firm faces demand curve $D(p) = 400(16 - p)$. What level of production maximizes its profits, and how should that level of production be divided among the three technologies?

9.12 A firm that makes a particular bulk chemical can use either of two processes. The first involves hydration and then distillation. The second involves a completely separate catalytic process. The inputs to the process are the raw materials (a different bulk chemical purchased at $1 per kilogram), labor time to run the processes, and time using the capital equipment. Specifically, to process a kilogram of raw materials in the hydration–distillation process requires 0.03 labor hours at $20 per hour, and to process a kilogram in the catalytic process requires 0.09 labor hours at the same wage rate. Suppose this firm can vary the amount of raw materials it purchases and the amount of labor hours it hires, but it cannot change the capacity it has for the two processes. It can run the hydration–distillation process at up to a level of 1000 kilograms of input per hour and the catalytic process at up to 500 kilograms of input per hour. For every kilogram of input to the hydration–distillation process, the firm gets out 0.4 kilograms of final output. For every kilogram of input to the catalysis process, the firm gets out 0.5 kilograms of final output.

What is the total cost function of this firm? Ignore the fixed costs of the machinery.

9.13 Consider the production process described in Problem 9.12. Draw the 200, 300, and 500 kilogram per hour isoquants (for the inputs of labor and raw materials).

9.14 (If you know linear programming, you might find it helpful to try to solve this problem by formulating the cost-minimization problem as a linear programming problem.) Suppose that we complicate Problem 9.12 as follows. We imagine that the firm cannot reduce its labor bill below 18 billed labor hours per hour of operation. It can, however, add to its labor bill (at $20 per labor hour) up to a level of 60 labor hours used per hour of operation. Beyond 60 labor hours per hour of operation, the firm must pay $30 per labor hour. What is the total cost function of this firm? Again ignore the fixed costs of machinery.

The final two problems are only for readers who know calculus and who have a taste for abstraction.

9.15 (a) Suppose a firm faces inverse demand function $P(x)$. Let $TR(x)$ be the corresponding total revenue function, and let $MR(x)$ be the marginal revenue function. Suppose as well that the firm has production function $f(y_1, y_2, y_3)$ for three inputs, whose prices (which the firm treats as given constants) are r_1, r_2, and r_3. We can formulate the firm's full profit-maximization problem without using the variable x as

$$\text{maximize } TR(f(y_1, y_2, y_3)) - [r_1 y_1 + r_2 y_2 + r_3 y_3]$$

subject to constraints that the levels of the three inputs are nonnegative. Characterize the profit-maximizing choice of inputs in terms of the functions $MR(\cdot)$ and $MPP_i(\cdot)$.

(b) Use whatever rule you come up with in part a to re-solve part b of Problem 9.5.

(c) Suppose that the firm is not a price taker in the markets for its inputs. Specifically, suppose that the price it pays for input i is $r_i(y_i)$, a function only of the amount of input i the firm uses. (Things get more complex if r_i is a function of y_1, y_2, and y_3.) Redo part a for this case.

9.16 In the text, the discussion of allocating production to independent-cost production facilities assumed that the total cost function of each facility has rising marginal cost and, if it has a fixed cost, the fixed cost is unavoidable. This problem addresses what happens if we drop those assumptions.

Suppose production facility i within an organization has total cost function $TC_i(x_i)$, where x_i is the amount of output produced by the facility. (Assume that total cost at facility i depends on x_i alone.) Suppose the firm announces to the manager of facility i that his facility's "contribution to firm activity" will be $qx_i - TC_i(x_i)$, where q is some transfer price for output that the central management announces and imposes on all facilities. (The facilities treat q as a given; they do not take into account their influence on the final value of q.) Corporate headquarters asks the manager of facility i to report back what quantity he would "optimally" supply as a function of q. In other words, it asks the manager of the facility to solve, for each value of q, the problem of maximizing $qx_i - TC_i(x_i)$, subject to the constraint that $x_i \geq 0$. Call the *set* of solutions to this problem, as a function of q, the set $X_i^*(q)$. Note that there might be multiple solutions to this problem at a given value of q for general total cost functions.

(a) Suppose for the moment that the total cost function of facility i, $TC_i(x_i)$, has rising marginal costs and, if it has any fixed cost at all, an unavoidable fixed cost. (You can assume as well that MC_i is a continuous function, although if you are trying this problem, you are probably capable of dealing with the case where TC_i has kinks, so MC_i "jumps.") Show that, for each value of q, the set $X_i^*(q)$ consists of a single number, which is 0 if $q \leq MC_i(0)$ and is otherwise the unique solution to the equation $q = MC_i(x)$.

(b) Suppose that the total cost function of facility i has rising marginal cost and a strictly positive fixed cost that can be avoided entirely if the facility chooses to produce no output. Let $AC_i(x_i)$ be the average cost function for facility i. We know from Chapter 8 that AC_i is bowl shaped. Let x_i^* be the efficient scale for facility i, and let q_i^* be the minimum average cost of facility i; that is, $q_i^* = AC_i(x_i^*)$. Show that the set $X_i^*(q)$ is given by $\{0\}$ for $q < q_i^*$, the unique solution to the equation $q = MC_i(x)$ for $q > q_i^*$, and

$\{0, x_i^*\}$ for $q = q_i^*$.

(c) Now return to the case of an arbitrary total cost function for facility i. Show that the sets $X_i^*(q)$ are "increasing" in q in the following sense: If $q' > q$, $x' \in X^*(q')$, and $x \in X^*(q)$, then $x' \geq x$.

(d) Suppose the firm has n facilities. Corporate headquarters collects from each facility i the facility's "answer" $X_i^*(q)$ for each value of q. Suppose the firm wishes to produce a total of X units of output and to divide this total among the n facilities in a cost-minimizing manner. It asks, Is there some transfer price q, and values $x_1, \ldots, x_n$, such that each $x_i \in X_i^*(q)$ and $x_1 + \ldots + x_n = X$? In words, is there some transfer price such that, if this transfer price is announced, the facility managers, on their own, maximizing for their own facilities, would be happy to produce in a manner that gives the corporation X units in total? If the answer is Yes, this is a solution to the product-allocation, cost-minimization problem.

(e) What does this have to do with the "horizontal summing" technique discussed in this chapter?

10. Multiperiod Production and Cost

Quality is free. Philip Crosby
There are no free lunches. Milton Friedman

This chapter concerns three aspects of multiperiod production:

1. Changing production plans can raise costs in the short run.
2. Some factors of production are long-lived capital assets. In theory, these are easy to deal with, but practice is harder. Accounting practices for dealing with durable assets—depreciation and the like—need a lot of explanation.
3. Actions taken today affect capabilities tomorrow.

In the early 1980s, one of the biggest fads in management was the experience curve, the notion that unit costs of production fall with experience. Management gurus and consultants preached that the winning strategy in industries with several firms was to accumulate production volume faster than one's rivals, to gain an ultimate cost advantage. In the early 1990s, Total Quality Management (TQM) was the fad of the day. The idea here is captured succinctly if a bit too simply by Philip Crosby's dictum that quality is free: A firm could improve its quality at no cost or even lower its unit costs by raising its quality.

Experience-curve strategies and TQM are a lot more than fads. They contain powerful and important ideas. But often they were used faddishly; adopted by managements that did not understand them, with predictably disastrous results. To be used wisely, they must be understood.

Both the experience curve and TQM concern the cost structure of a firm, and so, in an economics textbook, understanding them ought to begin with economic models of cost, the subject of Chapter 9. But, if you juxtapose the experience curve or TQM with concepts like total cost or production functions or isoquants, *as defined in Chapter 9*, there appears to be no connection. Why? Because, in Chapter 9, the firm's technological capabilities are static. The firm has certain technological capabilities and exists in a market environment with given factor costs and facing a given demand curve; it makes input and output decisions to maximize its immediate profit. The experience curve and TQM concern dynamic production effects, where production decisions taken today affect the firm's technological capabilities tomorrow.

The experience curve and TQM, while important, are only a part of the story of dynamic production. In this chapter, we discuss three general categories of dynamic production phenomena:

1. Today's production routines constrain, at least for a while, what the firm can do tomorrow. It can repeat what it is doing today fairly easily, but *changing* a production technique or level may temporarily raise the costs of production; in a word, changing production routines may engender *friction*.

2. Some inputs are durable. The list of *durable inputs* begins with physical capital, such as metal lathes and oil refineries, but goes on to include harder to measure assets such as the firm's human capital, and even extends to such intangibles as its reputation and relationship with suppliers.

3. Perhaps the least tangible productive asset is *know-how* or technology itself. Production decisions taken today can affect the firm's technological capabilities tomorrow. The firm can engage in direct R&D concerning its products and processes and it can learn by doing, which is what the experience curve and TQM are ultimately all about.

The dividing lines between *friction*, *durable productive assets*, and *know-how* are fuzzy: Friction can result from the inability, at least in short run, to procure or redeploy durable factors of production. Know-how is often embodied in the human capital assets of the firm. Still, when modeling dynamic production, these three categories are treated somewhat distinctively and so provide the structure of this chapter.

Dynamic production is a very complex, important subject. This is where basic microeconomics meets courses in Corporate Finance, Managerial Accounting, Production/Operations Management, and Human Resources. We cannot do justice in one chapter to all the nuances of those subjects. But we can—and I hope we will—begin to make connections, so when you study those subjects, you'll see the connections among them and with the economic notions of production and cost.

10.1. Profits Today, Tomorrow, and Next Year

Before getting to the different categories of dynamic effects, we first must confront the firm's basic objective: profit maximization.

In a single-period story, profit is revenue minus (economic) cost. This is clearly defined and one-dimensional; we know what constitutes greater profit. But, with multiperiod production, decisions can be taken that raise net cash flow—gross receipts less gross expenditures—tomorrow, or next year, or 5 years from now, but mean lower net cash flow today. Is $5 more in

5 years "worth" $1 less in this year's cash flow? Is it worth $4 less this year? How do we model the resulting trade-offs?

The standard model in economics assumes that, in place of profit maximization, the firm chooses among alternative streams of cash flows to maximize the market value of its net cash flows; that is, the amount of money that would be paid in the market to own the net cash flows. Moreover, and based on the theory of financial markets, the market value of a firm's stream of net cash flows is the sum of present values of those net cash flows, discounted at rates derived from the market price of debt. (I assume you know about discounted present values. If this is new to you, please consult a textbook on corporate finance.) So, in the spirit of the earlier assumption that the firm maximizes its profit in a single-period setting, in multiperiod settings, we assume that the firm makes choices with the objective of maximizing the present value of its stream of net cash flows.

10.2. Friction

Suppose that the Boeing Corporation currently produces 747s at a rate of three per month, at a monthly cost of $60 million per month. We want to know, What will it cost Boeing per month to increase the rate of its production to, say, six per month?

If you asked this question of Boeing engineers and production specialists, they probably would respond, "It depends." One thing that it depends on is, How soon does the change have to be made? It is a lot more expensive per month for Boeing to move to a production rate of six next month than to move to this production rate in 6 or 12 months. Indeed, it may be impossible for Boeing to double its rate of production in a single month.

(Engineers at Boeing would tell you as well that Boeing's production technology has a strong experience-curve effect. I ignore this for now; an explanation will be offered in the final section of this chapter.)

Think back to the terminology and symbols of the last chapter, where we deal with the firm's total cost function $TC(x)$. If we talk about the total cost per month of producing 747s and x is the rate of production of 747s per month, the data in the first paragraph of this section would seem to say that $TC(3) = \$60$ million. The point of the second paragraph is that if we ask, What is $TC(6)$? there is no simple answer. In particular, the value of $TC(6)$ might be infinite if we want to know the monthly cost for next month, and it is impossible to double production rates within a month. In general, $TC(6)$ has different values depending on whether we mean, in 3 months, 6, or 12.

Therefore the total cost (per month) of producing six 747s per month is not entirely well defined. It depends on how long we give Boeing to get to that level of production, as well as where Boeing is in terms of its production routines at the outset.

Economists, trying to model this complex situation, speak in terms of short-run, long-run, and sometimes intermediate-run production changes. They imagine a firm that has been producing at a given rate—called the *status quo*—for quite a while, then talk in terms of the short-run total cost of different production levels, perhaps the intermediate-run total cost function, and the long-run total cost function. Letting x_0 denote the status quo level of production, SRTC$(x; x_0)$ means the total cost of producing at the rate x *in the short run*, starting from x_0 as the status quo, and LRTC(x) means the total cost of producing at the rate x in the long run.

- How long are the short run, the long run, and—if there is one—the intermediate run? There are no pat answers to these questions; they depend on the context.

- While we wrote SRTC$(x; x_0)$, indicating that the short-run total cost of producing at the rate x depends on x_0, the status quo level of production, we wrote LRTC(x) for the long-run total cost, without indicating any dependence on x_0. The long run, however long it is, is supposed to be long enough that the old status-quo level of production has no impact on costs incurred producing, in the long run, at level x.

The Typical Relationship between
Short- and Long-Run Total Costs

In economic models of friction and different runs, the following two assumptions are typically made:

1. For every status-quo level of production x_0 and new level x, the short-run total cost of producing x is at least as high as the long-run cost of x. Or, in symbols,

$$\text{for all } x, \text{LRTC}(x) \leq \text{SRTC}(x; x_0). \tag{10.1}$$

2. The short-run total cost of producing the status-quo level x_0 is the same as the long-run cost of producing this level. Or, in symbols,

$$\text{LRTC}(x_0) = \text{SRTC}(x_0; x_0). \tag{10.2}$$

The rationale for these assumptions is simple: Anything the firm can do to achieve production level x in the short run it can do in the long run but not necessarily vice versa. Hence the firm, seeking to minimize its total cost, will do no worse in the long run than in the short, and it may do better. This gives inequality (10.1). But if the firm does not change its rate of production—if it continues to produce x_0—then there is nothing to change, and it will do just as well in the short run as in the long run, which gives (10.2).

These are assumptions, not laws of nature. They might fail. For instance, some firms can, in the short run of a few weeks or months, increase labor utilization by putting current workers on overtime. But, in the longer run, the existing workforce would be unable to sustain the overtime efforts, and new workers must be hired, trained, paid benefits, and all the rest. Insofar as overtime for old, experienced workers is cheaper than training and benefits for new workers, short-run increases in output obtained by increasing labor input may be less costly than long-run, permanent increases. In a similar vein, suppliers may be willing on a short-run basis to increase or decrease supply of components at the current price, but longer-run changes may call for renegotiation of the price, which could leave the firm worse off than at current prices.

The rationale for (10.2) supposes that the firm, at the status-quo level of production, produces that level as cheaply as possible. But, for some questions we might study, this may not be true. For instance, consider the example of Boeing and suppose that the status quo is $x_0 = 3$; that is, Boeing has been making three 747s per month. Suppose we are interested in the question, What would Boeing do, if its costs of skilled labor suddenly increased dramatically? We can imagine that Boeing has selected the optimal mix of skilled labor and, say, robots, at the old wage rates, for the status quo production rate $x_0 = 3$. But when wage rates rise dramatically, *even if Boeing chooses to stay at the production rate $x_0 = 3$*, the company would want to make some changes. In particular, it would probably substitute some robots for the suddenly more expensive skilled labor. If, in the long run, Boeing could do more substituting than in the short—for instance, because Boeing cannot obtain many robots in the short run—then, even at the status-quo production rate, Boeing's total cost of producing three 747s per month in the short run exceeds its total cost of producing three 747s in the long run.

To tell whether, in a particular context, assumptions (10.1) and (10.2) are valid, we must go into greater detail about what the firm is doing, the length of the short-run time frame, the constraints the firm faces in the short run that it may not face in the longer run, and so forth. A few examples of more detailed stories—some leading to satisfaction of (10.1) and (10.2) and some not—are presented in the problems at the end of the chapter.

Rather than debate the validity of (10.1) and (10.2) here, we examine their implications. To begin, their consequences for short-run and long-run total cost functions are captured in Figure 10.1. Assuming rising total costs, we have short-run total costs above long-run total costs except at the status-quo point, where the two touch. Assuming both functions are smooth (no kinks), they must be tangent to one another at the status-quo point.

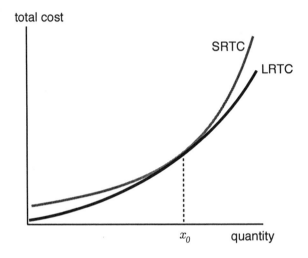

Figure 10.1. Long-run and short-run total cost, given the two assumptions. Assuming short-run total cost is at least as large as long-run total cost at all production levels and they are equal at the status-quo level of production x_0, we get the picture shown here. Note that SRTC and LRTC are tangent at the status-quo level of production.

Short-Run and Long-Run Average Cost

Figure 10.1 immediately gives us Figure 10.2, for the short-run and long-run *average* costs. Short-run average cost is always above long-run average cost, with the two touching at the status quo and tangent to one another there (if cost functions are smooth). This is a simple consequence of Figure 10.1:

$$\text{LRAC}(x) = \frac{\text{LRTC}(x)}{x} \quad \text{and} \quad \text{SRAC}(x) = \frac{\text{SRTC}(x)}{x},$$

and so short-run average cost exceeds long-run average cost wherever short-run total cost exceeds long-run total cost, and the first pair is equal precisely where the second pair is equal.

Short-Run and Long-Run Marginal Cost

Now for the part that sometimes causes difficulty. Assume both total cost functions are smooth. Then, if the two assumptions hold, the short-run and long-run marginal costs are equal at the status quo and short-run marginal

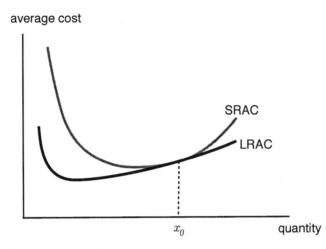

Figure 10.2. *Long-run and short-run average cost, given the two assumptions.* If the two assumptions hold, and therefore long-run and short-run total costs appear as in Figure 10.1, long-run and short-run average costs appear as in this figure.

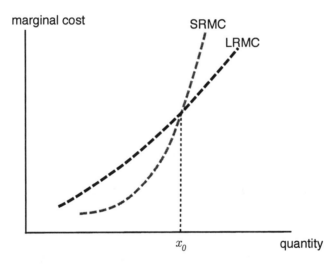

Figure 10.3. *Long-run and short-run marginal cost.* SRMC equals LRMC at the status-quo level of production, reflecting the tangency of long- and short-run total costs at that level. SRMC exceeds LRMC for increases from the status quo and is less than LRMC for decreases from the status quo.

cost is steeper than long-run marginal cost, at least for small changes in output level from the status quo. The picture is Figure 10.3.

The first part—equality of the short- and long-run marginal costs at the status-quo level of production—simply restates that the two total cost functions are tangent at the status quo. For quantities greater than the status-quo level, SRMC exceeds LRMC: short-run total costs rise more quickly for additions from the status quo than do long-run total costs, and the X-run marginal cost tells us how much X-run total costs must rise with each additional unit.

As for quantities less than the status-quo level, the X-run marginal cost tells us how much X-run total costs fall as the number of units declines. Short-run total costs exceed long-run total costs, so short-run total costs fall less than long-run total costs. Therefore, short-run marginal costs are less than long-run marginal costs for quantities less than the status quo.

This last part can be very hard to grasp. The key to understanding it is to keep reminding yourself that marginal cost measures the rate of *change* in total cost. And moving from the status quo, long-run cost increases *less* than short-run cost if production levels are increased, and long-run cost falls *more* than short-run cost if production levels are decreased. Keep that firmly in mind and you'll get it.

Putting All Three Figures Together

Look at Figure 10.4. It looks gruesome, but it is simply a recapitulation of Figures 10.1, 10.2, and 10.3. The two total cost functions are graphed in panel a, reproduced from Figure 10.1. Three output levels are indicated: the status quo x_0 as before, and two levels labeled LRES and SRES in panel b. These stand for the long- and short-run efficient scales, respectively, the levels where long-run and short-run average costs are minimized.

In panel b, the two average- and marginal-cost functions are graphed together. Note: (1) LRAC = SRAC and LRMC = SRMC at the status-quo level of production, (2) LRAC = LRMC at the long-run efficient scale (LRES in the figure); and (3) SRAC = SRMC at the short-run efficient scale (SRES).

Reacting to a Shift in Demand and Marginal Revenue

To put this model of friction to use, imagine a firm whose long-run profit-maximizing price and quantity, for a given demand function, are p_0 and x_0, respectively. Suddenly, the demand function facing this firm shifts inward, causing marginal revenue to shift inward as well. How does the firm react, in the short run and in the long run? Follow along on Figure 10.5.

Assume that the firm, in the short run, chooses production level x_{SR} that maximizes short-run profit, which equals revenue less short-run total cost; and in the long run, it chooses the production level x_1 that maximizes long-run profit, which equals revenue less long-run total cost.

If we make this assumption, the firm equates short-run marginal cost and marginal revenue in the short run, and it equates long-run marginal cost and marginal revenue in the long run. Since short-run marginal cost is steeper than long-run marginal cost, the firm produces more in the short run than in the long run; that is, $x_{SR} \geq x_1$. Therefore prices are lower in the short run than in the long run; prices rebound after a big fall. Nothing is profound

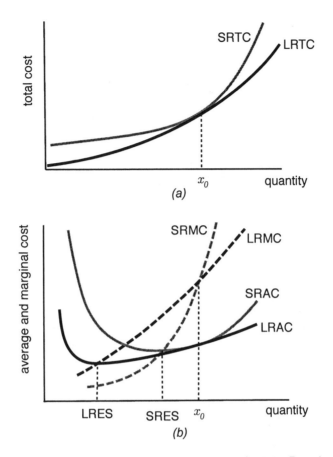

Figure 10.4. Putting together Figures 10.1, 10.2, and 10.3. Panel a replicates Figure 10.1, showing the long- and short-run total cost functions under the two assumptions. Panel b superimposes on a single graph the long- and short-run average and marginal cost functions. Note the production levels LRES and SRES, the long- and short-run efficient scales.

here: The firm, in maximizing its profit given the friction it faces gradually shifts its production quantity downward. The price falls dramatically at first, but rebounds as the firm continues to lower its production quantity in response to the fall in the demand.

Should the Firm Act as We Assume?

We assume in this story that the firm maximizes short-run profit in the short run and long-run profit in the long run. This deserves some commentary. Suppose, for example, that the short run is a month and the long run is half a year. Suppose as well that what differentiates the short run from the long run is an inability, in the short run, to add or discharge workers from the workforce. Suppose finally that the shift in demand is itself temporary, forecast to last 8 months or so.

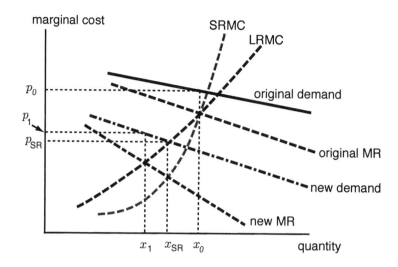

Figure 10.5. Reacting to a downward shift in demand and marginal revenue. At the original demand and marginal revenue, the firm produces x_0 and charges p_0. The demand and accompanying marginal revenue functions suddenly shift inward. In the short run, the firm cuts production back to x_{SR}, charging p_{SR}. In the long run, it cuts quantity still further, to x_1; the price rebounds to p_1.

In this context, we assume that, in the first month or so (in the short run), the firm shifts its production quantity somewhat, cutting back on the amounts of materials used to obtain a lessened output. As the months pass, the firm also discharges workers, so that, after 6 months (in the long run), it has a smaller workforce and is producing even less. Two more months pass, demand picks up, and the firm ramps up its production quantity, a little bit at first, and then more and more, as it is able to add workers back to the payroll.

Is this sensible? If the firm could forecast that the decrease in demand is temporary, it might decide—to maximize the discounted sum of its monthly cash flows—not to discharge workers at all but instead to ride out the lessened demand, making short-run adjustments only. The assumption that the firm, in chasing a shift in demand, shifts its labor force makes sense if the shift in demand is expected to persist long enough so that the establishment of a new status-quo point would not have to be undone too quickly. In essence, in our model of short- and long-run adjustments from the status quo, the firm's environment is relatively stable, so the firm reaches the long-run cost-minimizing production plan at the status quo, then shifts suddenly and unexpectedly, and is expected to remain constant for a substantial period of time. To the extent that shifts in the environment are temporary, predictable, or gradual, it takes a lot more analysis to figure out what short-term and longer-term actions are in the best interests of the firm.

A New Status Quo

To finish the story of adjusting to a change in demand, as time passes and the firm shifts in the long run to x_1, this establishes a new status-quo point, which gives a new set of short-run cost curves. To reiterate from before, for every status-quo level, we have a different set of short-run cost curves. The long-run cost curves, on the other hand, do not change with changes in the status quo, unless there is a very long run to worry about. A typical picture is Figure 10.6, where in panel a we have total cost functions and in panel b, the average and marginal cost functions, each for the long run and two short runs, for two different status-quo points.

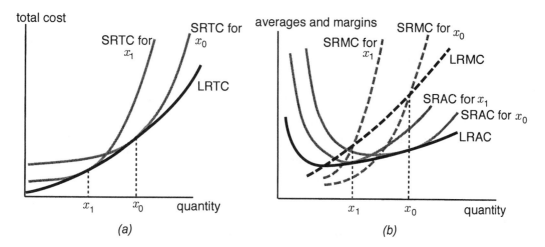

Figure 10.6. *Long- and short-run cost curves for more than one status-quo point.* For different status-quo levels of production x_0 and x_1, we have different short-run cost functions.

The Intermediate Run

Next chapter, we use the model of friction and short- and long-run responses to changes in the firm's environment, which we created here, in a context where many firms interact. When we do this, we sometimes add an intermediate-run response to the story. The intermediate run (IR) is just that, intermediate between the short run (SR) and the long run (LR), with all the intermediate-run cost functions fitting between the short- and long-run cost functions. In particular, intermediate-run marginal costs lie between short-run and long-run marginal costs: All three meet at the status-quo level of output: otherwise, the short-run marginal cost function is the steepest, and the long-run marginal cost function is the flattest. Figure 10.7 gives the picture.

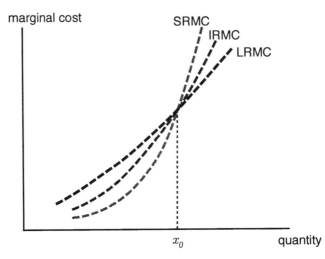

Figure 10.7. LR, IR, and SR marginal costs. If we add an intermediate run to the story and extend the two assumptions in the obvious manner, we get this picture for long-, intermediate-, and short-run marginal cost functions.

Kinks in Total Cost, Giving Discontinuous Marginal Costs

We assume in the model that the total cost functions are smooth or differentiable at the status-quo level of production. But imagine a firm that cannot freely vary its labor supply in the short run. It can add workers by paying them overtime—overtime that is more expensive than regular time, even taking into account benefits and the like—and it can lay off workers but must pay severance pay for a while. If you chase this model down— Problems 10.3 and 10.4 give you that opportunity—you'll discover that the corresponding short-run total cost function may be kinked at the status-quo level of production. This means a discontinuous short-run marginal cost function, and it may give some interesting short-run responses to shifts in demand and so forth.

10.3. Durable Assets

We turn now to the second sort of multiperiod effect in production: durable assets. This change in topic is accompanied by a change in style; we eschew functions and pictures for chat.

The Range of Durable Assets

The range of a firm's durable assets is huge. Obviously included here are real assets, such as buildings and land; large fixed assets such as blast furnaces, stamping machines, and assembly lines; and more temporary equipment, such as jigs, fixtures, and tools. But the list of durable assets contains a lot more than these obvious items. It includes:

- Human capital, or the stock of skills, training, and so on held by the firm's workforce.

- Goodwill, including the goodwill of suppliers, employees, union officials if the workforce is unionized, government officials, and so on.

- Demand-side assets, such as a strong reputation with a customer base built up from years of high-quality production and service or from a strong advertising campaign.

The firm doesn't hold legal title to its workers' human capital but often effectively controls it.[1] And while goodwill and reputation are largely intangible, they can be very valuable and powerful, as we discuss in Chapter 24.

Including Durable Assets in Economic Models

The whole point of durable assets is that they are useful for more than one production period. Money is spent today, to purchase the asset, and "value" from it accrues in later periods. Moreover, assets—whether physical or less tangible—can depreciate as time passes, at a rate that is usually somewhat, and sometimes mainly, under the control of the firm. So expenditures on maintaining or enhancing assets today—paying to keep the tools in good repair, to enhance a machine's performance, or to maintain a firm's reputation for producing high-quality goods—subtract from today's cash flows but add to tomorrow's. Depreciation here does not mean accounting depreciation but rather real depreciation, a temporal change in the asset's ability to contribute to the production process. Physical assets tend to *de*preciate in this sense, while intangible assets, such as human capital and customer goodwill can and often do *ap*preciate.

In theory, durable assets are easily dealt with. In a multiperiod setting, rather than speak of the profit of a firm, we work with the stream of net cash flows. We assume that the firm chooses its production plans, including which assets to invest in and how to maintain them, to maximize the sum of appropriately discounted net cash flows.

Therefore, the decision whether to purchase a particular blast furnace—or invest in worker training or customer goodwill—amounts to a present-value calculation: The blast furnace involves an immediate expenditure but provides increased revenues or decreased production cost, hence increased net cash flows, in future years. The blast furnace is purchased if the purchase decision increases the overall net present value (NPV) of the firm's stream of cash flows.

---

[1] See J. Baron and D. Kreps, *Strategic Human Resources* (New York: Wiley and Sons, 1999), Chapter 4.

As many readers know from experience, firms sometimes employ other techniques, such as internal rates of return or payback periods, to evaluate whether to employ a particular durable asset. I leave it to finance textbooks to explain why NPV calculations are superior.

As many readers also know and the rest can guess, the less tangible is a durable asset, the harder it is in practice to do these calculations. What would be the impact on the future cash flows of an investment in the goodwill of suppliers? What would be the impact of an investment in training workers or putting up a gym where they can play basketball at lunchtime? To reiterate, durable assets are easy to deal with *in theory*. In practice, the NPV prescription can be hard to fill, and managers have to rely on their instincts about what would or would not add value to the enterprise.

Accounting Depreciation and the Construction of Income Statements

Suppose durable assets could be evaluated in this fashion in practice. Compare the notion of computing the NPV of the stream of cash flows with accounting procedures and, in particular, the strange accounting practice of depreciating durable assets, where firms "recognize" depreciation in their income statements by taking a charge against current income for depreciation of assets, using rules such as straight-line depreciation.

- What, if anything, does accounting income have to do with economic profit?

- Why do accountants depreciate assets?

- From an economic perspective, what sins of omission or commission do accountants commit?

Let me say at the outset, these are difficult questions, and the various concerned communities—accountants, economists, lawyers, managers, regulators, and tax authorities—argue vociferously about answers. Completely satisfactory answers are impossible, and even reasonably satisfactory answers require concepts that we ignore until late in the book. But this is a good place to begin a discussion of these questions.

To answer these questions, we first discuss the uses to which income statements are put. There are several uses and I focus on only the most important: Income statements provide information to outsiders—especially outside investors—about the "ongoing health" of the enterprise. This provides outsiders with the information they need to do business with and in the enterprise. A potential investor in XYZ Corporation wants some indication of how well XYZ is doing, and this investor turns first to XYZ's annual report and income statement.

Suppose that XYZ is offered a license to produce a given product for the next 5 years. Suppose the firm can make excellent use of this license, because it has established channels of distribution that are ideal for the product. Purchasing the license is a good deal; the present worth of the incremental net cash flows from buying the license is substantially positive. But the license costs the firm a lot of money up front, with the incremental revenues coming only in the future. Purchasing this license ultimately generates value for shareholders but, insofar as the license must be paid for immediately, it *depresses* the firm's current-period cash flow.

In an ideal world of very smart investors, XYZ Corporation would issue the following information: "We have bought a license costing us N this period that, we believe, will add an extra M per year to our bottom line for each of the next 5 years." Investors check on the bona fides of this claim, compute the sum of the discounted incremental cash flows, and are happily impressed by the wise decision of the managers of the firm.

Unhappily, investors, instead of doing these calculations, look at "reports" in which all the firm's current activities are summarized into a single consolidated income figure. So, how should XYZ report the financial consequences of its license purchase?

Suppose XYZ takes the purchase price of the asset and charges it against the firm's cash flow a bit at a time; say one-fifth of the purchase price for each of the 5 years the license runs. In this way, in each of the 5 years, if those rosy claims are correct, the firm will realize positive cash flow from using the license more than sufficient to cover that year's portion of the purchase price of the license.

Accountants call this *straight-line depreciation*. Instead of charging the full purchase price of the license against current income, the license is depreciated in the accounting sense over its lifetime, with a fraction of its purchase price charged against income in each period it runs.

This is not ideal on at least two grounds: First, if credit is to be given for a good management decision, why not "recognize" the full NPV in year 1, when the license is purchased? Second, suppose that the incremental cash flow from the license will be very large in years 4 and 5, but not much at all in years 1, 2, and 3. Then, charging years 1 through 3 with one-fifth of the license fee makes those years look worse than they really are.

Why settle for the less-than-ideal procedure of straight-line depreciation? The reason is that accounting numbers, to be useful to the investing public, have to be somewhat objectively produced. Firms often have an incentive to paint a rosier picture of their situation than is true. If income figures were produced entirely subjectively, they would be unreliable. There must be rules and standards for how accounting numbers are produced, and there usually must be an independent authority—the external auditor—willing to vouch that those rules and standards were applied correctly, if investors and other parties are to trust the income statement.

Of course, the more formulaic and objective are the rules, the less well the accounting numbers reflect how the firm is doing in this period. Straight-line depreciation of an asset, for instance, is a good all-purpose rule that fits fairly well in a wide variety of circumstances and reduces the degrees of freedom of those generating the income report, *but therefore* it fits very few circumstances perfectly.

When accountants debate the rules of their profession—the Generally Accepted Accounting Procedures (GAAP), what the International Accounting Standards Board (IASB) or its national counterparts permit—the debates should be and often are framed along these lines. First, for the item under discussion, what is an ideal measure of its impact on the long-term profits of the firm? Then, to the extent that the ideal would allow for manipulation by management, what objective and formulaic rules can be devised that do rough justice to the wide range of specific situations that arise?

That is the basic story. I close with three remarks:

1. Some accountants and accounting theorists would dispute the notion that income should measure how current decisions affect the flow of profits to the firm, now and in the future. The other major category of information provided by accountants is the *balance sheet*, a statement of the firm's productive assets and liabilities. Income, by this alternative perspective, should be a measure of the current flow of realized "profit"; if management makes a wise purchase of an asset whose value to the firm is more than its purchase price, the value of the asset should be recognized on the balance sheet. I have a lot of sympathy for this philosophical position. But it does make it harder to understand some accounting procedures that go into the determination of income; why not just report cash flow and recognize the value of the asset on the balance sheet?

2. In the late 1990s, so-called dot-com companies posed a challenge to accounting conventional wisdom. These companies had substantial market value, even when they were showing quarter after quarter of accounting losses. If accounting income is meant to be a measure of how well its management is doing, this measure did a poor job for the dot-coms.

    The problem was that the dot-com companies invested heavily in "assets" that traditional accounting procedures have a hard time with, such as market share, channels of distribution, customer base, know-how, and human resources. These assets might pay back some day, and pay back handsomely, or so the market believed. But expenditures for them appear as immediate, direct charges in the current income statements. Accountants "ought" to have counted such expenditures as investment, with depreciation charges (only) appearing as appropriate on income statements. But they did not do this, and companies that consistently showed accounting losses simultaneously had substantial market capitalization.

3. I cannot resist closing with a slap at the terrible job done by most countries—or at least the United States—in accounting for assets when it comes to the national budget. No serious attempt is made, at least in the United States, to take into account whether yearly expenditures are for infrastructure, such as highways, or for expendibles, nor is depreciation seriously measured. This is not a book in macroeconomics—and I'm far from an expert on that mysterious branch of economics—but I think I know enough to say that, when people start talking about the federal budget surplus or deficit, without regard to the formation or degradation of long-lived national assets within the budget, they are not engaged in either meaningful or intelligent debate.

10.4. Know-How

The third sort of multiperiod effect we discuss concerns know-how. In a sense, know-how is a durable productive asset, and it could be dealt with in the same way as human capital or customer goodwill: An investment in know-how improves future cash flows, and whether a particular investment in know-how is undertaken or not should depend on whether it improves or degrades the net present value of the firm's cash flows. Know-how should, but rarely does, turn up on the firm's balance sheet, and charges for the depreciation of know-how, or credits for its appreciation, should appear on the income statement.

But know-how is placed in its own category, because, while we certainly think of production functions with arguments such as metal lathes, blast furnaces, and skilled labor, know-how *is* the production function itself.

Some forms of investing in know-how are fairly tangible and direct. A manufacturing firm might purchase a license that gives it access to a patented production process; the license should, and often does, go on the firm's balance sheet, and its cost should be amortized over the lifetime of the license. Other forms are direct if not so tangible, such as expenditures on R&D. But among the most interesting forms of investment in know-how are indirect investments, such as the experience-curve effect and TQM.

The Experience Curve

In the manufacture of aircraft, computer chips, and a host of other products, a remarkable empirical regularity is that direct costs of production fall a fixed percentage when cumulative output doubles, at least on average. If you are told that a certain manufacturing process follows an 80% learning or experience curve, this means that the firm can expect the 2000th unit it makes to cost 80% of its 1000th unit, and the 3000th to cost 80% of unit number 1500. There are all sorts of fancifications of this idea, concerning how unit costs decline for firms with multiple plants, how they change when a firm moves from a less-advanced to a more-advanced model of the same general product, and so on, but the basic idea is fairly clear. Firms, if they pay attention, learn by experience less costly ways of producing whatever they produce, and the sequence of unit costs falls in a very predictable pattern.

The consequences can be substantial. In the late 1970s and early 1980s, management consulting firms did quite well pushing the idea of the experience curve, which was loosely translated to say that the long-term profitable firms are those with the largest market shares. In infant industries or early in a product life cycle, firms should be willing to sell their products for less than their current direct costs, because by so doing they are riding down the experience curve, to a point, sometime later, when large positive cash flows would be realized. In bidding to sell a brand new model of aircraft, aircraft manufacturers often bid very low relative to their current direct costs in order to ride down the learning curve: The suppliers of military aircraft plan to take a loss on their initial sales in the hope of making profits on reorders or orders to foreign governments; and the suppliers of civilian aircraft chase initial sales very aggressively to build up the volume of production.

Whenever the experience curve is operating, production in and of itself is an investment in lower production costs, hence higher profits in the future. From the perspective of a proper economic calculation, losses incurred in early periods, measured in terms of revenue less the direct cost of production, may not be losses at all, since some of the cost of production is really an investment in knowledge. A controversy on this point arose concerning the sale of dynamic random-access memory chips (DRAMs) by Japanese firms in the United States. American manufacturers insisted that the Japanese were dumping DRAMs on the American market, where *dumping* means selling at a loss to forestall domestic (American) producers from entering. Certainly the Japanese were selling their DRAMs at prices well below direct manufacturing costs, and as the Americans were quick to argue, this non-profit-maximizing approach to price setting could only be for some nefarious purpose. The Japanese manufacturers retorted that using direct costs of manufacture is not economically correct; they claimed that they were simply pricing their chips in the way that would maximize their overall long-term profits, whether the American manufacturers were in the market or not.

Modeling the Experience-Curve Effect

Modeling the experience-curve effect requires rethinking the concept of a total cost function. Up to this point, whenever we write $TC(x)$, we think of the variable x as the *rate* of production, the number of units made during a specific time period, such as a month or a year. Thus we forcus entirely on the extent to which costs are driven by the rate of production. But, with an experience-curve effect, the total cost of producing x units in a given production period is a function of x *and* the cumulative amount produced before the current production period, which we denote temporarily by X. Writing $TC(x, X)$ for this total cost function, we assume that TC is increasing in x and decreasing in X.

In the simplest form of the experience curve, things are even simpler. It is claimed that unit costs fall a set percentage with each doubling of cumulative output, *no matter what is the rate of production*. This is rather incredible, because for one thing, it means that the cost of the 10,000th unit is the same whether the firm takes 5 weeks or 5 years to produce 10,000 units. Notwithstanding the (in)credibility of this claim, it means that $TC(x, X)$ can be simplified as follows:

- The cost of producing unit n is given by c_n, whenever unit n is made.

- If the firm produces X units prior to the current production period and x units during this period, total costs this period are $c_{X+1} + c_{X+2} + \ldots + c_{X+x}$.

- Moreover, for some $\gamma < 1$, $c_2 = \gamma c_1$, $c_4 = \gamma c_2$, $c_6 = \gamma c_3$, $c_8 = \gamma c_4 = \gamma^2 c_2 = \gamma^3 c_1$, and so on.

- *Therefore*, if the firm has produced X units prior to the current production period and x units during this period, total costs this period are (approximately)

$$\frac{c_1[(X + x)^\beta - X^\beta]}{\beta}, \quad \text{for } \beta = \frac{\ln(\gamma)}{\ln(2)} + 1.$$

That last step takes more math than I expect readers to know, so just take it on faith, or see the derivation in the *Student's Companion*.

The Formula Meets the Real World

This is a pretty remarkable model, on two grounds. It says that the rate of production is unimportant to costs: whether Boeing produces 10 747s a year for 10 years or 20 a month for 5 months, the cost of the 101st plane is the same and independent of Boeing's production rate when the 101st is produced. Further, costs fall in such a regular pattern that we can determine the unit and total costs of any unit from just two parameters: the cost of the first unit and the steepness of the experience curve.

In fact, this is a bit too remarkable; the world is not quite simple. Costs depend on rates of production as well as on cumulative experience. Experience lowers costs but at rates that vary with time and are somewhat random. Previous experience can count and there are spillover effects: Boeing did not start a new experience curve when it began producing 747-300s but profited from its experiences producing 747-100s and 747SPs. Different parts of a large product have different experience-curve rates; for instance, the rate of decline in costs for wings is larger than for cabins. Moreover, this price reduction is not free: Firms can take specific actions that increase or reduce the rate of cost reduction, which in just a few paragraphs takes us to TQM.

Still, the idea that costs are lowered by cumulative output means that a firm chasing maximal profits should "overproduce" and "underperform" in terms of revenue less cost early in a product's life cycle. Put in terms that hearken back to earlier chapters, MC = MR remains true, but the computation of marginal cost can be tricky. To see this fleshed out, try the exercise Pricing Down the Experience Curve? in the *Student's Companion*.

Natural Resource Extraction

In contrast to the experience-curve story, where costs fall with the level of cumulative output, in some cases production costs *rise* with cumulative output. The most prevalent case is that of natural resource extraction—for instance, extracting oil reserves, coal mining, or ore mining—where it becomes harder and more expensive to extract resources as the pool or vein is depleted. In this case, the "cost" of extracting the easy-to-get resource (oil, coal, or ore) should be thought of as greater than just the cost of physical extraction, insofar as this extraction imposes higher costs on later production periods. The economics of the situation, and models of cost structures, is the same as that of the experience curve, except that $c(x, X)$ —the cost of extracting x units in the current period if X units were extracted previously—increases in both x and X.

Total Quality Management

If the experience curve was to be found in every nook and cranny of the management press and management education in the early 1980s, the big buzz words 10 years later were *Total Quality Management*. There is no single form of TQM but rather a number of varieties and variations. Moreover, a number of other buzz words or terms are used somewhat interchangeably with TQM: *world class manufacturing, lean production systems, kanban systems,* and the *Toyota production system.* These share the following characteristics:

> Management and workers together must strive incessantly and continually to improve the production process, pursuing products of higher and higher quality, measured by conformance to specification. The production process and product specifications should be carefully and systematically documented, and conformance to spec should be watched especially carefully. Problems related to quality or production process should be dealt with as they occur; they should not be papered over or left for some other day. Workers must take responsibility for their own product quality; they must know how to recognize quality problems and be able—both in terms of a wide knowledge of the entire production process and the authority to implement changes—to solve problems as problems arise. The production process should be continuously subjected to increasing stress, in the form of lower work-in-process inventory, shorter production runs and more frequent changeovers, and so on, because stress gives the workers and managers the opportunity to see and correct problems in the production process. Suppliers must be tightly integrated into the production process and part of the TQM effort.

In traditional (economic) discussions of quality choice by a firm, it is assumed that the firm pays increased costs to obtain higher-quality output. Firms may be willing to pay those costs, if higher-quality output means a better reputation with consumers of the output and thus even higher revenues. But increased quality means increased total cost, to be traded off against increased revenues.

In contrast, the purported advantage of TQM is succinctly captured in a slogan coined by one of its developers, Philip Crosby: Quality is free. Crosby's slogan denies the existence of a trade-off between higher revenue and higher costs from higher quality. He claims that if the firm pursues better quality, using the general scheme of management he details, then higher quality costs the firm nothing. In fact, the firm might find that it costs less to produce at higher quality.

Economists respond reflexively to statements that *X is free* with the aphorism *There are no free lunches.*[2] So, in the early days of TQM, economists

---

[2] This phrase was coined with reference to the "free lunches" offered by saloons in the 1800s; customers who thought that they could eat for free were quickly disabused of the notion. Robert Heinlein, in *Stranger in a Strange Land,* popularized the phrase There ain't no such thing as a free lunch, or TANSTAAFL. Independently, the economist Milton Friedman brought the

tended to dismiss TQM as a sham; nothing is free, certainly not quality. But TQM should not be dismissed; viewed correctly, it makes good sense, even economic sense, which is not inevitably the same thing.

From the perspective of economics, the magic at work in TQM—if and when TQM does work—comes from the idea that the firm's production technology can be improved if the firm invests in product and process improvements. This involves learning how to make existing products more efficiently and reformulating product design so that the products are more manufacturable. The way to obtain the knowledge needed to improve product and process is to understand deeply the existing process and learn from mistakes or flaws that come up when employing the existing process. By chasing higher quality or greater conformance to specification, one focuses on the cases where conformance to specification is poor, which is precisely where the product or process needs to be and can be improved. Hence chasing higher quality in the form of greater conformance to specification is precisely chasing the sort of product and process improvements that, in the longer term, mean both higher quality and lower cost.

TQM is a lot more than this. The ways to invest most effectively in improved process and product design involve the management of work-in-process inventory, where the terms *kanban* and *lean production systems* come in, workforce practices that give workers knowledge and authority, tightly integrated relations with suppliers, and so on. Those details are what makes TQM effective or not, because they are the means by which one will or will not succeed in obtaining knowledge about process and product design. The essence of TQM lies in these details, details I do not get into here. (Chapter 24 discusses aspects of supply-chain management under TQM.) But, from the point of view of basic microeconomics, TQM is about an investment in know-how, involving a trade-off between today's cash flow and tomorrow's. Crosby's quality is free, in this respect, should be reformulated as *quality is a great investment in know-how that will quickly pay for itself*, even if it involves a rise in today's costs.

Executive Summary

- This chapter looks at some issues concerning multiperiod production.

- In place of profit maximization, we assume firms maximize their market value, which is operationalized as maximizing the sum of the discounted net cash flows. The justification for this operationalization, as well as the identification of the

---

phrase into the lexicon of economics, as a guiding principle of the Chicago School of economics.

appropriate discount factors, is part of financial market theory and corporate finance.

- The first dynamic effect considered is friction in production, a higher cost in the short run than in the long run for changes from the status-quo production plan.

- If SRTC is at least as large as LRTC for every level of production, and if they are equal at the status-quo level of production, then SRMC = LRMC at the status quo, SRMC $\geq$ LRMC for increases from the status quo, and SRMC $\leq$ LRMC for decreases from the status quo.

- The second dynamic effect considered is the role of durable productive assets. Most of the discussion here concerns the accounting measure of income and, more specifically, depreciation. Accounting income is meant to be a single-dimensional measure of how the enterprise is doing, used to inform investors and other outsiders. But, so that outsiders can trust these numbers, they must be computed in reasonably objective fashion, which compromises accuracy. Depreciation takes the cost of durable assets, at least some durable assets, and distributes that cost over the useful life of the asset.

- The third dynamic effect concerns the special durable asset know-how. Two specific "models" of the indirect accumulation of know-how—the experience curve model of production costs and total quality management—are described.

Problems

10.1 Consider a firm using two factors of production, m and l, with production function given by $f(m, l) = m^{1/3}l^{1/6}$. In addition, this firm faces a fixed cost of $300 per period. The price of m is $1 per unit, and the price of l is $4 per unit. The firm faces the inverse demand curve $P = 160 - 2x$. (This is Problem 9.6.)

In this case, the firm's total cost function is $TC(x) = 300 + 3x^2$, and the firm maximizes its profits by producing 16 units per period, at a price of $128 apiece. To produce the 16 units, the firm optimally uses 64 units of l and 512 units of m.

To add long-run and short-run considerations, imagine that the firm can adjust both m and l in the long run, so that $300 + 3x^2$ is its long-run total cost function. But, over the short-run period of a month, it cannot change the level of l it employs.

(a) Starting from the status-quo level of 16 units of output, made with 64 units of l, what is its short-run total cost function?

(b) The answer to part a is, $SRTC(x) = 556 + x^3/8$ (for the status-quo level of production $x_0 = 16$, $l_0 = 64$, and $m_0 = 512$). Using Excel or some other spreadsheet program, graph the long-run and short-run total cost functions on one graph, and the long- and short-run average and marginal cost functions on a second. Use the ranges $0 \leq x \leq 24$ for total costs and $3 \leq x \leq 24$ for average and marginal costs. Do you get the sort of picture you expect from Figures 10.1 and 10.4?

(c) Suppose from the status-quo position described the firm sees inverse demand shift suddenly from $P = 160 - 2x$ to $P(x) = 180 - 2x$. Compute the short-run and long-run output levels, prices charged, input-utilization levels, total costs, and profits, assuming the firm maximizes short-run profit in the short run and long-run profit in the long run.

10.2 Consider the firm in Problem 10.1, with production function $f(m, l) = m^{1/3}l^{1/6}$ and additional fixed cost of $300 per period. As in Problem 10.1, the short run is defined as a period in which m but not l can be changed. The firm is assumed to be sitting at a status-quo production level of 16 units of output, employing 64 units of l and 512 units of m. Suppose that the price of l suddenly rises from $4 per unit to $6. What are the new long-run and short-run total cost functions? If inverse demand does not shift, but stays at $P = 160 - 2x$, what are the firm's short-run and long-run responses to this shift in an input price?

10.3 We continue with the firm from problems 10.1 and 10.2, where l is labor and m is material. The reason for naming them is that the fixity of l, or labor, in the short run is easily explained: It takes time to hire and train workers, especially skilled laborers; and labor contracts, especially when dealing with a union, often forbid discharging workers without sufficient prior notice. Faced with sudden and unanticipated changes in demand conditions or wage rates, this may mean that the level of l is fixed in the short run. But sometimes l is less than completely fixed.

Return to the case where $r_l = 4$ and suppose that, from the status-quo production of 16 units, the firm cannot discharge any labor in the short-run—it must use the status-quo 64 units—but can add labor by adding overtime at $6 per hour, up to a total of 16 units of overtime or 80 labor units altogether. In the long run, the firm can add or subtract labor as it likes, at $4 per unit.

(a) What are the firm's long- and short-run total cost functions?

(b) Under these circumstances, how will be firm react in the short run and in the long run if inverse demand suddenly shifts to $P = 180 - 2x$?

10.4 Consider a firm with a fixed-coefficients (and constant returns to scale) production technology, in which x units of output require $3x$ units of the first input, m, and $x/5$ units of the second input, l.

(a) Suppose that factor prices of m and l are $1 and $10 per unit, respectively. What is the total cost function?

(b) Suppose that this firm faces inverse demand curve $P(x) = 23 - x/5$. What is the profit-maximizing level of production, what price does the firm charge, and what is its profit?

(c) Suppose that, in the short run, the firm can freely vary the amounts of m it can employ but cannot vary l. What does its short-run total cost function look like? How will the firm react (in the short run and in the long run) if inverse demand suddenly shifts to $P(x) = 23.5 - x/5$?

(d) Suppose that, in the short run, the firm can freely vary the amounts of m it employs. It can vary l to some extent: It can hire more l at a cost of $15 per additional unit and discharge all the l it wishes to, but must pay a "layoff" wage of $5 for every unit of l it discharges. What are its short-run total and marginal cost functions? How will the firm react (in the short run and in the long run) if inverse demand suddenly shifts to $P(x) = 23.5 - x/5$? How will it react (in the short run and the long run) if inverse demand suddenly shifts to $P(x) = 25 - x/5$?

(e) In part d, you should find that overtime pay leads to a kink in short-run total cost at the status-quo quantity. Compare this with part d of Problem 10.3. Why are we finding a kink in total cost in this case?

For a fairly long and complex problem about the experience curve, please see the *Student's Companion*, following the solution to Problem 10.4.

11. Competitive Firms and Perfect Competition

This chapter is a turning point in the book; the focus shifts from optimization to equilibrium. After some general commentary about this turn, we begin with perfectly competitive markets.

- We explore how a competitive firm, one that takes prices as given, responds to different prices for its output.
- These supply responses are summed to give the market supply function; then supply equals demand is used to find the equilibrium.
- Short- and intermediate-run equilibrium dynamics are explored.
- Next, the entry and exit of firms to and from the industry in the long run are studied.

The chapter ends with a brief discussion of monopolistic competition, a model of market structure not subsequently used in this book. It is included here for completeness, but you may skip it without compromising comprehension of anything that follows.

Beginning with this chapter, the book's focus changes dramatically. Up to this point, we have been concerned with the actions of single entities, firms and consumers, pursuing their own goals. The key concept has been *maximization*.

In our models, firms and consumers exist within an environment that defines and limits what each can do. For instance, a firm might face a price of $10 for one of its inputs. Where did this price come from? Why $10 and not $5? In some cases, the environment within which firms and consumers seek their private ends is determined by the interactions of many firms and consumers. In other cases, the environment is determined by the interactions of a small number of parties. But, in almost every case, the *interactions* among and between parties determine and limit what each can do.

Starting now, the focus shifts from the actions of single parties to their interactions. The key idea is equilibrium. An *equilibrium*, in general, is an array of behaviors by entities (consumers or firms), wherein each entity does as well as it can for itself, given the choices of all other entities.

This basic concept of an equilibrium must be adapted to specific situations. We begin in this chapter, and the next three, with the simple setting of a competitive market, the stuff of the most famous picture from Chapter 2.

Then we slowly pile on more and more complications: Uncertainty enters the story in Chapter 15, private information and moral hazard in Chapters 18 and 19, dynamics and small-numbers interactions beginning in Chapter 20. In other words, we begin with buying and selling commodities, where the market price is all anyone needs to know about the actions of others. By the time we finish, we examine complex dynamic transactions, such as the long-term relationships among Intel, Microsoft, and Dell Computer.

Market Structure and Beyond

The main plot for the rest of this book is *piling on the complications in economic exchange*. Simultaneously, a second plot develops. Not all markets are the same. In some markets—for instance, the market for wheat—many sellers and buyers interact. The commercial airframe industry is dominated by two sellers, Boeing and Airbus, and a variety of buyers, some of whom are quite large and powerful. When it comes to operating systems for personal computers, Microsoft has had a virtual monopoly, although Linux, not really owned by anyone, may be weakening Microsoft's hammerlock on the industry. Internet marketing has many competing firms, but unlike in the wheat industry, Internet firms often have their own niches, within which they have market power.

Microeconomics, in view of this variety, has traditionally dealt in four paradigmatic models of markets:

1. In a *monopoly*, a single seller deals with many buyers, who are typically summarized by a demand curve for the product. The monopoly firm sets the price and quantity to maximize its profit. This is largely old business; Chapters 8 through 10, constitute f Chapters 8 through 10, constitute, as executives at Microsoft can tell, really, the firms face difficulties that we have not begun to the term *monopoly* means the classic and setting a profit-maximizing price. In Chapter 23, we some real-life problems facing monopoly firms.

2. market associated with the most commodity items, many relatively small buyers and sellers, and lots of information. This is the main topic of this chapter and the next three.

3. *Monopolistic competition* describes a market with many buyers and sellers, but where the goods being sold are sufficiently differentiated that each seller retains some market power and is affected by competitors only in

terms of the competition's aggregate or average behavior. The editor of
this book, reading this description, asked me to give an example. At the
end of this chapter, we discuss both the model and why I am unable to
comply with this very reasonable request.

4. An *oligopoly* is a market with a few powerful sellers and a large number of relatively powerless buyers. Automobile manufacture is a reasonably good example. Oligopoly involves a lot of the complications we
   go into later—in fact, the discussion of oligopoly drives many of those
   complications—so it takes the stage only in Chapter 20.

These four paradigmatic types do not exhaust the possibilities. There are
markets with one buyer and one seller, so-called bilateral monopolies. A
market with many sellers and a single large buyer, such as labor markets
in small towns with a single dominant employer, is called a *monopsony*.
Perhaps most important for business-to-business situations, some markets
have a few powerful suppliers and a similarly small number of buyers; the
commercial airframe industry, with Boeing and Airbus on one side, and
major airlines and aircraft leasing companies on the other, is an example.
I suppose *bilateral oligopoly* is the right term, although I have never seen it
used. Other industries, such as passenger air transport, resemble oligopolies
but, at least in some markets, have a fringe of many small competitors. We
have things to say about these other cases as well, particularly in Chapters
22, 23, and 24.

Beyond markets are all sorts of exchanges that take place in quasi-market
or nonmarket settings. While our focus is on markets for the most part, the
techniques we develop, especially in the last several chapters of the book,
can be used to study outside-of-market transactions, including political and
some forms of social exchange. (But wait until you read the final chapter
before taking this assertion too seriously.)

With this prologue, we move to competitive firms and perfect competition.

11.1. The Supply Decision of a Competitive Firm

Imagine a firm that produces a single good. Let $\mathrm{TC}(x)$ denote the total cost
to the firm of producing and selling x units of the good.

Suppose this good is a commodity. Many firms supply a nearly identical
product, and customers care little from which firm they buy. Moreover,
customers look for the best price they can find and are very well informed.
Hence there is a *market price* for the good. Any producer or seller who tries
to sell for more than this price is left with no customers, and any firm that

sells for this price, or a bit less, gets as many customers as it wishes. The firm we focus on sells, if at all, at this market price. (Examples are given at the end of this subsection.)

Let p denote the market price of the good. Assume that our firm acts as if, at any point in time, the decisions that *it* makes have no effect on p. The firm, in other words, takes the price p as given; in Economese, recall, we say that the firm is a *price taker* or that it is *competitive*.

Is there any firm whose production decisions have no effect on the price it receives for its output? Even for a small firm selling a commodity item, it seems unreasonable to suppose that the firm has absolutely no impact on its product's price:

- Even if the firm contemplates a small net addition to or subtraction from the total industrywide supply of the good, this has a *small* impact on price. If it did not—if no small change ever had an effect on price—then big changes, which are the sum of small changes, could have no effect, which is ludicrous.

- The firm could contemplate a production decision that would yield an enormous change in the supply of its product; say, the firm decides to sell an amount equal to 10 times the total supply of the product from all firms that sell this product. This would cause a large change in industrywide supply and hence a change in the price the good commands.

The basic answer to both objections is that price taking is a modeling abstraction rather than an absolute truth. It is approximately true in some situations. We hope and, based on empirical evidence, expect that models based on this ideal provide useful insight into and predictions about situations where the assumptions are met approximately. Dealing more directly with the two objections:

- Even if firms have an impact on price, if the impact is small enough, their actions are virtually indistinguishable from the actions of a firm that is precisely price taking.

- We have in mind situations in which massive changes in the production level of a single firm are ruled out, either because no single firm has the resources needed to make such changes of scale or because the costs of changing scale to that extent are prohibitive.

This leaves the empirical question, Are there industries that, even approximately, meet the assumptions of perfect competition? In fact, there are many such. Agricultural commodities, such as wheat and pork bellies, and natural resource commodities, such as natural gas, crude oil, and copper wire, are the most obvious examples. To take a slightly more interesting example—more interesting because things are less clear—downtown office space in a large metropolitan area approximates a commodity item, holding fixed floor, quality of construction, and so forth. This is not to say that a prestige address, a high floor, or a great view does not command a higher rent. But a lot of office space is pretty close to undifferentiated, and business real estate agents speak in terms of "the price per square foot" of standard downtown office space.

Marginal Cost Equals Price

If a firm assumes that it can sell as much as it wants at the price p and none at any higher price, its total revenue function is $TR(x) = px$. Hence, the firm's marginal revenue is p. The usual profit-maximizing condition, that marginal cost equals marginal revenue, simplifies to

$$\text{marginal cost equals price, or } MC(x) = p.$$

The Supply Function of a Price-Taking Firm, Part 1:
The Supply Function "Is" (Almost) the Marginal Cost Function

If the firm takes p as given, how much does it produce and supply to the market as a function of p? This amount, regarded as a function $s(p)$ of the price p, is called the firm's *supply function*.

Begin with a firm that has no fixed cost—$TC(0) = 0$—and rising marginal cost. Facing price p, such a firm chooses $s(p)$ so that the marginal cost of unit $s(p)$ is p or, in symbols,

$$s(p) \text{ is defined by } MC[s(p)] = p.$$

This is pretty simple graphically. Panel a of Figure 11.1 depicts a firm's total cost function; panel b, its marginal cost function. For any price p on the vertical axis in Figure 11.1(b), the quantity the firm supplies is the quantity x with this marginal cost, so the supply function $s(p)$ is as depicted in Figure 11.1(c). (In Figure 11.1(c), the argument of the function is price, which goes on the vertical axis.) *The firm's supply function "is" (almost) the firm's marginal cost function.*

We have quotes around *is* because $MC(x)$ and $s(p)$ are not at all the same function. Marginal cost gives a dollar per unit (cost) figure as a function of quantity. The firm's supply function gives quantity as a function of dollars per unit (price). More precisely, one function is the inverse of the other. But they look the same in terms of the picture, so it is typical, if a bit sloppy, to say that supply "is" (almost) marginal cost.

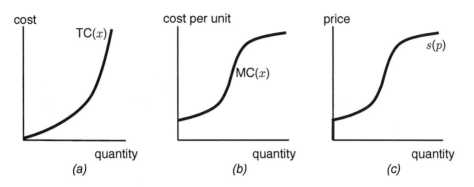

Figure 11.1. *Case 1: The supply function for a firm with rising marginal cost.* Panel a depicts the total cost function for a firm with rising marginal cost and no fixed cost; panel b depicts the corresponding marginal cost function. The firm's supply function is shown in panel c.

Why (almost)? Because, in Figure 11.1(c), we have the heavy line segment along the vertical axis as part of the supply function, which is not part of the marginal cost function. At prices below the lowest marginal cost the firm faces, $p = MC(x)$ cannot be solved and the firm supplies nothing.

The Supply Function of a Price-Taking Firm, Part 2:
Rising Marginal Cost with a Positive Fixed Cost

Now suppose the firm has rising marginal cost and a positive fixed cost. Assume that this leads to the standard bowl-shaped average cost function, as in Figure 11.2(b).

Nothing changes in this case for prices below the minimum marginal cost—the firm supplies 0 at such low prices—or at prices above the minimum average cost, where the firm's supply runs along with the marginal cost function. But writing p^{**} for the minimum marginal cost and p^* for the minimum average cost, the story is more complex for prices between p^* and p^{**}. Moreover, this more complex story depends on the answer to the question, Can the firm, by producing nothing (or otherwise going out of business), avoid its fixed cost?

If the fixed cost is unavoidable, then it is irrelevant to the firm's supply decisions. The firm's supply is just as in Figure 11.1(c), which is repeated in Figure 11.2(c).

Suppose, on the other hand, that the firm completely avoids its fixed cost by producing 0. Then at prices below p^*, the firm produces 0: To produce any positive amount means negative profit—the price is less than the minimum average cost, so it is less than average cost at whatever scale of production the firm chooses—while producing 0 means a profit of 0. And, at p^* specifically, the firm either produces 0 and earns a profit of 0 or it produces

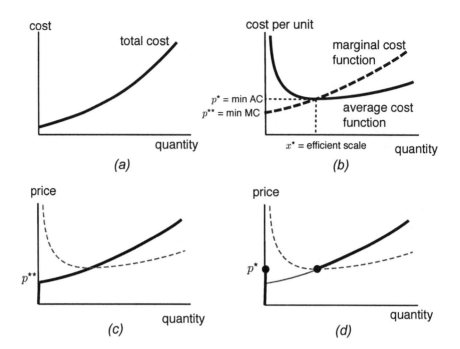

Figure 11.2. *Case 2: Rising marginal costs and a positive fixed cost.* Panels a and b depict the total, marginal, and average cost functions. Supply below p^{**} is 0 and above p^* it lies along the marginal cost curve, but what is it between p^{**} and p^*? If the firm must pay the fixed cost even if its production level is 0, then supply runs along the marginal cost curve for these prices, as in panel c. If the firm can avoid the fixed cost by producing no output, then supply at these prices is 0, as in panel d. And at the crucial price p^*, which equals minimum average cost, supply is either 0 or at efficient scale.

at its efficient scale, which also gives a profit of 0. Production at any other level means negative profit, so the only two possibilities are producing 0 or producing at its efficient scale. This is depicted in Figure 11.2(d).

The possibility remains that, by producing 0, the firm can avoid some but not all its fixed cost. I leave it to you to puzzle through this case; see Problem 11.1.

The Supply Function of a Price-Taking Firm, Part 3: Constant Marginal Costs

In a third case, the firm has no fixed cost and and linear total cost, so that marginal cost is constant. In this case, we get extreme behavior by the firm. At any price below its constant marginal cost, it supplies nothing. At any price above its constant marginal cost, it supplies infinite amounts, because believing as it does that it has no effect on price, it believes that it can make ever-increasing profits with ever-increasing output. At a price equal to its constant marginal cost, it is happy with *any* level of supply. See Figure 11.3.

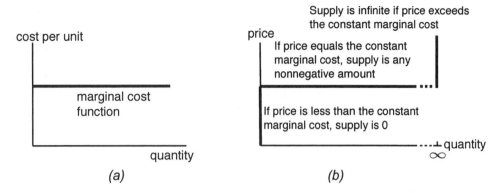

Figure 11.3. Case 3: The case of constant marginal cost and no fixed cost.

Do not be too impressed by Figure 11.3. The extreme behavior it depicts comes from taking the model much too seriously. Marginal cost cannot be constant forever, and even if it is, the firm will realize that eventually, at some scale of production, it will drive prices down. A model that says the firm will go from supplying nothing at the price $p - \$0.01$ to supplying any amount at p to supplying infinite amounts at $p + \$0.01$ should be thought of as an idealization of a firm whose supply responses vary enormously over a small range of prices.

Other Cases

In all the algebraic examples we deal with in this book, marginal cost is either rising or flat and, if flat, the fixed cost is 0. So this covers all the cases we will see later. But what about, in real life, the other possibilities? The key to an industry's being perfectly competitive is that at any price that is a reasonable candidate for the equilibrium price, individual firms maximize their profits at a scale that is small relative to the size of demand at that price. This is consistent with marginal costs that fall and then rise, for instance, as long as marginal costs for each firm rise fast enough. The mathematics in such cases is a little harder than the three cases we have explored, but most of the important insights we'll develop over the rest of this chapter continue to hold.

Sometimes, however, the technology of production simply does not support a perfectly competitive market. Imagine, for instance, that marginal cost is constant or falling for levels that are large relative to market demand, and firms also have a substantial fixed cost. Examples include electric power and natural gas distribution and, at least prior to the development of cell phone technology, local phone service. This is a case of a *natural monopoly*: One firm can serve the market efficiently; a second firm would have to pay the fixed cost without gaining a marginal cost advantage. Hence, a monopoly is natural both in terms of efficient production and as the result of market competition: The largest firm can always undercut the prices charged by its rivals. Industries in which the technology favors relatively large firms simply aren't consistent with perfect competition. But they do exist, and governments have to worry about them. In Chapters 12 and 13, we briefly discuss such industries, with specific reference to antitrust law and regulated monopoly.

Supply from Consumers

Not all supply comes from firms. Sometimes consumers are a source of its supply. Think, for instance, of the market for unused coupons in the GM truck coupon story. Supply there comes from old-truck owners who do not wish to purchase a new GM light truck.

In our examples in this chapter and the next three, supply always comes from profit-maximizing firms. But, especially for some of the conclusions we reach next chapter, you may want to ponder how price-taking consumers determine how much to supply. If you are curious, see Problem 11.4.

11.2. Equilibrium with Competitive Firms

Now we can look at the equilibrium of a *perfectly competitive market*, in which all the buyers and sellers are price takers. The setting is a market for some commodity item. Demand for this good is given by a demand function. We assume that demand slopes downward, but we say no more about where it comes from.

All supply comes from competitive firms. If there are N firms in the industry and, for $n = 1$, 2, and on up to N, $s_n(p)$ is the amount supplied by firm n at the price p, then the industrywide supply curve is given by

$$S(p) = s_1(p) + s_2(p) + \ldots + s_N(p).$$

That is, the total supply at any price is just the horizontal sum of individual firm-level supplies at that price. Why *horizontal*? Because when we graph these things, we always put price on the vertical axis, so just as with demands, we fix a price and sum quantities horizontally.

Three Examples

Three examples illustrate this. First, imagine that the good in question is supplied by 50 firms. Suppose that each firm has a total cost function given by $\text{TC}(x) = 2x + 0.01x^2$. Fixed costs are 0, and each firm's marginal cost function, $\text{MC}(x) = 2 + 0.02x$, is an increasing function that equals 2 at $x = 0$.

Because these firms have rising marginal cost and no fixed cost, each firm supplies nothing below its minimum marginal cost of 2 and a positive amount for prices above 2. At a price $p > 2$, the supply of the firm is the solution to price equals marginal cost, or

$$p = 2 + 0.02s(p) \quad \text{or} \quad p - 2 = 0.02s(p) \quad \text{or} \quad s(p) = 50p - 100.$$

Industry supply is the sum of the supplies of the individual firms. Since all 50 firms are identical, supply at any price p is just 50 times the supply of any single firm. So, at prices $p \leq 2$, industrywide supply is 0. At prices $p \geq 2$, supply is

$$S(p) = 50s(p) = 50(50p - 100) = 2500p - 5000.$$

In the second example, we complicate matters by supposing 100 firms supply the good. Fifty have the total cost function just given, and so the supply function of those 50 is as computed. The other 50 have total cost function $\text{TC}(x) = 3x + 0.005x^2$. So for these other 50, $\text{MC}(x) = 3 + 0.01x$. Hence, each of these firms supplies 0 at prices below 3, and at prices above 3, each supplies the amount $s(p)$ that solves

$$p = 3 + 0.01s(p) \quad \text{or} \quad p - 3 = 0.01s(p) \quad \text{or} \quad s(p) = 100p - 300.$$

Thus industrywide supply comes in three pieces: At prices p below 2, no firm supplies anything, so $S(p) = 0$. At prices p between 2 and 3, each of the first 50 firms supplies $50p - 100$ and each of the second 50 supplies nothing, for a total of

$$S(p) = 2500p - 5000.$$

At prices p that are 3 or more, each of the first 50 supplies $50p - 100$, or $2500p - 5000$ in total, and each of the second 50 supplies $100p - 300$, or $50(100p - 300) = 5000p - 15,000$ in total. Hence, at prices 3 or more, total supply is

$$S(p) = 2500p - 5000 + 5000p - 15,000 = 7500p - 20,000.$$

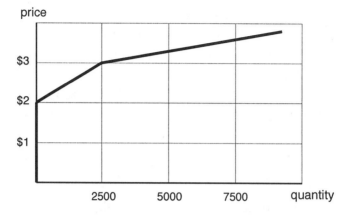

Figure 11.4. The supply function in the second example. This example has 50 firms with the marginal cost function $2 + 0.02x$ and 50 with the marginal cost function $3 + 0.01x$. No firm has any fixed cost. The first 50 firms begin to supply at the price $p = 2$, and the second 50 begin when the price reaches $p = 3$, giving the kinks shown.

A graph of this total supply function is shown in Figure 11.4. Note the kinks at $p = 2$, when the first 50 firms suddenly kick in and start producing, and at $p = 3$, when the second 50 begin producing.

A real-life lesson lurks in this toy example. If the equilibrium price in this industry is \$2.50, we would see 50 firms producing. If, in trying to construct the supply curve of this industry, we consider only these 50 firms, we would not come up with the supply curve in Figure 11.4, because we would miss the second 50 firms that would *enter* this industry if price exceeds 3. In constructing industrywide supply curves, you must consider whether firms will enter (or leave) the industry in response to changes in price and, if so, what would be the impact on supply.

The third example introduces firms with avoidable fixed costs. Specifically, imagine that the industry consists of 50 identical firms, each of which has the total cost function

$$TC(x) = 100 + 2x + 0.01x^2 \quad \text{for} \quad x > 0, \quad \text{and} \quad TC(0) = 0.$$

The fixed cost of 100 is paid only if the firm produces a strictly positive amount. Then, from our earlier analysis, we know that the firm's supply curve traces along its marginal cost curve $MC(x) = 2 + 0.02x$ *as long as the price exceeds the firm's minimum average cost.* If price is below the minimum average cost, then the firm supplies nothing.

We can find the firm's minimum average cost by employing Solver, by differentiating average cost and setting the derivative equal to 0, or by equating average and marginal cost. I do the last of these three: Average cost is

$$AC(x) = \frac{100}{x} + 2 + 0.01x,$$

so average cost equals marginal cost where

$$\frac{100}{x} + 2 + 0.01x = 2 + 0.02x \quad \text{or} \quad \frac{100}{x} = 0.01x \quad \text{or} \quad 100^2 = x^2,$$

which is $x = 100$. Plug this value of x back into the average or marginal cost function, to find that the minimum average cost is

$$AC(100) = \frac{100}{100} + 2 + 0.01(100) = 1 + 2 + 1 = 4.$$

The supply of a single firm, therefore, is: 0 if $p < 4$; either 0 or 100 if $p = 4$; the solution to $p = 2 + 0.02x$, which is $50p - 100$, if $p > 4$.

The industry supply curve is the horizontal sum of 50 of these supply curves. At prices $p < 4$, $S(p) = 0$. At prices $p > 4$, $S(p) = 2500p - 5000$. And, the hard part, at $p = 4$, $S(p) = 0, 100, 200, \ldots, 4900$, or 5000. The idea here is that, at $p = 4$, we can have any subset of the firms supplying 100 apiece and the rest supplying nothing. If k of the 50 firms supply 100 apiece, total supply is $100k$. And k can be 0, 1, 2, on up to fifty. The picture is Figure 11.5

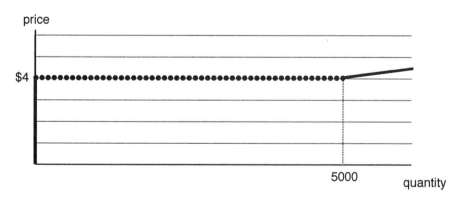

Figure 11.5. Supply in the third example. The third example has 50 firms with rising marginal and avoidable fixed costs. These firms have efficient scales of production of 100 units, at which point their average cost is \$4. Therefore, each firm would supply nothing if price is below \$4, along its marginal cost function if price is above \$4, and, if $p = \$4$, either 0 or 100. Hence, at $p = \$4$, supply is a succession of "dots"; supply is 0 if all 50 choose 0, or 100 if 1 chooses 100 and the other 49 choose 0, or 200, 300, up to 5000 if all 50 supply 100.

Equilibrium

Now for the punchline. A demand function is specified. The industry supply function is computed. Equilibrium is where the two intersect.

For instance, in the first example, with 50 firms, each of which has the total cost function $TC(x) = 2x + 0.01x^2$, industrywide supply is

$$S(p) = \begin{cases} 0, & \text{if } p < 2, \text{ and} \\ 2500p - 5000, & \text{if } p \geq 2. \end{cases}$$

If demand is given by $D(p) = 10{,}000 - 500p$, the equilibrium price is where supply equals demand, or

$$10{,}000 - 500p = 2500p - 5000,$$

where we must worry what to do if this gives us $p < 2$. This is

$$15{,}000 = 3000p, \quad \text{or} \quad p = 5.$$

At this price, supply equals demand equals 7500, which means that each of the 50 firms supplies $7500/50 = 150$ units. We can also work out each firm's total revenue, total cost, and profit: total revenue is $150 \times 5 = 750$, total cost is $2 \times 150 + 0.01 \times 150^2 = 525$, and profit per firm is $750 - 525 = 225$.

What If There Is No Intersection?

In some models we build, a problem arises at this point: Supply does not intersect demand anywhere. This can happen in a number of ways, but I have in mind the following: Go back to the third example of a supply function, where supply at the price $4 is 51 dots, as depicted in Figure 11.5. Suppose that demand is a continuous decreasing function and demand at $p = \$4$ is 3560. Then, supply does not intersect demand: At prices above $4, demand is less than 3560 while supply is at least 5000. At prices below $4, supply is 0 and demand exceeds 3560. While at $4 precisely, demand "falls between the dots": 35 firms producing 100 apiece gives us too little supply and 36 gives us too much. It does not do to have 35 producing 100 apiece and one producing 60, since at $p = \$4$, a firm would see substantially negative profit if it produced 60 units.

When we meet a model with this characteristic, the solution is simple: We stop taking the model so seriously. I explain what this means soon.

11.3. Short- and Medium-Run Analysis

Suppose that demand suddenly shifts in a competitive market that had reached equilibrium. In the spirit of the first third of Chapter 10, the firms supplying this good have differing capabilities to respond, as time passes. What pattern of equilibrium prices will result?

Assume that firms in this industry have available short-run responses, and a richer variety of intermediate-run responses. (We reserve the *long run* for later purposes.) Following the discussion in Chapter 10, we suppose that each firm has short- and intermediate-run total and marginal cost functions, the two marginal cost functions cross at the firm's status quo level of production, and the short-run marginal cost function is steeper than the intermediate-run marginal cost function. Ignore the possibility of fixed costs, or, even better, imagine that any fixed costs are unavoidable, hence irrelevant, in both the short run and the intermediate run.

The picture of a stable equilibrium is Figure 11.6. Firms' supply functions trace their marginal cost functions, and industry supply is the horizontal sum of firm-level supply, so we get short-run and intermediate-run industry supply curves that cross at the status-quo level of industry production, with the short-run supply curve steeper than intermediate-run supply.

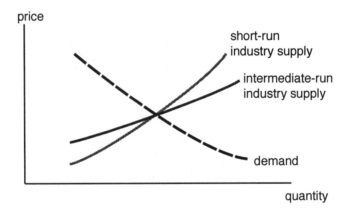

Figure 11.6 *Short-run (SR) and intermediate-run (IR) supply, in a stable equilibrium.* Mimicking the shape of the firm-level short- and intermediate-run marginal cost functions, short- and intermediate-run industry supply functions cross at the status-quo equilibrium, with short-run supply appearing more vertical than intermediate-run supply.

The use of *steeper* here might cause some confusion. The supply curve gives quantity as a function of price. But we graph price on the vertical axis. So does *steeper* mean that the derivative of the short-run supply function is larger? Or does it mean that if you look at a picture like Figure 11.6, short-run supply appears on the page closer to vertical?

I mean the latter. Short-run supply looks closer to vertical, because supply responses to changes in price in the short run are smaller. The derivative of the short-run supply function is smaller, and the derivative of short-run inverse supply (the price needed to call forth a given level of supply) is larger; on the printed page, the curve is closer to vertical.

When demand suddenly shifts out, price rises. (Follow on Figure 11.7.) As price rises, the firms supplying the good increase their output, moving along the short-run supply curve. A short-run equilibrium is attained where the new demand function and short-run supply curve intersect, at a price–quantity pair that is higher than before.

As time passes, firms make adjustments unavailable to them in the short run. At the new short-run equilibrium price, this would lead to an overabundance of supply. So prices begin to slip back toward their initial level. The intermediate-run equilibrium is achieved when demand intersects intermediate-run supply, at a price between the old equilibrium price and the short-run equilibrium price and at a quantity larger than both.

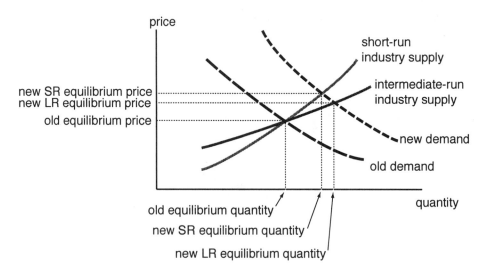

Figure 11.7. Dynamic price and quantity adjustment to an upward shift in demand. After demand shifts out, in the short run, the price rises and supply increases. In the intermediate run, supply continues to rise so the price drops back toward its original level.

That is how things work out in a model. In real life, of course, no single "short run" or "intermediate run" applies consistently to all the firms. Some firms in the industry can adjust their production levels more quickly, given an economic incentive to do so; others respond more slowly. But what we see in the model is, somewhat smoothed out, what would be observed in real life: If demand suddenly shifts out, the equilibrium price of the good rises dramatically. This motivates suppliers to increase their supply, which they do quickly or slowly, depending on their capability. As supply increases, the price begins to decline. An animation would have price jumping up to the new supply curve and then sliding down it, as supply increases. As long as intermediate-run supply slopes upward, price will not decline back to its starting point, but will decline some from its original sharp increase.

11.4. The Long Run, Entry, and Exit

If there is a short run and an intermediate run, there must be a long run. In the model, new firms can enter the industry in the long run, and firms in the industry can liquidate all their obligations and exit. We assume firms enter when they see the opportunity to make an economic profit, and they exit, eventually, if they take economic losses.

Economic Profit versus Accounting Income

The term *economic profit* needs explanation. Profit to an economist is total revenue less total cost. Included among the costs that make up total cost is a charge for the capital bound up in capital equipment, land, and so forth. If the firm borrows funds to finance its capital, interest on the borrowed funds is the appropriate charge. But suppose, moving from models toward the real world, the firm raises funds for capital purchases by issuing equity. The firm's accounting income statement contains no charge for equity capital, because accounting income is supposed to measure what is left over for equity holders, after all other claimants on the firm's revenues have been paid. In this very important respect, accounting income is *not* the same thing as economic profit.

Bear this distinction clearly in mind when evaluating the assumption that *firms enter the industry if economic profit is positive and leave if it is negative.* An economic profit of 0 does not mean no accounting income. An economic profit of 0 requires enough accounting income that equity holders are "satisfied" with their investment, so that their return on their investment matches the overall market rate of return. The assumption that firms enter when economic profit is positive means, essentially, that an industry whose equity holders are getting more than the market average rate of return is likely to attract investment. And the assumption that firms leave when economic profit is negative translates into this: Industries that provide equity holders with subpar returns see capital being withdrawn. Keep the distinction between economic profit and accounting income clear, and our assumptions about entry and exit are quite reasonable.

Back to the Story

This entry and exit process adds a third supply curve to the picture of Figure 11.6, which appears even less steep than the intermediate-run supply curve.

If we imagine, in the spirit of Figure 11.7, a sudden increase in demand, we would expect to see (1) a sharp rise in price and a smaller increase in quantity in the short run, (2) then a fall in price to above the original equilibrium level and a continued increase in quantity in the intermediate run, and finally, in the long run, (3) a further increase in quantity and a further fall in price to a level still no smaller than the original equilibirum price, driven by the entry of new firms.

Can There Be Profits or Losses in a Long-Run Equilibrium? Free Entry with the Best Available Technology

Suppose for the time being that, *in a particular industry, no firm has an advantage over any other in terms of its technological capability.* Whatever technology is available to any firm is available to all, including to potential entrants. Further suppose that *there is an unlimited supply of potential entrants.*

The italics are to get your attention. These are assumptions, which may or may not be true, even approximately, in specific cases. For instance, in agriculture, there is better farmland and there is worse, and there is a limited supply of the better. Since the quality of the land determines to some extent the yield, farmers lucky enough to own better land have a "more productive" technology. On the other hand, in the manufacture of relatively cheap clothing, done in Southeast Asia, say, for markets in the richer economies of Western Europe, North America, and Japan, there is a vast supply of potential manufacturers, all of whom have access to the lowest cost technology, fueled by cheap labor. (This assertion is descriptive, not normative.)

Under these assumptions, firms cannot earn positive economic profits in a long-run equilibrium. If one firm earns a positive economic profit, potential entrants just as capable as this firm observe the market price, compute that they can make a positive economic profit at that price, and therefore enter the market, causing the price to decline. This process continues as long as positive economic profits are being earned. The process of entry stops only when the price falls to a level at which no firm makes a positive economic profit. Similarly, if firms incur economic losses, they depart, and they continue to depart until all make an economic profit of 0.

This story is perhaps clearest and cleanest if the technology gives a U-shaped average cost curve because of a fixed cost that can be avoided (only) by leaving the industry. Then, firms make positive profits when price is above minimum average cost and take losses when price is below minimum average cost. So, as long as price is above minimum average cost, firms enter. When price is below minimum average cost, firms depart. The long-run equilibirum must be as follows:

> If the best technology in an industry is freely available to all producers, unlimited numbers of potential entrants are ready to enter the industry using this technology, and this best technology has U-shaped average costs, then the only long-run-equilibrium price in a perfectly competitive market is at the level of minimum average cost. At the long-run equilibrium, each active firm produces at efficient scale and earns an economic profit of 0.

Pictures of This

How does this look in pictures? What are the dynamics when there is a shift in demand? Consider Figure 11.8. Suppose the technology of the single firm is as in panel a with U-shaped average costs, with minimum average cost p^*. The long-run equilibrium price must equal p^*. So, if we have the demand curve shown in panel b, the equilibrium must be as indicated. Note that the efficient scale is marked at q^*; imagine that at the long-run equilibrium, N active firms each produce q^*. (What if demand at the price p^* is not an integer multiple of q^*? We get to this in the next subsection.)

Suppose firms in the industry can respond in the short run in limited ways to shifts in demand; the average cost function in panel a reflects the full range of possible actions that they can accomplish in an intermediate run shorter than the time it takes new firms to enter or existing firms to exit the industry. Thus the average cost function in panel a is the intermediate-run average cost function for a firm in the industry. We label it and the corresponding marginal cost function as such in panel c and add the short-run average and marginal cost functions, under the "usual assumptions" from last chapter.

Short-run and intermediate-run supply functions for the industry are shown in panel d. These are the horizontal sums of the short- and intermediate-run marginal cost functions, for the N active firms. Transferring these to panel e and superimposing a demand curve that suddenly shifts outward, we have the dynamics: an initial sharp rise in price, as incumbent firms make short-run adjustments; a fall in price back toward, but not all the way to, p^*, as incumbent firms make intermediate-run adjustments; finally, as prices above p^* attract new entrants, a new long-run equilibrium with the price back at p^*, all active firms again producing at the efficient scale q^*, and the number of firms increased by whatever number M it takes so that the quantity demanded along the new demand function at price p^* is $(N+M)q^*$.

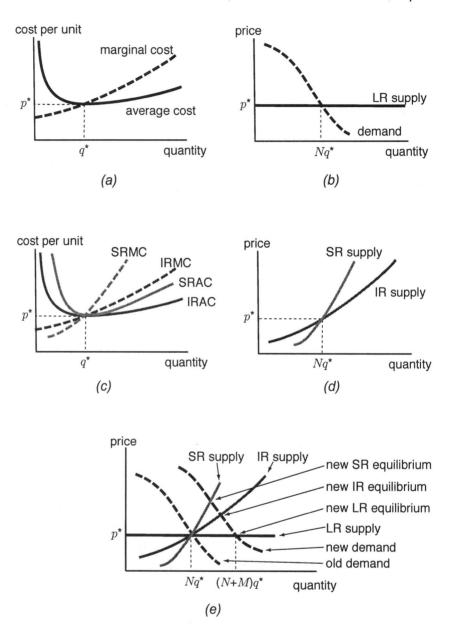

Figure 11.8. Dynamic adjustment to an increase in demand in the short, inter-mediate, and long run. Take an industry in long-run equilibrium, with a queue of potential entrants all of which have access to the best technology. In any long-run equilibrium, active firms must make an economic profit of 0; the number of active firms adjusts so this is so. If demand suddenly shifts out, the price rises sharply in the short run and then falls back toward its original level, just as in Figure 11.7. In the long run, the higher price attracts entry and increased supply, pushing the price down further. If minimum average cost for the active firms stays the same, price must return to its original level; new entrants serve the increased demand for the product.

Although it not shown in panel e, please note that once a new long-run equilibrium is reached, with $N + M$ active firms, the short-run and intermediate-run supply curves shift outward; they become the horizontal sums of $N + M$ times the respective single-firm marginal cost curves.

Again, What If There Is No Intersection?

What happens if demand at p^* does not precisely equal an integer multiple of q^*? This is relevant because, while I drew long-run supply as a horizontal line in Figure 11.8, I really should draw long-run supply as a sequence of separated dots, in the spirit of Figure 11.5, except that the dots continue forever, since an unlimited number of firms is ready to enter and produce at efficient scale q^* if the price is p^*. If $D(p^*)$ is not an integer multiple of q^*, then demand does not intersect long-run supply.

What happens here, in terms of the model, is that the industry is slightly unsettled. Suppose $D(p^*) = 34.3q^*$, so 34 firms are too few and 35 are too many. Then, if 34 firms are in the market, each makes a small profit. This attracts entry, and a 35th firm enters. This causes each of the 35 to take small losses, so one of the 35 leaves. This pushes profits slightly into the black, attracting a new entrant, and so on.

In real life, where firms are not completely, precisely identical, we are apt to see something slightly different: The 34 most efficient firms (ranked by their minimum average cost) are in the market, making slightly positive economic profits. Suppose the next most efficient firm can make a profit at the price that clears markets with these 34 firms. If it understands that its impact on prices, while slight, will be enough to cause it to sustain a loss, it will not enter. If it doesn't realize this, it may enter, and the experience of entry will teach it this lesson. Hence, we will probably settle out with 34 firms, each making an economic profit so small that no other firm is sufficiently motivated to enter. Which, from the point of view of predictions about price and equilibrium quantity, is virtually what the model, taken literally, predicts.

Rents

True or false? *In the long run, in a competitive industry, (economic) profits of all firms are 0.* Of course, the answer is, False, in general. This is true *if* there is unimpeded entry into the industry and *if* all firms, whether active or potential entrants, have access to the same technology. But these assumptions are approximately true in some cases and quite false in others. If, say, a farmer owns a particularly fertile piece of land—one that allows the farmer to harvest a large crop at less cost—then this farmer will earn positive profit in the long-run equilibrium.

Economists are so fond of the italicized slogan in the first paragraph, however, that they sometimes reduce it to a tautology. This bit of semantic legedermain works as follows: If the fertile land owned by the farmer in the previous paragraph is capable of higher crop yields, it is valuable land and should command a higher *rent* than less fertile land. If the farmer owns the land, so there is no question of rent actually changing hands, we should still think in terms of the rent the land could command if the owner rented it out instead of farming it himself. How much rent? The economic definition of *rent* is "just enough so that the italicized slogan is correct."

When it comes to farmland, the term *rent* is particularly appropriate. But the term *rent*, or sometimes *quasi-rent*, is also applied in cases where an industrial firm owns a patent on a particularly cost-effective technology or even when the technology is not patentable but still superior to the technology held by competitors. This fortunate firm does not make positive economic profits; instead, its patents, or just its production technology, earn rent, just enough rent that the firm's profit is 0. The term is applied whenever some input to production—land, a patented process, superior technology—is in relatively fixed supply, so that the process of entry does not "compete away" the value generated by the input for its owners. The term *rent* is used because this terminology, like most economic terminology, was set (in English) in 18th and 19th century England, when the chief example was in fact agricultural land. (Filers of income tax in the United States: If you ever wondered why rents and royalties are covered by the same laws and reported on the same form, this is the economic rationale. I leave it to you to discover the etymology of the term *royalties*.)

This is simply semantics. When you hear people (who speak Economese) talking about economic rents, this is what they have in mind. And when you hear an overenthusiastic economist say that, in competitive markets, economic profits must be 0, understand that this bit of semantics—in which any economic profits are relabeled rents to whatever input or technology other firms cannot match—may be all that is involved.

Do Firms Produce at Their Efficient Scale?

In Chapter 8, when I introduced the notion of efficient scale, I pooh-poohed the idea that a profit-maximizing firm must produce at its efficient scale. A profit-maximizing firm produces where marginal cost equals marginal revenue, which can be above or below its efficient scale.

When we look at competitive markets, however, the notion that a firm produces at its efficient scale gets a new lease on life. Any profit-maximizing *competitive* firm making an economic profit of 0 must be producing at its efficient scale, and what is more, the equilibrium price must be equal to its minimum average cost. This does not depend on free entry: If the price is below the minimum average cost, the firm cannot be active and sustain a nonnegative profit. If the price is above the minimum average cost, at some scale of production it will make a strictly positive profit. Zero profit thus means the price equals the firm's minimum average cost, and the only place the firm can make that 0 profit, aside from being out of the industry, is at its efficient scale.

So, to the extent that a competitive firm makes an economic profit of 0, it must be producing "efficiently." Moreover, a profit-maximizing competitive firm that turns a strictly positive profit must produce *above* its efficient scale. (See Problem 8.11.)

Is Long-Run Supply Flat?

(Skip or skim this subsection on a first reading, as it goes into some fairly subtle matters.)

Suppose the very best technology for making some product is freely available to all firms. Is the long-run-equilibrium supply curve really horizontal? It was drawn that way in Figure 11.8 and will continue to be so in models in which the least-cost technology is available to a vast horde of potential entrants. Why? If all firms have access to the same technology, including hordes of potential entrants, then equilibrium price in the industry must be the minimum value of average cost. At any higher price, firms make positive profits, attracting entry. At any lower price, firms sustain losses and depart.

This bit of reasoning is not perfect, however. Long-run costs depend on technology *and* the prices of inputs. If the long-run supply of inputs is not flat—if the price of an input rises with its usage by the industry in question—then, as the scale of industry production rises, each firm's long-run average cost function rises, minimum average cost rises, and the long-run supply curve of the industry is not flat. Long-run profit will stay at 0 in such a case. But the price needed to achieve a long-run profit of 0 for each firm must rise, to cover the increased cost of the inputs.

To be clear here, to say the supply of inputs is not flat is not to say that individual firms act as if they have market power in the input market. As long as all firms are relatively small, they regard their purchases of the input as on a scale that does not appreciably affect the input's price. But when all those competitive firms expand their demand for the input, the scale is sufficient for the input's price to rise. This is exactly parallel to the idea that, while each firm inside the industry might regard itself as a price taker in the output market, the industry as a whole can and does affect the price of that output.

This means that industrywide supply is not (really) the horizontal sum of individual supply functions. Indeed, this could be true even assuming that entry into or exit from the industry is not possible. Individual firm supply functions are drawn assuming that input prices are fixed, which they are, at least approximately, for small individual firms. But this may not be true for the industry as a whole.

Think, for instance, of grain farming, which is as close to a competitive industry as you can find. No individual farmer—not even an agribusiness giant—can have much of an impact on the price of fertilizer. Thus individual firm supply functions take the price of fertilizer as constant. But the industry as a whole makes tremendous demands on the fertilizer industry, demands that can push up the price of fertilizer as more land is brought under cultivation or land already cultivated is cultivated more intensively, using more fertilizer to increase yield. Thus industry supply is "steeper" than the horizontal sum of individual firm supply functions.

To try a (relatively!) simple example that illustrates this, see the discussion in the *Companion* following the problems for Chapter 11. Let me assure you, this is tough stuff, and if you can work your way through that discussion, you have command of this chapter.

11.5. Why Do We Care about Perfect Competition?

You now probably know more than you ever wanted to know about perfect competition. Indeed, most people studying economics for the first time react to all this by claiming that the first bit of knowledge was probably more than desired, since there are no perfectly competitive industries in the world.

This claim is incorrect. Some very important industries come close enough that the model is a good predictor, at least over some time frames. Broad classes of examples include many sectors of agriculture, some sectors of labor markets, and reasonably heavily traded financial securities. The case of financial securities is especially interesting, because prices are set in highly organized exchanges, exchanges that engage in activities, such as the disclosure of financial information, to make their markets come closer to the competitive ideal.

Beyond direct applications, which by themselves justify study of this sort of market, perfect competition provides a very good benchmark for markets and industries that are less than perfectly competitive. For instance, an important recent innovation in economic thinking (which we do not get to in this book) concerns what is called a *perfectly contestable* market, which is a model of a market in which the threat of entry makes firms react in some ways like perfectly competitive firms. This theory, which sets off from the starting point of perfect competition, was particularly influential in setting policy for airline deregulation in the United States.

The model of perfect competition is important for another reason. It provides the clearest statement concerning the efficiency of markets, which is where we are headed next, almost.

11.6. Monopolistic Competition

Before moving on to this next topic, I want to say a limited number of words about monopolistic competition. I explain why the number is limited—but not 0—after a brief introduction to the subject.

A monopolistically competitive industry or market comprises many suppliers (producers) and many demanders, but unlike perfect competition, the good in question is not a commodity but differentiated. That is, different consumers are more or less interested in the variety produced by a particular producer. Think, for instance, of a street lined with restaurants of various types, some serving Indian food, some serving Chinese, some Italian, and so forth. And the Indian-cuisine restaurants are differentiated: Some serve food from northern India, while others specialize in the cuisine of southern India. A given consumer might have a preference for northern Indian food over everything else, and then rank Sechuan Chinese food second, followed by Sicilian Italian cuisine, then Mandarin Chinese, and so forth. A different consumer might prefer Lebanese cuisine most of all, followed by southern Indian, and so on.

In this environment, there is no reason to believe that a single market price must prevail for "lunch." If the northern Indian restaurant raises its price above the prices charged by the other restaurants, it loses some business. But consumers with a strong preference for northern Indian cuisine will pay the higher price. Despite the many suppliers, each restaurant has some market power, each faces a downward sloping demand function, and each maximizes profit by equating marginal cost and marginal revenue.

Of course, demand at any one restaurant is affected by the prices charged by all the others. If a northern Indian restaurant, call it the Tandoor, charges $10 for lunch, and all the other restaurants charge $5, the Tandoor is going to sell fewer lunches than if all the others charge $12. The question is, How do the prices other restaurants charge affect the demand faced by the Tandoor?

In monopolistic competition, the demand facing any one producer, such as the Tandoor, depends on the full distribution of prices the others charge. If, say, Vesuvio, the Italian restaurant adjacent to Tandoor, lowers its prices, this has almost no effect on the demand at Tandoor. But, if all the other restaurants lower their prices, demand at the Tandoor falls. And, if new restaurants enter the market, this causes demand at the Tandoor to fall. At the same time, no matter what prices other restaurants charge or how many other restaurants there are, the Tandoor retains some market power; its demand function does not flatten out.

What does an equilibrium in this sort of market look like? Each firm is assumed to maximize its own profit, so each sets its price and quantity to equate its marginal cost and marginal revenue. Moreover, it is usually assumed that there is free entry into the industry, entry drawn by the lure of positive economic profit. And firms exit if they can (at best) make a loss. Suppose, then, for simplicity, that all firms have U-shaped average cost curves. In a long-run equilibrium, with free entry and exit, the marginal (producing) firm must make 0 profit. *This means that the demand function facing this marginal firm must intersect the firm's average cost curve*—otherwise, the firm would be unable to make nonnegative profit and would exit—*but the demand function cannot cross through the firm's average cost curve*—otherwise, the firm could make positive profit and other firms like it would enter. In other words, the (marginal) firm's demand function must be tangent to the firm's average cost function, as in Figure 11.9. Since, by assumption, the firm faces downward sloping demand, it must be producing at less than its efficient scale.

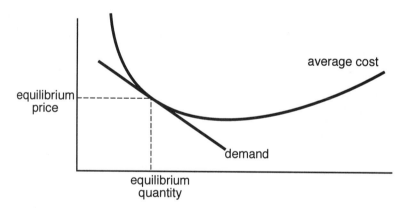

Figure 11.9. The marginal firm in a monopolistically competitive industry. The firm on the margin between entering and exiting must make 0 profit. This implies that the demand function it faces must just touch its average cost function, and since it faces downward sloping demand, it must be producing at less than its efficient scale.

That is the basic idea. There is competition and free entry, but firms retain market power. This, the theory tells us, leads firms to produce below their efficient scale. (This is true for the marginal firm on the cusp between entry and exit. If we play semantic games with the concept of rent, it is true more generally for all firms in the industry.)

I go no further with monopolistic competition, because I find it hard to give real-life examples of industries that conform to its assumptions. Specifically, the notions that demand facing a firm remains less than perfectly elastic, but no other firm's prices affect (by much) the first firm's demand, seem unlikely. A firm retains market power if its product is differentiated from the products of competitors; the Tandoor indeed has its own clientele. But the basis of that differentiation—location, perhaps, or cuisine style—means that "close competitors" have a sizeable impact on the demand facing the Tandoor. If the restaurant next door to the Tandoor or the northern Indian restaurant a block away changes its price, that has an impact on demand at the Tandoor. And once we suppose that this is true—that, to anticipate terminology from later chapters, the Tandoor is part of a local oligopoly—then the economic tools appropriate for finding an equilibrium in the restaurant market change. (We see what they change to in Chapter 22.)

I cannot say that the assumptions underpinning the theory of monopolistic competition are empirically vacuous. There may be industries for which these assumptions are good approximations. It is possible that electronic commerce (marketing over the Internet) gives rise to some approximate examples. But my sense is that if such industries exist, they are few and far between—in fact, I cannot name one—which makes the theory little more than a theoretical curiosity. In comparison, many important industries approximate the assumptions of perfect competition.

Why bother you with this theory at all? The models of monopolistically competitive markets possess features that make them very useful in some economic contexts, most notably in macroeconomic theories of trade and economic growth. You may run into these models in a course in macroeconomics, and to avoid angering your macroeconomics professor, I include this brief introduction. But, until you encounter monopolistic competition in some other course, my suggestion is to forget everything covered in the preceding discussion. You certainly do not need these ideas in this book.

Executive Summary

- A competitive (price-taking) firm believes it can sell as much or as little as it wishes at a going market price.

- For a competitive firm, MC = MR is replaced by *price equals marginal cost*, or $p = $ MC, since a competitive firm's marginal revenue is the price it faces. This implies that, for a competitive firm with no fixed costs and rising marginal cost, its marginal cost function "is" its supply function. If it has rising marginal costs and a positive and avoidable fixed cost, its supply is the marginal cost function but only at or above its minimum average cost.

- In a competitive market, aggregate supply is the horizontal sum of the supply functions of individual firms.

- Equilibrium in a perfectly competitive market is found by equating supply and demand.

- In an industry with free entry and exit, firms enter if they can earn a positive economic profit, and they exit if they are in the (economic) red.

- If the best technology is available broadly to firms in the market and to a host of potential entrants and entry and exit are free, the long-run equilibrium price must equal the minimum average cost of the best available technology, active firms will produce at their efficient scale, and all firms will earn 0 economic profit.

- Since economists like the idea that competition results in 0 economic profit, they invented the concept of *rent*, a return to superior technology or input to production, making economic profits of 0 a tautology.

- Even with free entry and exit at the best available technology, long-run supply can slope upward if changes in industry output affect the prices of inputs to the industry. If we imagine no change in the prices of inputs, long-run supply is horizontal.

- Perfect competition is interesting because some important industries are close to perfectly competitive; it is also interesting as a benchmark, especially as we turn, in the next chapter, to issues of economic efficiency.

- Monopolistic competition concerns industries with lots of competition but in which firms retain market power. The model is useful in certain branches of macroeconomics but not in the rest of this book.

Problems

11.1 A competitive firm has total cost function $TC(x) = 5$ million $+ 5x + x^2/10,000$. Regarding its fixed cost of \$5 million, \$4 million can be avoided if the firm produces 0, but \$1 million is completely unavoidable: Even if the firm ceases production, it must pay this \$1 million. What is the supply function for this competitive firm?

11.2 A competitive firm has marginal cost function $MC(x) = 3 + x/20,000$. The total cost function for this firm is $TC(x) = F_1 + F_2 + 3x + x^2/40,000$, where F_1 and F_2 are fixed costs: The firm can avoid paying F_2 if it produces 0, but it cannot avoid F_1. (That is, $TC(0) = F_1$.) Efficient scale for this firm—the level of x that minimizes average cost—is $x = 60,000$. This firm supplies positive levels of output for all prices above \$5. What are the values of F_1 and F_2?

11.3 A competitive firm has the marginal cost function $MC(x) = 8 - x/10 + x^2/2000$ and the total cost function $TC(x) = 8x - x^2/20 + x^3/6000$. What is this firm's supply function? Suppose the firm has a fixed cost of $10,000, and the entire fixed cost can be avoided if the firm produces 0. What is the firm's supply function in this case?

11.4 A consumer with the money-left-over utility function $u(x) + m = 10\ln(x + 1) + m$ is endowed with 100 units of x and $1000. This consumer can buy or sell the commodity in question, depending on its price. If, for instance, the price of x is $4 per unit and the consumer sells 25 units, she ends up with 75 units of the good and $1100 in money left over, for an ending utility level of $10\ln(76)+1100$. If she buys 25 units, she ends with 125 units of the good and $900 in money left over, for an ending utility of $10\ln(126)+900$. Given the price p of the good, the consumer buys or sells, doing whatever makes her ending utility as high as possible. As a function of the price p, what will this consumer do?

11.5 Suppose a particular perfectly competitive industry has 10 identical firms, each with the total cost function $TC(x) = 4x + x^2/2$. There is no possibility of entry into or exit from this industry. If demand for the item in question is given by $D(p) = 10(20 - p)$, what is the equilibrium in this market?

11.6 Suppose that, in a perfectly competitive industry, every firm has total cost function $TC(x) = 10$ million $+ 2x + x^2/100,000$. Demand is given by $D(p) = 500,000(42 - p)$.

(a) If the industry consists of five firms, with no possibility of entry or exit, what is the equilibrium?

(b) If there is an unlimited number of potential entrants for this industry and firms can enter or exit freely (and pay the fixed cost only if they are actively producing), what is the equilibrium?

11.7 Suppose that, in a particular perfectly competitive industry, the technology for making the product (by any single firm) has the total cost function $TC(x) = 100 + 3x + 0.04x^2$. An unlimited supply of firms could enter this industry, all with that total cost function. Firms incur the fixed cost only if they are in the industry.

(a) If demand for the product is given by $D(p) = 200(10 - p)$, what is the long-run equilibrium in this industry? What is the price of the good in equilibrium, how much is traded, how many firms are active, how much does each firm produce, and what profit is made by each firm?

(b) Suppose demand for the product suddenly shifts to $D(p) = 200(12-p)$. In the short run, firms cannot change their production quantities at all. What is the new short-run equilibrium? In the intermediate run, firms in the industry can change their production quantities according to the total cost function just given. What is the intermediate-run equilibrium in this industry? In the long run, firms can enter and leave the industry. What is the new long-run equilibrium in this industry?

11.8 Suppose, in the industry of Problem 11.7, four firms have a superior production technology, which gives each the total cost function $TC(x) =$ $50+x+0.04x^2$. An additional eight firms have the cost function from Problem 11.6. There are no other possible entrants into this industry.

If demand for the product is given by $D(p) = 200(10 - p)$, what is the equilibrium in this industry?

I have not told you whether the fixed costs of the 12 firms can be avoided. Does this matter to the answer to this problem? How?

11.9 Suppose that, in Problem 11.8, instead of eight firms with the cost function from Problem 11.7, an unlimited number of firms possess this cost function. Assume that all fixed costs can be avoided if a firm produces no output. If demand for the product is given by $D(p) = 200(10 - p)$, what is the equilibrium in this industry?

12. Market Efficiency

This chapter has two objectives:

- It presents the concepts of *consumer* and *producer surplus*, dollar-valued measures of the value that consumers and producers receive from participating in market exchange.
- Using these concepts, it shows why economists rhapsodize about markets and prices: Competitive markets are *efficient*, meaning they lead to the largest possible level of total surplus. But this statement must be qualified, and many of the qualifiers are discussed here as well.

This can be a frustrating chapter; the arguments given are more abstract than anything else in the book. If your skills of logical and mathematical proof are relatively weak, you may find it hard going. If so, at least understand what is being claimed, if not the arguments that support the claims. In the next chapter you get plenty of opportunity to see how these concepts and ideas are applied in more concrete settings.

If you surveyed the general populace, asking people to name phrases that economists use, *supply equals demand* would be the hands-down winner. But a contender for second place would probably be *the invisible hand*.

The invisible hand, a phrase coined by the father of economics, Adam Smith, refers to the role prices play in achieving a good allocation of resources in the economy. Economists, or at least economists who respect markets, are fond of rhapsodizing about the price mechanism. "Imagine," one of them might say, "many consumers and producers, with many conflicting preferences and capabilities, whose activities need to be coordinated. And the price mechanism does this so well, telling consumers the 'cost' of a particular item while telling producers the 'value' of the item in the marketplace." Warming up to her subject, our market-respecting economist explains, "Prices and the market mechanism are like an invisible hand that correctly and efficiently coordinates consumer desires and producer activities, achieving an unimprovable result."

Indeed, and with some justice, the invisible hand is sometimes cited as one reason that Soviet-style communism failed. The former Soviet Union was run as a centrally planned and administered economy. That is a pretty big operation to run from headquarters; and without in the least disparaging the talents of the commissariat and others who did the planning, the planning did not always work well.

In comparison, in price-driven economies, prices decentralize the planning process. To be very clear about this, decentralization is what gets the good results. Individual consumers have a lot of information and the time and incentive to process it, as they seek to maximize their utility. Firms have a lot of information and the time and incentive to process it, as they chase higher profits. Prices play an informational role: They sum up very concisely everything profit-maximizing firms and utility-maximizing consumers need to know about each other's desires and capabilities. Firms and consumers, guided by equilibrium prices and their own self-interest, reach an overall outcome that centrally planned and administered economies seemingly cannot touch.

Needless to say, there is a lot more to why Soviet style communism failed. The corrupt political system played a role, as did a lack of incentives for individuals to take risks and innovate. But there is little doubt that running by fiat an economy the size of the former Soviet Union's or even one the size of, say, Portugal is a daunting task. The central planners sitting in Moscow may have been able to decide how many shoes to make for sale in Minsk. But they probably had no clue about styles. And, if they got the styles wrong, the shoes might sit on the shelves of shoe stores in Minsk, as the consumers of Minsk made do with their somewhat worn old shoes. In comparison, the owner of a private shoe store in Zurich has a very strong incentive, and the time required, to learn what would be deemed a stylish pair of footwear in Zurich. Even if the bureaucratic planner sitting in Moscow had the incentive to follow the latest fashion trends in Minsk, which is doubtful, he still would have lacked the time and opportunity to glean the required information. Prices—or more properly, the decentralization of decision making and information gathering, allied with the incentives provided by the market system—get the job done.

What does the invisible hand accomplish, precisely? We discover in this chapter that the invisible hand, *if certain conditions are met*, produces an *efficient* outcome but not necessarily one that is *equitable*.

One more introductory thought, and we can begin. Economists attack this general issue in a number of different ways. One important dimension along which the attacks vary is the scope of the analysis: We can look at a single market, such as the market for shoes—what is called *partial equilibrium analysis*—or we can try to think about the whole economy, all at once—which is known in Economese as *general equilibrium analysis*. We have been developing tools appropriate for the first sort of attack, and so we look at these questions in the context of a single market. But, in the *Student's Companion*, following the solutions to problems for this chapter is a brief introduction to the general equilibrium approach to these questions.

12.1. Consumer and Producer Surplus

For most of this chapter, we look at a perfectly competitive market, where all supply comes from firms and all demand comes from consumers.

Figure 12.1 depicts the usual supply-equals-demand picture, with the equilibrium price and equilibrium quantity at the point where supply intersects demand. Note the two shaded regions. The darker region is bounded by the equilibrium price and the demand curve to the left of the equilibrium quantity. The area of this region is called the *consumer surplus*. The lighter region is bounded by the equilibrium price and the supply curve, to the left of the equilibrium quantity. The area of this region is called the *producer surplus*. I assert the following:

> Consumer surplus measures, in dollars, the benefits consumers obtain from trading in this market. Producer surplus measures, in dollars, the benefits producers obtain from trading in this market. Hence, these two quantities when summmed measure in dollars the value generated by the existence of this market.

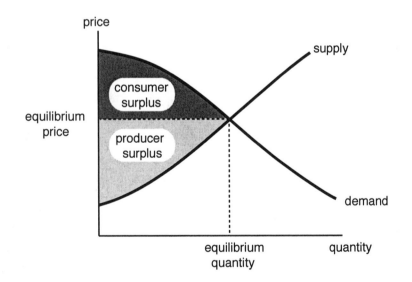

Figure 12.1. Consumer and producer surplus. Consumer surplus (the area of the darkly shaded region) measures in dollars the benefits that consumers obtain from the equilibrium outcome. Producer surplus (the area of the lightly shaded region) measures in dollars the benefits to producers of this market outcome.

Let me immediately qualify these assertions: they are not strictly true all the time. To understand them, we have to be a lot clearer about the term *benefits*. The next two sections indicate what these statements mean, when they are true, and why.

12.2. Producer Surplus

Producer surplus is, more or less, just a fancy way of saying *the profits of the firms in the industry*.

Assume for now that all firms in the industry have no fixed cost and rising marginal cost. Figure 12.2 graphs the marginal cost function of a single producer, which is also a graph of the producer's supply function. Suppose the equilibrium price and corresponding supply decision of the firm are as shown. In the first panel of the figure, the shaded rectangle's height is the price and its length is the firm's level of output; its area is the producer's total revenue. In the second panel, the shaded area under the marginal cost curve, up to the firm's level of output, is the integral of marginal cost, which is the total cost of the producer. So the difference between the areas of the two shaded regions, shaded in the third panel, is total revenue minus total cost, or profit.

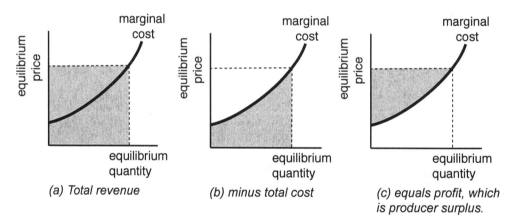

Figure 12.2. *Producer surplus = profits for a single producer.*

This is for a single producer. Now we extend to multiple producers. Suppose this industry has m firms, numbered 1, 2, ..., m. Write $s_j(p)$ as the supply function of firm number j, so that total industry supply is $S(p) = s_1(p) + \ldots + s_m(p)$.

1. The shaded area in the third panel of Figure 12.2 represents the profits of a single firm, say, firm number j. Remembering that supply is a function of price—so turn either your head or the page by 90°—this area is $\int_0^{p'} s_j(p)\,dp$, where p' is the equilibrium price and we correctly regard $s_j(p) = 0$ for prices p that are so low that the firm does not supply a positive amount at them.

2. The total industry producer surplus can likewise be written as $\int_0^{p'} S(p)\,dp$.

3. But then producer surplus, or $\int_0^{p'} S(p)\,dp$, is just

$$\int_0^{p'} [s_1(p) + \ldots + s_m(p)]\,dp \;=\; \int_0^{p'} s_1(p)\,dp \;+\; \ldots \;+\; \int_0^{p'} s_m(p)\,dp,$$

which is the sum, firm by firm, of the firms' profits.

Fixed Cost and Producer Surplus

What if one or more of the firms in the industry has a more complex total-cost function? I am not going to be completely general, but let me at least state the result for firms with a rising marginal cost function and, possibly, a positive fixed cost. Divide the fixed cost of each firm into avoidable and unavoidable portions.

> Producer surplus for the industry—the area bounded by the industry supply function and the equilibrium price, out to the equilibrium quantity—is the sum of the profits of the firms in the industry gross of (not counting) their unavoidable fixed costs.

The part *gross of unavoidable fixed costs* is easy: Take one firm. Its unavoidable fixed cost, being unavoidable, has no impact on its supply decisions. Hence, it has no impact on the firm's supply curve. If we redid the argument of Figure 12.2, we would conclude that the shaded area in the third panel is the firm's profit gross of the firm's unavoidable fixed cost.

Suppose the firm can avoid some or all of its fixed cost. Figure 12.3 tells the tale. Panel a shows the firm's full marginal cost function. In panel b, the firm's supply function is shown; it traces marginal cost above a price level p^* and quantity x^*, but is zero for lower prices. Moreover, we know from Chapter 11 that the price–quantity pair p^* and x^* are the price and quantity at which the firm just covers the avoidable portion of its fixed cost. That is, the firm's variable profit gross of all fixed cost at p^* and x^* (the shaded region in panel c) just equals its avoidable fixed cost. So, in panels d, e, and f, for some price and production level (p', x') along the firm's supply curve, producer surplus (panel d) is the firm's total revenue (panel e) less the sum of its total variable cost (the heavily shaded region in panel f) and avoidable fixed cost (the lightly shaded region in panel f).

Putting this together, for a single firm with a rising marginal cost function and a positive fixed cost, its producer surplus area is its total revenue less the sum of its total variable cost and avoidable fixed cost, which is its profit gross of any unavoidable fixed cost.

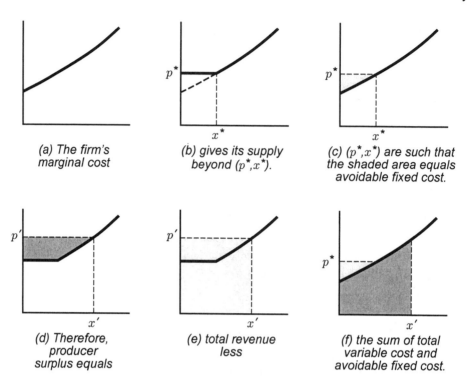

(a) The firm's
marginal cost

(b) gives its supply
beyond (p^*,x^*).

(c) (p^*,x^*) are such that
the shaded area equals
avoidable fixed cost.

(d) Therefore,
producer
surplus equals

(e) total revenue
less

(f) the sum of total
variable cost and
avoidable fixed cost.

Figure 12.3. Producer surplus with partially avoidable fixed cost.

That is for a single firm. For several firms, simply repeat the argument with all those integral signs. As you do, remember that *profit* in the previous subsection becomes *profit gross of unavoidable fixed cost* in this one.

Unavoidable Fixed Cost and Different Periods

For most purposes, that producer surplus is gross of unavoidable fixed cost is unimportant. If the fixed costs of producers are unavoidable, then they are unavoidable in any institutional arrangement, and society simply bears them. But the presence of unavoidable fixed costs can cause confusion when we apply the idea of producer surplus in analyses of short- and longer-run responses to things like taxes and price ceilings. (I use *longer-run* instead of *long-run* to cover the case of intermediate-run analysis as well.)

Figure 12.4(a) presents the typical picture of short- and longer-run supply in a competitive industry: Short-run supply is less elastic than longer-run supply, and the two supply functions cross at the status-quo production level X^*.

In Figure 12.4(b) we reproduce short-run supply, and using the status-quo production level X^* and price p^*, we shade in the area that gives producer surplus. In Figure 12.4(c), we repeat this, but using the longer-run supply curve. So the shaded area in Figure 12.4(b) represents short-run

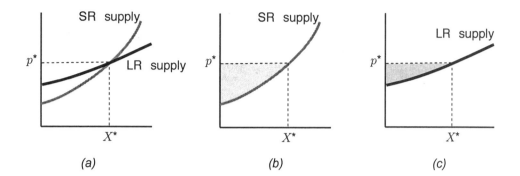

Figure 12.4. *Short- and longer-run producer surplus.* Panel a shows short-
and longer-run supply; panel b the short-run producer surplus; and panel c the
longer-run producer surplus, where in panels b and c, the quantity and price are
the longer-run status-quo levels. Short-run producer surplus exceeds longer-run
producer surplus. Does this mean that profits are higher in the short run than in
the longer run? See the text for the explanation.

producer surplus = short-run producer profit, and the shaded area in Figure
12.4(c) gives longer-run producer surplus = longer-run producer profit. Because longer-run supply is flatter than short-run supply, the shaded area in
Figure 12.4(b) is larger than the shaded area in Figure 12.4(c). So, it would
seem that short-run producer profit is *greater* than longer-run producer profit
at the status-quo level of production. In all our discussions of short-run and
longer-run costs, short- and longer-run cost were equal at the status-quo
level of production, so something seems amiss here.

Actually, nothing is amiss. The problem is that unavoidable fixed costs
are higher in the short run than in the longer run, and the shaded areas
represent profits gross of unavoidable fixed costs.

To keep things simple, assume all fixed costs are unavoidable. Then
Figure 12.5, depicting a firm's short-run and longer-run *total costs*, tells the
tale. The firm's short-run and longer-run total costs are equal at the its
status-quo level of production, and longer-run total cost is otherwise less
than short-run total cost. Clearly, then, the short-run total cost at production
level 0—or the short-run fixed cost—exceeds the longer-run total cost at
production level 0, which is just the longer-run fixed cost.

Indeed, Figures 12.4 and 12.5 show how to find the difference between
short-run and longer-run unavoidable fixed costs for the industry as a whole,
from the short-run and longer-run industry supply functions. The two total
costs are equal at the status-quo production quantity, so the area between the
short-run and longer-run industry supply functions, out to the status-quo
level of production (the triangular area in Figure 12.4(a)) is the difference in
fixed costs.

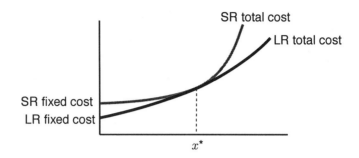

Figure 12.5. Short- and longer-run total cost functions.

In applications, questions arise such as these: If a tax is imposed on the industry or a price ceiling is enforced, how do producer profits change in the short run? How do they change in the long run? We cannot tell the absolute levels of fixed costs from the industry supply curves, so we cannot tell what is the absolute level of profits in any run. But, if we want to talk about the *change* in producer profits, fixed costs net out. The change in producer surplus equals the change in producer profits, whether the producer surplus measures net profits or profits gross of unavoidable fixed costs. Comparisons based on changes in producer surplus are completely legitimate, if you are careful: When you want to measure changes in profits in the short run, use the change in short-run producer surplus, based on the short-run supply curve. When you want to measure changes in profits in the longer run, use the change in longer-run producer surplus, based on the longer-run supply curve. In this way, any unavoidable fixed costs for the appropriate time frame will net out of the comparison. (Try Problem 12.3.)

Producer Surplus in Other Cases

We have been studying the concept of producer surplus exclusively in the context of a perfectly competitive industry, at the equilibrium outcome. Notwithstanding this single focus, the concept—essentially the sum of profits of producers, with some allowance made for various categories of fixed costs—is entirely general.

A nice thing about the context of a competitive market equilibrium is that producer surplus can be "seen" on the picture of supply and demand; it is the area of a recognizable region. In other contexts, this continues to be true. Most notably, in a monopoly industry, it is relatively easy to find producer profit gross of all fixed cost on the usual marginal cost–marginal revenue diagram, and you can find profit net of fixed cost if you have the average cost function on the graph. (See Problem 12.4 for where to find these.) But, in other contexts, it can be difficult to "see" producer surplus.

When we deal with producer surplus, we deal almost exclusively with competitive market equilibria or monopoly industries, so we nearly always can "see" producer surplus. But when you encounter other contexts, you will need to take considerable care in identifying producer surplus with some area on some graph.

Supplier Surplus When Suppliers Are Consumers

What if supply comes not from firms, but from consumers selling out of their endowment?

I do not take you through the details, but in this case, if we relabel producer surplus as *supplier surplus*, this area gives a dollar-valued measure of the benefits to suppliers of participating in the market, even if some or all the suppliers are consumers. The way to show this is (1) to figure out the supply function for an individual consumer who is selling out of his or her endowment, and (2) mimic the arguments we are about to make about consumer surplus. If you are worried about this, consult an advanced textbook in economics; but my advice is not to worry about it.

12.3. Consumer Surplus

Now we turn to consumer surplus. To begin with an admission, in general, the more heavily shaded area in Figure 12.1 is not precisely a dollar-valued measure of the benefits consumers take from consuming this good. Instead, this area gives an *approximation* of these benefits. I do not try to explain what this means: how a dollar–valued measure of benefits for a general utility is created, the nature of this approximation, when the approximation is particularly good. These are hard things to do, involving many hard-slogging pages of derivatives, which is in neither your interest nor mine. So you have to take my assertion on faith or consult a doctoral-level book on the subject.

You don't get off quite that easily, however. In a special case, the area in question provides a precise measure of these benefits. This is the case of *linear-money-left-over utility*, utility functions of the form $u(x_1, \ldots, x_k) = v_1(x_1) + \ldots + v_k(x_k) + m$, where m is money left over. You already read the argument for a single consumer back in Chapter 5 (consult pages 124–5) and taking the argument from one consumer to a set of consumers is one more application of the sum-of-integrals argument from pages 294–5.

Consumer Surplus for the Reservation-Demand Model

I complement the argument from Chapter 5 with a case that is, I hope, particularly transparent. This concerns a very special model of consumer demand, known as the *reservation-price* model. In this model,

- For the good in question, each consumer wishes to consume either precisely one unit of the good or none at all.

- In dollar terms, for each consumer, consumption of 1 unit of the good is worth an amount r, called the *reservation price* of the good for the consumer. If the consumer pays p for the good and consumes 1 unit of it, her utility, measured in dollar units, rises by $r - p.

- Therefore, the consumer's decision whether to buy the good is simple. If the price of the good is less than her reservation price, buy. If the price is more than her reservation price, do not buy. If the price equals her reservation price, she does not care whether she buys the 1 unit or not.

For example, imagine 10 consumers, whose reservation prices for the good in question are, respectively, $16, $4.50, $3, $10, $8, $2, $8, $4, $6, and $5. If the price of the good is $9, the first and fourth persons will buy units and the other eight will not. The utility gain to the first person, measured in dollars, will be $16 - $9 = $7, and the gain to the fourth will be $1. At a price of $4.40, the 1st, 2nd, 4th, 5th, 7th, 9th, and 10th consumers will purchase, with gains, respectively, of $11.60, $0.10, $5.60, $3.60, $3.60, $1.60, and $0.60. This gives us the demand function shown in Figure 12.6.

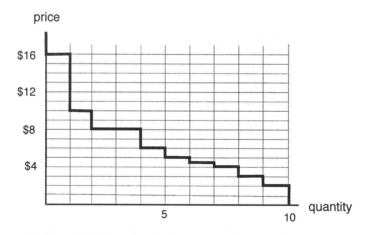

Figure 12.6. Demand in the case of reservation prices.

Usually we think of there being many more than 10 customers, with reservation prices scattered over a range. This gives a demand function that looks like a staircase with very tiny steps. Figure 12.7 shows such a staircase demand function, along with a supply function and three of the consumers whose reservation prices are $9.50, $8.50, and $6.80. The equilibrium quantity is 24 and the equilibrium price is $4.

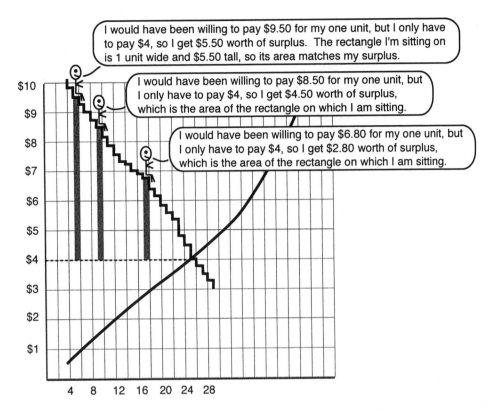

Figure 12.7. Supply, demand, and the surpluses enjoyed by three consumers.

Consider the consumer whose reservation price for the good is $9.50. Since she has to pay only $4, she is better off by the amount $5.50. As she tells you in the figure, this *surplus* that she enjoys is the area of the shaded rectangle on which she sits. The other two consumers make similar statements.

In Figure 12.8, all the consumers are brought together. If we add all their utility gain or surplus rectangles, we get the shaded area that we called the *consumer surplus*.

Consumer Surplus in Nonequilibrium Situations

As with producer surplus, we sometimes want to apply the concept of consumer surplus in contexts other than the supply-equals-demand equilibrium of a competitive marketplace. The concept does not change in the least when applied to a monopoly industry, where the monopolist serves a given demand function, or indeed to any setting where a price for the good is taken as given by consumers, who then buy as much as they desire at that price. Slightly more complex are contexts in which the good is sold using a price-discriminating scheme, but usually these can be "figured out" if you are careful. For instance, in the ideal-for-the-seller world of first-degree price

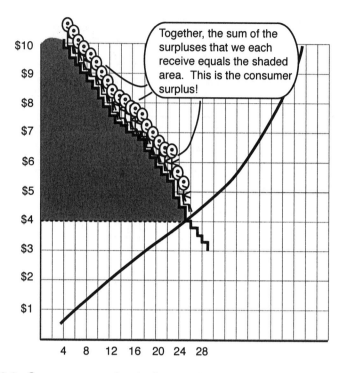

Figure 12.8. Consumer surplus is the surpluses enjoyed by all the consumers.

discrimination, consumer surplus is, by design, $0.

Other contexts can be hard to deal with. Suppose, for instance, the government nationalizes the shoe industry and produces 10 million pairs of shoes. Suppose further that the price per pair that would give demand of 10 million pairs is $50 per pair, but the Commissar for Shoes decides that a price of $10 per pair is more equitable. (Of course, a commissar would be dealing in a currency other than dollars.) Demand at $10 per pair is presumably significantly more than 10 million pairs, and so the 10 million pairs must be rationed among consumers. Queues form at the shoe department. Bribes are paid to shoe salespersons. A black market in shoes springs up, where people sell or barter shoes they do not want for things they do. And, as an economic analyst, you must work out the consumer surplus engendered by the 10 million pairs, sold—at least officially—for $10 per pair.

You cannot carry out this task without making a lot more assumptions. Even assuming linear-money-left-over utility functions, you need to know on whose feet those shoes will eventually be found, because you need to know how much benefit the shoe wearers get. As we are about to discover, a nice thing about competitive markets is that the folks who "value" the items for sale the most—who are willing to pay the most—get the items. (The quote marks around *value* will be explained later.) This allows for the computation of consumer surplus. But, when nonmarket allocation schemes are used, unless we know the identity of the folks who get the goods and the dollar-valued utilities they receive from those goods, we are stumped. For more on this, see Problem 12.6.

Firms as Customers

In the story so far, demand has come entirely from consumers. For the remainder of this chapter and the next, we maintain this assumption. But in real life, demand arises as well from producers, who purchase inputs to their production process. What about them?

It takes too long to grind through the details, so I simply assert this: For a firm that purchases some good for use in its production, where the firm takes the price of this input as given, the area under the firm's demand-for-the-input curve, down to the price, out to the quantity it buys (the area of the "consumer surplus" region) is the gain in profits accruing to the producer from being able to purchase and use the factor input. When part of demand comes from firms, the term *consumer surplus* is no longer appropriate. But, if we call it *customer* or *purchaser surplus* instead, the heavily shaded area in Figure 12.1 measures just the right thing.

12.4. Competitive Markets Maximize Total Surplus

Now that we have standards by which to judge the benefits received by consumers and producers from particular market outcomes, we can see in what sense the equilibrium achieved by a perfectly competitive market is ideal. The result is simple to state: *A competitive market equilibrium maximizes the sum of consumer and producer surplus.* This result is true in substantial generality but requires some assumptions; in particular,

- Each consumer's utility from consumption depends only on his or her own level of consumption and not on how the goods are produced or what other consumers get to consume.

- Also, each firm's total cost of production depends only on what the firm itself produces.

In Chapter 14, we learn that this pair of assumptions is crucial if the invisible hand is to perform ideally; to use the language of Chapter 14, this assumes that there are no consumption or production *externalities*.

While the argument is true in substantial generality, proving it is true takes a somewhat abstract argument. So, instead of giving the general argument here, I provide a simple argument, based on the assumptions that firms have rising marginal cost functions and no fixed costs and consumers have linear-money-left-over utility functions $v(x) + m$ where v moreover is concave.

With these assumptions, the argument runs as follows. In any plan for production and consumption, consumers consume amounts of the good in exchange (presumably) for cash, while firms take in cash in exchange for producing the good. The amount of cash received by firms must equal the amount of cash paid by consumers (monetary transfers must balance) and the amount of the stuff consumed must equal the amount produced. If consumer i gets x_i units of the good in return for m_i money, his consumer surplus is $v_i(x_i) - m_i - v_i(0)$. And if firm f gets m^f money for producing x^f goods, its surplus is $m^f - TC_f(x^f)$. (I use subscripts on x such as x_i for consumer i's consumption level and superscripts on x such as x^f for the firm f's production quantity.) Therefore, the sum of everyone's surpluses is

$$\sum_i [v_i(x_i) - m_i - v_i(0)] \quad + \quad \sum_f [m^f - TC_f(x^f)],$$

where the first sum is over all the consumers and the second sum is over all the firms. But the monetary transfers from consumers to firms must balance—that is, $\sum_i m_i = \sum_f m^f$—and so the sum of everyone's surpluses simplifies to

$$\sum_i [v_i(x_i) - v_i(0)] \quad - \quad \sum_f TC_f(x^f). \tag{12.1}$$

Time for the first major conclusion:

> The problem of maximizing the sum of surpluses is the problem of finding the production levels for the firms and the consumption levels for the consumers that maximize the expression (12.1), subject to the requirement that what is consumed equals what is produced, or $\sum_i x_i = \sum_f x^f$.

What is the solution to this problem? This is a constrained maximization problem, very much like the problem solved in Section 9.3, in that the variables enter the constraint in a one-for-one tradeoff. The rule for this optimization problem, ignoring complications for x_i or x^f that are 0, is this:

> At the solution to this problem, all the marginal costs should be equal, all the marginal utilities should be equal, and they should all be equal to one other.

In brief, if one firm has a higher marginal cost than another, we could re-arrange production and get the same amount of stuff at a lower total cost. If one consumer had higher marginal utility than another, we could rear-range their consumption and increase the utility of the first more than we decreased the utility of the second. And if Consumer A's marginal utility was, say, more than Firm B's marginal cost, we could have B make more, give it to A to consume, and raise A's utility more than we increased B's cost; the case where B's marginal cost exceeds A's marginal utility calls for decreasing A's consumption and B's production.

Such equating of margins is precisely what happens in a competitive market equilibrium. The key is the equilibrium price p. Recall that, in the introduction, I said that the role played by prices was informational. Now I can elaborate on this: The equilibrium price tells producers what their product is worth *on the margin* to consumers. It tells consumers what it costs *on the margin* to make the item. Of course, consumers and producers do not think in those terms: They maximize utility or profit. But as they do so, they cause the marginal cost of production to equal the marginal value of the good in consumption, and that is what maximizes total surplus. That is the invisible hand.

Breaking This Down: Production Efficiency; Consumption Efficiency; and the Right Total Quantity

I hope the argument just given is clear, but in case it is not, let me break this down. Step 0 in the argument is that, when we look at the total surplus, transfers of money do not matter. A dollar more or less in one party's pocket is a dollar less or more in another party's; these all net out of the total surplus calculation. What matters is the *physical goods outcome*, which consists of three things:

1. The total amount of the good, X, produced and consumed

2. The total cost incurred in producing X units of the good, which in turn depends on how this total production quantity is allocated among pro-ducers

3. The total utility generated for consumers who get to consume the good, which depends on how the X units are allocated among consumers

Then, with reference to these three:

- The cheapest way to produce X units is the way a competitive market does: Find the price p that gives supply X and let profit-maximizing firms choose how much to produce at price p.

- The greatest sum of consumers' utilities that X units of the good can produce is obtained by allocating the X units in a competitive market: Find the price p that gives demand X and let utility-maximizing consumers choose how much to consume at price p.

- The quantity X where supply equals demand maximizes the sum of utility generated in consumption less the total cost to the entire industry of production.

Or, paraphrasing, perfect competition minimizes the cost of production, maximizes the total utility obtained in consumption, and correctly sets the quantity produced and consumed.

Fairly general proofs of these propositions, more general than those given before, are provided in the *Student's Companion*.

This Does Not Work When Firms Have Market Power

What if the market is not perfectly competitive? Suppose it is served by a single profit-maximizing firm that faces a downward sloping demand function. Figure 12.9 presents demand, marginal revenue, and marginal cost. There is no supply function in this case, because a firm facing a downward sloping demand function sets the market price of its output rather than responding to an exogenously given market price.

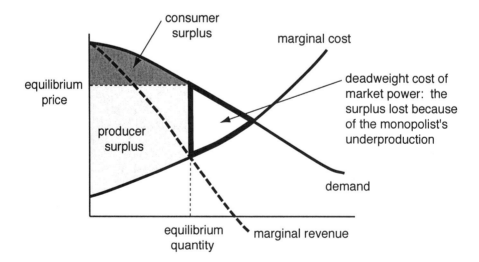

Figure 12.9. *Surplus with a monopolist.* A firm facing downward sloping demand produces where marginal cost equals marginal revenue, which is less than where marginal cost equals the marginal utility to the last consumer of the good. The loss in total surplus to society, relative to the best society could achieve, is the heavily outlined triangle, the so-called deadweight cost of market power.

The market equilibrium in this case is determined by the intersection of marginal cost and marginal revenue, giving the quantity and price marked on Figure 12.9. The area of the darkly shaded region is the amount of consumer surplus, and the area of the lightly shaded region is the firm's profit, gross of any fixed cost the firm faces. (See Problem 12.4.) Therefore, the combined shaded area is the total surplus generated in this market. It falls short of the maximal amount of surplus that could be generated by the area of the heavily outlined triangle. *The firm, in pursuit of maximal profits, produces at the level where its marginal cost equals its marginal revenue. This is less than the level that maximizes total surplus, where the firm's marginal cost equals the marginal utility or inverse demand.*

What About the Government's Share?

So far in this book, money that changes hands goes from firms to consumers or, more likely, from consumers to firms, with each dollar going out of one pocket winding up in another. But, in the next chapter, a third category of "player" is added to the story: There are firms, consumers, and the government, which may impose taxes or provide subsidies and the like. In the next chapter and Problem 12.7, when we evaluate outcomes that involve net inflows or outflows of cash from or to the government, we treat net government revenue on a dollar-for-dollar on-par basis with consumer and producer surplus. That is, the total surplus equals the net consumer surplus, plus the net producer surplus, plus the government's net revenue. In Chapter 14, we begin to question whether and why a dollar in the government's hands might be worth more or less than a dollar held by the private sector of the economy.

12.5. Efficiency versus Equity

So subject to some qualifications—that stuff about no externalities, which we explain in Chapter 14—competitive markets maximize total surplus. But is total surplus a good standard of comparison for social outcomes? What does it capture and what does it miss?

In any arrangement that causes the good to be produced and assigned to consumers, with money changing hands, two qualities to look for are efficiency and equity.

Efficiency measures whether the right amount of the good is produced in terms of the marginal costs and benefits of the good to society as a whole, whether it is produced by the low-marginal-cost producers, and whether it gets into the hands of the high-marginal-valuation consumers. *Equity*, on the other hand, concerns whether the combined transfers of goods and money result in a fair distribution of the surplus that could be created by production and exchange.

The sum of consumer and producer surplus measures efficiency without paying heed to equity. There are many ways to make this point; here are four:

1. When it comes to total surplus, only the physical good transfers matter. Any transfer of money is a wash. If we took $100,000 from every other consumer and divided the money in equal shares among all the firms and the other half of the consumers, total surplus would be unchanged. I doubt that many people would believe that the equity of outcome would be unaffected.

2. In computing total surplus, we add consumer and producer surplus on equal terms. We presumably attach value to profits because they are eventually returned to shareholders of the firm. But, insofar as shareholders tend to be wealthier as a group than consumers, some would argue that firms' profits ought not to be weighted as much as consumer benefits. Institutional arrangements that, say, increase consumer benefits or surplus by the equivalent of $10 million and decrease firms' profits by $20 million may be judged to improve equity, even though this means a $10 million loss in total surplus.

3. When measuring total surplus, we measure each consumer's utility in dollar terms and exchange one consumer's utility for another's, dollar for dollar. Suppose we have two consumers, one quite rich, a second very poor. Suppose we have some item, a bag of groceries, say. We ask each consumer: How much *money*, on the margin, is this bag of groceries worth to you? The rich consumer, being quite rich, gets little value on the margin from her money; she's bought nearly everything she wants or needs. Still, flush with cash and nothing to spend it on, she is willing to pay $100 for the bag. The poor consumer has little cash and many needs—housing, clothing, and so forth—so he cannot afford to give up so much cash for the bag: He is willing to pay only $50 for the bag of groceries. Then, maximizing consumer surplus means giving the bag to the rich consumer. This is not very equitable. Put it this way. Many and perhaps even most people would say that taking $1000 from a rich consumer to distribute equally among 100 poor consumers increases equity, because $10 is worth more to the poor than it is to the rich. But, *by definition* in the measure of efficiency we are using (dollar-calibrated utility), $10 is worth the same "utility" to each consumer.

4. As a final demonstration that efficiency misses a lot that goes into judg-

ments of equity, consider a monopoly firm interested, so it says, in maximizing total surplus: "It is true," it begins, "that when I set marginal revenue equal to marginal cost, I am underproducing relative to the amount required by total surplus maximization. This makes me feel rather bad. So permit me, if possible, to engage in first-degree price discrimination. In return for this right, I promise to produce at the quantity that maximizes total surplus." Our friendly and generous monopoly firm can be counted on to do just what it says, if it is allowed to engage in first-degree price discrimination. But it does this *because it is going to take every bit of the surplus for itself.* It goes to each of the little stick consumers, perched on the demand curve of Figure 12.8, and offers to sell to them their unit of the good for precisely their reservation price, up to the last consumer from whom it can make money on such an arrangement, which is the last consumer whose value for the good exceeds its marginal cost. Very efficient, to be sure, but very inequitable, by almost any standard, and certainly far from generous.

Economists are not very happy when asked to evaluate the equity of a given institutional arrangement on the basis of economic principles. They may have their own notions of equity, but they tend to leave to philosophers the question of how to measure equity formally. Philosophers are ready to take up this challenge; John Rawls and Robert Nozick, two modern philosophers, staked out strong and fairly opposing positions on what constitutes equity. But this is economics, not philosophy, so in this book, we use total surplus as a formal measure of the efficiency of institutional arrangements, leaving trade-offs between efficiency and equity to informal judgment.

Do not misunderstand. Just because something is formalized does not make it important, nor those things that lack formality unimportant. We separate equity and efficiency, and, using total surplus, we speak formally about efficiency. But do not feel in the least bit restrained from sacrificing a bit or even a lot of efficiency to serve equity. What we do in this chapter is provide the tools that let us measure how much efficiency is being sacrificed.

12.6. Other Aspects of Welfare and Efficiency

Since we began this chapter speaking vaguely of the triumph of capitalism over state socialism, I should say a few more things regarding this topic.

This chapter concerns "static efficiency," the ability of of the price system to achieve an efficient level of production and distribution of goods and services in a "settled" economy. The main result is that if firms and consumers respond to prices by maximizing profit and utility—and if firms and consumers are price takers and there are no externalities—then prices direct the economy to efficient production and distribution. This is not to say that a commissariat could not do just as well. But it is easy to believe that by decentralizing decisions on matters such as the number and styles of shoes to have available in shops in Minsk, markets (and profit and utility-maximization motives) outperform central planning.

But the story we've told in this chapter is inadequate for some other aspects of "efficient" economies. For instance, a large portion of what makes for material wealth is innovation and the creation of new products. A quite different story about incentives for innovation would have to be spun here. In particular, the story about static efficiency told in this chapter seems to imply that governments, to improve efficiency, should increase the level of competition. Antitrust activity seems to be clearly indicated. And things that stifle competition by protecting intellectual property, such as patents, would seem to be a bad idea. But innovation is spurred when innovators have the prospect of enjoying the fruits of their innovative activities. Some political economists would argue that the triumph of capitalism was not because the market-driven economies of the West resulted in a better assortment of shoes on the shelves of shoe stores in Los Angeles and Zurich than in Minsk. Instead, the triumph followed because capitalism and private enterprise (with protections built in for private property, including intellectual property) provide innovators the incentive to innovate and investors the incentive to seek out and finance worthwhile innovations.

We lack the tools needed to flesh out this sort of story at this point. We will be in reasonable shape to do so nearer the end of the book, although we will not do it. But it is worth noting that seeming implications of the story told here—about antitrust activity, patents, and the like—*may* be muted and even reversed when the process of innovation is added to the mix.

Another important aspect of economic efficiency concerns the ability of individuals within the society to transact with one another in a relatively low-cost manner. We take up this topic right at the end of the book, in Chapter 24. For now, it is probably useful to say that transactional efficiency may not be maximized by "Darwinian" economies, in which each firm and consumer is concerned solely and strictly with his, her, or its own welfare, so much so that an ends-justify-the-means mentality rules.

Finally, efficiency depends on what individuals value. We have used models of firm and consumer behavior in which self-interest is paramount. But, in real life, individuals have a positive taste for things like equity and providing for those less fortunate. In formal economic terms, when consumers have these sorts of tastes, we say that there are externalities in consumption. We deal with externalities in Chapter 14 and see there that they can cause real problems for the rosy picture this chapter paints. For now, record that the clear division between equity and efficiency relied on in this chapter is not entirely realistic.

Executive Summary

- In a perfectly competitive market, producer surplus (the area between the price per unit and the industry supply curve out to the level of production) gives the sum of profits of suppliers of the good, gross of any unavaoidable fixed costs.

- Consumer surplus (the area between the demand curve and the price per unit out to the level of consumption) gives a dollar-valued measure of the benefits consumers take from purchasing and consuming the good. This measure is exact in cases of reservation-demand utility and money-left-over utility, where the money left over enters as $\ldots + m$. Otherwise, it is an approximate measure.

- In a perfectly competitive market, the market equilibrium maximizes the total surplus generated in the production, exchange, and consumption of the good in question.

- The good is produced in an overall cost-minimizing manner by the industry, with the marginal cost of the last unit produced equal to the equilibrium price.

- The good is consumed in an overall sum-of-benefits-maximizing manner by consumers, with the marginal utility of the last unit consumed equal to the equilibrium price.

- The cost of the marginal unit produced matches the utility its consumption engenders, because each is equal to the price: The right amount is being produced.

- The transfer of money from consumers to producers is a net wash in terms of total surplus.

- In Economese, this is phrased as, A competitive market equilibrium is efficient. This is how *the invisible hand* works. However, keep in mind the following three points.

- Efficiency is not equity. Economists are usually informal about measuring equity, but this does not mean that it is wrong to sacrifice some efficiency to achieve a more equitable outcome.

- A firm that faces downward sloping demand and sets its price rather than taking price as given, sets its marginal cost equal to its marginal revenue: Since marginal revenue is less than price (for downward sloping demand), which equals marginal utility, this means that too little is produced to achieve full efficiency.

- Externalities complicate the story and can affect the basic conclusion (see Chapter 14), as can considerations of dynamic efficiency and the process of innovation (Chapter 23), transactional efficiency (Chapter 24), and consumer tastes for equity (Chapter 25).

Problems

12.1 Suppose the supply of a particular good is given by $S(p) = 1000(p-4)$, while demand is given by $D(p) = 3000(20 - p)$. What is consumer surplus at the equilibrium of this market? What is producer surplus?

12.2   Problem 11.9 described a perfectly competitive industry with four firms having the total cost function $TC(x) = 50 + x + 0.04x^2$ and an unlimited supply of firms having the total cost function $TC(x) = 100 + 3x + 0.04x^2$. In all cases, fixed costs are avoided by not producing. Suppose demand is given by $D(p) = 200(10 - p)$. What are the consumer and producer surpluses at the competitive market equilibrium of this industry? How does producer surplus relate to the profit levels of the firms?

12.3 Refer to Problem 11.7. An industry has free entry and exit for an unlimited number of firms, each having total cost function $TC(x) = 100 + 3x + 0.04x^2$. The industry demand is initially given by $D(p) = 200(10 - p)$, and the long-run equilibrium has price $7, total quantity 600, 12 active firms each producing 50, with $0 profit per firm. In the short run, firms cannot change their production quantities. In the intermediate run, the 12 active firms can change their production quantities. In the long run, firms can enter or leave. In Problem 11.7, we found the short-, intermediate-, and long-run equilibria if demand shifts to $200(12 - p)$. Compute the consumer and producer surpluses for the original equilibrium and then for the short-, intermediate-, and long-run equilibria following the shift in demand. Warning: To make meaningful comparisons with the status-quo situation, when you compute the status-quo level of producer surplus, do it *three times*. (Making sense of that last sentence is, more or less, the whole point of this problem.)

12.4 Figure 12.10 depicts the average and marginal cost functions for a firm with a fixed cost and rising marginal cost. It also gives a demand function and marginal revenue function for the firm, assuming this firm serves the market by itself and (therefore) has market power. Find the regions whose areas are the firm's profit gross of its fixed cost and net of its fixed cost, when it chooses price and quantity to maximize its profit. (Refer to Figure 12.9 if you need a hint for part of this.)

12.5   Imagine a monopoly whose marginal cost function is $MC(x) = 4 + x/1000$, facing a demand function given by $D(p) = 3000(20 - p)$. What pro-

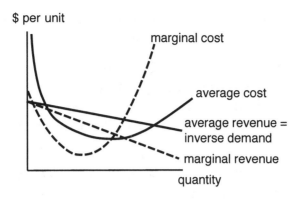

$ per unit

marginal cost

average cost

average revenue =
inverse demand

marginal revenue

quantity

Figure 12.10. Problem 12.4: The situation facing a firm with market power.

ducer and consumer surpluses result if the monopoly maximizes its profit? Compare your answers with the answers to Problem 12.1.

12.6 Suppose the demand for pairs of shoes in the People's Republic of Slynavia is given by $D(p) = 250{,}000(90 - p)$. (To keep the discussion simple, assume that each consumer wishes to buy at most a single pair of shoes.) The Commissar for Shoes can produce 10 million pairs of shoes to sell. A price of $50 per pair would lead to demand for 10 million pairs. But the commissar decides that a price of $10 per pair would be more in keeping with the government's ideology. At this price, 20 million pairs are demanded; hence, the shoes must be rationed.

(a) Suppose, in the rationing scheme employed, each of the 20 million consumers who wish to purchase a pair of shoes at $10 per pair has an equal chance of getting 1 of the 10 million pairs available. That is, each has a 0.5 of getting a pair, *which he or she then wears*. What measure of consumer surplus is appropriate for this outcome?

(b) To explain the italicized *which he or she then wears*, the rationing outcome described has some consumers who value a pair of shoes at $80 without shoes, while others who value a pair at $20 wearing a pair. It seems likely in such cases that a black market in shoes will spring up. Suppose this is a well-functioning black market, where an equilibrium black-market price emerges and trades are made at that price. What is an appropriate measure of consumer surplus generated by the sale of shoes (by the state, for $10 per pair) for the eventual outcome?

12.7 Imagine a market for a good in which demand is given by $D(p) = 10{,}000(10 - p)$. Twenty-five identical firms supply this good, each of which has the total cost function $TC(x) = 4x + x^2/200$. All these firms are competitive; they act as if they have no impact on the prices they face.

(a) What is the equilibrium price and quantity? At this equilibrium, what are the levels of consumer and producer surplus?

(b) The government imposes a tax of $1 per unit on this good, collected from the manufacturer. That is, if the firm produces x units of the good for sale, it must give the government $\$x$. What is the impact of this tax in terms of price, quantity, producer surplus, and consumer surplus?

(c) Add together producer and consumer surpluses from part a. Add together producer surplus, consumer surplus, and government net revenue from the tax in part b. Why is the second sum less?

13. Taxes, Subsidies, Administered Prices, and Quotas

In the last chapter, we developed the tools to discuss efficiency and inefficiency connected with market outcomes. In this chapter, we use those tools to study the impact on markets of a variety of government "interventions": taxes, subsidies, price floors, price ceilings, and quotas on imports.

- For many years, Japan has blocked the importation of rice from the world market by setting extraordinarily stiff quotas. In 1985, for instance, the quota on imports of rice from the United States amounted to 20,000 tons of rice, or less than 1/5 of 1% of Japanese rice consumption. These quotas were aimed at protecting Japanese domestic rice producers, who, relative to the rest of the world, were strikingly inefficient; the ratio of the world price of rice to the price in Japan at times has been worse than 1:5. But Japanese rise producers are politically very powerful, and the Japanese government has steadfastly resisted allowing massive imports of rice into Japan.

  The politics and economics of rice importation to Japan are very complex, and I make no attempt to analyze a realistic model here. But I do want to ask the following question: Assume that Thai rice production is among the most efficient in the world. Contrast two possible quota situations: The Japanese government permits the free importation of rice into Japan, or Japan allows for substantial importation but sets quota levels at roughly 40% of the Japanese market in rice, allocating licenses to import to foreign producers administratively. Suppose Thai producers, in the second scenario, are given licenses amounting to, say, 20% of rice consumption in Japan, while they would take about 50% of the market if free importation were allowed. Should the Thai government, acting on behalf of Thai producers, press for free importation? The answer, perhaps surprisingly, is that Thai producers may make substantially greater profits if Japan sets the total quota at 40% of its total market than if it allows free importation, even if this means the Thai rice industry would export less than half as much rice into Japan.

- In years past, the European Economic Community (EEC) maintained the prices of certain foods, such as butter, at artificially high levels through a price-support program in which quantities of the foods were purchased by the EEC and put into storage. For example, for a while, the EEC was the proud owner of a so-called butter mountain, a huge stock of butter that, one presumes, slowly went rancid.

What was the impact of this price-support program? What did it cost consumers and taxpayers, and how much did it benefit farmers? Would some other strategy provide as much benefit to farmers, at less cost to consumers and taxpayers?

- To raise revenues, state governments often resort to taxes on items such as cigarettes and liquor. Why cigarettes and liquor? One story is that these are somewhat less than completely savory goods, so taxing them is more likely to be acceptable. But are there other reasons for imposing taxes on these goods? And who pays these taxes, consumers or manufacturers? If a $0.50 per package tax is imposed on cigarettes, will prices rise only a little, so that this cuts into the profits of manufacturers, or will prices rise by nearly the full $0.50, so that consumers bear the brunt of the tax?

- Rent control programs impose a ceiling on the rent that can be charged for a dwelling or the percentage increase permitted in rent per year. Rent control is usually advanced as a program that saves renters from being gouged by property owners. Is this correct? What is the impact of rent control, in the short run and the long run? Who benefits, who loses, and by how much, when rent control is instituted?

This chapter concerns how economists answer these questions, by studying the impact—especially on producer, consumer, and total surplus—of taxes, subsidies, price supports, price ceilings, and quotas. The focus is on competitive markets, but we also look at monopoly markets, to see what changes.

A virtually unlimited number of questions can be investigated in these domains. A chapter five times as long as this one would not cover everything. The point of this chapter is to provide a taste of how this sort of analysis goes, looking at a few specific questions and stories. If you wish to understand the impact of some specific government policy or other, you'll probably have to construct your own model.

Why would you seek such understanding? If you are involved in the formation of public policy, the answer is evident: Actions you take affect people, and the tools here help you understand those effects. But, even as a manager in the private sector, your life is affected by such policies, and to the extent that you understand their impact, you may be able to influence the debate about their desirability.

13.1. Taxes

We begin with taxes. To keep matters simple, we consider taxes of a fixed amount per unit of the good, regardless of the price of the good. This is distinct from a percentage sales tax, where the dollar amount of the tax depends on the price of the item. Examples include taxes on liquor, cigarettes, and gasoline, at least in the United States. I also assume that it is up to the seller of the good to reimburse the government out of its revenues; the seller reports to the government the number of units that it has sold and encloses a check for that number times the per-unit amount of the tax. The price of the good includes the tax: If a unit of the good carries a tax of, say, $1 and the price of a unit of the good settles at $5, then $1 per unit sold goes to the government and $4 goes to the seller.

Thus, if TC(x) is the total cost of the good excluding the tax and the per unit tax is t, the posttax total cost to the seller is TC(x) + tx, and its marginal cost function becomes MC(x) + t. The tax raises marginal cost by the amount of the tax, which, in a competitive industry, raises the supply curve of each firm by the amount of the tax—to keep the story simple, we assume that there are no avoidable fixed costs—and therefore it raises industry supply by the amount of the tax.

When I say that a tax of size t raises the supply curve, I mean graphically, on the printed page, viewed with both your head and the book upright. Really, the inverse supply function is raised by the amount of the tax. If you are told—or if you compute from marginal cost functions and the like— that the supply function for a particular industry is $S(p) = 2000(p - 4)$ for prices above $4—supply is 0 for prices below $4—and if a tax of, say, $0.50 is imposed per unit, you *do not* add 0.5 to the supply curve. Instead, to deal algebraically with the tax and raise the supply curve by 0.5, you have to, first, invert supply, to get inverse supply, or $P(x) = 4 + x/2000$; then add 0.5 to inverse supply, getting $P(x) = 4.5 + x/2000$; and finally, reinvert to get back to supply, $S(p) = 2000(p - 4.5)$, for prices p above $4.50.

Follow along on Figure 13.1. Panel a shows the demand and old supply curves, and new supply, which is the old supply shifted up by the amount of the tax, t. The new equilibrium price and quantity are also marked.

- The equilibrium price (the price consumers pay) rises, although by less than the amount of the tax. (If supply is perfectly elastic or demand is perfectly inelastic, then the price rises by the full amount of the tax.) We denote the original price by P_0 and the new price by P_1, and we write ΔP for the rise in price, or $P_1 - P_0$.

- Reflecting the higher price to consumers, the quantity sold falls somewhat. We denote the original equilibrium quantity by X_0, the new equi-

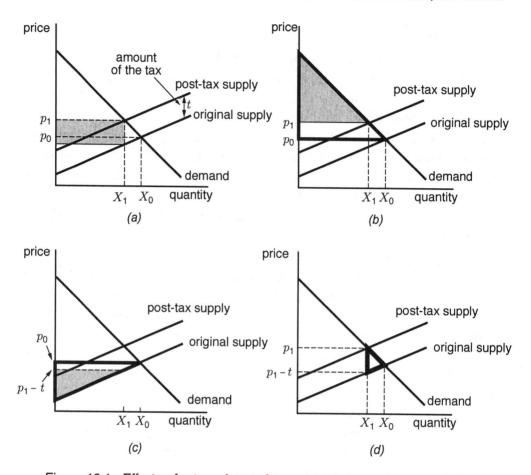

Figure 13.1. Effects of a tax. A tax of t per unit is imposed on a product in a competitive industry. This raises the inverse supply function by the amount of the tax. Price rises and quantity falls, the consumer and producer surpluses both fall (panels b and c), and total surplus declines by the area of the heavily outlined triangle in panel d.

librium quantity by X_1, and the change in quantity by $\Delta X = X_0 - X_1$. Note that the subtraction is done so that ΔX is positive, the amount by which quantity *falls*.

- Tax revenues for the government are, obviously, $t \times X_1$, the tax per unit times the new equilibrium quantity. This is shown as a shaded rectangle in panel a.

- Consumer surplus falls. Panel b shows original consumer surplus as a heavily outlined triangle and the new consumer surplus as a smaller, shaded triangle. The decrease in consumer surplus is the area of the left-over right-angle quadrilateral, $\Delta P(X_1 + X_0)/2 = \Delta P(X_1 + \Delta X/2)$.

- Producers receive only $P_1 - t$ per unit produced after they pay the tax;

their average revenue falls by $P_0 - (P_1 - t) = t - \Delta P$. Panel c shows the old producer surplus as a heavily outlined triangle and the new producer surplus as a shaded triangle. The loss in producer surplus is the area of the left-over quadrilateral, $(t - \Delta P)(X_1 + X_0)/2 = (t - \Delta P)(X_1 + \Delta X/2)$.

- Add together the new consumer surplus, producer surplus, and government tax revenues posttax, and compare the total with the sum of consumer and producer surplus pretax. The difference is the area of the heavily shaded triangle in panel d, called the *deadweight cost of the tax*, which equals $t\Delta X/2$.

Total surplus falls because the tax results in a fall in quantity, from X_0 to X_1. The socially efficient level of production and consumption (the level that equates the marginal value in consumption with the marginal cost of production) is X_0, the amount obtained by an invisible hand that is not pestered by the government. When the tax is imposed, a smaller quantity X_1 is produced, because a "gap" the size of the tax opens up between the marginal utility of the last bit consumed and the marginal cost of production of that last bit. The loss in total surplus (the deadweight cost of the tax) is precisely the lost utility less the cost of the units from X_1 up to X_0.

Please note that all this talk about triangles and quadrilaterals is something of an approximation. It is exact only if supply and demand are linear. If supply and demand are smooth—no kinks or jumps—these formulas give good approximations for small values of the tax per unit.

These formulas can be reexpressed very nicely in terms of the elasticities of supply and demand or in terms of their slopes. It is probably easiest to express them in terms of the slopes of inverse demand and inverse supply. I abbreviate the slope of inverse supply as Slope_{IS} and the slope of inverse demand as Slope_{ID}. Since demand slopes downward, the slope of inverse demand is a negative number. So, in what follows, you see a lot of $|\text{Slope}_{ID}|$, the absolute value of the slope of inverse demand. With this prologue, we can write some formulas:

- The reduction in the equilibrium quantity is

$$\Delta X = \frac{t}{|\text{Slope}_{ID}| + \text{Slope}_{IS}}.$$

- The amount of the tax passed on to consumers in the form of higher prices is

$$\Delta P = \frac{|\text{Slope}_{ID}|}{|\text{Slope}_{ID}| + \text{Slope}_{IS}} \times t$$

- The deadweight cost of the tax is

$$\frac{1}{2}\frac{t^2}{|\text{Slope}_{\text{ID}}| + \text{Slope}_{\text{IS}}}.$$

- The *relative burden of the tax on the consumers, relative to firms,* is both the ratio of the loss in consumer surplus to the loss in producer surplus and $\Delta P/(t - \Delta P)$, the ratio of the rise in the consumers' price to the fall in the producers' average revenue. Whichever definition you use, the relative burden of the tax on consumers is

$$\frac{|\text{Slope}_{\text{ID}}|}{\text{Slope}_{\text{IS}}}.$$

All these formulas are exact for linear supply and demand. When supply or demand is nonlinear, they still give good approximations as long as the amount of the tax is small and supply and demand are smooth.

Before you do anything else, use these formulas to evaluate the impact of a tax of $0.30 on a good whose (pretax) supply is given by $S(p) = 2000(p - 4)$ for prices 4 and above and whose demand is given by $D(p) = 1000(10 - p)$. See the answer to Problem 13.1, to check your work. (Hint: The slope of inverse demand is the inverse of the slope of demand and similarly for supply. For instance, since the slope of demand is -1000, the slope of inverse demand is $1/(-1000) = -0.001$.)

These are not magic formulas. They involve some very simple geometry and a bit of algebra. Derive them on your own or see them derived in the solution to Problem 13.2 in the *Student's Companion*. Do not memorize them. It may pay to have them copied somewhere handy, just in case they turn up on an exam. But, if you find yourself needing to figure out things like the new price or quantity and have mislaid them, don't despair. Simply raise inverse supply by the amount of the tax and solve for the posttax equilibrium price and quantity.

The formulas tell us about the economics of a tax:

- *Who bears the brunt of a tax?* This depends on the relative slopes of inverse supply and demand. Steep slopes for either side are bad for that side. If the absolute value of the slope of inverse demand is three times the slope of inverse supply, consumers are going to suffer, relatively: The price will rise by 75% of the amount of the tax, and the ratio of the loss in consumer surplus to the loss in producer surplus will be 3:1.

- *How large is the impact of the tax on equilibrium quantity?* The impact is larger the more elastic are supply and demand. If either one is relatively inelastic, the impact on quantity will be small, but if both are elastic, the change in quantity can be large indeed.

- *How large is the deadweight cost?* The deadweight cost is half of the product of the tax and the quantity reduction; so for a given tax, deadweight cost is small when the reduction in quantity is small, which, we just learned, is when either—or, better, both—supply or demand is highly inelastic.

Why are taxes often imposed on items such as alcohol or cigarettes? As noted previously, one reason often given is that the government wishes to discourage the consumption of these items, on paternalistic or other grounds. A second reason is that demand for these goods is often quite inelastic, which implies that the deadweight cost will be small. Figure 13.2 illustrates these ideas.

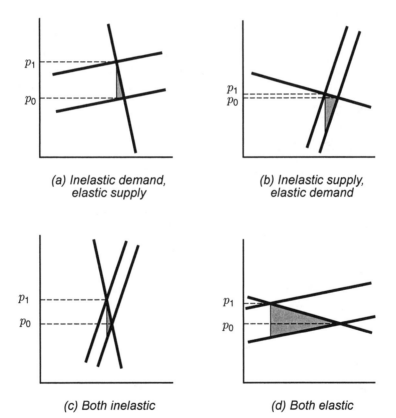

(a) Inelastic demand, elastic supply

(b) Inelastic supply, elastic demand

(c) Both inelastic

(d) Both elastic

Figure 13.2. Taxes and the elasticities of supply and demand. For an equal-sized tax, the four panels illustrate that the brunt of the tax is borne by whichever side has a more inelastic response to price shifts and that the deadweight cost is high when both supply and demand are elastic, fairly low when either is inelastic, and very low when both are inelastic.

Percentage Taxes, Prices Gross of the Tax, and Taxing the Buyers

We assume in the above discussion that the price is net of the tax. But, in many cases, the posted price of the good does not include the tax: If something costs $10 and there is a 6% sales tax on the good, the consumer remits $10.60 to the seller, who then transfers the $0.60 to the government. The fact that the price is gross and not net of the tax changes the formulas but not the essential economics: The consumer pays a net price that differs from the revenue the firm takes in by the amount of the tax.

It is usual for the seller of a good to be responsible for transferring the tax to the government, but, in some cases, buyers have this responsibility. For instance, the buyer of a used car from a private individual in California must pay the applicable sales tax when registering the car and transferring title. This is entirely irrelevant to the economics of the situation. The seller's net revenue is the posted price, and the buyer must pay the posted price plus the amount of the tax. (This ignores administrative costs, which are normally very small.)

Percentage taxes complicate the story a bit. Since firms are price takers, they take the tax amount as given, but you do not know how much to raise the inverse supply function until you know where the raised supply function intersects the demand function. But, while the algebra is a bit more complicated, the economics are the same.

Taxes on a Monopolist

What about a tax imposed on a monopolist (or any firm with market power)? Assuming a fixed tax per unit, paid by the producer, this shifts the firm's marginal cost curve up by the amount of the tax, leading to a new intersection of marginal cost and marginal revenue. The general formula for the amount of the tax passed on to the consumer is quite complex; see the solution to Problem 13.4. But there are easy special cases: If the demand function is linear and the marginal cost is constant (which, in a competitive case, would mean that 100% of the tax would be borne by the consumer), the price rises by exactly half the amount of the tax. See Figure 13.3.

Taxing a monopoly-supplied good results in a substantial deadweight cost. Figure 13.4 depicts the general situation. The heavily shaded region gives the posttax consumer surplus, the medium shading shows the new producer surplus, and the lightly shaded "tube" at the bottom gives net revenues from the tax. So, instead of a triangle for the deadweight cost, we have the heavily outlined quadrilateral. The difference is significant: In the case of perfect competition, the deadweight cost is (roughly) half the size of the tax times the reduction in quantity caused by the tax. For a small tax, the reduction in quantity is small, and so the deadweight cost is the product

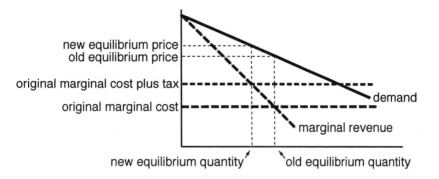

Figure 13.3. The effect of a tax on a monopolist. In the case of constant marginal cost and linear demand, half of any tax is passed on to the consumer.

of two small numbers. But, in Figure 13.4, the deadweight cost is, more or less, the reduction in quantity caused by the tax times the difference between average and marginal revenue. The reduction in quantity is small for a small tax, but the difference between the average and marginal revenue functions is relatively large unless demand is very elastic. Thus a tax on a firm with market power has substantial deadweight costs relative to a similar-sized tax imposed on a competitive industry.

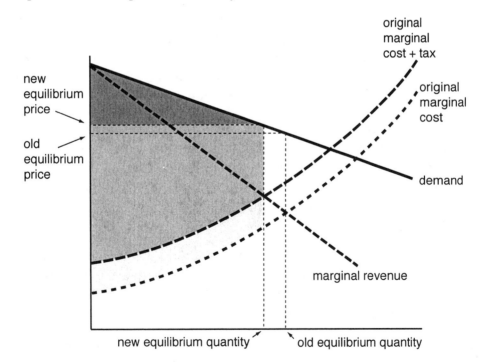

Figure 13.4. The effect of a tax on a monopolist. The shaded regions are (from top to bottom), the new consumer surplus, the new producer surplus (profit), and the tax receipts. The heavily outlined quadrilateral is the deadweight cost of the tax.

Subsidies

Direct subsidies are like negative taxes. Most of the analysis we did for taxes can be repeated for subsidies, and similar pictures emerge. Problems 13.5 and 13.6 give you the opportunity to replicate for subsidies the analysis done for taxes. But,

- When the production of a good is subsidized for a competitive industry, the good is overproduced relative to the level of output that maximizes total surplus; the true cost of the last few units exceeds the marginal value of those units in consumption, which generates a deadweight cost.

- In terms of total surplus, a subsidy to a monopolist can increase efficiency, because it increases production, getting the industry closer to the quantity where marginal cost equals marginal utility. This has interesting consequences on how, for instance, a government should handle concessions at places like national parks. See Problem 13.6.

13.2. Price Supports

Governments can do other things than impose taxes or give subsidies for specific goods. They can, and sometimes do, support the price of a good at a prespecified level, or they can put a ceiling above which the price may not go. We look at price supports in this section. In particular, we constrast two different ways that prices can be supported, with vastly different consequences for the deadweight cost of the support program.

1. The government can set an artificially high price for the good, above the price that would prevail if the market were left to find its own equilibrium. At this artificially high price, supply exceeds demand, and the government buys up the excess supply, putting it into storage or destroying it. This is how, for instance, the European Economic Community created a butter mountain.

2. Or the government can set two prices. Producers are paid an artificially high price for the good by the government, then the government resells everything it purchases from producers at a price low enough that demand equals this supply.

Figure 13.5 shows these two programs side by side. We begin with the usual supply and demand diagram. Note the equilibrium price p_e. We imagine that the government decides for some reason that p_e is too low. For instance, if the market is for agricultural goods, the government might wish to maintain a high price for the good to prevent farmers from going bankrupt, either on political grounds or to keep agricultural workers from flooding into urban areas. For whatever reason, the government decides to set a price floor of $\hat{p}$. At this price, producers will supply $\hat{X}$.

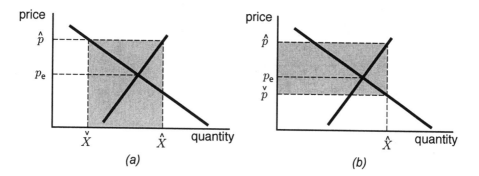

Figure 13.5. *Two means for setting a price floor.* In a market where the competitive market equilibrium price is p_e, the government decides to set price $\hat{p}$, which results in production at the level $\hat{X}$. (a) The government can charge consumers $\hat{p}$, giving demand $\check{X}$, with the government destroying or storing the difference $\hat{X} - \check{X}$, costing the government a gross $\hat{p}(\hat{X} - \check{X})$. (b) Or the government can set the price to consumers at $\check{p}$, which causes consumers to buy the amount $\hat{X}$, at a gross cost to the government of $\hat{X}(\hat{p} - \check{p})$.

If the government charges consumers $\hat{p}$, demand by consumers is $\check{X}$, far below the quantity $\hat{X}$ produced. The government then purchases the excess supply $\hat{X} - \check{X}$, destroying this excess supply, storing it, or shipping it off to some needy third-world nation. The expenditure by the government, excluding any storage cost, is $\hat{p}(\hat{X} - \check{X})$, the shaded region in panel a.

Or, as in panel b, the government can charge consumers the price $\check{p}$, far below $\hat{p}$, which causes consumers to consume $\hat{X}$. The government's expenditure is $\hat{X}(\hat{p} - \check{p})$, excluding the cost to the government of administering the program. This gross cost is shaded in panel b.

It isn't clear which program requires less government expenditure. The buy and store or destroy program requires very little expenditure if both supply and demand are inelastic and enormous expenditure if both are elastic. The level of expenditure in the two-price system is at least $(\hat{p} - p_e)X_e$ but will be not much more than this if demand is elastic and supply is inelastic.

There is no question, though, which program is better in terms of total surplus generated. The two-price system always wins. Figures 13.6 and 13.7 show why. Figure 13.6 computes the loss in total surplus from the buy and store or destroy program, while Figure 13.7 computes the loss in total surplus from the two-price system. Clearly the latter is less, and it is not hard to see why: In terms of total surplus, the dollar transfers net out. All that matters is the physical goods outcome of the two programs. Both have the

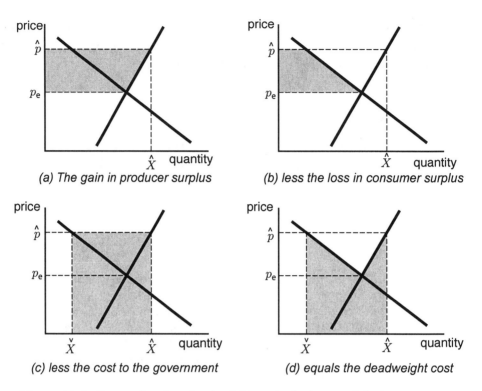

Figure 13.6. Computing the deadweight cost of a buy and destroy program.

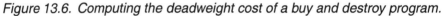

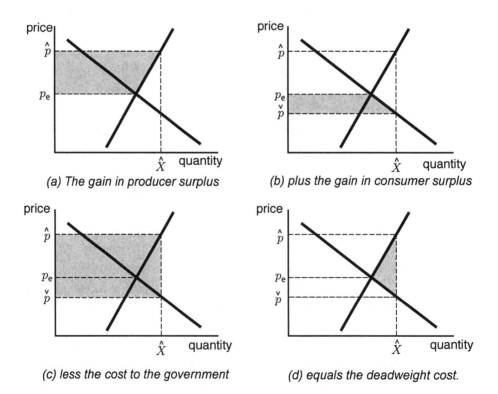

Figure 13.7. Computing the deadweight cost of a two-price price support system..

same amount being produced. But in the buy and store or destroy program, everything being stored or destroyed gives no consumption value. In the two-price system, the stuff that otherwise would be stored or destroyed is consumed. The difference in deadweight costs in Figures 13.7 and 13.8 is clearly just the consumption value of the excess supply.

Given the difference in deadweight costs, why would any government or body such as the European Economic Community choose the buy and store or destroy program over the two-price system? For one thing, the government's expenditure for the buy and store or destroy program might be less—inelastic demand tends to this result—making the first program more acceptable politically. And, in real-life applications, there may be external trade considerations to worry about. Suppose, for instance, some of the butter sold in the EEC came from outside the community. If the EEC sold highly subsidized domestic butter at a low price, foreign producers might find their market gone. It might make sense for, say, Canadian dairy farmers to sell their butter in the EEC at 10 FF per kilo but not if the price is 5 FF per kilo. To keep the Canadian government happy, the EEC might offer to buy a set amount of Canadian butter at the original price of 10 FF per kilo, then resell it cheaply to its domestic consumers, but one can imagine the domestic political uproar that this would occasion: French and German tax money going to subsidize Canadian butter producers! The "butter mountain" scheme, on the other hand, pushes the consumer price of butter up to 15 FF per kilo. The Canadian butter producers are happy; indeed, they want to increase the amount they sell in the EEC at this supported price, and the Europeans might want to impose a quota equal to the old amount of Canadian butter imported into Europe. The Canadian government might not like the quota, but its producers are better off than before, so the EEC can hope that Canada will understand and not retaliate. Of course, European dairy farmers are happy. And even a pretty penny can be made in manufacturing refrigeration units. European taxpayers just have to suffer. And as for European consumers, a bit less butter is probably good for their health

These are not the only sorts of programs one could imagine. A third alternative would be to ration the scarce demand to suppliers. That is, give dairy farmers quotas for their production, sufficiently severe to hold the supply down to the level of demand at the supported price. Or pay dairy farmers to "retire" some of their production. The implications of this sort of program are a bit hard to develop, because farmers can find ways around such limits on their production. So I leave this story here.

13.3. Price Ceilings and Rent Control

A price ceiling establishes a maximum price for some good. Typically, this is done on grounds of equity (the naturally occurring equilibrium price is held to be unjustly high) or interest-group politics. If the price ceiling has an impact (if it is less than the equilibrium price), demand for the good exceeds supply. This leaves the agency that wishes to enforce the ceiling with two basic options: It must either increase supply, by producing the good itself or by compelling producers to supply more than they would choose, or it must ration the supply among consumers.

Rent control is an excellent example. I use a model of perfect competition to study rent control and, indeed, in most metropolitan areas, the rental market is fairly competitive. Owners of a particular apartment or house face competition from owners of similar apartments or houses. The market does not fit the model of perfect competition perfectly, because apartments and houses vary in size, location, and amenities. But, usually, competition extends to most varieties of rental housing.

Suppose that the supply and demand functions for rental units are as given in Figure 13.8. I draw supply as fairly inelastic, because rental units are, more or less, in fixed supply. What is a landlord going to do except rent the unit at the best price he can get? He cannot live in all those units at once. (But things are not quite this simple, as we see in a bit.)

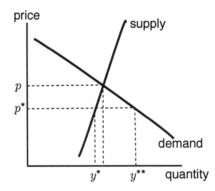

Figure 13.8. Imposition of a price ceiling, as in rent control. If a price ceiling is set below the equilibrium price, demand at that controlled price exceeds supply.

Suppose it is decided that the equilibrium price p is too high on grounds of equity, and a price ceiling p^* is imposed through legislation. Since supply is fairly inelastic, this does not cause much of a decrease in the amount of housing supplied; supply falls to y^*. But demand at p^* is y^{**}, which is considerably in excess of supply. A large number of consumers who would like to find housing at the controlled price are unable to do so. The right to rent housing at the controlled price becomes a valuable possession. In most cases, this right, once it is bestowed on an individual, is retained by the individual. Sometimes these rights are passed on by word of mouth; someone who is leaving a rent-controlled apartment tips off a friend, who asks for it the moment the vacancy becomes known to the landlord. It is not unknown—although it is often illegal—for potential renters to pay something to an incumbent renter for the "right" to take over the property. Or the unit may be sublet at a much higher price than the controlled price, with the difference going into the pocket of the lucky individual with the right to rent at the controlled price. It is not unknown for landlords, faced with a surfeit of demand, to use this as an opportunity to discriminate against some categories of individuals or demand under-the-table payments.

These "corruption" costs of rent control are hard to quantify, so I will assume them away, concentrating instead on how an ideal rent-control program affects the distribution of surplus. Specifically, I make the rose-tinted assumption that the available apartments are rationed in a way that gets the available units into the hands of those consumers who value them most highly. This means that, since y^* is the amount supplied at the controlled price p^*, the surplus obtained by consumers is the shaded area in Figure 13.9(a). Comparing with consumer (renter) surplus prior to the imposition of rent control, the impact of rent control is that consumers gain the rectangle in Figure 13.9(b) but lose the small shaded triangle in that figure. This is a considerable gain.

Landlords, on the other hand, are substantially worse off. The loss in producer (landlord) surplus is the shaded area in Figure 13.9(c). Note that most of this is the rectangle in Figure 13.9(b); landlords lose that rectangle plus a small triangle off on the right-hand side. So the deadweight cost of rent control is the sum of the two triangles in Figure 13.9(d).

Assuming supply is fairly inelastic, this is not much of a deadweight cost. Presumably the purpose of the rent control program is redistribution of surplus from landlords to renters and that certainly has been accomplished. Of course, the corruption and other costs of the rationing scheme must be considered, as must the hidden costs of having apartments held by people who do not value them as highly as those who are left out. But this picture makes it look as though, as a redistributive program, rent control accomplishes what it sets out to do with small loss in terms of efficiency.

Opponents of rent control argue that this picture is too rosy, however, because it assumes the supply of housing is inelastic. This may be true in the short run. But, in the longer run, landlords do not maintain rental units or withdraw them from the rental market where possible. Where the population is rising so that demand shifts out through time, rent control

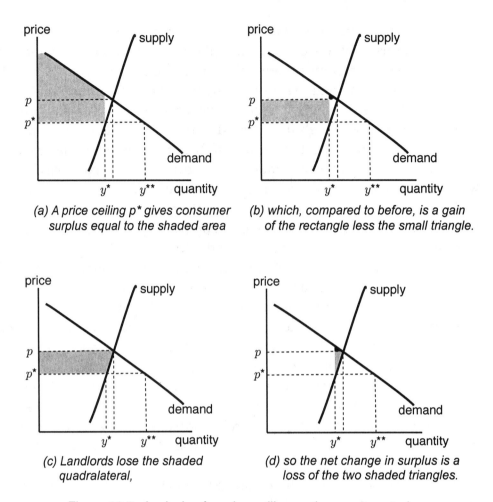

(a) A price ceiling p* gives consumer surplus equal to the shaded area

(b) which, compared to before, is a gain of the rectangle less the small triangle.

(c) Landlords lose the shaded quadralateral,

(d) so the net change in surplus is a loss of the two shaded triangles.

Figure 13.9. Analysis of a price ceiling such as rent control.

means that supply is not increased; new rental units are not built.

If supply is fairly elastic (in the long run), the picture of Figure 13.9 becomes much worse. Panels b and d of Figure 13.10 tell the tale. Now the gain by renters is the rectangle in panel b less the triangle in that panel; and while it looks as if the rectangle is larger, it is not larger by very much. Indeed, if rental demand is highly inelastic, the triangle becomes quite large; renters could lose surplus overall as a result of the decline in the available housing stock. And, per panel d, the deadweight cost is quite large.

Opponents of rent control argue that the progression from Figure 13.9 to 13.10 is typical when rent control is instituted. In the short run, renters are made better off at the expense of landlords, and the deadweight cost is small. But, in the longer run, the housing stock declines, renters as a class lose their benefits, and the deadweight cost becomes large. The opponents argue that it is better to avoid rent control from the start.

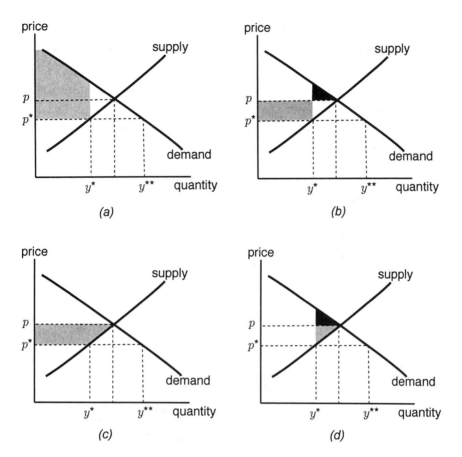

Figure 13.10. *Figure 13.9 with a more-elastic supply.* If supply is more elastic, the picture is not so rosy. The gain in consumer surplus (the rectangle less the triangle in panel b) may be small or even negative, while the deadweight cost (panel d) may be substantial.

If this is so, why does rent control persist? Why do renters not see what is going on—if indeed it is going on—and repeal rent control? Opponents of rent control give two answers. First, the repeal of rent control does not cause supply to return, unless potential landlords are convinced that rent control will not be reinstated as soon as the housing stock improves. Renters, seeing this is so, are stuck with a small housing stock, and make the best of it by keeping it under rent control. Also, say the opponents, the class of potential renters is a diffuse group, not well organized. The well-organized group consists of individuals who are lucky enough to be in rent-controlled units already. They are getting the benefits of the price ceiling—they are the folks "in the rectangle"—while the losers are consumers who would rent if there were increased rental stock. The political forces favor the entrenched renters, so rent control persists.

Price Ceilings and Monopolists

Price ceilings imposed on monopolists look very different. They can *enhance* efficiency while simultaneously enhancing equity. See Figure 13.11. Panel a depicts the usual picture of a monopoly equating marginal cost and marginal revenue. The shaded areas give the consumer and producer surpluses, and the heavily outlined triangle shows the loss in overall surplus that arises from the monopolist exercising its market power.

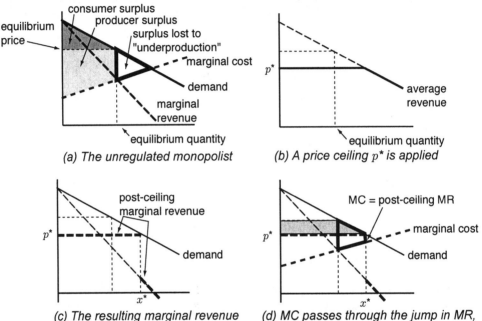

(a) The unregulated monopolist

(b) A price ceiling p^* is applied

(c) The resulting marginal revenue function is discontinuous

(d) MC passes through the jump in MR, the monopolist chooses x^*, consumers are better off, and total surplus increases

Figure 13.11. *Price ceilings imposed on a monopolist.* Panel a depicts the situation before price ceilings. In panel b, a price ceiling of p^* is imposed, giving the average revenue function shown by the heavy line. Panel c shows the marginal revenue function that goes with the average revenue function in panel b, and panel d puts marginal cost back in. The monopolist charges the ceiling price and produces x^*. The shaded area shows the gain in consumer surplus and the heavily outlined quadrilateral shows the gain in overall surplus.

Suppose the government imposes a ceiling price p^* on the monopolist somewhere between the old equilibrium price and the price at which marginal cost equals demand. Let x^* be the level of demand at the price p^*. This means that the monopolist faces the *average revenue* curve shown in panel b: As a function of the quantity produced x, total revenue is p^*x for $x \leq x^*$ and total revenue is the old level of total revenue for $x \geq x^*$. Thus, we get the marginal revenue curve shown in panel c: Marginal revenue is p^*

up to x^*, then jumps down and follows the original marginal revenue curve. Panel d shows the new equilibrium price and quantity: The monopolist in this case supplies x^* and charges p^*. Since x^* is closer to the point where marginal cost equals demand, total surplus goes up; consumer surplus rises quite a lot (the heavily shaded region in panel d), and producer surplus falls by a smaller amount. The fall in producer surplus is harder to see, being the difference between two areas—can you tell which two?—so I do not indicate it on the figure. But the gain in total surplus is easy to find; it is the area of the heavily outlined quadrilateral.

This pleasant picture assumes that the ceiling price is above the level at which marginal cost equals demand. Work your way through the picture that results if (1) the ceiling price is at less than this level, but above the level where marginal cost cuts through marginal revenue and (2) if the ceiling price is at less than the level where marginal cost hits marginal revenue. (In the second case, the price ceiling reduces overall surplus, although the distributional consequences are very large.)

Natural Monopoly, Regulation, and Deregulation

A *natural monopoly* is an industry in which, on both efficiency and competition grounds, it is natural for the industry to be served by a single producer. The most prevalent case is where the technology involves a very large fixed cost, so large that the efficient scale is large relative to the market as a whole. Electric and telephone utilities are typically cited examples, because of the need for a large local "network" to distribute electicity or phone messages.

When technology leads to a natural monopoly, promoting competition is either wasteful or impossible. But, allowing a monopoly to charge whatever price it wishes leads to inefficiencies (production will not reach the level where marginal cost equals marginal utility) and is inequitable. Hence, governments often resort to the regulation of natural monopolies; in terms of Figure 13.11, on efficiency grounds, the government seeks to set the ceiling price at the level where marginal cost hits demand. Two problems emerge in achieving this ideal: Regulators may have a hard time assessing the firm's marginal cost function, and if the fixed cost is very large, setting price at this level may mean the firm is compelled to charge less than its average cost.

To add further complications, natural monopolies have sometimes been extended by the monopolist into realms where competition would otherwise be feasible. For instance, electric utilities have used their natural monopoly in the distribution of electricity to construct monopoly positions in the generation of electricity. In the not so distant past, the Bell Telephone System used its monopoly in local phone service to construct monopolies in long-distance service and even in the manufacture of telephone equipment. Public policy over the past few decades has aimed at preventing this, by deregulating industries in which competition is economically feasible and stopping natural monopolies from using their monopoly position to extend their market power.

It would take another book to do justice to the issues of natural monopoly, regulation, and deregulation. If you are interested, such books exist and you have most of the tools required to tackle them.

13.4. Quotas and Tariffs

A quota is a program in which the importation of a particular good is limited. Quotas are imposed for a variety of reasons, including retaliation in trade disputes, but the primary direct reason for a quota is to protect a domestic industry. The protection can aim at helping the industry develop, especially if it is a relatively new industry and production costs have an experience-curve effect, or to protect an old, inefficient industry. For instance, Japan has for many years limited the importation of rice to protect its "traditional" and politically very powerful rice farmers.

As noted in the introduction, issues connected to current policy and trade disputes over Japanese rice imports are quite complex. I do not attempt a realistic model of the situation, but I want to indicate that the economics of such quotas can sometimes lead to surprises. In particular, I want to explain why rice exporters (to Japan) might prefer a system of quotas, where Japan permits only, say, 40% of its domestic rice consumption to be imported, instead of free importation.

The key is to ask, What determines the price of rice in Japan under the two scenarios? If free importation of rice is allowed to Japan, the price of rice must fall to meet the supply of rice on the world market. The domestic market in rice in Japan is fairly large, but the world rice market is quite a bit larger; and while the world supply of rice is not flat—it slopes somewhat upward—allowing free importation of rice into Japan would not raise rice prices worldwide by all that much.

But if a quota were set at 40% of the Japanese domestic market, then the marginal supplier of rice in Japan would be a domestic producer. Some domestic producers are reasonably efficient, but in comparison with international producers, Japanese rice growers have fairly high marginal costs. One can imagine, under this scenario, that the price of rice in Japan, driven by domestic marginal costs of production, would be two or even three times the international price.

That would make importation of rice into Japan very lucrative. Profit margins in the world market, because of the very high level of competition—

that is, the very elastic supply—are quite thin. With a 40% total quota, those international producers lucky enough to get the right to import into Japan would be looking at profit margins over 100% (of marginal cost).

Of course, this would make the right to import rice into Japan very valuable, and one can imagine all manner of—what's a polite way to say it?—activities devoted to getting a slice of the quota.

Three remarks are worth making here:

1. Instead of a quota on rice imports, the Japanese government might consider imposing a tariff on rice imports, or it might use a combination of tariffs and quotas. In that way, it could extract some of the profit that would otherwise accrue to international producers.

2. These quotas mean Japanese consumers pay a tremendous price in foregone consumer surplus. In fact, if you assume that the supply function for rice in the international market is fairly flat, the benefits to domestic producers of quotas or to producers and the government of tariffs and quotas are less than the benefits that would accrue to consumers if free importation were allowed. (If you do not see the argument, try Problem 13.9.)

3. In the 1980s, the Japanese automobile manufacturers voluntarily restricted the number of cars they exported to the United States, in what was called the voluntary export restraint (VER) program. The new car market is not perfectly competitive, and economists continue to try to estimate the impact of the VERs on American consumers, the U. S. domestic producers, and the Japanese producers. These estimates are controversial. But, by all accounts, this restriction did not hurt the Japanese manufacturers, and some analysts insist that the Japanese manufacturers made money out of the VERs: By administratively restricting their imports to the United States, the Japanese car manufacturers restrained their internecine competition and pushed up the price of Japanese cars in America, thus increasing profit margins on a smaller number of cars by enough to keep profits where they would otherwise have been or even to improve those profits.

Executive Summary

- Concerning taxes imposed on a competitive industry, the burden of a tax is borne relatively in proportion to how inelastic is supply or demand. Also, the deadweight cost of a tax is large when both supply and demand are elastic, and it is small if either supply or demand is inelastic. If the tax is small, the amount of revenue raised by the tax is large relative to its deadweight cost.

- Concerning taxes imposed on a monopoly, the burden of the tax is fairly complex in general, but for constant marginal cost and linear demand, half the tax is passed on to the consumers. And the deadweight cost depends on the "gap" between the average and marginal revenues: The deadweight cost is on the same order of magnitude as is the revenue raised by the tax.

- Concerning price supports, programs in which "excess production" is stored or destroyed are inevitably less efficient, in terms of the deadweight cost, than programs where the government buys from producers at one price and sell to consumers at a lower price, to get the same level of price support. But the comparison in terms of government expenditures is unclear.

- Concerning price ceilings (such as rent control), for a competitive market, an immediate question that must be answered is, How is the limited supply going to be rationed? There are hard-to-quantify and often hidden costs of rationing schemes, such as black markets, to worry about. Assuming the rationing problem is solved efficiently, a deadweight cost of underproduction remains. The size of this cost depends on the elasticity of supply; more inelastic supply means lower deadweight cost. This sort of program involves a transfer from sellers to buyers. Buyers benefit a lot when the supply is inelastic, but they can lose out in net if supply is sufficiently elastic. The short-run and long-run impacts on buyers therefore can be very different, as is often the case in rent control. But the beneficiaries are easier to organize politically, which is an important reason these programs persist.

- Price ceilings for monopolists can be much more benign; such programs can raise total surplus while they distribute surplus from the monopolist to consumers.

- Quotas on imports are often enacted to protect domestic producers but can benefit foreign producers as well by pushing up the domestic price of the good. They are paid for, by and large, by domestic consumers.

Problems

13.1 Consider a good for which the supply function is $S(p) = 2000(p - 4)$ (for prices 4 and above) and the demand function is $D(p) = 1000(10 - p)$. What are the equilibrium price and quantity for this market? If a tax of \$0.30 is imposed on the good, what are the new equilibrium price and quantity? How much is the deadweight cost of the tax? What is the relative burden of the tax on consumers, relative to the burden on producers (and how do you measure "burden")? What is the loss in consumer surplus, and what is the loss in producer surplus? You can answer most of these questions by solving for the equilibrium price and quantity with and without the tax, or you can use the formulas given on pages 319 and 320. Take your pick, although it would be ideal if you did both, just to check that the formulas really work.

13.2 If you did Problem 13.1, you know that the formulas really do work. So now the question is why. Derive the formulas. The key is to draw the right picture.

13.3 Suppose, in a competitive market, the supply function is $S(p) = 5000(p-2)$ and the demand function is $D(p) = 2000(16-p)$. If a tax of $0.70 is placed on the good, by how much does the equilibrium price rise? By how much does the equilibrium quantity fall? What is the deadweight cost of the tax? Do you need to solve for the equilibrium price and quantity to answer these questions?

13.4 In the chapter, we asserted (and showed in a picture) that, in the case of a monopolist facing linear demand with a constant marginal cost, half of any tax is passed on to the consumers in the form of higher prices. In the general case of a competitive industry, the percentage of a tax passed on in higher prices is a relatively straightforward function of the relative slopes of inverse supply and demand. So the obvious question to ask is, In the general case of a monopolist facing a downward-sloping inverse demand function $P(y)$ and having a nondecreasing marginal cost function $MC(y)$, how much of a (small) tax on the good is passed onto consumers in the form of higher prices? (This is very hard; the answer involves both the derivative of marginal cost and the second derivative of inverse demand.)

13.5 Derive formulas similar to those on pages 318–20 for a subsidy on a good produced by a perfectly competitive industry. You may assume that the production of the good is subsidized; that is, producers receive from the government a payment equal to the fixed size of the subsidy times the number of units the firm makes and sells.

13.6 (a) Consider a monopoly firm that faces the inverse demand function $P(x) = \$1000(100 - 0.01x)$ and has a constant marginal cost of production equal to $20. The government decides to subsidize the production of this good, offering the firm $4 for every unit of the good the firm manufactures and sells. What is the impact of this subsidy program on consumer, producer, and total surpluses?

(b) National and state governments often "privatize" the provision of concession services at national or state parks and recreation areas. The concessionaire is chosen by a competitive bidding process; firms that wish to hold the concession bid for the right to do so. An issue that often arises is the level of "services" the government provides the eventual consessionaire; in effect, the government can subsidize the costs of running the concession. Assume that the government does not wish to regulate the prices set by the eventual consessionaire. It is then sometimes asserted that the government should charge the concessionaire for all marginal cost items the government provides. Why might this argument be wrongheaded?

13.7 Rufus T. Firefly, prime minister of the country of Freedonia, faces an economic crisis. The citizens of his country are demanding the free importation of sorghum, and sorghum producers are threatening to vote en masse for his rivals if he allows this.

For the citizens of Freedonia, sorghum is a crop with a long tradition. The ancient folk fables of the Freedonian people stress the importance of sorghum to the tribes that established Freedonia. National rituals are built around the ceremonial use of sorghum. In addition to its ceremonial uses, sorghum is an important ingredient in the national staple, sorghum pancakes.

Demand for sorghum in Freedonia is given by the demand function $D(p) = 5000(10 - p)$, where p is the price of a kilogram of sorghum in the local currency and quantities are in kilograms. There is not much good sorghum growing land in Freedonia, and the supply function of sorghum from domestic sources is $S(p) = 25,000(p - 4)$ for prices $p \geq 4$. (Sorghum suppliers are perfectly competitive.) If the price of sorghum is less than 4 per kilo, domestic supply is 0. Sorghum imports are currently banned. (If this sounds like Japanese rice, the resemblance is entirely intentional.)

(a) What is the current equilibrium (price and quantity) in the sorghum market. Assuming sorghum producers have fixed costs of 0, what are the profits of sorghum producers?

The world price of sorghum (in local currency) is 3. If Freedonia allowed the free importation of sorghum, the world price of sorghum would be unaffected: Freedonians could purchase as much sorghum as they wish at 3 per kilo.

(b) What would happen if Freedonia allowed the free importation of sorghum? What would be the new equilibrium price and quantity? What would happen to the domestic suppliers of sorghum? By what amount would consumer surplus rise?

(c) Owing to the unhappy consequences for domestic suppliers of sorghum that you found in part b, Prime Minister Firefly considers subsidizing domestic sorghum producers. For each kilogram of sorghum sold by a domestic producer, the producer would receive a fixed amount. At the same time, the free importation of sorghum would be allowed. Firefly wishes to set the level of this subsidy so that domestic sorghum producers sell just as much sorghum as they did in the initial equilibrium of part a. What level of subsidy accomplishes this? At this level of subsidy, what is the market equilibrium in sorghum?

(d) In the market equilibrium of part c, if you take into account the welfare of consumers (measured by consumer surplus) and domestic producers (measured by producer surplus) and account for the cost of the subsidy program, are Freedonians in sum better or worse off than in the equilibrium in part a?

13.8 Suppose that, in the situation of Problem 13.7, Prime Minister Firefly considers a different course of action: He would allow the importation of some sorghum, by granting to each of 10 good friends and political supporters the right to import up to 1000 kgs of sorghum. These friends would be able to purchase their sorghum at the world price of 3 per kg, then resell it at whatever price the domestic market would bear. Any supply of sorghum above the 10,000 kgs imported by this method would be provided for by domestic sorghum producers, who would receive no subsidy from the government. What would be the result of this in terms of the equilibrium in the sorghum market? Relative to the market equilibrium computed in part a of Problem 13.7, are domestic consumers better or worse off and by how much? Are domestic sorghum growers better or worse off and by how much? What profits are enjoyed by the 10 friends of Prime Minister Firefly? Combining the welfare of domestic consumers, domestic producers, Firefly's friends, and the government (in terms of any subsidy costs or tax revenues), under which of the three programs (no imports, free importation combined with subsidized domestic production, or a quota on imports with licenses given to domestic importers) are Freedonians best off?

13.9 In the chapter, I asserted that, if the world supply curve of rice is nearly flat, it is clear that foregone Japanese consumer surplus from any combination of quotas and tariffs is greater than the surplus gains of Japanese domestic producers and the government. Hence, these quotas and tariffs must be the result of interest-group politics. I doubt that the second conclusion surprises you, but what the logic underlies the first assertion?

13.10 Go back to the GM truck coupon analysis of Chapter 1. I assert that a positive Q (the cost of the coupons in the transferred-coupon market) acts like a tax on GM, and a positive k (the additional, frictional, cost paid by buyers of a transferred coupon) acts like a tax on third-party buyers. Why is this? (Once you see that $Q > 0$ or $k > 0$ is like a tax, it should be clear, following this chapter, why larger Q and larger k are both "bad news" for GM.)

13.11 Suppose that a particular perfectly competitive industry has 10 identical firms, each with the marginal cost function $MC(y) = 4 + y$. Suppose that the demand function for the item in question is $D(p) = 10(20 - p)$.

(a) What is the equilibrium in this market?

(b) Suppose that, of the 10 firms in the industry, 5 are polluters and 5 are not. The government, to cut down on the amount of pollution, imposes a tax of $1 per unit produced on the five polluters and gives a subsidy of $1 per unit produced to the five others. What is the equilibrium after these taxes and subsidies are imposed? Do revenues from the tax on the five polluters equal the subsidies paid to the five nonpolluters?

(c) Continuing with part b, suppose that the total social surplus in this situation is computed as the sum of producer surplus (profits), consumer surplus (in the usual fashion), and net government revenues (tax revenue less subsidies paid), less $2 for each unit produced by a polluter, which you can think of as the loss to society from the pollution. Compute each of the four components separately, then compute total social surplus for the equilibria of parts a and b. How do they compare?

14. Externalities

This chapter concerns externalities, instances where the activity of one party affects the welfare (utility or profit) of another. When externalities are present, market outcomes need not be efficient, and a case can be made for government intervention into markets to promote efficiency. We

- Define and give examples of externalities.
- Discuss why they can result in market inefficiency.
- List various means for dealing with them.
- Discuss the regulation of a specific externality, pollution.
- See how the concept of externalities applies broadly to most large, complex organizations.

Advocates of smaller government and less government interference in the marketplace typically cite the argument of Chapter 12 (that the invisible hand of the market maximizes market efficiency) and point to the sorts of inefficiencies we saw in the last chapter to make their point. But proponents of government activity respond by citing four qualifications to that argument:

1. *Efficiency is not equity.* Redistribution from the haves to the have-nots may be warranted.

2. When producers have *market power*, the market may not provide an efficient outcome. Wherever possible, the government should promote competition, curtailing market power and preventing its accumulation. Natural monopolies should be regulated. The same is true for buyers with market power, particularly in the context of labor markets.

3. For market outcomes to be efficient, all sides to the transaction must have access to good *information*. This is obviously necessary when it comes to information about alternative possible trading partners. But it applies as well to cases in which one side to the transaction lacks information that the other side may have, such as about the quality of the goods being traded. We get to these issues only in Chapter 18, but for now, suffice it to say that this provides a rationale for things like insider trading laws, disclosure laws, and consumer protection legislation.

4. There may be *externalities* in production or consumption. That is the subject of this chapter.

If you are headed for a job in the public sector or a private-sector industry such as power generation, the material in this chapter, concerning externalities such as pollution and government and other interventions to deal with them, probably seems relevant to you. But for most aspiring private-sector managers, this material might seem of general interest only. This is incorrect: The ideas of this chapter are broadly relevant in the private sector. I cannot conveniently explain why this is so until the end of the chapter. But I beg your patience; the ideas—if not their application to government regulation of externalities—touch the work lives of almost every manager.

14.1. What Are Externalities?

When the economic activities of any entity, whether a firm or a consumer, affect the welfare of another entity, the first activity generates an *externality*. When the second party benefits, the externality is *positive*; when the second party is hurt, the externality is *negative*:

- Someone smoking a cigarette in an elevator probably generates a negative externality for anyone unlucky enough to be riding at the same time.

- When my neighbor spends hours and hours cultivating her front garden, she generates a positive externality for me, because I enjoy looking at her garden. And if I fail to tend my own front yard, I generate a negative externality for her.

- When a firm with a factory on a river discharges effluent into the river, it generates negative externalities both for downriver consumers and firms that use the river water and must now expend resources cleaning it before using it.

Beyond these straightforward examples of externalities are other less obvious but important categories:

Network and Standards Externalities

Network externalities are generally positive. Stanford University's decision to join in a communications network generates a positive externality for other members of the network, since being able to communicate with Stanford is presumably good for institutions already on the network. Similarly, the decision by an electronics firm to build its products in conformance to some industry *standard* benefits other firms whose products conform, since this increases the base over which the standard is valid.

Congestion Externalities

Suppose, leaving work or school today at rush hour, you take a highway on your way home. By so doing, you increase by a small amount the amount of time it takes others who have chosen to drive on the same highway. By adding to the *congestion* on the highway, you generate negative externalities for others. Of course, the time of day can be important: If you drove home at 3 A.M., you probably would not measurably affect anyone else.

Congestion externalities are important, for instance, at airports. For a variety of reasons, airlines flying the transatlantic route from Kennedy Airport in New York to western Europe prefer to leave Kennedy in the evening. But as anyone who has sat on a runway at Kennedy at this time of day knows, not everyone can take off at once. And, as folks who live in the vicinity of Kennedy Airport know, this desire adds to congestion on the highways leading to the airport in the late afternoon and early evening.

Commons Problems

A category of negative externalities very close to congestion externalities consists of *commons problems*. The name comes from the practice of allowing privately owned sheep to graze on the village common. If my sheep are eating grass on the common, the amount of grass available for your sheep is lessened; my sheep are generating a negative externality for you and, contemporaneously, your sheep are as well for me. A very significant example of this concerns fisheries, where each party's private interests are to overfish the fishery.

Public Goods

A *pure public good* in Economese is a commodity whose consumption by one party in no way hinders its consumption by another party. The good can be consumed by anyone who cares to do so, without affecting the enjoyment that others take in its consumption.

It is hard to think of anything that is a pure public good. Clean air, national defense, the services of a lighthouse, turnpikes, and national parks and recreation areas are all sometimes used as examples, although there are clear congestion effects to contend with in at least the cases of turnpikes or national parks. Still, these examples capture the flavor of a public good.

The public good has the possibility of *exclusion* if we can control the entities who take advantage of the good. For example, we can restrict access to turnpikes and national parks, so insofar as these approximate a public good, they approximate public goods with the possibility of exclusion. But it is hard to stop residents of some area from enjoying clean air, if clean air is provided at all.

The provision of a public good is an activity with very strong and substantial positive externalities. If I provide clean air, by cleaning air that is dirty or by failing to pollute, I generate positive externalities for others. Because so many others enjoy the clean air—because clean air approximates a public good—the amount of positive externality I generate can be huge.

Market Power

When a firm with market power uses that market power to, say, raise the price of its own good, it affects the welfare of its customers. When Intel lowers the price it charges for its processors, it adversely affects the welfare of Motorola and positively affects the welfare of Dell. Are these externalities? As a matter of formal economics, I think they count as externalities. But I do not push the point here; we do not talk about the exercise of market power as something that generates externalities in this chapter.

14.2. Why Do Externalities Lead to Inefficiency?

When firms or consumers generate externalities, the outcome of a market equilibrium may not maximize total surplus, even assuming that markets are perfectly competitive. To see why, review the argument from Chapter 12. In a competitive-market equilibrium, when there are no externalities, the marginal consumer benefit equals the equilibrium price, which equals the marginal cost of production. This leads to efficient outcomes.

But this involves the equation of the marginal *private* consumer benefit and the marginal *private* cost of production. When consumption by an individual generates externalities, the marginal *social* benefit of the consumption activity (the marginal impact on overall surplus) is not the same as the marginal private benefit to the consumer in question. And, when the production activities of a firm generate production externalities, the marginal *social* cost of production is not the same as the marginal private cost of production. To be efficient, we want to have marginal social benefits equal to marginal social costs. A market equilibrium does not necessarily achieve this.

Suppose, for instance, a firm generates negative externalities for consumers and other firms by polluting. When it pushes its private marginal cost to equal price, it does not take into account the amount by which its pollution lowers the utility (or surplus) of consumers generally or the profit (surplus) of other firms. It probably produces more output than is socially optimal, unless it is made to take into account, to internalize, the externalities it produces.

14.3. Dealing with Externalities

Externalities are dealt with in a number of ways.

Social Norms

Social norms can sometimes control externalities. My front garden, if well tended, generates positive externalities for my neighbors, as do their front gardens for me. If each of us maximizes his or her own private utility, each of us would spend less on our front gardens than is socially optimal. But we can fall into an arrangement where each of us spends more time because of the social pressure to do so; if I suddenly let my front garden go to seed, so to speak, my neighbors would quit speaking to me, stop pruning bushes that lie along our common property lines, and so on, to signal to me that my behavior is unacceptable. In fact, since I value the good opinion of my neighbors, I keep up my front garden even if they do nothing tangible to punish me for not doing so.

There is an important point here, which concerns us near the end of the book, so I briefly foreshadow it here. I just told two stories about norms of behavior. The first is that I conform to the norm of a well-tended front yard because, if I do not, my neighbors will take actions that adversely affect me. The second is that I conform to the norm because I *internalize* my neighbors' good opinion: Being in their good graces is directly valuable to me, increasing my utility. A variation on the second story is that I internalize conformance to the norm simply because it is a norm, and conformance to norms per se increases my utility. Whichever story appeals to you is fine; each works in different contexts and, as we see near the end of the book, the most powerful institutional arrangements are often those that enlist them simultaneously.

Property Rights and the Coase Theorem

A second method for dealing with externalities involves the establishment of clear and unambiguous "property rights." If an upstream firm pollutes a river, society might decide (1) that the downstream parties have a property right to clean water or (2) that the upstream party has the right to dispose of its effluent as it sees fit. Property rights can be established either way. But, once the property rights are clearly established, individuals bargain over how they exercise those rights. If downstream parties have the right to clean water, then the upstream firm can offer to pay them a sum of money to be allowed to dispose of its effluent in the river. If the upstream firm has the right to dispose of its effluent as it sees fit, then downstream parties can offer to pay the upstream firm to restrict its pollution. Of course, the establishment of property rights has substantial distributive consequences; the upstream firm wants the right to dispose of its effluent, so if it restricts its pollution, it is paid for that, rather than having to pay to pollute. In either case, as long as property rights are clearly and unambiguously delineated, the story goes, we can trust that parties bargain to a socially efficient outcome.

This approach to externalities is known as the *Coase theorem*, after its originator, Ronald Coase, who asserted that if property rights are clearly established, the problem of externalities vanishes. The approach of the Coase theorem to dealing with externalities (clearly establish property rights, then let "markets" [bargaining] determine the outcome) has been fashionable among economists and legal theorists recently, but it is not without problems. One problem concerns the costs of bargaining. Suppose we give the firm the property right to pollute and leave it to the parties downstream to bargain over abatement. If many parties are downstream, each will want the others to offer the upstream polluter money to reduce pollution, each will want a free ride on the efforts of the others. You can think of this problem as resulting from the inability of one party to exclude others from the enjoyment of some good. If I pay the upstream party to refrain from polluting the stream, I cannot exclude your enjoyment of the clean water that results, so you benefit from my efforts. To deal with this, we might try to give all the downstream parties the right to clean water, so that the firm must compensate each for any pollution it causes. Then a different sort of bargaining problem occurs: Downstream parties have private information about the value they place on an unpolluted stream, and each wants to claim that the cost to it is higher than it really is, to increase its compensation. Also, if we establish that downstream parties have a right to unpolluted water and the stream is polluted, we may have a problem ascertaining who is responsible for the pollution, hence who must pay compensation.

The Coase theorem is a useful starting point for analysis. It tells us to think of all problems of externalities as problems in which there are "missing markets" because of unassigned or hard-to-assign property rights; if property rights were assigned, then markets would be created to facilitate the bargaining. But it is often impractical to assign property rights and have the parties bargain. Hence, we move to a third category of answers to the problem of externalities, namely collective action

Collective Action

Some forms of collective action are informal, such as boycotts against or social sanctions imposed on entities that generate negative externalities. Groups such as the Audubon Society or the Kiwanis often engage in the provision of positive externalities. But the majority of collective action is taken more formally, by political collectives (governments):

1. Public goods are provided, using revenues raised from broad-based taxes.

2. The provision of positive externalities is encouraged, often through tax incentives or subsidies.

3. Activities that generate negative externalities are either directly regulated— proscribed entirely or subject to limits—or discouraged through the imposition of fines and fees.

14.4. On the Regulation of Pollution

That is the general theory of externalities. To illustrate this theory and, in particular, both formal (government) regulation of externalities and practical uses of the Coase theorem, consider how a government might regulate the pollution of a natural resource such as a river or the air.

Imagine a firm, sitting upriver from other firms and consumers, that disposes of effluent in the river. This pollutes the river and affects the welfare of the firms and consumers downstream.

Controlling pollution generates benefits *and* costs. If pollution lowers the welfare of consumers downstream, lowering or abating pollution raises external welfare, a benefit. But abating pollution has a cost, usually borne privately by the polluter. Following the usual marginal this and that logic, the social optimum is where the *marginal external cost of pollution* equals the *marginal cost of abating pollution*. We can use pictures to illustrate this.

The firm's overall profit depends on its level of pollution, as shown in Figure 14.1. Panel a graphs the profit of the firm as a function of its level of pollution. This function hits a maximum, then turns over; profit falls as pollution rises when the effects of pollution are so severe that they damage the firm's profit, say, by affecting the health and well-being of its workers. Panel b shows the firm's marginal profit as a function of the level of pollution, or the derivative of the profit function. Marginal profit is 0 where profit is maximized. In the figure, the marginal profit function is decreasing, because the profit function is (assumed to be) concave.

The marginal profit function in Figure 14.1(b) has a second name, *the marginal cost of abatement*. This function describes the marginal cost to the firm of decreasing or abating its level of pollution by a unit, which is just its marginal profit from increasing pollution by the same unit. The term *the marginal cost of abatement* is used because, in many contexts, it makes sense to think of the cost of reducing pollution, in terms of water filtration plants, smokestack scrubbers, or whatever, instead of thinking in terms of the marginal impact on profit from polluting more. However, do not be put

profit

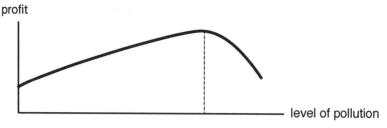

(a) Total profit as a function of the firm's level of pollution

marginal profit

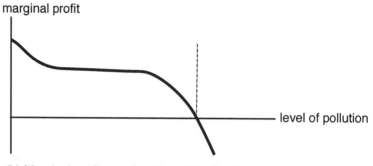

(b) Marginal profit as a function of the firm's level of pollution, which equals the firm's marginal cost of abatement

Figure 14.1. Profit and the marginal cost of abatement. Panel a shows the profit level of the firm as a function of its level of pollution; panel b shows the derivative of this, the marginal profit function. Since the cost to the firm of abating a unit of production is the same as the marginal profit it gives up by this action, another name for marginal profit is the *marginal cost of abatement.*

off by the semantics. This is just the derivative of the function in Figure 14.1(a).

Figure 14.2(a) shows the surplus of the external population as a function of the level of pollution. This is a dollar-valued measure of the welfare of everyone downstream of this firm as a function of the pollution put by this firm into the river. For consumers, this includes a measure of the loss in their welfare from the pollution. For firms, this takes into account their lost profits, because they now must clean up the water they use, for example. It is a heroic assumption to think we can assign a dollar value to the welfare of consumers and firms, as a function of the level of pollution. As a practical matter, finding this function—or even trying to get a sense of its approximate value—is enormously complex. Imagine, for instance, pollution that might result in permanent damage to the environment or extinction of a species: How do we associate a dollar value with that? But suppose it can be computed. Then we have a function, as in Figure 14.2(a), that decreases as the level of pollution of the upstream firm increases.

The negative of the derivative of this function is graphed in Figure

14.2(b). This is the marginal external cost of the pollution or, alternatively, the marginal external benefit from abating pollution.

In Figure 14.3, panel a superimposes the profit of the firm and the surplus of the external population. Panel b graphs the sum of profit and the surplus of the external population. And, in panel c, the marginal external cost of pollution and the marginal cost of abatement are superimposed.

Note that, in the middle panel, the sum of the two rises at first. Going up to the top panel, you see that this is so because the rate at which the surplus of the external population is falling, the marginal external cost of pollution, is less than the rate at which profit is rising, the marginal cost of abatement. The sum of the two continues to rise until the rate of decrease in the surplus of the external population equals the rate of increase in profit. At this point, the sum is as great as it is going to be; thereafter, falling external surplus outweighs any increase in profit. Eventually, profit falls as pollution increases, accentuating the decrease in the surplus of the external population.

Of course, this maximizing point in terms of the sum occurs where the two margins are equal; see Figure 14.3(c).

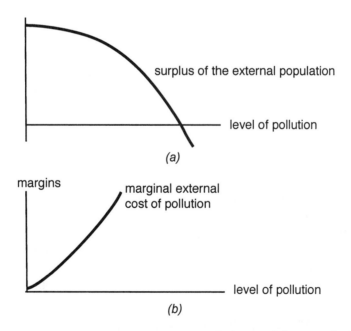

Figure 14.2. The surplus of the external population and the marginal external cost of pollution. The dollar-valued surplus of the external population, depicted in panel a, falls as pollution rises, and in the figure, it falls more rapidly, the greater is the level of pollution. Thus, the marginal external cost of pollution (panel b), which is the same as the marginal external benefit from abating pollution, is an increasing function of the level of pollution.

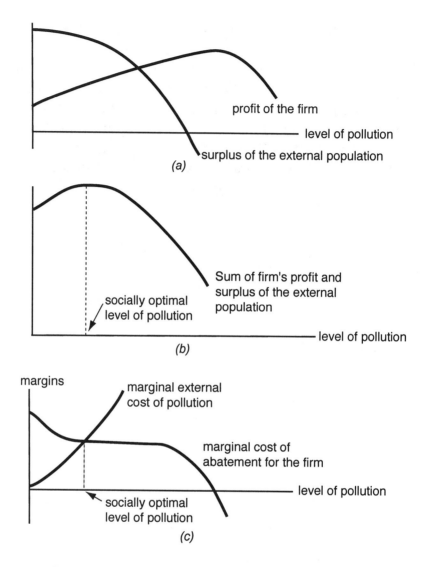

Figure 14.3. Superimposing direct and external effects, both totals and margins. Total surplus involves summing the profit of the polluting firm and the external surplus, both as a function of pollution. Panel b shows the sum, which is maximized at a lower level of pollution than the level at which profit is maximized. This level (the socially optimal level of pollution) occurs where the marginal external cost of the pollution equals its private marginal cost of abatement (see panel c).

Analysis of the Regulation of Pollution

Now that we have these graphs, we can proceed to some analysis. First, suppose the picture is as in Figure 14.4. If we engage in a *laissez-faire* economic policy (meaning that we do not interfere in the firm's activities), a profit-maximizing firm would choose the level of pollution at which the marginal cost of abatement is 0.

But if we choose the socially optimal level of pollution, we would go to the point where profit plus external surplus is maximized, the point where the marginal external cost of pollution equals the marginal cost of abatement.

This is the sense in which, when there are externalities, the unfettered marketplace fails to produce a social optimum. The firm does not take into account its external effects on the welfare of others. In this case, it pollutes more than is socially optimal.

How can the government enforce this social optimum? Two policy instruments are available. We can regulate directly the level of pollution that the firm is allowed to put into the river or we can charge the firm a fee or fine per unit of pollution (see Figure 14.4). If we tell the firm that it can pollute only to the point marked the *socially optimal level of pollution*, that is what the firm will choose to do. Or, if we charge the firm a fee per unit of pollution equal to the *socially optimal fee for pollution*, then it will pollute to the point where the marginal cost of abatement equals this fee, which is again the socially optimal level of pollution. Either instrument works.

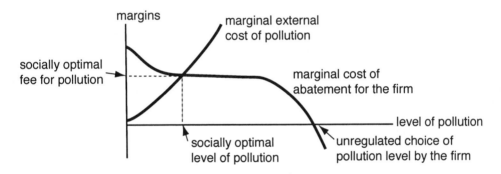

Figure 14.4. Setting an optimal level of pollution or an optimal fee for pollution. If the marginal cost of abatement and marginal external cost of pollution functions are known, then the socially optimal level of pollution is where they cross. This can be implemented by directly regulating the level of pollution or by setting a fee for pollution equal to the optimal pollution fee shown.

In reality, however, we do not know precisely the position of these curves. Each is estimated by analysis and data collection. The details are complex; we do not go into them. But the point is that the government will try to estimate the position and slope of these curves. Then, if we mis-set the standard of pollution allowable or the fee for pollution, what will be the social cost? If we set the standard too lax, at a higher-than-optimal level of allowable pollution, we have a social cost equal to the area of the shaded triangle in Figure 14.5. A similar picture, but with the triangle on the other side of the intersection of the two curves, results if the standard is set too stringently.

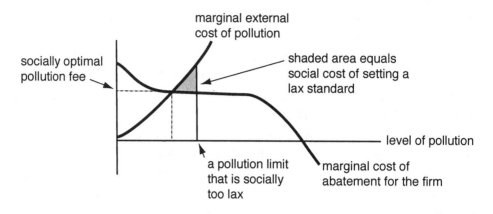

Figure 14.5. Mis-setting a pollution standard. If the firm is directly regulated and the level of allowable pollution is set too high relative to the social optimum, a net social cost equal to the area of the shaded triangle results.

On the other hand, if we mis-set a fee for pollution, we get the sort of picture shown in Figure 14.6. Here we set the fee too high, and the firm responds with a suboptimally low level of pollution. Again we get a shaded triangle as the social cost of setting the pollution fee incorrectly. (A fee lower than optimal would produce a welfare triangle as in Figure 14.5.)

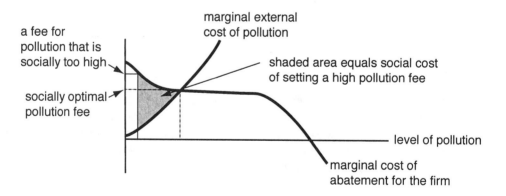

Figure 14.6. Mis-setting a pollution fee. If a fee for pollution is used, and if it is set too high relative to the optimal pollution fee, the firm responds by abating pollution more than is socially optimal, with a net social cost equal to the area of the shaded triangle.

Which is better, fees or standards? This depends on how well the government knows the shapes and positions of these two curves, as well as their slopes. Suppose, for example, the government has a very good idea of the marginal social cost of pollution and, moreover, this cost is relatively flat. Then we can impose a fee equal to the marginal social cost (firms pay society for the pollution they cause) and let the firms find the optimal level of abatement. On the other hand, when the marginal social cost of pollution is relatively low up to some level and then very steep and the government is unclear on the firm's marginal costs of abatement, so that it cannot tell how much firms will abate pollution given a pollution fee, then fixing the allowable level of pollution is likely to be a safer course of action.

Resaleable Licenses to Pollute

Do not be misled by the simplicity of these pictures. A lot of the ongoing debate centers on how to measure the external costs of pollution. What value do we put on the the the destruction of species in the water? What weight should be put on the welfare of unborn generations? How do we value unforeseen changes in the environment, in the case of things such as the greenhouse effect? Until such issues as these are settled, it may seem a bit silly to worry about the issue of fees vs. licenses. However, once these primary issues are settled—usually on political grounds—questions about the mechanism for controlling externalities can be tackled with this sort of analysis. Then, to control pollution most efficiently, market mechanisms that employ Coasian logic can be fruitfully employed.

For example, the U.S. government regulates the amount of sulfur emissions by electricity-generation facilities with resaleable licenses to pollute. The government has decided on an amount of pollution of this sort that it will permit. The "level of permitted pollution" is set by cost analyses similar to those sketched in the previous subsections but also is based on a substantial amount of political and interest-group lobbying. Essentially, the government started from existing levels of pollution and is gradually tightening what is permitted.

The government has decided how much pollution of this sort it wants to allow in total. Therefore, it makes sense to hand out pollution quotas rather than setting a pollution fee. Then the problem arises: Given a total amount of pollution it wishes to permit, how should it divvy up this quota among the various polluters? Ideally, the government wants to set pollution levels for each polluter in a manner that equates the polluters' marginal costs of abatement. At least, this is ideal from the point of view of maximizing the social surplus, given the fixed amount of total pollution allowed. But the government is not particularly well informed about the marginal costs of abatement of the various firms that pollute. Suppose, for instance, Public Service Electric and Gas (PSE&G) of New Jersey, because of its installed technology for generating electricity, can abate pollution more cheaply on the margin than Consolidated Edison (Con Ed) of New York. From a social surplus point of view, the government should give Con Ed a break and let it pollute, while turning the screws on PSE&G. But the government does not know these things. The government can ask the firms involved what are their marginal costs of abatement, but the firms, knowing how these data will be used, have a strong incentive to overstate their costs. Moreover, is it fair to penalize PSE&G and reward Con Ed, because PSE&G has technology that can abate pollution cheaply relative to that of Con Ed?

Hence, instead of setting quotas for each company, the government gives each polluter a number of licenses, each of which gives the holder the right to send so many tons of pollutant (oxides of sulfur) into the atmosphere. And, the novel part, the companies can trade these licenses among themselves. The idea is this: If PSE&G holds, say, 1000 tons' worth of licenses and can, at relatively little cost, abate its pollution to only 400 tons per year, it would probably increase profit by selling 600 tons' worth of licenses to firms, such as Con Ed, that find abatement expensive. Assuming the market in these licenses is well run and competitive—in fact, it is both—an equilibrium market price in licenses to pollute will become established, so that each firm abates to the point where its marginal cost of abatement equals the equilibrium market price. Of course, this has a very strong Coasian flavor: The government gives each company a property right to pollute to a given level, a property right that can be traded in the market.

The program has a further interesting feature. The pollution licenses establish a maximum amount of permitted pollution. But imagine that some broad-based conversation group, the Sierra Club, say, decides the government has allowed too much pollution. To the extent that the Sierra Club can raise the necessary funds, it can enter the market for licenses, buy up a number of them, then "retire" them by sitting on them. In fact, this has happened. And, if the government believes that groups like the Sierra Club face substantial free-rider problems when they try to raise money for this sort of thing, it could offer some "assistance," by using the tax laws, for instance.

This description of resaleable pollution licenses is somewhat simplified, but it conveys the program's basic structure: With this program, the government solves the allocation problem (how to divvy up the amount of pollution it wishes to permit) by letting the market solve the problem for it. This is an excellent example of how government regulation of externalities can use the "invisible hand" to advantage, in situations where full regulation might screw things up.

Does Intervention Help?

A caveat is in order at this point. Because of externalities and the three other reasons given at the start of this chapter, market outcomes may fall short of society's ideal, where the ideal mixes efficiency and equity. In such instances, government or other nonmarket action *might* improve matters. But there is no guarantee that government or nonmarket action *will* improve matters. Trying to improve on market outcomes through government action or legislation can lead to corruption, rentseeking or interest-group activity, or even granting the government or legislature is entirely noble and benign, worse outcomes, because legislation and regulation cannot generally match the information-processing capabilities of markets allied with self-interest. It is not enough to say that governments *might* improve matters. Proponents of such actions should offer convincing arguments that, on net, improvements will be realized.

Over the past 20 years or so, even relatively strong proponents of government intervention in markets have recognized the limitations of administered as opposed to market systems. Increasingly, governments examine specific situations to see where market mechanisms can be enlisted. The resaleable licenses to pollute are an excellent example. To take another, which addresses market power, telecommunications were long thought of as a natural monopoly because of the required network of telephone lines. Therefore, governments resorted to nationalization or regulation of large phone companies. To some extent, recent changes in technology provide alternatives to a physical large-scale network. But, even before these recent changes, governments understood that, as long as access was guaranteed, at regulated rates, competition in telecommunications that enlisted the strength of market forces was more likely to produce good outcomes than administered regulation.

The moral is clear: There may be good reasons to intervene in market outcomes, but the strengths of the market system should not be forgotten.

14.5. Externalities within Organizations

Unless you aspire to manage in the public sector or an industry subject to some form of government regulation, you might have concluded that this chapter is not of more than general interest. But the basic ideas of this chapter, repackaged just a bit, are often of great interest to aspiring managers, when the repackaging concerns externalities within organizations. Think in terms of a large, multidivisional firm. Often, to allow for efficient decentralization of decision making, divisional management is given the authority to make operating decisions for its own division. Divisional earnings are measured, and division top management is rewarded based on the performance of the division in terms of these measures.

The problem is that each division, seeking to maximize its own earnings, may lower the earnings of other divisions. To the extent that this is true, the first division exerts a negative externality on the second, and earnings maximization by each division leads to lower profit for the firm as a whole.

How can one division's activities affect the profit of another? One obvious mechanism involves competition among divisions for customers. When the Chevrolet division of General Motors advertises heavily to sell its cars, it presumably depresses the sales and earnings of the Pontiac division. Or different units within a corporation may compete for scarce factors of production. It is not unheard of, for instance, for one division to compete with other divisions for specific human resources. Division A may hire away from Division B an employee crucial to Division B but merely useful to Dvision A, offering the employee a promotion or higher salary or both.

To take a concrete example, imagine a corporation with three identical divisions that have a shared service facility. We let y_i for $i =$ 1, 2, and 3 be the level of services received from this shared facility by Division i. We imagine that the gross benefit to Division i in terms of improved divisional earnings is given by the function

$$y_i - 0.25y_i^2 - 0.1(y_1 + y_2 + y_3)$$

measured in millions of dollars. The key is the last part of this expression, $-0.1(y_1 + y_2 + y_3)$, which is meant to model the idea that the greater is the level of total demand placed on this facility, the smaller the value received by each division fixing its own service demands. In addition, the shared service facility must be paid for; if the demands placed on the facility are y_1, y_2, and y_3, the facility costs 0.5 in fixed costs plus $0.2(y_1 + y_2 + y_3)$ in variable costs.

(This is not a very realistic functional specification of a congestion effect. A more realistic model would say that the degradation in service quality is fairly low until the total demands on the facility approach the facility's capacity, at which point degradation rises very quickly. But dealing with a realistic model of congestion is difficult mathematically, so I illustrate the basic ideas with the simple model proposed here.)

What are the best utilization levels from the perspective of the entire corporation? You can solve this problem using a spreadsheet (see sheet 1 of CHAP14). But instead of using a spreadsheet, we employ calculus: Taking into account the divisional benefits and the cost of the facility, as a function of y_1, y_2, and y_3, total benefits to the corporation are

$$y_1 - 0.25y_1^2 + y_2 - 0.25y_2^2 + y_3 - 0.25y_3^2 - 0.3(y_1 + y_2 + y_3) - [0.5 + 0.2(y_1 + y_2 + y_3)],$$

which, collecting terms, is

$$0.5y_1 - 0.25y_1^2 + 0.5y_2 - 0.25y_2^2 + 0.5y_3 - 0.25y_3^2 - 0.5.$$

Maximizing this in the three variables gives $y_1 = y_2 = y_3 = 1$, for a net gain to the corporation of $0.25 million.

Now imagine that the firm allows each division to choose its own level of service. Imagine, first, that the firm does not charge the divisions anything for the service and each division chooses its utilization level to maximize its gross divisional earnings, taking as fixed the demands put on the facility by the other divisions. The divisions are identical, so we can figure out what happens by focusing on Division 1: It chooses y_1 to maximize $y_1 - 0.25y_1^2 - .1(y_1 + y_2 + y_3)$. Since y_2 and y_3 are outside of this division's control, the problem is to maximize $0.9y_1 - 0.25y_1^2$, which gives $y_1 = 1.8$. By symmetry, we also get $y_2 = y_3 = 1.8$. And, if you do the math, this gives each division a gross benefit of 0.45, against a cost to the firm in providing these services of 1.58. Therefore, the net benefit to the firm is $3 \times .45 - 1.58 = -0.23$ (millions of dollars). The firm actually loses money from providing this service.

Of course, it is clear why this is happening: The divisions do not internalize the variable cost $0.2(y_1 + y_2 + y_3)$ of providing this service. The firm should charge divisions a "transfer price" of 0.2 times the demands they place on the facility, in the accounts maintained on divisional profit. And if the firm does this, Division 1 chooses y_1 to maximize $y_1 - 0.25y_1^2 - 0.1(y_1 + y_2 + y_3) - 0.2y_1$, which comes down to maximizing $0.7y_1 - 0.25y_1^2$ in y_1, which is $y_1 = 1.4$. Divisions 2 and 3 are symmetric and also come up with this utilization level. And net earnings gain for the firm is $0.13 million. (Do the math if you are unsure where this number comes from.) This is better than in the previous paragraph but still not as high as we got two paragraphs ago; the divisions still overutilize the shared facility.

Why? Because while each division now internalizes the direct variable costs incurred by the firm in providing the service, the division fails to take into account the impact of its demand on the quality of service received by the other two divisions.

What are the remedies? Just as in the regulation of pollution, two basic remedies are available. The firm can dictate the utilization levels for each division, rationing each division to 1 unit of service. Or it can raise the transfer price for the service to a level sufficiently high that each division internalizes the external effects it has on its fellow divisions. This means raising the transfer price from 0.2 per unit to 0.4 per unit. If it uses this transfer price, each division, on its own, chooses $y_i = 1$, and the firm's total profit is maximized.

In this ultrasimple example, corporate headquarters can work out both the amount of the service to "dictate" to each division and the size of the transfer payment that causes each division, on its own, to "do the right thing." But in real life, where there is uncertainty in the mind of headquarters about the costs and benefits attending to this sort of problem, one instrument or the other may be preferred. More specifically, to the extent that headquarters cannot accurately estimate how valuable the shared service is directly to each individual division but it has a rough handle on the size of the externality each imposes marginally on the others, using transfer prices and decentralizing the decision is better. However, there are a lot of suppositions in the previous sentence; the most that can be said in general is that headquarters has to be aware of these sorts of externalities and, in some fashion or another, be ready to deal with them. For more on this story, see Problem 14.4.

Executive Summary

- When the actions of one economic entity (consumer or firm) affect the welfare measured in the utility or profit of another, the first imposes an *externality* on the second. The externality is positive if the second party's welfare is improved and negative if the second party's welfare is diminished. Examples of externalities include some obvious cases, such as pollution, but also network, standards, congestion, and shared-commons externalities.

- Public goods provide extreme cases of externalities: A public good is a good that can be consumed simultaneously by as many people as wish to do so without diminishing the welfare other consumers receive from the good. True public goods are hard to find, but things like clean air come close. The provision of a public good generates substantial positive externalities because of the large number of beneficiaries.

- The argument that says that a competitive market equilibrium maximizes surplus does not hold when there are externalities, because in a competitive market equilibrium, consumers and firms pay attention to the private utilities and profits they garner and do not take into account the full impact of their activities on social costs and benefits. Thus, when externalities are present, there is scope for beneficial government intervention in markets. But saying there is scope for beneficial government intervention is not the same thing as saying the government intervention will be beneficial.

- Externalities can be dealt with informally, through social norms. In theory, they can be dealt with through the assignment of property rights and reliance on markets and bargaining. Often, they are dealt with through government or legal action; governments provide public goods using tax revenues, they promote the provision of positive externalities, and they regulate the creation of negative externalities.

- In the regulation of specific negative externalities, the government can either directly set limits to the externality-generating activity (Firm X can put only N tons of sulfur dioxide into the atmosphere) or impose fees on the activity (Firm X must pay $\$M$ for every ton of sulfur dioxide it puts into the atmosphere).

- The resaleable-pollution-licenses program is an example of the regulation of a negative externality that takes advantage of market processes to allocate efficiently a fixed amount of allowable pollution.

- This sort of problem is not only a matter for governments regulating the economic decisions of individual consumers or firms; it can also be found in large organizations, where decentralized decision making combined with intraorganizational external effects can lead to suboptimal (less-than-profit-maximizing) decision making.

Problems

14.1 The business district of the capital of Freedonia, Freedonia City, sits on an island. Most of the people who work in this district commute from the mainland. Specifically, 400,000 people make this commute. Freedonians are in love with their cars, so each of the 400,000 people drives to and from work in a private car; there is no carpooling.

There are two routes from the mainland into (and out of) the business district, the Rufus T. Firefly Bridge and the Chicollini Tunnel. The times it takes to commute across the bridge and through the tunnel depend on the number of individuals n_B and n_T who take the bridge and the tunnel, respectively. Specifically, if n_B people come via the bridge, the commute time via the bridge is $30 + n_B/20{,}000$ minutes, and if n_T people come via the tunnel, the commute time via the tunnel is $40 + n_T/5000$ minutes.

(a) Suppose each of the 400,000 people who make this commute takes either the bridge or the tunnel; that is, $n_B + n_T = 400{,}000$. People choose whether to take the bridge or the tunnel depending on which takes less time, so in equilibrium, the numbers n_B and n_T are chosen so that the two commute times are equal. What are n_B and n_T?

(b) We define the total commute time as n_B times the commute time via the bridge plus n_T times the commute time via the tunnel. In your answer to part a, what is the total commute time?

(c) Suppose the Freedonia City mayor could control the number of people who come via the bridge and via the tunnel. She chooses these numbers to minimize the total commute time. How would she allocate the 400,000 commuters between the bridge and the tunnel to minimize total commute time?

(d) Except for the congestion on the bridge and tunnel, there is 0 marginal cost of getting consumers across the bridge and the tunnel. For this reason, transit across the bridge and through the tunnel have been kept free. But the mayor and City Council of Freedonia City are considering whether to impose a toll on one or the other. If a toll of t_B is imposed on the bridge and t_T on the tunnel, consumers will rearrange their commute so that $10t_B+$ commute time across the bridge (in minutes) equals $10t_T+$ commute time through the tunnel (in minutes). In other words, 10 minutes of commute time is worth $1 to commuters. Find values for t_B and t_T, where one is 0, so that, facing these tolls, commuters arrange their commute in the manner that minimizes total commute time.

14.2 The Freedonian people love fish caught in Lake Bella, a large lake in the middle of Freedonia. This fish is a great delicacy, and Freedonians are willing to pay quite a lot for it. In addition, the life of a Lake Bella fisherman has deep roots in Freedonian folklore. (In Freedonia, all fishermen are in fact men; this society is decades behind the times.) Each fisherman requires a boat, which has a fixed cost of $10,000 and otherwise spends $(10 + X/1000)x + x^2/100$ to catch x pounds of fish, where X is the total amount (in pounds) of fish caught in Lake Bella by all the fishermen. (That is, the more fish caught in total, the more expensive it is for a single fisherman to catch x lbs. of fish.) Fishermen choose how much fish to catch based on the price p for fish (per ton), which they regard as fixed (they are price takers); they understand their costs and take the total catch X from the lake as fixed and outside their control. Demand for fish from Lake Bella is given by the demand function $D(p) = 5000(60 - p)$.

(a) Suppose that precisely 10 fishermen fish Lake Bella. (They can neither enter nor exit and they cannot avoid the fixed cost of the boat by refusing to fish.) What is the market equilibrium in the Lake Bella fish market?

(b) Suppose there is free entry to and exit from this market. What is the long-run equilibrium in the Lake Bella fish market? What are consumer and producer surplus?

(c) Suppose the Freedonia Fish and Game Department imposes a $6 per pound tax on fish caught in Lake Bella. This tax is paid for by fishermen.

What is the (free entry and exit) equilibrium in the Lake Bella fish market? Compare total surplus in this equilibrium (including government net revenues) with total surplus in the answer you got to part b. Can you explain the answer you are getting?

14.3   Consider a firm with the sort of shared resource–congestion problem sketched in the final section of this chapter. Imagine that the shared facility has a capacity for, say, 500 units of work per month. Congestion (and concomitant service degradation) is minimal if demands placed on the facility total 450 units or less but becomes substantial as total demand on the facility approaches 500 and skyrockets if demands on the facility total more than 500. The firm is determined, therefore, to limit demands on the facility to 450 units per month.

Five divisions place demands on this shared facility, so the firm thinks first of dictating to each that it (the division) can use the facility up to 90 units of service per month. But headquarters worries that this is a suboptimal allocation of the 450 units available. Perhaps one division gets more (marginal) benefit out of its 150th unit of service, than another gets from its 70th.

How, in the spirit of resaleable pollution licenses, can the firm mitigate against this problem? If headquarters can increase the capacity of this facility at a cost per unit per month that it knows, but it is unsure of the value of the facility to its divisions, how can it decide whether to increase the capacity?

14.4   We do not discuss public goods in any depth in the chapter, but for those who are interested, here is a problem to acquaint you with some of the issues involved. In the *Student's Companion*, the solution to this problem is accompanied by further discussion about the issues connected to public goods.

We are interested in a good provided in an economy consisting of 5 million individuals. Every individual in this economy has a linear-in-money-left-over utility function for this good, taking the form $v_i(x_i) + m_i$, where the subscript i refers to the particular individual, x_i is amount of this good consumed by i, and m_i is the money i has left over. Moreover, each v_i takes the form $k_i \ln(x_i + 1)$ where k_i is a constant specific to individual i: $k_i = 24$ for 1 million individuals; $k_i = 12$ for another 1 million; $k_i = 6$ for 1 million individuals; $k_i = 1$ for 1 million individuals; and $k_i = 0.5$ for the final 1 million individuals. The marginal cost of production of this good is a constant \$3.

(a) Suppose this is a private-consumption good, the sort analyzed and discussed in the book prior to this chapter. How much of the good should be produced, and how should it be divided among the 5 million consumers, in an efficient (surplus-maximizing) arrangement?

(b) Suppose for the remainder of the problem that this is a public good. This means that, if X units of the good are produced in total, each consumer can consume X units of the good, without affecting the consumption or utility gain of any other consumer. How much of the good should be produced in an efficient (surplus-maximizing) arrangement? (Since this is a public good, there is no issue of dividing the good among the individuals.)

(c) Suppose we provide this good using private contributions. That is, each individual in the economy decides on an amount to contribute, the contributions are summed, and if the total amount contributed is C, the amount provided is $X = C/3$. How much an individual chooses to contribute depends on how much he or she anticipates others contribute. Suppose, therefore, that one of the first million consumers believes that all the other individuals contribute nothing. In this instance, how much will this one individual contribute? And if she contributes that amount and the other 4,999,999 individuals anticipate that she will, how much does each of them contribute?

(d) Suppose the good is provided by the government: It levies a tax t on each individual, raising $\$5,000,000t$, and it provides $5,000,000t/3$ units of the good. If t is set so that the government provides the socially optimal level of the good (your answer to part b) will any members in this society be worse off than if none of the good was provided?

(e) Suppose the good in question is a public good with the possibility of exclusion. The good is supplied by a monopolist, which announces that it will supply X units of the good, and any citizen willing to pay $\$p$ can enjoy the good. What levels of X and $\$p$ maximize the profit of this monopolist?

15. Risk Aversion and Expected Utility

This chapter introduces the expected utility model, the premier descriptive model of individual choice under uncertainty. First, we catalog common behaviors observed when people choose actions with uncertain consequences, then we introduce and develop the expected utility model, and finally we see how well the model captures the cataloged behaviors.

Uncertainty is a major fact of economic life. For individuals, major decisions concerning education, career, housing, saving, and investment have substantially uncertain consequences. For firms, this is true concerning which products to develop and market, technologies to employ, and employees to hire. And these are only partial lists. Vitally important markets—in securities, insurance, options, and futures—exist largely to help individuals and firms deal with the uncertainties they face.

Yet here we are, over 360 pages into a book about microeconomics, and nary a formal word about uncertainty. On occasion we have discussed uncertainty informally. But it has not turned up formally in any of the models we constructed or analyzed.

Beginning with this chapter, we rectify this glaring omission. And the first step is to model the choices made by individual consumers when they face choices with uncertain consequences.

15.1. How Do Individuals React to Uncertainty?

Individuals do all sorts of things, some crazy and some quite sensible, when facing uncertainty. A complete list of these behaviors is impossible, but a catalog of some behavioral patterns observed fairly broadly is worth compiling.

How Choices Are Framed Matters to What Is Chosen

Imagine you are advising the staff of the public health agency of your country (such as the Centers for Disease Control in the United States) concerning an immunization program that deals with a prospective flu epidemic. You are given a choice between two options that are described to you as follows:[1]

---

[1] These examples are taken, although not quite verbatim, from D. Kahnemann and A. Tversky, "Prospect Theory: An Analysis of Decisions Under Risk," *Econometrica*, Vol. 47, 1979, 263–91.

If nothing is done, the prospective flu epidemic will result in the death of 600 people. (Either death or complete recovery is the outcome in each case.) You can undertake either of two possible vaccination programs, and doing one precludes doing the other. The first will save 400 people with certainty. The second will save no one with probability 1/3 and 600 with probability 2/3. Which do you recommend?

You might wonder why you, a specialist in management, are being asked for advice concerning this sort of life-and-death·medical question. But decide how you would choose, if the choice were yours to make. Then try the following:

As an advisor to the staff of your country's public health agency, you are informed that a new flu epidemic will hit your country next winter. To fight this epidemic, one of two possible vaccination programs is to be chosen, and undertaking one program precludes attempting the other. In the first program, 200 people will die with certainty. In the second, there is a 2/3 chance that no one will die, and a 1/3 chance that 600 will die. Which do you prefer?

This pair of questions was put to a large number of medical professionals, and the modal pair of responses was to choose the first program in the first formulation of the question and the second program in the second formulation. My experience has been that the modal student of management makes the same pair of choices. In the first formulation of the question, it seems better to be sure of saving someone, while in the second formulation, it seems better to avoid consigning anyone to certain death. But, if you think about it, you'll see the questions are, in terms of actual consequences, the same. The first options in each formulation are the same (400 live with certainty and 200 die), and the second options in each are identically a 2/3 chance of no deaths and a 1/3 chance of 600 deaths. If you prefer the first option in the first question and you think in these logical terms, you should prefer the first option in the second question. But, as the data indicate, the different ways the questions are framed confuse many people; choices do depend on how the possible options are framed.

Framing effects are observed in all sorts of contexts, not only when matters of life and death cloud judgment. A very significant example involves the so-called *zero illusion*. Ask yourself, Would you rather pay $300 or take a gamble based on the flip of a coin, where you will lose $600 if the coin comes up heads, but you neither win nor lose anything if it comes up tails? Then reask this question, framing the outcomes in terms of your bank account balance. I do not know the level of your bank account balance, but if it is, say, $24,220, the question framed this second way is, Would you rather have a bank account balance of $23,920 for sure, or flip a coin where your bank account balance will be $23,620 if the coin comes up heads or $24,220 if it comes up tails? You can fill in your own answers, after adjusting the numbers to reflect your current bank account balance. In a significant number of cases, people prefer the gamble if the choices are framed in the first way, but they prefer the sure thing in the second framing. The explanation of this is usually that, in the first framing, the individual focuses too heavily on the zero point, hence the name zero illusion: Rather than accept a loss for sure of $300, the individual is willing to gamble, since this presents an even chance of losing nothing. But when framed in terms of bank account balances, the psychologically loaded term *loss* is missing and the choice reverses.

Better to Gamble with "Known" Odds Than When the Odds Are Unknown

Imagine an urn with 300 colored balls of equal size and weight. One hundred are colored red. Some of the other 200 are colored blue, while the remaining balls are green. It is unknown how many are blue and how many are green, only that the blues and greens total 200. An individual is paid $100 if a ball drawn at random from the urn has a specified color. Do people prefer that the specified color is red, blue, or green? A substantial number of people, facing this choice, say that they are indifferent between blue and green but strictly prefer red. They say that this is because, with red as the specified color, the odds of winning are clearly 1/3, while with blue or green, the odds aren't clear. "On average," these people might say, "the odds of blue or of green are 1/3, just like red. But I prefer a gamble with known odds to gambles the odds of which are unknown."[2]

Sometimes the likelihood of the different possible outcomes are "known," at least to sophisticated individuals. This prominently includes cases of gambling in casinos. In other cases, the possible outcomes are known, but the probabilities of those outcomes are a matter of subjective judgment. Think of betting at a racetrack. A bettor will know that a $2 bet on Old Rust Bucket to win will pay $25 if Old Rust Bucket wins the race. But the probability of this outcome is a matter of subjective judgment, about which people disagree. And in other contexts, including many important economic contexts, not only are the probabilities a matter of subjective judgment, but the range of possible outcomes is not fully known by the decision maker.

---

[2] This example is loosely adapted from D. Ellsberg, "Risk, Ambiguity, and the Savage Axioms," *Quarterly Journal of Economics*, Vol. 75, 1961, 643–69.

Economists use the following terminology: When a decision must be taken with uncertain consequences but where the possible consequences and their probabilities are objectively known, the situation involves *risk* or *objective uncertainty*. When the possible outcomes are known but their probabilities are not objectively known, the situation involves *uncertainty* or *subjective uncertainty*. And when the list of possible outcomes is not at all well known, the situation involves *ambiguity* or *unforeseen contingencies*. In these terms, the colored balls in the urn example illustrates aversion to subjective uncertainty. Individuals also tend to be averse to gambles with unforeseen contingencies

Aversion to Risk

The remaining behavioral patterns that we describe are most easily posed in terms of the simplest of settings: decisions made under conditions of objective uncertainty. So in what follows, we describe various options in terms of the prizes or outcomes that might be received and their objective odds. Moreover, these phenomena are most easily described in situations where the possible outcomes or prizes are monetary. Hence, we discuss things like a gamble that gives the decision maker $100 with probability 0.3, $50 with probability 0.2, nothing with probability 0.4, or costs the decision maker $200 with probability 0.1. To avoid writing out all the details, we use *chance node* depictions of such gambles. For instance, the four-outcome gamble just described is depicted as in Figure 15.1.

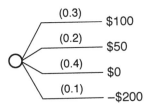

Figure 15.1. A chance-node depiction of a gamble. The gamble depicted has four possible outcomes, listed at the end points of the four branches of the node. The probability of each outcome is given in parentheses along the respective branch.

For any gamble with monetary prizes and objectively known probabilities of the possible prizes, we can compute the gamble's *expected monetary value* (EMV), sometimes called its *mean*, by multiplying each possible prize by its probability and then adding.

Suppose we offer an individual a simple dichotomous choice of a gamble or its EMV. For instance, we ask an individual, Would you rather have the gamble depicted in Figure 15.1 or a sure-thing payment of

$$(\$100)(0.3) + (\$50)(0.2) + (\$0)(0.4) + (-\$200)(0.1) = \$20?$$

Many individuals, in many situations, prefer the EMV for sure. When this happens, we say the individual is *risk averse*. An individual who is indifferent between a gamble and its EMV is *risk neutral*. And an individual who prefers a gamble to its EMV is called *risk seeking*.

Risk aversion is more widespread and more pronounced the greater is the scale of the gamble: Offered a gamble with prizes $50 or $0, with probabilties 0.6 and 0.4, respectively, many people would be close to indifferent between the gamble and its EMV, $30. But if offered a gamble with prizes $50,000 or $0, with probabilities 0.6 and 0.4, or a sure-thing payment of $30,000, many people would have a strong preference for the sure thing. And, if the scale is in millions of dollars, the preference for the sure thing becomes quite strong. This is such an important phenomenon that all of Chapter 17 is devoted to its economic consequences.

Risk aversion is widespread, but it is by no means universal. Indeed, in some specific situations, risk-seeking behavior is frequently observed. Two specific situations are these:

1. People gamble to avoid losses, especially when they suffer from a zero illusion. Such people prefer a gamble with prizes −$600 or $0, with probabilities 0.5 apiece, to being forced to pay $300 for sure.

2. People gamble to achieve a large prize, albeit with small odds, if the alternative large-probability loss is small. This is one explanation for why people buy lottery tickets. The typical lottery ticket gives a chance of a number of prizes, but these tickets are generally characterized as small chances at gains of various sizes, a virtually infinitesimal chance at a huge gain, and a large chance at a loss (the cost of the ticket) with the EMV of the package less than 0. It seems clear that people buy these tickets for the virtually infinitesimal chance at the huge gain; witness the buying frenzies that take place when the jackpot of a particular lottery is unusually large.

Risk aversion is, of course, a matter of individual taste, opportunity, and experience. Everything else held equal, a student on a tight budget is more likely to be risk averse and more risk averse than a well-paid executive of a large corporation. Someone who rarely faces gambles is more likely to be risk averse and more risk averse for a specific gamble than someone who routinely gambles on his or her own account.

Some important terminology goes along with the phenomenon of risk aversion and, more generally, with any choice among gambles with monetary prizes. Given any gamble, we can imagine asking an individual who owns the gamble, Would you prefer the gamble or X for sure? Depending on the size of X, the individual might prefer the gamble or the sure thing. When X is set at the precise amount that makes the individual indifferent between the gamble and the sure thing, we say that X is the individual's *certainty equivalent* (CE) for the gamble.

In this terminology, risk aversion means a certainty equivalent less than the expected monetary value, or CE < EMV; risk neutrality is CE = EMV; and risk-seeking behavior is CE > EMV.

Assuming risk aversion, so that CE < EMV, the difference between the certainty equivalent and the expected monetary value, or EMV − CE, is called the individual's *risk premium* (RP) for the gamble. The larger the risk premium, the greater is the distance between the gamble's EMV and the subjective value of the gamble to the individual, its CE, and thus, roughly, the greater is the individual's level of risk aversion for the gamble in question.

Decreasing (Absolute) Aversion to Risk

For a particular risk-averse individual, how does the individual's level of risk aversion change, as the individual becomes richer or poorer? A way to measure this is to see how the risk premium for a given gamble changes as the individual's overall level of wealth increases. It is by no means a universal truth, but the general tendency is for the individual to become less risk averse the richer he or she becomes. In other words, one's risk premium for a gamble decreases the more wealth one possesses. This sort of pattern is known as *decreasing (absolute) aversion to risk*.

The Certainty Effect

Probabilities close to 1 or to 0 give rise to some common behavioral patterns. For instance, how would you choose between the two gambles depicted in Figure 15.2(a)? How would you choose between the two gambles depicted in Figure 15.2(b)? A commonly observed pattern is that Gamble B is preferred to Gamble A and Gamble C is preferred to Gamble D. The explanation is that Gamble B offers the certainty of a substantial prize, making it preferable to the risky Gamble A. But both C and D are risky (neither offers a certainty), and given the odds and prizes, C is better than D.

To see why this might be problematic, compare the *compound* Gambles E and F in Figure 15.3. In each, there is a 0.1 chance that the prize is 0, and a 0.9 chance that you get either Gamble A, if you choose E, or Gamble B, if you choose F. If you focus your attention on the 0.9 chance that your choice

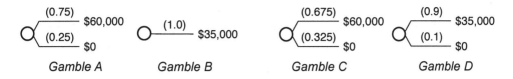

Gamble A   Gamble B   Gamble C   Gamble D

(a) Do you prefer Gamble A or Gamble B?   (b) Do you prefer Gamble C or Gamble D?

Figure 15.2. The certainty effect. Many people prefer Gamble B to Gamble A in panel a and Gamble C to Gamble D in panel b.

makes a difference and so frame the choice between E and F as really a choice between A and B, then perhaps F is better, because B is. But Gamble E gives a $0.9 \times 0.75 = 0.675$ chance of $60,000, and F gives a 0.9 chance at $35,000. Framed this way, Gamble E is identical to C, and Gamble F is D. So shouldn't anyone who prefers C to D also prefer E to F?

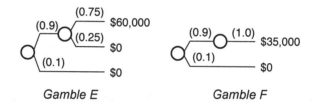

Gamble E   Gamble F

Figure 15.3. The certainty effect, continued. Then how do Gambles E and F compare? Should a preference for B over A in Figure 15.2(a) mean that F is better than E? Or should a preference for C over D mean that E is better than F?

I do not want to emphasize the framing issue here, although it is certainly interesting. Instead, I want to emphasize how the "certainty" of a positive prize in Gamble B makes it so very attractive psychologically, at least to some people. This is known as the *certainty effect*.[3]

Overweighting Small Probabilities

On the other side of the probability spectrum, where probabilities are close to 0, consider choosing between Gambles A and B in Figure 15.4(a), between C and D in Figure 15.4(b), and between E and F in Figure 15.4(c). Of course, all these judgments are subjective, but a commonly observed pattern in the first two is B over A in panel a and C over D in panel b. But then, in comparing E to F, is the difference between them that E gives

---

[3] The certainty effect and overweighting small probabilities are described in Kahnemann and Tversky, "Prospect Theory," and are special cases of the Allais paradox, first described in M. Allais, "Le Comportement de l'Homme Rationnel devant le Risque, Critique des Postulates et Axiomes de l'Ècole Americaine," *Econometrica*, Vol. 21, 1953, 503–46.

you A with probability 0.04 (and nothing otherwise), while F gives you B with probability 0.04? If so, shouldn't the original preference for B mean a preference for F over E? On the other hand, if you multiply out probabilities, E gives a 0.01 chance at $100,000, which is precisely C, while F gives a 0.02 chance at $60,000, which is precisely D. So should a preference for C over D translate into a preference for E over F?

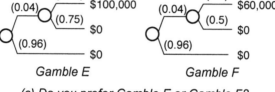

Gamble A   Gamble B   Gamble C   Gamble D
(a) Do you prefer Gamble A or Gamble B?   (b) Do you prefer Gamble C or Gamble D?

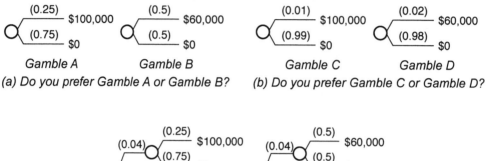

Gamble E   Gamble F
(c) Do you prefer Gamble E or Gamble F?

Figure 15.4. Overweighting small probabilities. In panels a and b, the pattern that B is better than A and C is better than D is often observed. How should a decision maker with this pair of preferences feel about E versus F?

The pattern of preferences B better than A but C better than D is rationalized as follows: In B and A, a careful and judicious study of the probabilities and prizes suggests to many people that B is better. But the chance of winning anything in either C or D is quite small. You win only if you are lucky. And as long as luck is running your way, why not win $100,000 instead of $60,000? This sort of psychology of preference is called *overweighting small probabilities*; a small probability event happens only if one is "lucky," and luck either happens or it doesn't. In other words, the decision maker does not feel that it takes "twice as much luck" to win in C as it does in D, although of course, objectively, it really does.

15.2. The Expected Utility Model

To review, when faced with choices that involve uncertain outcomes, individuals exhibit a variety of behaviors. The previous section catalogs some commonly observed patterns of behavior. To model the economic choices of individuals facing uncertain outcomes, we would like models of behavior that allow for these phenomena.

That is what we would like to have. What economic theory or, rather, mainstream economic theory delivers is something distinctly less. The model used overwhelming by economists to model individual decision making where outcomes are uncertain is the *expected utility model*. It is robust enough to accommodate some of the phenomena listed previously, but it misses some others. For ease of exposition, first I outline the model, and then I go back to what it does and does not permit in terms of behavior. To begin, I describe how this model works for gambles of the fashion of Figure 15.1: chance nodes with given objective probabilities and monetary prizes.

The individual's preferences among such gambles are essentially given by his or her *utility function*, a function that assigns to each dollar-prize level a corresponding number, the utility of the prize. (How does this use of the term *utility function* square with its use in Chapter 5? We get back to this question at the end of the chapter, but for now it is probably best to forget Chapter 5.) An example of such a utility function is the function U depicted in Figure 15.5.

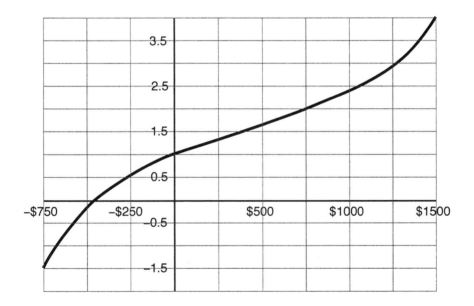

Figure 15.5. A utility function.

Now suppose this individual faces a choice among gambles. More specifically, suppose the individual has to choose among the three gambles depicted in Figure 15.6. Faced with this choice problem, we assume that the decision maker

1. Uses his or her utility function U to convert each possible prize in each of the available gambles to its corresponding utility level. For instance,

the first prize in the first gamble is $750. Assuming for purposes of illustration that the decision maker's utility function is the function in Figure 15.5, he or she notes that $750 has utility level 2.0.

2. Computes each gamble's *expected utility*: Fixing one of the gambles, the probability of each prize is multiplied by the utility of the prize, and these products are summed. So, for instance, the first gamble has prizes $750 and $0, with respective probabilities 0.7 and 0.3. The utility of $750 is [2.0], and the utility of $0 is [1.0]. So the expected utility of the first gamble is (0.7)[2.0] + (0.3)[1.0] = [1.7]. (I put utility levels in square brackets, in such computations.)

3. Chooses the gamble that has the highest expected utility.

Gamble X   Gamble Y   Gamble Z

Figure 15.6. Three gambles. Which gamble will a specific individual choose, if she must choose one (and only one) of the these three gambles? (See Figure 15.7 for the answer.)

In Figure 15.7, you see the computations carried out. The expected utility model says that a decision maker with the utility function of Figure 15.5 and a choice of the three gambles in Figure 15.6 would choose the first of these three gambles, since of the three, the first has the highest expected utility.

This is an as-if model, just like the model of utility-maximizing consumer back in Chapter 5. Individuals facing risky decisions do not actually compute expected utilities and choose according to the results of those calculations. But, in the economic models we build, we will suppose that individuals act *as if* they did this.

This as-if model, applied to a specific consumer and choice, is essentially specified by the utility function that characterizes the decision maker's attitude toward risk. The adverb *essentially* is added on two grounds:

1. The decision maker's behavior is characterized by the utility function *and the modeling hypothesis that his or her choices conform to maximizing expected utility.* The second half of this should not be ignored.

2. The specific utility function is important only to the extent that ordinal rankings of expected utilities are preserved. This is fancy talk for the

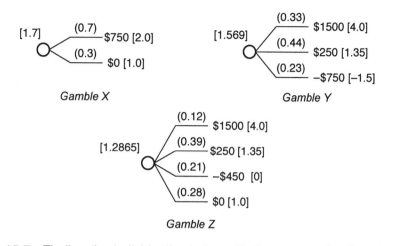

Figure 15.7. Finding the individual's choice with the expected utility model. If the individual choosing among the three gambles in Figure 15.6 has the utility function in Figure 15.5, he or she would choose the first gamble, because it has the highest expected utility.

notion that, if U is a utility function that (together with the hypothesis of expected utility maximization) characterizes the choices of a particular individual, then the function V defined by multiplying U by a positive constant and adding some other constant gives exactly the same choices. Utility is measured in imaginary, intangible units that are often called *utils*, and the scale on which utils are measured can be shifted up or down, and stretched or compressed, as long as the stretching or compression is uniform along the scale, without changing the modeled behavior of the individual in any problem involving choice under uncertainty. In particular, a utility level of 0 has no cardinal significance.

Nonmonetary Prizes

That is how the model works for monetary prizes and objective probabilties. We get to the extension to subjective probabilities in a bit, but the extension for nonmonetary prizes is simple: Whatever is the range of possible prizes, the utility function U assigns to each prize a utility level, and each gamble's value is measured by its expected utility, the sum over all the prizes in the gamble of the probability of each prize times the prize's utility.

In this model, a "prize" is the full bundle of items received. If you imagine that prizes are, say, a certain level of money received plus a particular market share (representing ongoing value), then prizes are *pairs*, such as $100,000 and a 10% market share, and the utility function associates to each such *pair* a level of utility. We do not have separate utilities for money and for market share that are added together.

Finding Certainty Equivalents from a Utility Function

For the three gambles in Figure 15.6 and the utility function in Figure 15.5, the first gamble has expected utility [1.7] and the second has expected utility [1.569]. Accordingly, the first is preferred by our decision maker. But how much better is the first to that person? There is no particular meaning to the difference (1.7 − 1.569 = 0.131) in expected utilities. Since the scale of the utility function (utils or whatever) can be stretched or compressed at will, it is hard to attribute any meaning to differences in expected utility levels.

In the case where prizes are monetary, we can get a measure of how much better the first is by converting these expected utility levels back to monetary amounts. This is done by reading the utility function backward. For the utility function in Figure 15.5, a utility level of [1.7] corresponds to a dollar level of approximately $525. (In other words, the first gamble in Figure 15.5 has a certainty equivalent of $525 or so.) A utility level of [1.569] corresponds to a dollar level around $425. So, to the level of accuracy possible in these rough measurements, the difference between the dollar-measured values of the first and second gambles is on the order of $100. This, it must be confessed, is not much of a difference, given the scale of the prizes or the level of accuracy implicit in these calculations. But it is worth knowing that the two look approximately the same in dollar terms.

(If your eyesight is not good enough to read that utility level [1.7] corresponds to $525 and [1.569] to $425, do not despair; neither is mine. I got these dollar values by linear interpolation, using $375 as the dollar value of [1.5] and $750 as the dollar value of [2.0].)

Properties of the Utility Function

The utility function in Figure 15.5 is typical of utility functions in economic models in two ways but atypical in an important respect. Figure 15.8 is very typical, possessing three properties:

1. It is an *increasing* function, which captures the idea that more money is better than less.

2. It is *continuous*, which captures the notion that the value of a gamble to the decision maker does not change dramatically when the prize levels change continuously. Continuity guarantees that every gamble has a certainty equivalent.

3. It is *concave*, which is equivalent to risk-averse behavior.

The first two properties are utterly noncontroversial, and you'll rarely if ever see a utility function without them. In particular, the utility function in Figure 15.5 has both.

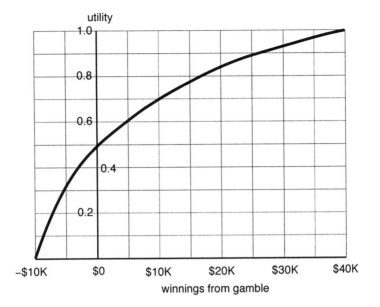

Figure 15.8. *A utility function typical of most economic models.* This utility function is typical because it is increasing, continuous, and concave.

But the function in Figure 15.5 lacks the third property, concavity, which implies risk aversion. I do not try to justify the assertion that concavity implies risk aversion and vice versa. (Readers with an excellent background in mathematics can prove this using Jensen's inequality.) Take my word for it, as well as for the following statements concerning risk neutral and risk-seeking behavior,

- A linear utility function is equivalent to risk neutrality.

- A convex utility function is equivalent to risk-seeking behavior.

These statements have interesting consequences for the utility function in Figure 15.5: It is concave up to a prize of approximately $500, and it is convex for prizes above $500. This means that, for a decision maker with this utility function and for any gamble with prizes all below $500, the gamble's certainty equivalent is less than the gamble's expected monetary value. But, for a gamble with prizes entirely above $500, the gamble's EMV is less than its CE. For gambles whose prizes span $500, we cannot be sure how its CE and EMV compare until we look at the specific gamble.

Therefore, the expected utility model is robust enough to capture the phenomenon of risk aversion: Simply use the model with a concave utility function. Moreover, while it can accommodate risk aversion, it does not require risk aversion: Depending on the shape of the individual's utility function, behavior that is risk neutral or risk seeking is consistent with the model.

What about the other items on our list of desiderata? By and large, the news is not good.

Framing Effects

There are a variety of different framing effects, but the ones we saw concern how the decision maker perceives the prizes and probabilities. Before getting to this, we should be clear on one thing: It is not enough to say that we put prizes or dollar values on the horizontal axis. Does $1000 on the horizontal axis mean a $1000 net gain from a particular risky venture or $1000 as the decision maker's final bank account balance after the gamble is over? Of course it matters, and we have to be clear what the dollars represent.

Then, turning to framing effect, we find problems even if you are careful to denominate the prizes in this fashion. Take the second example of framing we gave. If a decision maker has $24,220 in his bank account, a $500 net loss from gambling is precisely the same outcome as a final bank account balance of $23,720. But we claimed that for some people at least, how this (identical) prize and the other prizes involved are framed matters to the individual's choices.

In a sense, the expected utility model is agnostic about such matters. If framing a gamble as net gains or losses from the gamble instead of as net bank account balance matters to the decision maker, then we must be careful in our models to employ the framing that the decision maker uses (that is, be sure that the utility function we use reflects that frame), and we are in business. This can be hard to do in practice, however, at least insofar as decision makers do not systematically adopt one framing of a particular choice or another. And, indeed, most economic models of choice under uncertainty ignore framing effects altogether, assuming instead that the decision makers in the models treat a net loss from gambling of $500 precisely as they treat a final bank account balance of $B - 500$, where B is the starting balance. Even if the model, in principle, is flexible enough to capture at least some framing effects, it has rarely been used that way.

Subjective Uncertainty, Ambiguity, and Aversion to Unknown Odds

So far we have discussed this model for situations with objective uncertainty. What about cases where the probabilities or even the range of possible outcomes are not known—that is, cases of subjective uncertainty and ambiguity?

In most models employed by economists, the possibility that the decision maker does not know all the possible outcomes is simply not admitted. We see near the end of this book that accounting for unforeseen contingencies is one of the big unsolved challenges facing microeconomic modeling.

As for subjective uncertainty, the standard procedure in economic models is to assume (1) the decision maker is perfectly willing to assign probabilities to the different possible outcomes, probabilities that sum to 1 and, having done so, (2) he or she treats subjective probabilities precisely the same as objective probabilities. That is, the decision maker computes expected utilities using a "best guess" at the probabilities, whether those best guesses reflect objective odds, vast experience, or rough-and-ready guesstimates.

In the case of the urn with 300 colored balls, a decision maker (she) faces a random event with three possible outcomes: The ball drawn is red, blue, or green. Because she knows that 100 of the balls are red, it makes good objective sense to suppose she regards that outcome as having probability 1/3. And then, per the standard procedures of economic modeling, she assigns probabilities to the two other outcomes that sum to 2/3, so the sum of the probabilities of all the outcomes is 1. It probably makes the most sense for her to assign probabilities 1/3 to each of the three outcomes—why should blue be more likely than green or vice versa?—but the assignment of probabilities is subjective, or in other words, up to her own best judgment. Hence the terms *subjective probability* and *personal probability* enter the language of economics. The point is, one of green or blue must then have probability at least 1/3, and whatever utility she assigns to money, she is going to regard a bet that pays off on that color to give her at least as much expected utility as one that pays off if the ball drawn is red. In this example and more generally, under the standard procedure, there is no place for a general aversion to gambles where the odds are unknown.

Some people—and my guess is that *some* here means a majority—are averse to gambles where the probabilities of the outcomes are subjective. Some people (a majority?) would rather bet on red than blue or green in the example. So the standard model, as a descriptive model of how people choose facing subjective uncertainty, is simply inadequate. This empirical critique of the standard model is sometimes known as the *Ellsberg paradox*, after Daniel Ellsberg, who first noted this deficiency in the standard model.

Some alternatives to the standard model give us the flexibility to model aversion to subjective uncertainty. But these alternatives are not much used in applications, and so we do not chase them down.

The Certainty Effect and Overweighting Small Probabilities

Concerning the certainty effect and overweighting small probabilities, the simple and sad fact is that the expected utility model does not accommodate those two phenomena. I do not give a detailed explanation why this is; try

Problem 15.5 if you are curious.

This deficiency in the expected utility model is known as the *Allais paradox*, after its discoverer, Maurice Allais. A number of alternatives to the expected utility model accommodate the certainty and overweighting-small-probabilities effects, perhaps the best known is Prospect Theory, by Kahnemann and Tversky (reference given earlier in this chapter). Notwithstanding a recent surge of interest in them, these alternatives are used very little in applications and we do not discuss them.

Decreasing (and Constant) Risk Aversion

The final member of our list of desiderata for a descriptive model is the notion that, as individuals become richer, their level of risk aversion decreases. Not every utility function within the expected utility model, even if the function is concave, gives this. But it is not hard to check whether a given utility function has this property.

Suppose we have a decision maker whose choices among monetary-prize gambles are given by maximizing expected utility for the utility function U. If U is smooth enough that it has two derivatives and the function

$$\lambda(x) = -\frac{U''(x)}{U'(x)}$$

is a decreasing function, then U gives choices that are decreasingly risk averse as the decision maker's base level of wealth rises. (In this statement U' is the first derivative and U'' the second derivative of U.)

I will not prove this to you here; readers who want a proof should consult an advanced book on choice theory or the economics of uncertainty, but let me try to explain. Risk aversion goes with concave utility functions—that is, utility functions that bend over. The level or degree of risk aversion has to do with how "quickly" the function bends or, in slightly more precise terminology, its curvature. Decreasing risk aversion results when the function is less curvy at larger arguments than small. And, for the mathematical magic, the curvature of a function at a point is given by the ratio of its second derivative to its first. (The minus sign in front of the ratio is there because U is concave, so its second derivative is negative.) Thus, decreasing risk aversion is decreasing curvature, which is that the function $\lambda(x)$ defined previously decreases.

An important special case of a risk-averse utility function is where this ratio is constant. This means that the decision maker's degree of risk aversion is unchanging. In other words, the decision maker's choice among any set of gambles, the prizes of which are added to his or her status-quo wealth level, doesn't depend on that status-quo level of wealth. (See Problem 15.3 for an example.) The question is, For what utility functions is this true? For which functions U is $-U''(x)/U'(x)$ a constant λ? Readers with a background in simple differential equations can solve this to discover that the functions U for which this is so are functions

$$U(x) = -A\,e^{-\lambda x} + B,$$

where A is a positive constant and B is any constant. (The constants A and B are just the constants of integration.) These utility functions are called *constant absolute risk aversion* utility functions and the constant λ is called the individual's *coefficient of risk aversion*. The larger is λ, the more curvy is the function and, correspondingly, the more risk averse is the individual with this utility function.

15.3. Concluding Remarks

Economists—and for the rest of this book, we—use the expected utility model as a descriptive model of how individuals choose when facing decisions with uncertainty outcomes. This model can capture the basic phenomenon of risk aversion, and it gives us the ability to discuss decreasing and constant risk aversion. We can fiddle with the expected utility model to capture some framing effects, although few economic models actually do this. But the model is not flexible enough to capture aversion to unknown probabilities or subjective uncertainty, the certainty effect, or overweighting small probabilities. It is not a perfect descriptive model by any means.

Still, it is a pretty good model, especially because it captures one other behavioral phenomenon, approximate risk neutrality for small-scale gambles, that is vastly important in economics, as we discuss in Chapter 17. And it serves another important role: It is the basis for a *normative* theory of decision making under uncertainty, which is the subject of Chapter 16.

Some alternatives to the expected utility model try to accommodate some of the things this model misses, and these are beginning to appear more and more frequently in the literature of economics. Other alternative models serve special purposes. In particular, if you take a course in finance or financial markets, you are likely to encounter something called the *mean–variance model* of choice under uncertainty. I do not discuss this here, but you will find some commentary on the mean–variance model in the *Student's Companion*.

A final issue concerns the relationship between this chapter and Chapter 5, where the model of the utility-maximizing consumer was presented. To understand the relationship, remember what these models are trying to do in general. *We are modeling the choices made by individuals who choose from among a set of objects.*

Let Z denote the collection of all the *objects* that might be within the choice set from which the individual is asked to choose. These objects can be many different sorts of things.

- We can think of each z as a *bundle of commodities*, written $(z_1, z_2, \ldots, z_N)$, where N is the number of commodities and the vector $(z_1, z_2, \ldots, z_N)$ represents the bundle consisting of z_1 units of the first commodity, z_2 units of the second, and so on. This sort of object was discussed in Chapter 5.

- We can think of each z as a bundle of commodities $(z_1, z_2, \ldots, z_N, m)$ where the last commodity m is the amount of money left over, precisely as we did in Chapter 5.

- We can think of each z as a *lottery or compound lottery with objective probabilities*. That is, there is another set X of possible prizes, and each z is a lottery or gamble that gives prizes in the set X. This sort of object is discussed in this chapter.

- We can think of there being a finite number of financial securities and each z is a portfolio of those securities: We write $z = (z_1, z_2, \ldots, z_M)$, and interpret this as z_1 dollars invested in the first security, z_2 dollars invested in the second, and so on. This is one sort of object you deal with in courses on finance and investments.

- We can think of the objects as cash flows from investments over time, where $z = (z_0, z_1, z_2, \ldots)$ represents z_0 dollars accruing from the investment today, z_1 dollars accruing next month (say), z_2 dollars accruing 2 months hence, and so on.

- We can think of each z as a different variety of some consumer product, such as a car, where $z = (z_1, z_2, z_3, z_4)$ represents the vehicle's body-type z_1 (for z_1 drawn from subcompact, compact, midsized, etc.), z_2 is the color, z_3 tells the size of the engine, and z_4 gives the fuel economy of the car. That is, we describe each car according to a list of its characteristics. This sort of representation of objects turns up in consumer marketing.

To model the individual's choice behavior, confronted with these objects, we use a utility function model, as described back in Chapter 5: We suppose that some function u associates to each object z from the set Z a numerical index, $u(z)$, and given a set of objects from which to choose, the individual chooses the element of the set that gives the highest utility. This is not to say, of course, that the individual actually computes utilities or consults a utility function. Instead, this is an as-if model, the rationale of which was given in Chapter 5.

Back in Chapter 5, when we dealt with money left over, we went on to assume that the general utility function u had a special form: We assumed that $u(z_1, \ldots, z_N, m) = u_1(z_1) + \ldots + u_N(z_N) + m$. And, if you go back to Chapter 5, you'll find a (rough) rationale for at least the $+m$ part of this specialization; this was justified by a story about how, if the amount of money that might be spent is small relative to the decision maker's overall wealth, her marginal value of money might be fairly close to constant.

We do something quite similar here. In this chapter, the objects of choice have a special structure: They are lotteries with prizes. If we look momentarily at lotteries where the prizes are dollar amounts and the probabilities are objective, we are looking at objects described by a list of the prizes, say $\{x_1, \ldots, x_N\}$, and a list of corresponding probabilities, say $\{p_1, \ldots, p_N\}$. And we assume that the utility used to model the individual's choices among lotteries takes a special (and simple) form:

$$p_1 U(x_1) + \ldots + p_N U(x_N),$$

for some "utility function" U whose domain is the set of prizes.

Back in Chapter 5, when we assumed that utility was linear in money left over, we were making a special assumption, that holds even as an approximation only sometimes. Here, we make a special assumption about the structure of the decision maker's overall (little u) utility function over gambles, an assumption that, for instance, rules out capturing the certainty effect. This assumption, because it simplifies the preferences we look at, makes life easier in specific models. But, by making this simplification, we miss some phenomena we might otherwise want to model.

The point is that we use the term *utility function* in two different ways. Back in Chapter 5, the (little u) utility function gave us, for each basic object that might be chosen, a direct measure of the individual's preferences for the object. In this chapter, the (big U) utility function is a piece in the construction of the measure of the individual's preferences for lotteries; $U(x)$ tells us something about the relative desirability of the prize x, to be scaled by the probability of x and then summed to get the overall measure of how desirable is a particular gamble.

Just as special models of utility are used for uncertain prospects or gambles, so you may find in specialized contexts other specific ways to compute utility. For instance, when talking about the stream of cash flows coming to a firm, it is typically assumed that firms value those streams as discounted cash flows, where the discount factors reflect the firm's cost of capital. The other two specializations mentioned previously, portfolios of risky assets and objects described by a vector of the object's characteristics, also get special handling in some applications; you'll probably meet the former in courses on finance and the latter in courses on analytical consumer marketing. When you meet these other specializations in other courses or books, the connection to basic economics will always be the same: The basic structure is as in Chapter 5, where each basic object is assigned a numerical index or utility and the decision maker is assumed to choose whichever option scores most highly on this scale. When the objects have specialized structure, we often assume the utility of a basic option can be calculated using that structure, as in this chapter.

Executive Summary

- Beginning with this chapter, we add uncertainty to the story. As a first step, in this chapter, we present the expected utility model, the leading model of individual choice under uncertainty in economics.

- We begin by cataloging behavior patterns that we would (ideally) wish to accommodate in a robust descriptive model: framing effects, aversion to subjective uncertainty and to ambiguity, aversion to risk but (often) decreasing risk aversion as wealth rises, the certainty effect, and the overweighting of small probabilities.

- In the expected utility model, a (big U) utility function assigns a utility to each possible prize; for each gamble, expected utility is computed (for each possible prize, the utility of the prize is multiplied by the probability of the prize, and these products are summed); and the gamble chosen is the gamble with the highest expected utility. No allowance is made for ambiguity, and it is assumed that the individual assesses subjective probabilities where necessary and uses them precisely as objective probabilities

- When the prizes are monetary, the utility function can be specified in a graph. The utility function (so graphed) is almost always increasing and continuous. In most economic models, it is also concave, which corresponds to risk aversion. (Linear functions = risk neutrality, and convex functions = risk seeking.) The value units of the utility function have no particular meaning, and the scale on which they are measured can be shifted and stretched or compressed uniformly.

- The expected utility model does not explicitly give us the ability to deal in framing effects. It entirely misses aversion to subjective uncertainty and ambiguity. It misses the certainty effect and overweighting small probabilities. But, for a concave utility function, the model captures risk aversion.

- If U is concave and if $\lambda(x) = -U''(x)/U'(x)$ is decreasing, the level of risk aversion decreases as wealth increases. If $-U''(x)/U'(x)$ is a constant λ, then the utility function has constant risk aversion; the individual's choice among gambles is unaffected by his or her level of wealth. These utility functions are $U(x) = -A e^{-\lambda x} + B$, for constants $A > 0$ and B.

- The utility (the little u) of Chapter 5 is the basic model of consumer choice, indexing each basic object with an ordinal measure of how good it is. The utility (big U) function of this chapter indexes prizes, as a step to computing the expected utility of a gamble, gambles being the basic objects of choice.

Problems

15.1 Consider the three gambles depicted in Figure 15.9 and three decision makers, each of whom chooses among gambles based on expected utility:

(a) Jo MBA, whose utility function for the range of prizes in these gambles is depicted in Figure 15.10.

(b) Professor David Kreps, whose utility function for the range of prizes in these gambles is given by $U(x) = -e^{-0.00001x}$, where x is the dollar value of the prize.

(c) Professor Sanjay Patel, who like Professor Kreps has constant risk aversion for this range of prizes but who is more risk averse than Professor Kreps. Professor Patel's utility function is given by $U(x) = -e^{-0.00002x}$.

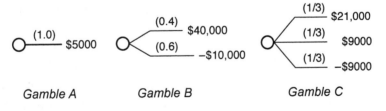

Figure 15.9. Three gambles.

For each of these three individuals, find the individual's certainty equivalent and risk premium for each of the gambles. (It is up to you whether you compute expected utilities.) How would each of these individuals rank the three gambles? You may find it helpful to use an Excel spreadsheet when dealing with Professors Kreps and Patel.

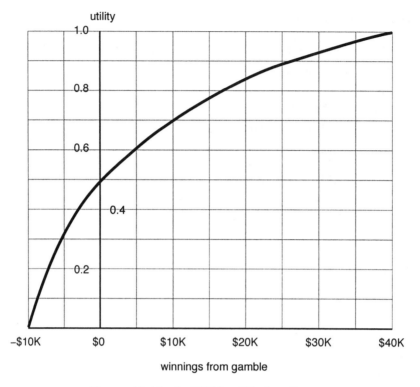

Figure 15.10. Jo MBA's utility function.

15.2 Suppose that Jo MBA, with the utility function depicted in Figure 15.10, is offered a gamble where a coin is flipped twice, and if two heads in a row result, she gets $40,000 (otherwise she gets $0). Would she rather have this gamble or $7500 for sure? What about Jack MBA, whose utility function, denominated in dollar winnings from this venture, is given by $U(x) = \sqrt{x + 5000}$? What about Jim MBA, whose utility function is given by $U(x) = \sqrt{x + 50{,}000}$? What are the certainty equivalents for each of the three for this risky gamble?

15.3 A decision maker faces the following decision under conditions of uncertainty. This decision maker has $1 million in assets. Most of those assets, $750,000, are the individual's equity in his house. The remaining $250,000 are absolutely secure. Unhappily, there is a risk that the individual's house will burn down in a fire, which would be a total loss of the $750,000. The individual can insure his house against the loss from this fire. The premium for the insurance is $40,000, and it will insure the individual completely; that is, if the individual chooses to purchase this insurance policy, his assets will be $960,000, whether or not there is a fire. (There is no mortgage on the house, so $750,000 is the full amount paid by the insurance company.) The probability of a fire is 0.05.

(a) What is the expected net earnings, the premium less the expected amount paid out to the client, to the insurance company from this policy?

(b) If the individual in question were risk neutral, would he buy this insurance policy?

(c) If the individual in question is an expected utility maximizer, with the utility function $U(x) = \sqrt{x}$ where x is the individual's total assets, would this individual buy the insurance?

(d) (Use Excel and Solver on this.) Suppose the individual of part c can buy partial insurance. Partial insurance works as follows: If the individual buys, say, α insurance, where α is a constant between 0 and 1, he must pay the premium $\alpha \times \$40,000$ up front. Then, in the event of a fire, the individual gets a payout from the insurance company of α times his loss or, in this problem, $\alpha \times \$750,000$. If the individual can insure partially and, in particular, can pick the level of insurance he purchases, what level of insurance would he select?

15.4 Suppose we offered Professor Patel from Problem 15.1(c) his choice of the following three gambles:

- Gamble A pays $50,000 with certainty.
- Gamble B pays $100,000 with probability 0.8 and $0 with probability 0.2.
- Gamble C pays $200,000 with probability 0.7 and $0 with probability 0.3.

(a) These winnings are added to Professor Patel's existing assets, which at the moment are $500,000. And Professor Patel's utility function $U(x) = -e^{-0.00002x}$ is in units of his total assets so, for instance, if Professor Patel chooses gamble A, his (expected) utility will be $-e^{-0.00002 \times 550,000}$. What is Professor Patel's choice? What is his certainty equivalent (in terms of net assets) from taking each of the three gambles?

(b) Suppose that, instead of $500,000, Professor Patel's initial assets were $1 million. What would be his choice in this case? What is his certainty equivalent (in terms of net assets) from taking each of the three gambles?

(c) Suppose that, instead of $500,000 or $1 million, Professor Patel's initial assets were $0. What would be his choice in this case? What is his certainty equivalent (in terms of net assets) from taking each of the three gambles?

(d) Professor Patel's twin brother, Professor Krishna Patel, claims he is twice as excitable and 100 units more optimistic than his brother. Therefore, he says, his (Professor K. Patel's) utility function is $-2\,e^{-0.00002x} + 100$. What choices does he make concerning these three gambles?

Problem 15.5 foreshadows the topic of Chapter 17; it is well worth trying. If you have problems with the exponential utility function, please see the discussion in the *Student's Companion*.

15.5 Jan MBA has the opportunity to take a gamble that will net her either a gain of $50,000 or a loss of $25,000, each with probability 1/2. Jan chooses among gambles to maximize her expected utility, with utility function

$$U(y) = 12.5859 - 7.4267\, e^{-0.0000211y}.$$

(a) Will Jan choose to take this gamble, if the alternative is a sure thing of $0?

(b) Suppose Jan could securitize this gamble, which means she prints up 100 "shares" in the gamble, each of which gives a 1/2 chance at a gain of $500 and a 1/2 chance of a loss of $250. Suppose Jan has 99 friends, each of whom has precisely the same utility function as Jan. Would one of those 99 friends be willing to pay Jan $100 for a 1% share of the gamble?

15.6 Verify that an expected utility maximizer, no matter what his utility function, would never exhibit either the certainty effect or the small-probabilities effect for the gambles in Figures 15.2 and 15.4. That is, an expected utility maximizer prefers A to B in Figure 15.2 if and only if he prefers C to D there, and he prefers A to B in Figure 15.4 if and only if he prefers C to D there.

16. Expected Utility as a Normative Decision Aid

This chapter explores the expected utility model as a *normative* model or decision aid. The protagonist of this chapter is not some abstract decision maker; instead, this chapter focuses on *you*.

- First we justify the expected utility model by presenting five qualitative axioms for behavior that, if you subscribe to them, imply you should make decisions under uncertainty by maximizing *your* expected utility.
- Then we discuss how to assess your own (subjective) utility function.
- We discuss some more-advanced procedures you can use, at least in some instances, to improve your assessment of your own utility function.
- We conclude by discussing three reasons why you might *not* want to use the expected utility model.

The purpose of this chapter is to help *you* make better choices when you face uncertainty. Whether in your personal or business life, you will some day face a choice among actions that have uncertain consequences, and you are likely to find that the choice is a hard one. A simple example illustrates how hard such a choice can be.

Imagine that I offer you the choice of the five gambles depicted in Figure 16.1. You can have only one of these. Which do you choose? How confident are you that your choice is the right one for you?

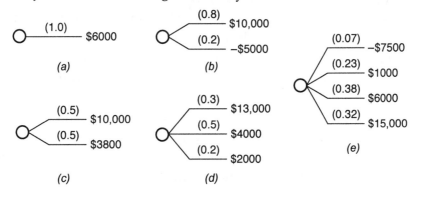

Figure 16.1. Five gambles. Given a choice of one of these five gambles, which would you select?

If you are like most people, this is no easy decision. It is hard because it requires that you integrate in your mind all aspects of a gamble with several prizes and probabilities like 0.07 and 0.38.

Suppose, though, I could convince you that you would like your choice concerning such gambles to conform to expected utility maximization. Further suppose I could direct you to an organization that, using an EEG (electroencephalogram, a device that measures brain-wave patterns), can plot your personal utility function. Then such decisions would become a simple matter of computing mechanically your expected utility—and, if you want, your certainty equivalent—for each gamble, choosing whichever gamble gives you the largest expected utility or CE.

I can almost deliver on this two-barreled promise. I hope to convince you that, subject to some important caveats, your choice in this sort of situation should conform to the conscious maximization of expected utility. And in place of the promised application of electroencephalography, I can show you how, making relatively simple subjective judgments, you can get a good approximation to your utility function to use in problems like this one.

16.1. Justifying the Expected Utility Procedure

The first step is to convince you that you want your choice to conform to the expected utility model. For the time being, I do this for gambles with objective probabilities. In my illustrative examples, the prizes always are monetary, but this is for expositional convenience only; what I say applies to gambles with objective probabilities and any sort of prizes.

I also throw into the set of possible objects of choice so-called compound lotteries or gambles. These are objects in which a sequence of random events may be conducted before you get a prize. For instance, I might roll a fair die. If the die comes up one or two spots (probability 1/3), I give you $500. If it comes up three spots (probability 1/6), I flip a fair coin: Heads, you get $400; tails, I flip again; and if heads this time, you get $500 and $0 if tails. If the original throw of the die comes up four, five, or six spots (probability 1/6 each), you pay me $10 times the number of spots. This compound lottery is depicted in Figure 16.2(a). (Ignore Figure 16.2(b) for now.)

I will ask you to make pairwise comparisons between gambles. Specifically, given any pair of gambles, I ask you to say whether you consider the first to be *as good as* the second and whether you think the second is *as good as* the first. About these preference judgments,

- I do not preclude the possibility that you say both things about a particular pair of gambles, in which case I will interpret your statements as saying that you are *indifferent* between them.

- I do not preclude the possibility, at least not yet, that you are unwilling to express a judgment either way.

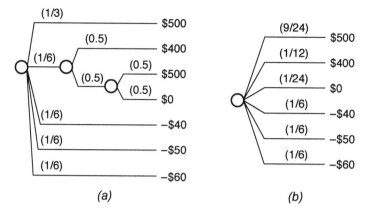

Figure 16.2. A compound gamble and the one-stage gamble to which it reduces. Panel a shows a compound gamble, a gamble that is conducted in several steps. This compound gamble reduced to the one-stage gamble in panel b by the rules of probability, so if you obey property 1 (reduction of compound gambles), you are indifferent between them.

- When you say that gamble A is as good as B, but you do not say that B is as good as A, I interpret this as you *strictly prefer* A to B.

Finally, I assume that you would like to connect your preference judgments and your choices as follows: If you must choose one gamble from a set of gambles, you choose one that you judge to be as good as everything else in the set.

What more can we say about your preferences? Here is a list of five properties that your preferences over gambles may or may not satisfy. As you read these properties, ask yourself whether they seem normatively desirable; that is, do you want your preferences to satisfy them?

Property 1. *Reduction of compound gambles.* You are indifferent between any compound gamble and the simple (one-stage) gamble to which it reduces using the rules of probability theory.

If your preferences satisfy this property, you are indifferent between the gambles in Figures 16.2(a) and 16.2(b), since if we multiply out branches and then add the probabilities of outcomes giving the same dollar prize in Figure 16.2(a), we get the gamble in Figure 16.2(b).

Property 2. *Completeness.* For any two gambles A and B, you are willing to judge A is as good as B, or B is as good as A.

That is, for any pair of gambles I choose, you are always willing to make a judgment one way or the other (or both, if you are indifferent between them). Do not agree to this property too quickly: For most people, expressing preference judgments is difficult in some cases. But the question here is whether you *want* to be able to express a judgment for every pair of gambles and not whether you *can*.

> **Property 3.** *Transitivity.*   If gamble A is as good as gamble B in your opinion, and B is as good as C, then you judge that A is as good for you as is C.

I assume you have no problem with transitivity.

> **Property 4.** *Continuity.* Suppose you feel that gamble A is strictly better than gamble B and that B in turn is strictly better than C. Construct two compound gambles: Let gamble D be a gamble in which you get the gamble A if 10,000 coins flipped in a row come up heads every time and you get the gamble C otherwise. Let gamble E be a gamble in which you get gamble C if 10,000 coins flipped in a row come up tails every time, and you get the gamble A otherwise. Then gamble E is strictly better than gamble B, which in turn is strictly better than gamble D. Or, if this is not true, some finite number larger than 10,000 makes it true.

What a mouthful. But the idea is simple. Gamble D is "almost" the same as gamble C, since it is gamble C with probability $1 - 0.5^{10000}$. Since you believe gamble B is strictly better than gamble C, gamble B ought to be strictly better for you than gamble D, the "almost gamble C" gamble. If it is not, then we can find some number bigger than 10,000 that will make it so. That is half of property 4; the other half does the same thing on the other side.

> **Property 5.** *Substitution.* Suppose you strictly prefer gamble A to gamble B. Take any third gamble C and any probability $p > 0$, and construct the following two compound gambles. Gamble D gives you gamble A with probability p and gamble C with probability $1 - p$. Gamble E gives you gamble B with probability p and gamble C probability $1 - p$. That is, the difference between the two compound gambles is that with gamble D, you get gamble A with probability p, while in E, you get gamble B with this probability. Since you strictly prefer the A to B and since $p > 0$, it must be (and this property says that it is) that you prefer D to E.

Do not worry about the names I give these properties and do not waste your time memorizing either the names or the properties themselves. Instead, concentrate on whether you find them to be *normatively desirable* rules for your preferences to satisfy? Would you like to make choices based on preferences that always satisfy these properties? If not, which one(s) would you be willing to violate?

I hope you think these are normatively desirable rules; you would like the choices you make to be based on preferences that satisfy these properties. Most folks, thinking about choosing among gambles, find these properties entirely reasonable, in most situations. (But do not be too fast to buy them. Wait at least until the end of this chapter.)

In the hope that you decide that these five properties are normatively desirable, I can give the punchline.

Mathematical fact. Any set of preferences among gambles that conforms to the preceding five properties is consistent with the expected utility model in the sense that one gamble is preferred to another if and only if the first gives higher expected utility, for some utility function U defined on the set of prizes. And any set of preferences that corresponds to maximizing expected utility for some utility function U must obey the five properties.

Therefore, if you find these five properties to be normatively desirable, you *want* to choose based on expected utility maximization for some utility function U. Please note carefully that in the last chapter, expected utility is advanced as an as-if theory. We do not see people computing expected utilities and letting those computations guide their choices; expected utility is a descriptive model to the extent that people choose *as if* they were doing this. But now, in a normative vein, there is nothing as if about this. I do not suggest the normative desirability of choosing *as if* you were computing expected utilities. I am selling—and if you find the five properties are desirable in terms of good decision making, you are buying—the *explicit* use of expected utility calculations to improve on your otherwise fallible decision making under uncertainty.

It remains to assess your personal utility function. Actually, a few things remain to say about the five properties and this basic conclusion, but it is expositionally easier to say those things after discussing how to assess your utility function.

16.2. Assessing Your Utility Function

If there were some way to have a machine discover your personal utility function U, choice among gambles would never be a problem for you, at least as long as you subscribe to the five properties. Unhappily, social scientists have yet to invent a machine capable of finding your personal utility function. *You* must do it. But there are ways to make this procedure *relatively* easy.

Suppose you must choose among a number of gambles. To be very concrete, suppose you had to choose among the gambles in Figure 16.1. First note that the range of prizes here runs from a loss of $7500 to a gain of $15,000. So we obtain your utility function for that range of prizes.

First, arbitrarily set the utility of −$7500 to equal 0 and the utility of $15,000 to equal 1. As discussed in the last chapter, utility functions can be translated and stretched or shrunk to fit any scale you wish; in practical terms, this means you can set the utility of any two dollar values as you like. Using a scale of 0 to 1, from the worst possible to the best possible prize, turns out to be convenient, so we do that.

Next ask yourself three questions:

1. What amount of money obtained for sure would be just as good as a gamble in which you receive $15,000 with probability 1/2 and you lose $7500 with probability 1/2?

You may object that this is a hard question to answer precisely. How can you tell precisely what is your certainty equivalent—that is what we ask you for—for the 50–50 gamble with prizes $15,000 and −$7500? The simple answer is that you cannot tell this precisely. But it is probably a lot easier for you to make this judgment than to choose among the five gambles in Figure 16.1. So suppose, for the sake of argument, that the answer you come up with is $2000. That is, if I offered you either the risky gamble or $2250, you would take $2250 for certain in preference to the gamble, but you prefer the gamble to $1750. Then we can continue,

2. What amount of money obtained for sure would be just as good for you as a gamble in which you receive $15,000 with probability 1/2 or you receive *$2000* with probability one-half?

Suppose for the sake of argument that the value is $7500. (Why is the 2000 in italic? I'll explain in a bit.)

3. What amount of money obtained for sure would be just as good for you as a gamble in which you lose $7500 with probability 1/2 or you receive *$2000* with probability one-half?

Since this gamble is probably worse than not gambling at all, I may have to amend the question to read:

3′. How much would you be willing to pay, to get out of having to take a gamble where you lose $7500 with probability 1/2 or gain *$2000* with probability 1/2?

If the answer to question 3 is $-\$X$, the answer to question 3' is $\$X$. Suppose that $\$X$ is $3000. That is, you would be willing to pay $2750 rather than take the gamble, but you would rather take the gamble than pay $3250.

The precise terms of questions 2 and 3 (or 3') depend on your answer to question 1. If your answer to question 1 is $1500, then question 2 would concern a gamble with prizes $15,000 and $1500 instead of $15,000 and $2000. That explains the italic: Where you see italics, substitute your answer to question 1.

Given answers to these three questions, we can begin to build your personal utility function. We set the scale so that $U(15,000) = 1$ and $U(-7500) = 0$. Therefore, the first answer you gave establishes that $U(2000) = 0.5$ on this scale. Why? Because a gamble where you get prizes $15,000 and −$7500, each with probability 1/2, has expected utility 0.5 on the scale we set. If this gamble is indifferent to $2000 for sure—and you said it was, or so we suppose, for sake of illustration—then $U(2000)$ must equal 0.5.

Similarly, your second answer establishes that $U(7500) = 0.75$ on this scale, and your third answer establishes that $U(-3000) = 0.25$. Why? Because if $U(2000) = 0.5$, then a gamble with equally likely prizes $15,000 and $2000 has expected utility $(0.5)[1.0] + (0.5)[0.5] = [0.75]$, and you said you were indifferent between this gamble and $7500 for sure. Similarly, the gamble that gives you −$7500 or $2000, each with probability 1/2, has the expected utility 0.25, and you are indifferent between this gamble and a sure loss of $3000.

So we can plot five points of your utility function, as in Figure 16.3(a). And then we can rough in a utility function for you, as in Figure 16.3(b). This is a pretty rough rough-in, but if you use this function to choose among risky gambles, you will probably get a pretty good approximation to your true preferences.

The murmurs I heard after step 1 are growing in volume: You may be thinking that this is crazy. You have to make choices among risky gambles, and this procedure is supposed make those choices relatively easy. But the procedure requires very fine judgments from you about indifference among risky gambles and sure things. What is gained by that?

The gain comes from the fact the very fine judgments I ask you to make are the simplest judgments of this kind you can be asked to make; you are asked to compare a gamble having two equally likely prizes with a sure thing. A difficulty most people have in choosing among risky gambles is that their judgment is no good with gambles having lots of prizes and probabilities

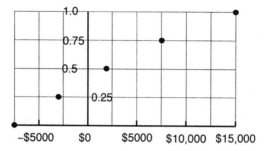

(a) Five points on your utility function, obtained
from answers to relatively simple questions

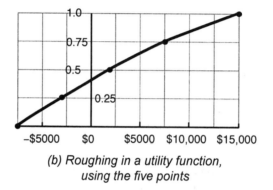

(b) Roughing in a utility function,
using the five points

Figure 16.3. Plotting your utility function. By asking you to supply certainty
equivalents for *relatively simple* gambles—with two equally-likely prizes—we can
construct a fairly good approximation to your utility function.

like 0.38 and 0.23. How likely is probability 0.23? If a gamble has four
different prizes, with probabilities ranging from 0.38 to 0.07, how are the
prizes to be combined and aggregated to get an overall sense of how good
is the gamble? It may not be *easy* to compare a gamble having two equally
likely prizes with a sure thing, but it is probably *easier* to do than to deal
directly with more complex gambles. You are probably going to come closer
to a sense of your preferences with simple comparisons than more complex
comparisons. The point is, if you find the five properties given earlier to be
normatively reasonable, then you can take judgments you make in *relatively*
simple situations and build from them your utility function U, which you
can then use to evaluate more complex choices.

    And make no mistake, the approximate utility function in Figure 16.3(b),
applied more or less mechanically to the five gambles in Figure 16.1, would
give you a pretty good sense of your preference among the five, *if* the answers
to the 50–50 gamble questions used to rough in this utility function reflect
your subjective judgment. Of course, it is possible that you made an error in,

say, the first judgment: Perhaps, your certainty equivalent for a 50–50 gamble with prizes $15,000 and −$7500 is closer to $1500 than $2000. But that error in judgment is more likely than not going to affect a comparison of the five gambles in Figure 16.1 somewhat uniformly. Moreover, any sensible use of a roughed-in utility function involves a computation of certainty equivalents, which gives you a sense of how much better (per your analysis) one gamble is than another. If the difference in CEs is small, then you cannot trust your analysis quite as much as if the difference is large. But, if the difference is small, you have less at stake if you follow the recommendations of your analysis and it is wrong.

Finally, we can do some relatively simple things to give you more confidence in the utility function you assess. I give you the three most common and powerful next.

A Consistency Check

The first way to improve your assessment is a simple consistency check. Suppose you gave the answers listed previously: On a scale where $U(-7500) = 0$ and $U(15,000) = 1$, $0.5 = U(2000)$, and then $0.75 = U(7500)$ and $0.25 = U(-3000)$. Now ask, What is your certainty equivalent for a gamble with prizes $7500 and −$3000, each with probability $1/2$?

Because the expected utility of this gamble is $(0.5)[0.75] + (0.5)[0.25] = [0.5]$, the answer consistent with your other judgments is $2000.

In most cases, people do not pass this consistency check the first time out. It takes some thinking and even a bit of fudging with the three subjective judgments until you are happy that the prize with utility 0.5 is the certainty equivalent of a gamble with equally likely prizes the utilities of which are 0.25 and 0.75. But this is a quick and easy way to check on your judgments.

Framing: Defeating the Zero Illusion

Although we did not say so explicitly, in our assessment of your utility function, the units on the horizontal axis were your net winnings or losses from this particular gamble. As noted in the last chapter, individuals are prone to a zero illusion when presented with gambles framed in this fashion.

Hence, as a practical matter, when assessing your own utility function, you should attempt to defeat, or at least check on, the zero illusion by framing and reframing questions.

You can often eliminate the illusion altogether if you frame all gambles in terms of your net bank account after the gamble is conducted. For instance, suppose you are offered a choice of the five gambles in Figure 16.1 and your net (liquid) asset balance is $24,220. Rather than thinking that the range of possible outcomes is −$7500 to $15,000, think in terms of a range for your possible net (liquid) asset balance between $16,720 and $39,220 or, probably better, a slightly larger range with even numbers for endpoints, such as from $15,000 to $40,000. Instead of beginning by trying to work through your certainty equivalent for a gamble with prizes −$7500 to $15,000, each with probability 1/2, try to decide what asset balance *for sure* would be just as good to you as the situation where, based on a coin flip, your liquid asset balance will be either $15,000 or $40,000. Frame everything in terms of your net asset balance, and you are likely to come up with numbers that more accurately reflect how you really feel about things.

Using Constant Risk Aversion

A final technique for improving the quality of utility function you assess is very powerful *when it can be applied legitimately*. I illustrate using myself as guinea pig.

Given the current state of my bank account and my prospects for future income, I think it is reasonable to assume that I have roughly constant risk aversion for gambles with prizes ranging from −$50,000 *to* $150,000. (This was written for the first time in 1996. By the time you read this, it will still be valid, although the range over which I am comfortable with constant risk aversion will have grown and my level of risk aversion in that range will have fallen, both consequences of the fact that I've done moderately well financially.)

The italicized sentence is the key to everything that follows. It has the following explanation: I am risk averse and I believe my level of risk aversion decreases in my total wealth. That is, the risk premium I attach to some given gamble would likely decrease if someone were to give me $1 million to keep. I am not quite sure what my attitude toward risk would be if my net asset position were close to $0, but as long as my assets stay roughly where they are, I do not believe my attitude toward a given risk would change much. The key question is, What does *stay roughly where they are* mean? Given the money I have in the bank and in other assets, I think a loss of $50,000 or a gain of $150,000 would not materially affect my attitude toward risk. A good test for this is, given recent gyrations in the stock market, I probably do not even know my net asset position to the nearest $50,000 or so.

This means that, over the range of prizes −$50,000 to $150,000, I have, roughly, exponential utility. That is, my utility function for winnings and losses in this range has approximately the form $U(x) = -A e^{-\lambda x} + B$, where x is my net from current gambles, to be added to my assets, and $A > 0$ and B are constants. The values of the constants A and B are irrelevant if I want to evaluate expected utilities to choose among gambles, so I set them to be $A = 1$ and $B = 0$. Then, *finding my utility function over the range from a $50,000 loss to a $150,000 gain comes down to finding my coefficient of risk aversion,* λ.

Now what? I give three intuitively derived CEs of my own. I intentionally pick three 50–50 gambles with different ranges of prizes but all prizes within the band of −$50,000 to $150,000:

- For a gamble with prizes $0 and $150,000, each with probability 1/2, my CE is approximately $60,000.

- For a gamble with prizes $0 or $10,000, each with probability 1/2, my CE is $4500.

- For a gamble with prizes $0 or $50,000, each with probability 1/2, my CE is $21,000.

Let me assure you that this is my best subjective judgment as to my CEs. I am not fudging these numbers

Take my first judgment, that my CE for $0 or $150,000, each with probability 1/2, is $60,000. Remember that I have constant risk aversion over this range, so my utility function has the form

$$U(x) = -e^{-\lambda x}.$$

Then the gamble has expected utility

$$(1/2)(-e^{-\lambda \cdot 0}) + (1/2)(-e^{-\lambda \cdot 150000}) = -0.5(1 + e^{-\lambda \cdot 150000}).$$

On the other hand, the (expected) utility of $60,000 for sure is $-e^{-\lambda \cdot 60000}$. If my CE judgment is correct, λ must be set so that these two utility levels are equal, or

$$-0.5(1 + e^{-\lambda \cdot 150000}) = e^{-\lambda \cdot 60000}.$$

EXCEL can solve for λ here (I cannot do it analytically), giving $\lambda = 0.00000548$. But my other two CE judgments are also sufficient to "determine" the value of λ. It should satisfy

$$-0.5(1 + e^{-\lambda \cdot 10000}) = -e^{-\lambda \cdot 4500} \text{ and } -0.5(1 + e^{-\lambda \cdot 50000}) = -e^{-\lambda \cdot 21000}.$$

The first equation gives $\lambda = 0.0000402$, and the second gives $\lambda = 0.000013$. Because we get different values of λ, my intuitive subjective judgment is inconsistent with the expected utility model *and* the maintained assumption that I have constant risk aversion over this interval of prizes.

This is hardly surprising. My intuitive judgment is fallible. Moreover, I am only approximately constantly risk averse over the interval −$50,000 to $150,000. But, as a normative aid to decision making, I find constant risk aversion a good working hypothesis, and my three CE judgments suggest that basing choices (for gambles in this range) with the utility function $U(x) = -e^{-\lambda \cdot x}$ for λ around 0.00001 will give me choices that are coherent (that is, that obey the five basic properties), have constant risk aversion, and are roughly in accord with the intuitive CE judgments I make.

Specifically, the value $\lambda = 0.00001$ gives me CEs for the three gambles of, respectively, $49,173, $4,875, and $21,907. Table 16.1 provides the three CEs, for four values of λ: $\lambda = 0.00000548, 0.0000402, 0.000013$, and 0.00001. Note that, as λ gets smaller, my CEs get larger; λ is called the *coefficient of risk aversion*, and the bigger it is, the more risk averse an individual is. Note also how my CEs respond to this parameter; there is little response (over this range of values) for the second gamble and the most dramatic response for the first.

lambda	CE1	CE2	CE3
0.00000548	$60,003	$4,932	$23,293
0.0000402	$17,183	$4,501	$14,115
0.000013	$43,087	$4,838	$21,007
0.00001	$49,173	$4,875	$21,907

Table 16.1. CEs for three gambles, for four levels of (constant) risk aversion.

Table 16.1 gives me the data I need to answer the question, How do I feel about $\lambda = 0.00001$? Essentially, this question is, How comfortable am I with CEs of $49,000 or so for the first 50–50 gamble, $4900 or so for the second, and $22,000 or so for third? Compared to my original estimates of $60,000, $4500, and $21,000, I am obviously fairly happy with the third. But am I certain that I would rather take the first gamble instead of $55,000? Am I certain that I would take $4800 over the second? It turns out (not surprisingly) that I am certain of neither of these, which is why I think $\lambda = 0.00001$ is a good "compromise" value.

Let me say again, *I am not a perfect chooser of gambles under uncertainty.* I expect my intuitive judgment to be somewhat flawed. The power of this approach is that I can look normatively at the five principles, and say, "In this context, I buy them." And I can look at the property of constant risk aversion for gambles in this range and say, "For me and for this range of prizes, roughly constant risk aversion makes sense." Then it follows logically that I want my choices to conform to maximization of expected utility, where $U(x)$ takes the form $-e^{-\lambda x}$ for some constant λ (and for x in this range).

I can then look at some intuitive judgments, get a rough handle on what λ might be, see how consistent my judgments are, and finally massage my intuitively derived CEs, to come up with more consistent numbers.

If I find the five qualitative properties plus constant risk aversion appealing on qualitative grounds, *and I do,* I am apt to give myself more credit for such qualitative judgment than I am for intuitive quantitative CE judgment, even for simple gambles. So when something has to give, I shade my intuitive quantitative judgment and end up more confident that I make a better choice, in consequence. That is how to use this model normatively. For more on this, see Problem 16.2.

16.3. What Sort of Behavior Is Sensible?

We discussed the justification for the expected utility model as a normative decision aid in the context of gambles with objectively known probabilities. What about problems with subjective uncertainty?

Recall from the last chapter that, as descriptive theory in such circumstances, economists use the expected utility model, assuming that the decision maker assesses subjective probabilities where necessary and then treats them on par with any objective probabilities that might be present. In other words, aversion to subjective uncertainty is not admitted into most economic models, which, since aversion to subjective uncertainty is a fact of life, is a deficiency of expected utility as a descriptive model.

As a matter of normative theory, we come to a different conclusion. It takes a different set of properties and a different, more general formulation of what is a gamble. But for properties just as reasonable as the five given previously, if you subscribe to the normative desirability of the expanded set of properties, the conclusion is that you should assess probabilities and use them as if they were objective. Uncertainty aversion (avoiding gambles that involve unknown odds simply because the odds are unknown) isn't normatively sensible.

I do not go into the details here. If you consult a more advanced book on microeconomics or choice under uncertainty, look for the theories of choice under uncertainty due to Savage and Anscombe–Aumann.

Framing Effects

It should be obvious from the discussion on defeating the zero illusion that, as far as normative theory goes, economics (or, rather, economists) assume that you *do not* want to be fooled by changes in how specific questions are framed. It is one thing—a true thing—to say that people can be fooled into changing decisions they might make, depending on how their options are framed. It is quite another thing—and one that I expect you would not agree to—to say that being fooled in this fashion is desirable. And if you agree that being fooled by framing is undesirable, this merely reinforces the admonitions made last section about being careful how you frame the questions that go into building your utility function.

The Certainty Effect and Overweighting Small Probabilities

Similarly, we observed in the last chapter that individual choices often exhibit the certainty effect and overweighting small probabilities, but we argue in this chapter for the normative desirability of using expected utility to make choices. Since the certainty effect and overweighting small probabilities are inconsistent with expected utility maximization, as asserted in the last chapter, I evidently assert that these are normatively undesirable behavior patterns you would do better to avoid.

In fact, it is not hard to see where this conclusion comes from. Go back to the descriptions of the certainty effect and overweighting small probabilities in the last chapter and, in particular, the three questions posed in discussing each. Then think through, in the context of those questions, the implications of properties 1 (reduction of compound lotteries) and 5 (substitution). If you grant the normative desirability of properties 1 and 5, you clearly find both the certainty effect and overweighting small probabilities to be undesirable forms of behavior.

Is Risk Aversion Sensible?

From the list of behavioral phenomena introduced in the last chapter as phenomena observed when people make choices with uncertain consequences, we now assert that framing effects, aversion to subjective uncertainty, the certainty effect, and overweighting small probabilities are all normatively undesirable. This leaves risk aversion and decreasing risk aversion as wealth increases. Is risk aversion also normatively undesirable?

Students sometimes argue that being risk averse is indeed normatively undesirable, or foolish, in the sense that, if you always pick the gamble with the largest expected value, the law of averages says that eventually you come out ahead. But this argument is nonsense. First, even if the law of averages applied—and I argue in a moment that it does not always—if gambles today provide a stake for your gambles tomorrow, then you would want to maximize the expected rate of growth of your fortune and not the additive increment obtained from any gamble. These are not the same. But, more important, the law of averages holds that *eventually* someone betting on the highest EMV gambles comes out ahead. How long is eventually? Ten years? Twenty? Ten thousand? Certain gambles in your life are not repeated five times, let alone the number of times necessary to put your faith in the law of averages; and there is nothing wrong with being risk averse in the face of those risks.

16.4. Reasons to Be Suspicious

There are, however, some good reasons to be suspicious of the normative desirability of following the expected utility model, and I want to mention the two most important here.

Portfolio Effects

Suppose you are engaged in some personal investments. In particular, suppose you hold a portfolio of stocks that includes a number of shares of Ford Motor Company. Your stock broker calls with a suggestion that you speculate on Ford Motor Company call options. If you buy these options, you would make money when your shares of Ford Motor Company are doing well and you would lose money when Ford's share price goes down.

If you followed the procedures outlined in this chapter, you might consider the consequences of this proposed speculation as a gamble and compare the expected utility of this gamble with the expected utility of doing nothing or investing your money in some other fashion.

This is not the right thing to do, however, because the payoff from this particular gamble is positively correlated with the value of your stock portfolio. In times when you are relatively richer, this gamble gives you a good return. In times when you are relatively poorer, this speculation provides poor returns. That is, this risk *compounds* the risk you already face. In such instances, you cannot evaluate this risk alone; you must consider it in conjunction with your entire portfolio of assets.

Investment advisors understand this problem very well. If you did not know better, you would be advised to analyze your entire portfolio of investments as a portfolio and not look at individual investments. But this problem is not limited to investments in financial markets. In most instances where probabilities are subjective, because they are probabilities of real-world things, the value of the prizes to you depend on the "state" in which the prize is received. For instance, if you are contemplating an entrepreneurial venture, involving the marketing of a new product, success is apt to be correlated to some extent with economic good times. But payoffs from this venture are probably worth more to you in economic bad times; putting it as negatively as possible, if your venture goes bust, you will need a job, and finding a job when the economy is growing slowly or even in a recession is more difficult than when the economy is going great guns. If you compare two entrepreneurial ventures that have exactly the same probability distributions of payoffs to you, but one pays off more when times are good and the other pays off more when times are bad, the latter is probably more valuable to you.

An extreme example of this concerns insurance. If you purchase, say, fire insurance on your house, the premium you pay exceeds the expected amount of money you will be paid. If you look at this purchase of insurance as an isolated gamble, it will look quite bad; it has a negative EMV and is risky as well. But that is not the way to look at insurance. The point of insurance is that it compensates you in circumstances when compensation is relatively valuable to you, for instance when your house burns down.

What happened to the five properties in these three instances? Why don't they work? None of the five properties is at fault; the entire approach to the problem is flawed. The starting point of this approach to choice under uncertainty is to say that, when you look at a gamble, all that matters to you are the prizes you receive and the probabilities with which they are received. That is incorrect in these instances. In these stories, the "state of nature" affects the value to you of the prizes you might receive. Two gambles with the same prizes and probabilities may look quite different to you, if they give their good payoffs in very different circumstances.

Two approaches can be taken to deal with portfolio problems. You can work out the value of the different prizes in the different possible circumstances the prizes might be received. This works great in theory, but it vastly complicates the assessment of your utility function. Or you can frame the decision problem on a scale large enough that the basic model works. For instance, look at the gamble on Ford call options not in isolation but in terms of your entire investment portfolio. Consider payoffs from insurance policies not in isolation but in terms of your net wealth with and without insurance, in case of fire or some other disaster.

Temporal Resolution of Uncertainty

The second caution has the fancy name of *temporal resolution of uncertainty*. Suppose I offered you three gambles. In the first, you get $500,000 with probability 1/2 and $0 with probability 1/2. In the second, you get $500,000 with probability 1/2 and $0 with probability 1/2. In the third, you get $500,000 with probability 1/2 and $0 with probability 1/2. No, my word processor didn't get stuck. These gambles are the same in terms of prizes and probabilities, but they differ in another fashion. In each case, if you win the $500,000 you will get the money precisely 9 months from today. In the first gamble, I flip a coin 9 months from today and tell you the outome then. In the second, I flip the coin today in the presence of a reliable witness and tell you the outcome in 9 months. In the third, I flip the coin today and tell you the outcome today, although you get the money in 9 months.

Most people prefer the third of these "gambles." Having the uncertainty resolve sooner is valuable, because it allows you to plan other activities. For example, if you know that you have $500,000 coming to you 9 months from now, you may change your vacation plans or your employment strategy. If I do not tell you whether you won the money or not for 9 months, you have to temporize in decisions you make in the interim.

The point is that these three "gambles" have the same prizes with the same probabilities. The expected utility procedure would necessarily rank them the same, since the expected utility procedure considers only prizes and their probabilities. But, in general, gambles that resolve earlier are more valuable because of the information they bring. This is something the expected utility procedure simply misses; when this effect is important, the expected utility procedure can be badly misleading.[1] In such cases, you must take a longer-term, broader view of the choices you have to make, including in a single model the full set of related decisions you must make.

If This Is Such a Great Idea, Why Haven't You Seen It Before?

Portfolio effects and problems with temporal resolution of uncertainty can complicate application of the expected utility model, but still, if you are aware of these problems and do not push the expected utility model where it is unsuitable, the model can be a remarkably powerful aid for making better decisions when you face uncertain consequences.

At this point, the big question is inevitable: If this is such a great idea, why haven't you seen it before? Or, put a bit differently, Do real managers ever use this procedure for deciding among the gambles they face?

There are cases in which this precise procedure is practiced. People who ply decision analysis make healthy salaries consulting on the uses of this technique. But, if you do not remember seeing this technique previously, you probably have not slept through meetings or failed to read memos you were supposed to read. This is not a widely used decision aid.

The reason for this—and a third and final reason to be suspicious of the expected utility model, applied in specific situations—is that this technique assumes that the risks involved in the gamble are borne by a single individual. Insofar as many risks taken by managers are risks taken on behalf of some firm or agency, the personal risk preferences of those on whose behalf

---

[1] When uncertainty resolves at a later date, this raises other problems for the expected utility procedure. Essentially, late-resolving uncertainty makes property 5 dubious. This gets very technical, so I do not go into details here. If you are interested, see Chapter 12 of D. Kreps, *Notes on the Theory of Choice* (Boulder, CO: Westview Press, 1988).

the decision is made are important, not those of the manager. Risks taken by firms, government agencies, and other organizations are often spread among many people. Risk sharing of this sort dilutes the risk in ways that we explore in great detail in the next chapter, so that risk aversion no longer plays an important role. More precisely, risk aversion plays a role, but it is risk aversion applied to something other than the immediate riskiness of the gambles being considered. *You do not see this procedure practiced much in the real world, because real-world settings are richer in opportunities for risk sharing than we have considered so far.* But

1. To understand those richer opportunities, you have to begin by understanding how you and other individuals react to risk, and this model, used descriptively, in the fashion of the last chapter, gives us a leg up on that.

2. In some cases, especially those involving entrepreneurial ventures, this technique used normatively, in the fashion of this chapter, can be very helpful, as long as it is blended with an understanding of opportunities for risk sharing and the like.

Executive Summary

- The expected utility model, used descriptively in the last chapter, is repackaged in this chapter as a normative decision aid, intended to help you make better decisions when facing a choice problem with uncertain consequences.

- The key to adopting this decision aid is to contemplate whether you agree that the five properties given in Section 16.1 are desirable for your preference judgment. If you find them desirable normatively, it follows logically that you want your decisions to conform to the expected utility model, for some utility function.

- The problem then is to assess your personal utility function. Using the simplest possible judgment of this sort (comparing gambles with two equally likely prizes to sure things) you can rough in your utility function. And a variety of techniques exist for refining the utility function so assessed.

- In some cases, the five properties are not normatively attractive, at least for simple-minded application. These include cases in which there are substantial problems with correlated risks (portfolio problems) and cases with temporal resolution of uncertainty.

Problems

16.1 Go back to the question with which the chapter began. Suppose you were offered a choice from the five gambles in Figure 16.1.

(a) Try to rank these five according to your unaided intuition about how good each is for you. If you can, figure out which in your ordering are "close" and where the significant gaps in quality (as far as you are concerned) occur.

(b) Assess (roughly) your own utility function for gambles with prizes between −$7500 and $15,000, using the techniques discussed in this chapter.

(c) Use this utility function to evaluate the five gambles and find their certainty equivalents as far as you are concerned. Compare these with the answers you gave in part a. Which technique, unaided choice or the technique of parts b and c, do you find more satisfactory?

16.2 Students sometimes object to the technique advanced for finding one's coefficient of risk aversion, once the judgment is made that, over some range, the individual has roughly constant risk aversion. More specifically, students sometimes object to the rather slapdash emergence of $\lambda = 0.00001$ for me, as described in the chapter.

But does the precise value of λ make a difference? Suppose I must choose from among the five gambles in Figure 16.1. Suppose I decide that my level of risk aversion is constant, more or less, for the range −$50,000 to $150,000, which more than covers the range of prizes of the five gambles. Then, by the methods discussed in the chapter, I decide that my coefficient of risk aversion was somewhere between 0.000005 and 0.000015, with 0.00001 as a "good compromise." How much would it matter if I had settled on 0.000012 or 0.000008? To answer this question, take the five gambles in Figure 16.1 and see how a decision maker would evaluate them, if the decision maker has constant risk aversion (for the range of prizes in these gambles) with a coefficient of risk aversion between 0.000005 and 0.000015.

17. Risk Sharing and Spreading: Securities and Insurance Markets

This chapter provides the major economic rationale for the existence of equity, insurance, and futures markets: By taking a risk and breaking it into pieces, with the pieces shared among many individuals—in other words, by *securitizing* the risk—risk aversion on the part of individual risk bearers is largely defeated. The main message of this chapter is just that, but after delivering this message, the chapter goes on with two caveats and an extension:

- Countervailing forces prevent risks from being shared completely, chief among which are adverse selection and moral hazard.
- Even if the risks are spread widely, the value of any share of a risk depends on how much riskiness it adds to the general portfolio of risk individuals bear.
- For a given risk and a fixed population of investors, the problem of sharing the risk efficiently is confronted.

During the late 1990s, the words *initial public offering* (IPO) were viewed as the key to fame and fortune for students of management. Students flocked to create entrepreneurial ventures, looking forward to the day when (1) the venture would be taken public, (2) money would roll in the door in wheelbarrows, and (3) the Porsche could be traded in for a Ferrari. At least, that was the dream.

More generally, securities, futures, and insurance markets are vitally important to managers of virtually every stripe. So it is imperative, at least for aspiring managers, to understand these markets as economic phenomena:

- What economic role do these markets play?

- How do they create value?

- What limits their ability to create value?

The academic discipline of finance is primarily concerned with these questions, and most students of management take at least one, and often a lot more than one, course in finance. I will not upstage the finance courses you might take or finance books you might read, but having introduced risk aversion, it makes sense to give the basic answers to these three questions.

At the outset, it must be said that these markets play several economic roles. In particular, security and other financial markets are the means by which firms obtain liquidity; that is, these markets allow firms to have cash on hand for current transactions, in anticipation of profits to be made later. I am not concerned here with the liquidity role of financial markets; instead I focus on the way in which these markets create value by sharing and spreading risk.

17.1. The Basic Idea

The story begins with one of the driving phenomena of the previous two chapters, risk aversion. Consider a gamble with equally likely prizes $50,000 and −$25,000. This gamble has a positive expected value of $12,500, but the chance of a loss is significant and the size of potential loss is large. Therefore, many risk-averse individuals would turn down this gamble if it were offered.

In particular, suppose this gamble is offered to Jan MBA, an expected-utility-maximizing decision maker with the utility function $U(x) = 12.5859 - 7.4267 \, e^{-0.0000211x}$. Jan computes the expected utility of this gamble:

- The prize $50,000 has utility level [10].

- The prize −$25,000 has utility level [0].

- Therefore, the gamble has expected utility $(0.5)[10] + (0.5)[0] = [5]$, corresponding to a certainty equivalent around −$1000.

- In contrast, if Jan does not take this gamble, she has prize $0 for sure, which has (expected) utility [5.1592].

So, Jan is better off declining this gamble.

Suppose instead that this gamble had equally likely prizes of $500 and −$250. Then Jan's expected utility from this gamble can be computed to be 5.1785, which corresponds to a certainty equivalent of $123.516. Jan would happily accept this scaled-down version of the original gamble.

Suppose Jan is smart enough to recognize that, while she would not be happy taking on the full gamble herself, she would be happy to take on a 1% share of it. How can she lay off 99% of the risk? One possibility is to find a bunch of friends and associates who, if they are about as risk averse as she, would each happily accept a small share of the gamble. More specifically, if she could find 99 friends whose utility function matched her own, she could give each a 1% share: All would be happy—this gift is worth $123.516 to each of them—and she is left with a 1% share worth $123.516 to her.

Should Jan give away 99% of the venture? Would it not be better for her to retain a larger share? In fact, you can use Excel and Solver to discover that, if Jan is giving away shares in this gamble, she does best for herself by retaining around 43.8% of the gamble, which gives her a certainty equivalent of $2684 (see Problem 17.1).

But Jan is even cleverer than this. Giving away shares in this gamble is giving away a valuable item. Perhaps she ought to *sell* shares in her venture. For instance, if she could find 99 friends and associates who have the same utility function as she, she could sell 1% shares in this gamble to each for up to $123.516. That is, if she sets a price for a 1% share at, say, $123, anyone with the same utility function that she has would be willing to pay this price; after paying this price, someone with the same utility function as hers would be left with a net certainty equivalent of $0.516. (Remember, this is an exponential utility function, so subtracting a constant from each prize in any gamble lowers the gamble's certainty equivalent by precisely that constant.) This means big bucks for Jan: If she sells 99 shares, each a 1% share in the gamble, for $123 apiece, she nets $99 \times \$123 = \$12{,}177$, to which we add her certainty equivalent of $123.516 for the 1% share she retains; overall, she is ahead by $12,300.516. And she was going to turn down the gamble!

A General Result about Small Risks

The story has Jan selling or giving shares to friends and associates who happen to have the same utility function as she. It is unlikely, to say the least, that she would find friends and associates with precisely her utility function. But the basic economic phenomenon illustrated by this story does not depend on finding folks with precisely the same utility function.

The general result here runs as follows: A risk-averse expected utility maximizer, presented with a gamble called Gamble A, has a certainty equivalent for the gamble that is no greater than its expected value. Normally, the certainty equivalent is less than the expected value. If we tried to sell Gamble A to this individual, he would usually be unwilling to pay the gamble's expected monetary value (EMV). Usually the individual would pay a good deal less. Indeed, even if Gamble A has a positive EMV, if it is very risky, with a substantial chance of a negative prize, we might have to *pay* the individual to assume it.

But pick some target percentage β less than 100%. Think of β as something like 98%, but any percentage less than 100% will do. *No matter how risk averse is the individual, there is a small fraction α such that if we offer the individual an α share of the gamble, the individual would be willing to pay $\alpha \times \beta \times$ the EMV of the gamble.* (To be mathematically precise, this is true as long as the decision maker's utility function is smooth—that is, differentiable—at the argument 0.)

The italicized sentence is the key to this chapter—and to securities, futures, and insurance markets—so do not pass it by too quickly. Let me be very concrete in interpreting and illustrating it. Think of Gamble A as Jan MBA's gamble, with equally likely prizes $50,000 and −$25,000, hence with an EMV of $12,500. Jan approaches some risk-averse expected utility maximizer and says, "I'd like to sell you a small share in my gamble, a share of size α. But you are going to have to pay me for this." An α share has EMV $12,500 $\times$ α, of course, but Jan is not greedy; she is willing to settle for, say, 98% of $12,500 $\times$ α as the price paid for the α share. (So in terms of the italicized statement, β = 98%.) What the italicized statement says is that, having fixed on the goal of recovering 98% of the EMV of the share sold, Jan can find a share α greater than 0, but probably not a lot greater than 0, such that the individual will be willing to pay 98% of $12,500 $\times$ α.

The size of the share α depends on several things. It depends on how risky is the initial gamble: The riskier it is, the smaller α will have to be. It depends on the target percentage β: The closer this is to 100%, the smaller α will have to be. And it depends on the person to whom this share is being sold: The more risk averse this individual is, the smaller α will have to be.

But, having set the target percentage β, Jan can flog a bit of her gamble on any risk-averse expected utility maximizer and get β of the EMV of the share. So, in a world filled with prospective investors, she can go around selling little bit after little bit, until she sells the whole gamble, at which point she winds up with β times the EMV of the whole gamble. As β gets closer to 1, she has to flog smaller and smaller shares to more and more people. But, in theory, she can recover the full EMV of the gamble (see Problem 17.2).

Securitization for Fun and Profit

In general, when risk-averse individuals, which is just about everyone, face substantial risk, they can improve their position by dividing the risk into pieces and selling it to outsiders, so the outsiders share the risk. Ignoring for now the transaction costs associated with the process of securitizing the risk and selling the shares, the theory suggests that any gamble, spread out among lots of people in this fashion, is worth nearly its EMV to its original owner. This is so even if the owner is risk averse. The owner's original risk aversion is unimportant, since in the end neither the owner nor anyone else bears much of the risk.

The basic idea of risk sharing is one with which you probably are already at least vaguely familiar, because it is a chief feature of modern capitalist society. Securities markets, where equity, somewhat risky debt, and instruments even more complex than debt or equity are traded, are precisely a manifestation of defeating risk aversion by risk sharing. Rather than have Henry Ford or his heirs bear all the risk of Ford Motor Company, Ford at one point took Ford Motor public, selling shares in this venture to the public, because the public was better able to bear the risk of the venture than he and his heirs could themselves. New examples appear every day, as privately held companies go public. Entrepreneurs share risk with venture capitalists, who provide capital to a venture in return for a share in the risky proceeds. You might argue that this is more a question of the availability of funds to the entrepreneur (that is, of generating liquidity); but if it were only a question of the availability of funds, then debt contracts, in which the payment to the venture capitalist does not depend on how well the venture does, would be the rule instead of equity arrangements, where the venture capitalist shares in good times and in bad. (Because of the law of limited liability—you cannot collect from a bankrupt—even nominal debt carries some risk, hence provides some risk sharing. But equity arrangements increase the amount of risk sharing, and their relative prevalence indicates that risk sharing is at least part of the motive for the venture capital arrangements we see.) Still another form of risk sharing via securitization are real estate investment trusts, which spread the risk (of both default and early repayment) of holding a single mortgage.

On the other side, when risks that individuals hold have negative expected payouts, we have insurance markets. Think of an individual who owns a house subject to risk of fire damage. Suppose, to keep it very simple, the house is either going to burn to the ground, a loss of $200,000, or not burn at all; and suppose that the probability it will burn to the ground is 0.001 in any given year. The EMV of the gamble facing the house owner is $(0.001)(-\$200,000) + (0.999)(\$0) = -\$200$. But, if the owner is at all risk averse, his or her certainty equivalent is likely to be a good deal more negative. When buying insurance, the owner pays a premium, say, of $300 per year to have the insurance company bear the risk of the $200,000 loss in case of fire. The insurance company is willing to bear this risk for a premium payment of $300 because it is close to risk neutral, and so the premium more than compensates it for the risk it assumes. *And it is close to risk neutral because it shares the risk out over many different shareholders in the company.*

A less obvious form of risk sharing involves futures markets. In the futures market for, say, wheat, one can buy or sell wheat for delivery some months hence. Consider a wheat farmer (he) whose crop is in the ground. This farmer faces two sorts of risks. First are the risks concerning his own yield: Will it rain? Will his fields be attacked by locusts? Second are the risks concerning the value of his harvest when it comes time to sell. If wheat sells $3.00 per bushel today, will its price be $3.00 or $3.30 or $2.70 in 4 months? Note that a $0.30 change in the price of a bushel of wheat means a 10% swing in the farmer's gross revenue, fixing his yield, which would mean an enormous swing in net income. The futures market gives this farmer a chance to "insure" against the second sort of risk, by selling a portion of his crop forward, while it is still in the ground, at a fixed price. On the other side, it allows large purchasers of wheat, such as mills, to buy forward and insure against rising prices.

This is the main message of this chapter. If you spread risk thinly, you defeat risk aversion, and in a world of risks, defeating risk aversion creates value. This is one rationale for securities markets, and it is the overwhelming rationale for futures and insurance markets.

Once you absorb this main message, you are likely to have come to the following conclusions:

1. *Risks should be spread out to such an extent that no risk averse individual is left holding a substantial fraction of the risk.* (Why? Because if anyone is left holding a substantial fraction of some risk, that person will value the risk at something less than its EMV. Spread it out, and this person will be able to capture the full EMV.)

2. *Thus, in consequence of conclusion 1, the value of any gamble to its initial holder is just its EMV, since this is its value in the market once it has been securitized and shared out.*

What a wonderful thing it would be if conclusion 2 were true. Having learned all that stuff about utility functions, we could forget about it and use expected monetary values, with the proviso that one should be sure to securitize and spread risk widely.

But, if you look at the real world, conclusion 1 is not true. The Ford family did not sell off all but a small fraction of their shares in Ford Motor Company. In general, many firms have significant fractions held by founders or their families. Other firms have significant fractions held by single investors. We see publicly held companies being taken private, through leveraged buyouts and the like. Why does conclusion 1 fail?

And even supposing conclusion 1 holds, conclusion 2 is not quite right.

The remainder of this chapter explores why conclusion 1 fails and, in cases where it holds, why conclusion 2 is not really right. Then we close with a subject that will be important in later chapters, efficient risk sharing.

17.2. Why Risk Is Not Always Spread Thinly

There are many reasons why conclusion 1 fails:

- There can be differences of opinion about the gamble a particular venture represents. Suppose Jan MBA believes that her gamble will yield $50,000 with probability 0.7 and −$25,000 with probability 0.3, while everyone else in the world thinks the odds are 50–50. Then she cannot sell the shares for more than $125 per percent. But, given her optimistic forecast, even at $125 per percent, she would want to retain 53.54%. (Can you replicate this 53.54%?)

- As something of a twist on the first reason, while the entrepreneur may be able to convince others that she is not unduly optimistic, to do so would compromise her venture. Suppose Jan could convince others that the probability of making $50,000 is 0.7, but doing so would expose her ideas to many potential competitors whose competition would destroy her profitable opportunity. She might then be willing to bear some of the risk of a profitable venture, even if, for the risk sharing she does, she gets less than what she knows to be the full value of the shares she sells.

- By retaining a significant share of a venture, an individual often retains or acquires controlling rights, such as a seat on the Board of Directors or, for a big enough share, the right to appoint the board. This has a value that may outweigh the gains from risk spreading.

- Transaction costs are associated with securitizing and selling pieces of a gamble. Some are fairly trivial in nature if not in expense, such as the costs of printing the securities, finding customers, and exchanging the shares for money. Beyond these more mundane transaction costs are two categories of transaction costs that are often both significant and subtle: the costs of *adverse selection* and *moral hazard*.

Chapters 18 and 19 concern adverse selection and moral hazard, so I do not give a complete treatment of these issues now. But, in the context of securitization of gambles, let me briefly indicate what are the issues.

Imagine that someone approaches you on the street, wanting to sell you shares in a gold mine. He represents to you that this is a risky venture; the prospectus he offers you gives you information from which you can construct a probability distribution for your returns. But you know that the prospectus is incomplete. Material facts are not given; for instance, the results of some preliminary borings that the seller might have done. So you wonder, Does this individual have information that is pessimistic in terms of the mine's prospects? You should worry about this, because if some gold miners have optimistic private information and others have pessimistic private information, those with pessimistic private information are more apt to want to sell their shares in the venture (see Problem 17.5). In other words, the gold mines being "sold on the street" are apt to be an *adverse selection* of all gold mines, in terms of their prospects.

Or imagine that someone approaches you on the street, wanting to sell you shares in her entrepreneurial venture. The prospectus she offers makes it clear that the returns from this venture depend very significantly on how much effort she puts into the development of the product this venture will produce. And you worry, Once she sells out a significant fraction of the venture, will she be motivated to put in the long, arduous hours needed to make the venture a success? She may promise to do so, but is a promise good enough? Even if you could be sure she would work hard, would she spend the venture's money on fancy rugs for her office, corporate planes, and the like? Would she spend her time and the venture's money creating a spin-off that she would leave to manage, leaving the venture in which you hold shares in the lurch? In this case, you face a *moral hazard*.

To summarize, we can see clear reasons why conclusion 1 fails in some cases. And as long as 1 fails, conclusion 2 is incorrect. If a risk-averse individual bears significant risk, the individual's risk aversion plays a role in determining the overall value of the venture.

17.3. Correlation between Gambles: Why Conclusion 2 Can Fail Even When 1 Holds

As if that were not bad enough, even if conclusion 1 holds, conclusion 2 can fail. The reason is that when a new risk is shared among lots of people, the new risk goes into a portfolio of risks the people already hold.

Imagine a centralized risk-sharing institution. Call it the NYSE or NAS-DAQ, if you wish. Anyone who has a risky venture can take it to this institution, where it is parceled out in small bits to people around the world. At any point in time, lots of people are holding on to little pieces of a whole lot of risky ventures. These risky ventures are not necessarily independent. Many are entrepreneurial and corporate ventures, most of which have a general tendency to do relatively well when the economy is doing well and relatively poorly when the economy is in recession. Therefore, when we look at the portfolio of risk, composed of many pieces of little ventures, held by any individual, there is some overall or systematic risk to that portfolio.

Along comes a new entrepreneur with some risk to share. If this new risk is independent of the systematic risk in everyone's portfolio, then the marginal impact of a little piece of the new risk on everyone's certainty equivalent is roughly the EMV of the little piece. Then conclusion 2 holds.

However, if this new risk is positively correlated with the value of everyone's portfolio (if it pays off well when, on average, the balance of other risks pay off well, such as when the economy is doing well), then even a little piece of the new risk compounds some of the risk in people's portfolios, and they do not see its incremental value as equal to its expected monetary value; its incremental value is something less.

On the other hand, if this new risk is negatively correlated with the value of everyone's portfolio (if it pays off well when, on average, the balance of other risks are paying off poorly, as might be true of a gold hoarding scheme, because the price of gold tends to rise when the economy is going sour), then the value of a piece of it for everyone can *exceed* its expected monetary value, because it provides insurance.

The point is that the valuation of a particular shared risk, in this world where all risks are shared, has to do with how the particular risk covaries with the risky portfolio all the risk sharers hold. Expected utility, which ignores the benefits of risk sharing altogether, is not right in isolation, and expected monetary value is not right either.

So, what is right? At this point, the modern theory of finance must be consulted. A pillar of the modern theory of finance is the capital asset pricing model (CAPM). Most treatments of the CAPM are done using mean–variance preferences instead of the expected utility framework we use here (see the discussion in the *Student's Companion* material for Chapter 15 on this point) but the conclusions of the CAPM (that the value of a share depends on its expected return and the correlation of that return with the market portfolio) is entirely in line with what we see here.

With this as an introduction, we could concentrate on large, perfectly competitive markets where the items for sale are shares in some risk. This becomes the theory of competitive financial markets, the domain of the CAPM, which I leave to your finance courses, books, and instructors. Instead, beginning with next two chapters, we go back to the list of reasons why conclusion 1 fails (why risk is *not* thinly spread), in particular, the problems of adverse selection and moral hazard. But, to do justice to these topics, first we attend to a final technical matter concerning risk sharing.

17.4. Efficient Risk Sharing

Suppose we have four individuals: John, Paul, George and Ringo. Each individual has a utility function and evaluates gambles according to their expected utility. The four utility functions might be the same, but I want to think more generally about the case where they are different.

The four face a "joint lottery," described by a probability distribution over dollar prizes. This joint lottery might just be the result of some joint venture they are taking or it might be gotten as the sum of lotteries that each of the four faces individually.

The four decide to form a *risk-sharing syndicate*, where they share the proceeds from their joint lottery. That is, if the lottery gives prizes, say, $1000, $2000, $3000, and −$4000 with probabilities 0.1, 0.2, 0.3, and 0.4, then they must decide on a sharing rule for dividing the outcome among them. One possible sharing rule is equal shares. A second would be to give John twice as much as the others, except if the prize is −$4000, in which case John pays $3000 and the others pay $333.33 each.

What sort of risk-sharing rule should they settle on? Each is probably interested in getting more for himself and less for the others, so we can expect some hard bargaining among them. But, at least ideally, we might hope that the four settle on a so-called *efficient sharing rule*. A sharing rule is efficient if no other rule makes each of the four at least as well off as with the first rule and one (or more) of the four strictly better off than with the first rule.

In general, when all four parties are risk averse, finding the efficient risk sharing rules can be quite a task. I get to the general procedure in a bit. Alternatively, in simple examples you can use Excel and Solver to solve this sort of problem (see Problem 17.7). But a special case is easier and will be important to things we do in later chapters, so we turn first to it.

Ringo Is Risk Neutral

Suppose at least one of the parties is risk neutral, and the rest are strictly risk averse. (Someone is strictly risk averse if, for any lottery in which there is nontrivial uncertainty—in which there is positive probability of two or more different prizes—the individual's certainty equivalent for the gamble is less than the EMV of the gamble. In terms of utility functions, a strictly risk-averse utility function is strictly concave, with no linear pieces at all.) In particular, suppose Ringo is risk neutral and the others are strictly risk averse. Then *every efficient risk-sharing rule gives John, George, and Paul shares that do not change with the outcome, and Ringo absorbs all the risk.*

In other words, in any efficient sharing scheme, John gets some fixed amount of money y_J, Paul gets y_P, George gets y_G, and Ringo gets what is left over: $1000 - y_J - y_P - y_G$ with probability 0.1, $2000 - y_J - y_P - y_G$ with probability 0.2, $3000 - y_J - y_P - y_G$ with probability 0.3, and $-4000 - y_J - y_P - y_G$ with probability 0.4. The four must negotiate the amounts y_J, y_P, and y_G, but any scheme that does not give the three fixed shares and load all the risk on Ringo is not efficient.

Why is this? Take any risk-sharing rule in which John bears some risk. Change the rule as follows: Give John a payment equal to the EMV of his share, no matter what is the outcome, taking this from Ringo; and give Ringo John's old share in addition to whatever he had before, less the EMV of John's share that he gives to John. Since Ringo is risk neutral, this change does not affect his overall expected utility; he gave away the EMV of the extra risk he takes on, which to him is a net wash. George and Paul are unaffected. But John is better off, since he replaces a gamble with its EMV; since he is strictly risk averse, he strictly prefers the EMV of any gamble to taking the gamble.

To summarize, when we have risk sharing among some people, some of whom are risk averse and others of whom are risk neutral, the efficient thing to do is to load all the risk on the risk-neutral folks.

Efficient Risk Sharing in General

What if none of the parties is risk neutral? I do not try to give complete answers or explain fully the answers I give, but we can make some progress on this. (This material will prove tough for readers without strong mathematical skills. If you do not follow this, it does not matter to anything we do in the balance of this book. But having devoted so much time to bang-for-the-buck stuff in earlier chapters, it seems a shame not to harvest a result here.) Let me be a bit more general in my notation: This syndicate has I members, each of whom is a expected utility maximizer. The utility function of the ith person is written U_i. I assume that each of these individuals is risk averse, with risk neutrality included as a special case, which means that each U_i is a concave function. I also assume that each U_i is strictly increasing and differentiable and write U_i' for the derivative of U_i. Because each U_i is a concave function, this means that that U_i' is a nonincreasing function. Because each U_i is strictly increasing, U_i' is strictly positive at all its arguments.

I assume that this syndicate holds a joint risky venture with total payoffs Y^1, Y^2, ..., or Y^N, with respective probabilities p^1, ..., p^N. (Note that superscripts enumerate the payoffs and subscripts enumerate the members of the syndicate.)

A sharing rule for the syndicate in this notation is an array of numbers $\{y_i^n\}$ for $i = 1, \ldots, I$ and $n = 1, \ldots, N$, where y_i^n is the share or payoff for member i if the total payoff is Y^n. The sum of the shares should equal the total, or $\sum_{i=1}^{I} y_i^n = Y^n$ for each n.

A sharing rule $\{y_i^n\}$ is efficient if and only if, for each i and j from 1 to I and for each m and n from 1 to N,

$$\frac{U_i'(y_i^n)}{U_i'(y_i^m)} = \frac{U_j'(y_j^n)}{U_j'(y_j^m)}.$$

Why? This is the bang-for-the-buck logic of earlier chapters at work. Fix two of the members of the syndicate, i and j. Hold fixed the sharing rules for everyone else in the syndicate and ask, If we hold j's expected utility constant (the constraint), what does it take to maximize the expected utility of i? Pick two outcomes, Y^m and Y^n. The contribution to i's expected utility of i's shares in these two states is

$$p^n U_i(y_i^n) + p^m U_i(y_i^m).$$

The contribution to j's expected utility of her shares is the same expression, but with j replacing i. So the marginal impact on i's expected utility of y_i^n is $p^n U_i'(y_i^n)$. Since a dollar more in state n for i is a dollar less for j (since everyone else's share is held fixed), the marginal impact on j's expected utility of y_i^n is $-p^n U_j'(y_j^n)$. The first marginal impact is the marginal impact on the objective (maximize i's expected utility). The second is the marginal impact on the constraint (hold j's expected utility at some fixed level). So, by bang-for-the-buck logic, the ratio of these two marginal impacts in state n should equal the ratio in state m, which, after canceling the probabilities in the numerator and denominator, is precisely the ratio condition given.

I close with three remarks:

1. Suppose one member of the syndicate, say, number 1, is risk neutral. This means that his utility function is linear; that is, the derivative of his utility function is constant. Therefore, for any efficient sharing rule, the ratio of the derivatives of the utility function of any other member of the syndicate, evaluated at any two of her shares, must be 1. Which means, if this other member is strictly risk averse (if her utility function is strictly concave), she must get a constant share. In other words, the special case of a risk-neutral Ringo is a corollary to the general case.

2. If you are a frustrated mathematician, here is a challenge: What is the form of efficient risk sharing when all members of the syndicate have constant risk aversion; that is, when $U_i(x) = -e^{-\lambda_i x}$ for each i? It is really not that hard if you use the equal-bangs-for-the-buck ratio condition.

3. Throughout this discussion, members of the syndicate have agreed about the probabilities of the different payoffs. Efficient risk sharing gets more complex when syndicate members disagree about the likelihood of the different outcomes. To see how this works, consult R. Wilson, "The Theory of Syndicates," *Econometrica*, 1972.

Executive Summary

- If you spread the risk of a gamble, giving a small share to each of many different risk-averse folks, since each share represents only a little risk, each share is worth nearly the expected monetary value (EMV) of the share to its holder. Thus, the value of gamble becomes nearly the sum of the EMVs of its shares, which is just the EMV of the original gamble.

- This idea (that risk spreading promotes value) is the raison d'être for all sorts of financial and insurance markets.

- However, if the shares are correlated with the portfolio of risks other folks hold, the value of the shares depends on that correlation. If the shares are uncorrelated, their value is their EMV. If the shares have positive correlation with the portfolio of other risks, their value is less than their EMV; if the correlation is negative, their value exceeds their EMV. A fully worked-out version of this idea is the capital asset pricing model, a pillar of modern finance.

- There are good reasons why it is hard to spread thinly all risks. Two of the most important categories of reasons—and the topics to which we move in the two chapters that follow—are problems of adverse selection and moral hazard.

- The general problem of efficient risk sharing (taking a given gamble and parceling it out efficiently among a fixed set of individuals) is quite complex. But, when one of the parties is risk neutral and the others are strictly risk averse, efficient risk sharing is simple: The risk-neutral party assumes all the risk.

Problems

These problems generally require the use of Excel spreadsheets and Solver. If you find that you cannot build the required spreadsheets on your own, in several of the problems I suggest a particular sheet of a spreadsheet to consult, to get started without seeing the entire answer.

17.1 Consider the plight of Jan MBA, who owns a gamble with two equally likely prizes, $50,000 and −$25,000. Jan is an expected utility maximizer with utility function $U(x) = 12.5859 − 7.4267\, e^{-0.0000211x}$. As we learned in the text, this gamble gives Jan a negative certainty equivalent. Suppose Jan was able to give away some percentage of this gamble. If θ is the percentage she retains, she then owns a gamble with equally likely prizes $50,000\theta$ and −$25,000\theta$.

(a) How does Jan's certainty equivalent change as a function of θ, the fraction she retains? Create a graph of this function.

(b) What percentage retained by Jan maximizes her certainty equivalent?

(c) Write $CE(\theta)$ for the function that gives Jan's CE as a function of γ. What is the slope of the function $CE(\theta)$ at the argument $\theta = 0$?

Hint: See sheet 1 of the spreadsheet PROB17.1 for a start on how to do this problem.

17.2 Suppose Jan from Problem 17.1 tries to sell an α share of the gamble to a risk-averse expected utility maximizer. No risk-averse person would pay "full EMV price," or $12,500\alpha$, for an α share (as long as $\alpha > 0$), but if Jan sets a target of getting back 95% or 98% or some percentage less than 100% of $12,500\alpha$ for an α share, she might succeed, if α is small enough.

(a) Suppose Jan has an associate with (essentially) the same utility function as she, $-e^{-0.0000211x}$. Would this associate buy a 10% share of Jan's gamble for 95% of 10% of the full EMV? (The answer is No, and the real point of this is to get started on what comes next. If you cannot see how to set up the spreadsheet to answer this part of the problem, look at sheet 1 of the spreadsheet PROB17.2.)

(b) Jan is set on obtaining 95% of the EMV of the gamble, so rather than lowering the price to her associate in part a, she decides to decrease the share she will sell to him. What is the largest share α Jan can sell to her associate at a price of 95% of $12,500\alpha$? Assume he buys as long as his CE for the full transaction is greater or equal to 0.

(c) Redo part b, if Jan decides to try for 98% of the EMV of the gamble. And find the shares needed to get either 98% or 95% of the EMV, if Jan sells to a second associate, whose utility function is $e^{-0.00001x}$. (Is this second associate more or less risk averse than the first?)

(d) (Optional, and the last part is difficult.) A third associate of Jan has utility function $U(x) = \sqrt{x + 50,000}$, where x is the associate's net from the transaction with Jan. Answer the questions of part c for this associate. Then evaluate, for this utility function U, the ratio $-U''(x)/U'(x)$ at the value $x = 0$. What does this tell you?

17.3 Suppose Jan MBA is convinced that her gamble will pay $50,000 with probability 0.7 (and lose $25,000 with probability 0.3). But everyone else in the world thinks the two probabilities are 0.5 and 0.5. Because of the latter fact, Jan can sell shares in her venture for no more than $125 per 1% (actually, she gets a bit less than this). Suppose, being very optimistic, she can get $125 per percent. What percentage share of her gamble would she wish to retain? (Look at sheet 1 of PROB17.3/4 for a hint on how to do this.)

17.4 Jan MBA's gamble does indeed pay off $50,000 with probability 0.7 (and loses $25,000 with probability 0.3). But to sell shares in her venture, Jan has to reveal some of the details of her venture. She can sell up to 10% of her venture without compromising too many details; if she sells 10% or less, the probability of the $50,000 outcome remains 0.7. But, if she sells between 10 and 30%, the details revealed may get to her competition; her chances of getting the $50,000 payoff are only 0.65. If she sells more than 30% but no more than 50%, the probability of the $50,000 outcome falls to 0.6. And if she sells more than 50% of her venture, the probability of the $50,000 outcome falls to 0.5.

Assume that, whatever share of the venture Jan sells, she gets 95% of the appropriate EMV. That is, if she sells 25% of the venture, she gets 95% of 25% of $(0.65)(\$50,000) + (0.35)(-\$25,000)$. What percentage share retained by Jan maximizes her certainty equivalent?

17.5 As an investor in the ventures of people like Jan MBA, you often are approached by MBA students with gambles that pay off either $50,000 or −$25,000. Inevitably, these individuals wish to sell you 1% shares of their gambles.

Half the MBAs who sell such shares have gambles where the chances of the $50,000 outcome are 0.6. The other half have worse gambles: For them, the chances of the $50,000 outcome are only 0.4. Note that, for the first group, the EMV of a 1% share of the gamble is $200, while for the second sort of MBA, the EMV of a 1% share of the gamble is only $50. Since you can't tell which sort of student you are dealing with—all these MBA students look alike—you assume that any 1% share you are offered has a 0.5 chance of paying off $500 and a 0.5 chance of paying off −$250; thus it has an EMV of $125. You are risk averse with utility function $-e^{-0.000015x}$, so the most you would pay to buy this gamble is $123.94. Happily for you, the market price of these 1% shares is $120. So you have been snapping up shares in these gambles. (You can trust all my numbers.)

To your unpleasant surprise, however, you seem to be having bad luck. Specifically, you find that you get the good outcome less than the expected 50% of the time. Instead, you are getting the good outcome only around 48.4% of the time (you do this a lot, so you are pretty confident about that number), and at that rate of success, the price of $120 for 1% does not cover the EMV, let alone the risk you take. Why is this happening?

17.6 Jan, Joe, and Jess MBA each own a gamble with equally likely outcomes of $500,000 and −$250,000. Each is attempting to sell 1% shares to friends and associates. But all the friends and associates of these three already possess portfolios that have some risk.

Specifically, imagine that Jan, Joe, and Jess approach Biff, who is an expected utility maximizer with utility function $U(x) = -e^{-0.00002x}$. Biff owns a risky portfolio, the value of which will be either $2 million or $1.8 million, each with probability 1/2. If you do the math (or consult the top box of sheet 1 of the spreadsheet PROB17.6), you'll find that Biff's certainty equivalent is $1,833,873.

If Biff buys a 1% share from any of Jan, Joe, or Jess, this is added to his current risky portfolio; that is, assuming he buys only one 1% share (an assumption we maintain in this problem), the possible outcomes for him are wealth levels of $2,000,500, $1,999,750, $1,800,500, and $1,799.750.

The differences between the gambles of Jan, Joe, and Jess concern how they covary with Biff's initial wealth portfolio. Specifically, Jan's gamble has outcomes independent of Biff's initial portfolio. Joe's gamble is positively correlated with Biff's portfolio. And Jess's gamble is negatively correlated. Even more specifically, conditional on Biff's initial portfolio being worth $2 million, Joe's gamble pays off $500,000 with probability 0.6, while Jess's gamble pays off $500,000 with probability 0.4.

What is the most Biff will pay for a 1% share of Jan's gamble, Joe's gamble, Jess's gamble?

17.7 John, Paul, George, and Ringo are partners in a venture that has four possible outcomes: $100,000 with probability 0.4, $200,000 with probability 0.3, $300,000 with probability 0.2, and $400,000 with probability 0.1. The Fab Four (as they are known to their business associates) must decide how to divide the results of their venture. Up to this point, they planned to divide the money equally, so, for instance, if the outcome is $300,000, each would walk away with $75,000.

(a) Each of the four is an expected utility maximizer, but they have quite different utility functions (and thus attitudes toward risk):

- John's utility function is $U_{John}(x) = \sqrt{x}$, where x is John's net proceeds from this venture.

- Paul's utility function is $U_{Paul}(x) = \sqrt{x + 100,000}$.

- George's utility function is $U_{George}(x) = x^{0.3333}$.

- Ringo's utility function is $U_{Ringo} = -e^{-0.00001x}$.

If we give them equal-division shares, their certainty equivalents would be, respectively, $46,968.70, $48,994.62, $45,925.83, and $47,041.85. To see how these were computed, check sheet 1 of the spreadsheet PROB17.7, which is depicted in Figure 17.1.

	A	B	C	D	E	F
					PROB17.7	
2						
3			state 1	state 2	state 3	state 4
4		Total	$100,000.00	$200,000.00	$300,000.00	$400,000.00
5						
6		John	$25,000.00	$50,000.00	$75,000.00	$100,000.00
7		Paul	$25,000.00	$50,000.00	$75,000.00	$100,000.00
8		George	$25,000.00	$50,000.00	$75,000.00	$100,000.00
9		Ringo	$25,000.00	$50,000.00	$75,000.00	$100,000.00
10						
11		probs	0.4	0.3	0.2	0.1
12						
13		John's utility	158.113883	223.6067977	273.8612788	316.227766
14		Paul's utility	353.5533906	387.2983346	418.3300133	447.2135955
15		George's utility	29.2303089	36.82703058	42.15585666	46.398079
16		Ringo's utility	-0.778800783	-0.60653066	-0.472366553	-0.367879441
17						
18			EU	CE		
19		John	216.7226249	$46,968.70		
20		Paul	385.9982188	$48,994.62		
21		George	35.81121196	$45,925.83		
22		Ringo	-0.624740766	$47,041.85		

Sheet1 / Sheet2 / Sheet3

Figure 17.1. Problem 17.7. Calculating the CE's of the Fab Four, for the equal-division sharing rule. This spreadsheet calculates expected utilities and certainty equivalents for John, Paul, George, and Ringo, assuming they split the proceeds from their venture in equal shares.

This does not seem efficient to Ringo, who wonders if there is not some better way to split the proceeds from the venture. Ringo wishes to know, assuming we give John, Paul, and George payoff shares that leave them, respectively, at the certainty equivalent levels $46,968.70, $48,994.62, and $45,925.83, how high can we push Ringo's certainty equivalent? Answer this question for Ringo. (Warning: I had some problems getting Solver to work on this problem. Everything worked once I asked for *Automatic Scaling* under the *Options* menu.)

(b) Suppose Ringo is risk neutral and John, Paul, and George are all as in part a of the problem. This would mean that Ringo's CE from the equal division shares would be not $47,041.85, but instead $(0.4)(25,000) + (0.3)(50,000) + (0.2)(75,000) + (0.1)(100,000) = \$50,000$. It seems unfair that Ringo has such a large CE while John, Paul, and George all have CEs under $49,000, so the Fab Four are looking for a scheme that gives John, Paul, and George CE's of at least $50,000, while making Ringo as well off as possible. What sharing rule scheme accomplishes this (and how well off can we make Ringo)?

18. Hidden Information, Signaling, and Screening

This chapter concerns economic transactions in which some parties have access to important information that other parties lack. This sort of *hidden information* can lead to substantial problems, including a breakdown of markets. The antidote to such difficulties is for the hidden information to be revealed, but when the information is revealed strategically, its content must be carefully considered. Among the applications discussed is *the winner's curse*, a phenomenon in competitive auctions in which winning bidders systematically find that they have bid more than the object at auction is worth to them.

Imagine an auction for the rights to extract minerals such as fossil fuels from a tract of land. Suppose the auction is conducted as a sealed tender auction: Bidders submit sealed bids, the bids are opened simultaneously, and whoever bids the highest amount wins the extraction rights, paying this bid. The winning bidder (he) can regret his bid on two different grounds.

1. Suppose that the winning bidder wins with a bid of $100 million, the tract turns out to be worth $120 million, and the second highest bidder bid $60 million. Even though the winning bidder winds up ahead $20 million, he suffers *winner's remorse* or leaving money on the table, because he bid more for the rights than was necessary to win the auction.

2. Suppose instead that the winning bid is $100 million, the next highest bid is $95 million, and the rights turn out to be worth only $60 million. Not much money was left on the table, but the winner is out $40 million. This is not necessarily the result of a bad decision. The amount of fossil fuel under the ground at a particular site is usually unknown at the time of the auction, and while the rights turn out to be worth only $60 million, at the time of the auction it might have been reasonable to assess that the rights would be worth $150 million on average. But suppose someone who bids repeatedly in such auctions finds the following "when winning" phenomenon: Averaging across *all* the auctions in which he participates, his bids on average are less than the objects being auctioned eventually prove to be worth. But averaging across those auctions *that he wins*, his bids exceed on average what the items turn out to be worth. This bidder is suffering from the *winner's curse*.

The winner's curse is much more than a hypothetical possibility. It is a common affliction among winners of auctions in which the bidders have access to different information about the value of the object being auctioned. This chapter is in part about the winner's curse, why it happens (and when it does), and what bidders must do to avoid it. More broadly, this chapter concerns economic transactions in which some parties to the transaction have information that other parties lack. Since the winner's curse is a relatively complex phenomenon, we begin with simpler situations with a single buyer who lacks information possessed by the seller of some object.

18.1. Hidden Information and Adverse Selection

Suppose you are a venture capitalist (VC). An entrepreneur (she) approaches you with a business plan and asks you to take an equity stake in the venture. In most cases of venture capital and entrepreneurs, the entrepreneur needs cash to fund her initial operations. Suppose, however, that this entrepreneur wants your participation only for risk sharing, as in the last chapter.

Could it ever make sense for you, as the VC, to be willing to pay $10 million for a 50% stake of the venture but be unwilling to pay even $5 million for a 90% stake? Assume that the entrepreneur retains whatever you do not buy.

The answer to this question is Yes; in fact, there are several reasons that the answer might be Yes. The VC (you) might be risk averse: We saw last chapter how a risk-averse person might have a negative certainty equivalent for a whole gamble but a positive CE for half of it. Something like that might be at work here, but to avoid this possibility, assume that you are so wealthy you are risk neutral.

The answer might also be Yes because the entrepreneur's efforts are crucial to the success of this venture, and you worry that an entrepreneur who retains only a 10% share has a greatly reduced incentive to put in the effort necessary. This is an issue of incentives and moral hazard, the topic of the next chapter.

A third reason the answer might be Yes, the reason that fits in this chapter, concerns things that the entrepreneur might know and you do not. To be very specific, suppose the venture's eventual economic success depends on whether a particular unproven technology can be made to work. If this technology works, the venture will be worth a lot of money, say, $100 million. But if it cannot be made to work, the venture has a net value of $0, counting in expenses.

Whether you would be willing to pay $10 million or even $5 million for an appreciable share of the venture depends on how likely it is that this technology can be made to work. Suppose you assess probability $\frac{1}{4}$ for this. As a VC, you are good at these sorts of assessments. Since we assume you are risk neutral, this makes the expected monetary value of the venture $25 million, and half is certainly worth $10 million.

Then why is 90% not worth $5 million? Imagine that the entrepreneur, who after all has been thinking about this project for a lot longer than you, had the opportunity to run some tests that would substantially resolve whether the new technology works. Specifically, if the entrepreneur had positive test results, then the odds that the technology works are 0.5, while if the test results were negative, the technology will not work. You know that the entrepreneur ran the test; based on the test results, her assessment that the technology works is either 0.5 or 0. But because you lack the information she has, you don't know which assessment she holds. You assess probability 0.5 that she has positive information and 0.5 that her information is negative (which means the marginal probability that the technology will work is 0.25, consistent with the previous paragraph).

And now for the point of all this: *If* the entrepreneur has negative information, she presumably would be happy to sell whatever share she can unload for any amount of money. But *if* her information is positive, she has a pretty good venture on her hands. Would she sell 90% of this for $5 million? Would she sell 50% for $10 million?

The answers to these questions are that it depends. Specifically, it depends on how risk averse is the entrepreneur. If she is very risk averse, she might well sell a 90% share for $5 million, even though the expected monetary value of the entire venture, if she has essentially positive information, is $50 million. (Would you give up a coin flip gamble with prizes $0 or $90 million for a payment of $5 million?) On the other hand, if she is risk neutral, she would want a lot more than $10 million for 50% of the venture.

But there are intermediate levels of risk aversion that would lead her to be willing to sell 50% for $10 million but not sell 90% for $5 million. Suppose you decide that this is her level of risk aversion. Then,

- If the test results she saw were negative, she would sell on any terms.

- If her test results were positive, she would not sell 90% for $5 million.

So a willingness to sell 90% for $5 million confirms that she must have negative information. In this case, the 90% you are about to buy is worthless. But a willingness to sell 50% for $10 million is consistent with her having either sort of information. Not knowing her information, this means you are back to assessing probability 0.25 that the technology works. In this case you would be willing to pay $10 million for 50% of the venture.

Adverse Selection

This is a contrived example, but it starkly illustrates the basic phenomenon of hidden information: In many transactions, one party has information that the second party lacks and that is relevant to the second party's evaluation of the transaction.

The simplest examples involve goods of different quality levels, where the seller has information about the quality of the good she offers for sale. The prototypical example concerns the sale of a used car, where the seller, having owned the car, knows things about the quality of the car that the buyer does not. A far more significant example concerns financial transactions—for instance, when a firm issues debt or equity to outside investors. The investors try to learn as much as they can about the prospects of the enterprise, but it is easy to imagine that insiders to the venture (the entrepreneur in a small venture, or management in a large, publicly traded firm) know a lot more than outsiders.

In these cases and in others, the good being bought and sold can be of high quality or low or somewhere between. If the seller, who knows the item's quality, is willing to sell, that willingness to sell is an indication that the item in question is more likely to be of lesser quality. This is not a sure indication, but on the general principle that owners of lesser-quality goods are more likely to want to get rid of their stuff, the indication is still there. Therefore, a buyer must figure that the item for sale is more likely to be of lesser quality or, in other words, an adverse selection of the entire population.

What is more, a vicious cycle often takes over. Buyers, not knowing the quality of the particular item they are buying, are willing to pay a price for the average quality in the population. But is this an average of the entire population? It is not, if the equilibrium price for an average draw from the full population is not high enough to induce holders of higher-quality goods to sell. This is the adverse selection. Now watch it get worse.

The price must be lowered to reflect this adverse selection. But, as the price lowers, owners of intermediate-quality goods begin to withhold their items, making the adverse selection worse. The price falls again, and the adverse selection gets even more adverse.

The Market for Lemons: A Stylized Example

A stylized example illustrates the vicious cycle.[1] Imagine that a variety of used cars is "out there," some good, some okay, some real lemons. Specif-

---

[1] This example is roughly drawn from the classic paper by G. Akerlof, "The Market for Lemons: Quality Uncertainty and the Market Mechanism," *Quarterly Journal of Economics* 89, 1970, 488–500, which began the economic literature on this general subject and for which Akerlof shared the Nobel Prize in 2001.

ically, there are used cars worth every price from $1000 to $3000 to new owners, with each price equally likely. Suppose as well that a car worth $x to a new owner is worth $x - 200 to its current owner. And suppose that a finite supply of cars can be found at each value level, while a much larger number of people stand ready to buy.

If the quality of a car were apparent to both buyer and seller, then the logic of supply equals demand would imply that cars worth $x to buyers would sell for precisely that price; competition among buyers would bid the price of these cars up to that level. Every seller of a used car would be willing to sell and pocket the $200 in surplus value thus created.

But the quality of a used car is rarely known precisely to buyers, while sellers have a very good idea what their cars are worth. Since this is a stylized example, I assume that buyers are incapable of seeing anything about the quality of a car, and they are willing to pay for the average quality of cars put on the market.

Since all the cars are sold if both buyers and sellers know the quality levels, we begin with the guess that all cars continue to be sold. That is, cars of value from $1000 to $3000 are put on the market by their owners. Then the average value of cars in the market is $2000, and that is the price the market establishes. Now adverse selection kicks in. If someone has a used car worth more than $2200 to buyers—hence worth more than $2000 to the seller—this seller takes that car off the market. Why sell a car for $2000 that is worth more than this amount to the seller?

Therefore, the only cars that would come on the market, if the market price is $2000, are those which are worth between $1000 and $2200 to buyers. But the average value of this set of cars is $1600, so that is the price. And adverse selection bites again: Owners of cars worth more than $1800 to buyers—hence, worth more than $1600 to sellers—withdraw from the market if the price is $1600. Now the only cars that come to market are those with values between $1000 and $1800.

So the market price drops to $1400. Now cars of value above $1600 drop out of the market, so the market consists of cars with values between $1000 and $1600, which means that the price drops to $1300, and more cars are withdrawn from the market, and the price drops again.

Where does all this end? What is a market equilibrium in this stylized model? Suppose that the market price is $1200. This means that cars worth $1200 or less to their current owners—therefore, worth $1400 or less to buyers—are brought to the market. Then the average value (to buyers) of cars on offer is $1200. This is the market price, and the market is in equilibrium.

What a crummy equilibrium. A scant 20% of the used cars in existence go onto the market, even though every used car is worth $200 more to a new buyer than to its current owner. Furthermore, this is not a random 20% but the 20% of worst cars. This is truly a lemons market.

Of course, reality is not this bad. Some buyers of fine used cars are forced to sell their cars, which improves the distribution of cars in the market, raising the price and bringing more cars into the market. Moreover, buyers can tell something of the quality of individual cars and can learn more by having the car inspected by a competent mechanic. As we'll see in a bit, the buyer or seller can do still more to signal or discern the quality of individual cars. The stark adverse selection problem of this stylized example is not found in reality. But the effect is there in real life, and it is particularly strong when (1) sellers have a hard time learning the value of the good they are buying and (2) the value of the object to prospective buyers is close to its value to prospective sellers.

18.2. Hidden Information on the Buyer's Side: Insurance and Contract Fulfillment

In the examples given so far, the seller knows more about the quality of the good than the buyer. But cases in which the buyer holds hidden information also arise, typically involving a service that the seller provides the buyer: The cost of providing the service is uncertain, and the buyer knows more about the cost than the potential service provider.

Life and health insurance are classic examples. In fact, the term *adverse selection* comes first from the literature of actuarial science. The cost of providing life or health insurance depends on how likely it is that the client will get sick or die. At any premium level, it is precisely the sick and nearly dead, assuming they know these sad facts, who are most anxious to buy insurance. Therefore, in terms of expected payouts on the policy, the insurance company faces an adverse selection of the population as a whole. This can lead to the sort of vicious cycle we saw before: Premium rates must be high, to compensate for the adverse selection problem. This leads the fairly healthy to go without insurance, and the selection of folks signing up for insurance becomes more adverse, raising premiums, worsening the adverse selection, and so forth.

This sort of problem arises as well in the context of outsourcing and service contracts. Suppose Corporation X requires a specific service at one of its facilities. It has the in-house capability to perform the service but has asked Contractor Y to take on the project, offering (say) $140,000. Contractor Y is unsure what it will cost to provide the required service, thinking that its cost will be somewhere between $100,000 and $170,000.

Contractor Y must ask itself, Why is Corporation X not using its in-house capability to provide this service? A good answer is, Because Y, being a specialist in this sort of service, can provide it more cheaply. In particular, suppose Y believes that it would cost Corporation X $10,000 more to do this project in-house than it would cost Y. But, *if Y believes that management at X knows what this project would cost X and X is offering $140,000, then the cost to X of the project is more than $140,000, which means the cost to Y is more than $130,000.* In this case, the relevant range of costs for Y is not $100,000 to $170,000 but instead $130,000 to $170,000. So perhaps Y should insist on a price of $155,000. But if X agrees to $155,000 as the price, then the cost to X must be more than $155,000, which means a cost of $145,000 or more to Y. And so forth, just as in the case of the used car market.

18.3. Problems of Average Selection

Imagine you are setting up a new manufacturing plant in a rural locale. Relative to other businesses in the area, your business involves a lot of on-the-job and off-the-job training of workers; your manufacturing technology demands skills that the local workforce lacks, and you will have to provide those skills to new employees. The training is costly, and to get a good return on your investment in training your employees, you want employees who will remain with your firm for a long period of time. Indeed, that is one reason you chose a rural location for your plant; people living in rural locations tend to be relatively less mobile than folks who live in urban or suburban settings. Also, you face less competition in the labor market for the people you train than you would in a more urban setting.

The problem is not that you get, among job applicants, an adverse selection of the population in terms of the quality you want, longevity on the job; it is that you get an average selection and you want to do better. Assuming potential employees have information that bears on their probable job longevity, you want to find a way to encourage them to "volunteer" that information, so you can select for employment and training the better-than-average selection of the whole population you desire.

18.4. Signals and Screens

The obvious response to situations where one party to a transaction has information that the second party lacks is for the second party to do what it can to get some or all the relevant information. Relevant information can come in many forms, among which are the following.

Freely Available Relevant Information

Relevant information is sometimes freely available, if the uninformed party knows where to look. Demographic information is often used in this manner. For instance, age and sex are important statistical indicators of mortality rates, useful to someone selling life insurance. If you are hiring for a rurally located plant, you might avoid young women, in the belief that they are more apt to get married or have children and then quit. (Please finish reading this section before deciding I am a male chauvinist.) Banks that sell mortgages sometimes engage in redlining (refusing to make loans on houses within certain geographical districts) because the default rate for homes inside the red line are historically high.

The use of demographic information in this manner is widespread, so much so that a caution is in order, on at least three grounds.

1. The basic statistical hypothesis can be incorrect, and the nature of the decision precludes learning this. For instance, professional partnerships sometimes discriminate against younger women in both initial hiring and promotion decisions, citing higher quit rates for family reasons. But careful empirical investigation does not support this hypothesis. Organizations that discriminate against women do not learn this, however, because too few women are hired or promoted to test the hypothesis. Compounding this are standard cognitive biases associated with making inferences from data: An organization that promotes only a few women and then sees one quit for family reasons might well overprocess this one piece of data, relative to its true statistical value.

2. Such hypotheses can be self-generating. Take a professional partnership that chooses not to promote young women to partner because of a perception that young women are more prone to drop out for family reasons. The partnership makes this choice because, it claims, it sees this pattern of behavior among its young woman associates. But this can be a vicious cycle: Young woman associates may be more likely to drop out precisely because they (correctly) perceive that this organization is less likely to promote them. Or in the case of redlining, if mortgage seekers inside the redlined area are forced to take loans with higher interest rates because of the perception that they are more likely to default, they may actually default more frequently because of the higher interest rates.

3. This form of discrimination raises legal and ethical questions. Is it fair to judge individuals based on membership in a demographic class that they can't control? Also, in response to its pernicious social effects, laws banning this form of discrimination are often enacted.

Legally Mandated Information

Direct and relevant information is sometimes available by legal or legislative mandate. For instance, good-faith disclosure of relevant information is required in the sale of real property: The owners of houses, who presumably know a lot about the hidden defects of the property, must disclose all known defects. An extremely important example is the legal requirement for publicly traded firms to disclose relevant financial information to protect potential investors. Of course, the recent spectacular case of Enron shows that legal requirements to provide information do not guarantee that the information will be revealed.

Information Required by an Independent Authority

Informed parties sometimes provide direct and relevant information to gain the certification of an independent authority. For instance, to be listed for trading on the New York Stock Exchange, firms must "voluntarily" reveal information beyond that required by government regulation. I put *voluntarily* in quotes here because the voluntary action is the decision by the firm to seek a listing on the NYSE; once that decision is made, the firm must reveal information about itself.

Information Provided Voluntarily

The final category is information provided voluntarily. For instance, when screening prospective employees, the employer might decide that possession of a high school diploma is a good signal of the employee's longevity prospects. That is, high school dropouts are more likely to be less accepting of authority on average, more likely to give up in the face of difficulty, and so forth. You might argue that the possession of a high school diploma is similar to demographic information—indeed, education level is often classified as demographics—but while an individual cannot change race or gender, the decision to stay or drop out of high school is at least partly voluntary.

Voluntarily provided information is a big category, covering a huge variety of cases and types. We define this category broadly, to include

- *Honestly volunteered information.* Many people, asked about problems they had with a used car or a house, will volunteer the truth, simply because they are honest. Of course, to trust such information, you have to be able to judge who is honest and who might be deceptive. But some people are pretty good at sizing up another person's character, especially when it comes to nonprofessional transactions, such as the sale of a used car from one individual to another. Social norms, supported by social structure, such as a small and tight-knit community, and backed by the threat of sanctions against those discovered to have broken with the community's norms, often guarantee honesty and openness. In some instances, individuals cultivate and then have the motivation to protect a reputation for honesty; we see how reputation works in Chapter 23.

- *Providing the uninformed party with an opportunity to procure information.* For instance, in the U.S. used-car market, it is standard for prospective buyers to take the car to their own mechanic for a checkup, with the prospective buyer paying the cost of the inspection. This is possible only if the seller permits the prospective buyer to borrow the car. Even more prosaically, sellers of used cars "permit" prospective buyers to look under the hood and take the car out for a spin.

18.5. Equilibrium Signaling

Of course, the value of a particular piece of information depends on how it correlates with the characteristic of interest to the uninformed party. For instance, if you are interested in finding new employees who are unlikely to quit over, say, a 5-year horizon and you screen on the basis of a high school diploma, the value of that screen depends on the strength of the statistical association between the diploma and longevity of employment.

When it comes to signals sent voluntarily, the information content of the signal depends on whether the informed party recognizes how the signal will be used. For instance, suppose one employer finds that employees in a local labor market are much more likely to last at least 5 years on the job if they have a high school diploma than if they do not. Accordingly, this employer begins to screen prospective employees in a local labor market based on whether they have a high school diploma. If this is one employer among many, not representing a significant fraction or a particularly desirable segment of employment opportunities in the region, students in high school are unlikely to change their dropout decisions. Hence the information quality of the signal (the statistical association between possession of a high school diploma and longevity of employment) will not change because the signal is being used by this one employer. But suppose this is a significant employer in the local labor market (it represents a significant fraction of local job opportunities, as in a rural mill town, or the "cream" of job opportunities) or suppose other employers in the area begin to apply the same screen. Then high school students in the area, or their parents, to the extent that the parents have any influence, may recognize how important a high school diploma is to future job prospects. This, in turn, may lead students who would otherwise drop out of school to remain, and thus it may weaken the informational content of a high school diploma. Please note that, in this case, the informational content of *no* diploma is likely to strengthen.

In equilibrium models of signaling, it is assumed that people who might send the signal recognize how the signal will be used and respond in whatever manner is best for them. Take the used-car market, for instance, and to make matters really simple, imagine that there are only two types of used cars: lemons, worth $2000 to buyers and $1800 to sellers; and cream puffs, worth $3000 to buyers and $2800 to sellers. Suppose as well that in the population of all used cars, three-quarters of the cars are cream puffs and that buyers learn nothing about a car's quality by driving or inspecting it.

In this model, adverse selection is a killer. Suppose all cars were brought to market. Then any single car has a 0.25 chance of being a lemon and a 0.75 chance of being a cream puff. The expected value to buyers of this "lottery" is a car worth, on average, $2750. Competition among buyers, assuming there are a lot of them, forces the price up to $2750. But then the owners of cream puffs would withdraw their cars from the market. The only equilibrium without signals is for the lemons only to be bought and sold for $2000.

Now suppose that sellers of used cars can, if they choose, voluntarily send a signal about the value of their car. Specifically, they can offer a limited warranty. Imagine that, for the owner of a cream puff, warranties cost $60 per month in expected value, for warranties up to 12 months. And warranties on cream puffs are worth $50 per month to buyers. But for lemons, warranties are worth $100 per month to buyers and cost sellers $200 for the first month, and $300 more per month, for every additional month the warranty runs.

With these assumptions, a signaling equilibrium exists on the following terms: used cars without warranties sell for $2000 apiece; a used car offered with a warranty of 5 months (or more) sells for $3250. In this equilibrium, all the lemons are sold for $2000 without a warranty and all the cream puffs for $3250, with a 5-month warranty.

Why is this an equilibrium?

- Imagine you own a cream puff. If you offer your cream puff for sale without a warranty, you net $2000. It is worth $2800 to you if you retain it. And if you sell it with a 5-month warranty, you gross $3250, from which the warranty cost of $60 × 5 = $300 must be subtracted, for a net of $2950. So you sell with a 5-month warranty.

- Imagine you own a lemon. If you offer your car for sale without a warranty, you net $2000. If you hold onto it, you have a car worth $1800 to you. And if you sell with a 5-month warranty, you gross $3250, against which the cost to you of the warranty ($200 + $300 + $300 + $300 + $300 = $1400) must be subtracted, for a net of $1850. So you do best to sell without a warranty.

- Imagine you are a buyer. Because of what we just saw, if a car is offered to you without a warranty, you know it is a lemon, and you would be willing to pay $2000 for it. If it is offered with a 5-month warranty, you know it must be a cream puff, worth $3000 plus 5 months of warranty, at $50 apiece, or $3250 in total. Assuming lots of buyers and a limited supply of cars for sale, supply equals demand leads to prices of $2000 and $3250, respectively, which is the asserted equilibrium.

There are two keys to this sort of signaling equilibrium. First, the signal sent must be more costly for low-quality car owners than for high-quality car owners, more costly enough that low-quality car owners are unwilling to send the signal, even knowing that to do so would elicit the price appropriate for high-quality cars. Second, the signal cannot be so expensive, relative to its value to the buyers of cars, that owners of high-quality cars are unwilling to send it.

For another example, go back to the case of hiring screens used by an employer. When high school students realize that possession of a diploma is used to screen prospective job applicants, the students may choose to stay in school, when previously they did not. If this happens, it is because students who would otherwise drop out are willing to pay the cost of staying in school (subjecting themselves to the arbitrary discipline of shop teachers and vice principals) to land a job. What the employer needs, then, is to find a signal that is very expensive for the prospective employees that are not desired but not very expensive for those desired and that, ideally, generates some positive payoff for the employer. Something like a tour of duty in the armed forces might fit the bill.

In the example of car warranties, there are only two types of cars, and the equilibrium signals *separate* the two types. In other signaling equilibria, called *pooling* or *partially pooling*, a single signal is sent by more than one type or quality level.

Signaling versus Screening

Imagine the buyer and seller of a used car meet, in a world with a 5-month warranty equilibrium. Does the seller take the initiative and say, "I want $3250 for my car, and I'm offering it with a 5-month warranty." Or does the buyer take the initiative and say, "I'll pay you $2000 for your car as it is, but I'll increase the price to $3250 if you give me a five-month warranty along with it. Take your pick." It would not seem to matter very much, but economists distinguish between the two: A *signaling* equilibrium is a situation in which the informed party takes the initiative. When the uninformed party offers the informed party a menu of choices, where the choice from the menu becomes the informative signal, economists say that we have a *screening equilibrium*.

Screening is especially prevalent in cases where the uninformed party provides a service for the informed party. For instance, in health, life, and casualty insurance, screens that are frequently employed include the size of the deductible, the percentage of the total loss insured, and reduced benefits for some period of time.

Economists see subtle distinctions between signaling and screening, but these distinctions are too subtle for most practitioners to see or care about. The leading reason you see one or the other is the cost of processing the required information. Take insurance, for instance. Insurance companies collect reams of data from many clients and use those data to assess fairly well how, say, the rate of payout on a health insurance policy varies with the policy's deductible. An individual, out to buy health insurance, is going to have a lot harder time fine-tuning the details of the contract offered to the insurance company. And, unless the client comes up with a standard proposal, the insurance company may be unwilling to evaluate the offer.

Multiple Equilibria and the Problem of Unexpected Signals

In the equilibrium involving car warranties, it takes a 5-month warranty to get a premium price. The reason for 5 months, instead of 4 or less, is that a 4-month warranty would not separate lemons from cream puffs, if the lemon owners catch on to the buyer's logic. Let me do the calculation: A 4-month warranty on a cream puff is worth $3200 (in total) to a buyer. A 4-month warranty on a lemon costs the old owner $200+$300+$300+$300 = $1100, so the owner of a lemon who can sell the car with a 4-month warranty for $3200 nets $2100. This is more than the owner gets ($2000) if the car is recognized as a lemon.

So we need at least 5 months of warranty. But longer warranties are used in other equilibria. In particular, consider the following terms: Cars without warranties sell for $2000 and cars offered with warranties of at least 6 months sell for $3300. You can do the calculations to check that this is an equilibrium in which all lemons sell for $2000 and all cream puffs for $3300: Owners of lemons want no part of a 6-month warranty on these terms; cream puff owners are happy to offer the 6-month warranty, if that is what it takes to sell their car at a decent price; and buyers are paying for each car what that car is worth.

While this is an equilibrium, it is worse for cream puff owners than the equilibrium with 5-month warranties; cream puff owners get $3250 less $300 or $2950 in net value in the 5-month warranty equilibrium, whereas in this new equilibrium, they net $3300 less $360 or $2940. And buyers and lemon owners are no better off in this second equilibrium. Buyers come away with zero surplus in either case, and lemon owners do just as well as before.

Why do cream puff owners settle for this worse equilibrium? Why does some enterprising cream puff owner (she) not offer her car with a 5-month warranty, expecting to get a price of $3250? Maybe this would work. But we cannot be sure. The key question is, What would buyers infer about a car offered with a 5-month warranty, in a world where 6-month warranties are the norm? Would they decide that the car must be a cream puff? Would they think, "I cannot tell, so I assess probability 0.25 that the car is a lemon, that being the overall population proportion"? Since the 5-month warranty signal is not being sent in the 6-month warranty equilibrium, we cannot tell what buyers will infer, so we cannot be sure that such an offer would be accepted.

Yet another signaling equilibrium, but without any signaling, has cars selling for $2000 no matter how long a warranty is offered. In this case, only lemons are sold; owners of cream puffs retain their cars. This is an equilibrium, and a particularly bad one for cream puff owners, because if the equilibrium doesn't involve warranties, buyers don't know what to make of them, and cream puff owners can't predict how buyers would react if offered a warranty. (Some economists argue that buyers should be able to figure out that owners of lemons would never offer a 5-month warranty if they can sell their cars for $2000, and so a 5-month warranty *must* mean the car is a cream puff. Therefore, equilibria that require more than 5 months of warranty or that do not involve warranties at all can be ruled out. This requires that buyers are quite sophisticated, however. Advanced treatments of market signaling will discuss this issue; look for the term *refinement of out-of-equilibrium beliefs*.)

As fanciful as this discussion may seem, it does attend to real-life phenomena. In the real-life used car market in the United States, when a car is sold privately by its owner, the practice is for prospective buyers to take the car to their mechanics for a diagnostic checkup. But in Israel, for instance, the seller of a used car gets a diagnostic report from one of a few well-known reputable sources for such reports, then hands out copies. It is pretty clear the U.S. system is relatively inefficient, because it involves the cost of multiple diagnostic checkups.

What would happen if the owner of a used car in the United States had her car inspected, had a report written up, and when buyers show up, handed out copies, pointing out how this saves prospective buyers the cost of an inspection, which ought to be reflected in the final price? I suspect that prospective buyers, unused to this way of doing things, would be unsure of what to make of the proffered report. At least, my inclination as a buyer would be to suspect that something is amiss. Why does the owner not want me to have *my* mechanic check out the car? How much did the owner pay this garage, to falsify this report? Well, perhaps I would not be that suspicious. But any suspicions along these lines would kill unilateral attempts to move from the less-efficient U.S.-style equilibrium to the more-efficient Israeli-style equilibrium. This is precisely the problem observed in the 6-month-warranty and the no-warranty equilibria. When a signal normally is not sent, receivers do not know what to make of it.

18.6. The Winner's Curse

We conclude with the *winner's curse*. I explore this phenomenon in the case of a sealed tender auction of some single object, whose value to the different bidders is unknown to them. Think, if you wish, of firms bidding for mineral rights or individuals bidding to purchase a week's vacation in Hawaii.

While no bidder can be certain about the value to himself or herself of the prize, each bidder forms an assessment of this value in the form of a probability distribution. For instance, imagine that Bidder A, based on her analysis and information, assesses that the expected value to her of the object being auctioned is $45 million.

Suppose that Bidder A learned the assessments of her rivals. Suppose, for instance, she learned that Bidders B, C, and D assessed expected values of $30 million, $38 million, and $25 million, as the expected values of the worth of the object to each of them, respectively. *Would this information affect Bidder A's assessment of the value to her?* Would she, for instance, on learning that her assessment is the most optimistic, have reason to temper her optimism?

The answer to this question depends on the context:

- If the object is a week's vacation in Hawaii, the value any bidder puts on the object is, probably, purely personal. Bidder A knows as much as anyone about what this vacation would be worth to her. She might be uncertain about the value (will it rain?) but the fact that Bidders B, C, and D attach different values to the vacation does not affect the value she attaches to it. This is not to say that she wouldn't like to know their valuations, because if she knew those, she might be better able to predict what they will bid and thus avoid leaving money on the table. But the question is not whether she wants to know their valuations. The question is, Does knowledge of their valuations change her own? In this case of *private values*, the answer is No.

- If the object is the right to extract minerals from a particular tract of land, the answer may be quite different. The value of the prize depends on exactly how much oil or gas or coal there is to be found and on how hard it will be to extract those resources. There is more to it than that (one bidder may be better equipped to exploit the resources than another) but there is a lot of *common value* in the object being auctioned. And different bidders probably have access to different information about the tract of land. They presumably did different geological surveys of the site. They may have run different seismic tests. They may have different experiences with similar, nearby tracts of land. For a variety of reasons, it is not hard to believe that Bidder A, based on her own private information, assesses an expected value of $45 million for the rights, *but were she told that all three rivals value the rights at less than $40 million, she would lower her expected value.* This is not definite: She might believe that her information is simply superior to theirs—she would not spend a dime to learn things that they know and she does not when it comes to determining her assessment of value of the rights at auction—and she believes her geologists are simply superior to theirs. But this is pretty extreme; probably, she would move her assessment in the direction of theirs, if she knew what assessments they were making.

We find the winner's curse in the second situation. Suppose that on the basis of an assessed value of $45 million, Bidder A bids $40 million. *Bidder A wins the auction when Bidders B, C, and D bid less than $40 million.* And B, C, and D are much more likely to bid less than $40 million when their respective assessments are values such as $30 million, $38 million, and $25 million than when their assessments are values on the order of $50 million, $75 million, and $65 million. *Bidder A, in consequence, wins the auction precisely in those instances where her colleagues are relatively more pessimistic. But in those instances, Bidder A should be more pessimistic than her own information indicates as well.*

The winner's curse occurs when unsophisticated bidders in an auction face this sort of statistical structure of information and valuation, forming their bids without taking into account that the winner of the auction is apt to be a party with relatively optimistic assessments. The major oil companies are quite sophisticated about this effect; they have come to understand the winner's curse through bitter experience and nowadays formulate their bids bearing in mind that the winner of an auction is going to be relatively optimistic and often the most optimistic of all the bidders. But less sophisticated or inexperienced bidders, who fail to understand this phenomenon, can find themselves cursed by winning.

How should you bid in a context where a possible winner's curse lurks? This is not a question that can be answered easily. Perhaps the only simple takeaway is that if you are involved in an auction that may possess a winner's curse and your rival bidders are unlikely to be sophisticated about this fact, find another place to do business: Unsophisticated bidders in this sort of situation are likely to overbid, and so the only way you can win the auction is by bidding more than parties who, on average, overbid. This is unlikely to lead to generous profits.

But beyond this simple advice, questions remain. What if your rivals are reasonably sophisticated? What if the object at auction is likely to be worth more to you than to other bidders; in other words, what if the auction mixes private value and common value features, so that even if your rivals are overbidding, you can still make a profit bidding more than they do? How do you find the optimal strategy for bidding in such cases, where the simple rule *Don't even try* is no longer valid? A detailed analysis of the auction is necessary, concerning the value of the object at auction to you, the values and assessments of other bidders conditional on the value to you, and often crucially, the bidding strategies employed by the other bidders. Optimal bidding strategies are rarely easy to find, and this is a place where a knowledgeable consultant can probably help a lot.

Executive Summary

- Problems of *hidden information* appear when one party to a transaction has access to information that other parties cannot access, if the information is relevant to the transaction.

- When items offered for sale are disproportionately drawn from the lower-quality end of the spectrum, because owners of higher-quality items are more likely to want to hold on to their items and where buyers cannot discern the quality, a problem of *adverse selection* exists.

- It is also a problem of adverse selection when, in markets for "services" such as insurance or contract fulfillment, high-cost-of-provision buyers (assumed to be better informed than the service providers about the cost of providing the service) are disproportionately represented in the population of buyers.

- In both types of adverse-selection problem, adverse selection can be a vicious cycle: Lower prices are paid because the average quality sold is low (or higher prices charged because high-cost-of-provision buyers are disproportionate in the population of buyers), which drives from the market goods of intermediate quality or clients of intermediate costs of provision, further driving the price of the goods down or the services up.

- Hidden information problems extend beyond adverse selection. For instance,

companies seeking to hire workers would like to get a better-than-average selection of the population applying for jobs. And the *winner's curse* refers to a
problem of hidden information that occurs in auctions of various types.

- Information revelation cures problems of hidden information. Very generally,
  this involves information freely available that is correlated with characteristics of
  interest, such as demographic information; information whose provision by the
  informed party is compelled by law; and information voluntarily provided by the
  informed party or elicited voluntarily from the informed party.

- To understand correctly information that is voluntarily provided, you must consider
  whether informed parties understand the uses to which the information will be
  put. In signaling and screening equilibria, it is assumed that informed parties fully
  appreciate the uses to which the information will be put and that they respond in
  a manner that is optimal for them.

- Signaling and screening equilibria can be *separating*, where differently informed
  parties take distinct actions, or *pooling*, where differently informed parties send
  the same signal.

- When information is voluntarily provided at the initiative of the informed party,
  economists call it a *signal*. When the uninformed party finds a means for eliciting
  this information, it is called a *screen*.

- In signaling equilibria, the presumed interpretation of signals that are not sent in
  the equilibrium can be crucial.

- The winner's curse refers to auctions in which different bidders have access to
  different information about the value of the item at auction to all bidders. The curse
  occurs when bidders do not take into account that in such circumstances, the
  winner of the auction is apt to be someone with relatively optimistic information,
  information that must in consequence be discounted.

Problems

18.1   At the Famous East Coast Business School (FECBUS), all MBA students want summer jobs working for investment banks in New York City.
They want this sort of job so much that, if they are not offered a position
of this sort, they refuse out of pride to do any other work. A summer job
with an investment bank carries a stipend of $50,000. Therefore, a student
at FECBUS who has probability p of landing such a job owns a lottery with
payoffs $50,000 or $0, with probabilities p and $1 - p$. Beyond the prestige
of having such a job or the shame of not having one, FECBUS students use

this money to help pay for their second year of school, and being risk averse, they consider the possibility of buying insurance against the contingency of no job. Specifically, Beantown Casualty, a local insurance company, has always provided catastrophic summer income insurance to FECBUS students. Beantown offers simple policies in which the student pays a premium P and Beantown reimburses the student Q if the student fails to land a job. If a student buys this policy, the outcomes are $50{,}000 - P$ with probability p and $Q - P$ with probability $1 - p$.

(a) Drake Duck is a typical FECBUS first-year student. His probability of landing a summer job at an investment bank is 0.7. His utility function, used for calculating expected utility, certainty equivalents, and the like is

$$U(x) = \sqrt{x + 40{,}000},$$

where x is the proceeds from summer employment, net of any premiums paid to Beantown Casualty and net of any repayments from Beantown if Drake fails to land a job. If the alternative is to go without insurance, would Drake be willing to pay a premium of $P = \$10{,}000$ for insurance that pays back $Q = \$30{,}000$?

(b) Suppose Beantown Casualty is risk neutral. Which policies could Beantown write for Drake, assuming Beantown knows his utility function and probability of finding a job, that (1) give an expected payoff no larger than the premium, (2) give Drake a higher certainty equivalent than he gets with no insurance, and (3) are efficient in terms of risk sharing?

(c) Unhappily for Beantown, it does not know, a priori, the probability with which any individual student at FECBUS will land a summer job. But, we assume, each student knows his or her own probability. Assume that the first-year class of FECBUS consists of 500 students. For 100 students, the probability of landing a summer job is 0.9. For 100, it is 0.8. For 100 more, it is 0.7. For 100 more, it is 0.6. And for the last 100 students, the probability of landing a summer job is $p = 0.5$. To keep the problem as simple as possible, suppose that all 500 students have precisely the same utility function as does Drake.

Suppose Beantown decides to offer a single policy providing full insurance; that is, $Q = \$50{,}000$. Since the "average" student at FECBUS has probability 0.7 of getting a summer job, Beantown decides to charge a premium of $0.3 \times \$50{,}000 = \$15{,}000$. Would Beantown make or lose money with this policy? Why? (Assume that a student who does not buy insurance from Beantown goes without insurance entirely.)

(d) Suppose that Beantown is convinced that offering a single full-insurance policy is the way to go. Is there any premium Beantown could charge for full insurance that would make a positive expected profit for Beantown? Which premiums do this?

(e) In part d, you should find that the only full-insurance policies that would make a positive expected profit for Beantown involve insurance for the 100 students with a 0.5 chance of landing a job. All the rest choose not to purchase insurance. Beantown would like to insure more members of the FECBUS class, even partially, and so Beantown thinks about offering a single policy with a premium of $14,000 and a payout of $30,000. What would be the response to this policy? How would Beantown do in terms of expected profits?

(f) Beantown Casualty is not interested in making a huge profit writing these insurance policies—they are regulated by the insurance commissioner of the Commonwealth of Baystateland, and in any event, the head of Beantown is an old FECBUS grad who would never try to profit at the expense of students from her old school—but it does see a value in selling some insurance to as many students of FECBUS as possible. Beantown is required by law not to offer any policy that has a negative expected profit; cross-subsidization of one policy by another is not permitted. Moreover, it is compelled to offer full insurance at terms that break even. Therefore, it is compelled, in this circumstance, to offer a full insurance policy (one that pays back $50,000) for a premium of $25,000. (See part c.)

Suppose that, in addition to this policy, Beantown offers a $10,000 insurance policy for a premium of $3500, a $2000 policy for a premium of $500, and a $200 policy for a premium of $20. What would happen? In particular, what would be Beantown's expected profit on each policy and altogether?

18.2 In a particular economy, all homeowners own identical homes worth $80,000 apiece. These homes are subject to complete loss via fire, and the Old Reliable Insurance Company (ORIC) offers policies against loss by fire. The chance of a fire at any particular home is a probability p, which is known to the homeowner but not known to ORIC. The values of p run from 0 to as high as 0.4. Homeowners have no control over the value of p; it is simply given. For instance, Peter Reece has a home on the edge of a forest, and for his house, $p = 0.1$. John Yost has a home in the suburbs, and for his house, $p = 0.03$.

ORIC is risk neutral and offers two different policies. The first is a complete insurance policy, which pays the homeowner back $80,000 in the event of a fire. The premium for this insurance policy is $11,600. The second policy offers partial insurance. It has a payback in the event of fire of $58,400, and a premium of $5900. This means that a customer who buys this policy and has no fire is out $5900. With a fire, the customer nets $58,400 − $5900 = $52,500.

All the homeowners in this society are expected utility maximizers and have the same utility function:

$$U(x) = \sqrt{x + 10{,}000},$$

where x is the net of this situation, including the value of the house, if there is no fire. For instance, a consumer who buys the second insurance policy and has no fire has utility $\sqrt{10{,}000 + 80{,}000 − 5900} = \sqrt{84{,}100} = 290$, while with a fire, the utility is $\sqrt{10{,}000 + 58{,}400 − 5900} = \sqrt{62{,}500} = 250$.

(a) Of the three options available (no insurance, full insurance, or partial insurance), what would be the choice of Mr. Reece? What would be the choice of Mr. Yost?

(b) For which values of p would consumers with that value of p choose no insurance? For which values of p would consumers with that value of p choose partial insurance? For which values of p would consumers with that value of p choose full insurance? You should answer so that, for any value of p between 0 and 1, we can tell what the consumer would choose. Don't worry about values of p for which there are ties.

(c) The actuaries at ORIC, based on historical experience, predict that ORIC will sell 100,000 partial insurance policies, with an average profit per policy of $1228. They predict that ORIC will sell 5000 full insurance policies, with an average *loss* per policy of $12,400. Therefore, their net profit from this business is

$$(100{,}000)(\$1228) + (5000)(−\$12{,}400) = \$60.8 \text{ million.}$$

What would be ORIC's net profit from this business if it offers only the partial insurance policy?

18.3 Selling life insurance to senior citizens is a business with an enormously powerful adverse selection problem: People who are ill or in poor health sign up for this sort of insurance. A natural response to this, used extensively by insurance companies, is to require a physical examination before insurance is sold.

You probably have seen TV advertisements for life (or extended care) insurance, marketed for senior citizens, that proudly proclaims that no physical exam is required and "you cannot be turned down." These policies sometimes charge premiums that depend on the individual's age, gender, weight, and so forth. Still, they would seem to be prime candidates for problems with adverse selection. So how do they cope? If you read the fine print, you discover that "benefits are drastically reduced for the first 2 years of the policy." What is the point of this?

18.4 Among the benefits offered by corporations, at least in the United States, is health insurance. One explanation for why corporations offer such insurance is that this benefit is tax favored: Companies can compensate employees with health-insurance benefits that are treated as nontaxable income. Also, health care providers and insurers (such as Blue Shield) have historically offered better rates to employers for their employees than to individuals who ask for the same coverage. Why is this?

Some companies offer so-called flexible benefits to their employees: Employees have a certain number of pretax dollars to spend on benefits and are allowed to choose the portfolio of benefits they wish. In terms of the prices charged employers by health care providers and insurers for their product, provided as benefits, what do you think is the effect of flexible benefit plans?

18.5 In some countries, title to an automobile includes a history of previous owners. And in those countries, the price for a particular car, holding fixed the car model and features, miles driven, and general (discernible) condition, is a decreasing function of the number of previous owners. Why is this, do you think?

18.6 In the 1980s and 1990s, a large number of first-tier firms offered no-layoff employment. These firms promised employees that, perhaps after a probationary period, an employee had a job for life; he or she would never be laid off. Some firms, such as IBM and Eastman Kodak, had made this promise for decades; in the 1980s and 1990s, this employment practice, as a piece of so-called high-commitment Human Resource management, became increasingly prevalent.

Such policies have substantial benefits when times are good, but they do not come for free. In particular, a firm that offers such promises and that faces economic difficulties must choose between breaking these promises and desirable reorganization. For instance, before the return of Steve Jobs to Apple Computer, Apple, which had prided itself on its no-layoff policy, found itself badly hamstrung by the policy. Apple needed to shed excess employees, but especially given its fairly young workforce, waiting for the natural process of attrition seemed much too slow.

So Apple decided to initiate a program of voluntary layoffs. It offered substantial inducements to employees to quit, including generous severance pay and excellent placement services for those who would consent to go. Apple found, to its dismay, that its program of voluntary layoffs had some bad repercussions. In particular, Apple top management, because of the voluntary layoff program, learned a lot about adverse selection. Precisely what sort of adverse selection problem did they learn about? And can you think of any way to put in place a voluntary layoff program that negates (or, at least, ameliorates) this problem of adverse selection?

18.7 In the U.S. real estate brokerage industry, brokers employed by large brokerage firms have traditionally worked for a portion of the commissions they generate. That is, if a house sale generates a 6% commission split equally between the brokers for the two sides (which is standard in many markets in the United States), the broker on one side might personally pocket 1.5% with 1.5% going to the firm for which the broker works. In return for a share in the broker's commissions, the firm provides the broker with an infrastructure, such as clerical support, phone services, and office space, and especially for new brokers, a base wage.

In comparison, RE/MAX, a national brokerage firm, permits its agents to keep 100% of the commissions they earn. The firm provides clerical services, phones, and the like, and charges its agents a fixed monthly fee for those services. RE/MAX is known for having the most aggressive agents in the business on average. If you want to find an aggressive, hardcharging agent, going to RE/MAX is usually a safe bet.

(a) Why does RE/MAX attract more aggressive agents?

(b) RE/MAX charges its agents more for the services it provides than it costs to provide those services. In fact, RE/MAX makes money by marking up the clerical and administrative services it provides to its agents. Why are aggressive agents willing to pay RE/MAX more for these services than it would cost them to procure the services independently?

(c) In addition to joining RE/MAX or a more traditional firm, realtors can go independent. How does this third option affect RE/MAX? How does it affect the more traditional firms? Put another way, would you expect a hardcharging, aggressive agent to remain with RE/MAX for the long haul? Does your answer to the question depend on aspects of the local real estate market; that is, would you give the same answer for, say, the Silicon Valley as you would for a prosperous county seat in South Carolina?

Questions about the winner's curse are generally quite difficult to pose. While very stylized, Problem 18.8 illustrates the phenomenon in about as simple a model as one can find. Problem 18.9 is more realistic, but it is very difficult to tackle and should not be attempted unless you have considerable skills in probability modeling and analysis.

18.8 Three construction firms, Ace, Base, and Case, are considering whether to declare their willingness to undertake a contruction project for the Freedonian government. The cost of fulfilling this construction project is very likely to be $100,000. But there is a chance that the cost will be $200,000. This cost does not change depending on the firm; if it is $100,000 for one firm, it is $100,000 for the other two.

The Freedonian government declared it will pay precisely $125,000 for this job. That is, the price paid to the firm doing the work is fixed in advance. The decision facing Ace, Base, and Case is whether to declare that it is willing to undertake this project. If no firm is willing to undertake the project, it will not be done. If only one of the three is willing, that firm will be awarded the job. If two firms are willing, one of the two will be chosen by a coin toss. And if all three firms declare their willingness, one of the three will be chosen at random, with each firm having a $\frac{1}{3}$ chance of getting the job.

The three firms must each decide and then declare simultaneously and independently whether it is willing to take the job. All three are risk neutral. You are advising Ace, and the management of Ace has told you that it is willing to take the job if the expected costs of construction are less than the fixed price of $125,000.

Each of the three firms initially assessed probability 0.8 that the cost of this project will be $100,000 and 0.2 that the cost will be $200,000. But each has a 0.75 probability chance of having learned the true cost. These 0.75 probability chances are independent of one another and independent of the true cost of the facility. That is, conditional on Ace learning the true cost, the probability that Base would learn it is still 0.75, and so on. And if we condition on the true cost being $100,000, the chance that Ace would learn this is 0.75.

In fact, the management at Ace told you that it did not learn the true cost, so it still assesses 0.8 that the cost will be $100,000. And it does not know whether Base or Case knows the true cost; it assesses binominal probabilities 0.75^2 that both rivals know the true cost (whatever that is), $2 \times 0.75 \times 0.25$

that one rival knows the true cost and the other does not, and 0.25^2 that neither rival knows the true cost.

Suppose that Base and Case both use the following decision rule to determine whether they should declare their willingness to take on this project:

> If the firm in question is certain that the costs would be $100,000, then declare that it is willing to take on the contract; otherwise, do not indicate a willingness to take on the contract.

Against two rivals whose decision rules are these, should Ace, which remains uncertain about the true cost, indicate a willingness to take on this project?

18.9 An object being auctioned by sealed tender to one of three bidders has a value V, which is common to all three bidders. The value V is also uncertain, and the three bidders assess, a priori, that $V = e^X$, where X is Normally distributed with mean 15 and variance 1. Each of the three bidders receives a signal about the value of X; the signal received by bidder i (for $i = 1, 2, 3$), denoted s_i, is Normally distributed with mean X and variance 1. Moreover, the signals are conditionally independent of one another, conditional on the true value of X.

Bidder 1 has received the signal $s_1 = 15.3$. Bidder 1 believes that bidder 2 will bid 70% of what bidder 2 believes to be the expected value of V, conditional on s_2, and that bidder 3 will bid 80% of what bidder 3 believes to be the expected value of V, conditional on s_3.

The auction is a first-price auction, meaning the high bidder wins the object, paying his or her bid. Bidder 1 is risk neutral and aims to maximize her net expected value for the auction, which is the probability that she wins times the expected value of V less her bid, conditional on her winning. What is the optimal bid of bidder 1 under these circumstances?

Suppose we change the story, so that bidder 3 learns not s_3 but the true value of X. Bidder 3 therefore bids $.8 \times e^X = .8V$. What is the optimal bid for bidder 1 under these circumstances?

19. Incentives

In many economic transactions, one party takes actions that affect the welfare of another party, actions that cannot be specified contractually. The actions chosen by the first party are determined by the *incentives* he or she faces, and the second party may attempt to structure the transaction so that these incentives lead to the choice that the second party prefers. Myriad examples exist; perhaps the most prominent is so-called pay for performance. This chapter explores some basic ideas about incentives. It begins with a fundamental tension between motivation and efficient risk sharing and goes on to a number of variations and extensions, including incentives for groups, in dynamic settings, and for screening.

- An insurance company sells a policy that insures a factory against fire and wonders whether the factory owner, now that she has insurance, will take care not to leave oily rags lying around.

- A company that manufactures large capital equipment employs salespersons who deal with the firm's clients. The sales effort takes place outside the view of top management of the manufacturer, which wonders whether its salespersons exert themselves in selling the product.

- A day laborer is hired to remove tree trunks from a field. His employer wonders whether, at the end of the day, she will find a large number of stumps removed or only a few, accompanied by tales of hard, rocky soil and a dull axe.

- The loan officer at a commercial bank, considering whether to make a loan to an entrepreneur, wonders whether the entrepreneur will be prudent with the funds provided or will gamble with the funds, hoping for a big win and a spectacularly successful initial public offering.

- Five lawyers form a partnership with the intention of splitting equally the profits of the partnership. Each wonders whether this arrangement would mean that all five spend more time on the golf course and less in the office.

These are examples of moral hazard, situations in which the actions of one party affects the welfare of others, where the interests of the parties diverge to some extent, and the actions chosen by the first party are not completely controllable. As these examples indicate, the range of contexts in which moral hazards can be found is wide.

The solution to problems of moral hazard is, broadly speaking, incentives. A variety of motivators or incentives can work on individuals and groups, including

- Intrinsic motivators, such as pride in a job well done.

- Reliance on norms of appropriate behavior, including the norm of keeping promises.

- The desire to elicit positive reciprocal actions from one's immediate trading partner(s) or to avoid future punishment or bad behavior.

- The desire to acquire and maintain a general reputation for good behavior, because such a reputation provides future benefits.

- For employees and contractors, the desire not to be fired.

- The desire not to be sued for breach of promise or contract.

- The prospect of promotion, desirable assignments, or lucrative future opportunities.

- Direct financial incentives based on measures of performance, such as sales commissions and other forms of pay for performance.

Intrinsic motivation and norms of behavior are discussed in Chapter 25. Chapters 22 through 24 discuss reciprocity, reputation, and the lure of future opportunities. This chapter focuses on direct financial incentives.

19.1. A Basic Trade-off: Risk Sharing versus Motivation

There are, potentially, two simple solutions to problems of incentives. *The first is to determine what choice of action is desirable and fix this contractually.* In the case of a factory owner, the insurance contract specifies that no insurance is paid if the owner does not store oily rags safely. A salesperson is provided no compensation if he does not exert himself to a prespecified level. The entrepreneur loses control of her business to the bank if she does not take prudent decisions. The problem with each of these is that it may be impossible, ex post, to verify that the contractual terms were met. It might be possible to monitor compliance with a contractual provision on the storage of flammable items, with spot checks. But how can a salesperson's level of effort be monitored? How can the level of prudence of an entrepreneur be measured? Even if these things can be monitored or measured, can this be done in a manner that a court could enforce? A commercial banker who loans money to an entrepreneur may know that decisions made by the entrepreneur were imprudent, but can a judge or jury in a civil trial be convinced of this? The problem, generally, is that often the desired "inputs" cannot be adequately measured or monitored or, if they can be, cannot be made part of an enforceable contract.

This takes us to the second potential simple solution. *Construct an arrangement that puts the onus entirely on the party choosing the action.* Do not offer fire insurance to the factory owner, so he bears fully the consequences of not storing oily rags carefully. Have the salesperson bear fully the impact of his effort decisions, by giving him a payment that equals (on the margin) the full effect of whether he makes the sale. Have the entrepreneur bear completely the consequences of her choice, by making a loan that guarantees a fixed amount of repayment to the bank.

The problem with these is that they imply no risk sharing between the parties involved. If the marginal profit from a sale is $10 million and a sale is uncertain even if the salesperson tries his best, will he be willing to bear that much risk in his level of compensation? Will the entrepreneur be willing to bear all the financial risk of her venture? (Given laws on limited liability, is it even legally possible to achieve this?) The problem is perhaps clearest in the insurance context: If the solution to moral hazard in an insurance context is not to offer any insurance, then the insurance business is dramatically curtailed.

(Another problem is associated with this second solution: What if more than one party takes an action subject to moral hazard? Suppose the salesperson must choose a level of effort to exert and, simultaneously, the firm must choose an uncontractable level of after-sales service to provide. The ability of the salesperson to make repeat sales depends on the firm's level of after-sales service and his own efforts. If he bears fully the consequences of his sales levels, the firm has no incentive to provide good after-sales service. But if the firm bears fully the consequences of the sales level, the salesperson loses incentive to exert himself in making sales. This situation of *simultaneous moral hazard* occurs in any situation where outcomes are influenced by the decisions of multiple parties, such as in the context of a legal partnership, and we take it up later in the chapter.)

A fundamental trade-off concerning incentives involves the confluence of three factors:

1. The desired actions cannot be specified contractually, because of problems of measurement, monitoring, or enforceability.

2. Even if the desired actions are taken, there is uncertainty about the consequences.

3. Loading the full consequences on the party taking the action is undesirable, because of the economic benefits of risk sharing among the parties.

To share risk efficiently typically means shielding the party choosing the action from at least some consequences of that choice, but doing so lowers the level of incentives. The trick is to balance risk sharing and motivation.

An Example: Salesperson Compensation

A simple model of salesperson compensation illustrates these ideas. Suppose that you employ a salesperson who is going to try to make a particular sale for you. If the person makes the sale, you will earn a profit of $60,000. If the person does not make the sale, you earn $0. These figures do not include wages you pay the salesperson.

This salesperson must decide on a level of effort to devote to selling for you. He can kill himself, he can work hard, he can try but not hard, or he can loaf. His level of effort affects the probability that he makes the sale. If he kills himself, he will make the sale with probability 0.5. If he works hard, the probability that he will make the sale is 0.4. If he tries but not hard, he makes the sale with probability 0.25. And if he loafs, he will make the sale with probability 0.05.

This salesperson has a utility function that depends on his wages and the amount of effort he puts into making the sale. If he is paid a wage of w, his utility is

$$\sqrt{w} - \text{disutility of effort},$$

where his disutility of effort is 40 if he kills himself, 20 if he works hard, 10 if he tries but not hard, and 0 if he loafs. If the salesperson faces uncertainty in his wages, this utility function is used to compute expected utility.

The salesperson's best alternative to working for you is a job in which, for the length of time this sales call will take, he will make $10,000 with no disutility of effort. So to get this salesperson to work for you, you must give him a contract where his expected utility is at least $\sqrt{10,000} = 100$. You are risk neutral. You want to maximize your net expected profit from this venture, net of wages you pay to the salesperson.

Before going further, I should comment on the assumption that you are risk neutral, while the salesperson is risk averse. This assumption is typically made in economic models of incentives, because it simplifies the analysis. But the assumption is more than a matter of modeling convenience. If we think of "you" in this story as a sizeable, publicly held firm, with shares widely dispersed among many shareholders, then it is reasonable to suppose that "you" are risk neutral (although see Section 17.3 and financial market theory for an important caveat). On the other hand, the salesperson is likely to bear entirely the risk in his own compensation, for which he is risk averse.

With this assumption in place, we come to an easy first conclusion. Suppose that you can contractually fix the level of effort the salesperson expends. That is, you are able to write and enforce a contract that reads, in essence, *The salesperson will exert effort level A and be paid X if a sale is made and Y if not.* Since the amount of money to be shared between you is random, you are risk neutral, and the salesperson is risk averse, efficient risk sharing would dictate that X should equal Y. The salesperson should be shielded entirely from risk.

To determine A and $X = Y$, reason as follows:

- If you wish the salesperson to put in no effort at all, pay him a wage w sufficient to get him to work at this level of effort; that is, w must satisfy

$$\sqrt{w} - 0 \geq 100, \text{ or } w \geq \$10,000.$$

The 0 on the left-hand side of the first inequality represents the disutility of loafing. (In these constraints, I assume that, if the utility and later the expected utility of the salesperson equals his next best alternative, then he will choose to work for you. If this is not so, then we have to sweeten the salary a little bit.) If you pay this person $10,000, your net profit is $(0.05)(\$60,000) - \$10,000 = -\$7000$; that is, you wind up losing money.

- If you wish the salesperson to try but not too hard, pay him a wage w sufficient to get him to work at this level of effort; that is, w must satisfy

$$\sqrt{w} - 10 \geq 100, \text{ or } w \geq \$12,100.$$

The 10 on the left-hand side of the first inequality represents disutility of trying but not too hard. If you pay this person $12,100, your expected net profit is $(0.25)(\$60,000) - \$12,100 = \$2900$.

- If you wish the salesperson to work hard, pay him a wage w sufficient to get him to work hard, which is

$$\sqrt{w} - 20 \geq 100, \text{ or } w \geq \$14,400,$$

where the 20 on the left-hand side of the first inequality represents the disutility of working hard. If you pay this person $14,400, your expected net profit is $(0.4)(\$60,000) - \$14,400 = \$9600$.

- And if you wish the salesperson to kill himself, pay him a wage w that is sufficient to get him to kill himself, which is

$$\sqrt{w} - 40 \geq 100, \text{ or } w \geq \$19,600.$$

(Your turn: Why is 40 on the left-hand side of the first inequality?) If you pay this person \$19,600, your expected net profit is $(0.5)(\$60,000) - \$19,600 = \$10,400$.

So the optimal thing to do is to write a contract in which you agree to pay this person \$19,600 in return for a killing level of work—A is "killing level of effort" and $X = Y = \$19,600$; for which you net \$10,400.

Now suppose that you cannot fix the salesperson's level of effort contractually, whether because you cannot observe his level of effort or this cannot be made a part of an enforceable contract. What do you do?

If the salesperson were risk neutral, the second easy solution could be used: Put the onus on the salesperson to take the right action by loading the consequence of the salesperson's actions squarely on his shoulders. In effect, you would give the salesperson the following sort of contract:

The salesperson has the right to choose his preferred effort level. If he makes a sale, he keeps the full marginal profit he generates, \$60,000. And to have this opportunity, he pays the firm (you) a fixed amount Z, regardless of whether he eventually makes the sale or not.

If the salesperson were risk neutral, this would be a fine solution. He can bear the risk as well as anyone, so put all the risk—and all the consequences of his effort choice—on him. But he is not risk neutral, and so at least some risk sharing is a good idea. Indeed, because he is risk averse and you are risk neutral, efficient risk sharing, taken on its own, means you should bear all the risk.

That does not work either. If he bears no risk (if his level of compensation is the same whether he makes a sale or not) what incentive does he have to put in any effort? The answer, at least within the model, is none. And we know already that if he expends minimal effort, giving a 0.05 probability of a sale, your net profit, after paying him what it takes to get him to take the job, leaves you with a negative net expected profit.

I can hear the protests: "What about pride in doing a good job?" "What about the salesperson's desire to make the sale just for the self-satisfaction this generates?" "What about extracting a promise of hard work from him, a promise he is likely to keep if he is at all the sort of person you want your company to deal with?" "What about the salesperson's concern to keep his job in your sales department?" "What about his desire to become a district sales manager?" "What about his concern for his general reputation as a salesperson?"

All these are good questions. They point out that motivating a sales-person, and more generally motivating anyone who faces a moral hazard, involves a vast complex of factors. We must evaluate these other factors in real-life examples to see how powerful they are. Perhaps they are power-ful enough that, in a particular context, efficient risk sharing can continue without causing the salesperson to loaf.

But, in this chapter, the focus is on extrinsic, explicit, and formal monetary incentives, so we assume all these away in our model. And, in that case, the conclusion we just reached (efficient risk sharing means no bonus means no effort) is correct. To motivate the salesperson, we have to give him some incentive to try, which means making the amount he is paid if a sale occurs greater than what he makes if he comes back without a sale. But we do not want to go too far in this direction, since that means loading too much risk on him. It is a matter of trading off incentives against risk sharing, trying to find the right balance.

We do not, in this chapter, push all the way to the optimal solution in this model. You can do that on your own, in Problem 19.1. But we start you toward the solution, with a bit of trial and error:

> Suppose you can write a contract for the salesperson that specifies that he gets a base wage of $9500, regardless of whether a sale is made or not, and in addition a bonus of $15,000 if he makes a sale. On these terms, would he take the job? If so, what level of effort would he put in? What would be your net expected profit?

He has the following five choices:

1. *If he chooses not to work for you at all,* he nets utility 100 in his next best alternative.

2. *If he chooses to work for you and loaf,* he receives income $9500 with prob-ability 0.95 and $24,500 with probability 0.05. He has zero disutility of effort, so his overall expected utility is $(0.95)\sqrt{9500} + (0.05)\sqrt{24,500} - 0 = (0.95)(97.468) + (0.05)(156.525) - 0 = 100.421$.

3. *If he chooses to work for you and tries but not too hard,* he receives in-come $9500 with probability 0.75 and $24,500 with probability 0.25. He has disutility of effort equal to 10, so his overall expected utility is $(0.75)\sqrt{9500} + (.25)\sqrt{24,500} - 10 = (0.75)(97.468) + (0.25)(156.525) - 10 = 102.232$.

4. *If he chooses to work for you and try hard,* he receives income $9500 with probability 0.6 and $24,500 with probability 0.4. He has disutility of effort equal to 20, so his overall expected utility is $(0.6)\sqrt{9500} + (0.4)\sqrt{24,500} - 20 = (0.6)(97.468) + (0.4)(156.525) - 20 = 101.091$.

5. *If he chooses to work for you and kill himself,* he receives income $9500 with probability 0.5 and $24,500 with probability 0.5. He has disutility of effort equal to 40, so his overall expected utility is $(0.5)\sqrt{9500} + (0.5)\sqrt{24,500} - 40 = (0.5)(97.468) + (0.5)(156.525) - 40 = 86.996$.

Among his five options, taking the job and trying but not too hard maximizes his expected utility (net of the disutility of effort). So we conclude that this is what he would do, if offered this incentive contract. Therefore, your expected profit, net of the cost of his wages, is

$$(\$60,000)(0.25) - \$9500 - (\$15,000)(0.25) = \$1750;$$

this is your expected gross profits, less his base wage, less the bonus times the probability that he earns the bonus.

That is not bad, but can you do better? To help answer this question, we use the spreadsheet CHAP19, depicted in Figure 19.1. Here is what it does: The base wage and bonus payment are placed in cells B1 and B2. Then the spreadsheet computes the gross (of the disutility of effort) levels of utility if a sale is made and if not; and for each of the four effort choices, it finds the

CHAP19

	A	B	C	D	E	F
1	base wage	$9,500				
2	bonus	$15,000				
3						
4	gross utility if sale	156.5247584				
5	gross utility if no sale	97.46794345				
6						
7		EFFORT CHOICE	DISUTILITY	PROB SALE	EU	Expected net profit
8		loafing	0	0.05	100.42	-$7,250
9		tries but not hard	10	0.25	102.23	$1,750
10		works hard	20	0.4	101.09	$8,500
11		kills self	40	0.5	86.996	$13,000
12		reservation level			100	
13						

Sheet1 / Sheet2 / Sheet3

Figure 19.1. A spreadsheet for analyzing different incentive contracts. This spreadsheet, sheet 1 of CHAP19, computes for a given base wage and bonus level the salesperson's expected utilities and the employer's expected net profit for each level of effort. Of course, the salesperson chooses whichever effort level gives him the highest expected utility, subject to the constraint that he must have a net expected utility of 100 to take the job at all.

net expected utility (EU), net of the disutility of effort, as well as the expected net profit, net of the salesperson's expected compensation, for that effort level. So, in Figure 19.1, we see the analysis we did for the contract with a base wage of $9500 and a bonus of $15,000: The highest EU for the salesperson is from trying but not hard; this beats the salesperson's reservation level of utility 100 and so is the salesperson's choice. With this compensation offer, you (the employer) have an expected net profit of $1750.

Note that, with the base wage and bonus levels of Figure 19.1, if the salesperson chooses to kill himself, the expected net profit for you rises to $13,000. But the nature of the moral hazard problem here is that you do not choose the effort level, the salesperson does. And in this model, he chooses his effort level (or whether to work for you at all) based on the incentives you put before him. With the contract of Figure 19.1, his choice is to try but not hard, and the only way you can induce a higher level of effort from him, intuition tells us, is to give him a bigger bonus if he makes the sale.

Will it be worthwhile for you to induce more effort from him? With the spreadsheet in hand, we can play with the base wage and bonus to find out. Suppose, for instance, you increase his bonus to $20,000. See Figure 19.2. Now his choice is to work hard. And having induced this level of effort, your expected net profit rises to $6500.

	A	B	C	D	E	F
1	base wage	$9,500				
2	bonus	$20,000				
3						
4	gross utility if sale	171.7556404				
5	gross utility if no sale	97.46794345				
6						
7		EFFORT CHOICE	DISUTILITY	PROB SALE	EU	Expected net profit
8		loafing	0	0.05	101.18	-$7,500
9		tries but not hard	10	0.25	106.04	$500
10		works hard	20	0.4	107.18	$6,500
11		kills self	40	0.5	94.612	$10,500
12		reservation level			100	
13						

Figure 19.2. Getting the salesperson to work hard with a somewhat larger bonus. By increasing the bonus to $20,000, the salesperson is motivated to try hard, which improves the employer's expected net profit.

Note that the salesperson's expected utility in the arrangement in Figure 19.2 is 107.18. You need to give him an expected net utility of only 100 to get him to work, so you are paying him more than his next best outside alternative. You can probably increase expected net profit by taking some wages away from him, and I tried to do this by decreasing his base wage. As I do this, I have to be careful that he continues to choose to work hard, but this did not seem to be much of a problem; I found that cutting the base wage to $8,000 kept him working and choosing to work hard, and it pushed your expected net profit up to $8,000. The numbers are shown in Figure 19.3.

	A	B	C	D	E	F	
				CHAP19			
	A	B	C	D	E	F	
1	base wage	$8,000					
2	bonus	$20,000					
3							
4	gross utility if sale	167.3320053					
5	gross utility if no sale	89.4427191					
6							
7		EFFORT CHOICE	DISUTILITY	PROB SALE	EU	Expected net profit	
8		loafing	0	0.05	93.337	-$6,000	
9		tries but not hard	10	0.25	98.915	$2,000	
10		works hard	20	0.4	100.6	$8,000	
11		kills self	40	0.5	88.387	$12,000	
12		reservation level			100		
13							

Figure 19.3. Reducing the salesperson's surplus relative to the contract in Figure 19.2. By reducing the base wage, you economize on how much you pay the salesperson, improving expected net profit. You can continue to do this until you reach the reservation expected utility of 100, which is almost done here.

The scheme in Figure 19.3 looks pretty good, but there is still some room for manuever. Note that working hard gives the salesperson an expected utility of 100.6, while the next best alternative level of effort (trying but not hard) gives utility 98.915. We continue to get the desired incentive effect (motivating hard work) and do better in terms of risk sharing if the bonus is decreased a bit. While we do this, we must add a bit to the base wage, to keep his net expected utility at or above the reservation utility level of 100. Figure 19.4 shows the best I was able to do with this, by hunting around: With a base wage of $8700 and a bonus of $17,000, the salesperson is just barely willing to work for the firm (100.089 vs. 100 for his next best alternative) and just barely prefers working hard to trying but not hard (100.089 vs. 100.033). This gives an expected net profit of $8500

There is one final thing to try. Expected net profit is better still if we get the salesperson to kill himself. Indeed, we know that this is the effort level to shoot for if we could directly monitor and contract on effort level. Can we increase the bonus enough that this is his choice, leaving us with a higher expected net profit? I found that getting him to choose to kill himself requires an enormous bonus. The best I could do by hunting is in Figure 19.5: a base wage of $1530 and a bonus of $56,500, which means an expected profit of $220. It looks like the optimal incentive scheme will not involve motivating him to kill himself.

	A	B	C	D	E	F
1	base wage	$8,700				
2	bonus	$17,000				
3						
4	gross utility if sale	160.3121954				
5	gross utility if no sale	93.27379053				
6						
7		EFFORT CHOICE	DISUTILITY	PROB SALE	EU	Expected net profit
8		loafing	0	0.05	96.626	–$6,550
9		tries but not hard	10	0.25	100.03	$2,050
10		works hard	20	0.4	100.09	$8,500
11		kills self	40	0.5	86.793	$12,800
12		reservation level			100	
13						

Figure 19.4. Fine-tuning the incentive scheme of Figure 19.3. By moving in the direction of better risk sharing (a lower bonus) while keeping hard work the choice of the salesperson (which includes meeting the reservation constraint that hard work gives an EU at 100 or above), expected net profit rises to $8500.

	A	B	C	D	E	F
1	base wage	$1,530				
2	bonus	$56,500				
3						
4	gross utility if sale	240.8941676				
5	gross utility if no sale	39.11521443				
6						
7		EFFORT CHOICE	DISUTILITY	PROB SALE	EU	Expected net profit
8		loafing	0	0.05	49.2042	–$1,355
9		tries but not hard	10	0.25	79.56	–$655
10		works hard	20	0.4	99.8268	–$130
11		kills self	40	0.5	100.005	$220
12		reservation level			100	
13						

Figure 19.5. Getting the salesperson to kill himself. A very large bonus is required to motivate the salesperson to kill himself, leading to a relatively small net profit. This is the best I could do in terms of net profit while motivating him to kill himself.

All I am doing in these exercises is hunting with my spreadsheet, trying to find successively better schemes, where better is measured by the effective expected net profit of the firm. I apply two general procedures in doing this: I try to see what is the best I can do in terms of expected net profit if I give the salesperson incentives to take each of the four actions. (Actually, I could give up on loafing from the start, since I know that loafing means an expected loss.) And for each level of effort in turn, I try to fine-tune the incentive scheme so that (1) the salesperson is brought as close to his reservation utility of 100 as possible (no need to give him extra surplus) and (2) he is shielded from risk to the maximum extent possible, consistent with keeping him at the effort level I am working at. I cannot be sure, since I am just hunting heuristically, that the scheme in Figure 19.4 is optimal. But I bet that it is pretty close.

You may be wondering why I hunt heuristically. Why not just use Solver? I will not take you through all the details, but with logical variables, the spreadsheet can be set up so that Solver can be employed. (Find the maximal EU, and set up a logical variable for each action that equals 1 if the action achieves the maximum and 0 otherwise, being careful about ties—not pleasant, but doable.) But Solver doesn't do well in general with maximization problems that involve logical variables; this might not work.

There is a better way to have Solver solve this problem. Indeed, this problem, viewed properly, can even be solved by hand. Problem 19.1 takes you through the drill, where you'll discover that the absolute best that can be done in this problem is to set a base wage of $8711 and a bonus payment of $16,890 (rounded to the nearest dollar), leading to an expected net profit of $8533. Figure 19.4 is within $33 of the optimum.

The technique described in Problem 19.1 is probably worth learning on conceptual grounds, and it is a favorite for exam questions on this topic. But it is not very practical, since you rarely know with precision the utility function of salespersons who work for you. What is more important is the qualitative insight generated by hunting for the answer heuristically:

> The basic trade-off in this problem is efficient risk sharing versus motivation. To motivate higher levels of effort, you have to pay a higher bonus. But as you pay a higher bonus, you load more and more risk on the salesperson, because the range of his incomes increases, bad for risk sharing. The optimal solution involves a compromise of these two opposing forces. In particular, you want a high-enough bonus to motivate the level of effort you target. But you want *just enough* motivation so this is true and no more. And you want to fine-tune the scheme so that the salesperson's utility of working for you just beats his next best alternative.

Of course, this is just an example. But, in all sorts of problems in which individuals must be given incentives to take desired actions, incentives based on noisy measures of the actions the individual does take, we see the same basic trade-off. To motivate the desired action, the individual has to be given more compensation in circumstances that indicate that the desired action was taken. If the individual cannot entirely control the outcome, this subjects him or her to risk, which typically compromises efficient risk sharing.

To take another example, suppose an insurance company ensures an individual's home against fire. The chance of a fire depends on how much care the individual takes, although even the most careful individual can face a risk of fire. Efficient risk sharing, assuming the homeowner is risk averse and the insurance company is risk neutral, means insuring the homeowner entirely against any loss; that is, the insurance company bears entirely the risk of fire, the homeowner is completely compensated for any loss. But, if taking care is costly for the homeowner and she is entirely insured against loss, she has no incentive to take care. The insurance company, to motivate her to take care, must "reward" her if there is no fire; that is, she must be better off if there is no fire than if there is. Typically, this is done by partial insurance or, equivalently, by insuring the house but with a substantial deductible. The prospect of losing the deductible if there is a fire motivates the homeowner to take care. But it necessarily means less than perfectly efficient risk sharing. For a worked out example of this, similar to the salesperson compensation problem, see Problem 19.2.

19.2. Sundry Comments, Qualifications, Extensions, and Variations

The salesperson compensation problem of the previous section and the fire insurance and venture capital models provided in Problems 19.2 and 19.3 are very good exercises for firming up one basic trade-off concerning incentives: efficient risk sharing versus motivation. But this trade-off is far from the end of the story. Incentives and motivation are complex and subtle phenomena, about which entire books have been written. To complement the basic insight from the previous section, this section has a selection from the most important comments, qualifications, extensions, and variations.

Continuous Effort Choice, Continuous Outcomes

In the model just presented, the salesperson is limited to one of four possible levels of effort and there are only two possible outcomes: A sale is made or it is not. A richer, more realistic model would allow for a continuous effort choice variable and permit more outcomes, such as the level of the sale made. With such a model, we could address more easily the following questions:

- Is it better for the employer to have a salesperson who is more risk averse or one who is less? How does the salesperson's level of risk aversion affect the level of effort put forth?

- How does the level of a salesperson's disutility of effort enter into the compensation scheme he or she is offered? If we compare two salespersons, one of whom is more effort averse than the other, should the second be given stronger incentives or weaker? Does the employer prefer the less effort-averse salesperson?

- In general, should you aim for effort levels greater than or less than the optimal level if the effort level can be enforced contractually? In other words, do problems of moral hazard mean that effort levels go up or that they go down?

- How does the level of noise affect things like the employer's expected net profit and the effort level by the agent?

In general, these questions have no simple answers. Even the question that seems most obvious—surely when incentives are a problem, the firm should aim for a lower level of effort—is not true in all cases. Optimal incentive contracts can be fairly wild things. The reason for this, if you can stand the math-speak, is that the key to optimal incentives is to reward the agent highly for outcomes whose likelihood, if he takes the effort level you desire, is relatively higher than the likelihood of that outcome if he takes his next best alternative level of effort. Since likelihoods (conditional probabilities of outcomes, conditioned on the agent's choice of effort level) can jump around a lot, so do optimal incentive contracts.

Still, it is possible to put together specific model formulations with continuous levels of effort and continuous outcomes, in which these questions can be answered. If you are interested, you can find one such model formulation and analysis in Appendix C of J. Baron and D. Kreps, *Strategic Human Resources* (New York: J. Wiley & Sons, 1999). I do not repeat that analysis here because it is several degrees more difficult than the model given previously, but if you can tolerate some difficult math, it is worth trying.

Robustness

Finding the optimal incentive scheme for a particular model, as done in the problems, is an interesting exercise in mathematics and logic. But do not put too much credence into such analyses, or rather, do not attach too much significance to the precise results of the optimization exercise. These analyses are predicated on the parties involved being very sophisticated about the environment they are in. For instance, the parties are assumed to understand fully the impact the employee's effort choice has on the distribution of observables, such as whether a sale is made or not. The employer is assumed to know perfectly the utility function of the employee, including the employee's precise attitude toward risk and level of aversion to effort.

These are nice assumptions when you are playing with a model. To be more precise, they are not terrible assumptions when your objective is to understand, say, the trade-off between motivation and risk sharing. But for real-life application, they are pretty silly as assumptions go. Real incentive schemes, at least those that are effective, are relatively simple and robust to perturbations in the basic data of the situation, because the parties involved lack the data necessary to fine-tune things.

This is not to say that incentive systems are never fine-tuned to the individuals who are meant to be motivated by them. So-called management-by-objectives (MBO) systems are based on the notion that incentives should be tailored to the specific situations of specific employees. But, even with MBO, when the incentives for a given employee are set by the boss, it is doubtful that the boss knows everything necessary to solve for the specific employee's optimal incentive scheme.

Instead, real-life incentive design looks a lot like the hunting we did with the spreadsheet, but without the instant feedback the computer gave us. Firms experiment with different incentive schemes, seeing what sorts of behavior result, and to the extent that they try to fine-tune, it is very much trial and error, blended with past experiences with similar situations.

Screening

Taking this a step further, do not lose sight of the fact that incentive schemes can serve several purposes simultaneously. They motivate individual employees, of course, but they also act as a screen for desirable employees.

In some cases, the two purposes push incentives in the same direction. Recall, from Problem 18.7, the case of the real estate network RE/MAX. RE/MAX offers its agent–employees a compensation scheme that is atypical of the industry: Individual agents retain 100% of the commissions they generate and pay a fixed fee for clerical and informational services and for the reputation gained by working for RE/MAX. This compensation scheme attracts able and aggressive agents, which gives RE/MAX a reputation for such agents, a reputation on which it is able to capitalize by charging its agents high fees for the services it provides. Agents in turn pay those fees because, by being RE/MAX agents, they are instantly branded as able and aggressive. This is a screening story. But at the same time, this sort of compensation scheme, which provides very little insurance for the individual agent, motivates each agent to work very hard, which is right in line with what RE/MAX desires.

Sometimes screening and incentive effects run in contrary directions. For instance, engineers in high-tech firms in Silicon Valley, during the boom years of the late 1990s, were often motivated by the lure of the big payoff. To motivate an engineer to work hard, high-tech firms had to offer compensation schemes that rewarded outstanding performance. To the extent that these firms wanted their engineers to take risks, they had to offer compensation that did not penalize failure too strongly. But firms adopting this sort of incentive scheme for engineers found that they were attracting engineers who were after the big payoff and willing to take risks to get there. This had drawbacks: A driver of success in Silicon Valley was the ability to retain key technical employees in a labor market with extraordinarily high rates of worker mobility. So, to the extent that a firm attracted engineers who would gamble for a big payoff, it attracted key technical employees who were inclined to leave when the next startup came along, offering a chance at a super payoff in the form of stock options and the like. As long as a firm retained its engineers, they were motivated to perform as desired, but the same incentives led to a workforce more likely to turn over, a highly undesirable characteristic.

Hewlett-Packard (H-P), which, at least until recently, has been one of the most successful firms in Silicon Valley, motivated its engineers differently. Instead of motivating engineers with the prospects of a big payoff, H-P rewarded engineers with the freedom and encouragement to pursue engineering projects and puzzles of interest to the engineer. By setting up its incentive system this way, H-P attracted engineers who were turned on more by technical puzzles and the freedom to innovate than by the chance of a big payoff. Turnover rates among technical staff at H-P were a good deal lower than the local industry average, which meant success overall.

My point is this: Calculating the optimal incentive scheme for a given employee is all well and good, but when incentive schemes screen as well as motivate, which is practically all the time, do not ignore screening by focusing your attention solely on the motivation half of the story.

Incentives Should Not Be Based on Irrelevant Noise

Imagine a firm that wishes to provide incentives for the manager of one of its plants. Imagine a very simple situation in which the plant manager's sole responsibility is to produce a given amount of a product as cheaply as possible. Suppose that quality of output is not an issue, nor the development of human resources at the manager's plant, nor any one of a host of other issues that afflict plant managers beyond unit cost. Unit cost is measurable ex post, and it is partially responsive to the manager's efforts in running the factory. But random factors creep in, such as the quality of raw materials and the weather, which cause unit cost to be a noisy measure of the plant manager's efforts.

Once the product is made, it is sold at a price the market will bear. The profit level of the firm depends on the unit cost of production but also on the state of the economy, the actions of the firm's competitors, and so forth.

To motivate the manager, the firm considers two sorts of incentive schemes. One would tie the manager's compensation to the measured unit cost of production at the plant. The second would tie the manager's compensation to the firm's overall level of profit. Which of these is better?

If we assume the manager is vastly less able to bear risk than the firm—an entirely sensible assumption when the firm in question is financed by widely spread, publicly traded equity—then on economic grounds, the first scheme is very likely to be better. On pure-risk sharing grounds, the firm wants to shield its vastly more risk-averse employee from risk wherever it can. The firm may have to compromise on this, to motivate the employee, by tying compensation to measures of employee performance not fully controlled by the employee. But tying the employee's compensation to uncertain variables that have nothing to do with the employee's level of effort simply loads unnecessary risk on the employee. (As we see in Chapter 25, however, there is more to this story than these economic considerations.)

Tournaments and Benchmarking

Return to the problem of motivating a salesperson. Why does the salesperson's level of effort not completely determine the outcome on any given sales call, measured, say, in terms of the dollar value of sales made on this call? Any number of factors, together with the salesperson's level of effort, influence the level of sales. Some factors are idiosyncratic to this particular sales call, things having to do with the particular customer to whom the sale is being made. But other factors outside the control of the salesperson are likely to influence similarly the level of sales achieved by other salespersons working for this firm; factors such as the quality of the product, the state of the general economy, the efforts of competitors to sell a rival product, and so on. If a salesperson does not make a sale or sells only a pittance, the product could be no good, the economy sluggish, or rivals cut the price of a similar good. But, if one of these factors is largely to blame for a poor result, it is more likely that other salespersons working for the firm do not do well on their sales calls. So the best evidence available that the particular salesperson (she) is trying hard may be that she books a large level of sales when other salespersons do poorly, and the best evidence that she is loafing may be that she fails when others do well. Note well, this may be the *best* evidence, but it need not be conclusive: Other idiosyncratic factors are at work on any single sales call.

Thus, a firm with multiple salespersons may be able to evaluate better the performance of each by comparing how each did with the others' results in the same time period; that is, the firm uses comparative evaluation. The firm might, for example, give its salespersons a base wage, then a bonus to the top seller in a given time period, or a bonus to the top 25%, or whatever. Schemes that tie compensation to purely ordinal rankings are called *tournament incentive schemes*. Relative to incentive schemes that tie the individual's pay entirely to how the individual does, tournament incentive schemes and schemes that use both absolute and relative performance data can do better, because they allow the firm to reduce the effective risk faced by the individual; the only risk left—if all salespersons are equally able or even if the abilities of each is known to others—is idiosyncratic risk related to the customers called on by that salesperson.

A number of problems arise with these incentive schemes: (1) They give individual salespersons incentive to collude against the firm; if all hold back on their effort, then each looks fairly good "in comparison" with the overall average. (2) They sometimes promote unhealthy competition inside the firm; salespersons spend some of their time trying to affect adversely the performance of their peers or fail to render assistance to one another that would improve the firm's profit. Of course, it is unlikely that you will face both problems for the same two salespersons at the same time; either they are colluding to hold down on the overall level of effort or each is spiking the efforts of the other. The standard ways to control these two problems is to isolate the employees in the comparison set and put a large number of employees in the set: The first precludes collusion by precluding communication and the second both makes collusion harder and gives smaller rewards to pernicious actions directed against the efforts of one or a few others in the comparison set.

Another way to control these problems is for Firm A to compare the performance of its salespersons with the performance of some external group, say, the salespersons of Firms B and C. Terminology in these matters is imprecise, but this is often referred to as *benchmarking*. For example, Firm A might benchmark its growth in sales revenue with that of several competitors, rewarding salespersons who do better than the "industry benchmark." This controls the twin problems of collusion and pernicious activities because:

1. It is much less likely that the salespersons in firm A will collude with those in Firms B and C, because more people must be in the collusive scheme and they have less opportunity to talk, scheme, and otherwise interact.

2. Firm A is probably less concerned if its salespersons act uncooperatively with the salespersons of its rivals.

On the other hand, the disadvantage of benchmarking against salespersons of another firm is that the comparison controls for fewer common factors. If we compare the sales results of two individuals selling the same product, we control for the quality of the product they sell, the prices charged by rivals, and the general reputation of the firm's products. When we benchmark the sales results in Firm A against what Firms B and C achieve, we no longer control for these things.

A third problem with tournament schemes, especially those that reward only the top performance, is that the prize must be increasingly large as the number of people in the tournament grows. If 500 salespersons all compete for a free dinner, they are unlikely to pay it much attention; for a 500-person tournament, it may take a week in the Bahamas to see much effect. To deal with this, it is often more effective to provide rewards to the top 10% of performers, rather than the top one (or two or three) individuals.

Related to this is the problem that arises when different participants in the tournament have different skill levels. If salesperson X is better than Y and Z, and all of them know it, or if X has a better client list, and all three know that, giving a prize to whomever sells the most may not have much of an impact. It may even have a negative impact, if Y and Z resent that they have little chance to win. Beyond this psychological risk, Y and Z may see increased effort as pointless, since X is bound to win. And if X anticipates that this is how Y and Z see matters, then X need not try very hard to win. In theory, handicapping the results can help here. But, handicapping, if done even somewhat subjectively, invites corruption; for instance, Z takes the boss to lunch, hoping to persuade her to favor him in the handicap scheme. If handicapping is done on a historical basis (X has won in the previous three quarters, so to win he must outperform Y and Z by more than 20% this quarter), then pernicious dynamic effects intrude; if X knows she will be penalized next period for doing well now, her incentives to perform well in this period are lessened. There are other important dynamic problems with tournaments; see the general discussion of dynamic effects in incentive schemes that follows.

Group Incentives and Internal Monitoring

At the other extreme from tournaments are situations in which incentives are tied to group performance. Each worker is a member of a work group, and the bonus the worker receives depends on how the group performs. The main negative associated with group incentive schemes is the free-rider problem: Because each individual has proportionately little impact on the final outcome, each has less motivation to try hard. Despite this, group incentive schemes are often used, for a variety of reasons:

- The production process may not be conducive to the measurement of anything other than group output. When production is on a continuous flow process or an assembly line, no single worker has much control over the level of output.

- Rewarding individual output may cause workers to look only to their own level of output, without regard to how others are doing. In situations where workers can assist each other to the benefit of the total outcome, some reward for offering assistance should be offered. Tying compensation to the level of output of the group promotes helping efforts within the group.

- Small groups have a great advantage in self-monitoring, especially when the group works together in close proximity to one another. By rewarding at the level of the group, the firm promotes monitoring of members of the group by other members.

At the risk of overdoing it, let me develop the third point further. Providing group-based incentive schemes, especially when the group is small, can be advantageous when three factors come together: good measures of the quality of group performance are available, members of the group can monitor each other's individual effort levels easily and accurately, and groups have at their disposal the means and the inclination to enforce a healthy group norm for hard work. The means can include the ability to punish slackers, either immediately or in future dealings, and the ability to enforce social sanctions on slackers. The inclination is trickier; one needs to watch out for groups that adopt a norm in which no one works hard, groups that have dysfunctional social relations, and groups that may scapegoat individual members.

Incentives in Dynamic Settings

Most incentive problems arise in settings that are more dynamic than the very stark, static setting of a single period of sales. Salespersons deal with not one customer but many, and they deal with their customers sequentially. Imagine, say, a tournament scheme in which the top salesperson over the period of a month gets an especially large bonus. If salespersons are able to keep track of how everyone is doing through the month, and if after the second week or so, one salesperson has built up a big lead, then that salesperson may coast, as may others; the others recognize that if they get close to the leader, the leader will speed up, while the leader is willing to sit on her lead. Everyone slows down, just what the firm does not want in terms of the incentives it provides. On the other hand, if the contest is close as the month comes to an end, those in or near the lead may take actions not in the interest of the firm, such as making sales to clients who are likely to default on their orders or their payments, simply to win the contest.

Dynamic effects arise as well when incentives are based on the performance of the individual only. Suppose I promise you a reward if you are able to sell $20 million or more over some fiscal year. Suppose that three-quarters of the way through the year, you have sold $21 million. You can safely coast for the rest of the year. Or, suppose that, three-quarters of the way through the year, you have sold $7 million. Now you "coast" for a different reason: There is no chance you will meet your goals so why struggle? The incentive effects of a bonus-if-hurdle-met scheme kick in largely during the early stages of the period and then very powerfully at the end, if the goal is in sight but not yet met. Even here there are problems: What will you do to make one final sale in the fiscal year if, with two workdays left to go in the year, your sales for the year sit at $19.8 million?

The effects in the previous paragraph result from the combination of two factors: The salesperson can monitor the likelihood of meeting the goal as the year progresses, and the reward scheme is discontinuous in the sense that there is a big jump in compensation if a particular hurdle level is met. The problems caused by these factors can be controlled to some extent— even to large extent—if the reward scheme is continuous; for instance, if the bonus is a flat percentage of sales generated for the entire period, or if the salesperson gets, say, 1% of sales for any sales over a $5 million total, rising to 2% for incremental sales beyond a $10 million total.

Another worry is, Where do target levels or hurdles come from? Often they are based on how the individual did the previous year; for instance, a salesperson (he) earns a bonus for improving his sales level from the previous year by, say, 5%. This sort of goal-setting procedure is subject to a host of problems, associated with the rubric of *the ratchet effect*.

1. The salesperson has an absolute disincentive to beat last year's sales figure by any more than 5%, since doing so will only make it harder for the next year.

2. Three-quarters of the way through the year, the salesperson who realizes that the 5% improvement will not be met has an incentive to go into the tank for the remainder of the year, to make the next year easier.

3. The salesperson who has a really good year acquires an incentive to get another job, because the hurdle for next year will be very high.

On the other side of this story, when individuals interact through time, we can use time and the promise (threat) of good (bad) treatment in the future to provide incentives. Executives in a corporation may need no incentive to work hard early in their career other than their career aspirations; there may be no need to tie their immediate compensation to their immediate performance.

Other-Than-Effort Incentives and Multitask Jobs

The notion that people must be motivated to work hard sometimes is relevant, for instance, for day laborers hired to pull tree stumps. In many cases of interest, however, it is not relevant at all. The issue is not motivating people to work hard but motivating them to direct their efforts in a manner that is best for the organization and to avoid motivating efforts that are ultimately counterproductive. For instance, in a piece-rate compensation system, a fixed amount, the piece rate, is paid for each unit produced. This motivates speed but not quality. Where quality is easily measured, it is easy to repair matters: The piece-rate is paid only for high-quality output, or the employee must rework (without additional compensation) defective units.

But what if quality is hard to measure? For instance, in the provision of a service, the number of clients served is easy to measure, but it is often much harder to obtain reliable statistics on whether the service provided was appropriate, clients were treated respectfully, and so forth. In such cases, and in all jobs that mix easy-to-measure and harder-to-measure tasks, a problem arises: If compensation is tied strongly to the easy-to-measure aspects of performance but not to the harder-to-measure aspects, the employee is motivated to ignore the harder-to-measure aspects. (In a simple piece-rate system, employees ignore quality to maximize quantity.) But to tie compensation strongly to both the easy-to-measure and the harder-to-measure aspects of performance is either expensive, if it is costly to measure the harder-to-measure aspects, or introduces risk into compensation levels, if the harder-to-measure aspects involve imprecise or noisy measures. The latter means a lot of risk inefficiently loaded on the employee. The only way out is to go easy on direct incentives altogether and deal with loafers by other means, such as with appeals to professional pride and so forth.

Stock Options for Top Managers

Top managers have jobs that are especially multitask in character, so that providing them with good direct incentives is especially tricky. On grounds that the value of shareholder equity is a good proxy for what is good for the organization, compensation for top managers is sometimes tied to the price of the firm's equity, often through the granting of stock options, which allow top managers to buy shares in the company at a fixed price.

Stock options given to executives have been controversial, in terms of how they should be reported in a firm's financial accounting statements and for the level of income they provide top managers. But their basic raison d'être has been pretty noncontroversial. They are meant to tie the compensation of top management to the fortunes of the enterprise, thus aligning the interests of top managers with those of equity holders. Stock options are used, the story goes, because the market price of equity most accurately captures how the enterprise is doing; market prices capture the value of the firm better than any formula because market prices are set by savvy investors interested in predicting the future value of the firm.

This is a nice story, but as events in 2002 have shown, the assumption on which this story is based (that the market price of equity reflects the true value of the firm) may be flawed. The market price of a firm's equity necessarily reflects the information that equity markets possess, and to the extent that top management can manipulate financial statements, top management may be able to manipulate, at least for a while, the price of equity. Thus stock options given to top management may contain the seeds of a classic multi-task incentives problem or, worse, a problem of *mal*aligned incentives. Top management, provided with options keyed to the market price of the firm's equity, are motivated to inflate that market price. Top management can, as originally intended, serve that incentive by improving the economic fortunes of the firm. But they can also serve that incentive by engaging in accounting practices that paint a rosier picture of the firm's prospects than is the truth, hoping to cash in the options and get their money before their misleading accounting practices have been discovered.

Psychological and Social Effects

This brings us to a brief closing comment about incentives and moral hazard problems, at least as discussed in this chapter. Except for some remarks near the beginning about intrinsic motivation and the like, the approach in this chapter has been resolutely economic in nature. We assume that, to motivate an individual, tangible incentives have to be put in place. Without those incentives, individuals loaf or otherwise take actions that serve their private agendas exclusively.

If you view them through the lens of social psychology and organizational sociology, you can get a very different take on many of these issues. Individuals are not so resolutely self-centered or selfish as economic models assume. They are sometimes motivated by an intrinsic pride in what they do. They can internalize the welfare of the organization for which they work. They avoid behavior they consider unethical. Moreover, and very important, the degree to which they are motivated by pride in what they do, by the fortunes of their organization, and by ethical considerations can be negatively affected by the extent to which they are subject to explicit, extrinsic incentive schemes. By explicitly tying someone's compensation to concrete measures of performance, the organization may legitimate actions that improve those measures, even if the actions mean a shoddy overall performance, a worse outcome for the organization, or bent ethical principles.

I do not want to delve too deeply into this now. We return to these and related points in Chapter 25. For now, the message I want to leave you with is that the analysis of this chapter is predicated on a particularly dim and simple view of human nature. It is not a view of human nature that is without foundation, but human nature is, in many cases, more complex than this chapter assumes. Before taking any of this too seriously, I suggest you read Chapter 25.

Executive Summary

- When a party to a transaction takes an action that affects the value of the transaction to the other side, a potential *moral hazard* exists: Will the action chosen by the first party be to the detriment of the second party? Means for dealing with problems of moral hazard include good will and honesty on the part of the first party, contractual enforcement of an agreed-to action, observability of the action chosen and a means by which the second party can reward the first if the action chosen is "correct" (see Chapter 22), general observability of the action chosen and a desire on the part of the first party to preserve that party's reputation (see Chapter 23), and direct and explicit incentives, based on some observable measure or signal of the action chosen.

- In many problems in which explicit incentive schemes are used, the individual subject to the incentive scheme does not fully control the observable measure or signal on which the incentive is based. Thus, to employ the incentive scheme subjects the individual to risk, which gives rise to a basic trade-off: Efficient risk sharing (usually) mandates shielding the individual from this risk, but unless some risk is imposed, there is no motivation.

- Beyond this basic trade-off of risk sharing (and shielding) versus motivation, incentives give rise to a host of complications and extensions. Incentive schemes should be robust to the characteristics of the individual being motivated and the situation in which motivation is being applied. Incentive schemes often screen as well as motivate. Tournament schemes and benchmarking can, if used carefully, help control the risk to which the motivated individual is subject. In some instances, group-based incentive schemes can be employed. Dynamic aspects of incentive schemes (where the choices of the first individual are taken over time) should be carefully considered. Most incentive schemes are found in situations where the individual being motivated has a multi-dimensional choice of "effort."

The impact of a given incentive scheme on the full choice of the individual—not only how hard to work but on what tasks in particular—must be carefully considered. Explicit incentive schemes have social psychological and sociological effects that should not be ignored (see Chapter 25).

Problems

19.1   This problem takes you, step by step, to the precise solution of the salesperson compensation problem of Section 19.1. In fact, we go through this twice, once using spreadsheets and Solver and then doing it by hand.

The key to both ways of solving the problem is to break the problem into pieces. First, for each of the four effort levels, you answer the question: What is the cheapest (in terms of expected compensation) way to motivate the employee to take that effort level? Then, once you have the answers to this question, combine your answers to find the optimal incentive contract.

So, to begin, take the spreadsheet CHAP19. For reference sake, Figure 19.1 is reproduced here as Figure 19.6. Pick one of the four levels of effort; say, tries but not hard. Ask Solver to maximize cell F9 (the firm's expected net profit if the salesperson tries but not hard) varying cells B1 and B2 (the base wage and bonus), subject to the constraints that E9 (the net expected utility from this level of effort) is at least as large as the three other levels of expected utility and the reservation utility of 100 (in cell E12). By telling Solver to keep E9 larger than E8, E10, E11, and E12, you effectively restrict Solver to incentive schemes (base wage and bonus pairs) that lead to *tries but not hard* as the level of effort chosen.

	A	B	C	D	E	F
1	base wage	$9,500				
2	bonus	$15,000				
3						
4	gross utility if sale	156.5247584				
5	gross utility if no sale	97.46794345				
6						
7			EFFORT CHOICE	DISUTILITY	PROB SALE	EU	Expected net profit
8			loafing	0	0.05	100.42	-$7,250
9			tries but not hard	10	0.25	102.23	$1,750
10			works hard	20	0.4	101.09	$8,500
11			kills self	40	0.5	86.996	$13,000
12			reservation level			100	
13							

Figure 19.6. A spreadsheet for analyzing different incentive contracts. This is sheet 1 of the spreadsheet CHAP19.

The result is shown in Figure 19.7: The best scheme has a base wage of $9506 and a bonus of $12,250, for an expected net profit of $2431.

	A	B	C	D	E	F
1	base wage	$9,506				
2	bonus	$12,250				
3						
4	gross utility if sale	147.5				
5	gross utility if no sale	97.49999968				
6						
7		EFFORT CHOICE	DISUTILITY	PROB SALE	EU	Expected net profit
8		loafing	0	0.05	99.9999997	-$7,119
9		tries but not hard	10	0.25	99.9999998	$2,431
10		works hard	20	0.4	97.4999998	$9,594
11		kills self	40	0.5	82.4999998	$14,369
12		reservation level			100	

CHAP19 — Sheet1 / Sheet2 / Sheet3

Figure 19.7. Finding the cheapest way to induce tries, but not hard. We ask Solver to maximize cell F9, varying B1 and B2, subject to the constraints that E9 is at least as large as E8, E10, E11, and E12. This is the answer it provides.

I said we would find the expected-compensation-minimizing scheme for inducing *tries but not hard*, then instructed Solver to maximize the expected net profit for that choice of effort. Recognize that, fixing the action, the two are the same: The expected net profit is just the probability of a sale given the chosen action (0.25 in this case) times the gross value to the firm of a sale ($60,000), less the expected compensation to the salesperson. In other words, since the gross contribution to the firm of this action is $(0.25)(\$60,000) = \$15,000$, when Solver reports that the maximized expected net profit is $1750, it is telling you that the minimum expected compensation to get that effort level is $\$15,000 - \$2431 = \$12,569$. Just to check this computation: The expected level of compensation is the base wage of $9506, plus the bonus of $12,250 paid with probability 0.25, or an expected $3062.50, for a total expected compensation of $12,568.50.

Now redo this for the other three levels of effort. Then combine the results to get the answer. (See the solution in the *Student's Companion*, if what I want you to do here is not obvious.)

As for doing this by hand, let me write B for the base wage and X for the base wage plus bonus; that is, X is the sum of B and the bonus. And let me write b for the square root of B and x for the square root of X. In other words, b and x are the gross levels of utility the salesperson gets, if he does not make or makes a sale, respectively.

We answer by hand the question Solver just answered: What is the cheapest way (in expected compensation) to induce the effort level *tries but not hard*? If the salesperson chooses to try but not hard, the chances of a sale are 0.25, and the disutility of effort is 10, so his expected utility is $0.25x + 0.75b - 10$. If we want the salesperson to try but not hard, this has to be at least as large as 100 (to induce work) and at least as large as the levels of net expected utility for the other three levels of effort, or $0.05x + 0.95b$, $0.4x + 0.6b - 20$, and $0.5x + 0.5b - 40$. We not only want the first of these expected utilities to be larger than 100 and larger than the other three, but we want B and X (or b and x) to be such that the expected compensation cost is as low as possible.

The discussion in the chapter suggests that at the optimizing values of B and X (or b and x), the salesperson gets no more expected utility than he requires to accept the job:

$$0.25x + 0.75b - 10 = 100.$$

And the bonus should just barely induce *try but not hard*. The least incentive to induce this is where the expected utility from *trying but not hard* is equal to the expected utility of the next lower level of effort, *loafing*. So we have the equation

$$0.25x + 0.75b - 10 = 0.05x + 0.95b - 0.$$

(In theory, the left-hand side of this equation should be greater than or equal to the net expected utilities from the three other possible effort level choices. Why is this one the binding constraint? See the solution in the *Student's Companion* for further discussion of this point.) This is two equations in two unknowns, so we can solve for x and for b. Do the algebra, and you'll come up with $b = 97.5$ and $x = 147.5$, and therefore, B, the base wage, is $97.5^2 = \$9506.25$, while the bonus is $X - B$, or $147.5^2 - 97.5^2 = \$12,250$. Compare this answer with what Solver told us.

Now redo this (by hand) for the other three levels of effort, combine your results, and you have the answer (by hand).

If you feel you know what is going on, try to finish off this problem both with the spreadsheet and by hand. If you are not quite there yet, consult the solution in the *Student's Companion*, then try Problems 19.2 and 19.3, which are solved the same way, although the contexts are insurance and venture capital.

19.2 As an insurance underwriter, you have been asked to write a policy that insures a factory against loss by fire for a period of 1 year. If the factory has a fire, it will be a total loss of $8 million. The owner of the factory is an expected utility maximizer, with (gross) utility function $\sqrt{x + 1 \text{ million}}$, where x is the value of the factory at year's end; that is, x = $8 million if there is no fire and x = $0 if there is a fire. Your insurance company is risk neutral.

The chance of a fire depends on whether the owner of the factory takes due care. If he does not, the chance of a fire over the 1-year period is 0.05. If he does take due care, the chance of a fire over the 1-year period is 0.01. To take due care is psychologically wearing on the owner and lowers his expected utility by 50. That is, if the factory owner's overall utility depends on both x and on his decision whether to take due care or not, with

$$U(x, \text{no due care}) = \sqrt{x + 1 \text{ million}} - 0 \quad \text{and}$$
$$U(x, \text{due care}) = \sqrt{x + 1 \text{ million}} - 50.$$

(a) If the factory owner cannot get insurance for the building, will he choose to take due care or not? What will be his overall expected utility?

(b) The insurance company wishes to maximize its expected profit from writing insurance for this factory owner. If it could contractually specify the level of care taken by the factory owner, what policy or contract would it write? (When the factory owner takes insurance, x in his utility function is adjusted down by the amount of any premiums he pays and up by any indemnification he receives from the insurance company in the event of fire.)

(c) Suppose the insurance company cannot contractually specify the level of care taken by the factory owner. Suppose as well that, in the pursuit of efficient risk sharing, the insurance company is determined to insure the building fully; that is, it will write a policy that pays the owner $8 million in the event of a fire. What is the best (profit-maximizing) policy of this sort the insurance company can write?

(d) The insurance company decides to investigate insurance policies with a deductible. That is, it will charge a premium P and, in the event of a fire, reimburse the factory owner $8 million less some prespecified deductible amount. What is the best (profit-maximizing) policy of this sort that the insurance company can write? Please do this by hand and not using Excel.

(e) Suppose that taking due care does not involve a "psychological cost" that lowers gross utility but instead comes at a dollar cost of, say, $100,000.

That is, in the factory owner's utility function $\sqrt{x + 1\text{ million}}$, x includes the value of the building, less any premiums paid for insurance, plus any indeminification from the insurance company in the event of fire, less $100,000 if the owner takes due care. This change in formulation makes the problem harder to solve (by hand). Why? Do not grind through the numbers unless you want practice using spreadsheets; simply redo the four previous parts of the problem with this reformulation, until you get to calculations that are too hard to do by hand.

19.3 An entrepreneur has a venture that will make either $100 million or $0. The chance that this venture will make $100 million depends on the effort level expended by the entrepreneur: If she tries hard, the chance of the $100 million outcome is 0.1. If she does not try hard, the chance of this outcome is 0.02. This entrepreneur is risk averse, with utility function

$$\sqrt{x} - \text{disutility of effort},$$

where the disutility of effort is 0 if the entrepreneur does not try hard and 500 if she does.

(a) Assuming this entrepreneur bears all the risk of this venture, will she try hard or not? What will be her expected utility, net of the disutility of effort (if any)?

(b) A risk-neutral venture capitalist is prepared to support this venture. Specifically, the venture capitalist will pay the entrepreneur a base amount B up front, in return for which the venture capitalist will retain X out of the $100 million the venture generates, if the venture succeeds. Assuming this venture capitalist is the entrepreneur's only alternative to going it alone (doing whatever you determined the answer was in part a), and assuming the venture capitalist can make part of his contract with the entrepreneur a specification of her effort level, what is the optimal contract of this sort for the venture capitalist to write? What will be the venture capitalist's net expected monetary value with this contract?

(c) Unhappily, the venture capitalist cannot contractually specify the effort level of the entrepreneur. If the venture capitalist wishes to motivate the entrepreneur to try hard, he must do this with the terms B and X in the contract he provides. What is the best contract for the venture capitalist to offer the entrepreneur, assuming that if the entrepreneur does not accept this contract, she is stuck going it alone on this venture?

20. Porter's Five Forces and Economics with Identities

This chapter, after a bit of introduction, concerns Michael Porter's *five forces*, a scheme for organizing facts about a particular industry that bear on how profitable firms in the industry will be. Porter suggests organizing the data into the categories of *rivalry, supplier power, customer power, substitute products*, and *barriers to entry*.

In 1974, the disposable diaper business in the United States, a very profitable business, was largely controlled by Procter and Gamble (P&G), which held a 69% market share.[1] Kimberly-Clark held another 17%, and 9% of the market took the form of private label sales. The business was extremely profitable for P&G; P&G's pretax income from diaper sales was estimated to be $55 million, a return on sales of 25%. (In comparison, P&G's income from all other lines of business was approximately $245 million, a return on sales of 6.9%.) Profits on this scale attracted entry into the industry, and the early 1970s saw entry by both Johnson & Johnson (J&J), the well-known health and baby care products firm, and Union Carbide, a major manufacturer of chemicals and plastics, which was aiming to expand into consumer products from a base in batteries. P&G regarded J&J fairly benignly, as an entrant not to be discouraged, if not exactly encouraged. But P&G had no desire to admit Union Carbide into the industry; and as Union Carbide tested the waters in the disposable diaper business, P&G pulled out all stops, competing viciously and successfully. Union Carbide was driven from the market.

Chapters 11 through 14 primarily concern perfectly competitive markets, markets with a large number of anonymous buyers and sellers. The items concerned are commodities; it does not matter to either buyer or seller who are their specific trading partners or who are their rivals.

But, as most parents who have used disposable diapers will tell you, disposable diapers are not commodity items. And, even more, from the perspective of P&G, competition from J&J is not the same as competition from Union Carbide. An economic theory that would be useful for understanding the interactions between P&G, J&J, and Union Carbide would not be a theory of impersonal, anonymous markets, but a theory in which the

---

[1] For details and all figures reported here, see "The Disposable Diaper Industry in 1974," Harvard Business School Case 9-380-175, revised 1981, reprinted in Michael E. Porter, *Cases in Competitive Strategy* (New York: The Free Press, 1983).

identities of competitors matter.

It is not simply a matter of competitors. The identities of suppliers matter, as we see in Chapter 24, where we discuss the Toyota system of supply-chain management through subcontractors. The identity of customers can matter; think for instance of the relationship between Intel and IBM. And the identity of firms that are not competitors, suppliers, or customers can matter, for instance, in the relationship between Boeing and General Electric, in GE's role as the manufacturer of jet engines.

All these are examples of economic relationships between large industrial firms. Identities also matter in more personal economic relations, as between, for instance, client and lawyer. Or consider the relationship between employer and employee, which I believe is the most interesting and important economic relationship of all.

This is not to say that the economics of large, impersonal, anonymous markets is unimportant. A large slice of the economy can be studied fruitfully with models of such markets. But, in an even larger slice of the economy, identities matter; and we need different models and tools for these situations.

This chapter and the next provide two very different sets of tools for dealing with pieces of economics with identity. The next chapter provides a general language and style of analysis, noncooperative game theory, that is very useful for framing and studying all sorts of economic situations where identity matters. But first, I want to discuss the important context of oligopoly, industries in which a few large firms compete.

This discussion is oriented around two sets of questions:

1. What determines how profitable are firms in an oligopoly? More specifically, what was it about the disposable diaper industry that made P&G so profitable?

2. What can a firm within such an industry do to improve its profits? What could P&G have done to ensure continuing high profits?

A lot of effort has gone into constructing and testing theories that address the first set of questions, with obvious implications for the second. The result of this effort is that we know a lot of variables that bear on profitability, but how those variables combine in specific instances—which variables are decisive and which unimportant—remains a matter of guesswork and inspiration.

Because so many variables bear on profitability, it can be hard in specific cases just to keep track. It is helpful, therefore, to have a filing system for sorting through the facts concerning a specific case. Perhaps the most popular and widely used filing system, applied to profitability of firms, is by Michael Porter, as formulated initially in *Competitive Strategy* (New York:

The Free Press, 1980). In Porter's framework, you examine the situation of a particular firm by looking at five groups of factors, the so-called *five forces*:

- *Rivalry* among existing firms in the industry, the discipline of competition among the firm and its direct rivals.

- *Potential entrants* (and barriers to entry and mobility).

- *Substitute products* (and complements).

- The bargaining power of *customers*.

- The bargaining power of *suppliers*.

Roughly, according to Porter, a firm is more profitable, the less intense is the rivalry in its industry; the less danger of potential entrants and the higher the barriers to entry; the fewer substitute products for what it sells, the more restrained the firms that sell those substitute products, and the more aggressive and numerous the firms that sell complementary goods; and the weaker the bargaining power of its customers and suppliers. In the practice of *industry and competitive analysis*, firms analyze their position along these dimensions and seek ways to shift environmental conditions to be more favorable to the firm.

The rest of this chapter puts some meat on this very bare skeleton. This consists of fairly loose verbal theorizing; unlike most of this book, symbols, algebra, and calculus play no role. I say a lot about what sorts of things are apt to increase or decrease profitability, without the benefit of a formal model of the situation. Indeed, before we are done with these ideas, we'll see situations in which the basic Porteresque theory needs to be qualified. In Chapter 24, for instance, we see a reason why strengthening the hands of suppliers can improve profits. So, take what you read in this chapter with a grain of salt. I use the case of disposable diapers to illustrate the concepts. Although the case concerns an industry almost 30 years ago, it remains one of the best vehicles for exploring these ideas.

20.1. What Is the Industry? What Are Important Niches?

In Porter's framework, the unit of analysis is the industry more than the individual firm. Firms within a given industry are differentially profitable, depending on firm-specific factors. But the first-level analysis concerns profitability of the industry as a whole. This is because Porter focuses on factors that affect all members of the industry; if those factors are favorable for one firm in the industry, they generally are favorable for all.

There is room for differences in profitability among firms inside the industry. In Porter's framework, we explain those differences by noting the different conditions facing different firms; we discuss *niches* inside the industry. For instance, in the handheld calculator industry, Texas Instruments inhabited the high-volume, high-quality niche, by virtue of which TI had low costs for having ridden the experience curve the farthest, leading to high profitability for TI relative to firms in other high-quality niches.

The initial task in carrying out a Poteresque analysis, then, is to define what constitutes the industry. Does the industry that includes Coca-Cola and Pepsi also include Royal Crown? Snapple? Vittel? Anheiser-Busch? Gallo? Seagrams? This list can be continued along a path that takes us, a step at a time to, say, Foster Farms, a producer of packaged chicken. It is relatively clear that Foster Farms is not in the same industry as Coca-Cola and Pepsi. But where is the line drawn? The question to address is, In terms of the five forces, which firms face roughly similar conditions and which exist in a different, if related, universe? There are no hard-and-fast rules here; you must rely on judgment in specific instances. And in some sense, drawing a single line is not logical; the world is not in or out but a matter of degree. Two things make drawing the line less than crucial:

1. If too expansive a definition is used, you can still use the notion of niches within an industry to get to a more useful unit of analysis.

2. If you draw the lines too tightly, the third factor, *substitute products*, captures firms you place outside the industry; wherever you draw the line, you do not ignore the impact of outside firms.

Example: Disposable Diapers

The major question concerning the definition of the industry in this case is whether to include cloth diapers, either washed at home or procured through a diaper service, in the industry. If we include either form of cloth diapers in the industry, then the disposables become a distinct niche. If we do not include them, then home-washed and diaper-service diapers are substitute products. In either case, the most useful unit of analysis is the firms that manufacture disposables, since the technology of manufacture, distribution, and use of cloth diapers is very different from disposables. There is no right answer to the question, Are cloth diapers in the industry or not? You can proceed either way. So we choose to rule them out of the industry: The industry is disposables, and cloth diapers are substitute products.

Having defined the industry, the five factors are examined one by one. I leave rivalry to the end, for reasons that will become apparent.

20.2. Substitute and Complementary Products

The force of *substitute products* reminds us that the ability of firms within an industry to make large profits through the imposition of high prices is limited, at least to some extent, by the existence of substitute products. In part, this is a simple matter of demand elasticities; the more and better substitutes there are for the product in question, the higher the elasticity of demand facing the industry and the lower the profits the firms within the industry can achieve. But, in looking at substitutes, one also has to think through the nature of firms in the substitute industry: Do they compete vigorously, trying to expand their market at the expense of the market in question? Or, if firms in the primary industry raise prices, will firms in the substitute product industry be restrained in their attempts to take advantage?

When looking at a particular industry, you should be pretty liberal in your use of the term *substitutes*. In practice, there is sometimes a tendency to look for tangible substitute products: Commerical airlines see bus, train, and highway transportation as subsitutes. But if the industry is, say, commercial air transportation between major European cities and a large fraction of that business or its profits comes from business travel, think at least prospectively of teleconferencing and other ways of doing business across a distance when you think of "substitutes."

While Porter's original list did not explicitly consider the impact of *complementary goods*, in some cases complements can be as important as or more important than substitutes. Software vendors such as Microsoft must concern themselves with the actions of microcomputer and chip manufacturers and vice versa. Makers of air-engines must be concerned with the actions of airframe manufacturers. In general, what is good for you concerning the producers of substitutes is bad concerning the producers of complementary goods and vice versa. For example, the air-engine manufacturers benefit from the cutthroat competition of Boeing and Airbus, because lower airframe prices mean increased demand for airframes, which means a more robust market for air engines.

Disposable Diapers, Continued

For firms in the disposable diaper industry, the obvious substitute products are cloth diapers, purchased by families that do their own laundry, and diaper service firms that provide laundered cloth diapers, picking up soiled diapers for cleaning and reuse.

Diaper services are a more convenient alternative to home laundry but also a more expensive alternative. The diaper-service industry was quite fragmented, which normally means a more competitive industry and bad for the disposable diaper industry, but the industry was typically quite concentrated on a local basis, with constant allegations of local price fixing, which is good for disposables.

The big advantage of disposables is convenience in use and disposal. This is particularly true when baby and parent(s) travel. Hence, a rise in general mobility acts as a complement to disposable diapers; airline deregulation was good for the disposable diaper business.

20.3. The Bargaining Power of Customers and Suppliers

The power of firms inside an industry to make substantial profits depends on how strong they are vis-à-vis their suppliers and customers. The seven sister oil refiners were once the epitome of a strong oligopoly, until OPEC came along and raised the price of crude oil. Major airlines and large airplane leasing companies are able to insist on preferential treatment from the airframe manufacturers Boeing and Airbus and from air-engine manufacturers, such as Pratt & Whitney, GE, and Rolls Royce, which erodes the profits of the manufacturers.

What makes a customer or supplier powerful? Among the factors are these:

- The supplier has a unique franchise on a particular product required by firms in the industry, protected by patents or some other barrier to entry.

- The supplier industry is not restrained by any close substitutes for its product.

- The supplier industry is concentrated (meaning very few firms) with firms that are not aggressively rivalrous with each other.

- The client industry is highly concentrated.

- The client industry takes a very large share of the products of the industry in question. For example, tire manufacturers are at a substantial disadvantage vis-à-vis the auto assemblers, because such a large percentage of their output is sold to the auto assemblers.

- The product being sold is inessential to the clients. (This is, more or less, the problem of substitutes all over again.)

- The cost of the product being sold is a substantial fraction of the client's total costs—or, if the client is a consumer, the client's budget—so that the client is apt to resist attempts to push up prices.

You will see many more items on lists like this one in more complete treatments of this subject. Sometimes you see items that are less than clear. For instance, it is sometimes asserted that a supplier is more powerful the less important the industry is to the supplier's overall demand. The reasoning is that, the less important the industry is to suppliers, the better able the suppliers are to tell the industry to "take it or leave it." But the more important the industry is to suppliers, the more attention the suppliers pay to the industry and the greater the efforts they expend to get as much out of the industry as they can. Put the other way around, suppliers may be unwilling to spend the effort required to get the most they can out of an industry that represents a small share of the suppliers' business. This may depend, in turn, on the extent to which the supplier's overall reputation is affected by what it does vis-à-vis this industry, a topic we discuss in Chapter 23. There are no easy answers, either theoretical or empirical, along this dimension.

Moreover, the notion that more powerful suppliers or customers means less profit is, perhaps, true on average. But under certain circumstances, empowering suppliers or customers can increase profits. The details, which involve a closer look at economic relationships, are supplied in Chapter 24. For now, simply note that there is more to this story than the straightforward admonitions to avoid powerful suppliers or customers and to avoid empowering either group.

Disposable Diapers, Continued

The position of the manufacturers of disposable diapers vis-à-vis their suppliers and customers was fairly strong, very strong in the case of P&G. Diapers are manufactured in a continuous flow process, using large, complex machines. The raw materials are the outer and inner liners and the fluff pulp filler that absorbs the "moisture." Paper and woodproduct firms, such as Kimberly-Clark, produced their own fluff pulp. P&G must buy it, but several large paper or woodproduct firms would welcome the business. Outer liners come from large plastics firms and are not extraordinarily specialized. Inner liners, which ideally let moisture cross in only one direction, are more specialized, produced by Kendall, J&J, Sterns & Foster, and Dexter Corporation, a fairly concentrated group but perhaps not as powerful as the diaper manufacturers. The diaper forming machines are crucial to low-cost production, and one might imagine that manufacturers of these machines have substantial bargaining power. But this power is substantially diluted because newly purchased diaper forming machines are not themselves very valuable. A brand new machine might produce 125 diapers a minute, but by making on-site improvements to a given machine, based on its own proprietary experience and knowledge, the diaper manufacuter could triple this rate of production. Other "suppliers" to the production process included transportation services (most firms in the industry had their own distribution systems) and labor, largely semiskilled. Overall, then, some suppliers have some power (the manufacturers of the forming machines and of the inner liners are the best bets here), but on balance the suppliers to this industry are probably not as strong as industry participants.

Diapers in 1973 were largely (70%) sold in supermarkets, with a small but dramatically increasing fraction of sales coming from mass merchandisers such as K-Mart. Sales to supermarkets and drugstores were via wholesale brokers on fixed commissions; sales to mass merchandisers were probably more likely to be direct. Supermarkets and drugstores, even the large chains, were much more fragmented than the producers of diapers, and it is easy to imagine that a consumer expendables manufacturer such as P&G had tremendous bargaining leverage with these outlets. P&G's bargaining power with a national mass merchandiser such as K-Mart was probably somewhat reduced, but it still seems likely that P&G would be at something of an advantage relative to those firms. (In 1973, warehouse distributers such as Costco and Price Club did not exist; it is interesting to contemplate how these outlets would have affected the wholesale margins received by firms such as P&G.)

Because disposable diapers take up enormous amounts of shelf space, they are expensive for retailers to stock. So, while P&G might be in a relatively strong bargaining position vis-à-vis retailers, one imagines that smaller firms or new entrants would have a harder time.

Going the final step in the distribution chain to consumers, disposable diapers, and specific brands of diapers, are somewhat addictive. Parents who begin with disposable diapers for newborns are likely to continue through toilet training, and parents who find success with a particular brand (success being defined as no leaks) are unlikely to switch brands to save a small amount of money. Therefore, profits to the manufacturers in this business are highest for diapers for toddlers; diapers for newborns are sold with much smaller margins and are even given away in gift-packs presented the parents as they leave the hospital with their new baby.

20.4. Potential Entrants (and Barriers to Entry and Mobility)

If the firms in an industry are profitable, firms outside the industry are likely to attempt to enter, to share in the good times. Insofar as this entry is successful, the good times worsen somewhat for the incumbent firms. Therefore, firms in a profitable industry remain profitable to the extent that barriers to entry impede potential entrants.

Tangible Barriers

Economists focus on two classes of entry barriers, tangible barriers and psychological barriers. Tangible barriers are anything that would put an entrant at a disadvantage in the competition that would ensue after entry takes place. These things tangibly determine the "rules" of the postentry game between incumbents and new entrants. Among the tangible barriers to entry are these:

1. *Scale-based cost advantages.* When production involves substantial fixed costs, large-volume producers have relatively lower average costs. If it comes to a fight or shakeout in the industry, such firms are better able to withstand price cutting. When firms in an industry are large and have substantial fixed costs, so that efficient scale is large, then size itself may be a barrier to entry.

   But this assumes a fight will ensue on entry. A firm with a large market may be unable or unwilling to compete with a small entrant that bites off a small piece of its market, for fear of losing profits in the bulk of its market. This can have particularly dramatic consequences when the large firm does not realize that the entrant will, eventually, become a powerful rival. When discount brokerage first appeared, the traditional stock brokerage firms by and large adopted a wait and see policy, preferring not to lower their very profitable brokerage rates. They waited, they saw, and they got crunched. In one of the more colorful dialects of Economese, this is known as the *fat-cat* effect.

2. *Scope-based cost advantages.* *Scale* refers to the volume of output of a particular good. Complementing scale-based cost advantages are scope-based advantages where certain (fixed) costs can be shared among a number of different products. In consumer marketing, for example, distribution can be cheaper for a firm that sells a wide variety of products. Alfred P. Sloan built GM on the basis of scope-based cost advantages, where the development of car technology in one division such as Pontiac could be shared with other divisions, say, Chevrolet. As noted in Chapters 3 and 9, Sloan also relied on scope economies in the sale of cars, getting repeat customers to stay within the GM family while trading up from Chevrolet to Pontiac or Buick to Oldsmobile and finally to Cadillac.

3. *Knowledge-based cost advantages.* Firms may hold proprietary information concerning how to do things cheaply and efficiently. This knowledge may be built up by experience or accumulated by years of R&D. Whatever its source, potential entrants that lack this knowledge may be impeded from entering, at least directly. For example, Boeing and Airbus have

(as of 2002) resisted entry by Japanese firms through their tight control of the "technology" of building large airframes. On the 777, Boeing subcontracts tail assemblies to Japanese firms, which one might think would give those firms an entrée into the business. But the most know-how-intensive portion of airframe manufacture is the manufacture of wings, and Boeing has resisted offers by Japanese firms to subcontract all or part of wing assembly.

In industries with substantial experience-curve effects, where unit costs fall with cumulative volume of production, cumulative volume can be a substantial barrier to entry. For example, in the early years of handheld calculators, Texas Instruments rode the experience curve to a ferocious cost advantage in basic calculators, which for a while kept them dominant in the market.

4. *Financial resources and extending market power.* When firms in an industry face entry, their ability to fight off that entry, by cutting prices and so forth, depends on the financial resources they can command. So the possession of financial resources inside the industry deters entry. Financial resources can be obtained from capital markets (having low debt to equity gives the firm leverage in raising capital quickly) or it can be obtained internally. In the latter case, we have *extending market power*: Firms that are powerful in some industries can use the financial resources this strength gives them to impede entry into other areas of their businesses.

5. *Favored access to particular resources.* If firms inside the industry have favored access to resources that are useful or even essential for efficient production, entry is impeded. Airlines, insofar as they make money at all, do so in large measure because they can control slots and counter space at particular airports. The classic competitive strategy of hub and spoke in commercial passenger air transport, in addition to having basic production efficiencies, also gives the airline a strong-enough presence at its hub to impede entry into that particular market by new carriers. Control of landing slots at favorable times by existing airlines is another barrier to the entry of new airlines.

6. *Favored access to distribution channels.* When a firm or firms in the industry can more easily reach the ultimate customers or impede competitor access to distribution channels, a formidable barrier to entry is created. For instance, Sabre, the chief computer-based information system concerning airline schedules and fares, was a creation of and, until 1996, a subsidiary of American Airlines, which American is alleged to have used to its considerable advantage.

7. *Customer goodwill and reputation.* A firm that has built up a loyal customer following has placed a substantial barrier to entry in the path of any potential entrant that, to be successful, has to wean the loyal customers away. This is the second half of Alfred P. Sloan's strategy for GM, where he tried to develop customer loyalty to GM. As a variation on this, a new entrant sometimes has difficulty being taken seriously by customers, since it has no track record in the business. Public accounting firms, for instance, rely on reputation with customers to impede competition from new entrants.

8. *Customer lock-in.* A slightly different turn on customer goodwill is customer lock-in, where customers of firm X tend to continue to source from firm X because of after-sale considerations, such as compatibility with existing equipment, economies in repair and maintenance, and so on. This barrier can be dangerous, however: If a firm tries to raise barriers by locking in its customers too strongly, those customers may go elsewhere from the start; see the story about Intel in Chapter 23.

9. *Legal and political restrictions.* Firms may be protected against entry by legal restrictions on entry; government certification or licenses may be required. Firms may also use political levers to impede entry. Examples include trying to obtain special assistance, such as subsidies and low-interest loans from the government and invoking the government to ban foreign competitors from entering.

Psychological Barriers

The list of "tangible" barriers to entry does not exhaust the category, but it gives you a flavor of the more important barriers. Note that *tangible* is in quote marks here; it is hard to see customer goodwill as something entirely tangible. Still, this is tangible compared to the second category of barriers to entry, which are psychological. The idea here is that entrants come to believe that, if they enter, the firms already in the business will react aggressively, regardless of any short-term losses that must be sustained, to force the entrant out.

Fighting off an entrant or two is perhaps the surest way for firms in an industry to gain a reputation for being willing to fight off entrants. (For U.S. firms, at least, it can also be a good way to attract the attention of the Antitrust Division of the Department of Justice, so it can be a mixed blessing.) But there is a question of credibility here, and often firms take tangible actions that add credibility to the psychological barrier they wish to erect. Keeping excess capacity on hand, for either production or distribution, often deters entry. Holding patents and products on the shelf, ready for use when and if needed, is another strong signal. Putting in place a high-fixed, low-variable cost technology is usually taken as a sign that the firm would react aggressively to protect its market share, to keep its capacity utilization high. Some analysts believe that capital structure can also be used to signal aggression—a highly leveraged firm is seemingly compelled to protect its market share, to be able to service its debt—but the evidence on this is mixed. High leverage may raise a psychological barrier, but it may simultaneously lower a tangible barrier; namely, access through the capital markets to a war chest in case war does break out. To threaten implicitly a particular firm that might enter, a firm in the industry may take steps to develop a foothold in the target firm's own backyard, sending the message, "If you invade my territory, your own 'homeland' will not go unscathed."

Mobility Barriers

Just as profitable industries attract entry unless entry is impeded, so do relatively profitable industry niches attract entry from outside the industry and, perhaps more interestingly, from within. Firms occupying a relatively profitable niche within an industry need protection from firms within the industry but outside the niche. To convey that this is within-industry movement, such barriers are called *mobility barriers*.

The list of potential mobility barriers is not much different from the list of entry barriers. But to add to that list, niches can be established by product differentiation when the differentiation is protected by some barrier or another. Patents or copyright production can be particularly useful here, as can specific channels of distribution, customer lock-in, the value (to customers) of dealing with a single supplier, and experience curves specific to the differentiated product. For instance, Apple Computer has been able to maintain relatively high margins for its Macintosh-based computers, relative to the margins obtained by Wintel computer manufacturers, by a combination of legal protections and customer lock-in. The downside of this has been that less software has been developed for Macs because of its relatively small niche, and while Macs continue to be strong in specific applications, such as desktop publishing, it is not clear that this niche strategy will, in the long run, prove to have been wise.

Mobility barriers that accompany differentiation or segmentation strategies may lower overall entry barriers: If companies A and B in an industry segment the market geographically, each is on its own if company X attempts to enter either segment. If A and B share the full market, potential entrant X must figure that either rival could trigger a price war, and the financial resources of both must be taken into account.

Erecting Barriers

Taking a normative message from the preceding discussion, firms inside an industry, to protect themselves, should construct barriers to entry. Firms within a specific niche should construct mobility barriers. There are limits to how much of this is possible (some barriers are fully outside the control of the firms in the industry or niche), but particularly in the psychological realm, barriers can be built and strengthened.

To take another important example, experience-based barriers are constructed out of a large level of experience. A firm that creates a new product or industry and wishes to protect itself from future entrants may, if the production process exhibits an experience-curve effect, increase its production, to build up experience, which means lower costs and higher barriers to entry subsequently. This is more than the investment in lower costs that we saw back in Chapter 10; we might even see a firm raising its prices to milk a market, after it has erected experience-based barriers so high that it need not fear entrants. The term *milking* here is particularly appropriate: This sort of strategy was advocated by the Boston Consulting Group in the early 1980s, where a product or business for which an experience-based entry barrier had been raised was known as a *cash cow*.

Disposable Diapers, Continued

In the disposable diaper business, entry barriers were formidable. The production process, oriented around the huge machine that makes diapers, requires significant capital investment. A strong experience curve takes effect as the manufacturer learns to get more out of a machine. Reputation with consumers is all-important; perhaps P&G accepted the entry of Johnson & Johnson without a vigorous fight because J&J had a natural franchise in anything having to do with babies and because P&G did not believe that J&J had the marketing muscle it would take to become a significant player in the high-volume, low-price part of the business that was P&G's strength. P&G certainly had favored access to channels of distribution, especially with its scope-based advantages on getting shelf space in supermarkets. In terms of shipping costs, P&G's huge market share gave it a cost advantage. Many potential customers (families with newborns) are introduced to disposable diapers in the gift-packs handed out at hospitals as the new parents depart with the baby; P&G had gone to great lengths to tie up that marketing channel. And P&G had cultivated, over the years, a strong reputation for being a vicious competitor, a reputation enhanced when it did everything it could to block Union Carbide as Union Carbide tried to roll out its line of diapers.

20.5. Rivalry

We come, finally, to rivalry. The basic story is simple. Good rivals, in terms of the profits of the industry, are rivals that are restrained in their competition. Taking a more normative approach, there are good rivals to have (firms that will follow your firm's lead; in a segmented industry, firms that are content to tend their own garden and leave you to cultivate your own) and there are bad. A firm, looking for profits, should encourage the former and discourage the latter.

P&G regarded Kimberly-Clark as an excellent rival, because Kimberly-Clark seemed entirely willing to accept its status as number 2 in the industry. P&G found Johnson & Johnson, prospectively, to be a good rival as well: J&J would likely be content with the high-quality end of the market, since that was consistent with J&J's overall image as a provider of high-quality baby products; and the production technology for disposable diapers has a steep experience curve, so such a strategy by J&J would not imperil P&G's position. (In fact, J&J found its volume and experience-based cost disadvantages too much to overcome, and it left the market relatively quickly.)   But Union Carbide was another story altogether.   On a number of grounds, P&G had good reason to regard Union Carbide as a prospectively bad competitor. Union Carbide had exhibited a desire to expand into all sorts of consumer products, such as cleaning agents from its toehold in batteries. Given Union Carbide's strong industrial base, it might eventually become a formidable rival to P&G. So P&G decided to spare no efforts in teaching Union Carbide that it (P&G) was not the sort of rival Union Carbide should choose to have. As it had at its disposal the tools (entry barriers) to oppose Union Carbide's entry, P&G took every opportunity to make sure that Union Carbide learned this lesson well.

20.6. Coming Attractions

To say that restrained rivals are good for profits and vicious rivals are bad is virtually to say that good profits are good for profits. What makes for restraint? Is it a matter of psychology? Are structural and economic factors at work?

To answer these questions and, indeed, to have a better understanding of how entry barriers work or when strengthening a supplier might actually improve profits, we need a better understanding of how firms compete, how trading partners cooperate, and so forth.   And, to understand these things better, we require a language and mode of analysis of competitive and cooperative interactions in which identities matter.

The language and mode of analysis that economists have used to study these things is noncooperative game theory. So, we take a one-chapter break in the discussion and develop some language and analytical skills.

Executive Summary

- This chapter begins a wholesale move from the economics of large, anonymous markets to the economics of interactions and transactions where identities are of paramount importance. This chapter concerns Michael Porter's *five forces*, a scheme for organizing the facts about a given industry or industry niche to get a sense of why firms in the the industry or niche are profitable and how they might improve their levels of profits. Porter suggests organizing salient facts into five boxes: the impact of substitutes and complementary products, the (relative) strength of suppliers, the (relative) strength of customers, entry barriers (both tangible and psychological), and rivalry among firms in the industry or industry niche.

Problems

The material in this chapter does not lend itself particularly well to problems. Instead, you can best learn this material by applying it to the study of specific industries, using cases. I already mentioned the disposable diaper case ("The Disposable Diaper Industry in 1974," HBS 9-380-175). Other cases that provide good exercise in the five factors include "General Electric vs. Westinghouse in Large Turbine Generators (A)," HBS9-380-128; "Crown, Cork and Seal Co., Inc.," HBS9-378-024; and "Rockwell International (A)," HBS9-383-019.

21. Noncooperative Game Theory

The remaining chapters of this book concern economic exchange and economic relationships where identities matter. This often involves situations in which a small number of intelligent parties interact. *To be a good strategist in such situations, try to see world the way your rivals or partners see it, understanding that they are simultaneously trying to understand the world from your perspective and that of each other.*

Economists use *noncooperative game theory* as a tool for framing and analyzing this type of situation. It is a very powerful and flexible tool, employed in many fields of economics applied to management, such as in finance, accounting, marketing, human resource management, and most of all, strategic management.

This chapter covers the basic ideas of noncooperative game theory:

- We discuss two ways to model multiparty interactions, so-called strategic-form and extensive-form games.
- We show how to analyze these models using dominance analysis and Nash equilibrium analysis.

The examples used in this chapter are chosen to be simple—to expose basic concepts clearly—and not to be managerially relevant. After we nail down basic ideas here, managerially relevant applications will appear in the next two chapters.

We begin with a very simple example that illustrates most, if not quite all, the basic ideas of this chapter. Two friends, Sam (she) and Jan (he), must decide independently where to spend a Tuesday evening after dinner. The three possible choices are a bar named Old Pros, an art museum, and a coffee shop named Cafeen. Sam and Jan have preferences over these three spots, but they also have a general desire to be together, rather than apart. More specifically,

- Sam's first choice is to be with Jan at Old Pros, second is to be with Jan at the art museum, third is to be alone at Old Pros, fourth is to be with Jan at Cafeen, fifth is to be at the art museum alone, and last is to be alone at Cafeen.

- Jan's ranking is, from best to worst, be with Sam at Cafeen, be with Sam at the art museum, be with Sam at Old Pros, be alone at the art museum, be alone at Cafeen, and be alone at Old Pros.

A model of this situation is shown in Figure 21.1. You see there a 3 ×

3 table. The three rows give Sam's three choices; the three columns give Jan's. In each of the nine cells in the table are two numbers. These numbers assign utilities to the nine possible outcomes (where is Sam, where is Jan) corresponding to the preferences for the two just outlined. The first number represents Sam's preferences, and the second gives Jan's. Please note that

- In the rankings given previously, six and not nine outcomes are ranked. This is because of an implicit (now explicit) assumption that, if the other person is somewhere else, it does not matter to Sam or Jan where is that somewhere else. Therefore, if Sam is at Old Pros (row 1), Sam gets the same utility (4) whether Jan is at the art museum or at Cafeen. Of course, Jan's utility does depend on which of these prevails.

- The rankings are an *ordinal* ranking of the outcomes. The translation in Figure 21.1 into numerical utilities is consistent with those rankings, but the exact numbers are otherwise entirely arbitrary; I simply assigned 6 to the best option, 5 to the second best, and so forth.

		Jan		
		Old Pros	art museum	Cafeen
	Old Pros	6,4	4,3	4,2
Sam	art museum	2,1	5,5	2,2
	Cafeen	1,1	1,3	3,6

Figure 21.1. The situation facing Sam and Jan. As described in the text, Sam and Jan must decide independently whether to go to Old Pros, the art museum, or Cafeen. Their utility depends on the choices each makes; in each cell, Sam's utility is listed first and Jan's, second.

Now for an assumption that is critical to the story: Sam and Jan must choose independently where to go, without knowing what the other party has done. Can they consult before making their choices? I leave this question open for now.

Sam Is Not Going to Cafeen. Is Jan?

Can we say, based on what we have done so far, what will happen? Can we say where Jan or Sam will go? Can we say for sure what will not happen?

If—and this is a big *if* in applications of game theory—we have the utilities of Sam right, we can be fairly sure that Sam is not going to Cafeen. No matter what Jan does, Sam is better off going to the Old Pros than to Cafeen.

Can we say anything more? Suppose—and this is a big *suppose*—Jan is familiar enough with Sam to know Sam's utilities for the nine outcomes. Then Jan should conclude, just as we did, that Sam is not going to Cafeen.

Once there is no chance of this, Jan's preferences are such that he prefers the art museum with or without Sam to being at Cafeen without Sam. So if (big *if*) we suppose that Jan comes to the conclusion of the previous paragraph, and if (another big *if*) we have Jan's utilities right, we know Jan would not choose Cafeen.

Two objections typically emerge at this point. (1) Being at Cafeen with Sam is Jan's first choice. If Sam and Jan are friends, is there no chance that Sam will sacrifice her own interests to please Jan? (2) If the two friends get together frequently, might not Sam sacrifice her own interests on this one occasion, expecting that Jan would reciprocate in the future? In real life, the answer to both questions is Yes, this is possible. But if these are possibilities, then: (1) We are unsure about Sam's utilities. If she prefers to please Jan and sacrifice her own selfish interests, then the ranking we assumed for her is incorrect. (2) If the two friends face this sort of situation repeatedly, the "game" they play is a lot more complex than a one-shot choice of a place to go. Repeated play can change everything, as we see at length in Chapters 22 and 23.

Can We Go Further?

So, after ruling out these two objections, we are left with the conclusions that Sam would not choose Cafeen and, if Jan realizes this, neither will he. But this still leaves Sam and Jan each with a choice of either the art museum or Old Pros. Now we reach an impasse. If Jan could anticipate that Sam would go to the art museum, the art museum is his best response. If he anticipates that she would go to Old Pros, Old Pros is his best response. The same is true of Sam; her best choice is to match whatever she anticipates he would do. Logic alone does not seem to answer the question, Where will they wind up?

Students sometimes assert that logic dictates that Sam go to Old Pros and Jan to the art museum. Why? Sam, not knowing anything more, chooses Old Pros because this guarantees her at least 4 units of utility. And Jan chooses the art museum, as this guarantees him at least 3. But is this logical? It cannot be entirely obvious that this would happen, because if it were entirely obvious, it would in particular be obvious to Sam. Then Sam, anticipating that Jan would choose the art museum, would choose the art museum also. I am not asserting that there is an obvious answer to the question, Where will they wind up? Rather, if that question has an obvious answer, it cannot be Sam at Old Pros and Jan at the art museum. At least, that answer cannot be so obvious that both parties will recognize it.

If we cannot say how Sam and Jan will coordinate their actions, can we at least predict that they will? That depends. If they could converse on the phone beforehand, it seems likely they will do so. If they have to guess at what each other will do, they might not.

Suppose Jan Moves First

All this analysis supposes that both Sam and Jan must choose where to go independently, without knowing what the other person has chosen. Suppose instead that Jan moves first. Specifically, Jan chooses a location, goes there, and phones Sam, saying reliably and credibly, "I'm at location X, and I'm not moving." Never mind the impoliteness of such an action; if we have the utilities right, what do we predict?

Jan reasons as follows: "If I go to Old Pros, Sam will follow me there. If I go to the art museum, Sam will follow me there. If I go to Cafeen, Sam will go to Old Pros. So predicting Sam's responses, I'm best off going to the art museum."

Fitting the Example to the Rest of the Chapter

This example illustrates much—but not all—of the content of this chapter. When Sam and Jan move simultaneously, they engage in a game in which their *strategies* are simple actions and thus Figure 21.1 represents their situation as a *strategic-form game*. When we rule out Sam going to Cafeen, we are applying a *dominance* argument. Jan's decision in consequence not to go to Cafeen is an application of *iterated dominance*. When we argue that it is not "the answer" for Sam to go to Old Pros and Jan to the art museum, it is because this *strategy profile* does not constitute a *Nash equilibrium*. This story gives us to little to conclude that the two wind up at an equilibrium, although the possibility of preplay communication (a phone call) makes it more likely that they reach one. And we have no basis on which to predict which equilibrium (both at Old Pros or both at the art museum) they would select, assuming they select one. If Jan gets to move first, though, and Sam, having learned Jan's choice, responds, then the game is converted to a simple *extensive-form game of complete and perfect information*, which is simple enough that we can apply *backward induction*, to conclude that Jan goes to the art museum and Sam follows. Now we flesh out all those italicized terms and add a few more.

21.1. Modeling Situations as Games

To apply game theory, first we model the situation as a game, then we analyze the model created. When modeling a situation as a game, we specify

- The list of individuals or parties involved, called the *players*.

- The rules of the game, or who has what options when, with what sort of information.

- For every possible play of the game, how well each player does, an assignment of utilities or *payoffs*.

We specify these things in two ways: strategic-form and extensive-form games.

Strategic-Form Games

In a strategic-form game, we begin with a list of players. For instance, in the preceding situation, we have two players, Sam and Jan.

Next, for each player, we list the player's *strategies*. A strategy is a complete plan for playing the game, for any one of the players. Depending on how complex the game is, strategies can be ferociously complex. But, in simple games, strategies are usually fairly simple. For instance,

- In the Sam and Jan game, Sam and Jan must choose independently where to go. Each has three choices, and so each has three strategies: go to Old Pros, go to the art museum, or go to Cafeen.

- Consider the game with the rules changed, where Jan chooses where to go first, goes there, and then Sam, knowing Jan's choice, responds. Jan has a simple tripartite choice of Old Pros, the art museum, and Cafeen. But Sam's strategies are more complex, because Sam has to plan what she will do contingent on what she learns about Jan's choice. One strategy for Sam is to go to Old Pros no matter what Jan does. A second is to go to Old Pros if Jan goes to Old Pros and go to the art museum if Jan goes to either the art museum or to Cafeen, and so forth. Since Sam has to choose one of three places to go and she must plan her choice in each of three "information states," Sam has $3 \times 3 \times 3 = 27$ strategies when she responds to Jan's choice.

For even moderately complex games, the number of strategies a player possesses can be enormous. But, at least conceptually, we can imagine listing out all the player's strategies. This list (one for each player) is what gives a strategic-form game its name.

Given a list of strategies for each player, the term *strategy profile* is used for a vector of strategy choices, one for each player. So, for instance, in the Sam and Jan game where the two must choose simultaneously, hence where Sam has three strategies and Jan has three, there are $3 \times 3 = 9$ strategy profiles, such as Sam goes to Old Pros–Jan goes to the art museum. If the rules specify that Jan moves first then Sam responds, so that Jan has 3 strategies and Sam has 27, then there are $3 \times 27 = 81$ strategy profiles; a typical profile is Jan goes to Old Pros–Sam goes to Old Pros if Jan does and goes to the art museum otherwise. Note that in this strategy profile, since we know the strategy employed by each player, we can work out what happens; namely, Sam and Jan both turn up at Old Pros.

The third piece of a strategic-form game is a specification of utilities for the players, for each strategy profile. Game theorists use the term *payoffs* instead of *utilities*, but the two terms mean the same thing.

When the game has only two players, as in the Sam and Jan game, all the data of a strategic-form game can be and often are represented by the sort of table you see in Figure 21.1: The strategies of one player are rows in the table, and the strategies of the other player are columns. Inside the cells of the table, we record payoffs, where the convention is that the first number in a cell gives the payoff to the row-choosing player and the second number is the payoff to the column-choosing player. Note that if the rules of the Sam and Jan game are that Jan moves first and Sam, having seen what Jan does, responds, so that Sam has 27 strategies, in place of the 3×3 table in Figure 21.1, we would have a table with 27 rows (assuming we let Sam pick the row) and 3 columns (see the solution to Problem 21.7 in the *Student's Companion*).

For three or more player games, tables such as Figure 21.1 are inadequate. For three players, for instance, we need a three-dimensional structure, much like a multistory parking garage, where one player's strategy choice fixes the east–west coordinate, a second player's strategy choices fixes the north–south coordinate, and the third player's choice fixes the level or floor of the garage. Each cell, given by east–west coordinate, north–south coordinate, and floor, holds three numbers, giving the payoffs in some specified order for the three players. I do not attempt to draw this.

In some games, for every strategy profile, the sum of the payoffs to the players is a some constant K. Such games are called *constant-sum* games. Old time game-theory books would take the constant to be 0 and call them *zero-sum games*, as in Lester Thurow's famous book, *The Zero-Sum Society*. Notwithstanding Thurow's book, most games in economic contexts are nonconstant sum, and we have little occasion to look at constant-sum games.

Extensive-Form Games

In extensive-form games, an alternative way to depict (model) a competitive situation, the emphasis is on the dynamic back-and-forth tactics of the players. To keep matters simple, I restrict attention for a while to a special case, where the rules specify an order of play and where each player, called on to move, chooses knowing full well what choices were made previously. So, for instance, if Jan chooses where to go first and then Sam responds, knowing how Jan chose, we have a game of this special sort. Such games are called *extensive-form games of complete and perfect information*.

The depiction or model that we use is a stylized tree diagram, as in Figure 21.2. The one open and several closed dots are called *nodes*. They represent positions in the game where some one player is called on to move. The one open circle is the starting position, all the rest are intermediate positions. Each node or position is labeled by the name of the player whose choice it is to move there. Coming out of a node are arrows. These are the options available to the player whose move it is; the player must choose one option. Each arrow or option leads either to another intermediate position, if there is a follow-on move, or to a terminal position, at which point the game is over. Terminal positions are marked by vectors of payoffs that the players receive if this is how the game ends. Each terminal position gives one payoff for each player, given in some specified order, such as Sam's payoff is always listed first.

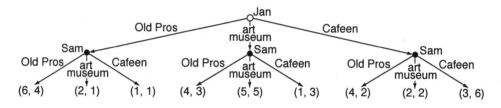

Figure 21.2. An extensive-form representation of the Sam and Jan game, if Jan moves first and Sam responds. Because Sam knows what Jan did when it is her turn to move, this extensive-form game has complete and perfect information. Sam's payoffs are listed first.

So, for instance, in Figure 21.2, Jan goes first (his name labels the open dot) and he must choose one of Old Pros, the art museum, or Cafeen. Each choice leads to an intermediate position at which it is Sam's turn to respond, choosing Old Pros, the art museum, or Cafeen. This second choice ends the game, and payoffs are recorded, first for Sam then for Jan.

Moves by Nature and Information Sets

How could we model with an extensive-form game the Sam and Jan game under the rules that they must choose independently, without knowing the choice of the other person?

It seems impossible. If they move simultaneously, then neither goes first; so who should we record as going first? But simultaneity is not the important issue. Suppose, for the sake of argument, that Sam lives further from all three locales, so in terms of the timing of decision, Sam does choose before Jan. If we put Sam's choice first and Jan's second, Jan does not know, when it is his turn to choose, what Sam chose. Of course, this makes a difference. How do we record this difference?

As we turn our attention from Sam and Jan to more managerially relevant situations, another complication intrudes. In all sorts of competitive situations, pure chance can play a part. When one firm engages in some speculative R&D, it is unclear whether the particular research will pan out. From the perspective of the firm contemplating the R&D, this is a random event. More complex still, suppose a firm engages in some speculative R&D and, after seeing the results of the research, must decide whether to enter a particular market. A rival must decide as well whether to enter the market. Imagine a situation where the second firm, prior to making its decision whether to enter, sees whether the first firm enters. While the first firm knows the results of its R&D, the second firm does not learn this, *except insofar as the entry decision of the first firm reveals this information.* How do we encode all this in an extensive-form game?

It can be done. The two basic tools are *moves by nature* and *information sets.* I illustrate this with a single example involving the two firms engaged in the previous story about R&D and entry. Firm 1 has to make an initial decision whether to engage in R&D on a particular process or not. If it does so, it learns whether or not a particular technology is feasible; suppose that a priori the probability that this technology is feasible is assessed to be 0.333. Firm 1, having learned whether the technology is feasible, if it invests in the R&D, must decide whether to enter a particular market. (Entry decisions are rarely as dichotomous as this, but this is just an illustrative example.) If firm 1 does not invest in the R&D, it must still make an entry decision. Then firm 2 must decide whether to enter the market, having observed firm 1's entry decision but not whether firm 1 did the R&D and, if it did, what it learned.

This fairly complex situation is depicted as an extensive-form game in Figure 21.3. The game starts (the open circle) with firm 1 deciding whether to undertake the R&D. If it does, then the next move belongs to *nature,* which chooses whether the technology is feasible. We mark the two branches coming out of nature's node with the probabilities assessed for them. Then, in each of three possible informational conditions—(1) firm 1 did not do the R&D and so does not know whether the technology is feasible, (2) firm 1 did the R&D and learned that the technology is feasible, (3) firm 1 did the R&D and learned that the technology is not feasible—firm 1 chooses whether to enter the market or not. Following firm 1's choice, firm 2 chooses whether to enter the market.

The move by nature is obvious in the figure. But what are information sets? Note in Figure 21.3 the two dashed lines that join together into two sets of three the six nodes where firm 2 must decide what to do. The dashed

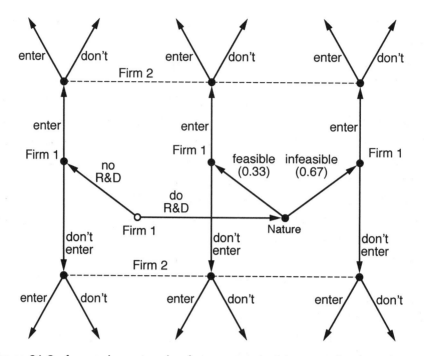

Figure 21.3. A complex extensive-form game. In this extensive-form game, you see how to represent random choices of nature (by assigning nodes to Nature and putting on the branches coming from those nodes the probabilities with which various possibilities happen) and how to represent what different parties know when it is their turn to move, with the sort of dashed line information sets shown. (The payoffs to the two firms are not included on this graph.)

lines are marked firm 2, rather than the six individual nodes. One set (the three on the top) consists of the three nodes where firm 1 decides to enter and the second set (the bottom three) consists of the three nodes where firm 1 decides against entry. These are firm 2's two *information sets*, meaning that, when it is firm 2's turn to choose, it knows whether it is in the first set of three or the second but nothing more. I have not supplied payoffs at the end of branches in Figure 21.3, but that is all that is needed to turn Figure 21.3 into an extensive-form game.

With information sets, we can capture the lack of information a party has about actions that precede its own choice, by tying together locations that the party cannot distinguish. We can artificially use this technique to model competitive situations where parties move more or less simultaneously: We draw one party as moving first, but the second has no information about what the first did when the second "responds." (Can you draw an extensive-form representation of Sam and Jan under the rules where they must choose without knowing the other's choice, using information sets? Hint: If you copy Figure 21.2, you are one small step from being done.)

21.2. Dominance and Strategic-Form Games

Having modeled a particular situation with an extensive-form or strategic-form game, the next step is to analyze the model and predict what will happen in the real-world situation of concern. This can be done to predict how actors behave, as descriptive economics, or more normatively, to help the analyst decide how to act in a particular situation.

For games in strategic form, one form of analysis is directed at the question, Can we confidently predict that certain strategies will *not* be employed by the players involved? Affirmative answers to this questions involve *dominance* arguments.

Figure 21.4 shows a two-player game in strategic form. The two players are Row and Col, Row's strategies are row 1, row 2, and so forth. Recall that we think of the players choosing strategies simultaneously and independently. Given this, can we rule out either strategy of Row? Can we rule out any of Col's three strategies?

		COL		
		column 1	column 2	column 3
ROW	row 1	7,3	3,1	0,5
	row 2	5,1	5,3	2,2

Figure 21.4. A strategic form game solved by iterated dominance. In this game, Column 3 dominates Column 1, so we predict that column 1 will not be selected. And if Row comes to this conclusion, Row 2 dominates Row 1—that is, Row 2 iteratively dominates Row 1—so iterative dominance leads to the prediction that Row 1 will not be selected. Then, if Col replicates this logic, he predicts that Row will choose Row 2, so by another round of iterated dominance, Col chooses Column 2.

- *Column 1 is dominated by column 3*: If Row chooses row 1, then Col is better off with column 3 than with column 1. If Row chooses row 2, then Col is better off with column 3 than with column 1. We say, therefore, that column 3 dominates column 1, and we predict that Col is not going to choose column 1.

   To be very clear about this, Col is better with column 1 if Row picks row 1 than he is with column 3 if Row picks row 2. If Col's choice of column could influence Row's choice of row, we could not rule out column 1. But if Row and Col choose strategies independently, Col's decision to choose column 3 cannot influence Row's choice, and whichever row Row selects, Col is better off with column 3 than with column 1.

- *Row 1 is iteratively dominated by row 2*: Suppose that Row is smart enough to replicate our argument that Col will not choose column 1. Whether Col chooses column 2 or column 3, Row is better off with row 2 than with row 1. Therefore, row 2 iteratively dominates row 1, following the first dominance argument that eliminated column 1. Based on an argument of iterated dominance, the prediction is that Row does not choose row 1.

Again taking this very carefully, row 2 does not dominate row 1, as long as column 1 is viewed as a possible choice for Col. But if we can confidently predict that column 1 will not be played, and if (a big *if*) we believe that Row understands this, then we can eliminate row 1 from consideration.

- Having eliminated row 1 from consideration, *column 2 iteratively dominates column 3*. After removing column 1 and then row 1 from consideration, column 2 is Col's clear best choice.

- Column 2 and row 2 are all that remain. *By iterated dominance, the prediction is that Row chooses row 2 and Col chooses column 2.*

Because the application of iterated dominance got us to a single strategy profile—more properly said, because it eliminated all strategies but one for each of the players—we say this game is *dominance solvable*. Dominance solvability is not always available; if you go back to the Sam and Jan game in Figure 21.1, you'll see that we eliminated Sam going to Cafeen by dominance and then Jan going to Cafeen by iterated dominance. But that is as far as dominance or iterated dominance take us in that game.

Are the Predictions of (Iterated) Dominance Believable?

That is how dominance and iterated dominance work, mechanically. But should you believe in them? Is it really the case that no one would ever play a dominated strategy? How about a strategy that is eliminated by iterated dominance?

Words like *never* and *zero probability* simply do not belong in a discussion of real-life behavior. Suppose you invited a sequence of individuals into a room and gave them a choice: "On the table in front of you, you see a $20 bill and a $1 bill. Choose one and leave." Run this experiment enough times, and someone will inexplicably walk away with the $1 bill. So, when you read a phrase like *no one would ever play a dominated strategy*, you should immediately translate this to "almost no one would ever...." If you get 90 or 95% compliance with a theory in economics, you are doing great.

That understood, the only way to answer the question posed is empirically. For instance, in preparing this book, I asked a collection of 330 or so individuals (first-year students in the Stanford MBA program) how they would play games like that depicted in Figure 21.4, translating the units of payoffs into money at some specified rate of exchange. In particular, for the game in Figure 21.4, I specified an exchange rate of $0.25 per one unit of utility, meaning that if one student, in the role of Row, chose row 2, while the student in the role of Col chose column 2, Row would be given $0.25 × 5 = $1.25, while Col would get $0.25 × 3 = $0.75. These questions were asked of students prior to a discussion of game theory or dominance, so they were somewhat neophyte subjects. Also, the questions were posed in a fashion that gave the students a (very small) incentive to take the questions seriously: Students were chosen at random and rewarded according to how they said they would play. For the game in Figure 21.4, 92% said that, if they were choosing a row, they would pick row 2, with 8% choosing row 1; while if they were choosing a column, 1% chose column 1, 36% chose column 2, and 63% chose column 3.

So dominance worked fairly well: A very small number of students (three out of 330) selected column 1. But iterated dominance fared a bit worse: 8% choose row 1. And iterated-twice dominance failed miserably: A majority chose column 3.

This should not surprise you. Dominance involves a single player and his or her own incentives. Iterated dominance, on the other hand, involves one player putting himself or herself in the shoes of the other player, deciding what the other player will do, which involves giving the other player credit for intelligence and responding according to one's own payoffs. And interated-twice dominance involves a player putting himself or herself into the shoes of the second player and imagining the second player puts herself or himself in the shoes of the first player, giving the first player credit for enough intelligence to choose according to his or her best interests, then responding according to her or his own best interests, then responding to his or her best interests in what remains. (If you find the last sentence hard to parse, that is precisely the point.)

The conclusion, backed by a lot of empirical evidence, is that dominance typically works fairly well; dominated strategies are not played (but see the next section). The predictive power of iterated dominance is not nearly as good, however, and it gets downright poor as you iterate a second time and beyond.

Payoffs Sometimes Reflect Things Other Than Money

In some cases, simple dominance fails empirically, providing the text for another lesson about using game theory to study the real world. Consider the game depicted in Figure 21.5, known as the *prisoners' dilemma*. For reasons to be given next chapter, it is the basis for an enormous literature in game theory. The story that goes with this game is that two individuals commit a crime (a burglary, say) and are apprehended by the police, but only after they have hidden the loot. The police know these two committed the crime but have no evidence and, lacking a confession by either one, must let both go free. So the police separate the two and say to each individually:

> "We are willing to make a deal with you. Confess to the crime, implicating your partner. If you confess and he does not, we will give you a suspended sentence for cooperating with the authorities and lock your partner up for a long time. You will go free and enjoy all the loot. Of course, if you both confess, you both go to jail, but for a shorter time. And if you do not confess and your partner does, he gets the suspended sentence and the loot, and you get a long spell in jail."

Although it is not part of the speech, both individuals know that if each remains silent, both will be let go, and they will split the loot. Moreover, each understands that the same speech is being made to his partner. So they recognize that they are playing a simultaneous move, two-player, two-strategy-apiece game, in which the strategies are *confess* or *remain silent*.

		Prisoner 2	
		remain silent	confess
Prisoner	remain silent	5,5	−3,8
1	confess	8,−3	0,0

Figure 21.5. The prisoners' dilemma. Two individuals who jointly committed a crime are held by the police and individually given the option of remaining silent or confessing to the crime.

The payoffs in Figure 21.5 reflect the following ranking of outcomes. Best is to confess and inform on one's partner while he remains silent: This gives no jail time and all the loot. Second best is for neither to confess: no jail time and half the loot. Third is both confess: moderate jail sentences and, presumably, a split of the loot when both get out. Worst is to remain silent while your partner confesses, informing on you: This gives you a long jail sentence and no loot.

You might argue with this ranking of the outcomes. But, given this ranking, confess dominates remain silent for both players. Application of simple dominance, with no iterations, predicts that both confess.

I asked the 330 Stanford MBA students how they would play the game in Figure 21.5 for money, where the exchange rate was one unit of utility equals $0.50 and with a change in labels: The strategies labeled *confess* in Figure 21.5 were labeled *fink* for the MBA students, and the label *remain silent* was changed to *cooperate* (with each other, not with the authorities). Notwithstanding that confess (fink) dominates remain silent (cooperate),

74% of the MBA students said that if asked to play this game against a classmate, they would remain silent.

Why? Because money is not everything. Finking gives more money to player 1 than does cooperating, regardless of what player 2 does. But, for students playing this game in public, it might be worth $1.50 to establish a reputation as someone who does not fink, but instead tries to cooperate. The payoffs for a player who has these preferences are not what is written in Figure 21.5, and fink does not dominate cooperate. The point is that, when writing down a model of a situation as a game, do not blithely assume that money equals payoffs for the players. It is not so, and if you assume it is, a game theoretic analysis can sometimes lead you astray.

Weak Dominance

To finish the discussion of dominance, consider the game in Figure 21.6. In this game, row 1 *weakly dominates* row 2: Against column 2, row 1 does strictly better than row 2, while against column 1, row 1 does just as well as row 2. Can we therefore conclude that row 2, which is weakly dominated, will not be chosen? Can we iterate on this and say that, once the column-selecting player concludes that row 2 will not be chosen (hence row 1 must be), column 2 will be the choice of the column player? Certainly the logic is less compelling than when we have the type of dominance discussed before, where one row or column is strictly better than another for every choice the opponent might make. (To distinguish from weak dominance, the form of dominance where one strategy does strictly better than another for every choice by the opponents is sometimes called *strict dominance*.) Once again, the answer to this question must be settled empirically; without going into detail, I simply assert that weak dominance, at least in some games, does not do nearly as well as strict dominance, and iterated weak dominance can do quite poorly. Be wary of analyses you see that invoke weak dominance.

	column 1	column 2
row 1	3,0	2,1
row 2	3,4	0,0

Figure 21.6. *Weak dominance.* Row 1 weakly dominates Row 2. Having eliminated Row 2 by weak dominance, iterated dominance eliminates Column 1, yielding the prediction that the players would choose Row 1, Column 2.

21.3. Nash Equilibrium

Economists employ dominance and iterated dominance, both strict and weak, whenever they can. But, in many economic contexts, such as the original Sam and Jan game, this does not get all the way to a predicted outcome. In such cases, the analysis turns to Nash equilibria. (Since the movie *A Beautiful Mind* won the Academy Award, I should note that this is the concept for which John Nash won the Nobel Memorial Prize in Economics. Regarding the movie, please see Problem 21.8.)

For a strategic-form game, a *Nash equilibrium* is a strategy profile (a specification of one strategy for each player from that player's list of strategies) such that no player, by changing his or her part of the strategy profile unilaterally, can improve his or her payoff. Here are some examples:

- In the Sam and Jan game of Figure 21.1, there are two Nash equilibria: Sam goes to Old Pros paired with Jan goes to Old Pros; and Sam goes to the art museum–Jan goes to the art museum. Look at the cell described by the strategy profile for each of these and ask, In that row, is there anything better for Jan, who chooses columns? In that column, is there anything better for Sam, who chooses rows? The answer is No to both questions for both strategy profiles, which makes them Nash equilibria.

- In contrast, look at the strategy profile Sam goes to Cafeen–Jan goes to Cafeen. This gives Jan a payoff of 6, and he can do no better than that. But Sam, by shifting to Old Pros while Jan sticks to Cafeen improves her payoff from 3 to 4. So this is not a Nash equilibrium.

- The strategy profile Sam goes to Old Pros–Jan goes to the art museum is not a Nash equilibrium, this time because both players have the incentive to deviate if the other sticks with his or her part of the profile: If Jan chooses the art museum, Sam is better with the art museum than Old Pros, and if Sam chooses Old Pros, Jan is better with Old Pros than with the art museum.

- As a final example, consider the prisoners' dilemma game, depicted in Figure 21.5. The sole Nash equilibrium of this game is confess–confess. Readers sometimes object to this, pointing out that if both parties shift to remaining silent, both are better off. This is certainly true, but in checking whether a strategy profile is a Nash equilibrium, the test is whether any player, deviating *unilaterally*, can improve his or her own payoff. If Col is going to confess, Row hurts herself by remaining silent, and vice versa. So confess–confess is a Nash equilibrium. On the other hand, remain silent–remain silent is not a Nash equilibrium, because if Col is going to remain silent, Row does better for herself by confessing.

What Does It Mean? Games with and without an "Obvious Way to Play"

Once you get comfortable with the definition, the formal idea of a Nash equilibrium is remarkably simple. But what does it mean? What good is it? The answer to these questions is somewhat lengthy, so your patience is requested. Look at the four strategic-form games depicted in Figure 21.7. For each one, ask yourself

- How would you play the game, matched against a peer (a fellow student, if you are a student), where you assume the role of Row or Col?

- Do you think you can predict with substantial confidence how a peer of yours, playing the game against you, would play?

- Suppose two individuals were selected from some population at random and asked to play the game. Can you predict, with substantial confidence, what each would do? Do you think that they could predict, with substantial confidence, how each other would play?

These are variations on the general question, Does the game have an obvious way to play? The general question is meant to encompass the players themselves, first of all. Do they see the game, and the role of each player in playing the game, as obvious? Then, if you are studying the game as an outside analyst or observer, can you discern that obvious way to play?

	column 1	column 2
row 1	0,0	5,5
row 2	15,15	0,0

(a) Easy coordination

	column 1	column 2
row 1	5,−10	10,10
row 2	15,15	−10,5

(b) Risky coordination

	column 1	column 2	column 3
row 1	−5,−5	10,10	−5,−5
row 2	15,5	−5,−5	−5,−5
row 3	−5,−5	−5,−5	0,30

(c) Harder coordination

	column 1	column 2
row 1	−10,−10	20,0
row 2	0,20	0,0

(d) Chicken

Figure 21.7. *Four coordination games.* For each of these four games, how likely is it that the players see an evident or obvious way to play?

For some games, the answer is No. For other games, the answer is Yes. For instance, I imagine that most people, looking at the game in Figure 21.7(a), called *easy coordination*, see row 2–column 1 as pretty obvious. You probably would play your part of this strategy profile if you were in the game and expect your rival (as long as he or she is relatively intelligent) to play the other part. As a third-party observer, you probably expect and predict row 2–column 1 to happen with high probability, and indeed it does. In my sample of MBA students, with payoff units of $0.25, less than 2% of the students indicated the intention of playing row 1 or column 2. Why? Because it is in the players' joint interest to coordinate their choices this way.

The game in Figure 21.7(b), called *Risky coordination*, is less clear. The two players can coordinate their actions with row 2–column 1 or with row 1–column 2. Since row 2–column 1 does better for both than row 1–column 2, the same "logic" that in easy coordination leads to the prediction of row 1–column 2 would seem to apply here. But in this case, additional benefits accrue from trying the other strategy: If Row picks row 1, she is guaranteed at least 5. And there are risks in going with row 2: If Col happens to go with the safer course of action for him, column 2, Row gets −10. Note that the logic of making the "safe" choice reinforces itself: Row is safer choosing row 1. Col is safer choosing column 2. And the risks of the unsafe choices grow the more each side thinks that the other side, thinking in this fashion, would choose to play safe.

The sample of MBAs, playing this game for units of $0.25, exhibited some of this behavior. Asked which row they intended to choose, 36% chose row 1 instead of row 2; and 32% said they intended to choose column 2.

The game in Figure 21.7(c), called *Harder coordination*, presents three ways for the players to coordinate: row 1–column 2, row 2–column 1, and row 3–column 3. The players do not agree which to choose: The person picking the row prefers the second, and the person picking the column prefers the third. My experience has been that most people who believe that they know what to do and what to expect, think that the "answer" is row 1–column 2, because it is the equitable thing to do; both sides benefit, more or less equally. But, while this logic is appealing to some folks, it is not appealing enough to describe row 1–column 2 as an obvious way to play the game; in my sample of MBA students only 44% said that they would pick row 1 in the role of Row (40%, row 2; 16%, row 3), while 60% expressed an intention to choose column 2 (28%, column 1; 12%, column 3). Based on these data, I do not think we can answer affirmatively the question, Does this game have an obvious way to play?

Finally we come to the game in Figure 21.7(d), called *chicken*. American students and, I expect, others recognize the name and the game as describing the popular pastime of preadolescent bike riders, who ride straight at one another, trying to see who will veer off first and win the undesirable reputation of a chicken. Both get this reputation if both veer off. If neither one does, they both get a trip to the first-aid station. The players can coordinate their actions in two ways: fold–dare and dare–fold, which have dramatically different consequences for the two players. Unless the two players know each other and, based on previous interactions, know which side should defer to the other, it is a question of how aggressive each is. I can report that Stanford MBA students are somewhat aggressive: 60% opted to dare their opponent, while 40% said they intended to fold.

So, of the four games in Figure 21.7, at least *when played by randomly selected students from the Stanford MBA classroom, with no preplay communication,* only the first seems to have an obvious way to play. To explain the italicized caveats, if the two can communicate beforehand, the answer we give may change. For instance, a small amount of preplay communication in risky coordination normally suffices to get the two to row 2–column 1. Preplay communication also can be quite effective in harder coordination, at least in the sense that preplay communication increases the odds that the two parties involved figure out some way to coordinate. (If preplay communication were allowed and the players could redivide their winnings after the game is over, then one begins to expect that they would settle on row 3–column 3, since that maximizes the sum of their prizes, giving them the most to split between themselves afterward. But that changes the rules of the game quite dramatically.) And identity matters: harder coordination and chicken, played by, say, a Japanese student and his professor are very likely to result in the student deferring to the professor, and the professor anticipating this deference. Either game played by some (not all) married couples or by siblings who have an understanding of who defers to whom are likewise more likely to be obvious to the two parties, if not to a third-party observer.

At the risk of overdoing this, here are two further examples. The first is a game for any number of players. Each player must simultaneously and independently write down a number, either 5 or 3. The choices are revealed, and payoffs are made by this rule: Each player gets the $5 if everyone picked 5; a player gets $3 regardless of what anyone else did if he or she chose 3 and −$4 if he or she chose 5 and anyone else chose 3. With two players who know each other well, my experience has been a vast proportion of time, both pick 5, expecting that of each other. When the number of people playing the game gets up to four or five, it is no longer obvious how to play: Everyone would like to coordinate on all 5. But can everyone trust that, in a group of four or five, no one would play it safe with 3? Lest you think that large numbers make it less obvious what to do, when we get to 15 or 20 players, it becomes obvious to all concerned that trying for all 5 is too risky, and everyone should choose 3.

Now consider the following two-player game, based on the following list of 11 cities in the United States: Atlanta, Boston, Chicago, Denver, Los Angeles, New York, Philadelphia, Phoenix, San Francisco, San Diego, and Seattle. One player is told to put his name on a piece of paper and then list some of these cities. His list *must* include Boston. The other is told to put her name on a different piece of paper and list some of these cities; her list *must* include San Francisco. Each is free to list as many or as few other cities as he or she desires. The lists are compared, and each gets $0.50 for each city that appears on only his or her list but loses $1.50 for every city on both lists. So, for instance, if she lists six other cities in addition to San Francisco, but two of her seven cities are on his list as well, she gets $7 \times \$0.50 - 2 \times \$1.50 = \$0.50$. To add social color to the situation, he is told to pretend he is an MBA student at Harvard Business School, and she is told to pretend she is an MBA student from Stanford. Finally, all the rules are explained to the two simultaneously, so each understands the rules and each understands that the other player understands the rules.

Before reading further, decide how you would play this game, against a randomly selected student from the Stanford MBA program. Assume you are given the role in which you must have Boston on your list. What other cities would you list, in addition to Boston? What cities would you expect your opponent to list? To be clear, what you want to do is to list any city you feel your rival would not. Given the numbers, if you want to maximize your expected payoff, you should list cities for which you assess probability less than $\frac{1}{3}$ your rival will list.

This is a game with a lot of ways to coordinate. Perfect coordination, which you might think is impossible, involves each of the nine "free" cities found on one list or the other but not both; there are 512 ways to do this. Despite the huge number of ways to coordinate, my experience has been that, in a significant fraction of the time (around 50%), Stanford MBA students either coordinate or come very close. Moreover, they coordinate (or come close) in a very specific way. Something in the description of the game suggests to them that the Mississippi River is a good way to divide the cities, so the Boston player chooses Atlanta, Chicago, New York, and Philadelphia (sometimes omitting Chicago, since it is not on the East Coast), while the San Francisco player chooses Denver, Los Angeles, Phoenix, San Diego, and Seattle. If both players are U.S. nationals and both know this and know that both know this, the odds of coordinating in this fashion rise. If I am nasty and substitute, say, Minneapolis for Atlanta, the odds of coordination decrease, not merely because Minneapolis is on the "border" but because its presence on the list suggests that dividing using the Mississippi River is not a good idea. The main point is that, in this very complex game, with a lot of ways to coordinate, we see something approximating an "obvious way to play" in a surprising number of cases.

These are just examples, but they suggest that some games, in some situations, can be assigned to the *clear-what-to-do-and-expect* category, while others cannot. What does it take for a particular game, played in particular conditions by particular players, to make it into this set? There are no exact answers, no test applies universally, but some obvious factors are the following:

- First, it is usually helpful, perhaps even essential, that all participants have a common understanding of the rules of the encounter, what options each has, and the like.

- Some games can be "solved" logically. Usually, logical solutions involve the application of dominance or a few rounds of iterated dominance: Player A would not choose her strategy X, and everyone realizes this. So Player B can safely eliminate his strategy Z from consideration. If player A and player B each have only two choices, that does it.

- Consultation before the players select their strategies normally help.

- When the participants have a long history of interacting with each other, especially in similar situations, and they know with whom they are interacting, predictability is usually enhanced. Think of two siblings, or two kids living on the same street, playing a round of Chicken. But repeated interactions can be tricky, as we see in Chapter 22.

- Small numbers of participants can be a plus if they know each other. But in some encounters, large numbers can be helpful, because large numbers and a good sense of how the population responds can be clarifying.

- Social conventions and norms that govern behavior in general can sometimes be applied to the specific situation. For example, think of a Japanese student and professor playing harder coordination.

- Sometimes we can apply nebulous principles of common understanding, which in Economese are called *focal point arguments*. Examples include broad principles such as *go for the joint maximum* or *split gains equally* and the sort of implicit understanding that leads students, in the 11 cities game, to use the Mississippi River as a dividing line.

This list of factors is not complete, but it does cover a lot of the territory. It is probably worth adding, in conclusion, that in situations of interest to managers, the most relevant and powerful of these are social roles and conventions, including organizational and professional norms, direct communication, and direct experience.

Nash Equilibrium?

In the analysis of situations modeled as games, the concept of a Nash equilibrium is used as follows: Having formulated the situation as a game, we ask, Is there any reason to believe that the participants to the game have a fairly good conception of how the game is played? Do they have experience with each other? Might they have consulted? Might they have gone through an elaborate ritual of signaling to each other their intentions? Can a social convention be applied? Can logic be applied? The answer to all these questions might be No. But, when the answer is Yes to one or more, we expect to see them play some Nash equilibrium of the game. If each participant can predict what the others do, each would maximize for himself or herself given those predictions, always assuming that the payoffs capture what is important to the players. Since this is meant to be true about all the participants, the predicted way to play must be such that no single individual, knowing what the others do, wants to deviate. Which is, precisely, the statement that the predicted way to play constitutes a Nash equilibrium.

Note well that the previous sentence reads *a* Nash equilibrium. The indefinite article *a* refers to two things here. First, many games have multiple Nash equilibria (you already have seen a number of them), and an obvious way to play, when one exists, must be one of them. The implication runs in one direction only. Although contrived, so I do not bother to give details, one can manufacture games with a single Nash equilibrium but no obvious way to play, in which almost no one ever chooses his or her part of the Nash equilibrium profile. Second, the logic of the previous paragraph is about the perceptions of the players in the game. They must have a clear understanding of how to play. It is a bonus when, as a third-party observer, an analyst studying the situation shares that understanding. But if you think about the Sam and Jan game played under conditions where the two can engage in preplay communication, you see that there are cases in which we believe the players in a game have a clear conception of how to play, which means a Nash equilibrium, but as outsiders, we await the data to see which one they choose.

Moreover, and most important, all this is predicated on the existence of a clear, common conception of how to play, at least for the players. If that is lacking or if we are unsure whether it is there, the concept of a Nash equilibrium is of no value or use regarding the specific situation. Unless you can say, with reasonable confidence, that the participants in the situation being modeled have, for some reason or other, a clear, common conception of how each acts, there is no point in launching into a Nash equilibrium analysis.

Following this chapter, as we apply game theory to situations of interest to managers, we say that this or that is a Nash equilibrium for a given model of a real-life situation. Whenever, in this book or elsewhere, you hear that said—whenever someone announces that, "Aha, here is a Nash equilibrium in the model"—respond with some skepticism. Unless you are convinced that the parties involved in the interaction have a clear conception of how to play, the fact that this or that mode of behavior is a Nash equilibrium is of little value. In fact, ideally, the analysis should proceed along very different lines. First, after modeling the situation, an argument should be given that some particular mode of behavior is anticipated by everyone. Then, a test of the consistency of that claim is that the predicted mode of behavior should be a Nash equilibrium. Or, less definitive but sometimes still useful, if an argument can be mounted that the parties have a common understanding of the obvious way to play the game, the common understanding lies in the *set* of Nash equilibria.

Mixed Strategies and Games Where It Pays to Be Unpredictable

Every game studied so far has been one in which, at some level, the players involved want to coordinate their actions. They may disagree about which particular brand of coordination is best—Sam would like to meet at Old Pros, while Jan, knowing that he cannot have Cafeen because Sam is not going there, would prefer the art museum—but if they can sort that out, they still want to coordinate. A different way to say this is that, in every game so far, each player would like to change the rules so that he or she moves first and rivals respond to that choice.

But, in some competitive situations, moving first is something to avoid. When choosing strategies simultaneously, players do not wish to be predictable. A very simple, standard example is the children's game rock–paper–scissors, in which two players simultaneously signal with their hands *rock* (a closed fist), *paper* (flat hand), or *scissors* (fore and middle finger make a V). If they choose the same sign, it is a tie. Otherwise, rock versus paper is a win for paper, paper versus scissors is a win for scissors, and rock versus scissors is a win for rock. As anyone who has played this game can tell you, you do not want your rival to guess what you will do. You certainly do not want to move first.

To take a richer example, most readers have played poker and know about the phenomenon of bluffing: When you have good cards in your hand, you want to bet aggressively. But if you bid aggressively only when you hold good cards, your betting behavior reveals the quality of your hand, and you wind up seeing your rivals fold their hands when they have mediocre cards and you are betting. So poker players bluff: They sometimes bet aggressively when they hold poor cards, with two objectives: They wish to to bluff rivals into folding, because the rivals see the aggressive betting as a sign that the party betting has a good hand. At the same time, by bluffing, a poker player confuses her rivals. When betting aggressively, she might be bluffing. So folding whenever she bets aggressively is a bad idea. Then the first player, holding a good hand, can bet somewhat aggressively and hope that her rivals do not fold, allowing her to win a fair amount of money from her good cards. In short, people bluff in poker to become unpredictable.

In business and managerial contexts, coordination and predictability are usually more important than unpredictability. But this is not always true, and so we might take a moment to consider whether the concept of Nash equilibria has anything to say about games where unpredictability is a virtue.

Such games pose a problem for Nash equilibrium; they seem to have none. Consider the game in Figure 21.8. In this game, if Row chooses row 1, Col would prefer to choose column 2. But if Col chooses column 2, Row wants row 2, which leads Col to switch to column 1, which takes Row back to row 1. No single strategy profile is a Nash equilibrium.

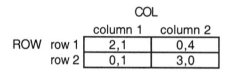

Figure 21.8. A 2×2 *strategic-form game in which unpredictability is a virtue.* This game has no pure-strategy Nash equilibria; from every cell, one player or the other wishes to deviate; both players prefer to be unpredictable.

In fact, a Nash equilibrium does exist if you are willing to extend the notion of a strategy for a player. So far a strategy is a definite choice of action, like scissors in rock–paper–scissors or row 1 in Figure 21.8, a so-called *pure strategy*. Suppose we imagine a player who chooses actions randomly, according to some probability distribution set in advance. For instance, in the game in Figure 21.8, Row can decide to play row 1 with probability $\frac{1}{3}$ and row 2 with probability $\frac{2}{3}$. Such a strategy is called a *mixed strategy*, and a *mixed-strategy profile* is a set of (possibly) mixed strategies, one for each player.

To deal with mixed strategies, some immediate technical qualifications are needed. Suppose, in the game in Figure 21.8, Row plays the mixed strategy in which she chooses row 1 with probability $\frac{1}{3}$ and row 2 with probability $\frac{2}{3}$. Is Col better off with column 1 or column 2? Column 1 guarantees a payoff of 1, while column 1 gives payoff 4 with probability $\frac{1}{3}$ and 0 with probability $\frac{2}{3}$. Which is better? When practicing game theory, it is universally assumed that the players are expected utility maximizers, and the payoffs are denominated in the individual's utility function, so the appropriate comparisons involve expected utilities: Column 1 means an expected utility of 1, while column 2 gives an expected utility of $\frac{1}{3} \times 4 + \frac{2}{3} \times 0 = \frac{4}{3}$. Thus, if Row chooses row 1 with probability $\frac{1}{3}$, Col is better off with column 2 than column 1.

Now consider the mixed strategy profile in which Row chooses row 1 with probability $\frac{1}{4}$ and row 2 with probability $\frac{3}{4}$, while Col chooses column 1 with probability $\frac{3}{5}$ and column 2 with probability $\frac{2}{5}$. Against Row's mixed strategy, you can compute that Col's expected payoff from choosing column 1 is 1, and his expected payoff from choosing column 2 is 1. He is indifferent between the two. So, in particular, mixing between the two is a best response for him to what Row is doing. If he chooses column 1 with probability $\frac{2}{5}$ and column 2 with probability $\frac{3}{5}$, you can calculate that Row has an expected payoff of $\frac{6}{5}$ with row 1 and an expected payoff of $\frac{6}{5}$ with row 2. So among her best responses is the mixed strategy where she chooses row 1 with probability $\frac{1}{4}$. We have a Nash equilibrium.

Is this sort of Nash equilibrium completely crazy? Sophisticated poker players who play other sophisticated players recognize that it is not. Good poker players bluff to appear random to their rivals—if rivals know when a bluff is being run, the bluff accomplishes nothing—and they bluff just enough that, seeing them bet aggressively, rivals on average are unsure how to respond. In response, rivals call bluffs unpredictably, just enough so that their rivals are indifferent between bluffing and not. This, of course, describes the essence of a mixed-strategy Nash equilibrium. (If you play poker, since most rivals you face at the poker table are unlikely to be sophisticated game theorists, take this with a grain of salt as practical advice.)

Do mixed strategies have any relevance for managers? Do we really expect a CEO to make an important decision based on a coin flip or the roll of a pair of dice? If she does, do we expect her to keep her job, if the decision turns out wrong? In situations where it pays to be unpredictable, the notion of a mixed strategy is relevant. But rarely is there a need for a manager—or a poker player—to decide what to do based on a coin flip or the roll of a pair of dice. The important thing is to act unpredictably from the perspective of one's rivals. And in most real-life applications, including poker, the player who seeks to be unpredictable has a lot of private information that, together with the actions of his or her rival, affects how well or poorly he or she does. As long as this information is private in the sense that rivals don't know the information, basing the decision on what to do on the precise "values" of the information makes the actions unpredictable.

It should be noted, finally, that mixed-strategy equilibria can be found in games where it pays to be predictable, but they are rarely relevant there. For instance, in the Sam and Jan game of Figure 21.1, suppose Sam goes to Old

Pros with probability 0.8 and to the art museum with probability 0.2, and Jan responds by going to Old Pros with probability 0.2 and to the art museum with probability 0.8. This is a mixed-strategy Nash equilibrium: In response to Sam's strategy, Jan's expected payoffs are 3.4, 3.4, and 2, from Old Pros, the art museum, and Cafeen, respectively; while Sam's expected payoffs in response to Jan's strategy are 4.4, 4.4, and 1, respectively. This mixed-strategy Nash equilibrium gives both players worse expected payoffs than if they manage to coordinate at either Old Pros or the art museum. This is a general phenomenon for coordination-style games: They have mixed-strategy equilibria, but they do worse for both players than the so-called pure strategy equilibria. Therefore, it would be remarkable in the extreme if one of them turned out to be the obvious way to play.

We do not deal in mixed strategies any further in this book. If you want to learn more about them and their interpretation, almost any textbook devoted to game theory will pick up the story from here.

Nash Equilibrium and Dominance

We have now seen two methods or modes of analysis of strategic-form games: dominance, including weak dominance and iterated dominance, and Nash equilibrium. It is natural to ask, How are the two connected?

- A strategy that is eliminated by iterated strict dominance can never be part of a Nash equilibrium. If we can eliminate all the strategies but one for each player by iterated strict dominance, the strategy profile that remains is the unique Nash equilibrium of the game.

- If you eliminate some strategies by iterated dominance, where some of the steps may use weak dominance, there is a Nash equilibrium for the entire game among the strategies that are not eliminated. Therefore, if we can eliminate all the strategies but one for each player by iterated dominance, where some of the steps may invoke weak dominance, the strategy profile that remains is a Nash equilibrium for the entire game, but it may not be the only one. An example is given later in this chapter.

21.4. Backward Induction in Extensive-Form Games of Complete and Perfect Information

The discussions of both dominance and Nash equilibria have so far concerned strategic-form representations of games. The analysis of general extensive-form games, in which moves by nature and information sets are found, can be quite difficult. But, games without these things (games of complete and perfect information) can be analyzed by a very simple technique, called *rollback* or *backward induction*. An example illustrates.

We begin with a game of complete and perfect information. For instance, consider the game depicted in Figure 21.9. The four players are Paul, George, John, and Ringo. Paul begins the game with a choice of either X or Y. If Paul chooses X, George must choose between A and B. If Paul chooses Y, it is John's turn to choose among a, b, or c. If John chooses b, it is Paul's turn again, and he chooses between k and l. And if John chooses c, then it is Ringo's turn to choose between x and y. All other choices end the game. The payoffs are given in the order Paul's first, then John's, George's, and finally Ringo's.

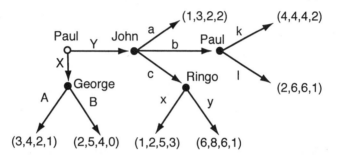

Figure 21.9. An extensive-form game. In this game, the payoffs for the four players are given in the order first Paul's payoff, then John's, George's, and finally Ringo's.

Now for the analysis. We begin by going out to some choice node for a player, where the choice, whatever it is, ends the game. There are three such:

- If Paul begins with the choice of X, George must choose between A and B and end the game. If George chooses A, his payoff is 2, while if he chooses B, his payoff is 4. It seems logical to believe that he would choose B. Note this means that, starting from George's choice, the payoff *vector* for the four is going to be (2,5,4,0).

- If Paul chooses Y and John responds with C, Ringo can choose either x, giving him (Ringo) 3, or y, which gives him 1. Ringo seems likely to end the game with x. So if Paul chooses Y and John chooses C, the game is going to end with the payoff vector (1,2,5,3).

- If Paul chooses Y and John responds with B, Paul chooses between k, netting himself 4, and l, netting himself 2. Paul is probably going to pick k, and the resulting payoff vector is (4,4,4,2)

Now find a node all of whose successors are either end points of the game, or nodes that have been "evaluated."

- For instance, if Paul chooses Y, John chooses between A, giving himself 3; or B, giving the move to Paul again, which we decided means a payoff vector of (4,4,4,2), or 4 for John; or C, giving the move to Ringo, which we decided means a payoff vector of (1,2,5,3), or 2 for John. Faced with this choice and given the predictions of what would happen given the possible choices, John's apparent best move is to pick B, give the move to Paul, and reap 4 for himself and the full payoff vector of (4,4,4,2)

- Now we are ready to figure out what Paul should do to start the game. His choices are Y, giving the move to John, which leads to a payoff vector of (4,4,4,2), as we discovered, or X, giving the move to George, which we earlier decided meant a payoff vector of (2,5,4,0). Paul is better off with Y, predicting that John responds with b and then Paul with k, for a payoff vector for the whole game of (4,4,4,2).

Take it a step at a time, working from the top of the tree (the tips of the branches) to the tree's bottom or trunk, and you can figure out what would happen, or so the theory says.

On a technical level, this technique of analysis is simple. The only possible complication is if a player, looking at his or her choices, sees more than one tied for best. We avoid such cases in this book—what you do then is a bit complex—so that, for our purposes, the technique is simple. But do we believe the results? There are two reasons why we might not.

Should We Believe the Predictions of Backward Induction?
1. Money Is Not Payoffs

First is a problem we met earlier, true payoffs may not equal dollar winnings. One example is called the *ultimatum game*. There are two players, A and B. A moves first and chooses to be either greedy or fair. If A is fair, each side gets \$0.50. If A is greedy, B must accept A's greed, giving \$0.90 to A and \$0.10 to B, or make a fair counteroffer, giving \$0.05 to each, or be greedy himself. If B is greedy, A must either accept, giving \$0.01 to A and \$0.09 to B, or reject, which leaves both players with no money at all.

This game, depicted as an extensive-form game, is shown in Figure 21.10, *with payoffs identified as monetary prizes*. If these are the payoffs, backward induction tells us this: If we get that far, A should accept B's greed. Therefore, B, given the choice, should accept A's greed—better to get \$0.10 than \$0.09 by being greedy. And thus A should be greedy.

This game and others like it have been the subject of a great deal of

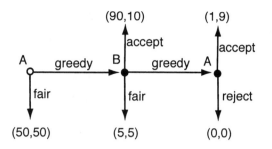

Figure 21.10. A version of the ultimatum game. (A's payoffs are listed first.) Backward induction leads to the prediction that A is greedy at the outset and B accepts this. But we do not find this to be true empirically, because for some individuals, the money prize is not everything.

empirical investigation: Often player A is fair at the start. When she is greedy, often player B fails to accept. And when B is himself greedy, often A rejects the offer. How often is "often" depends on the scale of payoffs and other factors, but "often" is almost always a nontrivial fraction of the time.

The explanation is quite simple: Money is not everything to the players. Player B, faced with a greedy A, may feel it worthwhile to lose up to $0.10 to teach A a lesson, or even just so that he (B) can feel he has not been taken advantage of. A, anticipating this, might decide not to risk the sure $0.50 she can get by being fair. She might even feel that being fair is worth more to her than the $0.40 she might extract by being greedy.

Should We Believe the Predictions of Backward Induction?
2. Too Many Iterations

A second reason to doubt the predictions of backward induction is that these predictions do poorly when the number of nodes along branches through the tree gets very large. Chess is a good example. The rules of chess are such that the game must end in a finite number of moves; if 50 moves pass without a pawn being advanced or a piece taken, the game is a draw, unless a forced mate is in progress. In theory, we could take the extensive-form game that describes chess and work our way back through the tree, to see how it would be played by completely rational players. If this were so, watching a chess match between two completely rational players would be boring. They would know that it is either a forced win for white, or for black, or a forced draw; and to save time, they would simply announce the result, shake hands, and go home. But the game tree of chess is very large, and no one has ever worked out the rational way to play nor is anyone likely to do so in the foreseeable future.

An example a bit more relevant to business applications is the centipede game. Two players are selected to play, designated as Players 1 and 2, and two dimes are put on the table. Player 1 has the first move; she can either take the two dimes, leaving Player 2 with nothing, or say "I pass." If she passes, a third dime is put on the table, and it is Player 2's turn to take the money, leaving Player 1 with nothing, or to say "I pass." If Player 2 passes, a fourth dime is put on the table, and we go back to Player 1. And so on, and so on. This continues until either one of the players takes the money off the table, ending the game, or the amount of money on the table reaches $2. When $2 is reached, it is Player 1's turn, and she can either take all the money or say, "Split it," in which case each player gets $1. Either way, this ends the game.

What does backward induction say about this game? On the last move, Player 1 can have either $2.00 or $1.00. If money equals payoffs, Player 1 takes the $2.00. Therefore, on the move before, Player 2 can either take $1.90 or give the move to Player 1, who will take the $2.00, leaving 2 with nothing. (Even if Player 1 says, "Split it," Player 2 gets only $1.) So Player 2 takes the $1.90, leaving 1 with nothing. Therefore, two moves from the end, Player 1 takes the $1.80, and three moves from the end, Player 2 takes the $1.70—and on the first move, Player 1 takes the $0.20, leaving Player 2 with nothing.

This is a nice theoretical argument, but when people play this game, the prediction that player 1 grabs the $0.20 fails miserably. In the population of MBAs, less than 10% in the role of Player 1 said they would grab the two dimes at the start. Around 35% said they would wait until the end and then offer to split the money, and most of the rest were willing to wait until the sum reached at least $1.60 before grabbing. On the other side, as Player 2, 25% were willing never to grab the money, and another 35% were willing to wait until at least $1.50 was on the table before grabbing.

It is clear that, for some of these players, money is not everything. If a player is motivated by money, there is no reason to split the money on the last move. And, in the role of Player 2, it is witless to wait until the end and hope for $1.00, when a move before you can be sure of $1.90 for yourself. Since 35% of the students were willing to wait until the end, then split the money, and 25% in the role of Player 2 were willing never to grab, a lot of "money is not everything" goes on here. But this is a game where the effect multiplies. Suppose you are Player 1 and money *is* everything to you. Should you grab immediately? Absolutely not. There is a 25% chance, if you accurately anticipate the strategies used by the rest of the population, that you can have $2.00 by waiting to the end and then taking it all, for an expected value of $0.50. Why not try for that instead of taking $0.20 for sure?

Then how about this? Suppose you move first. Suppose money is every-thing to you. Suppose you know for a fact that money is everything to your rival. And suppose your rival does not know that you know that money is everything to him. Then if you say, "I pass," your rival will think to himself, "Maybe my rival does not know that money is everything to me. If so, she is likely to pass for quite a while. Perhaps, then, my best action is to pass back to her, rather than grabbing." What are the odds that your rival thinks this way? Even if the odds are only, say, 1 in 4, you are probably better off passing for while; you can grab $0.20 right away, but perhaps there is a 1 in 4 chance you can get the total up to, say, $1.60. If so, planning to grab at $1.60 is the better deal.

The backward induction argument is predicated on an *assurance* that, on the last move, Player 1 will grab all the money. The more iterations of backward induction you apply, the more important a small probability that this is not true becomes.[1] Conclusions drawn from many-iteration backward induction arguments are rarely robust to small changes in the model, concerning what motivates some of the players, with small but positive probability, and you should take such conclusions with boulder-sized grains of salt.

21.5. Nash Equilibrium in General Extensive-Form Games

For all extensive-form games, both games of complete and perfect informatio, and more general games with information sets and moves by nature, the notion of a Nash equilibrium can be applied. The basic definition holds: A Nash equilibrium is a profile of strategies, one for each player of the game, such that no player by deviating unilaterally (by changing his strategy) can improve his or her (expected) payoff.

The difficulty in applying this definition, even mechanically, comes in verifying that no player can improve his or her payoff by changing strategy. For general extensive-form games, and even for games of complete and perfect information, the set of strategies that a player possesses can be quite complex. In essence, a strategy for a given player specifies for that player what action the player would take in every situation in which the player has a move. More formally, a strategy specifies an action for a player at every one of the player's information sets. That is fairly complex for all but the simplest of extensive-form games. In chapters to follow, we look at some very complex games, and I simply assert that this or that strategy profile constitutes a Nash equilibrium. Most of the time when this happens, I hope

---

[1] The formal argument that this is so is very complex, even in examples. If you want a taste of high-powered game-theoretic reasoning, try the discussion of this point in Section 14.6 of D. Kreps, *A Course in Microeconomic Theory* (Princeton, NJ: Princeton University Press, 1990).

my claims seem reasonable, but I do not go through the difficult verification; you'll generally need to take my word for it.

Nash Equilibrium and Backward Induction in Games of Complete and Perfect Information

For games of complete and perfect information, then, we have the backward induction technique for predicting play, and we can examine Nash equilibria. How do they compare? An example illustrates the connection.

Consider the game depicted in Figure 21.11(a). The players are A (she) and B (he). B must decide whether to challenge A. If B does not challenge A, A gets a payoff of 2 and B gets 0. If B challenges A, A must respond by either acquiescing or fighting. Fighting costs A one unit and B two units (the payoffs are −1 and −2, respectively), while acquiescing gives a payoff of 1 to each.

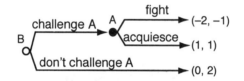

(a) The game in extensive form. B's payoffs are listed first.

		Player A	
		fight	acquiesce
Player	challenge	−2,−1	1,1
B	do not challenge	0,2	0,2

(b) The game in strategic form. B chooses a row and A, a column.

Figure 21.11. A game in extensive and strategic form. Panel a depicts the game in extensive form and panel b depicts the corresponding strategic form. You can see two Nash equilibria in panel b, namely challenge–acquiesce, and do not challenge–fight. The second, though, involves the weakly dominated strategy fight for A. This corresponds to the fact that, in the extensive form, it is not credible that A would fight, if B challenges A.

Should B challenge A? If he does, A must choose between payoffs of −1 and 1. Surely A would acquiesce. So it seems that B can safely mount the challenge. That is just backward induction.

Now turn this into a strategic-form game. Both A and B have two strategies: B can challenge or not, and A can fight or acquiesce. Map pairs of strategies into outcomes and payoffs, and you get the strategic-form game in Figure 21.11(b). Note that

- Challenge–acquiesce is a Nash equilibrium. Backward induction generated a Nash equilibrium.

- But do not challenge–fight is also a Nash equilibrium. Player A can "afford" to fight because, if there is no challenge, she does not incur the costs of actually fighting: If A threatens to fight and B is coerced by the threat, then A need not carry out the threat. But this threat has credibility problems. If B calls A's bluff and challenges, would A really fight?

- You can see the credibility problem by noting that this Nash equilibrium involves a weakly dominated strategy; acquiesce weakly dominates fight for A. As we just said, the threat to fight costs A nothing if the threat works: Fight does just as well as acquiesce for A against do not challenge. But if there is a challenge, acquiesce is strictly better than fight.

This example illustrates the general principle that, when converting an extensive-form game into a strategic-form game, you often go from a single backward induction "answer" to a lot of Nash equilibria. The solution obtained by backward induction is a Nash equilibrium. The other Nash equilibria involve strategies that can be eliminated by iterated weak dominance. In fact, the iterations are the steps in the backward induction. Do we believe the results of backward induction? Do we believe the consequences of iterated weak dominance in general? The issue here is not simply technical. It goes to the question, What makes for a credible threat or promise, made by one party to another? There is a lot of economics to this question, so we leave it here, to be revisited in Chapter 23.

Backward Induction in More Complex Extensive-Form Games?

For general extensive-form games, with things like information sets and moves by nature, we employ Nash equilibrium analysis. But, as just seen, some Nash equilibria are based on incredible threats. For games with complete and perfect information, backward induction helps us recognize these incredible-threat equilibria. It would be nice to have something such as backward induction for general extensive-form games.

In fact, this sort of thing does exist. But to develop the concepts would take a full-fledged textbook in game theory. I hope that the applications of game theory in the next few chapters convince you to tackle a course in game theory. If you do, the concepts of perfect equilibrium and sequential equilibrium are what to look for, in this regard.

Executive Summary

- When studying a competitive or cooperative situation or when engaged in one, whether as analyst or as participant, try to see the situation from the varying perspectives of all participants. We use noncooperative game theory to do this, modeling and analyzing situations in which various parties with conflicting interests interact.

- Noncooperative game theory uses two general sorts of models, strategic-form and extensive-form games, and employs two general sorts of analysis, dominance and Nash equilibrium analysis.

- A strategic-form game is specified by a list of players, for each player a list of strategies, and for each strategy profile (choice of a strategy for each player), a vector of payoffs obtained by the players.

- Extensive-form games give a dynamic picture of the game, with players moving and responding to one another's moves and to information they receive. In extensive-form games of complete and perfect information, players take turns moving; and at any point in the game, the player moving knows the choices made by those who moved earlier, as well as the information possessed by those who moved earlier. The notion of an information set can be used to study extensive-form games with simultaneous moves or where one player acts in ignorance of what other players know or have done previously.

- One strategy for a player dominates another if, no matter what strategies the player's opponents choose, the player does better with the dominating strategy than with the dominated strategy. The force of this definition is, We do not expect a player to use a dominated strategy.

- If the player does strictly better with the first strategy than with the second, for every set of strategy choices by the opponents, we say the first strategy strictly dominates the second. If there are ties for some strategy choices by the opponents, we have weak dominance.

- After eliminating from consideration some strategies for some players by the application of dominance, it may be possible to eliminate other strategies for other players using dominance in the "game that remains." This sort of procedure is known as iterated dominance.

- Predictions of the form *a player would not play a dominated strategy or one eliminated by the iterated application of dominance* do not always work empirically. For one thing, the payoffs in the model may not capture what really motivates the players. Beyond this, players sometimes play weakly dominated strategies, believing their rivals are sure to play a strategy selection that makes the weakly dominated strategy as good as the dominating strategy. As we iterate dominance, more and more assumptions about what each player is thinking about what others think and do are bundled in, making the conclusion less and less robust.

- A Nash equilibrium is a strategy profile, one strategy selection for each player, such that no player can improve his or her payoff with a unilateral deviation. The force of this concept is that, *if* players have an "obvious way to play," in the sense that it is obvious to them, it is obvious to them that it is obvious to each other, and so forth, then that way to play must be a Nash equilibrium. A variety of reasons can be offered for why a game might possess an obvious way to play, including the application of logic by players, preplay communication and negotiation, specific experience with one another, general social experience in this sort of situation, and most vague, a sense that this is what everyone would do, based on the notion of a focal point. When a game in a specific context and with specific players does not possess for those players an obvious way to play, then the concept of a Nash equilibrium is of little use or value.

- In some games, such as poker, players are better off if they are not predictable. Game theory uses the notions of a randomized strategy and Nash equilibria in randomized strategies in such cases.

- The connections between Nash equilibrium and dominance are that no strategy eliminated by the iterated application of strict dominance can be part of a Nash equilibrium. In a game that is strictly dominance solvable (where the application of iterated strict dominance eliminates all strategy profiles but one), the remaining strategy profile is the game's unique Nash equilibrium. If the application of iterated dominance, weak or strong, results in everything but a single strategy profile being eliminated, the remaining profile is a Nash equilibrium (but there may be others).

- To analyze extensive-form games of complete and perfect information, we use backward induction analysis: Work from the ends of an extensive-form game to figure out what each player would do given the backward-induction predictions of what his or her successors would do. Absent any ties in the backward-induction procedure, this gives a unique prediction of what happens if the game is played. This prediction is not always supported empirically, because both the payoffs in the model may not capture the players' true objectives and rolling back many times essentially involves each player piling on assumptions about how other players think and act.

- The concept of a Nash equilibrium applies unchanged to extensive-form games. For games of complete and perfect information, backward induction yields a Nash equilibrium of the game, but there may be other Nash equilibria that involve threats that are not credible.

Problems

21.1   (a) In the game in Figure 21.12(a), is row 1–column 2 a Nash equilibrium?   (In all the strategic form games in these problems, the payoff of the person selecting the row is given first.)

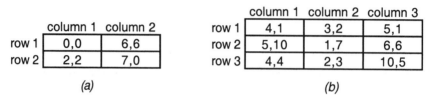

	column 1	column 2
row 1	0,0	6,6
row 2	2,2	7,0

(a)

	column 1	column 2	column 3
row 1	4,1	3,2	5,1
row 2	5,10	1,7	6,6
row 3	4,4	2,3	10,5

(b)

Figure 21.12. Problem 21.1: Two strategic-form games.

(b) Find all the Nash equilibria in the game in Figure 21.12(b).

21.2   Find all the Nash equilibria in the game in Figure 21.13.

	column 1	column 2	column 3	column 4
row 1	1,9	2,9	2,8	7,3
row 2	3,3	4,4	1,1	6,3
row 3	0,10	1,7	2,9	2,1
row 4	2,2	0,0	3,3	1,0

Figure 21.13. Problem 21.2: A strategic-form game.

21.3   Apply iterated dominance to the game in Figure 21.14.

	column 1	column 2	column 3	column 4
row 1	6,1	2,1	5,2	2,3
row 2	8,0	10,1	4,5	1,2
row 3	4,4	10,0	3,0	1,1

Figure 21.14. Problem 21.3: A strategic-form game.

21.4 Apply iterated dominance to the game in Figure 21.15.

	column 1	column 2	column 3	column 4
row 1	1,9	2,9	2,8	7,3
row 2	3,3	4,4	1,1	6,3
row 3	0,10	1,7	2,9	2,1
row 4	2,2	0,0	3,3	1,0

Figure 21.15. Problem 21.4: A strategic-form game.

21.5 A common procedure for selling a single indivisible object is a sealed-bid auction. In sealed-bid auctions, all prospective buyers are given the opportunity to examine the object, then each places a "bid" in a sealed envelope, which is given to the auctioneer. After all the bids are collected, they are opened and revealed. In the most common form of sealed-bid auction, the object is awarded to whoever bid the highest amount, in return for a payment equal to the amount this person bid. This is known as a *first-price* auction. In a less common form, the object is awarded to whoever bid the highest amount, but this person must pay only as much as the second highest bid. This is known as a *second-price* or *Vickrey* auction.

Imagine you are taking part in an auction, where the object being auctioned is a vacation trip. There are 15 other prospective buyers in addition to you. You have determined that the trip is worth $2000 to you: You would rather have the trip and pay some amount less than $2000 than to miss the trip (and pay nothing), but you would rather miss the trip (and pay nothing) than take the trip if it costs more than $2000. You are indifferent between missing the trip and paying nothing and going on the trip if it costs $2000. To be very specific, your payoff is 0 if you do not win the auction (and pay nothing) and it is $2000 - P$ if you win the trip and pay P.

You have very little idea how much the trip is worth to the other 15 bidders or how they bid.

(a) Suppose this is a first-price auction. Why does the strategy of bidding $1950 weakly dominate the strategy of bidding $2000 for you? Can you compare (using dominance) bidding $1950 or bidding $1960? Can you compare (using dominance) bidding $2000 and bidding an amount more than $2000?

(b) Suppose this is a second-price auction. Why does the strategy of bidding $2000 weakly dominate *every* other strategy for you?

21.6 Figure 21.16 shows two extensive-form games of complete and perfect information: the threat game in panel a, and the trust game in panel b. Solve each by backward induction. Then, do you think that your peers, playing the games in, say, units of $1 equals one unit of payoff, would follow the prediction of the Nash equilibrium analysis?

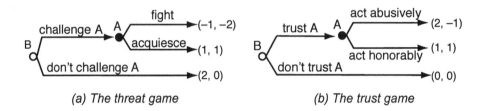

(a) The threat game   (b) The trust game

Figure 21.16. Two extensive-form games of complete and perfect information. A's payoff is listed first in each case.

21.7 Consider the Sam and Jan game, in the variation where Jan chooses first and Sam responds. An extensive-form representation of this game is shown in Figure 21.2.

(a) Carry out the backward induction analysis of this game.

(b) In this game, Sam has 27 strategies. List them.

(c) Draw the 27×3 strategic-form representation of this game, complete with all the payoffs. Find the cell that corresponds to the analysis you carried out in part a. Is it a Nash equilibrium?

(d) Can you find other Nash equilibria in this strategic-form game?

(e) What does an (iterated? weak?) dominance analysis of this strategic-form game tell you?

(f) If you followed the discussion about information sets, what would an extensive-form representation of Sam and Jan look like, if Sam and Jan chose independently rather than sequentially? To repeat a hint from the text, if you start by copying Figure 21.2, you are almost done.

21.8 In the movie *A Beautiful Mind*, John Nash is depicted as inventing the concept of a Nash equilibrium while in a bar with some male friends, trying to decide on a technique for meeting some unattached women. The story in the movie does not quite capture the idea of a Nash equilibrium, but here is a version that does. Two friends, John and Joe, in a bar, spy three unattached women, Mary, Jane, and Sally. John and Joe are interested in meeting the women, but the mores of their society are such that each can approach only one. If, say, John approaches Jane and Joe approaches another woman, John's probability of "success" is p_{Jane}. The same is true of Joe. If they both approach Jane, each has probability $p_{Jane}/2$ of success. Sally is very beautiful, and a successful meeting with her is worth 10 units of utility, compared to 7 units of utility for a successful meeting with the quite cute Jane or Mary. But, being very beautiful, Sally is apt to decline the approach of these gentlemen: $p_{Sally} = 0.2$, while Jane and Mary are a bit more approachable: $p_{Jane} = p_{Mary} = 0.3$. An attempted meeting, if unsuccessful, means a payoff of 0. Convert this story into a strategic-form game and find the various Nash equilibria. If John could move first and then Joe responds, what do you predict would happen?

21.9 Imagine two firms, labeled A and B, producing products that are substitutes but not perfect substitutes. The inverse demand functions for their two goods are

$$p_A = a - x_A - bx_B, \quad \text{and} \quad p_B = a - x_B - bx_A$$

for a positive constant a and for $0 < b < 1$, with the same constants a and b appearing in both inverse demand functions. Each firm has a constant marginal cost of production c.

(a) Suppose the two firms must simultaneously and independently choose quantities to produce, each without knowing what the other has chosen. What are (or is) the Nash equilibria of this game?

(b) Suppose that the two firms must simultaneously and independently choose prices to charge, each without knowing what price the other has chosen. What are (or is) the Nash equilibria of this game?

(c) Suppose firm A can choose its production quantity first. Firm B sees this choice, then chooses its production quantity. What do you predict would happen?

(d) Suppose firm A can choose its price first. Firm B sees this choice, then B chooses its price. What do you predict would happen?

22. Reciprocity and Collusion

This chapter concerns reciprocity and cooperation in repeated interactions: How and when do repeated interactions allow essentially selfish parties to cooperate? After answering this question somewhat abstractly, we apply the answers to the subject of implicit and explicit collusion in oligopolies.

Large electric turbine generators are enormous, expensive pieces of capital equipment that turn mechanical energy into electricity. They are essential to the production of electricity by large electric utilities, in applications where fossil fuels are burned, where steam is produced by nuclear reactors, and in large hydroelectric facilities. In the late 1950s, large turbine generators for the U.S. market were produced by three large industrial firms, General Electric, Westinghouse, and Allis-Chalmers.[1]

A Porteresque five forces analysis of this industry as of the 1950s and 1960s leads to the conclusion that, at least potentially, this could be a very profitable industry. There were very few economical substitute products. Suppliers were weak. Customers were relatively weak; even better, because of the way most customers' businesses were run (as regulated utilities), the customers were not very price sensitive. Entry barriers were absolutely formidable.

In the 1950s, the three firms reaped tremendous profits. But in the early 1960s, they were much less profitable. In fact, in the early 1960s, their levels of profit were so low that the smallest of the three, Allis-Chalmers, was driven out of the industry, leaving GE and Westinghouse to share very low levels of profit. By 1970, GE and Westinghouse were once again earning enormous profits.

The wide swings in profitability were due to changes in the nature of rivalry in the industry. In the 1950s, GE, Westinghouse, and Allis-Chalmers found a very clever—and entirely illegal—way to coordinate their prices, leading to high profits. How did they do it? To understand their scheme, you first must understand that, in this business, a customer (typically a large electric utility like Consolidated Edison of New York or Pacific Gas and Electric) in need of a turbine generator would make a formal announcement of this fact, complete with specifications to be met, asking for potential

---

[1] The story of the large turbine generator business related here is taken from "General Electric vs. Westinghouse in Large Turbine Generators (A, B, C)" (HBS9-380-128, 129, 130), which should be consulted for a lot of extraordinarily interesting detail.

suppliers to submit bids. At the moment such a formal solicitation of bids was made, the three suppliers would consult a lunar calendar. On Days 1 through 17 of the lunar month, with the New Moon counting as Day 1, GE was understood by the three firms to "own" the contract; GE would make a bid at a relatively high price, and Westinghouse and Allis-Chalmers would put in bids at even higher prices. If the solicitation of bids occurred on days 18 through 25 of the lunar month, Westinghouse was understood to "own" the contract. And if it occurred on days 26 through 28, Allis-Chalmers was understood to "own" the contract. (I am not certain about the precise apportioning of the lunar month, but this gives market shares of around 60% to GE, 30% to Westinghouse, and 10% to A-C, which is about the share that each had. If I am off, it is probably only by a day or so.)

To be very clear, this was a price-fixing conspiracy. It was in direct violation of the Sherman Antitrust Act. It was so blatant a violation of U.S. antitrust law that, when the U.S. Department of Justice figured out the scheme, it pursued criminal charges against executives of the three firms and jail time was handed down. But, because the people at the Department of Justice did not think to consult a lunar calendar, they did not figure out how the three firms were coordinating their bids for quite some time, and for that length of time, the three made sizeable profits.

In the early 1960s, after Allis-Chalmers dropped out, rivalry between GE and Westinghouse was intense. Then, in 1963, GE made a strategic move that permitted it and Westinghouse to return to relative benign rivalry, and profits shot up. In this chapter I do not discuss either the events of the early 1960s or GE's strategic move; I suggest in the strongest possible terms that, after you read this chapter, you get the GE–Westinghouse A and B cases and try to figure them out. Roughly, the A case explains why competition was so intense in the early 1960s, and the B case describes GE's 1963 opening gambit. The C case describes what happened over the following decade or so, up to the next move in the "game" by the U.S. antitrust authorities. Although the case is quite old, there is no better vehicle for understanding the concepts we discuss here. I do not want to spoil the story for you or your instructor, but I will say this: GE's actions in 1963 may have been in violation of the spirit or letter of antitrust law and for that reason may not be something to be admired generally. (To the best of my knowledge, the courts have come to no definitive ruling whether GE's actions were in violation of the law, so the *may be* is accurate.) But, setting aside the legality of GE's actions and looking at them solely as an attempt to bend the rules of a "game" in a fashion favorable to the party doing the bending, this was simply magnificent, the Beethoven's *Ninth Symphony* of business strategy. The cases are fascinating.

Rather than discuss the post-phases-of-the-moon period, I want to address the question, Why did the phases of the moon scheme work? Suppose it is Day 25 of the lunar month, and Con Ed of New York solicits bids for a generator. Westinghouse owns Day 25 according to the agreed-to scheme. So Westinghouse prepares a bid that leaves it with a substantial profit, expecting GE and A-C to make even higher bids. Imagine you are the CEO of Allis-Chalmers. Your market share is, on average, around 10%, because you own only 3 days out of 28. Moreover, the luck of the draw, combined with a slow market, may mean that you have not seen a order (that is, one that you own) for a year. Why not defect from the agreement and steal this order from Westinghouse? After all, if Westinghouse's bid is going to leave it with a substantial profit, there is plenty of room for you to capture the order and still make a fair piece of change. You need not fear that Westinghouse will take you to court for breaking an oral contract. Since the deal is illegal, it is not enforceable in court. Why do you adhere to the deal?

This main subject of this chapter is the answer to this question or, more precisely, the answer to the question, Under what conditions will parties to this sort of arrangement adhere to the deal they struck? The general topic is reciprocity in repeated interactions: How and when can we get cooperation from folks who are essentially selfish?

22.1. A Game-Theoretic Analysis of Reciprocity: The Folk Theorem

The story starts with the prisoners' dilemma game from last chapter. I reproduce the game in Figure 22.1, with the prisoners now named ROW and COL, and with the two strategies called *fink* and *cooperate*. Let me remind you what we said about this game: Finking is a dominant strategy for each side, and thus fink–fink is the only Nash equilibrium of the game. This isn't a very happy conclusion for the two prisoners, because they wind up with payoffs of 0 apiece, rather than the 5 apiece they could get if only they could find a way to sustain the cooperative outcome where each remains silent. This is the prisoners' dilemma: How can the two attain this cooperative outcome, when the selfish interests of each leads each one to fink?

		COL	
		remain silent	confess
ROW	remain silent	5,5	−3,8
	confess	8,−3	0,0

Figure 22.1. The prisoners' dilemma.

One way to escape the dilemma is to form a legally enforceable agreement to cooperate. But, if this is not possible, there is another possibility. Suppose the two are involved in this situation repeatedly. To be precise, imagine that they play the game once, with the results revealed at the end of play. Then some random event is conducted such that with probability 0.8, the two play a second time; while with probability 0.2, the encounter ends. After they play the second time, if they do, the results are again revealed, and again the random event is conducted independently, so the probability of going on to a third round of play is 0.8, and so on. After each round of play, the chance of proceeding to another round is 0.8 and the chance that the encounter ends is 0.2, independent of what has happened in the past. Assume that payoffs for a string of plays for each player are just the sum of their payoffs in each round; and insofar as a player is uncertain what payoffs he or she will get, for instance, because of uncertainty how long the game will last, the player seeks to maximize the *expected value* or probability-weighted average of his or her summed payoff.

In this case cooperation *can* be sustained as *a* Nash equilibrium. To see how, consider the following strategy for ROW:

> Begin by cooperating. As long as the game continues and as long as both players have cooperated at every previous stage, cooperate. If ever either player finks, in all subsequent stages, as long as the game continues, fink.

This is a strategy on an entirely higher plane than fink or cooperate. Those are actions available in any single round of play and hence are strategies if the game is played once. This is a strategy for the repeated interaction between the two players, in which ROW's action in one round depends on what happened in earlier rounds.

What is COL's best response to this strategy by ROW? Suppose COL responds by always cooperating. Then each side would cooperate in each round of play, for as long as the game goes on. COL would get 5 in the first round, 5 in the second, if there is a second round, and so on. COL's *expected* payoff is

$$5 + (0.8)(5) + (0.8)^2(5) + \ldots = \frac{5}{0.2} = 25.$$

To explain, the first 5 in the sum is COL's payoff in the first round. The second term, $(0.8)(5)$ is the payoff in the second round, 5, times the probability 0.8 that there is a second round. The third term $(0.8)^2(5)$ is the payoff 5 in the third round times the probability $(0.8)^2$ that there is a third round, and so on.

The right-hand side, seeing that the infinite sum gives the total $5/0.2 = 25$, is just a mathematical formula.

Would COL do better to fink in the first round? If he does, he gets a payoff of 8 in the first round, but if ROW follows the outlined strategy, COL does no better than 0 in any subsequent round, because ROW finks forever after. Therefore, the best COL can do if he finks in the first round is the expected payoff

$$8 + (0.8)(0) + (0.8)^2(0) + \ldots = 8.$$

This is worse than always cooperating: *If COL anticipates that ROW is playing the outlined strategy, then COL is better off responding with any strategy that has him cooperating forever than with any strategy that involves finking in the first round.*

It takes a bit of mathematics, but it can be shown that COL's best strategic response overall to the given strategy for ROW is any strategy that has him (COL) cooperating as long as ROW does. Many strategies for COL satisfy these conditions, including the following three:

1. Always cooperate, no matter what.

2. Cooperate at the start, and continue to cooperate as long as ROW does. If ever ROW finks, then fink forever after.

3. Cooperate at the start. After this, do in round t whatever ROW did in the previous round, $t - 1$.

To give these three strategies names, we call the first *naive cooperation*, the second *grim cooperation*, and the third *tit for tat*. The first and third names are probably clear; the middle strategy is called *grim cooperation* because, if ever the player using it is finked on, he or she grimly finks forever after, never forgiving or forgetting.

Suppose ROW plays grim cooperation and COL plays naive cooperation. Is this a Nash equilibrium of the repeated interaction? We already asserted that COL's strategy is a best response to what ROW is doing, but the reverse is not true: If COL is always going to cooperate no matter what ROW does, then ROW does better to fink in every round.

On the other hand, grim cooperation against grim cooperation is a Nash equilibrium, as is grim cooperation against tit for tat. In the first pair of strategies, each side has the incentive never to fink; each is playing a best response against the other. This is also true in the second pair, although to convince you of this, we must demonstrate that, against tit for tat, it is better not to fink than to fink at any point of play. It turns out that this is so for the numbers we are using; one round of punishment for finking is adequate to keep the other side in line.

What is going on here? It is nothing very profound. Because of the repeated nature of the interaction, each side can threaten the other that any breach of cooperation would be met with reciprocal noncooperative behavior. The threat of punishment for a breach in cooperation is adequate to keep each side cooperating. Doubtless, in some ongoing interaction in your life, you have participated in this sort of reciprocally cooperative scheme, where you did not take short-term advantage of someone with whom you have ongoing relations because you feared the other would then punish you to the extent he or she could. Most children learn this early in life: Bobbie shares her toys with Tommy or waits patiently for Tommy to move first if it is his turn, so that Tommy will reciprocate later on.

There are several things to note about this:

- In the story told, the 0.8 discount factor represents the probability of making it to another round. We could tell a different story in which there is probability 1 that the interaction takes place over and over again but the payoffs are accrued with a sufficient time delay that the overall payoff from a stream of rewards is given by their discounted sum. As long as the discount factor is 0.8, we get exactly the same analysis.

- We describe one Nash equilibrium that results in perpetual cooperation, but other Nash equilibria in this situation give very different outcomes. For example, suppose each player chooses Fink in every round, no matter what has happened in the past. This gives a Nash equilibrium in which perpetual finking is the outcome. This is a Nash equilibrium because, if ROW always finks, the best COL can do is to fink and vice versa. Neither player, changing his or her strategy alone can do better. Of course, both players are better off with the grim against grim equilibrium than with the always fink against always fink equilibrium. But always fink against always fink is a Nash equilibrium, because neither side has an incentive to change what it is doing *unilaterally*.

- Equilibria that involve cooperation (such as grim vs. grim) require a significant probability that the two will continue to play and stakes that are somewhat balanced from one round to the next. Cooperation is based on a calculation that the short-term advantages from finking are outweighed by the longer-term advantages of keeping a cooperative arrangement going. If, for example, the probability of continuing for another round after each was only 0.1 and ROW played grim cooperation, then COL calculates, "If I cooperate, I net 5 in each round, for an expected payoff of

$$5 + (0.1)(5) + (0.1)^2(5) + \ldots = \frac{5}{0.9} = 5.556.$$

But if I fink, then in the very first round I get 8 and I can guarantee that I never get less than 0 after that. Clearly I am better off finking."

Or suppose that the size of the stakes changed from round to round, and in the third round of play, the stakes increase 30-fold, with little chance they would ever be that high again. Then, in the third round each side has a very strong incentive to deviate to finking in the short run, even if this destroys cooperation in all subsequent periods. In this situation, it jointly behooves the players to try to take advantage of opportunities for cooperation that exist in other periods. Although always fink versus always fink is an equilibrium, in other equilibria the two parties cooperate except in the third round. For instance, suppose each chooses the strategy cooperate in all rounds but the third, as long as both have always cooperated in the past except for the third round. It is as if the two say to one another, "We can't trust each other to cooperate in the third round. Our selfish interests lead us each to fink, and no threat that either of us makes against the other will stop that. So let's be mature and ignore what happens in round 3."

The Folk Theorem of Game Theory

The basic idea in the preceding example is formalized in what is known as the *folk theorem* of noncooperative game theory. It is called the *folk theorem* because it seems always to have been known. No one is brash enough to take credit for such a simple idea.

The formal setting is as follows. We have a simple game played by some number of players. This game is played once, then a second time, a third, and so on. Each player receives as total payoff from the sequence of plays the discounted sum of his or her payoffs in each round, discounted with some discount factor $\alpha < 1$. You can think of α as reflecting the time value of money, a probability of continuing, or both. It does not matter.

For each player, we compute the player's *max–min* payoff. This is the worst punishment that all the others can inflict on the player, if the player anticipates what the others will do. For example, in the prisoners' dilemma, each player's max-min payoff is 0, because by finking each player can get at least a payoff of 0 no matter what the other player does.

The Folk Theorem (roughly). Take any outcome of the game that gives to each player a payoff that exceeds the player's max–min payoff. Then, if the discount factor α is close enough to 1, a Nash equilibrium of the repeated-interaction game gives this outcome round after round.

This is a rough version of a precise mathematical result. You can see the precise result in textbooks on game theory, but the statement here conveys the basic idea. As long as the future matters enough (the discount factor is close enough to 1) any outcome that gives players more than their max–min payoff can be sustained as an equilibrium. In fact, it is easy enough to describe the Nash equilibrium: All the players play the chosen outcome as long as no one deviates. If someone deviates, everyone else punishes the deviator to the fullest extent possible, putting the deviator at his or her max–min payoff level. This is a Nash equilibrium because, if the future matters enough and the chosen outcome gives each player more than he or she gets if punished by the others, it is better for the player to go along with the deal than to deviate and be held afterward to his or her max–min payoff.

A number of questions arise about this result. For instance, can a particular outcome that gives each player more than his or her max–min be sustained as an equilibrium for a particular discount factor, such as 0.8? The theorem says that, if the discount factor is close enough to 1, the outcome can be sustained. But, is 0.8 close enough? Also, will the players carry out the mandated punishment of a deviator? Is the threatened punishment credible? What happens if more than one player deviates from the scheme? In formal treatments of the folk theorem, all these questions are addressed without affecting the basic result. Rather than presenting the details, we take an applied point of view, stressing the basic idea. The basic idea is already clear from the example of the prisoners' dilemma, but so is the chief weakness of the idea.

Too Many Equilibria and No Way to Predict Which Would Be Used

The chief weakness of this rather neat idea is that it gives us too many Nash equilibria. We began by wondering if there were some way to sustain cooperation in the prisoners' dilemma game. Repeated play answers this desire; cooperation can be sustained if the discount factor is close enough to 1. But repeated play answers this desire with an embarrassment of riches. Cooperation is an equilibrium. So is continual finking. So is alternating between the two. So is alternating between cooperate–cooperate and fink–cooperate, where we give ROW's action first. So is *anything* that gives to the players more than they get by continual finking, which gives the max–min payoffs in this case. When we get to applications, sorting through this embarrassment of riches to figure out what will happen, is the first order of business.

Finite Horizons

A second weakness is that the formal game theoretic construction does not work when, on both intuitive and empirical grounds, it seems that it should. To explain this cryptic remark, imagine two individuals playing the prisoners' dilemma game precisely 10 times. The two begin knowing they will play 10 times, and when they get to the 10th round, they know it is the last.

If we look for Nash equilibria in this setting, cooperation flies out the window, at least theoretically. In the 10th round, both players know that this is the last round of play. Whatever transpired earlier, if they play to maximize their payoffs, they do better to fink than to cooperate. So in the final round, both fink.

Now consider round 9. If both are sensible, they see the logic in the preceding paragraph, and each knows that the other will fink in round 10, no matter what has happened in previous rounds or in this round. Since cooperating in the current round cannot affect the future and cooperating in the current round is worse than finking in terms of current payoffs, whatever one's rival does, the only equilibrium response in round 9 is to fink.

Then in round 8, if both see the logic in the preceding paragraphs, there is no point not to fink. And there is no point not to fink in round 7, and 6, and so on, all the way back to the start.

You may sense a family resemblance here with the discussion of the centipede game from last chapter. Actually, it is the same basic idea. We can sustain cooperation in repeated play as long as both sides believe that the negative future consequences of finking outweigh the positive current consequences of this action. When we put a definite horizon in place, there comes a time where there is no future, and the whole thing unravels.

But, just as we rarely see the first player grabbing the money in the first round of the centipede game, in a 10-round repetition of the prisoners' dilemma, we often do not see perpetual finking. We see this sometimes, but in other cases, the players cooperate for a while, with cooperation breaking down somewhere near the end. The strong prediction of the theory (no cooperation) is empirically wrong. Cooperation is sometimes sustained by some means *beyond* that provided for in the folk theorem argument. Of course, when the prisoners' dilemma game is played only once, we sometimes see cooperation. We rationalized such observations in the last chapter by saying that money is not everything to the players. I make a different point here by asserting that even if the payoffs are right, we still might see some cooperation in early rounds of a 10-round version of the game.

As far as the folk theorem is concerned, this is a sin of omission, not commission. The folk theorem argument is fine as far as it goes, but it misses something that works even when the horizon is firm, as in a 10-fold repetition of the prisoners' dilemma game. Economists have a number of working theories as to what the missing something is. Chase down the reference given in the discussion of centipede game, to see what it is.

Noise and the Breakdown of Cooperation

In the prisoners' dilemma–folk theorem construction of a cooperative equilibrium, it is important that each side observes what the other does. The prospective punishments that hold together cooperative outcomes are inflicted on a deviator following observation of the deviation, which requires that the deviation is observed.

In many applications, however, deviations from an agreed-to code of conduct are not so clearly observed. In the real world, individuals do not choose between unambiguous finking and cooperation. They take very complex, multidimensional actions, which are sometimes less than perfectly observable by their rivals. Participants have a rough idea of what others are doing but only a rough idea. Observations are made that are consistent with deviations from a cooperative scheme but also consistent with behavior that is faithful to the scheme. What happens then?

To shed light on this question, models have been investigated in which individuals obtain noisy indications of what others intended to do. The formal investigation of these ideas becomes very complex very quickly and, once again, I do not attempt to give precise formulations or detailed calculations.[2] But the basic ideas behind the formal details are relatively easy and intuitive:

Imagine A (she) and B (he) playing the prisoners' dilemma game repeatedly, with the following change in the rules. In each round, A and B simultaneously and independently choose their *intended* actions, either to fink or to cooperate. Then, with a given probability, say, 0.9, what they intend is what transpires. But with complementary probability 0.1, what transpires is the reverse of what was intended. And what transpires (not intentions) both determines the players' payoffs and is observed by the other player.

In this new setting, what happens if the two players attempt to always cooperate? Things proceed smoothly for a while, with cooperate–cooperate the outcome. But then, on round 4, say, B's apparent and observed action is fink. B claims that this is a mistake; he intended to cooperate, but against his will, his intentions were reversed by the forces of nature. He implores A not to resort to finking, which hurts both of them. Should A accede to B's arguments? If she does so, then she is open to wholesale finking by B, who

---

[2] See Section 14.3 in D. Kreps, *A Course in Microeconomic Theory* (Princeton, NJ: Princeton University Press, 1990).

can always claim that he intended to cooperate. Should A permit a certain amount of finking by B? If she does, then B has the incentive to fink just that amount. At some point, A must meet finking with punishment or B will fink all the time, and A must do this even if she is relatively sure that B's finking was unintentional. To do otherwise is to invite B to fink intentionally.

How does A punish B? The sort of punishment given by the grim co-operation strategy, finking forever after being sufficiently provoked, is not a good idea, since this punishment leaves B no alternative but to respond with finking; then cooperation can never be restored. A better punishment would be something like this: When sufficiently provoked, A should start finking, and she should restore cooperation only after B has cooperated for some number of times while she is finking. In other words, she should de-mand some payback. But the amount of payback is delicate: If she insists on too much, it will take too long to restore cooperation and B will be unwilling to invest in the relationship; once cooperation breaks down, he will say "To heck with it" (or something stronger), and resort to permanent finking. But if she does not insist on enough payback, then B loses the incentive to avoid finking altogether; that is, he finks until she initiates punishment, pays her back the small amount it takes her to restore her cooperation, then goes back to finking.

Moreover, as the level of noise rises (if instead of a 0.1 chance that in-tended actions are reversed, the probability becomes 0.2 or 0.3), it becomes harder and harder to sustain cooperation. More time is spent with one side or the other requiring payback, which lowers the value to both sides of the cooperative scheme, which lowers the amount of payback that can be re-quired without causing the other side to give up on the relationship. And, as the amount of payback that can be obtained decreases, the point is reached where neither side can be kept honestly cooperating, and cooperative equi-libria die altogether.

22.2. Collusion in an Oligopoly

One of the most important applications of these ideas is to collusion in oligopoly. To begin, we connect oligopolistic competition to the prisoners' dilemma. In general, firms in an oligopoly make many different decisions about how to compete, concerning prices they charge, advertising, location of facilities, characteristics of products they offer, and so on. In the prison-ers' dilemma, the players have a single, discrete decision: whether to fink or cooperate. Nonetheless, the strategic aspects of oligopolists' decisions often have the general flavor of the prisoners' dilemma: Oligopolists can decide whether to compete in a restrained fashion—charge a high price; advertise in restrained fashion; avoid the territory, whether geographic or in terms of product specification, of rivals—or aggressively. If one firm in an oligopoly competes aggressively, *with no response from its rivals*, then that firm is better off and its rivals are worse off. But, if all compete aggressively, all are worse off. I do not mean to denigrate the added difficulties brought on by competition on many dimensions; indeed, we return to those difficulties in just a bit. But the *basic* strategic structure of the prisoners' dilemma captures to a first approximation the strategic structure of rivalry in an oligopoly.

Once you grant this, the first-order extension of the folk theorem to rivalry in oligopoly is fairly obvious. The folk theorem indicates the possibility of sustainable collusion, either implicit or explicit. I should define this bit of Economese. Oligopolists collude when all restrain their competition with one another. This collusion can be explicit, based on discussions among the oligopolists. In some cases, such as OPEC, it can be both explicit and more or less public, in which case the oligopolists collectively form a *cartel*. But, in the United States, the European Community, and many other places as well, to stay within the antitrust laws, collusion must never be discussed but somehow implicitly agreed to, which gives us *implicit collusion*.

Whether implicit or explicit or even explicit and public, the issue addressed by the folk theorem is the same. Even if there is an explicit agreement among the oligopolists, each has a short-run interest in abrogating the agreement and competing aggressively, where by the *short run* we mean a period of time so short that rivals are unable to respond. What balances this is the long-run interests of the oligopolists, who fear that if they compete aggressively, in very short order their rivals will respond aggressively and they will be left worse off than if they had continued to collude.

The logic, if not the implementation, is clear for explicit collusion. Go back to the case of large electric turbine generators and the phases-of-the-moon scheme. Suppose an electric utility invited bids from the three manufacturers to produce a generator, formally announcing the request for bids on the 25th day of the lunar month. This order, therefore, belongs to Westinghouse. Allis-Chalmers could, if it reneged on its agreement, underbid Westinghouse, land the order, and make a pretty nice profit. But both GE and Westinghouse would know that A-C had reneged, because it is clear in the scheme that this order belongs to Westinghouse. So, perhaps for some period of time, GE and Westinghouse would compete fiercely, driving prices down and draining away the profits that A-C made from sticking to the deal. Of course, for this to be sustained, it must be that the future is worth more to A-C than what it can get by a single reneging, but that is just the folk theorem in action: When the future is worth more than a one-time renege, taking into account the punishment that would be meted out after a party reneges, collusion is sustained.

Implicit collusion is a good deal more difficult than explicit collusion, because the firms involved must find their way to a tacit understanding of what each should do. This is harder than playing the prisoners' dilemma repeatedly, because in the real world, the choices are not discrete and the situation is not symmetric. Member firms in an oligopoly often have a long history of dealing with each other, however, and implicit understandings sometimes emerge. This may involve one of the firms to act as an industry leader, announcing a particular policy and expecting others to follow. (Usually the leader is the firm with the largest market share, but that is not always the case.) Often it involves signaling through the trade and general press and through actions such as an announcement of higher prices or a plan for capacity expansion. But do not think that, because the participants cannot talk directly about it, it cannot be done. If the stakes are high enough, *if the general economic situation is supportive,* and *if the participants have a predisposition to try to collude,* collusion can be sustained.

Note well the two italicized qualifications. Economic conditions must be conducive to collusion and the participants must be predisposed to trying to collude. To take the second of these first, the statement is that collusion *can* be sustained, not that it *will* be. In the repeated game of prisoners' dilemma, grim cooperation against grim cooperation or tit for tat against tit for tat are two equilibrium strategy profiles that lead to perpetual cooperation. But always fink against always fink is also an equilibrium. So it is with oligopolies. Some oligopolies attain nice, stable collusion; that is, nice for them and bad for the consumers. Others never get there, despite the theoretical possibility that they could. A good example of a failure to collude is Boeing vs. Airbus. In this oligopolistic industry, *most* of the the conditions necessary for sustaining collusion are present (see the following). But much to the delight of the airlines, these firms have fought fiercely over orders, cutting prices, and sometimes with the support of their respective governments, offering financing at below-market rates. In part, this reflects the political pressures on the different firms. In part it reflects some economic conditions. And part (a large part in this case) is simple dislike; the folks at Boeing do not like the folks at Airbus, a dislike that is returned at least in equal measure. I do not say that Boeing would be happy to file bankruptcy papers as long as Airbus is forced into bankruptcy 6 months earlier, but perhaps.

Moving on the first qualification, I want to highlight a few of the more important ways in which economic conditions can either help or hinder collusion. In the end, each of these concerns the basic trade-off that sustains collusion: the long-term loss from a breakdown of the scheme must outweigh the momentary gains from defection.

Large Momentary Gains

Momentary gains can be large for a variety of reasons. The civilian airframe industry provides good examples. When Boeing or Airbus launches a new plane, it competes especially hard at getting a big initial order, to "make" the program for the new plane: Airframe manufacture exhibits a strong experience curve effect, and sale of a new plane to a major carrier induces others to rush to order to avoid being backlogged. Indeed, trying to get the initial launch customers can sometimes warp an entire program. The story, roundly denied by Boeing, is that when Boeing launched the 757, it was so anxious to get a large initial order from American Airlines that it added 20 seats to the basic design, making a plane that came rather too close in capacity to its own 767, which it was launching at the same time. On the other side of the coin, when one manufacturer tries to launch a new aircraft, its rival will try hard to prevent it from getting orders. For instance, in 1998, Boeing made some very attractive offers on advanced model 747s, trying in vain to keep Airbus's superjumbo out of the air. Needless to say, aggressive attempts to launch one's own new plane or to deny customers for one's rival's new plane are not helpful to trying to collude implicitly.

It is always alluring to an oligopolist to try a single, brilliant move that blows the competition out of the water and converts an oligopoly into a monopoly or into an oligopoly with one fewer rival. The creativity that can go into these moves can be substantial. A competitive encounter between Pratt and Whitney and Rolls-Royce concerning aircraft engines illustrates this. Rolls-Royce wanted to develop an advanced model of an existing air-engine, which was to be hung on 757s and 767s. Needing development capital to finance the upgrade, it approached the British government, which was willing to help as long as Rolls-Royce could show some orders. Pratt and Whitney decided to try for a knock-out blow; it offered all purchasers of P&W engines that their engines would be 8% more fuel efficient than any Rolls-Royce engine that derived from the currently existing engine. If P&W's engine was not that much more fuel efficient, then P&W would pay the difference in fuel costs. The point of this was that, if it could knock Rolls-Royce out of the market with this one move, then the British government would not provide the development capital for the upgrade, there would be *no* improved Rolls-Royce engine, and so P&W's 8% guarantee would be against a benchmark of the existing engine, which would not present P&W much of a problem.

It was a neat knockout strategy, but it did not work. Of course, with this guarantee on the table, all the airlines ordered P&W engines. But the British government took umbrage and gave the development funds to Rolls-Royce anyway, and Pratt and Whitney took a bath on the guarantees it had given.

The point is that the urge to try for a single knock-out blow destroys the delicate balance necessary for sustaining collusion. When knock-out blows seem possible, collusion is harder to sustain.

The Future Must Be Significant

Recall the discussion concerning the prisoners' dilemma played exactly 10 times. In particular, recall that in the 10th and final round, both sides have no future to trade off against the current payoffs, and so both (probably) fink. Recall also that, in the version where there is always a chance of another round, if the probability of continuing is not 0.8 but instead 0.1, then the incentive to play cooperatively is much less. If you fink in the current round, assuming your opponent is playing cooperatively, you get 8 instead of 5. The loss is that you will get 0s in the future, versus 5s if you keep to a cooperative strategy. If there is only a 0.1 chance of surviving from one round to the next, the immediate gain of 3 outweighs the loss of those future 5s: The number you get is likely to be very low if you get any at all.

In real-life settings, these simple observations attend to two points. First, the "reaction" time of each rival, or the time until the next encounter, must not be too long. If two oligopolists compete over some project today and there is a chance they will compete again in 2 or 3 years' time, but not until then and maybe not then, it will be harder to sustain collusion than if they compete day after day. Take the three turbine generator manufacturers, for instance. Imagine that, because of a downturn in the economy, orders for large turbine generators are fairly rare, say, an average of six per year. Imagine that the downturn has lasted for a while and A-C's luck in landing orders has been bad, so that A-C is finishing the last order it has on its books. Without another order and soon, A-C must either discharge some of highly skilled workers or pay an idle workforce. Because A-C "owns" only 3 days out of each month, its chances of landing any particular order is $\frac{3}{28}$. With six orders per year, A-C would have to wait on average approximately a year and a half before it would get an order according to the scheme. Its rewards for sticking to the scheme are far off in the future. At that pace, and given the uncertainties in the business and its current condition, A-C is likely to find very attractive a decision to renege and steal a particularly attractive order that belongs to Westinghouse or GE. Sure, there would be consequences. But this could well look to A-C like a case where something is better than nothing.

Similarly, in an industry that is declining or otherwise facing a deadline (for instance, because of an impending change in law or the anticipated arrival of some new competitor who will upset everything), collusion is harder to sustain. Does this mean that growth industries are the best places to find collusion? Not necessarily. In a growing industry, the opportunities for knockout blows tend to be more prevalent. Also, participants in the industry are less likely to have come to an understanding of what the collusive scheme means for each. (This is discussed further on.) Collusion is most prevalent in mature, stable industries.

Entrants Must Be Kept Out

If oligopolists sustain collusion, they will be profitable. If they are profitable, the industry will invite entry. New entrants are bad for collusion on several grounds:

- They cause the pie to be divided into more, and hence skinnier, pieces.

- It may take a while for them to "learn" how to behave.

- They may not be willing to fall into the ongoing collusion scheme. Stable collusive schemes can founder with the arrival of an entrant that refuses to play along. Indeed, even a change in ownership in one of the firms already in the industry can have this effect, as when Rupert Murdoch bought the *London Times* and upset a longstanding pattern of restrained competition among England's national broadsheet newspapers.

- Anticipating the arrival of entrants causes momentary advantage, however fleeting, to look more inviting relative to the future; and this anticipation can cause collusion to break down.

Entrants are generally bad news for collusion, and successfully collusive industries are generally those that can erect substantial entry barriers. We discussed entry barriers at length in Chapter 20 and get back to them in Chapter 23, so I leave this here.

Compliance with the Scheme Must Be Observable

This issue here corresponds to our theoretical discussion of the effect of noise on cooperation in the repeated prisoners' dilemma. If collusion is sustained by the threat that transgressions would be punished in the future, participants have to be able to observe transgressions. If it is hard or impossible to observe what one's rivals are doing, then it becomes hard to sustain collusion. Even if one's rivals keep to the scheme, if there is a wall of noise between rivals' actions and what each sees, they may "see" transgressions that are not there and set off punishment. A vicious cycle of punishments, all based on a misunderstanding, may result, leading to unrestrained competition. Indeed, the threat of such punishment can cause more chiseling on the agreement, making punishment a self-fulfilling prophecy.

An excellent example is OPEC. OPEC is a completely explicit, public cartel. The oil ministers of the OPEC nations meet at a fancy hotel in Geneva, emerging to let the world know that they have arranged quotas for each member nation that mean oil prices are going up. And the prices do go up, for a while. But, while OPEC can assign its members extraction rates, it cannot monitor compliance precisely. There are ways to get crude oil into the commodity markets that are hard to trace. And member nations of OPEC have an incentive to try to slip a few hundred thousand barrels out unnoticed, since prices are very high. When some member nations give in to this temptation, prices begin to erode. Members of the cartel see the slowly deteriorating market price of oil and know that someone is probably cheating. They may even have a fairly good idea who it is. But nothing can be proven. Everyone begins to anticipate that the Saudis, who are the enforcers of OPEC, will have to initiate punishment, which in this case means that the Saudis will pump a lot of oil to depress the price. In anticipation of this, a deadline effect takes place; all the cheaters rush to do a bit more business before the hammer comes down. This depresses prices even more and accelerates the time when the Saudis start the pumps. Prices fall precipitously and stay very low for a while, until everyone is sufficiently remorseful; then the oil ministers can meet at a fancy hotel in Monte Carlo to start the dance all over again.

Noisy observables do not imply that collusion cannot be sustained at all, but collusion is harder to sustain and less can be gotten out of it. Successful collusive schemes therefore are based on observable actions by participants; the most successful collusive schemes are those constructed in forms that support observability of what each party does. There are many ways to do this. Collusion that partitions the market geographically or by product characteristics is generally easier to enforce than a scheme in which each participant is entitled to a certain market share, because in the first sort of arrangement, it is easier to see when one firm poaches in another's territory.

But market segmentation along these lines can be less stable if the segments grow at different rates or have differing implications for technological advance. Put another way, market segmentation based on market niches may have an advantage in observability but be disadvantageous to one or more of the parties, so it may be simply unacceptable to some participants. And, as noted in Chapter 20, market segmentation strategies can adversely affect the barriers to entry for the industry as a whole.

Understanding the "Agreement"

We already remarked that the real world of oligopoly is vastly more complex than the world of the repeated prisoners' dilemma. Firms compete along many lines, in terms of price, quality, advertising, product characteristics, and so on. Moreover, market conditions are constantly in flux.

For firms to collude, they must know when others transgress on the collusive scheme. As a precursor to this, they must know what *is* the collusive scheme: which firms are entitled to what market share or which market niches, what sort of advertising is legitimate and what sort is overly aggressive, what terms can and cannot be offered to different customers. None of these things is engraved in stone; they must be negotiated by the participants. Even if explicit negotiation is allowed, this can be difficult, because no negotiated agreement covers all the contingencies. When the scheme must be "negotiated" indirectly, by press releases, statements, responses by one side to actions of the other, and so on, the potential for misunderstanding and confusion rises dramatically.

To deal with this, it is advantageous to arrange collusion on schemes that have discrete divisions of the market. (As noted in the preceding subsection, this also helps observability.) There is less to settle and less chance of confusion if we break up markets along product type or geographic lines. But, as noted previously, for such schemes to be acceptable to all concerned, they must not give too much of an advantage to one party. When a simple, discrete partition of the market can be found that is stable, it can be a substantial boon to effecting collusion.

Small Numbers, on Two Grounds

Finally, it is helpful for collusive schemes that the number of firms in the industry is relatively small, on at least two grounds.

1. The more participants there are, in general, the harder it is to observe what each is doing, the harder it is to come to agreements, and the greater the chances of misunderstanding. More participants typically increases the risk that someone will defect, triggering a price war that hurts everyone, thereby lowering the future expected value of collusion. And, typically, the gains from defection for a single participant do not fall as quickly as the gains from collusion; a defector might, temporarily, take a huge share of the market, while in the collusive scheme, the individual participant must be content with its proportional share.

2. Cartels and collusive schemes often live with a fringe of smaller firms that choose to stay out of the cartel. OPEC again provides a good illustrative example. If OPEC succeeds in holding down the production of all the members of the cartel, a small oil producer (say, Colombia, if Colombia produces any oil) would benefit. Colombia benefits even more if it refrains from joining the cartel: It need not pay dues or send its

Minister of Natural Resources to OPEC meetings and, most important, it need not accept any restrictions on the amount of oil it supplies to the market. The big oil producers often do not respond when a fringe country like Colombia pumps a lot of oil, because disciplining these marginal players is not worth the cost. Saudi Arabia can certainly pump enough oil to punish Colombia for its high rate of production. But, if Colombia's level of production is relatively small, Saudi Arabia and OPEC are apt simply to ignore it. The larger the fringe of outsiders, the less effective is collusion by the insiders.

The Public Interest

When collusion, whether explicit or implicit, is attained, it comes at the expense of the customers of the industry. In many cases and in many economies, preventing collusion is a matter of law and public policy. Sometimes the motivation for such laws and policies is distributional: It is held to be inequitable for producers to charge high prices. Sometimes these laws and policies are motivated by efficiency concerns: Collusion among manufacturers leads to prices above the marginal costs of the goods being sold, lowering overall surplus.

In some cases—most notably in the case of labor unions—laws and public policy work the other way around, allowing "collusion" among sellers. A common story in such cases is that this is needed to redress the too-powerful position of employers. And, in some cases, governments allow some collusion on grounds of standards setting, technological efficiency, or to prevent "ruinous" competition. At least these are the stories; as is almost always the case in such matters, the public policies we see mix in various proportions good economic intentions, stories of good economic intentions, and interest-group politics.

Still, the balance of such policies and laws runs against collusion. Especially when facing examples of implicit collusion, courts and, ultimately, legislatures face some difficult issues. Certainly it was illegal for representatives of General Electric, Westinghouse, and Allis-Chalmers to meet clandestinely and divide the market using the lunar calendar. But suppose competitors, with no overt discussion, fall into a pattern of charging similar prices, with one of the competitors leading the way by announcing price and service policy changes that others in the industry nearly immediately follow. Suppose, in a particular industry, the firms involved fall into a pattern of geographic segmentation, where each company "controls" the market in some region, largely unchallenged by its rivals. Suppose entry into a particular industry, especially an industry characterized by one of the preceding two patterns, is met by vicious price cutting, driving the entrant out, and for reasons we discuss next chapter, erecting psychological barriers that keep other potential entrants from entering. If legal authorities see such behavior, should they act? If legal authorities believe that the law does not give them weapons sufficient to deal with such actions, should legislatures provide them with weapons?

Taking the perspective of the firms involved, suppose legal counsel for the firm advises management that actions directed at implicit collusion with rivals are not expressly illegal; either the laws are insufficient to forbid those actions or the law is sufficiently murky, without binding precedents, so that the case is not clear. If management is nonetheless clear that the actions under consideration would be expressly directed toward implicit collusion with rivals and the spirit of the law forbids collusion, is it ethical to pursue the actions?

Regulatory authorities also face ethical dilemmas. Imagine that a very strong firm in one national market seeks to merge with some rival, which will make it formidable internationally. The authorities charged with maintaining a competitive market in a different national or international jurisdiction believe that this will cause grave harm to firms in its jurisdiction. If the law concerning whether the merger is, in fact, anticompetitive is murky, should those authorities "misuse" their power to prevent the merger, to protect home-grown firms? Should they use the threat of regulatory action to wring concessions from the merging firm, concessions that do not go directly at the merger itself but protect home-grown firms?

Do not expect to find easy answers to these questions. The line that divides legal from illegal conduct is fuzzy, and the line that divides ethical from unethical conduct is fuzzier still. Management has a responsibility to the public, but it also has a fiduciary responsibility to protect and increase the value of its equity. Regulatory bodies, being essentially political, face very severe conflicts of interest. Where the law is unclear, because of legitimate conflicts of interests on both sides, ethics are as well. These are issues that modern economies address daily, with a great deal of controversy.

While I can supply no ultimate answers to any of these questions, I would like to be clear on one point: Students with an interest in public policy, on reading this section, sometimes assert that it should be titled "How to Break the Law Against Collusion." As such, they assert that the discussion itself is unethical. I respectfully disagree, on two grounds:

1. In many cases, the law is unclear and management has a fiduciary responsibility to the holders of its equity. I am certainly uncomfortable with the position that management should push the law whenever and wherever it can. But I am also uncomfortable with the position that man-

agement should forebear from perfectly legal actions that would enhance the value of equity.

2. Effective antitrust and anticollusion enforcement begins with an understanding of how collusion and, to look ahead to next chapter, predatory entry deterrence works. Legislators who draft the laws and regulatory authorities that administer them should understand how implicit collusion can be achieved and what structural impediments can be placed in its way. If you feel that you just read "How to Break the Law Against Collusion," perhaps a more sympathetic reading would be "How Colluders Collude, and What You Can Do to Make It Difficult for Them."

22.3. Other Applications of the Folk Theorem

Oligopolistic collusion is an important application of the basic idea of the folk theorem, but it is far from the only application. Another important application involves long-term trading relations between firms. Imagine two firms, one that bottles soft drinks and another that makes glass bottles. Because of the costs of transporting empty bottles, it makes sense for the bottle manufacturer and the bottler to locate facilities close to one another. Indeed, it makes sense for them to have adjoining plants, with a conveyor belt that moves empty bottles right onto the bottling line of the soft-drink bottler.

But each firm has to worry: Once it has invested in a facility next door to the other party, perhaps the other party will try to take advantage. Perhaps, the bottle manufacturer worries, the bottler will insist on cutting the price it pays for the bottles. Once the bottle-manufacturing plant is built, what recourse does the bottle manufacturer have?

If each side to the transaction has substantial assets at risk, each can threaten the other. The bottle manufacturer can refuse to accept the demanded low price for its bottles; then the bottler must buy its bottles from a bottle manufacturer some distance away and pay for shipment. So, the bottler may be reluctant to try to take advantage of the bottle manufacturer.

Think of the relationship between Microsoft and Intel. Each firm "needs" the other to behave itself, to maintain its profitability. So these two firms maintain a wary and respectful friendship. Of course, a stealth attack from either side is always possible: Microsoft could be secretly working with Motorola to get a second source of processors that use Windows. And Intel could be secretly working with, say, Sun, on developing a processor and software that use Linux. Each side has to be fearful of the other trying for the very attractive knock-out blow that will turn the balance of power into a one-sided contest. This may have a corrosive effect on their attempts to cooperate. And it gives each firm some incentive to allow the other to monitor what it (the first) is doing. But, as long as each side can hurt the other sufficiently, wary and respectful trust and cooperation can ensue. We get back to this story, with some important elaboration, in Chapter 24.

What is true for firms is true for countries that are trading partners. At least in the days before GATT and the World Trade Organization (WTO), countries like the United States and Japan maintained relatively open trading relations because each knew that, if one tried to take advantage, by slapping on a tariff, say, the other could respond quickly, to the detriment of both sides. So why have GATT and the WTO? Because there are decided inefficiencies to having a welter of bilateral trading relationships, uniformity in trade rules makes a lot more sense. And the WTO, by enlisting the unified might of all its members, is better able to punish a miscreant. Bolivia may not have the muscle to keep, say, Japan in line, in the trading relationship between those two countries. But if Bolivia can invoke the might of all the members of the WTO to take action against Japan, if Japan misbehaves with Bolivia, then Japan is rather strongly constrained. Why does Japan accept this contraint? Because it wants access—on fair terms—to the Bolivian market.

A firm whose workforce is organized and the union that represents its workers provide another example. Without going into all the details, it may surprise you to learn that, in the United States, the presence of a labor union in a firm has a slightly positive impact on firm productivity on average, controlling for obvious factors. The story behind this is, more or less, the folk theorem: The ongoing relationship between the labor union and management allows each side to trust the other, with a positive impact on productivity. Each party can trust the other, because each can powerfully harm the other, if the other tries to take advantage. It is worth noting, though, that this is an average effect with a lot of dispersion around the mean. Some labor–management relationships are cooperative and positive, like the grim cooperation versus grim cooperation equilibrium in the repeated prisoners' dilemma; other labor–management relationships are destructive, like an always fink–always fink equilibrium in the repeated game.[3]

A final example concerns peer pressure in small work groups or partnerships. Imagine a situation in which a number of individuals have to exert themselves for the common good. If A works hard, she generates benefits for the entire group, but she bears all the costs of working hard. The same is

---

[3] This is a much more complex story than this simplistic rendition would indicate. For a fuller analysis, including citations to the data of the unionization effect on productivity, see Chapter 7 in J. Baron and D. Kreps, *Strategic Human Resources: Frameworks for General Managers* (New York: John Wiley, 1999).

true of B, C, and D. Suppose that A, while she is working, can observe how hard B, C, and D are working and they can observe her. If this group falls into a behavioral pattern where everyone works hard for the common good, all benefit. And this sort of pattern can be sustained, as long as B, C, and D have a way to punish A for slacking off.

One way to punish A, of course, is for B, C, and D to slack off themselves. But often, in small work groups, even better ways to sanction slackards exist. Small workgroups often form social groups. Each member of a well-functioning, well-constructed work group values the social interactions he or she has with other members. So if A slacks off, B, C, and D can punish her by denying her the social interaction she values. Moreover, people usually have a taste for the good regard of their peers. When A slacks off, B, C, and D can show her by word and deed that they think she is a, well, several words come to mind, but I do not want to commit any to paper. Both the threat of social sanctions and the prospective loss of the regard of her peers keeps A's nose to the grindstone and keeps the group, as a group, cooperative and productive.

In this regard, social homogeneity in a small work group can be positive. Worker A is more likely to be careful about incurring social sanctions of her fellow group members, if they all bowl at the same bowling alley or drink at the same pub. Moreover, A is more likely to be concerned with the good opinion of B, C, and D if they are socially similar to her. This is not to say that social homogeneity is the be-all and end-all of small work groups. There are often very good reasons to strive for social diversity in such groups, but there are also some reasons why social homogeneity is valuable. If the reasons to have socially diverse groups are strong, it may make sense for management to build a sense of social identity among members of the work group. Management may want to build social ties where, unaided, they would be weak, say, by putting the team through a shared experience, building diverse teams that share some common hobby or life experience, or by promoting after-hours social interaction.

But do not forget the embarrassment of riches provided by the folk theorem. A small, socially homogeneous work group may adopt an equilibrium—a specialist in organizational behavior would use the term *work norm*—of hard work to provide all with lots of compensation. But in a different equilibrium, hard work may be frowned on as "rate busting." Work groups of this sort do not guarantee high levels of effort. They make this outcome possible, but the question of the predisposition of the parties involved still must be considered.

These other applications begin with the folk theorem but do not end there:

- We already signaled in several places that credibility and general reputation can be significant factors to consider.

- The governance of relationships in these applications (who makes what decisions when) is very important and requires further analysis.

- The story throughout this chapter has been predicated on selfish, self-serving individuals, who cooperate with one another only because there is, at least potentially, something in it for them.

These three issues conclude the book.

Executive Summary

- Cooperation can emerge in repeated interactions if the parties engage in self-interested reciprocity: A does nice things today for B and C, because of the good things they will do for her later if she does or because of the bad things they will do to her later if she does not.

- The formal, game-theoretic expression of this simple idea is the folk theorem: An outcome of the game that gives to each player a payoff that exceeds the player's max–min payoff can be sustained as a Nash equilibrium if the discount factor α is close enough to 1.

- The chief weakness in the folk theorem, and in this basic idea, is that it makes too many outcomes into potential equilibria: The psychology of the parties involved can then be decisive.

- Other problems for the formal argument involve finite horizons and, especially important for applications, the destructive impact of noisy observables: To sustain cooperation, each party must know when other parties violate the cooperative agreement.

- An important application of this basic economic idea concerns collusion, both explicit and implicit, in oligopolies. For collusion to work, the members of the industry must be inclined to collude. But beyond a willingness to collude, important structural conditions must hold: momentary advantage cannot be too decisive, the future must hold enough promise to keep current actions in check, entrants must be kept out (or domesticated), compliance must be observable, the number of members cannot be too large, and the "agreement" must be clear.

- Many other applications of the basic idea are found in economics, including long-term trading relationships between companies and countries, efficiency in work settings with organized labor, and peer pressure in small work groups.

Problems

This chapter has been conceptual rather than computational. Some very nice models of the concepts can be developed (you got a taste of some of them in Section 22.1), but the mathematics necessary for an analysis of them, dynamic programming, is probably not in the arsenal of most readers. If you know dynamic programming and wish to build your understanding of these concepts by working through some models, try the problems in Chapter 14 of D. Kreps, *A Course in Microeconomic Theory* (Princeton, NJ: Princeton University Press, 1990). Meanwhile, here are two problems that are more conceptual than computational.

22.1 (The details given in this problem are simplified for pedagogical purposes. Assume that these details are descriptive of the real estate business, even if you know that they are not entirely accurate.) In the United States, real estate brokerage fees for private residences are usually 6% of the gross price of the property. That is, if a property is sold through a broker for $200,000, then $12,000 is paid to the broker(s) involved, either by the buyer or by the seller. (It is a matter of negotiation between the buyer and the seller who pays the fee.) If both buyers and sellers have their own broker, then this fee is split, usually 50–50, between the two brokers.

Brokers provide many valuable services. Because they maintain a network among themselves, they can match prospective buyers and sellers. To help sellers, they can screen out nonserious buyers; and to help buyers, they can select houses that, according to information they are given by the buyer, match the requirements and tastes of the buyer. They help sellers present their properties effectively, and they help buyers recognize important factors to consider when evaluating a particular property. Most agents are members of the Board of Realtors, a professional body that provides arbitration services when a dispute arises between agents or between an agent and client. The Board of Realtors also provides a clearinghouse for information, so individual agents are well informed about what properties are on the market. And it provides a code of ethics for agents.

Another service provided by the Board of Realtors, at least in some states of the United States, is that it registers all sales made through its members. It has a listing of recent sales that describes the property, the purchase price, mode of financing (in some cases), and all commissions and fees. Commission and fee data are made available as a service to the public, so that prospective buyers and sellers can evaluate what will be the net cost of buying or selling property and can understand what are common practices, such as whether buyers or sellers pay particular fees, in the area.

Especially in areas where housing prices have increased dramatically, far above the general rate of inflation, it is something of a mystery why broker-age fees continue to stay at 6%. The marginal cost of providing brokerage services would not seem to rise linearly with the price of property and there are many brokers, so that the brokerage service market seems fairly competi-tive. One might expect in consequence that commissions on more expensive properties would be less than 6%, and that, as housing prices inflate faster than general inflation, the average commission percentage would decrease, but this has not happened to any great extent.

You are advising a state legislator about this. The state legislator wishes to promote competition in real estate brokerage, to benefit consumers. Why, do you think, competition has not forced down commission rates? What can the state legislator do to promote competition in this industry?

22.2 Recall the Porsche dealership case from Chapter 6. We assumed there that the dealer held a monopoly in a given area. In fact, in most urban and suburban areas (at least), multiple dealers sell Porsches. Healthy com-petition among these dealers would reduce the mark-ups they charge and effectively solve the double-marginalization problem. But, will the dealers compete? Porsche must be, and is, concerned that its dealers in a particu-lar area engage in implicit collusion, setting fairly high prices for their cars. Given that Porsche is unable to "disenfranchise" its dealers, what concrete steps can Porsche take to prevent or at least impede implicit collusion among its dealers?

23. Credibility and Reputation

This chapter concerns two linked phenomena: credibility and reputation. First we ask, What renders a promise or a threat credible? Several answers are given, but we dwell in particular on the role that reputation—and the desire to protect it—can play in lending credibility to a promise or threat. After discussing these phenomena somewhat generally, we apply them to the problems facing real-life monopolists and oligopolists.

Monopolists are rarely the object of sympathy or pity. After all, according to the standard theory of monopoly, a monopolist examines the demand function for its product, determines what price maximizes profit, declares this to be the price, then watches profit roll in. What other subspecies of economic animal has a board game named after it?

The life of a real monopolist is not so smooth, however:

- When the 086 chip, the central processor of the original IBM PC, was first developed and sold by Intel, personal computer manufacturers were wary of designing computers that would use the chip. They were concerned that once they built a product around the 086 chip, had software developed for it, and established a base of customers who used the chip, they would be at the mercy of Intel, which could raise prices and thereby extract any profits the manufacturer might earn in the PC business. *How could Intel convince computer manufacturers that, once they were hooked on the 086 chip, they would not be subjected to rising prices?*

- In the early days of the copier business, Xerox had a virtual monopoly on the manufacture and sale of plain paper copiers. The technology was vastly superior to available alternatives—how many readers remember the days of carbon paper?—and some potential users, such as law firms, were willing to pay a premium price for a copier. But Xerox encountered some resistance: Potential customers anticipated that Xerox, having sold its copiers to such high-end users at a premium price, might then cut prices for the next tier of users. Anticipating this, many high-end users waited for prices to fall. *How could Xerox convince its high-end customers that it would not allow prices to fall if it saturated the high-end-customer segment of its potential market?*

- For many years, Polaroid enjoyed a virtual monopoly in the instant photography segment of the photography industry. To be sure, instant photography was small potatoes compared to standard photography, but if Polaroid's position was limited, it was enviable. Then, in 1976, Kodak announced that it was going to enter this line of business. Kodak tailored its entry strategy in a way that left Polaroid somewhat protected: Profits in instant photography come from selling film rather than cameras, and Kodak entered with a camera–film package incompatible with Polaroid's cameras and film and with a fairly expensive camera. Kodak was as much as saying that it wanted to share in the market and not drive Polaroid out. Polaroid had to choose: It could respond in "businesslike" fashion, accommodating itself to Kodak's entry, which would probably have left it with substantial profit. Or it could choose to go to war against Kodak, an expensive and uncertain proposition, especially given Kodak's immense financial strength. *Both to protect its monopoly against this incursion by Kodak and to forestall other entrants, how should Polaroid react?*

- In the mid-1970s, Boeing, McDonnell-Douglas, and Lockheed almost simultaneously introduced the first jumbo jets, the 747, DC-10, and L-1011. While the DC-10 and L-1011 were quite similar in operational characteristics, the 747 was something unique. It was larger, of course, but it also had some range advantages, especially the 747SP, which compromised size for a very impressive flight range. As a result, Boeing had a niche in the civil air transport business all to itself. Yet, despite this very impressive position in the market, major customers of Boeing continued to insist on favored treatment. *How could Boeing convince these customers that, by virtue of being a monopolist, it would set the price for its widebodies?*

This chapter examines two intertwined topics that bear on these four problems: credibility and reputation. Section 23.1 discusses the basic issue of credibility and some solutions that work in specific instances. In the course of this discussion, we further examine the cases of Intel and Polaroid. Section 23.2 discusses the economic model of reputation, emphasizing how reputation can—sometimes—repair problems of credibility. To illustrate these general ideas, we return to cases of problems facing real-life monopolists.

23.1. Credibility

Consider the extensive-form games depicted in Figure 23.1. In this game, called the *threat game*, Player B (he) must decide whether to challenge Player A (she). If there is no challenge, B nets 0, and A gets 2. But, if A is challenged, then she must decide whether to fight or acquiesce. Acquiescence nets 1 for

A, while fighting costs her 1, so it seems likely that A would acquiesce if challenged. Thus, Player B can safely challenge A and get a payoff of 1.

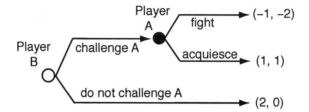

Figure 23.1. The threat game. Player B must decide whether to challenge A. If B challenges A, A must decide whether to acquiesce or to fight. Fighting is bad for A once A has been challenged, but if B is convinced that A would fight, B does not challenge A, which is good for A. Therefore, A would like to threaten B that she would fight if challenged. But is this threat credible? (A's payoffs are listed first and B's second.)

Or can he? What if, as he starts to issue the challenge, A bares her teeth, growls, and issues a warning that, *even though* it will cost her 1 to fight, she will fight if challenged. If he believes this threat, he stays out, and she gets 2. Since it does not hurt her to make such a threat—talk is cheap—she can growl away. But precisely because talk is cheap, Player B probably should disregard this threat as mere posturing. Assuming we have the payoffs right, Player A's threat lacks credibility.

Now consider the extensive-form game depicted in Figure 23.2. This game, called the *trust game*, has the same basic structure of moves as the threat game, but the payoffs (hence the names of the moves) are quite different. Player B must decide at the outset whether to trust A. If B does not trust A, both sides net 0. If B trusts A, A must choose between treating B fairly, netting 1 apiece, or abusing B's trust, which nets 2 for A and −1 for B.

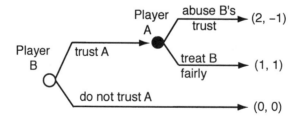

Figure 23.2. The trust game. Player B must decide whether to trust A. If B trusts A, A must decide whether to treat B fairly or be abusive. Abuse is best for A once she gets B's trust, but if B anticipates this, he will refrain from trusting A, to the detriment of both. Therefore, A would like to promise B that she will not abuse him. But is this promise credible? (A's payoffs are listed first and B's second.)

In this game, if B trusts A, A gets a higher payoff by abusing him than by treating him fairly. Seeing this, B would not trust A, to the detriment of both. So, before he decides, perhaps she should smile at him, make soothing noises, and tell him that she promises no abuse. Perhaps she can convince him to trust her. But is this credible? If A plans to abuse B, would she not smile and offer a promise of no abuse? This sort of promise is cheap talk once again, lacking credibility.

These two examples are two sides of the same coin. In each case, B must take an action, forecasting A's response. In each case, the best action for A once B has acted is clear. And, in each case, to elicit a particular initial action from B, A wishes to convince B that she would not act in her own best ex post interests. How can she do this credibly?

The term *credibility* has a number of meanings in English. In this chapter, we use the term as follows: We are always concerned, as in these games, with what some parties (call them Bs) expect, anticipate, fear, or hope would be the future actions of some other party (A). To induce desired behavior by others today, A wants to influence the expectations, anticipations, and, in some cases, fears or hopes of the Bs. Intel wanted to convince potential clients that it (Intel) would not dramatically increase the price of its microprocessors, once it has "hooked" a client base. Xerox wanted to convince potential high-end clients that it would not lower the price of its copiers in the future. Boeing wanted to convince its clientele that it would not bargain over the price of 747s. Polaroid wanted to convince prospective entrants such as Kodak that entry into Polaroid's domain of instant photography would be an unpleasant, unprofitable experience for the entrant. Is any of this credible? Unless it is, Bs cannot reasonably be expected to adopt the desired expectations, anticipations, fears, or hopes.

So the question becomes, How can A render credible what she wants to be credible?

Tying Your Own Hands, Alone

Notwithstanding their differences, the promise and threat games point out the basic conundrum: What is credible, in most cases, is what is in the interests of A when it comes time for A to choose. And, in many situations, A's interests when it comes time for her to choose are different from what she would prefer ex ante to be credible. A simple promise or threat is insufficient, when the promise or threat does not change A's ex post incentives.

The most obvious way for A to render credible the actions she wants to be credible is to redesign the situation so that those actions are in her interests ex post. She can take steps that improve the payoff to herself if she takes those actions or worsen her payoff if she does anything else. Since it is typically harder to improve one's payoffs from one action than it is to worsen them from another, we look for steps A can take that effectively tie her own hands, by substantially worsening her payoffs if she takes the "wrong" action.

Contracts promising specific performance are the most obvious examples of this. If the contract is enforceable by the courts, if it is clear that the Bs will avail themselves of court enforcement, and if the penalty for breach is substantial enough, party A, by entering into a contract, can render the promise of contractually stipulated performance quite credible. Do not go past the first two *ifs* in the previous sentence too quickly, however. Contracts work only to the extent that the courts enforce them, which requires first of all that the aggrieved party sees it in his interests to take the matter to court (see Problem 23.1).

Contracts are promises secured by court-enforced penalties in the event of breach. But they require third-party enforcement, which can be costly. Rather than enter into a contract, party A may simply structure matters so that the Bs, on their own, can punish A for misbehavior or malfeasance.

Consider, for instance, the problem facing Intel, which was to reassure its potential customers that it would not increase microprocessor prices once they were hooked. Intel could write a contract guaranteeing customers access to a certain number of microprocessors at a certain cost, but such a contract would either be extraordinarily rigid (unable to adapt to changes in the cost conditions facing Intel, technological innovations, or changes in the demands of customers) or, if it attempted to be flexible to these things, too complex to be enforceable.

Instead of offering rigid or unenforceable contractual guarantees, Intel simply licensed production of its microprocessors to several competitors. This reassured potential customers that, *if* Intel raised prices or rationed supply, the customers would have alternative sources. Intel could not successfully hold up its clients, and so it had no incentive to try.

(The Intel story is more complex than this quick recapitulation indicates, however, because for later generations of the 086 microprocessor, Intel drew back its licenses. Specifically, Intel licensed the 086 chip to 12 other manufacuters and, in fairly short order, was left with only a 30% market share in these chips. For the 286 chip, Intel cut the number of licensees to five and retained a 75% market share. And for the 386 chip, only IBM was given a license, to produce only for IBM's own computers. To the substantial extent that clients of the 086 chip were thereby addicted to subsequent generations of X86 chips, Intel's initial assurances provided by the licenses did not, in the end, provide all that much protection. It is doubtful that potential clients, when deciding whether to adopt the Pentium, would have been very reassured had Intel licensed broadly production of the first generation of Pentiums. So why has Intel not engaged in the holdup originally feared? The stories in the next section, about reputation, may be the answer. And some of Intel's clients might argue that, to some extent, Intel has taken advantage of its very strong position as a monopoly supplier of a good to which many downstream manufacturers are somewhat addicted.)

A second example involves the actions of James Casey, the founder of the United Parcel Service, the leading package delivery company in the United States. When Casey first organized UPS, his plans for the business put a premium on getting the cooperation of the truck drivers, who would be largely unmonitorable, since they work out of the eye of any supervisors. To reassure his employees that he would not take advantage of them once they entered employment and set down roots, Casey invited the Teamsters labor union to organize his workforce. This happened at a time when management in the United States was generally extremely hostile to efforts by their workforce to organize. But Casey reasoned that, by inviting the Teamsters in and, from the start, building a constructive relationship with the union, he would give his workforce a hammer with which to pound UPS if UPS management tried to take advantage of the workforce. Therefore, the workforce could trust that UPS management would not try to take advantage, which in turn would benefit the company.

The punishment for misbehavior or malfeasance need not be rendered by a court or the injured party. To make a particular sort of behavior credible, party A might enlist social sanctions. The idea, roughly, is to set things up so that, if A acts badly, she is guilty of the violation of a social norm and will be punished socially accordingly. Promising good behavior in the presence of witnesses—and being demonstrative about this—can sometimes work. Promises made within a family-owned business are generally held to be fairly credible, because breaking a promise to a family member often results in social sanctions from the family. Although there are obvious problems with business done solely in an old-boy network or (only) with "members of the club," promises made within such a closed and close social circle can gain credibility on similar grounds.

Tying Your Hands, So You Must Fight

Notions of contracts and the examples of Intel and of UPS concern situations strategically similar to the trust game: Party A wishes to ensure the Bs that she would not abuse them in the future. On the other side of the coin are situations resembling the threat game, where party A wants to render credible the threat that she will fight any B that challenges her. *Tying your hands*, in this context, means constructing the situation so that, when challenged, it is more costly to acquiesce than to fight. The idea usually is not that A makes fighting more attractive but that she makes acquiescing so unattractive that she must fight.

For instance, the threat game is a parable for entry deterrence: A potential rival (B) must decide whether to enter a market; and if it enters, the incumbent firm (A) must decide whether to accept the entry or fight, which is costly to both firms. In this context, the incumbent firm might choose a production technology that has very high fixed costs; it might commit to irrevocable agreements to purchase expensive raw materials, turning variable costs of inputs into fixed costs; it might load up on debt that can be serviced only if it maintains market share; or it might convenant its debt so incumbent management loses control of the firm if its market share slips. Then, the incumbent firm's back is to the wall, and it will fight.

A model of this is given by the game in Figure 23.3. Party A moves first, choosing between an optimal technology and a high fixed-cost (FC) technology. The word *optimal* here means that the first choice is better than the second, *fixing the action of Player B*. To see this, simply compare the payoffs to A in the top and bottom halves of the game tree.

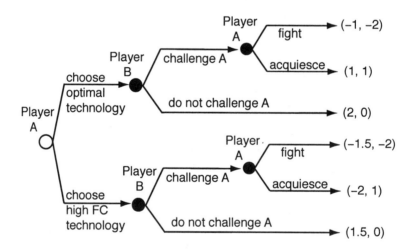

Figure 23.3. *Making fighting credible by choosing a suboptimal technology.* By choosing the high fixed-cost technology, A lowers its own payoffs at the end of each branch. But, because this choice is extremely harmful to A's payoffs if it acquiesces to entry, B is convinced that A would fight, and so B chooses not to challenge A.

The virtue of choosing the high FC technology for A is that it is particularly costly if A acquiesces to B's entry, so costly that, if A chose the high FC technology, it would rather fight than acquiesce to entry. If A chooses the high FC technology, B expects a fight if it enters and so chooses not to enter. Since the cost of maintaining the high fixed-cost technology (if it guarantees no entry) is not high relative to using the so-called optimal technology and suffering from entry, the so-called optimal technology is not optimal at all.

This, in essence, is a Porteresque entry barrier, one that lies on the interface between tangible and psychological barriers. A standard interpretation of an entry barrier is some action that makes entry unattractive to a potential entrant by lowering its payoffs if it enters; for instance, firms in the industry might lock up favored resources or channels of distribution, so that an entrant's costs would be high. What we see here is that it may work equally well for firms in the industry to take actions that commit them to a post-entry course of action costly for the entrant. In the game, A's choice of technology has no direct impact on B's payoffs; B's payoffs in each half of the tree are identical. But B's evaluation of whether to challenge A changes decisively in the top and bottom parts of the game, because of the effect of A's choice of technology on A's payoffs.

This sort of strategem is not danger free. Choosing a high fixed-cost technology can be a good move *if* it keeps at bay rivals, who fear that the technology compels the incumbent to fight. But no such strategem comes with a guarantee. Suppose A chooses the high FC technology then finds that B enters anyway. Party B might do this because its cost structure is such that it prefers to enter, even if it knows a fight will ensue, because it has its own reputation to protect (see the next section) or even out of pique. Then A is in a worse state for having tried to make its threat credible by these means.

If this warning sounds fanciful, please recall the story from Chapter 22 about Pratt and Whitney's unsuccessful attempt to knock Rolls-Royce out of a particular segment of the air-engine market. The game involved a third player, the British government, but the idea was not that different: Pratt and Whitney issued fuel-efficiency guarantees that would be costly for it *if* Rolls-Royce developed an upgraded engine. Since these guarantees starved Rolls-Royce of orders, they should have ensured that Rolls did not develop the upgraded engine, and thus they should not have been costly. This was a brilliant strategic move, *except* that the British government took umbrage and, notwithstanding the economics of the situation, gave Rolls-Royce the money it needed to develop the upgrade, moving Pratt and Whitney to a particularly bad outcome. Or, to cast this in classical military terms, burning your bridges behind you can be a great strategy if it convinces your rival not to attack, because you cannot retreat and your army, realizing this, would fight ferociously. But, if your rival attacks anyway and your ferociously fighting army loses the battle, burning those bridges would look pretty stupid in the history books.

Tying Your Own Hands, and Everyone Else's

The major chemical firms in the United States, such as Dow or Monsanto, are among the strongest lobbyests for tough safety and evironmental standards. Since these standards increase the costs of these firms, we might ask, "Why do these firms lobby for such tough standards?"

One explanation, based on the discussion in the preceding subsections, is that the firms are trying to make a credible promise to various constituencies that they conduct safe, environmentally clean operations.

This is not the only possible explanation, however. Legislation of this sort binds not only the major chemical firms but also their domestic competitors. Compliance with these sorts of regulations is generally an activity with a substantial fixed-cost component, so it is an activity relatively less expensive for the biggest firms than for smaller competitors. By supporting this sort of legislation, the big firms impose on smaller domestic competitors average costs substantially higher than the costs they impose on themselves.

This strategy (tying your own hands to tie those of your competitors) can go beyond lobbying for government regulations. Go back to the story of Jim Casey, inviting the Teamsters to organize the UPS workforce. One reading of Casey's intentions was given earlier: By empowering his workers, his promises that he would not try to take advantage of them gained credibility. Another reading is that he felt that his management style and business plan was particularly well suited to an empowered workforce; and he had the ability to work in businesslike fashion with the Teamsters, more so than his competitors. His recognition of the Teamsters did not guarantee that the union would subsequently be able to organize his rivals, but it increases the odds that his rivals would find their workforces organized, which, relatively, would be to UPS's benefit.

What If Cheap Talk Is a Little Expensive?

In the preceding discussion of both the trust and the threat games, it was asserted that growling and hissing in B's direction as he decides whether to challenge A in the threat game and smiling at B as he decides whether to trust her in the trust game are unlikely to be effective. These things cost A nothing, and if they were at all efficacious, A would do them regardless of her intentions for subsequent action. So they are meaningless; and B should disregard them. In the language of game theory, they are *cheap talk*, as in "talk is cheap," with the implicit corollary that, when talk is cheap, only actions mean anything.

Having said this, it must be admitted that cheap talk does work on some individuals. Individuals in the role of party B sometimes are impressed by hisses and growls or smiles. So, in real-life encounters, don't forswear these apparent indications of your intentions. Maybe your rival will be impressed, even if a game theorist would not be.

This presumes that the hisses, growls, and smiles are costless. In fact, they sometimes cost something, especially when the party who issues them subsequently acts in a manner at variance with her earlier expressions of intent. The cost might be psychological or trace from a loss in general reputation. Abusing a trading partner after smiling at him might, if the smile were observed by others, excite social sanctions. Growling and then backing down might cause a loss of self-esteem or exposure to ridicule.

If the cost of the hisses, growls, and smiles is high enough to guarantee that, once issued, they guarantee the desired subsequent behavior (if, for instance, to back down from a challenge after growling is so costly that, having growled, one is ready and willing to fight), then we are back to the sort of story told earlier. These are actions that, by changing A's payoffs enough, render credible promises of good behavior following smiles or threats of an aggressive response to a challenge in the wake of growls and hisses.

But what if these actions, while costly, are not so costly as to lend full credibility to the desired action? Do they then have any impact? This is a difficult and subtle question. The answers suggested by a game theoretic analysis are not entirely satisfactory. But a game theoretic analysis indicates that they may have an impact. Let me briefly illustrate this point by working with the threat game or, more precisely, the variation depicted in Figure 23.4. Prior to B's decision whether to challenge A, A can take an action, called *costly growling*, that decreases her payoffs everywhere in the game but decreases them in particular if B enters and A does not fight.

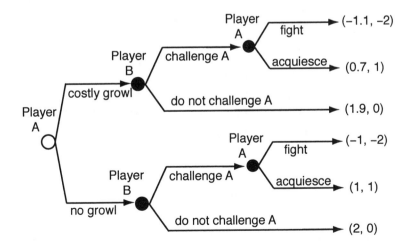

Figure 23.4. Is irrational growling rational? By choosing to growl, A lowers her payoffs at the end of each branch but not by enough that growling makes a fighting response credible. So what impact does growling have? (See the text.)

Compare Figure 23.4 with Figure 23.3, where costly growling is identified with high FC technology. In both cases, a choice of costly growling–high FC by A lowers A's payoffs relative to no growls–optimal technology. In both cases, B's payoffs are unaffected. But the crucial difference is that, while costly growling is more expensive to A if she does not fight than if she does, the relative expense is insufficient to make fighting better than acquiescing in the event of a challenge. Growling is costly, but not so costly that it makes a fighting response credible.

So what does a simple rollback of the game tree tell us? Player A would acquiesce if challenged in either half of the tree. Hence, B should enter in either half. Hence, there is no point to costly growling.

Now imagine you are Player B. You have done the analysis just given. You confidently await a lack of throaty noises from A, following which you will enter—then A growls. What do you make of this? How do you respond?

Your worry as B is that A would fight you if you challenge her. You were relatively sure she would not do so, because it is not in her interests ex post to do so. But this assurance is predicated on a presumption that A is not a crazy person who might strike out irrationally. And if A is not crazy—if you can be assured that she would acquiesce to entry—why did she engage in this pointless, costly growling? Maybe this is a sign that she is crazy. Maybe you should, on this basis, pick your fights with someone else.

Except, if this growling causes you to forgo the challenge, then growling is an entirely rational thing for A to do. In which case, you should read nothing into it and confidently challenge her. Except, if that is right, then growling is not rational.

To carry out a full analysis of this situation, you need a few techniques from the arsenal of game theorists that I have not introduced. In particular, you need to be able to put within your model the possibility (at least the possibility in the mind of player B) that A might be a crazy person who, notwithstanding the costs of fighting, is willing to fight if challenged. Further, you need to introduce into the model the notion that, if A is crazy in this fashion, she is likely to be growling. Interested readers can consult more advanced textbooks on game theory to see the ideas worked out.

On Kodak's Entry into Instant Photography

Without going into the technical details, I can still give a case history that illustrates the conundrum faced by B, when to his surprise, he hears growls from A. When Eastman Kodak attempted to enter the instant photography business, which had been completely monopolized by Polaroid, it entered in a particularly gentle fashion.[1] Its strategy seemed tailored to reassure Polaroid that Kodak would not use its immense financial and marketing strengths to knock Polaroid out of the market. In particular, Kodak designed cameras and film that were incompatible with Polaroid's cameras, so that Polaroid would be relatively reassured that it (Polaroid) would be able to continue to make money, selling film to its established customer base. In many ways, this constituted a tying our own hands strategy by Kodak.

Based on any reasonable financial calculations, it seemed better for Polaroid to acquiesce to Kodak's entry than to fight. This did not seem a fight that Polaroid could win, except by knocking Kodak out of the game with a legal victory in a patent infringement suit. Kodak had enormous financial and marketing strengths, and if the two firms went to war, it was hard to see how a "win" for Polaroid would, on financial grounds, be anything other than a loss.

Notwithstanding these considerations, Polaroid chose war. It launched patent infringement actions. It lowered the prices of its cameras. It brought to market a sequence of improved products, which it had been saving "on the shelf," presumably for just such a situation. And, right at the outset, Polaroid trotted out its founder, Edwin Land, who was quoted in the *New York Times* (April 28, 1976) as saying,"This is our very soul ... our whole life. For them, it's just another field."

It is not hard to imagine Kodak looking at Land's statements and Polaroid's actions and wondering what was going on. Trotting out Land was not entirely cheap talk. If Polaroid planned to accommodate Kodak's entry, putting Land on display would mean a somewhat painful backing down. So if Polaroid were going to accommodate Kodak, why send Land out in this fashion? Taking into account the patent infringement suits, the new products, and the lowered prices, Kodak had to wonder whether Polaroid was willing to defend its "turf," even at the cost of ruining the company's financial position. Should Kodak be influenced by this? Should it back away from what was beginning to look like a costly fight? If it could be pushed out by such saber rattling, then the saber rattling was rational after all, in which case Kodak should expect Polaroid to back down. But, if Polaroid were going to back down, why rattle those sabers, at some immediate expense, in the first place?

In the event, Polaroid's saber rattling worked. It took quite a while, but every time Kodak tried to signal its firm intentions to stay, Polaroid took what seemed to be another warlike action. In the end, Kodak folded its hand,

---

[1] For details of this case, see the HBS case study *Polaroid vs. Kodak in Instant Photography*, HBS 9-376-266.

leaving instant photography to Polaroid, a monopoly Polaroid maintained until the advent of digital photography revolutionized the industry.

23.2. Reputation

We now take up the notion of reputation. As with credibility, I have something fairly specific in mind when I use the term. Imagine you are engaged in an encounter with some other party, whom I label B. You wish to predict how B would act in a particular circumstance. Of course, your prediction is influenced by the specific circumstances of the current situation: What specific options and payoffs are open to the other party? What might he reasonably expect you to do? Beyond this, it is entirely natural for you to study his past behavior, especially in similar situations, as a guide to what he will do next. A consistent pattern of his past behavior that helps you to predict how he would behave in the current situation is his *reputation*.

Reputations are usually fairly compact descriptions of predicted future behavior. *Procter & Gamble has the reputation of fighting entry fiercely* is shorthand for P&G has fought most (perhaps not all) entrants fiercely and can be expected to do so again. A less compact version would explain the caveat—for instance, P&G has in the past shown itself willing to accommodate entrants that would not threaten its particular market niches—and in so doing sharpen the prediction conveyed by the reputation.

Also, when I use the term *reputation*, I have in mind actions taken with a conscious appreciation for how they will be looked at in the future. Suppose, for instance, that in the Sam and Jan game of Chapter 21, Jan consistently alternated his Tuesday nights between Old Pros and the art museum. Then Sam would have no difficulty in knowing where to go on any particular Tuesday, assuming she knew where Jan went the week before. But do we say that Jan's *reputation* is that he alternates between the two destinations? It is probably more appropriate to say that this is Jan's *habit* or *pattern of behavior*.

United States Supreme Court Justice Potter Stewart once famously wrote, "I shall not today attempt to further define pornography, ... but I know it when I see it." So, to some extent, it is with reputation: To understand what I mean by reputation, concrete examples are needed.

A Reputation for Trustworthiness

Imagine that A (she) and B (he) play the trust game repeatedly. To be very specific, suppose that, after each round of play there is a 0.2 chance that the just-completed encounter was the last and a 0.8 chance that they play at least one more time. The payoffs from the sequence of encounters they have is just the expected sum of payoffs. (In exactly the fashion of Chapter 22, you could alternatively imagine that they play the game infinitely many times, with a discount factor 0.8 used to compute net present values.)

As we saw earlier, the only Nash equilibrium in this game played once has B refusing to trust A, because A would abuse B if B were foolish enough to trust to A's good nature. But if we repeat the game in the preceding fashion, the folk theorem kicks in and lots of other outcomes are part of equilibria. For instance, suppose that A and B adopt the following pair of strategies:

B trusts A in the first round and continues to trust A as long as A respects that trust by treating him fairly. But, if A ever abuses B's trust, B grimly refuses to offer trust ever again.

A treats B fairly in the first round and for as long as she has done so in the past. But if she ever—by mistake, presumably—abuses B, she will abuse him in all subsequent rounds given the chance.

Computation shows that these two strategies constitute a Nash equilibrium for the repeated game. The crucial computation is, Will A treat B fairly when trusted? She can do so and continue to do so, garnering payoffs of 1 in each round, for as long as the game persists. This gives her an expected payoff of

$$1 + (0.8)1 + (0.8)^2 1 + \ldots = 1/0.2 = 5.$$

Or she can act abusively, netting an immediate payoff of 2. But then she would never be trusted again, getting 0 in all subsequent rounds, for an expected payoff of

$$2 + (0.8)0 + (0.8)^2 0 + \ldots = 2.$$

It is pretty clear that she prefers to stick with her part of the equilibrium. And, fixing her strategy, the optimality of A's strategy for him is clear.

Now let me rephrase those two strategies:

B will trust A in any round if A has the reputation of a trustworthy individual. But B will not trust A if A's reputation is that she is untrustworthy.

A lives up to her current reputation. She treats B fairly if her (A's) reputation is that of a trustworthy person. But she acts abusively if her reputation is that she is not trustworthy.

A's reputation begins as a trustworthy person and remains that way as long as she never abuses B's trust. If she does abuse B, she gains a reputation for being untrustworthy, a reputation that can never be shed.

Note that the two players' strategies are described somewhat implicitly here: The actions of A and B both depend on this mysterious new thing, A's reputation. Then the "rule" by which A's reputation evolves is specified. You can turn this into a standard pair of strategies if you wish—in which case you get the strategies just given—but the point is to phrase things in terms of A's reputation, which is a product of her past.

Of course, since the strategies defined here implicitly are the strategies given before, which form a Nash equilibrium, this is just another way of describing an equilibrium.

The key to this being an equilibrium is the answer to the question, When A has the reputation of being trustworthy, why does she protect this reputation? Why does she forgo the short-run payoff of acting abusively? Preservation of her reputation, while it sacrifices short-run payoff, is better in terms of A's long-run payoff. Protecting her reputation is A's ticket to getting B to trust her, which means good payoffs in the future. In general, a good reputation is worth something, even if it means sacrifice in the short run, if it elicits behavior from others that sufficiently improves the reputation holder's long-run prospects.

Of course, this is not the only equilibrium in the repeated encounter. The folk theorem guarantees that there will be a lot more. For instance, consider the reputation-based decision rules just given, but replace the rule for the evolution of A's reputation with *A's reputation is that she is not trustworthy and never will be.* This gives Nash equilibrium strategies where B never trusts A and A would abuse B any time B is silly enough to trust her. There are other equilibria: where B trusts A and A acts fairly on all even-numbered rounds; where A is trustworthy, hence trusted, on all rounds whose number is not prime; and so forth. When you deal with the folk theorem, you gets lots of equilibria.

A Sequence of Trading Partners

The folk theorem, as related in Chapter 22, depends on the folks involved playing the game repeatedly. Specialized to this encounter, the notion is that B, if abused by A, punishes A by refusing to trust her in the future. Suppose instead that A plays the game with one B; call him B1, for the first B. Then, if there is a second round, A plays the game with a different individual, B2. B3 is the other party in the third round, if there is one, and so on. Does this really matter to the equilibria we described?

It does not. Let me restate the first equilibrium for this context, using the language of reputation. Not much changes:

> Bn will trust A if A has the reputation of a trustworthy individual and not otherwise, when and if round n comes along.
>
> A behaves in conformance with her reputation, as before.
>
> A's reputation evolves as before: A is perceived at the outset as a trustworthy person, and this remains her reputation as long as she never abuses any B's trust. But, if she does abuse some B, she loses her reputation for trustworthiness, a reputation that can never be reclaimed.

Even though the Bs change, this is still a Nash equilibrium. Now the language of reputation is even more appropriate, since we can imagine Bn asking Bs with earlier experiences with A, "How did she treat you? What's her reputation?" In fact, as long as each Bn asks his immediate predecessor these questions and passes on the information according to the reputation rule, everything works.

To tie this back to credibility, in the promise game played once, according to the payoffs in Figure 23.2, it is not credible that A, if trusted, would treat B fairly. The payoffs facing A motivate her to act abusively once trust is given. Credibility of fair treatment can be restored by a contractual guarantee (backed by the threat of court-ordered sanctions and punishments if A breaches the contract) or by some other structuring of the situation that makes abuse relatively less attractive to A than fair treatment. *Giving A a reputation stake in a repeated game situation is one way that abuse can be made less attractive than fair treatment.* If she is trusted at some date, A does better in the short run by abuse. But traded off against this is the long-run value of her reputation, *assuming* (1) her reputation is valuable, because it induces future Bs to trust her, and (2) abuse would shatter or, at least, damage that reputation. A's desire to protect her reputation, because of its value and fragility, makes fair treatment in any single encounter a credible action.

A Reputation for Toughness: Making Threats Credible

Next imagine that A and B play the threat game repeatedly. As before, suppose that, after each round of play, there is a 0.2 chance that the just-completed encounter was the last and a 0.8 chance that they play at least one more time. The payoffs from the sequence of encounters they have is the expected sum of payoffs.

Played once, the equilibrium (obtained when you consider how credible is a threat that A would fight) has B enter and A acquiesce. Repeating the encounter opens other possibilities; consider, for instance, the following strategies for A and B, done up in the language of reputation:

As long as A has a reputation for being tough, B will not challenge her. He will challenge A if ever A's reputation is that she is a wimp.

A will fight any entry that occurs, as long as she has a reputation for being tough. She will acquiesce if her reputation is that of a wimp.

A's reputation at the outset is that she is tough. It stays that way unless she acquiesces to some entry, after which her reputation is irrevocably that of a wimp.

This holds together as an equilibrium. Moreover, it is an equilibrium where A's threat to fight is now credible. To see this, suppose B challenges A. If A fights, she loses a unit of utility this round but preserves her reputation. Assuming B reverts to the strategy of no entry, this gives a stream of payoffs of 2, the expected value of which is

$$-1 + (0.8)2 + (0.8)^2 2 + (0.8)^3 2 + \ldots = 7.$$

(Trust me on the calculation.) If, on the other hand, she acquiesces, she nets 1 immediately, destroys her reputation, and gets a payoff of 1 for the rest of the game, as long as it lasts. This gives her an expected payoff of

$$1 + (0.8)1 + (0.8)^2 1 + \ldots = 5.$$

It is a near thing, but A is better off protecting her reputation than acquiescing and losing it. And if A is going to fight to protect her reputation, B's best response is not to challenge her.

Once again, it is not necessary that one A play one B repeatedly. It suffices that A plays repeatedly, even if A plays a different B in each round, as long as B in round n bases his entry decision on A's reputation, A's reputation evolves as given, and (presumably) B in round n, prior to his entry decision, asks B in round $n - 1$, "What sort of reputation does A have? What happened in the last round?"

As in the first example, we see reputation providing credibility. Player A's threat to fight is credible because if she does not fight, she faces a much bleaker future than if she does. Acquiescence is relatively more expensive, not in the short run but overall, which is what it takes to make the threat to fight credible.

Sometimes objections to this equilibrium are heard. If the equilibrium describes how the game is played, then A never faces any entry and never has to fight. Put it this way: In the one A against a sequence of Bs version of the game, the answers given by B in round $n - 1$ to B in round n are, "A is tough; she'll fight if you challenge her. But I don't know this from personal experience, because I respected A's reputation and failed to challenge her." Hearing this, B in round n might ask, "Has anyone ever seen A fight?" To which, in the equilibrium described, the answer is, "Nope. She's never been challenged." How did A manage to get this very convenient reputation for toughness? Two answers to this question can be offered:

1. Suppose that a certain fraction of the Bs (say 10%, on average) challenge A no matter what is her reputation, because even if abused, they are better off than if they fail to challenge her. Then, every so often, A faces a challenge, which she must fight to maintain her reputation. A calculation is needed here. If A faces challenges 10% of the time on average no matter what is her reputation and she fights all challenges to forestall others, then instead of averaging 2 per round, she expects to get $(0.9)2 + (0.1)(-1) = 1.7$. If challenged and she fights, her expected payoff is $-1 + (0.8)(1.7) + (0.8)^2 1.7 + \ldots = 5.8$, versus $1 + (0.8)1 + (0.8)^2 1 + \ldots = 5$. The reputation is still worthwhile, but only barely so.

    We see this in real life. Procter & Gamble has a reputation for aggressively fighting entrants into its markets. This reputation forestalls most potential rivals, but not all. Those entrants that challenge P&G soon learn that P&G is willing to defend its reputation—which, in the end, is the real source of P&G's very valuable reputation.

2. The equilibrium describes a situation in which A has her reputation. At the outset of the sequence of encounters, she has to work to obtain it. This might mean facing entry one or two times and fighting that entry to obtain the desirable reputation; the point is that the reputation–acquisition phase describes a situation where her rivals do not know what to expect from her; hence, it is not described by an equilibrium.

One Enduring Player versus Two

In the two examples we explored, reputation works in the general fashion of the folk theorem, but both sides to the encounter need not be enduring. It is important that A is enduring, because her credibility is at stake.

Do not conclude from this that everything the folk theorem gives us can be gotten with just one enduring player, facing a sequence of rivals. For instance, imagine one enduring player playing a sequence of prisoners' dilemma games against a sequence of rivals, each of whom plays once. The short-lived players have no reputation at stake, hence they follow their short-run interests and fink. Because they do, the enduring player has no reason to do otherwise. In the repeated prisoners' dilemma game, it takes two enduring players to get away from fink–fink.

On the other hand, when two enduring players are in a conflict situation, the fact that each has a reputation stake has different consequences. Consider the threat game. Do we really expect an enduring A, playing a sequence of threat games, to be able to acquire and defend a reputation for fighting entry? If an enduring A plays a sequence of Bs, each of whom plays only once, this seems entirely plausible. The Bs, since they play only once, have no long-run incentive to press A; each is concerned with what A will do only in their one round of play. Because A has a reputation at stake and the Bs do not, A would seem to have the upper hand. But if A plays a single, enduring B, that B might seek to acquire a reputation for *never backing down* from a fight by challenging A. If B can convince A that he cannot be cowed by a fighting response by A, A has no incentive to fight. When an enduring A meets an enduring B in the repeated threat game, it seems natural to suppose that a war of attrition would start the encounter, where B challenges A and A fights, until one or the other side "gives in" to the superior staying power of the other. (If you consult the advanced literature of game theory, you'll find substantial theoretical support for these intuitions.)

Reputation and Simultaneous Play with Many Partners

In these reputation stories, either A faces a single rival repeatedly or a sequence of rivals, each of whom conditions his choice of action in his own encounter on A's previous behavior. This establishes a possible long-run vs. short-run trade-off for A, which is the basis for A's reputation.

In some instances, instead of facing the Bs in sequence, A faces them simultaneously, but in encounters that themselves take a while to develop. In such cases, A can be restrained by a desire to maintain a good reputation with all her trading partners simultaneously.

For instance, Toyota deals with many suppliers. For most of these suppliers, Toyota is an extremely important client. Toyota's dealings with its suppliers constitute an ongoing matter, but in many instances, especially since Toyota insists on double sourcing most subassemblies, the balance of power between Toyota and any single supplier is entirely in Toyota's favor. That is, Toyota's good behavior is not really guaranteed by the folk theorem applied to the two-player game involving Toyota and the single supplier, because an individual supplier lacks the muscle needed to hurt Toyota, if Toyota misbehaves.

But collectively Toyota's suppliers can punish Toyota. Toyota's network of subcontracting relationships is highly efficient because it is remarkably flexible, flexibility that derives from the fact that the "contracts" between

Toyota and its suppliers are very simple, essentially providing that contingencies will be met with goodwill as they arise. If Toyota used this lack of contractual detail and its superior muscle to abuse one of its suppliers and the other suppliers learned of this, their natural response would be to insist on detailed contracts spelling out how the parties would deal with contingencies that might arise. Toyota would lose a lot of the flexibility it has under the current system, at great cost and inconvenience.

That is the point. Toyota maintains a reputation for being a tough-but-fair client of its suppliers. It has the power to be tough and unfair in any single case, but it does not exercise that power because to do so would compromise its reputation with all its suppliers. Its desire to maintain this reputation, to preserve its relationships, is what protects individual suppliers. (We return to this story in the next chapter.)

Noise in Reputations

In the two examples given at the start of this section, the games are simple and the ability to observe what A does in each round is total. There is neither noise in observables nor ambiguity about what A's reputation is for. In the real world, both noise and ambiguity abound, and both can be killing to reputation equilibria.

Take the trust game; more specifically, take the repeated trust game with an enduring A facing a sequence of short-lived Bs. Imagine that, every time a B trusts A, A chooses between abuse and fair behavior. But these are only A's intentions: Even if A intends to treat Bn fairly, there is a probability that the Bs see A's actions in round n as abusive.

If A *seemingly* abuses a given B, subsequent Bs must punish A to some extent or A has an incentive to abuse all the Bs and blame it on happenstance. But the punishment inflicted on A should not be more severe than necessary to keep A in line. A should be given the opportunity to show contrition if possible. She should be able to get her reputation back, after the punishment. And A and the Bs should jointly look for ways of constructing A's reputation so that it can be monitored relatively noiselessly, to avoid all or at least most of the costs of noise.

Although it is a bit more complex than the model of A and a sequence of Bs, consider in this regard public accounting firms that audit the financial reports of publicly held firms. The "trusting party" in these transactions is the community of investors in the companies being audited, which must trust the auditor to put in the long hours it takes to unravel what is going on at the firm being audited. If the auditing firm works hard and honestly, it is being "fair." If it slacks off or shades its report because of, say, the consulting work it might get from the audited firm, it abuses the trust of the investing community. But, even if the auditing firm works hard and honestly, it might miss something. When that something comes to light, the auditing firm may appear to have abused the public's trust. To be more precise, the investing public would not be able to tell if the undiscovered facts were the result of abusive behavior or honest error. To let the flawed audit go by invites auditors to spend less effort on their audits or worse. But, if too little punishment invites abuse, punishment that is too harsh can also be counterproductive: If the auditors lose their reputation completely after the first honest mistake and such mistakes do happen, then *take the money and run* can become the optimal strategy. In this regard, two observations are worth making:

1. Public accounting firms protect their reputations to garner economic re-wards, which arrive in the form of continuing audit engagements, based on a reputation for trustworthiness. In recent years, audit engagement fees have become much lower, as competition in the audit business has become more fierce. This has lowered the value of a good reputation, which means less incentive to behave.

2. An auditor that seems to have missed something defends itself, ex post, by showing that it followed standard auditing procedures. But to verify this means that the standard auditing procedures have to be somewhat formulaic, with less room for subjective judgment by the auditor about what to do at a particular engagement. The same phenomenon appears in the practice of medicine, where the increasing prevalence of malpractice suits (more severe punishment for a seeming abuse of a patient's trust) means greater reliance on the practice of medicine "by the book," instead of using the physician's best subjective judgment.

The general phenomenon of noise enters into the reputation construc-tions in a second way. In the theoretical analysis of the repeated trust game, it was assumed that each B, when it is his turn to decide whether to trust A, is able to learn how A acted in previous encounters with earlier Bs. More gen-erally and more robustly, it is enough that the behavior of A can be credibly communicated from one generation of Bs to the next. Reputation, in other words, passes by word of mouth, modified perhaps by the current actions of A. But suppose B in round n cannot see how A acted previously and either has difficulty in comprehending what B from round $n-1$ is passing along or finds that testimony less than fully credible. Insofar as A can anticipate these difficulties, A has less incentive to treat fairly B in round $n-1$, as it is less likely that abuse of this B would hurt A's prospects with the next B. If this is so and the Bs anticipate this, then they have less reason to trust A. In other words, in a reputation construction, we must worry about both noise in observing A's actions and, when reputations are communicated by word of mouth, noise in the process of communication of reputation.

In real life, this leads to three further considerations:

1. Reputation constructions, especially of the sort that involve trust, work best when successive generations of A's trading parters can communicate effectively. A common language and a shared culture among the Bs is a plus on these grounds.

2. It is generally in the interest of A to facilitate this sort of communication among the Bs, because A's reputation is the basis on which the Bs trust A; if A's reputation does not work, there is no trust. Hence, we have examples such as Toyota, facilitating communication among its suppliers.

3. While it is often in A's interest to facilitate communication among the Bs, the interests of the Bs to allow for this communication is more complex. If the repeated encounters are like the trust game, then both A and the Bs benefit from clear communication channels. But if the interactions are more adverserial, as in the threat game, then the Bs want to cut channels of clear communication; they do not want A to gain the sort of backbone that preservation of her reputation gives her.

Ambiguity

Ambiguity presents problems as well. Imagine a version of the repeated trust game where, instead of a dichotomous choice between fair treatment and abuse, A has a continuum of choices to make, all of which affect her own payoff and B's. Suppose as well that objective conditions of the game change from round to round. And suppose A wants to cultivate a reputation for being fair but not generous; she is fair enough to merit the trust of B but does not overdo it. Toyota's reputation is precisely this; it is fair with its suppliers, but it certainly is not generous.

The problem is, What does *fair but not generous* mean? What are reasonable demands for Toyota to make of its suppliers? What is a fair level of compensation for them? I do not assert that these things cannot be specified to the satisfaction of the parties concerned; after all, the Toyota-supplier network works quite well. But it is easy to see how, in a real-life example, coming to terms and then keeping to those terms is not easy. When serious ambiguity enters, especially when entirely novel situations arise that call for renegotiating terms, reputations and relationships can founder.

Reputation and Multiple Constituencies

In the real world, actions taken by a particular entity are observed by multiple constituencies. An ideal action in terms of reputation with one party may cause problems in the relationships with other parties. For instance, some firms like to project to their employees an image of being a "family" rather than a business. Such firms eschew organization charts, visible signs of status differentiation, large pay differentials, and so forth. An example of such a "family" is Ben and Jerry's. If such a company decides to expand its operations and needs to raise the capital to do so externally, it has a delicate problem to solve: Bankers and others need to be reassured that the firms they lend money to mean business. Few bankers see the commune atmosphere of a Ben and Jerry's and think, "Now there's a tight ship, run on sound business principles." Accordingly, one typically sees businesses with this sort of family or commune culture run on internally generated capital, and such businesses typically are closely held.

How Fragile Is a Reputation?

In the specific reputation equilibria discussed at the start of this section, A's reputation was extremely fragile. If A ever abused a B in the trust game, no B would trust A again. If A ever acquiesced to B in the threat game, every subsequent B would enter.

Are reputations in real life so fragile? If A damages her reputation by one abusive action or in a moment of weakness, is it really gone forever? Of course not. If, say, A acquiesces to some B in the threat game but then abuses the next 10 or so Bs in a row, A is likely to reacquire a reputation for fighting. A would have a harder time restoring her reputation in the trust game, since no subsequent B would, in the equilibrium, trust her and she would never have the opportunity to show that she is not abusive. In real life, she might obtain the trust of some trading partners, at least some of the time, giving her the opportunity to resuscitate a reputation soiled by a previous action.

When noise, ambiguity, or multiple constituencies enter the story, this consideration becomes crucial, because these factors imply that A will sometimes be perceived as taking actions inconsistent with the reputation she wishes to project. Then it is essential that she be able to repair the damage.

Having said this, let me drop the other shoe. While, in real life, reputations can be repaired, if it is too easy to do so, the reputation becomes worthless. When a soiled reputation is easily repaired, preserving the reputation is less of a concern to the indivdual who holds it, and thus it provides less in the way of credibility. Powerful reputations often gain their power *because* they are fragile, which gives the reputation holder the greatest incentive to maintain the reputation.

Inertia and Reputation

The way to gain and maintain a particular reputation is to act in that fashion. It can be useful to talk about what you are doing in the press, through a website, and so forth, especially to explain the underlying principles that govern specific actions you take. But actions usually speak a lot louder than words in this domain.

As a consequence, it can be hard to change a reputation whenever a change suits you. A firm that projected a dog-eat-dog, take-no-prisoners, the-market-is-a-jungle-and-we-mean-to-survive attitude for years will have a hard time if management determines that a change of heart is called for. Going the other way, a company that has not been tough on suppliers in terms of timeliness of deliveries or quality of materials will have a hard time convincing those suppliers that times have changed.

This is not to say that change is impossible. Accompanied by symbolic acts, often including changes in top management or done in a period of crisis, reputations can be turned around. But it is not easy, and it is especially hard to shift reputation in some respects without undesirable consequences for other pieces of the reputation.

The Bottom Line on Reputation

A firm's various reputations—with suppliers, workers, rivals, customers, investors, and the local community it inhabits—are often vitally important to its smooth and efficient functioning, both because it sets the expectations of others who deal with it and because it can lend credibility to the firm's intention to act in one way or another. In fact, we see in the final chapters of this book that what has been said so far concerning reputation probably understates its general importance.

But, as important as reputations are, it is not easy to "dial in" to the desired setting or make your reputation do what you want it to. This is also a point reinforced in the last two chapters.

23.3. The Tribulations (and Salvation) of Monopolists

To illustrate the ideas of credibility and reputation, we close with a discussion of the economics of being a monopolist. Recall the classic theory of monopoly: The monopolist faces a demand curve from which it can choose the price that maximizes its profit. Customers, who are many and fragmented, take that price as given and buy what they will. The monopolist's customers could band together and use the coercive powers of the state to regulate the monopolist, specifying what price can be set. If this happens, all bets are off. Also, going the other way, the monopolist can use clever schemes of price discrimination to do even better than to set a single price. But set aside the possibilities of regulation and price discrimination and we come back to the question, Can a monopolist really set a price and then, essentially, ram it down the throats of customers?

Customers That Want to Bargain

If you ask the Boeing Corporation, it will tell you that the world does not always work that way. As of 2001, Boeing holds, and has held for many years, a fairly unique market niche with its 747 aircraft. That monopoly position was coming to an end with Airbus's development of its superjumbo. But even when Boeing held this unique niche, it faced substantial resistance from important customers. You might imagine Boeing explaining to its customers that it holds a monopoly on planes with the 747's capability, and all the economics textbooks in the world insist that it can name the price it wants to charge. But big customers such as British Air are unimpressed by economics textbooks. They argue back that they hold a monopoly on something Boeing wants, their money, and if Boeing wants some of that money, it must bargain.

British Air is a very powerful customer, so it is not surprising that it resists when Boeing tries to set a price. What about other, smaller customers? What makes us think that any monopolist can set a price and stick to it, deaf to the demands for a bargain from customers large and small? What gives credibility to the monopolist's proclamation of a particular price? Here are five answers:

1. *Numbers and the costs of bargaining.* One source of the monopolist's bargaining strength may be that it is simply too costly to bargain with most individual customers. It posts a price and tells customers to send in their orders. If a customer tries to bargain, it shrugs its shoulders and says that it has no time for this; the profit on a single sale is too small to be bothered about; it has many more important and profitable things to attend to. This is credible because bargaining with small customers takes time that it truly cannot afford. It does better to walk away from any customer that insists on bargaining.

2. *Finite capacity.* Suppose the monopolist has only a limited supply to sell. Faced with a demand that it negotiate, it can argue credibly that *if* it sells one of its very valuable pieces of merchandise at a low cost, it loses the opportunity to sell it at a high cost. New car dealers use this argument a lot; it is particularly effective when the car in question is being rationed among dealers. Of course, this works only insofar as the monopolist's capacity comes close to matching the profit-maximizing quantity that it

wishes to sell. Whenever the monopolist can find a way to commit to the production level it desires, it is safe against demands to bargain.

3. *Resale.* If the good in question can be resold, the monopolist can say to a customer who wants a low price that it cannot afford to sell at that price, because the buyer will only resell the good to some customer that would otherwise pay its high price. This is like the finite supply argument, although the issue is not that the monopolist would lose the unit it could sell to another customer; rather, it would lose the customer by providing its own competition.

4. *Most-favored-customer guarantees.* The monopolist can strengthen its case with customers that want to bargain if, with each item it sells, it includes a most-favored-customer guarantee, which says that it will rebate the customer the difference between the price this customer paid and the (lower) price paid by any other customer it deals with. This may sound like a good deal for the customers, and it is to the extent that it protects them against price discrimination. But, if the monopolist is worried about customers that want to bargain, such guarantees are good for it and bad for bargaining customers. The monopolist that provides customers with such guarantees can say entirely credibly that although it would be happy to bargain, if it sells for a low price, it is going to cost a bundle. Since it cannot charge different customers different prices, it must sell for some single price. Obviously that price is going to be the single price that maximizes its profit.

5. *Reputation for no bargains.* Suppose the monopolist does not offer most-favored-customer guarantees, it has unlimited supply or can make the product in short order, and the good cannot be resold. It can still credibly refuse to bargain if it is cultivating a no-bargains reputation. While it is in the monopolist's immediate interests to bargain with this particular customer, to do so would puncture its reputation for not bargaining with enormous adverse consequences: Every customer would want to bargain, at prohibitive cost. Note that individual customers that want to bargain see it in their interest, on these grounds, to conduct negotiations behind closed doors, in secret. The monopolist would want to make sure that all deals are public.

For these reasons and others, it is generally held to be a reasonable assumption that the single monopolist, dealing with many small customers, can get away with naming a single price and sticking to it. This does not mean that Boeing can mail a copy of this subsection to British Air and escape negotiating with it. But had Boeing established its marketing policies and reputation on a somewhat different basis than it did (had it hung tough in its initial negotiations, which would have taken a lot of nerve, since at the outset of the 747 program, Boeing did not really know what a goldmine it had in its possession), it might have been able to hold the line on this sort of thing better than it has done.[2]

The Coase Conjecture and Durable Good Monopolies

Suppose the monopolist is one and its customers are many and disorganized, so it need not worry about being forced to negotiate with them. Even so, it faces a possible foe that may be too much to overcome: itself.

This was Xerox's problem. When the first Xerox copiers were produced, Xerox identified some high-end customers who were willing to pay premium prices, if the alternative was not to buy copiers at all. Once the demand from those high-end customers was satisfied, Xerox would still face an unsatisfied demand for copiers at lower prices. So, ex post, it made sense for Xerox to sell more copiers at lower prices.

Indeed, if the customers of Xerox consistently believed that Xerox's price quotations of the moment were the best price Xerox would ever offer, Xerox could engage in first-degree price discrimination. Xerox would begin by quoting a fantastically high price, then lower the price it charged. Imagine a customer just willing to buy a copier for $100,000. When Xerox's price had fallen to, say, $99,999, *if this customer believed that Xerox would not lower price further*, it would buy a machine, then curse its decision when, a few minutes or days later, Xerox cut the price to $99,499.

The problem, from Xerox's perspective, is that its prospective customers, if they are at all intelligent, can work this out. Even if not, they would see a pattern emerge if Xerox continually lowers its prices, day after day. Even if you are willing to spend $100,000 for a copier, why not wait the weeks or months it will take for price to fall to, say, $10,000? Xerox, attempting first-degree price discrimination by starting at a very high price and letting price decline, would wind up getting no sales at high prices, as everyone waits for the seemingly inevitable price drops.

We cannot blame this entirely on a desire to engage in first-degree price discrimination. Suppose demand for copiers is given by the demand function $D(p) = 100,000 - P$, and Xerox's marginal costs are a constant $10,000. Then, as a classic monopolist with no intention of engaging in price discrimination, Xerox would charge $55,000 per copier, selling 45,000 copiers. What happens after those 45,000 copiers are sold? Xerox has another 45,000 customers willing to pay prices between $55,000 and the firm's marginal cost of

---

[2] An excellent book on this subject in the context of civilian airframes is *The Sporty Game* by John Newhouse (New York: Knopf, 1982).

$10,000. Perhaps a price of $32,500 should be tried next. But then those of the first 45,000 customers who anticipate this would not buy at $55,000 but wait for the price drop.

The monopolist's dilemma arises from the fact that customers want to wait for it to lower the price, as it chases after demand by unserved segments of the market. For this to work, it is necessary that the customers who would otherwise pay a high price be willing to wait for prices to come down. If those customers need the item quickly, then perhaps the monopolist gets back the power to name a high price and sell some of the item. Put another way, its ability to get some sales at a high price will depend, to some extent, on the impatience of its customers. The more patient they are, the harder it is for the monopolist.

Accordingly, this particular problem is felt to be most acute for monopolists who sell *durable goods*, items like cars, refrigerators, or copiers that last a long time. When the monopolist sells a durable good, its customers are more apt to be able to wait. When it sells, say, a service that must be received at a given time to be of value to the customer, it is in a much stronger position.

In the extreme case of a very durable good and very patient customers, the monopolist, according to this logic, really falls afoul of its own subsequent interests. Ronald Coase[3] advances the conjecture, the Coase conjecture, that absent some other sort of market friction, a monopolist selling a very durable good to very patient customers has no monopoly power: It essentially is forced to sell the product at marginal cost.

What saves monopolists from the dire fate conjectured by Coase?

- *Most-favored customer clauses* work well here, since when the monopolist sells units at a high price accompanied by a most-favored customer guarantee, it no longer has the incentive to chase lower-valued customers: To make sales to them, it has to give money back on the high-price sales already made.

- To return to the Xerox story, some durable good monopolists control the problem by refusing to sell their product. They *rent* it instead, with short-term leases. This practice, used for many years by Xerox in the copier market and by IBM in main-frame computers when they were close to being monopolists, works because it means that to charge lower rental rates for some customers would entail lower prices for all. (Short-term leases make it harder to convince a customer to pay the setup costs of getting used to new equipment, if the customer is not guaranteed that

---

[3] Winner of the Nobel Memorial Prize in Economics in 1991, Coase is also responsible for the notion that, to deal with problems of externalities, one should assign property rights and let the parties bargain, discussed in Chapter 14.

it could continue to rent the equipment at reasonable cost. To solve this problem, short-term leases are constructed that give the lessee the right to renew the lease at a given cost more or less indefinitely, but that does not give the same rights to the lessor. Thus, the lessee has the option to renegotiate a lower rate but cannot be held up for one higher.)

- Finally, *reputation* can play a role in defeating the logic of the Coase conjecture. There are two ways this can work. The monopolist sets a price and sticks to it, because if it ever drops its price to chase unfilled demand, its customers would believe that further dramatic price drops are coming and would wait for those very low prices.

  Second, imagine that the manufacturer faces this problem repeatedly, because it produces many generations of products. Then it is possible to refrain credibly from lowering prices for the product currently being sold, despite a large unserved market waiting for lower prices, because to do so would signal to customers for later generations of products to wait for prices to drop.

  A variation on the reputation story concerns the problem faced by artists, whose work is valuable in part because of its rarity. For this reason, for example, an artist producing a set of castings literally "breaks the mold," so that, after a given number have been produced, no more can be made. More subtly, consider the problem faced by Pablo Picasso, who could produce a prodigious number of paintings in a very short time. If he made and sold only a few, he could obtain high prices for them, because if there are only a few Picassos, each is rare and thus more valuable. But, if it is known that he could turn them out by the hundreds, his buying public would be wary. A Picasso is very nice on the wall, but it loses some of its value if enough Picassos are in circulation to put one on every wall. Picasso solved this problem by hiding the bulk of his work. Only after his death did it became clear how many Picassos there are to be hung. (Their value fell accordingly, although Picassos are so nice to hang on one's wall, that the value of each did not fall all that much.)

Intel's Problem: A Promise Not to Hold Up Clients

Boeing's problem with customers was that they wanted to bargain. Xerox's problem was that customers might hold off making a purchase, in anticipation of price declines as Xerox served lower and lower segments of its demand curve. Intel's case history illustrates a third problem monopolists can have with customers, an unwillingness to purchase an "addictive" good without some sort of assurance that the monopolist would not try to hold up its clients, once they are addicted.

We already discussed how Intel used licensing (providing itself with competitors) to provide its clients the assurances they desired, at least in the early days of the 086 chip. Since those early days, though, Intel has pulled back on licenses. Some of Intel's clients believe that Intel nowadays is actively gouging addicted clients. But on at least three grounds, Intel is still restrained from fully exploiting its monopoly position:

1. Intel's ability to hold up its clients is directly connected to its lack of competition. Insofar as it lacks competitors, the Antitrust Division of the U.S. Justice Department can pursue antitrust action against it. Intel knows it is being watched, and it has to restrain itself, in consequence.

2. The microprocessor business is an ongoing business, with new generations of microprocessors arriving at breakneck speed. Intel therefore has the opportunity to cultivate a reputation for restraining itself, a reputation that works to some effect because its clients have options for changing microprocessor suppliers as entirely new generations of chips arrive.

3. The threat of entry restrains Intel. If it abuses its clientele badly, other major players in the industry, such as Microsoft, might see real advantage to enabling a competitor to Intel.

Entry Deterrence

This takes us, finally, to the threat of entry and entry barriers. In this regard, Intel is in a fairly anomolous, delicate position. Clearly Intel does not like entrants invading its markets, and it has not been reluctant to use patent infringement suits as a weapon against firms it feels are getting too close to its market. But, to the extent that Intel relies on the threat of entry against it to reassure its clients that it would not engage in gouging, it does not want its barriers to be too high.

Whether this is correct (whether Intel benefits on the customer front by keeping alive the possibility that it may face competition), most monopolists and oligopolists have a primary interest in erecting stout barriers against entrants. We discussed entry and mobility barriers in Chapter 20, so only a little needs to be said here. But it is worth noting the connections among credibility, reputation, and what was called *psychological barriers to entry*.

An entrant that contemplates entering an industry, whether an oligopoly or a monopoly, must decide if it can be successful in the postentry competition. In part, its success is determined by tangible factors: access to channels of distribution, access to resources, technology, costs relative to those of firms already in the market, and so forth. But equally, the potential entrant has to evaluate how forcefully incumbent firms would respond. Sometimes incumbent firms must fight ferociously to survive. And the need to fight to survive in itself is a tangible entry barrier, because it makes credible the implicit threat of the incumbent firm to fight ferociously.

Often, though, the economics of the industry are such that incumbent firms do best for themselves by accommodating the new entrant. They have the power to drive the entrant from the market, but the exercise of that power would cost them more than they gain back, once the entrant is gone. In other words, the threat by the incumbent firm(s) to fight is not credible, based on economic calculations.

Still, incumbent firms in this sort of situation can successfully threaten potential rivals; this, essentially, is a *psychological barrier to entry*. The question to be answered is, On what basis are threats to fight, notwithstanding the economic consequences, still credible?

Reputation can play an important role here. When a small-time crook invades Mafia turf, it may be costly for the organized criminal element to take "corrective actions." But if the local Mafia organization allows hood 1 to invade its markets, it essentially invites hoods 2 through 1000 to do the same. It is as if the Mafia enforcer is saying to hood 1, "I'm not breaking your legs to discipline you—it's more expensive for me to do this than it would be to live with you—but by breaking your legs, I convince others that this is how we do business." Because this makes breaking the legs of hood 1 a credible threat, even if the direct costs exceed the direct benefits, it is sufficient to deter hood 1 from encroaching on Mafia territory.

The same argument extends to entirely legitimate businesses. When Union Carbide attempted to enter the disposible diaper business, it decided on a rollout strategy: It entered one local market, which was to be developed into a region (New England), to be followed with a national rollout of the product. Moreover, Union Carbide made no bones about the fact that it was interested in general in consumer expendibles, the bread and butter of Procter & Gamble, and it was willing to experiment with diapers as an initial foray. It cost P&G rather a lot locally, but it responded by bombing UC's initial area with coupons, point-of-sale discounts, and everything else it could think of. Had UC decided to enter massively, P&G might have seen the battle as one that was lost or, at least, that could be won only at too high a price and might have accommodated itself to UC's presence. But with a rollout strategy, UC might as well have worn a sign saying, "Kick me, because I can be convinced to abandon this fight," which made P&G's willingness to fight region by region entirely credible. (UC gave up fairly quickly, in the actual case.)

In any discussion of this sort, it should not go unsaid that the U.S. government, the European Community, and other, similar bodies take a dim view of actions intended to create or preserve a monopoly (or a collusive oligopoly). The legal limits of entry-deterring actions (predation) change as case law develops. So before you take too seriously some of the prescriptions offered here for forestalling entry, you might want to consult lawyers, as well as your conscience.

Executive Summary

- A credibility problem arises when some party, which must take an action in the future, wishes to be perceived ex ante as planning to take an action that, ex post, runs counter to its own interests. In some instances, typified by the trust game, the problem is that the party wishes to be perceived as planning to be "good," even though "bad" behavior is in its interest ex post. In other instances, typified by the threat game, the party wishes to be perceived as ready to be "bad," even though the ex post costs of being bad outweigh the ex post benefits.

- A variety of methods can be used to solve such credibility problems. The party can tie its own hands, typically by increasing the ex post costs of the action that it does not wish to be perceived as its optimal response. This can be done by signing an enforceable contract, or by noncontractual actions, including actions that empower to partners, rivals, suppliers, or customers. Threats or promises may be effective, but these often lack credibility because they cost nothing. (When threats or promises are somewhat costly but not costly enough to ensure they will be carried out, the analysis becomes very subtle.)

- Reputation can lend credibility to threats or promises, if the reputation will be valuable in the future. This is very much like the folk theorem of last chapter: A party behaves in a way that not optimal for it in the short term, because the long-term benefits of behaving in this fashion (maintaining its reputation) outweigh short-term costs. Reputation can work in cases in which a party deals with one other party repeatedly, the party deals with a sequence of other parties, or the party deals with a number of others simultaneously. As with the folk theorem, noise and ambiguity can kill reputations. This includes noise or ambiguity in the transmission of the reputation from one generation of partners or rivals to the next. A reputation that is easily soiled is often more powerful for being so fragile. It can be difficult to shift from one beneficial reputation to another; reputations are often fraught with inertia.

- Notwithstanding the textbook theory of monopoly, which assumes monopolists set a price and watch the money roll in, a real-life monopoly firm has a host of problems connected to credibility: (1) It must convince customers that it will not bargain. (2) Especially for durable goods monopolies, customers may anticipate prices that fall through time, as the monopolist pursues unserved portions of the market; the monopoly must convince its customers that it will not act in this fashion. (3) When the good the monopoly sells is "addictive," or requires the customer to make sunk cost investments in using the good, the monopoly may have to take action to convince customers that it will not hold them up for higher prices once they have become addicted or incurred the sunk costs. (4) To protect a monopoly position or a market niche in an oligopoly, a monopoly (or oligopoly) must deter entry into its business, which often involves convincing potential entrants that it (the monopoly) would respond vigorously to any attempted entry.

Problems

One problem captures most of the ideas of this chapter.

23.1 Two firms, Yaki Industries and Zenith Enterprise, are contemplating a joint venture. Yaki owns a proprietary technology that, unfortunately for Yaki, is unpatentable. This technology, if made available to Zenith Enterprise, could improve Zenith's profit by $20 million, in a market that Zenith serves and that is not connected to any of Yaki's ventures. But, once Zenith has access to this technology, it could use it to invade Yaki's own market as well, which would be very costly to Yaki and quite profitable to Zenith. Zenith proposes to Yaki that it (Yaki) give Zenith access to the technology for a $10 million fee. Zenith issues solemn promises that it will use the technology only in the market it currently serves, netting for it (Zenith) a net $10 million: the $20 million gain mentioned previously, less the $10 million fee. But Yaki is concerned: If Zenith were to renege on its promise and invade Yaki's market with this technology, Yaki would lose a net $10 million (including the $10 million fee), while Zenith's net gain (from both markets, net of the $10 million fee) would be $20 million.

(a) Diagram the "game" played by Yaki and Zenith, where the sequence of actions is this: First Yaki must decide whether to accept Zenith's offer and then, if Yaki accepts the offer, Zenith must decide whether to restrict its behavior as promised or invade Yaki's market. Use rollback to analyze how this game would be played. Of the games discussed in the chapter, which does this resemble?

(b) In part a, you should have come to the conclusion that Yaki would not accept Zenith's offer, because Zenith could not be trusted to keep its promise. In light of this, Zenith decides to offer Yaki a contract that includes the promise. That way, if Zenith invades Yaki's territory, Yaki can take Zenith to court. The contract would be written so that, if Zenith is taken to court by

Yaki and Yaki wins its suit, Zenith must pay Yaki damages of $20 million, which is the amount of damage that Yaki would in fact incur.

This sounds good to Yaki, but it has two concerns. The first is whether it would actually take Zenith to court in the event of a breach of contract. It would receive the $20 million, but there are court costs to consider, costs for which it would not be compensated. The best estimate is that these costs would be $12 million. Zenith's court costs would be $9 million. Assume that, if Zenith breaches the contract and Yaki takes Zenith to court, Yaki is sure to win its case. Does this sort of contractual guarantee make Zenith's promise not to invade Yaki's market credible? Can Yaki sign the contract with Zenith in this case?

(c) Unfortunately, Yaki is not convinced that, if Zenith breaches the contract and Yaki takes it to court, Yaki would win its case. The contract is necessarily a bit murky (what does it mean, precisely, that Zenith invaded Yaki's market?), and the interpretation would be up to a civil-suit jury. In fact, Yaki assesses the probability of only 0.3 that it would prevail in a court case. Assume that the two sides pay their own court costs, win or lose. Also assume that each party is an expected-monetary-value maximizer; that is, both sides are risk neutral. Under these circumstances, would the contract work, in the sense that it provides sufficient guarantees for Yaki to sign?

(d) Suppose we modify part c as follows. If Yaki takes Zenith to court and Yaki wins, the courts might award Yaki punitive damages. The amount of punitive damages will be three times the compensatory damages of $20 million. The odds of getting punitive damages awarded, conditional on Yaki's winning the suit (which has marginal probability 0.3), is $\frac{2}{3}$. Under these circumstances, will the contract work, in the sense that it provides sufficient guarantees for Yaki to sign?

(e) Suppose punitive damages, instead of being awarded to the successful plaintiff, were given to charity. That is, a losing defendant must pay the punitive damages, but the plaintiff receives only the compensatory damages. Under these circumstances, would the contract work, in the the sense that it provides sufficient guarantees for Yaki to sign?

(f) Taking the case of part e, how might reputation in some form or other help get Zenith to a deal, where Yaki would be willing to sign? Think expansively here: The first question to ask yourself is, Whose reputation and for what?

24. Transaction Cost Economics and the Theory of the Firm

- What is the economic rationale for a firm?
- Where do we draw the boundaries of the firm and why? Why conduct some transactions within a firm, while others are conducted across a market interface? How do we structure the firm internally?
- What makes a firm more or less efficient?

The ultimate objective of this chapter is to address these questions. We first study a branch of microeconomics known as *transaction cost economics*, which aims to understand the structure of complex economic transactions. Then we use this to provide some initial answers, focusing on two revolutionary innovations in industrial management: Henry Ford's system of mass production and the Toyota production system.

Throughout this book, firms are modeled entities devoted to the single-minded pursuit of maximal profits. Reiterating from Chapter 3, this model is not perfect, but for most of the questions studied in this book, it has been quite acceptable. Now we tackle some questions for which this model is anything but acceptable. The easiest way to frame these questions is with two concrete examples from recent economic history.

The automobile industry is one of the largest and most important in the world. More than that, at least twice in the 20th century, the automobile industry was the setting for truly significant revolutions in production, the mass production system pioneered by Henry Ford and the Toyota production system. There is a lot to each of these revolutions, but for current purposes, I want to focus on Ford's and Toyota's practices with regard to vertical integration.

Imagine a "tree" diagram that describes a car (see Figure 24.1). At the root is the finished car. At one level up the tree trunk are several major branches: the engine, the electrical system, the drive train, the body, the braking system, the wheels, and tires. The body, in turn, is subdivided into the frame (if the car has one), the panels, the seat assemblies, the glass, and so forth. Seat assemblies divide into the frame, the cushioning, upholstery, control systems, and so on. Somewhere up the tree from the seat frame are springs, and from the springs (perhaps immediately) is steel wire. You get the point: A car is assembled from an enormous number of pieces, tracing back to sheet steel, steel wire, rubber, glass, and so forth. And, to gild this

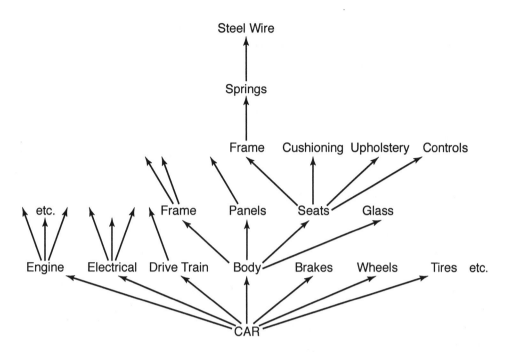

Figure 24.1. A tree diagram of a car. The trunk of the tree is the whole car. Branching off from this are the major subassemblies of the car, each of which splits into smaller and smaller subassemblies.

lily, to make the steel we need iron and coke; to make the coke, coal is needed, and so on.

When Henry Ford entered the industry, the number of parts that went into a car was fewer than today but still impressive. The standard technology for assembling cars at the time was for the assembler to purchase or fabricate most of the pieces and assemble them. When Ford pioneered his machine-paced production line, he integrated into his firm, the Ford Motor Company, the manufacture of many of the parts and pieces that went into his cars. He did not go as far as mining his own coal, but before he was finished, he made his own steel and rubber. The Ford Plant at River Rouge, Michigan, was a wonder of the industrial world, with (actual) raw materials delivered at one end of the plant and finished cars rolling out of the plant on the other end.

Why did Ford integrate all these manufacturing operations into his company? One reason was the simple belief that he could, with his superior systems for management and engineering, perform all this manufacturing more efficiently than any would-be suppliers. But there were two other, more specific reasons why he integrated vertically:

1. *Quality control.* Ford felt that purchasing parts and pieces from outside vendors gave him insufficient control of the quality of his inputs. His

assembly-line technology, as well as his general reputation for dependable cars, required a level of quality that he could get only if he controlled the manufacture of such parts.

- *Timely deliveries.* Ford's machine-paced assembly line required, to run well, the timely delivery of parts and pieces. In a "job shop" assembly operation, labor can be assigned flexibly to perform tasks that are both needed and for which the inputs are on hand. But, with an assembly line, the pieces have to be there on time. Ford could, and did, buffer uncertainties in supply with inventories of the parts and pieces. But these inventories represented unproductive capital, and Ford felt that to get a measure of timeliness in his deliveries, he needed to control of the manufacture of all sorts of subassemblies.

Jump ahead 40 years or so, to the 1960s and 1970s. Toyota pioneered a number of practices in how cars are made. Two of the most important pieces of the Toyota production system were zero defects and reduced work-in-process (WIP) inventory on the line.

- Toyota moved from the very high quality control standards of companies such as Ford and General Motors, which still allowed for a small rate of defects, to a policy that accepts no defects at all. Whenever a defect appears on the line, the production line stops and restarts only when the cause is identified and corrective action is taken.

- In what is colloquially called the Kanban system, after the inventory control tags that drive the levels of WIP inventory, Toyota gradually removed from the production line nearly all the buffering WIP inventory, inventory that keeps the line moving when deliveries to the line are not precisely on time.

In other words, Toyota has increased emphasis on the two concrete motivations Henry Ford had for massive vertical integration. Simultaneously, Toyota exists with a level of vertical integration very much lower than that of the Ford Motor Company of Henry Ford. In terms of the tree diagram, Ford of the 1920s and 1930s is outlined in the solid line in Figure 24.2, while Toyota's boundaries are given by the inside dashed line. (The Ford Motor Company today has moved dramatically toward the Toyota level of vertical integration, although not as far as Toyota or the other major Japanese car manufacturers, all of whom substantially resemble Toyota in this regard.)

Ford created a firm that was very broad and "large" in terms of the process of manufacturing cars. Toyota has a much smaller, tighter concept of what goes into Toyota and what is kept outside. Both Ford and Toyota,

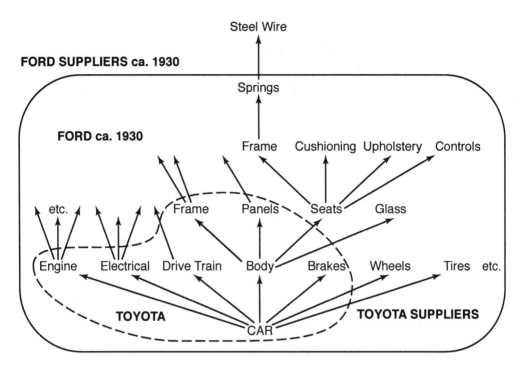

Figure 24.2. Toyota today, and Ford of the 1930s. In terms of the "tree" of a car, Ford in the 1930s took in most of the tree, while Toyota takes in much less.

in different times and under different conditions, found different answers to some basic questions:

- What is the economic rationale for a firm?

- Where do we draw the boundaries of the firm and why? Why conduct some transactions within a firm, while others are conducted across a market interface? How do we structure the firm internally?

- What makes a firm more or less efficient?

These are central questions for practicing and aspiring managers to answer. If microeconomics is going to speak to the main concerns of managers, it should have a lot to say about these questions. To say that a firm is a profit-maximizing entity is to avoid these questions entirely; to answer them, we have to dive into the "innards" of a firm, to see what makes it tick and tick well.

The agenda for this chapter is first to provide the economic tools for answering these questions, then to apply those tools to get answers. The economic tools we develop, transaction cost economics, are applicable more widely, answering as well questions such as these: How should two firms structure a joint venture? When and why does it make sense to let employees make decisions? When and why might it make sense, notwithstanding Michael Porter, to empower suppliers or clients? These are complex and subtle questions, and it would take another book to do them justice. So we only scratch the surface in terms of answers.[1] But, if you exit this chapter understanding the Ford and Toyota strategies concerning vertical integration, you'll be on your way.

24.1. Transaction Cost Economics

We begin with an outline of the basic tools and concepts of transaction cost economics.[2]

1. Many important transactions are complex in a variety of ways. They take time to complete, with the parties to the transactions having multiple opportunities to act. They often involve uncertainty, hidden information, and moral hazard.

2. The parties to these transactions are unable, either at the outset or during the transaction, to imagine all the possible contingencies that may arise or the consequences of those contingencies that they do imagine. To use terminology you will hear at cocktail parties filled with economists, the parties are *boundedly rational*.

This is not perjorative. We do not say that the parties to the transaction are not very intelligent. No one, no matter how smart, can foresee all the future contingencies and adaptations to those contingencies in transactions that stretch out for years.

Some commentators decry the notion that individuals are unable to think through all the contingencies that might occur and their consequences. Instead of being unable to do this, these commentators claim, individuals are *unwilling* to do so, because the cost in time and effort to do so would exceed the benefits that would accrue. It is better and cheaper to cross bridges when and if they are encountered than to expend the resources required to work out some grand and all-inclusive plan for how every bridge that might be encountered will be crossed. (This interpretation is one of the reasons for the name, *transaction cost economics*.) As a practical matter, though, it does not

---

[1]   After you finish this book, my strong recommendation to learn more about these issues is P. Milgrom and J. Roberts, *Economics, Organization, and Management* (Englewood Cliffs, NJ: Prentice-Hall, 1992).

[2]   This account of transaction cost economics borrows heavily from the work of Oliver Williamson. For a fuller and more nuanced treatment, I recommend his book, *The Economic Institutions of Capitalism* (New York: The Free Press, 1985).

matter whether you think some future contingencies cannot be foreseen—it is a matter of *ability*—or you imagine that folks, to avoid the costs of planning, are *unwilling* to take the time to foresee and plan for them. What matters is that the terms of the transaction are not specified at the outset, which leads to the third basic principle of transaction cost economics.

3. Both at the outset and as the transaction unfolds, the ultimate terms of the transaction are unclear. Those terms are worked out as time passes and contingencies arise. In the jargon of Economese, the terms of the transaction are initially *incomplete*, and the parties *adapt* as time passes and adaptation is required by circumstances.

For instance, when a car assembler contracts with a firm to produce seat assemblies, both parties hope for a long and mutually profitable relationship. At the outset of the relationship, neither can predict the volume of cars to be manufactured; when the workforce of either firm, if organized, will go on strike; or what sort of cars will be in vogue 5 or 10 years down the line. So, at the outset, the exact terms of trade for this transaction are unclear. As time passes and the future unfolds, the two parties must negotiate over things such as prices, product specification, volumes, delivery times, and special adjustments if one workforce or the other goes on strike.

4. To say all this is not to say that the parties enter the transaction blindly. They may be quite sophisticated in their attempts to structure the transaction in a way that is likely to lead to efficient adaptation.

It is not, "We cross bridges we come to, when we come to them." And it is not, "There are streams and rivers out there, but we have no idea what they will be like, so we just have to confront them when we find them." Instead, the notion is that the parties undertake their transaction thinking, "There are streams and rivers out there, and our experience and the experience of others gives us some idea what sorts of bridging and fording tools to bring with us. Based on those experiences, we set out provisioned in a general sense for what we think we are likely to find. Of course, we might be completely blindsided sooner or later. In fact, we are more likely than not to be blindsided eventually. But we set out ready, to the extent that we can be, for the sorts of rivers and streams we expect to have to cross."

"But," you may ask, "what sort of structuring of the transaction do we have in mind here? What sorts of 'tools' are used in this situation?" That is the main point of the theory, which we get to momentarily.

Among the transactions described to some degree by these statements are most forms of employment, education, partnership arrangements, joint ventures, professional service relations (such as legal, banking, medical, and accounting services), and long-term business-to-business vendor–customer relationships (for example, between a car manufacturer and a firm that makes seat assemblies for the manufacturer's cars).

I call the multiyear "thing" between the car manufacturer and seat-assembly manufacturer a *transaction*. But, is this a transaction? Isn't the transaction a 6-month arrangement between the two parties to provide a certain number of seat assemblies of a specified type at a specified price? Isn't the multiyear thing between the car manufacturer and seat-assembly manufacturer more properly called a *relationship*?

If you go by dictionary definitions, I believe the term *relationship* is probably more appropriate than transaction for the multiyear thing, a relationship in which the parties engage in a long, complex sequence of separate transactions. But whether you call the multiyear "thing" a *relationship* or a *transaction*, one dimension along which such transactions–relationships vary is crucial. Two examples illustrate this dimension.

For the past 27 years or so, I have done an overwhelming percentage of my food shopping at a local, family-run market. I visit this store three or more times a week; we have a relationship consisting of a long sequence of transactions. A lot of uncertainty is involved: I have some notion what I will want to buy in the future, but there is a lot I do not anticipate. Prices sometimes change in ways I do not expect, and every so often the owners of the store surprise me by dramatically changing the store's layout. So it is very much an adapt-as-we-go relationship.

Over about the same period, I have been an employee at the Graduate School of Business at Stanford University. This is another trading relationship (I provide labor services in exchange for pay) that consists of a long sequence of transactions. A lot of uncertainty is involved in this relationship as well; the set of tasks I do changes as circumstances change and contingencies arise in ways that neither the school's administration nor I can anticipate beyond a horizon of a few months, except in very broad terms. So this is another adapt-as-we-go relationship.

In at least one respect, though, these two relationships consisting of a sequence of transactions are quite different. They vary in the extent to which market pressures determine the terms of trade as time passes. I shop at the market by choice and because of some relatively minor benefits that accrue to me: I know and like the people who work there, I know where to find items I want, and especially, I know what I can and cannot get from the butchers behind the butcher counter. If this market closed tomorrow, I would certainly regret it, but I could transfer my allegiance to another store at relatively little cost. More to the point, if the owners of the market suddenly raised their prices, so those prices were out of line with the prices of similar goods in the area, I would transfer my allegiance without much thought or cost.

On the other hand, I am somewhat stuck at Stanford University. This is not to say that I could not find a job elsewhere, I probably could. But no other, similar universities are in the immediate vicinity. Moving to a suitable job elsewhere would entail substantial costs, including the costs of relocating my family, changing my children's schools, losing close personal relationships that I formed over the years, and losing that portion of my human capital especially well suited to the particular tasks I do at Stanford. Indeed, when I recently considered moving to a job that I thought would be better for me, precisely the objections of family members kept me at Stanford. Put it this way: If I ever change employers, the new job would have to hold the prospect of being substantially better than the job I have today, to cover both the costs of moving and the loss of those specific advantages that my current job confers.

Because of this, the Stanford administration, in its dealings with me, is less restrained by market forces than my local grocery. The administration could heap duties on me, fail to give me market-level raises, or otherwise take advantage of me and I would not be so quick to move to a new employer. This is not to say that I am defenseless. To a lesser extent, I can put a (figurative) gun to Stanford's head and hold it up. I do not have, perhaps, quite the hold on it that it has on me. But, having spent 27 years working at Stanford, I have developed a peculiar mix of skills that it would find difficult to replace.

For another example, imagine an MBA student at an excellent school of business. The student, periodically through the year, remits a sizeable tuition check. What has the student bought for this money? An "education" is a remarkably ambiguous good, the dimensions and qualities of which become apparent only as time passes and contingencies arise. After the first few weeks or months, the student is remarkably at the mercy of the school's administration. Perhaps, 12 months earlier, she had the choice of several fine MBA programs. But now that she has chosen and enrolled, a substantial amount of her tuition is unrecoverable. It is unclear that, if she leaves her current institution, she could move to some other program that recently was eager to have her business. So she is unlikely to leave, except for a truly major disappointment or adverse circumstance.

Transaction cost economics is not about me and my grocery store, but me and the Stanford GSB or this MBA student and her school.

5. Parties to the transaction–relationship, in varying degrees, are increasingly held hostage by their trading partners, as time passes and the transaction–relationship matures. The parties (each) stand to lose things

of value, if the transaction–relationship is sundered. The cost of a sundered relationship includes both incidentals, such as relocation costs, lost personal relationships, and the like, and the loss of more direct efficiencies that develop in the relationship and require a continuing relationship to be realized. In the jargon of transaction cost economics, the parties to the transaction develop *transaction-specific assets* that are of value only in this transaction and would be lost if the transaction ends prematurely.

6. To the extent that this is true, a party with transaction-specific assets at risk is potentially the victim of a *holdup* by the other side. That is, when it comes time to work out the terms of the deal left open at the outset, the other side might demand terms of trade that are onerous but not so onerous that the first party would willingly forfeit the value of those transaction-specific assets by taking its business elsewhere. In other words, market discipline—"If you don't give me market-level wages or conditions, I'll walk"—is lost.

Relocation costs and lost social relationships are real, important examples of the costs of a sundered relationship. But they are often just incidentals in comparison to the loss of more directly productive transaction-specific assets, including tangible investments made by one party to serve more efficiently the needs of the trading partner. Take the car manufacturer and seat-assembly manufacturer. To serve the car manufacturer most efficiently, the seat-assembly manufacturer locates a seat-assembly plant in close proximity to the car-assembly plant. The seat-assembly manufacturer may invest in dies specific to the seats that fit in this manufacturer's cars. If the car assembler practices just-in-time production methods, the seat-assembly manufacturer may invest in an electronic communication system that links its seat-assembly operation to the production line or production scheduling program of the car manufacturer. At the same time, the car manufacturer invests in the relationship with the seat-assembly manufacturer. Perhaps the car manufacturer pays for dies that fit on the stamping machines of the seat manufacturer or for the communications system. The car manufacturer may spend considerable resources educating the seat manufacturer in the car manufacturer's methods. It may spend considerable resources educating itself about the technology and capabilities of the seat manufacturer. One or both might spend considerable resources on designing seats that fit into the cars of this particular manufacturer. Much of this constitutes sunk-cost investments in the relationship. These are important investments to make if the economic relationship is going to be conducted efficiently, but they are investments that one party or the other makes and that, thereafter, puts the parties somewhat at risk of a holdup by the other side.

The confluence of these different factors—complex transactions, boundedly rational individuals, therefore incomplete transactions, and transaction-specific assets that remove market discipline and give rise to the possibility of a hold-up—characterizes the subject matter of transaction cost economics:

- If people were infinitely rational, they could specify all aspects of the transaction before it was consummated, at terms more or less determined by market forces that are binding before transaction-specific assets are created.

- If not for the complexity of the situation, even individuals moderately endowed with intelligence might be able to draft a sufficiently complete contract.

- If not for transaction-specific assets, the parties could always "appeal to the market" to determine the terms of trade as the sequence of smaller transactions that makes up the relationship takes place, much as I do when dealing with my local food market.

When the situation is complex and the parties are boundedly rational, the full terms of trade are not specified at the start; that is, the transaction is incomplete. Then, because of the development of transaction-specific assets, the impersonal discipline of the market is replaced by a truly personal relationship. The questions then are, Who calls the shots, as time passes and contingencies arise? Who determines a posteriori what those a priori unspecified terms of trade are?

7. Essential to any incomplete transaction where the parties have transaction-specific assets at risk are the rules, conventions, and procedures by which the terms of the transaction are adapted to contingencies that arise. Those rules, conventions, and procedures typically mix legal rights, contractual terms, and custom to varying degree. Those rules—in the jargon, the *governance of the transaction*—are what makes one transaction efficient and another hopelessly inefficient.

Now we are at the heart of the matter: What makes for a more efficient transaction? There are several crucial factors.

8. A transaction, generally, is more efficient
   a. the less it costs at the outset to set up and the less it costs while ongoing to arrive at the necessary adaptations and to enforce them. (This often means, the less the costly services of lawyers are required, in initial negotiations, in subsequent renegotiations, and in subsequent adversarial litigation.)

    b. the more willing are the parties involved to invest in transaction-specific assets that increase the joint surplus the transaction generates.

    c. the more willing are the parties to meet contingencies that arise with a flexible give-and-take attitude, where one party gives up something of value today if doing so is jointly beneficial, in the legitimate expectation that the favor will be returned or reciprocated.

    d. the greater is the extent to which the inevitable adaptations to changed or unforeseen contingencies meet those contingencies in an efficient manner.

What does it take for these sorts of efficiencies to be realized? We focus here on two crucial elements: who decides what and trust.

9. So that adaptations meet changed or unforeseen contingencies efficiently, decision-making authority on any particular issue is best left to the party best informed and with the best judgment about what should be done, *everything else held equal*.

10. Trust by both parties—trust that each side will act equitably, refraining from holdups and the like—is crucial.

    a. The greater is the level of trust, the less the services of costly lawyers are required, the less the amount of costly preplanning for contingencies is needed, the greater the level of flexibility that can be built into the relationship, the more likely that the parties are willing to make efficiency-enhancing transaction-specific investments, and the more likely that parties engage in efficient give and take.

    b. While, *everything else held equal*, it is sensible to place decision-making authority in the hands of the party whose information and judgment is superior, this requires that a party lacking decision-making authority trust that the decision maker will not abuse that authority.

I italicize *everything else held equal* because superior information and judgment are not enough. If the better-informed, wiser party is not trusted to use that information and wisdom in a fair manner, giving that party decision-making authority does not, in general, lead to efficiencies. Information and judgment are important factors, to be weighed carefully, but so are the reasons why trust can be given.

11. There are many sources of trust. One party may be trustworthy because its own selfish interests are aligned with the interests of the other party. It may be trustworthy because it obeys norms of behavior that lead to equity. It may be trustworthy because it has, through one means or

another, internalized the welfare of the other party. As in Chapter 22, it may be trustworthy because it needs the continued cooperation of the other party. Or, as in Chapter 23, the source of trust may be a concern for reputation in general. And, as in Chapter 19, trust may be induced by incentives that cause a relative alignment of interests.

Unified Governance: Why Henry Ford Vertically Integrated

To reiterate from the start of the chapter, in the early years of the automobile industry, at least in the United States, the major manufacturers engaged in massive vertical integration. At one point, the Ford Motor Company produced its own steel, made its own glass, and manufactured its own tires. The reason Henry Ford at Ford Motor (and nearly contemporaneously, Alfred P. Sloan at General Motors) engaged in such extreme vertical integration was precisely to economize on transaction costs. Rather than have to deal at arm's length with an autoglass manufacturer or a tire fabricator, risking holdups and other disruptions to a smooth production process, Ford and Sloan decided to centralize decision-making authority in most facets of automobile manufacture and assembly.

In the jargon of transaction cost economics, Ford and Sloan chose *unified governance* as the economical way to organize automobile manufacture. In general, the term *unified governance* refers to situations where one party takes ownership of physical assets and such intangible assets as patents, designs, and so forth. Since ownership generally implies the right to use assets as the owner sees fit, the owner can deploy the assets as it wishes, in the face of contingencies that arise. Costly negotiations and renegotiations between two or more parties and threats by one to hold up the other are eliminated. And other transaction cost advantages are provided by at least a measure of unified governance: To put pressure on suppliers or customers, a firm may integrate vertically partially; for instance, oil refiners may maintain a network of company-owned and operated gas stations, to influence the actions of gas stations which they supply.

Unified Governance: The Major Cost

Unified governance is not a panacea, however. Because human assets cannot be bought and sold, a firm that buys out a supplier cannot purchase that supplier's management or workforce. It might find new managers and workers to run the now integrated supplier operation. Or it might transact with the old managers and workforce, who become employees. Whichever it does, governance of the employment transactions becomes important, bringing with it a new set of issues and costs.

Chief among the new issues and costs is, in the jargon, the loss of *high-*

powered market incentives, replaced by *low-powered intraorganizational incentives*. The idea is a lot simpler than the jargon. If Automobile Manufacturer X buys seat assemblies from Seat Manufacturer Y and the seat manufacturer does not do a good job, the car manufacturer can take its business elsewhere. It may be costly to do so—some transaction-specific assets may be lost—but the threat is there and credible. At least, the threat is more credible than if the car manufacturer has integrated vertically into seat manufacture. Then the seat-manufacture operation is a part of X Corporation, staffed by employees and run by managers from X Corporation, who often are "on rotation." It is usually a lot easier to change nonperforming suppliers across a market interface than to fire the management and workforce of a poorly performing internal division. Insofar as the managers and workers in the internal seat-assembly operation know that they probably would not be fired quite so quickly, the threat of this drastic action, being less than fully credible, imposes no high-powered incentives on them, the way the threat of being "fired" as an outside supplier motivates the outside supplier.

This is not quite so pat as I make it sound. If X Corporation owns all the capital equipment used for making seat assemblies—if that operation is part of X Corp—then top management at X Corp can fire its seat-assembly managers and workers and replace them without losing control of the physical capital. If X Corp deals across a market interface with Y Seat Manufacture Company and it decides to change its supplier, the value of the transaction-specific physical capital would likely be lost. In this respect, unified governance lends more credibility to X Corp's threat to fire nonperforming employees than to its threat to "fire" a nonperforming supplier. But notwithstanding this, it usually is the case that the incentives for employees of a firm are not as sharp as are the incentives for a supplier to the firm.

The Alternative: Relational Contracting

An alternative to unified governance is relational contracting. Here the parties stay economically separate entities but they have a long-term relationship held together by aligned interests, goodwill, mutual threats, or one party's or the other's (or both parties') desire to maintain a reputation for being a good trading partner. Relational contracting can take the form of *hierarchical governance*, where one party calls the shots for how the relationship adapts to contingencies; various types of *balanced bilateral governance*, where the parties either share decision rights or have decision rights apportioned among them; or *trilateral governance*, where independent, neutral third parties are called on to adjudicate disputes or resolve dilemmas.

For instance, the relationship between an automobile manufacturer and one of its franchised dealers is balanced bilateral. The manufacturer chooses the design of its cars, their wholesale prices, and special incentive plans offered both to dealers and directly to purchasers of its cars. Typically, the manufacturer also coordinates regional advertising to which all dealers are required to contribute. But the area dealers have some say over the nature and character of regional advertising. And, very important, dealers decide how many vehicles to buy for resale and how to price those vehicles.

In this case, the parties to the transaction have specific decision rights—things that each has the authority to decide. In others, decision rights are shared and a measure of unanimity is needed to change things. An example of this is the system of *codetermination* in Germany, where representatives of workers at a firm and equity holders must agree before major strategic decisions are taken by the firm.

In hierarchical relationships, one party has most of the relevant decision rights. Of course, virtually never does one party have an absolute monopoly on all decision rights: Unless we move to unified governance, parties generally retain the ability to sever the relationship, albeit at some cost. So there is more of a continuum from hierarchical to balanced-bilateral relationships than distinct categories.

An example of a largely hierarchical relationship is that between a student seeking education and an MBA at a business school. As said already, the contract is remarkably incomplete: Students do not know at the outset what courses they can take, who will be their teachers, what cases will be covered, and so forth. At the same time, students very quickly develop substantial transaction-specific assets, which tie them to the school at which they begin. How are decision rights distributed? Of course, the school consults with the students about their interests. Students are allowed a fairly large amount of discretion, in the selection of electives, for instance, and in how hard they choose to work on particular courses. But, by law and common practice, in the event of a dispute, most decisions are a matter of administrative discretion. Students make requests, and deans and other administrators make decisions. Students have the right to appeal those decisions, but administrative discretion is usually affirmed, unless the student demonstrates particular malice or caprice in the decision.

Nearly every relationship has some aspects of trilateral governance: The courts or other legal or administrative authorities exist to adjudicate disputes. For instance, the courts can have a lot of say in specific franchise relationships in the United States. A disgruntled student can take her university to court. But, in some contexts, trilateral governance is more than somewhat default reliance on outside authority to interpret the law, contracts, and so forth: Sometimes specific contracts call for binding arbitration by independent authorities in the event of disputes.

Efficiency in Relational Contracts

Who gets which decision rights in relational contracts? Why is the structure balanced bilateral in one case and hierarchical in another? When might trilateral governance be a good idea, and when is it particularly inefficient? We already covered the basic principles but, to reiterate, decisions should be placed, to the extent possible, in the hands of parties that have the information and expertise necessary to make those decisions well. At the same time, decisions should be placed in the hands of parties trusted by the other side not to abuse the decision-making authority.

Begin with the case of the MBA student and her school. Here, the school administration, with years of experience in the process of education, is usually in a better position informationally to make decisions about the student's education. Of course, the individual student has a better sense of her own interests and abilities. To the extent that there is no conflict, students are given substantial freedom to structure their own educational programs. But, in case of conflict and in the important matter of setting requirements, the administration, with its relative monopoly of experience and general information, has all the decision-making authority. What about student trust, if administrators have most of the decision-making authority? For one thing, school administrators are rarely malicious or capricious by nature. Often they have an emotional attachment to the students. They enjoy good social relationships and strive to please students, at least to some extent, to create an atmosphere of good feeling. Backstopping this, the school's administrators have a fairly strong reputation stake in their decisions. Schools prosper or die based on their reputation with outside parties, and they have a significant interest in maintaining a good and accurate reputation. If the administration of a school acts capriciously or maliciously, this would dramatically and adversely affect the school's reputation. Therefore, to protect its reputation, the school will try to avoid malicious or capricious decisions.

Employment is usually thought of as being hierarchical, with the employer or hierarchical superior directing the efforts (having the decision-making authority) of employees. Indeed, employment law sanctifies this to some extent; employees can be fired "for cause" if they refuse the legitimate and legal direction of their employers. But, in some forms of employment, the employee acts as the hierarchical superior, if one defines an employee as someone who provides labor services for monetary compensation. For instance, according to this general definition, lawyers and physicians are employees of their clients. But lawyers and physicians typically decide what tasks to perform and even what bill to submit for services rendered. Why? Because (1) a physician or lawyer has specialized skills and knowledge, so that he or she is best placed to make the necessary decisions, and (2) the physician or lawyer has a much greater *reputation* stake in the matter than the individual client. Note carefully here that while the client or patient has more at stake in general, the *reputation* stake of the lawyer or physician is greater.

In a balanced-bilateral relational contract, especially one that requires unanimity, it is important that both sides have the knowledge required to make good decisions and some motivation to act constructively and fairly. For many years, works councils (the representatives of workers) of German firms fulfilled both conditions; workers were well informed and, as a collective, they pursued policies that were good for the enterprise as a whole. As long as these conditions were met, the system of codetermination was very efficient and much admired. But, in recent years, in part under the stress of the reunification of Germany, relations between management and works councils have been less constructive. There has been less trust, and thus a significantly lower level of efficiency in the system.

The advantage of trilateral governance (bringing in an outside, independent "expert") is that the third party is disinterested and, so, generally felt to be equitable. This is not automatic. Third-party arbitrators might be corrupted by one side or the other, and so the best and most successful third-party arbitrators are those that have a significant reputation stake in appearing to be fair and neutral. For many years, for instance, labor arbitration in the United States was conducted by a very small number of extremely well-paid, well-known figures, who were widely used precisely because they were so well paid that they would not risk their reputation for neutrality by taking some sort of bribe in a single case. On the other hand, the weakness of trilateral governance, at least in many cases, is that the third-party arbitrator is the least well-informed party in the negotiation and, therefore, the least able to make an efficient decision. To address this weakness, binding arbitration procedures are often designed to elicit from the informed parties as much information as possible. For instance, the well-known procedure in which an arbitrator must accept in toto the proposal made by one side or the other encourages reasonable, well-informed proposals by both sides.

Toyota's Supplier Network

Toyota, as noted, is not nearly so vertically integrated as the Ford Motor Company of Henry Ford or, for that matter, Ford or GM of fairly recent vintage. Toyota, in essence, rejects unified governance as the most efficient solution to the transactions cost problems it faces.

Instead, Toyota embraces a textbook example of relational contracting. A supplier to Toyota, such as Johnson Controls, which supplies Toyota in the United States with seat assemblies, reasonably expects a long, relatively profitable relationship with Toyota.[3] At any point in time, Johnson Controls and Toyota have a very simple, short-term contract. But Toyota's reputation is as a client that continues to work with its suppliers, *as long as they comport themselves in a manner that is appropriate for a Toyota supplier.* What is appropriate comportment? The supplier must deal with quality control issues the way Toyota does internally. The supplier must integrate its operations into Toyota's and maintain very timely delivery of its product, so that Toyota can run an operation that is very lean in terms of WIP inventory. The supplier is expected to allow Toyota full access to its own production facilities and cost structure. Toyota determines product volume rates and what it pays for the product. Toyota does not accept rigid contracts; Toyota suppliers are expected to deal on the basis of simple contracts, few if any lawyers, and a whole lot of trust in Toyota.

Suppliers are, of course, allowed to make suggestions. Suppliers that have performed particularly well are given the right to design the subassemblies they ship to Toyota, subject, of course, to Toyota's approval. (Newer suppliers and those who have not earned this level of trust work on the basis of designs formulated by Toyota.)

On net, Toyota runs a very hierarchical relationship with its suppliers, with Toyota the hierarchical superior. For instance, Johnson Controls supplies seat assemblies to the Toyota assembly plant in Georgetown, Kentucky. At one point, Toyota had a single assembly line at this facility, and so Johnson Controls had a "monopoly" on supplying seat assemblies to this factory. Johnson Controls was a model Toyota supplier, so when Toyota opened a second assembly line in Georgetown, Johnson Controls requested that it be allowed to supply this line as well. But Toyota's longstanding practice is to double-source subassemblies whenever possible, and it rejected Johnson's request. Instead, Toyota asked Johnson to form a joint venture with one of Johnson's competitors, which would go into business supplying the second assembly line. That is, Toyota asked Johnson to use its expertise as a Toyota supplier, to teach a competitor how to be a better competitor to Johnson. And the nature of the relationship between Toyota and its suppliers is such that Johnson saw little choice but to accede to Toyota's remarkable request.

Why does Johnson accept all this? Why does it risk so much, serving virtually at Toyota's whim? We briefly touched on the reason in the last chapter: Toyota's very strong reputation as a client. This reputation is for

---

[3] In this subsection, I abridge drastically the description of the Toyota supplier network and, in particular, Toyota's relationship with Johnson Controls, as given in the case "Johnson Controls, Inc.—Automotive Systems Group, the Georgetown, Kentucky Plant", Stanford University Case BE-9, 1997. A reading of the case to get a richer and fuller picture of this story is highly recommended.

being an extremely demanding client but one that provides its vendors with very steady and moderately profitable work, as long as the vendors live up to their end of the bargain. The system is very good for Toyota, and Toyota would be loathe to fracture its reputation and lose the benefits this system provides. So Johnson's best assurance of good behavior by Toyota is Toyota's concern to maintain its reputation as a demanding but fair client. Two important features of the Toyota system support this:

- Johnson Controls, by itself, probably could not hurt Toyota very badly, if Toyota abused Johnson Controls. Toyota's good behavior is guaranteed by the threat of defensive or even hostile action by all its suppliers. Thus, Johnson's guarantees arise not from its one-on-one ongoing relationship with Toyota, in the manner of Chapter 22, but from Toyota's concern for its general reputation, in the manner of Chapter 23. For this sort of reputation to provide credible guarantees, Toyota must be sure that its actions vis à vis Johnson Controls and other individual vendors are observed and understood by all its vendors. Therefore, Toyota takes a very active role in promoting communication among its vendors. It has created associations of vendors, in which the different vendors meet together frequently, discussing what Toyota is doing and learning from one another. By doing this, essentially forming a "union" of Toyota suppliers, Toyota significantly empowers its suppliers. In Porteresque terms, it takes weak suppliers and strengthens them. But this then promotes the sort of trust that the Toyota system requires, which ultimately redounds to Toyota's benefit.

- Toyota's reputation for being demanding but fair is not easy or cheap to maintain. To give firms like Johnson Controls a fair level of profit on its business, Toyota must understand the technology and cost structure of Johnson. So Toyota employees are constantly on the factory floor of Johnson Controls, taking notes and observing. Johnson is not concerned that Toyota might use the information so obtained to Johnson's detriment by, say, leaking it to a competitor or creating an internal seat-assembly operation: Toyota's reputation, secured by its desire to have this reputation, is that it does not do that sort of thing. Instead, Johnson and other Toyota suppliers understand that Toyota, to set a fair price, requires this information. So the Toyota employees on the Johnson factory floor are welcome visitors.

This takes us to the final and, ultimately, the key question about the Toyota system. Suppliers such as Johnson Controls are so integrated into Toyota's operation, that they might as well be part of Toyota. Why does Toyota maintain a stable of suppliers, rather than go for the unified-governance solution chosen by Henry Ford 40 years earlier? To be clear, there seems little doubt at this point that the Toyota way of doing business is, in the current environment, superior. What is the source of that superiority?

It is the issue of high- versus low-powered incentives, mentioned earlier. The "deal" between Toyota and Johnson Controls, and between Toyota and its other suppliers, is that Toyota will be demanding but fair, giving steady work at a moderate profit, as long as the supplier performs up to the demanding standards of a Toyota supplier. If a supplier falls short, in terms of quality, timeliness of deliveries, or achieving the rate of cost reductions that Toyota feels is appropriate, the supplier quickly becomes an ex-supplier. Indeed, Toyota's reputation for being *demanding* is at risk here: If it papered over or accepted less-than-Toyota-standard performance from one of its suppliers, others would probably learn this and have less incentive to perform at Toyota-level standards. Hence, Toyota is doubly motivated to drop badly performing suppliers. This puts a lot of motivation into the management of Toyota suppliers, motivation that likely would not be so strongly there, in the unified-governance solution of Henry Ford.

24.2. The Firm

What, then, is a firm? What makes a firm more or less efficient? The preceding discussion suggests at least four answers.

1. Firms Are the Legal Embodiment of Unified Governance

Firms have a legal status, which is particularly important in terms of liability and tax law.[4] This legal status also involves the ownership of physical and financial capital, which in turn is a powerful force in terms of governance. For instance, when a car manufacturer buys out an independent seat-assembly manufacturer, it takes title to the physical plant and equipment of the manufacturer and a fair amount of intellectual property. If, for one reason or another, the car manufacturer decides it must discharge the management or the workforce of the seat-assembly operation, it retains control of the physical plant, equipment, and intellectual property.

The legal status of a firm is also a contracting convenience in conducting multilateral transactions on multiple bilateral basis. This means that, when building and selling a car, a huge number of "entities"—assembly-line

---

[4] Legal and tax considerations often drive the structuring of firms, and they sometimes interact with the more fundamental economic concerns we discuss here. For a tax-oriented analysis of the structure of firms and their strategies, see M. Scholes and M. Wolfson, *Taxes and Business Strategy* (Englewood Cliffs, NJ: Prentice-Hall, 1992).

workers, engineers, marketing specialists, and suppliers of all sorts—are involved. The firm provides a legal entity with which each of these entities can contract bilaterally (or nearly so); the line worker has a contractual relationship with the firm (and his or her union, which is the reason for the previous parenthetical caveat), the tire supplier does as well, and so forth. It is hard to imagine how the many parties involved would arrange themselves contractually, without this "center" to their activities.

2. Firms Provide a Focus for a Reputation Stake

In our description of the relationship between Toyota and Johnson Controls, we used phrases such as "Toyota decides what price it will pay to and what quantities it requires from Johnson Controls." That is shorthand for "Managers at Toyota decide..." Toyota is not a sentient being; it can make no decisions. Managers who work for it make decisions on its behalf.

This is important because, when a manager at Toyota makes a decision, the impact of the decision is primarily on *Toyota's* reputation and not the reputation of the manager. At least, this is true concerning Toyota's reputation with its suppliers. When they get together, they speak of Toyota's reputation, Toyota's actions, and the Toyota way of doing business.

Reputation, to work effectively, to lend credibility, requires wide-ranging and frequent application. If Manager X (he) plays the trust game of Chapter 23 against one party B or against one party B per year, X is not strongly motivated to protect his reputation for being fair. Therefore, the Bs have little reason to trust X or, at least, X's desire to protect his reputation is no reason to trust X. But, if X bands together with a group of somewhat similarly situated individuals, each of whom plays a trust game, if the Xs link their reputations, creating a "brand image," and each X benefits if the "brand" is strong, then each X can be credibly expected to act honorably. In just this fashion, Toyota Manager Y, making decisions on behalf of Toyota concerning its relationship with Johnson Controls, probably does not deal with very many, if any, other suppliers. But if we can tie Y's economic interests to the fortunes of Toyota generally, and Y understands that her individual actions affect the overall reputation of Toyota, then the reputation-borne credibility comes alive.

The firm's role is to be the brand image. It is the focus of the reputation stake, and because "its" reputation is frequently on the line, as long as we appropriately align the interests of those who make decisions in its name with its long-run success, reputation-based credibility can take off.

3. Firms Provide a Focus for a Specific Reputation

Toyota treats its suppliers in one fashion; General Motors, in another. If you went to managers in firms such as Johnson Controls, which supplies both

Toyota and GM, you would find that they have very well-formed opinions about how the two differ as clients, what sort of behavior can be expected from each, and what sort of behavior can be ruled out. Consistency in the actions of managers making decisions on behalf of a single firm is valuable because it enables trading partners of the firm to understand what the firm's reputation is for. The role of the firm here is to provide a consistent and coherent focus for reputation.

Readers are sometimes fuzzy on the distinction between this answer and the one of the previous subsection, so let me put it this way. Imagine an individual A, who plays against a single B the trust game of Chapter 23. Because A plays only once, she has no ability to use a reputation, to gain credibility for not being abusive. So A looks for other folks to join in her "brand." She finds some As engaged in games like the threat game. She finds other As engaged in games like the trust game, but in utterly different economic contexts. *In theory*, if she can find a way to join her economic outcome to how well all those other As do and join theirs to hers, she can use this to create a credible reputation stake. She will not abuse her trading partner B, because to do so, for instance, causes another A's B to challenge this other A in a threat game, which would hurt this first A's financial fortunes. And her B, recognizing this, can trust her; it is now credible that she will not be abusive. This is the answer of the previous subsection: The brand or firm joins together the interests of a diverse population, giving them a collective reputation stake.

But this is a theoretical construction only. How likely is it that a completely diverse group of individuals could successfully form a reputation, a reputation that one member of the group is not abusive, a second fights entry, a third does some third thing, and so forth? How likely is it that such a complex reputation equilibrium would take hold? The answer is, Not very likely. Successful reputations, like successful brands, are those easily communicated and understood by their intended audiences. The first A, looking to form a collective reputation stake, is more likely to succeed in obtaining the outcome she wants if she "incorporates" with similar As involved in similar transactions with similar Bs. This is the answer of this subsection.

4. Firms Create Roles That Affect Expectations and Tastes

Roles affect how individuals relate to one another, in terms of what they expect and how they behave. This lies at the heart of why we see higher powered incentives across a market interface than within a firm; on average, forgiveness for poor performance within a firm is more likely and more forthcoming than forgiveness across a market interface. Moreover, expectations and tastes are organization specific. Employees A and B of a firm that has a familylike culture of cooperation relate to each other differently than employees A' and B' of a firm that has a marketlike culture of dog eat dog. Of course, many social characteristics affect what A expects of B, how A regards B, and what sort of treatment A thinks is appropriate for B. But firms have a role to play here, the more so the more intense is the firm's internal culture.

The Corresponding Challenges of Management

These four answers have immediate implications for the challenges to management of firms. First, managers must know where to draw the boundaries of the firm, trading off the benefits of unified governance of property and relatively low-powered incentives for individuals against a lack of control of physical assets but more high-powered, market-based incentives for individuals. Henry Ford was a great manager for a number of reasons, among them that he saw how, in his time and context, unified governance (extensive vertical integration) was a key to efficient assembly-line production of automobiles. Toyota's management, in a different time and context, achieved managerial distinction (and riches) by seeing how it could use relational contracting effectively to get back some of the high-powered incentives Ford's design lacked.

Second, top managers must find ways to link the economic futures of individuals who make decisions on the firm's behalf to the fortunes of the firm. We said previously that, when an individual manager at Toyota makes a decision about the price Johnson Controls will get for its seat assemblies, the reputation that is most affected is that of Toyota. But the decision also affects the reputation of the individual manager. How is the latter reputation effect manifest? The reputation of the individual Toyota manager is probably much more internal to Toyota. The individual manager at Toyota has a reputation at stake: his or her reputation with upper-level managers, which affects promotion prospects and the like.

At the same time, decision rights within Toyota for decisions that affect Toyota's reputation must be carefully crafted. A firm such as Toyota often finds it helpful, to protect its collective reputation from injury by individuals making decisions in its name, to require a substantial level of consensus before decisions are made. Instead of giving the decision rights on how much Johnson Controls will be paid to a single manager, Toyota can give those rights to a committee of its managers, who are more likely to weigh properly the impact this single decision would have on Toyota's general reputation.

Third, managers must manage the specific reputation of their firm to satisfy a number of goals. The reputation must be strong and easily communicated to trading partners. It must be easily communicated to employees of the firm whose actions are meant to align with the reputation. And it must be robust to the sorts of dilemmas and problems the firm will face. Note the conflicts here: A firm with a wide-ranging business, which faces a great diversity of dilemmas and problems, wants a fairly general reputation, one that is adaptable to the great diversity of problems. But the broader and less specific is the reputation, the harder it is to communicate and the weaker the guarantees it provides. For these reasons, managers often limit the scope of what their firm will take on, finding a niche that can be adequately served by a strong, specific reputation.

Fourth, managers must manage the internal culture of the firm, promoting efficient intrafirm transactions. For instance, in organizations where performance is easy to measure, the "technology" of production involves few and controllable interdependencies among workers, and productivity requires substantial effort, a marketlike culture within the organization probably works well. If work is interdependent and individual performance cannot be measured, a culture of cooperation is probably favored.

As you might imagine, these thoughts only scratch the surface of the challenges facing managers, once you think of a firm or other sort of organization in these fashions. We are rapidly reaching the end of this book, so surface scratching is all we can manage, but don't despair. You are very likely to pick up these ideas and move ahead on them—now that you are equipped to do so—in courses on strategic mangement, human resource management, and the like.

24.3. Transaction Costs and Ethical Behavior

In summer 2002, the business pages of the newspapers and news magazines were filled with stories of allegedly unethical and perhaps illegal behavior by top management of large corporations. The scandals concerned management hiding relevant information from the financial markets through the use of creative accounting, but they went well beyond this in some cases. In general, the scandals involved *pushing the envelope*: Managers are allowed a certain amount of discretion in what they do and what and how they report what they have done. Some actions and some sorts of reports are proscribed by law, but there is always a gray area, and in many of the cases in the news, management stood accused of pushing as far into the gray area as it could, perhaps going beyond the gray area, but in any event using its skills and creativity to circumvent the spirit of the law. Certainly any willful and knowing violations of the law (at least, of these sorts) is unethical. But most commentators asserted that simply pushing the envelope, without crossing the line, is also unethical.

Is pushing the envelope in this fashion unethical? This may involve an ethical dilemma: Pushing the envelope may serve the interests of shareholders, to whom management has a fiduciary responsibility, although it harms the interests of other stakeholders, such as workers, suppliers, customers, and the general public. Just as in the question of whether implicit collusion is unethical, management sometimes has to balance its responsibility to shareholders with its other responsibilities. But this type of dilemma did not seem to be present in many of the cases in 2002, where management was, if anything, taking actions that hurt outside shareholders as well as other stakeholders, to line its own personal pockets. Stipulating that this is so, can we say that this sort of pushing the envelope is unethical?

One sometimes hears, in connection with sports, that it is right to push to the edge of rulebreaking; it is the responsibility of the rule makers to provide rules that outlaw undesirable behavior, and it is the responsibility of athletes to do everything they can within the rules to win.

Management, however, is more complex than sports, chiefly because economics is not a zero-sum competition. Doing anything and everything as a manager that is not specifically excluded by law—pushing the envelope to try to see how far you can go—can lead to substantial inefficiencies. The story here involves transaction costs. Parties to complex transactions have myriad opportunities to take advantage of others. Moral hazards and hidden information abound. These opportunities can be dealt with by formal "contractual" safeguards. But each formal, explicit safeguard comes at some cost, in terms of specifying and enforcing the safeguard and in transactional rigidities and maladaptations caused by formal, specific safeguards. To the extent that certain behaviors are "off the table" because they are regarded as unethical, the parties involved in a specific transaction can economize on transaction costs.

This is the instrumental case for ethics and ethical behavior. If ethical behavior, suitably defined, is guaranteed, then transaction costs can be lowered. For instance, if top management could be trusted to draw up income statements that did not try to paint an overly rosy picture or otherwise mislead investors, less would have to be spent on auditors, there would be less need for rigid accounting rules and procedures, and capital markets would function more effectively. But, as events in 2002 indicated, ethical behavior, at least defined in this fashion, is not guaranteed.

Indeed, when managers can line their own pockets by issuing misleading reports, why would they behave ethically? In the face of clear and direct incentives to engage in unethical behavior, what prevents an epidemic of it? The answer is that several extrinsic motivators may be at work:

- Getting close to the line may take you over it, with criminal and civil penalties imposed by the courts.

- The risk of social opprobrium for those caught pushing the envelope, reinforced by social sanctions, can motivate individuals to stay well within the bounds of acceptable practices.

- Acquiring a reputation as someone who sometimes behaves unethically can mean the loss of economic opportunity in the future, say, because potential trading partners are less willing to trade with someone with a poor reputation or because potential trading partners would insist on contractual safeguards.

The strengths of these motivators are endogenous to the social setting: Laws can be changed, and indeed they were in summer 2002. The extent to which unethical behavior excites social opprobrium and sanction depends on society's distaste for the specific behavior. And an unwillingness to trade with someone with a poor reputation for ethical behavior depends at least in part on the availability of alternatives who behave more ethically.

The point I wish to emphasize here is that these are all extrinsic motivators. They work in the fashion of other motivators we studied in this book. In particular, the latter two would seem to fit very well within this chapter and Chapters 22 and 23, in terms of their "economics."

I venture to say that most people—at least, most people who are not trained as economists—will read this section with increasing disdain. The case for ethics made here is not that behaving ethically is the right or noble thing to do, but that ethics are an instrument for reducing transaction costs. And I assert that ethical behavior does not come from within the individual but must be motivated extrinsically. The perspective on human beings and their behavior that this suggests, a perspective that seems part and parcel of economics, is pretty bleak.

This takes us to the final chapter of the book.

Executive Summary

- This chapter, essentially, completes a journey begun around Chapter 15, moving from the simple, market- and price-mediated transactions of Chapters 1 through 14 to transactions and long-term economic relationships that involve the complexities of uncertainty, hidden information, moral hazard, dynamics, and identity (instead of anonymity). As those complexities pile up, we are less and less able to imagine transactions where everything is provided for ex ante; we move to incomplete contracts. Add to this a lack of ongoing market discipline, because of transaction-specific assets, and one's focus when studying an economic transaction or relationship shifts from the specific terms of the transaction to how it will be governed: Who has which decision rights? How will adaptations be made? Efficiency in transactions requires "intelligent" adaptation, but it also requires trust. Therefore, in looking at governance, we ask, Who has the information and judgment required to make good decisions? From where, if at all, does trust between the parties come?

- Applied to the automobile industry of the 20th century, this perspective on complex transactions and economic relationships helps us understand both why Henry Ford choose a very high level of vertical integration (to gain control of important parts of the production process) and why and how Toyota led the way to much lower levels of integration (to reimpose high-powered market incentives).

- This set of ideas, known as *transaction cost economics*, can be used to analyze a wide variety of complex transactions. In particular, it provides the basis for the analysis of firms as institutions rather than as profit-maximizing entities.

25. Economics and Organizational Behavior

Many, if not most, students of management, around the time they study economics, take courses with titles such as Organizational Behavior, which present models of individuals and institutions that seem utterly different from what economics teaches. These courses present concepts and notions from the disciplines of social and cognitive psychology and organizational sociology, which seem to share little, if any, common ground with economics. But in "managerial" courses such as strategic management and human resource management, students are asked to blend these different perspectives on human motivation and behavior. The purpose of this chapter, after reviewing where we have been, is to discuss how these seemingly different perspectives can be blended as complements rather than contrasted as substitutes.

25.1. Thirty Takeaways and the Big Picture

In 600 or so pages, we have covered a lot of ground and a lot of economics. A lot of specific messages and takeaways have been provided. Without pretending to be an exhaustive list, here are 30 specific takeaways that, I hope, you absorbed. (These takeaways are cross-referenced with the chapters in which they occurred, in case you skipped some chapters.)

1. You are not at the top of a hill if the ground under your feet slopes up in one direction or another. By itself, this is not much of an insight, but it should remind you to think in terms of margins rather than averages; for instance, think marginal cost and marginal revenue, not average cost and price. And, when you think about marginal cost or marginal revenue, think in terms of the marginal impact of a decision on all your revenue and cost terms. (Chapter 3)

2. The amount of a good demanded by a consumer relates to the marginal utility that item provides and not the total utility. But, to the extent that consumers can be faced with entry fees or take-it-or-leave-it offers, the amount of money that can be sucked out of them depends on the total utility they get from a product. (Chapters 5 and 7)

3. In marketing a product, each layer in the chain of distribution adds a markup as the organization at that layer extracts its piece of the profit, diminishing both the total amount sold and the amount of benefit ob-

tained by the customer. However, if a manufacturer can charge re-
sellers a fixed fee for the right to buy its product (and resale of the good
can be controlled), the manufacturer can control this problem of multi-
marginalization. (Chapter 6)

4. The protection offered under law to franchisees is not simply a matter of
political power and rentseeking by the franchisees, nor is it an unalloyed
bad for franchisers. It protects the franchisees from being held up after
they make sunk-cost investments and, in this way, helps franchisers by
inducing franchisees to make those sunk-cost investments. (Chapter 6)

5. If you can find ways to separate more-elastic-demand demanders from
more-inelastic-demand demanders and can charge the second group
higher prices, you make more money than charging a single price. This
general principle finds expression in a variety of ways: discrimination
by group membership, couponing, third-degree price discrimination (using product characteristics to separate groups, as in hard- and soft-cover
books, availability as a function of time, and airline ticket provision), and
second-degree price discrimination (quantity discounts or discounts for
the first few units purchased). Related to this are schemes for extracting
"surplus" from customers with entry or up-front fees leading, ideally, to
first-degree price discrimination. (Chapter 7)

6. The profit-maximizing level of production is generally greater than the
level of production at which profit per unit, or profit margin, is maximized, because you "make it up in volume." (Chapter 8)

7. The level of production that minimizes average costs (called *efficient scale*)
has no particular connection to the level of production that maximizes
profit, unless you have a competitive industry with free entry and exit
at the best available technology. (Chapters 8 and 11)

8. *The bang-for-the-buck principle:* When you maximize or minimize some
objective subject to a single constraint, look at the ratios of the marginal
impact on the objective of a variable to the marginal impact on the constraint of the same variable. Subject to caveats about nonnegativity constraints, these ratios are equal at the solution of the constrained optimization problem. (Chapter 9)

9. Accounting procedures that involve depreciation are an attempt to measure current "profit flow." Most procedures employed do this imperfectly, because accounting measures are governed by a general prejudice
in favor of conservatism (give accountants no leeway to make things look
rosier than they are) and the (auditing) need to be able to reconstruct ac-

counting procedures ex post, to be sure that no funny business took place. Also, remember that accounting earnings differ from economic profits in a second important fashion: Accounting earnings do not include a "regular charge" to equity holders for the use of their resources. (Chapters 10 and 11)

10. When current production activities lower future production costs, as in the experience curve or activities such as TQM, "marginal cost" is not the additional current cost for making another unit. At least a portion of current costs is an investment in better technology and should be treated as the investment activity that it is. (Chapter 10)

11. Economic profits earned by firms in a given industry attract entry into that industry; losses induce exit. At the extreme, in competitive industries with free entry and exit and where many producers have access to the most efficient technology, the equilibrium is where economic profits are 0, firms produce at their efficient scale, and the price is the minimum average cost. As a practical consequence of this, when trying to forecast how an industry will respond (at least in the long run) to changes in conditions such as a change in supply or demand or the imposition of a tax, take into account the powerful impact of entry and exit. In particular, the relevant industry includes not only the currently active firms but potential entrants. (Chapter 11)

12. In competitive markets, firms equate their marginal cost to price and consumers equate their marginal utility to price. In this fashion, the price mechanism is Adam Smith's "invisible hand," leading to efficient levels of production and consumption. But, in imperfectly competitive industries, where marginal cost is equal to marginal revenue, which is less than price, market equilibrium generally leads to too little production. And, in markets with externalities in production and consumption, competitive markets lead to equal private marginal costs and private marginal benefits but not social marginal costs and benefits, which may be inefficient. (Chapters 12 and 14)

13. In competitive markets, government intervention in the form of taxes, subsidies, price ceilings, price floors, and quotas introduces a "wedge" between the prices facing consumers and producers, leading to an inequality between marginal cost and marginal utility, leading in turn to inefficiencies. Such instruments can have positive distributional consequences, however; and they can enhance efficiency in imperfectly competitive markets or situations with externalities. (Chapter 13)

14. In a competitive industry, the relative impact of a tax or subsidy on

producers and consumers depends on the relative elasticities of supply and demand. Everything else held equal, the impact is felt more strongly the more inelastic is supply or demand, relative to the other. But inelastic supply or demand (or both) lessens the deadweight loss associated with a tax or subsidy. This is the efficiency-based motivation for so-called sin taxes, on items such as alcohol and cigarettes for which demand is inelastic, and for taxes on real property, for which supply is inelastic. (Chapter 13)

15. In theory, to remove the inefficiencies caused by an externality, establish clear property rights and let the parties bargain. But the bargaining process often introduces inefficiencies, making this theoretical solution impractical. Otherwise, in the regulation of specific externalities, both quotas and fines (for positive externalities, subsidies) can be used; the choice often depends on the distribution of information among the regulators and the parties being regulated. Programs such as resaleable pollution licenses mix quotas with a Coasian market-allocation mechanism, leading to more efficient solutions than could be obtained by pure quotas or pure fines for pollution. In intrafirm contexts, this suggests setting transfer prices using a marketlike mechanism. (Chapter 14)

16. Faced with choices with uncertain consequences, individuals are usually averse to risk and ambiguity in the odds. They tend to overvalue certainty and overweight small probabilities. And they are very susceptible to being "manipulated" by how the consequences of their decisions are framed. (Chapter 15)

17. Risk aversion is normatively a reasonable behavioral characteristic, but aversion to ambiguity, overvaluation of certainty, overweighting small probabilities, and manipulation by framing are usually less reasonable normatively. The expected utility model can be a useful normative tool to avoid these pitfalls and make difficult choices under uncertainty from relatively simpler judgments. (Chapter 16)

18. When individuals are risk averse, risk sharing and spreading are powerful devices for creating value. When a gamble is uncorrelated with other risks people face and is thinly spread, its "value" approaches its average or expected value. When it is positively or negatively correlated with other risks, its value depends on those correlations: Usually, positive correlation decreases value, while negative correlation increases value because of an insurance effect. This story is picked up in the subject of finance, in the form of the capital asset pricing model. (Chapter 17)

19. A host of factors limit the extent to which the value created by risk shar-

ing or spreading can be enjoyed: Differences of opinion, the need to protect proprietary information, the value of control, adverse selection, and moral hazard problems all intrude. For organized security exchanges, both legislatively mandated disclosure and voluntary disclosure of audited financial accounting data are vehicles to combat the problems of adverse selection and moral hazard, so that the gains from risk sharing or spreading can be taken advantage of more widely. (Chapter 17)

20. Adverse selection can greatly inhibit markets, especially as the problem of adverse selection is often a vicious cycle: As high-quality goods are pulled off the market, the average quality of the goods that remain falls, so the price buyers are willing to pay falls, causing more high-quality goods to be withdrawn. (Chapter 18)

21. The cure for adverse selection is information, whether obtained by statute or voluntarily. The key to an effective voluntary signal or screen is that the signal or screen is *relatively* cheap for goods of higher quality, so it separates quality levels. (Chapter 18)

22. Competitive bidding situations, where the prize has uncertain value with a substantial common-value element and different bidders have access to different information about that value, hold the possibility of a winner's curse. Knowing how to behave in a situation with a potential winner's curse is generally complex, especially when the other bidders are sophisticated enough to know about the winner's curse, but at least this much is clear: If you face a winner's curse situation and the other bidders bid without taking this into account, hence too aggressively, you should probably forgo the auction. If you win, you will almost surely lose. (Chapter 18)

23. In situations of moral hazard, risk sharing, taken to an extreme, can diffuse individual motivation; a fundamental conflict exists between risk sharing and individual motivation. (Chapter 19)

24. Beyond this fundamental conflict in incentive systems, consider, for any incentive system, dynamic effects, multitask questions, and the screening impact of the system. (Chapter 19)

25. In attempting to discover how profitable are firms in an industry, consider Porter's five forces: barriers to entry, substitute and complementary products, the power of suppliers, the power of customers, and rivalry within the industry. (Chapter 20)

26. In situations where your welfare is affected by the actions of specific others, while your actions affect them, analyze the situation by trying to

understand how each party (you and others) sees the situation. In other words, think through the situation as a game. (Chapter 21)

27. Cooperation built on reciprocity requires that each party be able to observe what the other is doing and have a clear understanding of what constitutes the "deal." (Chapter 22)

28. Individuals and organizations often face a conflict between their ex ante and ex post interests. The ability to control or restrict one's later options (through choice of technology or cost structure, contractual guarantees, reputation concerns, regulations, or laws) can be a blessing ex ante, if it induces others to act in a way that the first party prefers. (Chapter 23)

29. For complex transactions that stretch out over time, the appearance of bounded rationality means that the terms of the transaction are not fixed at the outset. Transaction-specific assets dull the power of the market to determine those terms of trade. Then the *governance* of the transaction (who makes what decisions when) becomes crucial to the efficiency of the transaction. In general, decisions should be made by the parties with the best information and ability to make the decisions *and* that will be trusted by the others involved. (Chapter 24)

30. In managing a supply chain in the manner of Toyota, notwithstanding Porter's admonition against strong suppliers, it may improve efficiency to empower your suppliers by giving them a forum in which they can share information and, potentially, organize. More generally, when a single party deals with many others and wishes to cultivate a particular reputation, facilitating communication among the others is generally a good idea. For those other parties, communication can be both a blessing (in cooperative situations) and a curse (in more adversarial situations). (Chapters 23 and 24)

The Big Picture

Beyond these specific takeaways is a much more general and, I hope, ultimately more important big-picture takeaway. Think the way an economist thinks: about individuals who act purposefully, pursuing some fairly well-defined goal, with conflicts of interest adjudicated by institutions that reach an equilibrium.

Economics and Organizational Behavior

Many if not most students of management, around the time they study economics, also study models of individuals and institutions that seem entirely different. Courses with titles such as Organizational Behavior present concepts and notions from the disciplines of social and cognitive psychology and organizational sociology. If you take such a course while studying this book, you might come away believing that these are such different perspectives that they share no common ground. Although 40 years old, a quip by the famous economist James Duesenberry is telling: "Economics is all about how people make choices; sociology is all about how they don't have any choices to make."[1]

This picture of disciplines in conflict is, however, changing. Increasingly, strong complementarities in the subjects are recognized. Often this happens in subjects that apply basic economics and the other social sciences, such as courses in strategic management and human resource management. But even in the basic disciplines themselves, a synthesis of these different perspectives is beginning to appear.

While it has yet to enter the mainstream, this synthesis is a natural development. Over the past 25 years, the topics discussed since Chapter 18 (information economics, game theory, and transaction cost economics) have entered the mainstream. But these developments tell an incomplete story. Having moved away from the simple models of anonymous market exchange and classic monopoly into more complex and personal transactions, economics is virtually forced to reexamine its basic models of individual behavior. This has moved economics toward the other disciplines.

25.2. What Motivates Workers?

Try the following. Here is an alphabetical list of eight general "motivators," categories of things that motivate employees to work and work hard on the job:

- *Benefits.*
- *Feeling good* about onself.
- The ability to learn and *grow.*
- *Pay.*
- *Praise* for a job well done.
- Job *security.*
- The opportunity to acquire and practice *skills.*
- The opportunity to do *worthwhile* things.

Think of yourself on the job. Which of these motivators is most important

---

[1] J. Duesenberry, "Comments on 'An Economic Analysis of Fertility'." In *Demographic and Economic Change in Developed Countries*, edited by the Universities–National Bureau Committee for Economic Research (Princeton, NJ: Princeton University Press, 1960), page 233.

to you? Which is least? Rank them in order, from the most important to the least, as far as your own motivation is concerned.

Now answer these questions: Which of these is most important to your peers? Which is least? On average, how do you think your peers rank them?

Suppose we assembled a collection of your peers and asked them to rank the eight, in terms of what is important to them. (That is, we ask a group of your peers the first set of questions.) Then we compute the average ranks of each. (That is, if *pay* is rated most important by 60% of the population, second-most-important by 30%, and third-most-important by 10%, then we compute for *pay* the average rank $(0.6)(1)+(0.3)(2)+(0.1)(3) = 1.5$). If we do all this, which of the eight, do you think, will have the lowest average, meaning it is highest ranked, on average? Which will have the highest average (lowest rank)? How will the eight be ordered, based on these average ranks?

I do not know how you rank these items for yourself, what you think motivates your peers, or what you think they would say motivates them, but questions like the first and the third were put to managers and customer service representatives at the international financial giant, Citibank (back before it become a piece of Citigroup) by Chip Heath.[2] Heath reports average responses as shown in Table 25.1.

	Managers, speaking for themselves	Managers, predicting how their peers would rank them	Customer Service Reps, speaking for themselves	CSRs, predicting how their peers would rank them
Most important	**Worthwhile**	Pay	**Skills**	Pay
2nd most important	**Skills**	**Skills**	**Worthwhile**	Security
3rd most important	**Feeling good**	Security	**Learning**	Benefits
4th	**Learning**	Benefits	Benefits	Praise
5th	Security	**Feeling good**	Security	**Feeling good**
6th	Benefits	**Learning**	**Feeling good**	**Skills**
7th	Pay	**Worthwhile**	Pay	**Worthwhile**
Least important	Praise	Praise	Praise	**Learning**

Table 25.1. Perceptions of on-the-job motivators. Managers and customer service representatives at Citibank were asked to rank eight on-the-job motivators, both for themselves and how they felt their peers would respond concerning their own motivation. Average ranks are shown, indicating that both categories of individuals felt that they were motivated by different factors than their peers.

It is clear that both managers and customer service representatives feel that they are different from their peers. Moreover, consider partitioning the set of eight motivators into two subsets, as follows:

---

[2] "On the Social Psychology of Agency Relationships: Lay Theories of Motivation Overemphasize Extrinsic Incentives," *Organizational Behavior and Human Decision Processes* 78 (1999), pp. 25–62. Table 25.1 is adapted from Heath's Table 2, page 36, and is reproduced here with the permission of Elsevier.

1. Feeling good, grow, skills, and worthwhile.

2. Benefits, pay, praise, and security.

I hope you agree that the first set would generally be considered motivators that are more intrinsic, stemming from internal satisfaction, while the second set are the more extrinsic motivators, based on materialistic concerns and status. In Table 25.1, I have listed the motivators in the first set in boldface, and if you accept this partition and the spirit in which it is offered, it is clear from the table: Both the managers and customer service representatives think of themselves as motivated largely by the first set, while their peers are motivated largely by the second.

How do we explain the difference between what these individuals think about their own motivation, and what they think about how their peers are motivated? One seemingly natural explanation for these data is that people naturally think of themselves as more noble than others. Although I do not go into details, Heath controlled for perceptions of "nobility" of these motivators, and even with this controlled for, individuals saw themselves as motivated somewhat differently than they believe their peers would see themselves.

This leaves us with two polar possibilities: Perhaps individuals misperceive how they themselves are motivated, but they have it right when they think (more objectively, perhaps) about others. Or perhaps individuals are accurately self-aware (they understand what motivates them) but incorrectly perceive what motivates their peers.

Which hypothesis is right? What really motivates these managers? In the end, are they motivated, as they think they are, by the less materialistic factors in the first set? Or are they motivated, as they think their peers are, by the factors in the second set? Of course, the answer is not a black or white one or the other. But does the truth lie more on one side or the other? Unhappily, that is a much harder piece of research to accomplish, and we do not know, at least not for these two sets of employees at Citibank.

The answer is very important. Suppose you were responsible for creating incentive systems, in the spirit of Chapter 19, for either these managers or customer service representatives. The tone and treatment of issues in Chapter 19 (entirely typical of economic approaches to these questions) seems to assume rather strongly that you motivate people with money and other materialistic rewards. In other words, if you take the ideas of Chapter 19 to the real world, you would probably be inclined to use as "levers" the second set of motivating factors. If the second hypothesis is right (if the stronger set of motivating factors is Set 1), then the motivators in Set 2 are the wrong levers.

In fact, while we do not know the ultimate answers for these two groups at Citibank, data have been developed on what motivates workers in a variety of settings, and intrinsic motivational factors such as those in the first set can, in some settings, play a very important role. Moreover, there are theories in social psychology that hold that offering extrinsic, materialistic motivation may dull employees' intrinsic motivation so much that the extrinsic incentives are counterproductive, lowering the quality of the employees' work.[3]

25.3. Beliefs, Perceptions, and Tastes

This is but one example of a very general situation, which can perhaps best be illustrated by moving to the subject of reciprocity-generated cooperation, as discussed in Chapter 22.

When two individuals play the prisoners' dilemma game repeatedly, it is relatively easy to see how they can sustain cooperation with strategies such as tit for tat. But in real-world applications, where the possible actions are many, the situation changes through time, matters are not symmetric, and the individuals involved carry a lot of baggage into their relationship from other relationships:

- How does each party form its *beliefs*, about what the other side will do, both at the outset and in response to actions the first party takes?

- As time passes and outcomes are recorded, how do the parties form their *perceptions* of what the other side is doing and how well or poorly they are faring?

- Given beliefs and perceptions, there is still the question of motivation or utility. What are the *tastes* of the parties concerning the possible outcomes? Are those tastes fixed or do they evolve through time?

All these are questions about which the economic theory in this book is silent. But the theory we presented—in particular, the theory in Chapter 22—makes abundantly clear that the answers to these questions are crucial to whether or not reciprocity-generated cooperation will emerge and persist. Chapter 22 and the folk theorem tell us that reciprocity-generated cooperation is often a possibility. The chapter tells us about structural factors (noise, a small chance of future encounters, a single round played for huge stakes) that may impede cooperation or even make it impossible to sustain. But,

---

[3] See Chapter 11 of J. Baron and D. Kreps, *Strategic Human Resources* (New York: Wiley, 1999), especially the section "The Case against Pay for Performance."

even if all such impediments are removed, the folk theorem says only that cooperation is possible and, in most real-world applications, can take many different forms. The folk theorem does not say what form the cooperative equilibrium takes or even that a cooperative equilibrium emerges. Only by answering the preceding sorts of questions can we predict more tightly what will happen.

Social psychology, cognitive psychology, and organizational psychology provide some answers to these questions. They also teach us that answers are not universal; what people believe, what they perceive, and what are their tastes depend a lot on the social context they inhabit. Here is a taste of what you can learn from them.

- Beliefs are often formed adaptively. People induce from the past into the future. First impressions and experiences can be vital. Beliefs are often based on stories and fables and the patterns they establish. Conformance to existing social patterns can be very important. Consistency with other social forms and patterns, such as general social status, can be very important.

- In assessing how well they are doing, individuals often make comparative judgments rather than absolute judgments. Someone making $90,000 per year in an organization where others at this individual's level are making $80,000 may well feel better treated than someone making $100,000, if others at this individual's level are making $110,000. Social comparisons to those above, below, and especially at one's own level are often the chief way in which perceptions of treatment are formed.

- Individuals internalize the welfare of others with whom they deal. The degree to which this happens evolves with the relationship and depends on the extent to which the parties involved perceive that their own behavior is motivated extrinsically or intrinsically. In a successful long-term relationship, where reciprocal cooperation is not directly and explicitly rewarded, the parties tend to embrace and protect each other's welfare, even at some personal cost, more than when the relationship has been less successful or where cooperation is motivated directly.

Let me say again, these are simply examples; and they are examples that apply in some contexts and not in others. But I hope they make the point: Beliefs, perceptions, and tastes lie outside of economic analysis as presented in this book, but they are crucial to the economic analysis of some situations. If we can import reasonable assumptions about these things from the other social sciences, our economic models are more likely to shed light on real-life situations.

Do These Things Make a Difference?

Economists have traditionally resisted the inclusion of such ideas into economics. I doubt you are much interested in why they have resisted, but one form this resistance has taken is worth addressing.

When we introduced the models of the profit-maximizing firm and the utility-maximizing consumer, we mounted the positive science, or "as-if," model defense: These are positive models of behavior. It does not matter that firms do not consciously maximize profit nor that consumers do not consciously maximize utility. The conclusions of our models are valid as long as firms act (approximately) as if they maximize profit and consumers, as if they maximize utility. Accordingly, we do not need tools from the other social sciences to explain beliefs, perceptions, and tastes; the standard models of these things used in economics are adequate as-if models.

This argument resisting the incorporation of other models of behavior is flawed in two ways. First, it simply fails to address the fact that standard economics gives us too little guidance in the sorts of situations we examined in Chapter 22, when the folk theorem applies, when it comes to predicting which equilibrium will ensue. If all these tools from the other social sciences do is fill in vacuums of standard economics, they are worth developing.

But the case for these tools is stronger than that: In some cases, "standard economics" assumptions concerning behavior can lead you badly astray. Individuals, in some situations, do not act "as if" they were conforming to standard economic models of behavior. For instance, one is hard pressed to predict, using standard economic models of behavior, that an employee paid $90,000 when all his peers make $80,000 would feel better treated, hence less likely to depart voluntarily, than an employee paid $92,000 when all his peers make $100,000. This is not to say a clever economist could not find some way to make such behavior consistent with standard economic models of behavior. Economists are extremely clever at contorting their models of behavior. But, a simpler path to follow is to understand the role that social comparisons play in individual assessments of fair and equitable treatment and, ultimately, satisfaction on the job.

Consider a conclusion drawn back in Chapter 19, that in motivating employees, one should shield them from extraneous and unnecessary uncertainty in compensation (see pages 463–4). In particular, tying the compensation of employees to the profit a firm earns is distinctly inferior to tying their compensation to more direct measures of individual and group performance; for instance, tying the compensation of employees at a particular facility to their facility's costs of manufacture, number of on-time shipments, and the like. Adherents of so-called high-commitment human resource management demur from this solid prescription of standard economic modeling, suggesting instead that tying employees' compensation to the firm's overall level of performance is consistent with other actions taken to cause employees to internalize the welfare of the firm, thus solving a host of otherwise quite intractable agency problems. The idea that employees can, by such means, be led to internalize the welfare of the firm, or their group within the firm—that they can essentially have their tastes changed— is far outside the realm of traditional economics. And, if it is true, it has profound implications.

Why the Post-Chapter 18 Material
Makes This Synthesis a High Priority

I earlier expressed the opinion that the synthesis of economics and organizational behavior is, more or less, impelled by economics' recent forays into information, dynamics (using game theory), and transaction cost economics. Let me explain why. Classic economics involves simple, discrete transactions. A good of known quality is produced and sold; produced and sold by firms that know what it costs to make the good and what price they can get for it; sold to consumers who know the utility the good will provide them and what it will cost. There is no need here to worry about beliefs, because all the relevant information is available, or perceptions, since there is nothing in the story to perceive. There is plenty of room here to worry about tastes; if we could explain why consumers like bananas more than grapefruit (if indeed they do), we could sharpen the predictions we make about the relative prices of bananas and grapefruit. But economists have long been accustomed to leaving tastes to other social sciences. *De gustibus non disputandum est* (there is no arguing about tastes) is probably the economist's second favorite bit of Latin, after *ceteris paribus*. Even though it would be helpful to be able to explain tastes, economists have regarded this as outside their capability; they take tastes as given and proceed from there.

Once we begin to introduce uncertainty in Chapter 15, beliefs and perceptions become an important part of the story. The tradition in economics has been to leave alone the question of the formation of beliefs. We do not say why someone believes the chance of a fire or a rising stock market is this or that; we simply take that as data. But already here, we have to confront seriously the question of perceptions, as in our discussion of framing.

When both dynamics and uncertainty are in the mix, then the question of how individuals forecast from the past to the future has to be confronted, especially where economic decisions and outcomes affect how much information individuals receive, how that information is presented to them, and the like.

As we move to more "personal" economics, where the identities of trading partners become consequential, the need to discuss beliefs and perceptions becomes even stronger. It is one thing to say that beliefs about where the stock market is going can be taken as exogenous. But, can we seriously regard beliefs about how, say, Procter & Gamble would react to entry, as forecast by a potential entrant, as exogenous? When notions such as psychological barriers to entry and reputation become central to the discussion, the formation of beliefs and the perceptual processes that individuals use are central to the story. We can, and until recently economists have, treated these as exogenous. But they become so much a part of the story that the story begins to lose credibility, if they are not taken seriously.

Finally, as we move from anonymous markets to contexts where identities matter, notions only beginning to enter the conversation of economists, such as pride, anger, revenge, and benevolence, ought to enter. There is no doubt these "emotions" affect individual actions, by affecting what the individual values. We might be able to get away with treating as exogenous someone's relative tastes for bananas versus grapefruit, but a taste for revenge or a willingness to sacrifice one's own immediate welfare to benefit someone else, *especially where those things are endogenously affected by economic decisions and outcomes*, ought to be part of the story. At least, when we get to the economics of identity and look at situations that are complex, dynamic, and involve individuals whose level of rationality is insufficient to foresee everything (when we get to transaction cost economics), we have a lot better, more powerful theory if we find ways to include these sorts of things rather than setting them aside.

Put it this way: I think there is no more important economic transaction than employment. I do not have handy the dollar value of wages relative to the dollar value of all exchanges in modern economies, but wages are certainly a substantial portion of the whole. Managing people, especially employees, is surely the ultimate challenge that faces managers. And, while employment is an economic transaction, it is equally a social transaction. Some people may work solely for the wages they earn, but in the context of a modern economy, where most managers will find themselves, work usually provides—and is motivated by—a lot more than wages. To do an adequate job understanding the economics of employment, you must come to grips with the social side of employment. That drives you toward a synthesis of economics and the other social sciences.

This does not mean that, having waded through this book, you can abandon the subject for social psychology or organizational sociology. Just as with economics, those subjects are "incomplete" lenses with which to study employment and other transactions. Economics brings to the table some crucial ideas, perhaps the most important of which is that individuals act purposefully, within limits perhaps, but still with a purpose in mind. If Due-senberry was correct in stating that sociology (say) is all about how people have no choices—if their behavior is totally a matter of social context and social forces—then sociology and economics are incompatible. If instead sociology and social psychology are about how social context and social forces shape beliefs, perceptions, and tastes—if the great social scientist Herbert Simon was right that boundedly rational behavior is behavior that is *intendedly rational*, but limitedly so—then economics and these other social sciences are indeed complementary, and the synthesis of them that we are beginning to see will make microeconomics, suitably enriched, an even more powerful tool of analysis and understanding for managers than it is today.

Index

Italicized page numbers refer to figures.